Herausgegeben von / Edited by
Cosima Rainer und / and Robert Müller

DER HAUSFREUND

Eine Wiederentdeckung des exzentrischen Werks von
A Rediscovery of the Eccentric Work of
FRIEDRICH VON BERZEVICZY-PALLAVICINI

Verlag der Buchhandlung Walther König

INHALT
CONTENTS

Vorwort / Foreword 3
Gerald Bast

Wi(e)der-Entdeckungen (Einleitung) 4
Counter-Rediscoveries (Introduction) 6
Cosima Rainer

Der Hausfreund 8
Cosima Rainer und / and Robert Müller

Die Kraft des Ephemeren 19
The Force of the Ephemeral 20
Brigitte Felderer

Wie im Champagnerglas.
Berzeviczy-Pallavicinis Raumgestaltungen . . 27
As if in a Champagne Glass:
Berzeviczy-Pallavicini's Interior Designs . . . 28
Anne-Katrin Rossberg

ABCs im Klassenkampf.
Was die „Dekorateure“ Federico Pallavicini
und Andy Warhol verbindet
(und was sie trennt) 43
ABCs and Class Struggle:
What Connects the Two "Decorative Artists"
Federico Pallavicini and Andy Warhol
(and What Separates Them) 44
Manuela Ammer

Ausstellungsansichten / Exhibition Views
Der Hausfreund (Wien / Vienna) 77

Insert: Ciphers of Regression
featuring *Der Hausfreund* 100

Ausstellungsansichten / Exhibition Views
Der Hausfreund (Berlin) 106

Künstler*innen der Ausstellungen /
Artists at the Exhibitions 153

Eine Chronologie 165
A Chronology 164
Sofie Mathoi

Werkliste / List of Works 180

Biographien / Biographies 184

Bildnachweis / Image Credits 189

Impressum / Colophon 191

Vorwort / Foreword

Gerald Bast

Die Ausstellung *Der Hausfreund* präsentiert die schillernde Figur des Künstlers Friedrich von Berzeviczy-Pallavicini (1909–89) als eine hochaktuelle Wiederentdeckung. Im Umfeld der Wiener Kunstgewerbeschule schuf Berzeviczy-Pallavicini einst Werke in einer manierierten und eigenwilligen Formensprache, die heute erstaunlich zeitgenössisch erscheint. In der Ausstellung werden wichtige Motive seiner Produktion, ausgehend vom umfangreichen Werkbestand der Sammlung der Universität für angewandte Kunst Wien, im Dialog mit zeitgenössischen Künstler*innen sowie mit historisch verwandten Positionen aufgegriffen, gespiegelt und neu interpretiert.

Die von der Sammlungsleiterin Cosima Rainer und dem Künstler Robert Müller kuratierte Ausstellung wurde 2019 in zwei unterschiedlichen Versionen in der Universitätsgalerie im Heiligenkreuzer Hof in Wien und im Österreichischen Kulturforum Berlin gezeigt.

Dass die Universität ihn wahrlich als Hausfreund bezeichnen kann, liegt an seiner großzügigen Schenkung von über 300 Arbeiten an die Kunstsammlung 1986, die der damalige Rektor Oswald Oberhuber und die Sammlungsleiterin Erika Patka mit Freuden annahmen. Oswald Oberhuber hatte Berzeviczy-Pallavicini bereits 1982 die neu geschaffene Ehrenmitgliedschaft der Hochschule für angewandte Kunst verliehen. Im Gegensatz zu anderen Sammlungen wurde in der Kunstsammlung der Universität für angewandte Kunst Wien Wert darauf gelegt, Künstler*innen, die in Österreich durch das Regime des Nationalsozialismus verfolgt oder aus anderen Gründen vergessen wurden, wieder in die Aufmerksamkeit zu rücken.

The exhibition *Der Hausfreund* presents the multifaceted artist Friedrich von Berzeviczy-Pallavicini (1909–89) as a highly topical rediscovery. Within the milieu of the Vienna School of Applied Arts, Berzeviczy-Pallavicini created works in an idiosyncratic and mannered formal language that appears surprisingly contemporary today. Drawing on the extensive catalogue of works in the university's collection, the exhibition examines, contrasts, and reinterprets relevant motifs from the artist's oeuvre in dialogue with contemporary artists and historically related works.

The exhibition, curated in 2019 by the head of collections Cosima Rainer and the artist Robert Müller, was shown in two different versions at the University Gallery in Heiligenkreuzer Hof in Vienna and at the Austrian Cultural Forum in Berlin.

The name of the exhibition, *Der Hausfreund* (literally "friend of the house"), is well-chosen in view of the artist's generous donation to the art collection in 1986 of over three hundred works, which the then rector Oswald Oberhuber and head of collections Erika Patka were delighted to accept. A few years previously, in 1982, Oberhuber had awarded Berzeviczy-Pallavicini the recently introduced title of Honorary Member of the University of Applied Arts. Unlike other collections, the art collection of the University of Applied Arts places special emphasis on raising awareness of artists who were persecuted in Austria during the Nazi regime or who have been forgotten for other reasons.

Wi(e)der-Entdeckungen
Einleitung von Cosima Rainer

Große Kunstsammlungen gleichen Eisbergen: Nur ein Bruchteil ihrer Masse ist sichtbar, das meiste verharrt oft still im Verborgenen. Für die Schulsammlung der Universität für angewandte Kunst Wien gilt dies im gesteigerten Maße, da sie weder über permanente Ausstellungsräume noch Werbemittel verfügt, ihre Schätze kommen nur sporadisch ans Licht. Doch wenn, dann offenbaren sie ein großes Potenzial für diskursive Verschiebungen und Neubewertungen. Denn der Reichtum der Sammlung an unterschätzten oder verdrängten Positionen der Kunst- und Gestaltungsgeschichte ist enorm und die kritische Auseinandersetzung mit dem etablierten Kanon durch Gegenerzählungen und Wieder-Entdeckungen ist ihr eigentliches Sammlungsprogramm.

Die mittlerweile mit 65.000 Werken bestückte Sammlung wurde erst in den 1980er-Jahren durch die Initiative des damaligen Rektors Oswald Oberhuber aktiv angelegt und bezog sich auf wichtige Entwicklungen und Protagonist*innen der k. k. Kunstgewerbeschule.

Tatsächlich war die einstige Gründungsinstitution in zahlreichen Bereichen Avantgarde: Sie setzte früh auf pädagogische Konzepte und Gestaltungsansätze, die mit den späteren Vorkursen des Weimarer Bauhauses vergleichbar waren. Ähnliches galt für die „moderne Raumkunst“[1], die von den Protagonist*innen der Wiener Werkstätte entwickelt wurde und auch den Ausstellungsraum als Ganzes als Gestaltungsaufgabe sah. Auch ließ die Kunstgewerbeschule bereits seit ihrer Gründung 1867 Frauen zum Studium zu – ganz im Gegensatz zu anderen Universitäten. Diesen Aspekten will die Sammlung seit ihren Anfängen in Form von Ausstellungen, Präsentationen und Diskussionen mehr Sichtbarkeit verleihen.

Das Institut umfasst heute die Kunst- und Designsammlung, das Oskar-Kokoschka-Zentrum, die Kostüm- und Modesammlung, eine Stiftung, die dem Designer Victor Papanek gewidmet ist, sowie das Universitätsarchiv. Geprägt durch wichtige Schenkungen und Nachlässe, verfügt die Sammlung u. a. über Schwerpunkte zu Fred Adlmüller, Friedl Dicker-Brandeis, Josef Hoffmann, Anton Kolig, Adele List, Elly Niebuhr, Franz Schuster, Margarete Schütte-Lihotzky, Emmy Zweybrück und den Wiener Kinetismus. Mit den historischen Sammlungen der frühen Kunstgewerbeschule und der Künstler*innen Mileva Roller und Rosalia Rothansl gehören außerdem seltene Kleidungsstücke zu den Beständen.

Oswald Oberhuber, für den Kunst immer im Spannungsfeld von Politik und Gesellschaft stand, ging es zudem stark um eine aus der Gegenwart perspektivierte Arbeit an Geschichte und um alternative Fortschreibungen ihrer ästhetischen Narrative im Sinne einer Pluralisierung des kunsthistorischen Kanons. Künstler*innen, die in Österreich durch das Regime des Nationalsozialismus ermordet oder vertrieben wurden, wurden von ihm in den Mittelpunkt der Aufmerksamkeit gerückt. Mit Ausstellungen und Publikationen wie *Die Vertreibung des Geistigen aus Österreich. Zur Kulturpolitik des Nationalsozialismus* (1986)[2] und frühen Einzelpräsentationen „vergessener“ Künstler*innen setzte er gemeinsam mit der damaligen Sammlungsleiterin Erika Patka wichtige Akzente.

Hierzu gehört auch die erste Übersichtspräsentation zu den Arbeiten von Friedrich von Berzeviczy-Pallavicini 1988 im Heiligenkreuzer Hof in Wien.[3] Im Kontrast zur disziplinierten Ästhetik der Wiener Werkstätte hinterließ Berzeviczy-Pallavicini Werke mit einer manierierten und eigenwilligen Formensprache. Heute ist seine schillernde Persönlichkeit nochmals auf ganz besondere Weise neu zu entdecken, mithin als widerständige Position gegen die etablierte „Klassik“ der autonomen, formalistischen oder konzeptuellen Kunst. Besonders sein künstlerischer Allround-Ansatz und seine ungebrochene Lust am Ornament

1 Plakolm-Forsthuber, Sabine, Die moderne Raumkunst: Wiener Ausstellungsbauten von 1898–1914, Wien 1986.
2 Oberhuber, Oswald, Koller, Gabriele, Die Vertreibung des Geistigen aus Österreich. Zur Kulturpolitik des Nationalsozialismus, Wien 1986.
3 Patka, Erika (Hg.), Friedrich von Berzeviczy-Pallavicini. Poesie der Inszenierung, Hochschule für angewandte Kunst in Wien, Wien 1988.

bieten heute einen interessanten Ausgangspunkt, um einen „externen Blick“ auf Bewegungen und Felder aktueller Kunstproduktion zu werfen.

Der Ausstellungstitel *Der Hausfreund* ist bewusst mehrdeutig: Einerseits bezieht er sich auf eine Entwurfsserie von grotesk-heiteren Figuren, die verschiedene Mehlspeisen darstellen, die Berzeviczy-Pallavicini für die Konditorei Demel 1970 zeichnete und die heute zum Nachlass seiner Arbeiten in der Sammlung zählen. Zugleich beschreibt er aber auch dessen besondere Beziehung zur Wiener Kunstgewerbeschule, in der er während seines Studiums und in Zeiten finanzieller Not, einer „Hauskatze“ gleich, immer Unterschlupf fand.

Die Ausstellung wurde in einem Dialog mit dem Künstler Robert Müller erarbeitet, der auch für das Display verantwortlich zeichnete. Seine Vitrinen und Konstruktionen wurden speziell für die Räume des Heiligenkreuzer Hofs, die einst dem Abt von Heiligenkreuz als Wohnung dienten, entworfen. Müller setzt diesem historischen Ambiente glitzernde Ketten und industrielles Acrylglas entgegen. Die Konstruktionen sind fragil, vieles wirkt provisorisch. Während damit formal einerseits Berzeviczy-Pallavicinis verträumte Leichtigkeit und laszive Verdichtung mit anklingen, wird andererseits jedes Objekt durch die Transparenz der Konstruktion zur Disposition gestellt. Für die Präsentation im Österreichischen Kulturforum Berlin leicht adaptiert, gewinnen sie hier im Zusammenspiel mit der Eklektik der Architektur Hans Holleins eine gänzlich andere Wendung. Mit ihrer „grimmigen“ Fragilität untersucht Müller Fragen der Form und Fallstricke des Biografischen, beispielsweise durch Verweise auf die Adaption fremder Handschriften. Seine Ausstellungsgestaltung für *Der Hausfreund* setzt auf die subtile Kombination unterschiedlicher künstlerischer und architektonischer Elemente, und bringt so die Objekte (mit verstellter Stimme) zum Sprechen.

Auch einige der teilnehmenden Künstler und Künstlerinnen wie Julian Göthe, Kamilla Bischof und Ulrike Müller wählten eigens Werke von Berzeviczy-Pallavicini aus der Sammlung für ihre Präsentation und Gestaltung aus oder verbanden diese mit eigenständigen Konstruktionen und führten so die Verschränkung der ästhetischen Diskurse weit über die zeitlichen Gräben hinweg fort – als dialogisches Gespräch zwischen einst oft strikt getrennten Feldern und ganz im Sinne der Sammlung.

Der vorliegende Katalog ist nach der Publikation Erika Patkas vor mehr als drei Jahrzehnten die erste Wiederaufnahme einer Auseinandersetzung mit dem vielschichtigen und spannungsreichen Œuvre Berzeviczy-Pallavicinis sowie dessen biografischen Eckpunkten und Bezügen. Vieles liegt noch im Dunkeln und bedarf einer erweiterten Auseinandersetzung und Forschung. Die vorliegenden Beiträge beleuchten jeweils Teilaspekte und Ansätze dieser Arbeiten und folgen dessen Motivationen, Umfeld und Konstruktionen durch die Jahrzehnte.

Anne-Katrin Rossbergs Text widmet sich den stilistischen und kulturellen Einflüssen der Raumgestaltung Friedrich Berzeviczy-Pallavicinis, insbesondere dessen Wirken im Wien der 1920er- und 1930er-Jahre unter dem Einfluss der Kunstgewerbeschule, und beleuchtet dessen Entwicklung und Eigenheiten. Brigitte Felderer folgt den Motiven und stilistischen Einflüssen Friedrich Berzeviczy-Pallavicinis und verortet sie in einem sozialen und kulturellen Milieu, das den Habitus und dessen Gesellschaftssprache als Zeichensystem aufschließt.

Der Beitrag von Manuela Ammer schließlich bespricht Pallavicinis Zeit im New York der 1940er- und 1950er-Jahre im Kontext der Arbeiten Andy Warhols und mit dem Schwerpunkt auf (Klassen-)Codes der Bildsprache der beiden Gestalter am Beispiel der jüngsten Erwerbung der Sammlung, eines (undatierten) Alphabetentwurfs, der in dieser Publikation erstmals abgedruckt vorliegt.

Counter-Rediscoveries
Introduction by Cosima Rainer

Major art collections are like icebergs: only a fraction of their mass is visible, while quite often the larger part of it remains hidden. This is even more true of the art collections of the University of Applied Arts Vienna. As an institution, it has neither a permanent exhibition space nor a significant advertising budget, and its treasures are only sporadically presented in public. When they are, however, its holdings offer huge potential for discursive reinterpretation and reassessment. The richness of under-appreciated or displaced positions in art and design history within the collections is enormous, and to question the established canon through "counter-re-discoveries" is their pivotal raison d'être.

Now comprising some 65,000 works, the collection of the University of Applied Arts Vienna was established in the 1980s at the initiative of the University's former rector Oswald Oberhuber. It was conceived to reflect major developments and protagonists of the Imperial and Royal School of Applied Arts.

From its earliest beginnings, the School was pioneering in many respects: It was an early advocate of pedagogical concepts and approaches to design that were later adopted in the preparatory courses of the Bauhaus in Weimar. The same applies to the concept of "moderne Raumkunst" (literally: "modern spatial art"),[1] developed by the protagonists of the Wiener Werkstätte, who regarded the design of exhibition spaces as an artistic task in its own right. Unlike other universities, the School of Applied Arts was already admitting female students right from its establishment in 1867. All of these are aspects the institution seeks to highlight in its exhibitions, presentations, and discussions.

The Collection and Archive of the University of Applied Arts Vienna currently encompasses the Art and Design Collection, the Oskar Kokoschka Center, the Costume and Fashion Collection, a foundation devoted to the designer Victor Papanek, and the University Archive. Thanks to major donations and legacies, the collection now has 65,000 items, with a particular focus on works by Fred Adlmüller, Friedl Dicker-Brandeis, Josef Hoffmann, Anton Kolig, Adele List, Elly Niebuhr, Franz Schuster, Margarete Schütte-Lihotzky, Emmy Zweybrück, and representatives of Viennese Kineticism, as well as some rare historical costumes preserved by the artists Mileva Roller and Rosalia Rothansl.

Oswald Oberhuber understood art as a reflection of both politics and society. He thus was eager to tackle history from a contemporary perspective and to develop alternative aesthetic narratives, i.e. to pluralize the art-historical canon. Artists who had been killed or expelled by the Nazi regime in Austria were given special attention, not least through exhibitions and publications such as *Die Vertreibung des Geistigen aus Österreich: zur Kulturpolitik des Nationalsozialismus* (1986)[2] and early solo presentations of "forgotten" artists, which he developed together with Erika Patka, the head of collections at the time.

These activities also included a first overview at Heiligenkreuzer Hof in Vienna in 1988 of the works of Friedrich von Berzeviczy-Pallavicini.[3] In contrast to the disciplined aesthetic of the Wiener Werkstätte, Berzeviczy-Pallavicini's work was notable for its idiosyncratic and mannered formal language. His multifaceted personality can now be rediscovered, not least as a contrasting position to the established "classicism" of autonomous, formalistic, or conceptual art. His all-round approach as an artist and his undiminished joy in ornamentation in particular offer an interesting starting point for an "external look" at movements and fields in today's art production.

1 Sabine Plakolm-Forsthuber, *Die moderne Raumkunst: Wiener Ausstellungsbauten von 1898–1914* (Vienna, 1986).
2 Oswald Oberhuber, Gabriele Koller, eds., *Die Vertreibung des Geistigen aus Österreich: zur Kulturpolitik des Nationalsozialismus* (Vienna, 1986).
3 Erika Patka, ed., *Friedrich von Berzeviczy-Pallavicini: Poesie der Inszenierung*, Hochschule für Angewandte Kunst in Wien (Vienna, 1988).

The exhibition title *Der Hausfreund* is deliberately ambiguous. On the one hand, it refers to a series of light-heartedly grotesque figures representing different types of pastry, which Berzeviczy-Pallavicini created for Konditorei Demel, the renowned Viennese confectioners, in 1970, and which are now part of his estate in the collection. At the same time, it also alludes to the artist's special relationship with the Vienna School of Applied Arts, where, like a family cat ("Hauskatze"), he was able to find shelter and support during his student days and in times of financial hardship.

The exhibition was devised in dialogue with the artist Robert Müller, who also designed the display. His showcases and structures were conceived specifically for the rooms in the Heiligenkreuzer Hof, once the residence of the abbot of Heiligenkreuz. Müller created a contrast to this historic setting with glittering chains and industrial acrylic glass; his structures are fragile and many seem temporary. While there are formal echoes of Berzeviczy-Pallavicini's dreamy lightness and lascivious concentration, the immediacy of each object is emphasized by the transparency of the design. Slightly adapted for presentation at the Austrian Cultural Forum in Berlin, they acquire a completely different meaning through their interaction with Hans Hollein's eclectic architecture. With this determined fragility, Müller examines questions of form and the pitfalls of biography, for example through references to the adaptation of other styles. His exhibition design for *Der Hausfreund* plays on the subtle combination of different artistic and architectural elements, letting the objects speak for themselves (albeit using a disguised voice).

Some of the participating artists, such as Julian Göthe, Kamilla Bischof, and Ulrike Müller, chose specific works by Berzeviczy-Pallavicini from the collection for their presentations and designs or combined them with their own structures, extending the overlap in aesthetic discourse across the chasm of time as a dialogue between once strictly separate fields, exactly as the collection itself does.

After Erika Patka's publication over three decades ago, this catalogue now resumes the discussion of Berzeviczy-Pallavicini's diverse and fascinating oeuvre and the main biographical features and references. Much is still unclear and needs to be researched and studied further. The essays in this catalogue shed light on aspects and features of these works and trace their motivations, settings, and structures over the years.

Anne-Kathrin Rossberg looks at the stylistic and cultural influences on the artist's spatial design, particularly the development and characteristics of his work in Vienna in the 1920s and 1930s, following his studies at the School of Applied Arts. Brigitte Felderer discusses Berzeviczy-Pallavicini's motives and stylistic influences, and places them in a social and cultural setting, revealing the habitus and social language as a system of symbols.

Finally, Manuela Ammer's essay discusses Pallavicini's time in 1940s and 1950s New York in the context of the work of Andy Warhol, with a focus on the (class) codes in the pictorial vocabulary of both artists, citing the most recent addition to the collection, an (undated) design for an alphabet, appearing in print for the first time in this catalogue.

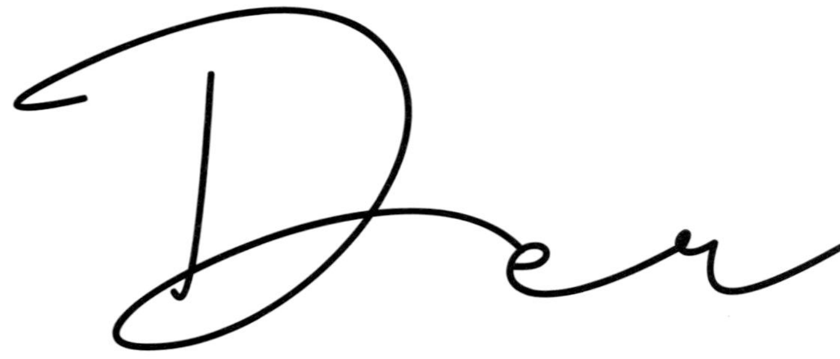

An exhibition by Cosima Rainer and Robert Müller

Friedrich von Berzeviczy-Pallavicini studied at the School of Applied Arts Vienna under Eduard Wimmer-Wisgrill during the 1920s. The influences of the "Moderne Raumkunst" (literally "modern spatial art") and the Wiener Werkstätte—especially Dagobert Peche's exceptional approach—are clearly reflected in his works, their playful and eccentric pictorial and formal inventions positioning them somewhere between applied and fine art. Berzeviczy-Pallavicini's oeuvre is a classic example of a graphic and painterly art that subscribed to a flamboyant unfurling of forms and a transgression of purist Modernist paradigms. By combining a lucid visual language with an exotic vocabulary oscillating between Rococo and Art Déco, Berzeviczy-Pallavicini celebrated a burlesque crossing of boundaries between tradition and Modernism that has regained currency today. He therefore represents "another Modernism," sometimes even an Anti-Modernism, as also evident in the work of Florine Stettheimer, Cecil Beaton, or in Andy Warhol's early work, but which, in the conflict between ornament and asceticism, or the "right form," was already an object of artistic discourse in fin-de-siècle Vienna.

Around 1900, in Vienna and elsewhere, the conflicting aims and interests in the art world culminated in an engagement with ornament. While some associated ornament with the emergence of modern art, others equated it with the bombast of Historicism. The 1902 Vienna Secession exhibition, to which Josef Hoffmann contributed an abstract, decorative overdoor relief, is paradigmatic for the temporary triumph of ornament. It clearly demonstrates how its forms migrated from the "realms of applied art to the realm of fine art."[1] In art history, the way for this development had been paved in Alois Riegl's *Stilfragen* (*Problems of Style*), published in 1893, which placed a complete history of ornament as an "art history without names" (Heinrich Wölfflin) alongside the established art-historical narrative. Riegl emphasized the "purely artistic" character of ornament and his aim was to release it from any connotations of inferiority.

But retaliation was not long in coming: Adolf Loos's polemical work *Ornament und Verbrechen* (*Ornament and Crime*) of 1908 is still highly influential, a work that is far more nuanced than its title would suggest. Although initially mainly a "malicious" battle cry raised against his professional rivals, such as Josef Hoffmann and the Wiener Werkstätte, its denigrations of ornament fell on fertile ground at the time and have continued to resonate throughout the twentieth century—whose Modernism was dominated by "functionalism" or a formal and abstract "autonomy"—and still holds sway even today.

It is along this historical fault line and this ideological rift, which only recently has begun to heal, that Berzeviczy-Pallavicini's oeuvre can be positioned, an art that is eccentric in every sense of the word.

Addressing this complex topic was also an implicit objective of this exhibition. *Der Hausfreund* is not only concerned with presenting the artist's rich estate in the collection of the University of Applied Arts Vienna. It also seeks to aesthetically examine the specific connotations permeating his oeuvre. The following text will further explore some of these motifs in relation to both Berzeviczy-Pallavicini's art and to the accompanying works by other artists in the exhibition.

When first encountering the artist's work, one may be surprised by the gentle dominance inherent in the high degree of creative subjectivation as well as by his seemingly unbridled delight in decoration. In his works, which make abundant use of coded motifs in a recurring system, a great deal of subconscious content is processed by his hand—which is at times accurate, at times slightly slapdash. However, interestingly, this aesthetic assertion of the "ego," for all its highly individual expression, does not come across as "original." Rather, the subjects and pictorial creations have a sense of the conventional, formulaic, and

1 See Markus Brüderlin, ed., *Ornament und Abstraktion*, exh. cat. Fondation Beyele, Riehen/Basel (Cologne, 2001), p. 120.

Hausfreund

Eine Ausstellung von Cosima Rainer und Robert Müller

Friedrich von Berzeviczy-Pallavicini studierte in den 1920er-Jahren an der Wiener Kunstgewerbeschule bei Eduard Wimmer-Wisgrill. Die Einflüsse der modernen Raumkunst und der Wiener Werkstätte, und hierbei besonders der exzeptionelle Ansatz Dagobert Peches, spiegelten sich intensiv in seinen Arbeiten wider, die sich mit ihren spielerischen und exzentrischen Bild- und Formfindungen im Spannungsfeld zwischen angewandter und bildender Kunst bewegen. Berzeviczy-Pallavicini steht somit paradigmatisch für grafische sowie künstlerische Verfahren, die sich einer ausschweifenden Entfaltung der Formen, aber auch einer Transgression modernistischer Reinheitsparadigmen verschrieben. Durch die Kombination einer klaren Gestaltungssprache mit einem exotischen, zwischen Rokoko und Art déco oszillierenden Vokabular zelebrierte Berzeviczy-Pallavicini burleske Grenzüberschreitungen zwischen Tradition und Moderne, die gerade heute wieder aktuell erscheinen. Er steht damit repräsentativ für eine „andere Moderne" oder bisweilen gar Anti-Moderne, wie sie sich auch in den künstlerischen Arbeiten etwa Florine Stettheimers, Cecil Beatons oder des frühen Andy Warhol zeigt und die bereits im Wien der Jahrhundertwende im Konflikt zwischen Ornament und Askese bzw. der „richtigen Form" Gegenstand der gestalterischen Diskussionen war.

Um die Jahrhundertwende kulminierten – nicht nur in Wien – die widersprüchlichen Bestrebungen und Interessen innerhalb des Kunstfelds vor allem in der Auseinandersetzung um das Ornament. War das Ornament für die einen mit der Entstehung der modernen Kunst verbunden, setzten es die anderen mit dem Schwulst des Historismus gleich. Als paradigmatisch für die zwischenzeitliche Durchsetzung des Ornaments gilt die Ausstellung der Wiener Secessionisten von 1902, zu der Josef Hoffmann ein abstrakt-ornamentales Supraportenrelief beisteuerte. An ihm zeigte sich prominent, wie dessen Formen von den „Gefilden der angewandten Kunst in das Gefilde der bildenden Kunst" wanderten.[1] Kunsthistorisch vorbereitet wurde diese Sichtweise bereits 1893 von Alois Riegl in *Stilfragen*, der eine durchgehende Entwicklungsgeschichte für das Ornament konstruierte und als „Kunstgeschichte ohne Namen" (Heinrich Wölfflin) neben die große Kunstgeschichte stellte. Riegl betonte in dieser Schrift das „rein künstlerische" Wesen des Ornaments und wollte es von den Konnotationen des Minderwertigen befreien.

Doch der Gegenschlag ließ nicht lange auf sich warten: Bis heute prägend wurde vor allem Adolf Loos' polemische (und wesentlich differenziertere als dem Titel nach anzunehmende) Schrift *Ornament und Verbrechen* von 1908. Obwohl sie zunächst nur eine „bösartige" Kampfansage gegen seine beruflichen Konkurrenten, unter anderem Josef Hoffmann und die Wiener Werkstätte, war, wirkten ihre auch im Zeitkontext auf fruchtbaren Boden fallenden Abwertungen durch eine vornehmlich im Verlauf des 20. Jahrhunderts „funktionalistische" oder von gestalterischer und abstrakter „Autonomie" geprägte Moderne bis in die Gegenwart.

An dieser historischen Bruchlinie entlang, deren Graben sich zunehmend in der jüngeren Zeit auch ideologisch zu schließen beginnt, verläuft nicht nur die im Wortsinn „*ex*zentrische" Praxis Berzeviczy-Pallavicinis. Die Thematisierung dieses Komplexes ist auch der implizite Gegenstand dieser Ausstellung. Das Anliegen von *Der Hausfreund* ist mithin nicht nur die Präsentation von dessen reichem Nachlass in der Kunstsammlung der Universität für angewandte Kunst Wien. Sie ist auch eine ästhetische Untersuchung der spezifischen Konnotationen, die dieses Lebenswerk durchziehen. Im Folgenden seien einige dieser Motive in Bezug auf Berzeviczy-Pallavicinis Arbeiten und die begleitenden Positionen in der Ausstellung eingehender besprochen.

Wer der Produktion des Künstlers zum ersten Mal begegnet, ist überrascht von der sanften Dominanz, die das

1 Siehe dazu Markus Brüderlin, (Hg.) *Ornament und Abstraktion*, Ausst.-Kat. Fondation Beyeler, Riehen/Basel, Köln 2001, S. 120.

reticent about them, as if decisive aspects of the message were dwelling beyond the picture in some shape or form that does not readily materialize. This paradox appears especially in the few "autonomous" pictures we know of, such as, for example, in *Portrait of a Young Woman*, thought to be from around 1950, in which a twig intrudes into the picture space from the right, evoking some hidden context, thus slightly unsettling this otherwise statuesque composition.

The painting *Doblando* of 1955, a bizarre, erotically charged image of a bullfight, is combined with motifs from Mexico's Día de Muertos (Day of the Dead), thereby merging the abstract-fantastical traits of the composition with highly coded structures of desire, while at the same time adopting an almost medieval style for its schematic figures.

It soon becomes apparent that these pictorial worlds are characterized above all by the presentation of a timeless narrative. No radio, television, or car serves to date these worlds. They invoke other codes and forms: fairy tales, myths, Orientalizing scenes, nursery rhymes, *fêtes galantes* reminiscent of Watteau, bouquets, masques, and balls define the pictorial program. Although the figures are mostly assigned clear functions and specific actions, these motifs nevertheless seem depersonalized. The frequently recurring variations of the same elements have something highly stylized and artificial. However, even their exaggerations have forerunners.

One example of this is the work of Berzeviczy's teacher Eduard Wimmer-Wisgrill (1882–1961). Long acknowledged as a key pioneer of Viennese fashion, he was in charge of the Wiener Werkstätte's fashion department from 1907. From 1918, he was also head of the Vienna School of Applied Arts' workshops for fashion design and textiles. Aside from clothes and fashion accessories, he also designed furniture and other everyday objects. Together with Josef Hoffmann he was an important supporter and patron of Berzeviczy-Pallavicini. In the 1950s, Wimmer-Wisgrill also emerged as a prolific painter, with portraits of young men central to this late oeuvre, two of which were shown in the exhibition. Visible in the background of some of these portrayals are the screens and works of his student and friend Berzeviczy-Pallavicini, clearly revealing his floral, eccentric style.

In these works—as in Berzeviczy-Pallavicini's early floral furniture designs that were also on display—the proximity to Dagobert Peche (1887–1923) is particularly apparent. Peche's work, deemed as overly flamboyant and decadent, was likewise forgotten for many years. From 1911, Peche worked in all departments of the Wiener Werkstätte, developing an unusually experimental approach to applied art. He evoked surreal atmospheres with the skill of a set designer, decorating whole museum spaces with swathes of fabric, with artfully positioned ornaments, and display cases adorned with frills. He countered the rationalist approach to architecture with his drawings of "fantasy architecture." In this, he was also referencing artists like Aubrey Beardsley with his salacious style and penchant for the grotesque.

In addition to reverberations of, and enthusiasm for, Dagobert Peche, many of Berzeviczy's motifs reveal clear overlaps with other protagonists from his era. The obligatory butterfly is a good example, appearing in the work of artists like Erté or Florine Stettheimer as well as Cecil Beaton, coupled with representational modes and conventions that share the enthusiasm and influence of early scenic presentations of Modernism, such as the costume designs by Léon Bakst.

Floral echoes can also be found in the early work of Josef Frank (1885–1967), one of the most significant architects and applied artists of Modernism, whose works, owing to their conceptual closeness between decoration and avant-garde architectural sculpture—which makes his art all the more fascinating today—were long considered as contrary to the heroic, "progressive" narrative of the avant-garde, a fate that he shared with Peche.

From 1919 to 1925, Frank was a teacher at the School of Applied Arts in Vienna and his designs and writings reveal him as an exponent of a less dogmatic Modernism. He was involved with Vienna's social housing movement and a champion of Garden Cities. In 1925, he founded the home furnishings company Haus & Garten, together with Oskar Wlach and Walter Sobotka. Besides printed linen and upholstered furniture, the company specialized in lightweight, individual pieces of furniture that could be flexibly arranged in the room. Josef Frank's fantastical fabric designs are legendary. Berzeviczy-Pallavicini probably also produced a number of designs for the Haus & Garten range.

It was not only in these early years that Friedrich Berzeviczy-Pallavicini varied his signatures, sometimes signing his work Fritz Berzeviczy, sometimes Federico Pallavicini, while still retaining his "telltale" and consistent style even in later years. These works, however, are often difficult to date. For one thing, they were increasingly created without connection to a particular publication, commission, or exhibition. Furthermore, as already mentioned, their style eludes any connection with current vogues and, even when conceived as "autonomous" works, they persistently hark back to variations on serial themes and motifs. These include cats, flowers, butterflies, seasons, zodiac signs, alphabets and occupations, whose depictions conjure up a kind of "Fourth Rococo," happily ignoring contemporary themes and stylistic trends (it is no coincidence that Pallavicini collected souvenirs from debutante balls and other courtly festivities as well as richly decorated, crystal Easter eggs).

Although Pallavicini was occasionally receptive to contemporary depictions, for example in *Doblando*, as already mentioned, or in his costume designs and drawings for the magazine *Flair*, this influence is only really noticeable in his very early works. For example, his interior designs and tapestries for *A Lady's Boudoir*—dating from 1929 when Pallavicini was still a student—combine design with Modernist, geometric décor, while the choice of material

hohe Maß der gestalterischen Subjektivierung einnimmt, aber auch von der scheinbar ungebrochenen Lust am Dekor. In seinen Arbeiten, die ein hohes Maß an codierten Motiven in einer wiederkehrenden Systematik verwenden, ordnet die mitunter akkurate, mitunter leicht nachlässig gezogene „Handschrift" vieles vom bisweilen ganz unterbewusst verhandelten Inhalt ein. Dieses ästhetisch ungebrochene „Ich", obgleich in hohem Maß individuell im Ausdruck, erscheint jedoch interessanterweise nicht als „originell". Den Sujets und Bildfindungen haftet vielmehr etwas Konventionelles, Formelhaftes und Verschlossenes an, als würden entscheidende Aspekte des Vermittelten in einer Form außerhalb des Bildes wohnen, die sich nicht ohne Weiteres materialisiert. Dieses Paradox tritt besonders in den wenigen uns bekannten „autonomen" Bildern auf, in denen sich, wie etwa in *Bildnis einer jungen Dame*, das vermutlich um 1950 entstanden ist, ein kleiner Zweig von rechts ins Bild schiebt und so einen verborgenen Kontext evoziert, der in der sonst statuarischen Komposition eine leichte Unsicherheit mitvermittelt.

Die Malerei *Doblando* von 1955, deren seltsam erotische Aufladung Handlungen der Corrida nachzuvollziehen scheint, paart diese dann mit Motiven aus dem mexikanischen „Día de Muertos" und verschränkt somit die gleichsam abstrakt-fantastischen Züge der Bildkonstruktion mit höchst codierten Begehrensstrukturen, bedient sich dabei aber zugleich einer fast „mittelalterlichen", schematischen Figuration.

Schnell wird klar, dass diese Bildwelten gerade durch die Aufführung von überzeitlichen Handlungen charakterisiert sind. Kein Radio, kein Fernseher, kein Auto erscheint darin und ‚datiert' diese Welten. Andere Codes und Formen werden hier angerufen: Märchen, Mythen, orientalisierende Szenen, Kinderreime, Fêtes Galantes à la Watteau, Bouquets, Masken und Bälle bestimmen das Bildprogramm. Auch wenn den Figuren zumeist klare Funktionen zugewiesen sind und sie spezifische Handlungen vollziehen, so erscheinen diese Motive dennoch depersonalisiert. Die immer wieder variierten und (wieder)verwendeten Elemente haben etwas äußerst stilisiertes, artifizielles. Aber auch ihre Übersteigerungen haben Vorläufer.

Eduard Wimmer-Wisgrill (1882–1961) beispielsweise, in dessen Klasse Berzeviczy eintrat, gilt bis heute als zentraler Pionier der Wiener Mode und leitete ab 1907 die Modeabteilung der Wiener Werkstätte. Seit 1918 war er auch Leiter der Werkstätten für Mode und Modezeichnen und der Werkstätten für Textilarbeiten an der Wiener Kunstgewerbeschule. Neben Kleidern und Modeaccessoires entwarf er Möbelstücke und andere Gebrauchsgegenstände. Gemeinsam mit Josef Hoffmann gehörte er zu den wichtigen Unterstützern und Förderern von Berzeviczy-Pallavicini. Ab den 1950er-Jahren schuf er eine Vielzahl von Gemälden. Porträtdarstellungen junger Männer, von denen zwei auch in der Ausstellung gezeigt wurden, sind ein zentraler Teil seines malerischen (Spät-) Werks. Im Hintergrund einiger Bildnisse kann man ebenjene Paravents und Arbeiten seines Schülers und Freundes Berzeviczy-Pallavicini erkennen, die den floralen, exzentrischen Duktus am besten zeigen.

Hier wird – neben den ebenfalls gezeigten frühen, mit Blütenformen spielenden Möbelentwürfen Berzeviczy-Pallavicinis – auch die Nähe zu Dagobert Peche (1887–1923) deutlich. Dessen Werk war ebenfalls lange Zeit wegen seines überbordenden, als dekadent bezeichneten Stils negiert und vergessen. Peche arbeitete seit 1911 in allen Bereichen der Wiener Werkstätte und entwickelte einen ungewöhnlich experimentellen Umgang mit dem kunstgewerblichen Material. Mit inszenatorischem Geschick erzeugte er surreale Stimmungen und dekorierte ganze Museumsräume mit Stoffbahnen, mit kunstvoll eingesetzten Ornamenten und rüschenbesetzten Vitrinen. Der rationalistischen Auffassung von Architektur setzte er seine zeichnerische „Phantasie-Architektur" entgegen. Dabei nahm er auch Bezug auf Künstler wie Aubrey Beardsley und dessen frivolen Stil und Hang zum Grotesken.

Neben Anklängen und Begeisterung für diesen finden sich bei vielen von Berzeviczys Motiven zugleich deutliche Überschneidungen mit anderen Protagonisten seiner Epoche; so etwa exemplarisch der obligatorische Schmetterling, der sich ebenso bei Künstler*innen wie Erté oder Florine Stettheimer wie bei Cecil Beaton findet, gepaart mit Darstellungsformen und -konventionen, die Begeisterung und den Einfluss früher szenischer Darstellungen der Moderne teilen, wie etwa die Kostümentwürfe von Léon Bakst.

Floralen Widerhall finden die frühen Jahre auch im Werk von Josef Frank (1885–1967), einem der bedeutendsten Architekten und angewandten Künstler der Moderne, dessen Arbeiten aber auch aufgrund einer konzeptuellen und heute umso spannenderen Nähe von Dekoration einerseits und avantgardistischer Bauplastik andererseits lange Zeit einer heroischen, „progressiven" Erzählung der Avantgarde entgegenliefen, ein Schicksal, das auch die Rezeption von Peches Œuvre lange Zeit teilte.

Frank war von 1919 bis 1925 Lehrer an der Wiener Kunstgewerbeschule und vertrat mit seinen Entwürfen und Schriften eine eher undogmatische Moderne. Er beschäftigte sich mit der Arbeiterwohnungsfrage und war ein Verfechter der Siedlungs- und Gartenstadtbewegung. Gemeinsam mit Oskar Wlach und Walter Sobotka gründete er 1925 das Einrichtungsunternehmen *Haus & Garten*. Neben bedrucktem Leinen und Polstermöbeln führte das Unternehmen vor allem leichte Solitärmöbel, die flexibel im Raum platziert werden konnten. Die fantastischen Stoffmuster Josef Franks sind legendär. Vermutlich fertigte auch Berzeviczy-Pallavicini einige Entwürfe für das Sortiment von *Haus & Garten* an.

Es ist aber in diesen frühen Jahren nicht allein Friedrich Berzeviczy-Pallavicini, der zwischen den Signaturen wandelt, mal mit Fritz Berzeviczy, mal mit Federico Pallavicini signiert, er behält dabei auch in späteren Jahren einen „verräterischen" und konstanten Strich bei. Diese Arbeiten

and composition show a strong interest in handmade, decorative luxury goods. These are rooms far removed from the International Style or any Constructivist influence. Their vocabulary remains a diverting adornment without questioning the established social order. It is still operating within the framework of the applied arts and not, as was contemporaneously the case at the Bauhaus, in an industrial context.

In the same way as Berzeviczy-Pallavicini's art, the work of Marianne "My" Ullmann (1905–95) and Elisabeth Karlinsky (1904–94) was first introduced to a wider public at the sixtieth anniversary exhibition of the School of Applied Arts Vienna. Elisabeth Karlinsky began her studies at the School of Applied Arts in 1921, where she designed a number of flamboyant costumes, which were shown in the exhibition. Later on she worked as an illustrator and designed window displays for the department stores Macy's and Gimbels in New York. Marianne "My" Ullmann, like Karlinsky, studied in Franz Čižek's department of ornamental form theory, where Viennese Kineticism was born. Ullmann's costume designs from her later student years reveal the influence of Frederick Kiesler's *International Exhibition of New Theater Technology*, held in autumn 1924, where she would have seen Oskar Schlemmer's figurines from the Bauhaus Ballet and the Russian revolutionary ballet. Her costume designs shown in this exhibition were created for the 1933 carnival ball at the Berlin School of Applied Arts. These themes have been further elaborated with works by other artists from then and now.

Ulrike Müller (born 1971) has for a long time been interested in perspectives suppressed from the modern canon and belittled as ornamental, folkloric, or decorative. She deliberately chooses materials like enamel or textiles, the traditional domain of women in the applied arts. In the exhibition she juxtaposed her enamel works with a selection of Berzeviczy-Pallavicini's designs for confectionery wrappers. The brightly painted floorplan forms, which appear to have been flipped into a vertical position, oscillate between functional sketch and unexplained shape.

The ornamental vase by Amelie von Wulffen and Nico Ihlein also engages in a provocative game with anti-Modern—in this case Baroque—formal vocabulary, venturing into the field of tension between applied and fine art. Using the medium of paint, Amelie von Wulffen (born 1966) deploys acerbic satire and astute analysis to examine what is repressed by society. Nico Ihlein (born 1972), meanwhile, works conceptually with bizarre, outmoded décor elements and materials. In his grotesque arrangements of vases, tables, wall hangings, and images, reminiscent of displays in home furnishing stores, the repressed hits back with a vulgar charm.

The works of Min Yoon (born 1986), on the other hand, reveal echoes of Berzeviczy-Pallavicini's floral eccentricity. He exhibits oversized leaves sewn from leather, complete with artificial rips and holes. Repeatedly, he resorts to techniques from "applied art" and uses the tools of art production—pencils, ballpoint pens, paint tubes, and canvas—as the self-referential subject of his pictures. Min Yoon playfully engages with moments of trompe l'oeil and mimicry. In his assiduous handiwork he pushes himself to the limits, thereby demonstrating the absurdity of aspiring to artistic mastery.

Julian Göthe (born 1966) references a formal repertoire familiar from Baroque and Rococo in his sculptures and drawings, in which he transforms candelabras, obelisques, and cartouches into monstrous figures. His approach recalls Giovanni Battista Piranesi (1720–78), who, with his *Capriccios*, playfully amassed classical shapes into whimsical architectural fantasies. Göthe's drawings are equally fantastical. They show surreal collages of anti-Modern ornamentation, psychedelically distorting and interpenetrating one another. Influenced by the film sets of legendary Hollywood Art Déco designers, he explores the margins of art and design history. Göthe's vitrine sculpture, created especially for this exhibition, displayed a selection of Berzeviczy-Pallavicini's abstract rug designs.

In Berzeviczy-Pallavicini's painted works, the spatial aspect holds a significant position. He created unusual folding screens, tapestries, and rugs, which oscillate between autonomous picture and functional spatial element. Kamilla Bischof (born 1986) works with similar approaches, albeit in reverse, as her paintings idiosyncratically occupy their surroundings in the form of stage-like interiors. Feminine beings and décor objects merge in her images to create allegories of burlesque eroticism. Together with Laura Welker (born 1985), she created a doll's-house sculpture to serve as a set for the film *Victoria's Secret Subtenants* (2018). The doll's house comprises elaborately decorated rooms dominated by an abundance of trashy found objects and hysterical pinks. The film shows two gloved hands that lasciviously and humorously perform erotic-esoteric scenes before eventually preparing pizza dough in a bathtub.

As an alternative approach to a visually encoded (social) space, Viennese artist Verena Dengler (born 1981) reiterates traditions from Austrian socialism, such as its formal traces in everyday items. "Fantastic Realism," which emerged in 1950s Vienna, is transformed into "Fantastic Socialism." On another occasion she adorned one of her room dividers with the well-known Gmunden Ceramic décor. In contrast to Berzeviczy-Pallavicini, however, Dengler explicitly uses her own biography as a marker and, based on a by no means classless popular culture, converts this into a living ornament. She transfers existing cultural conditions into the realm of the visible, without sparing her own physical self.

sind allerdings oft schwierig zu datieren. Nicht nur entstehen sie zunehmend ohne konkrete Publikation oder zuordenbare Beauftragung oder Ausstellung, sie entziehen sich auch gestalterisch, wie schon erwähnt, aktiv einem modischen Bezug oder greifen auch dort, wo sie „autonome" Produktion nachstellen, auf seriell verhandelte Thematiken und Motive zurück und variieren diese beharrlich.

Zu diesen Motiven gehören Katzen, Blumen, Schmetterlinge, Jahreszeiten, Sternzeichen, Alphabete und Berufe, deren Darstellung gewissermaßen eine Art „Viertes Rokoko" herbeizitiert und an aktuellen oder zeitgeschichtlichen Themen oder Gestaltungstendenzen unbeeindruckt vorübergeht (nicht ohne Grund war Pallavicini ein Sammler von Hofballcotillons oder reich dekorierten, kristallenen Ostereiern).

Auch wenn Pallavicini bisweilen empfänglich war für zeittypische Darstellungen, etwa beim bereits erwähnten *Doblando* oder den Kostümentwürfen und Zeichnungen für das Magazin *Flair*, so wird doch ein starker Einfluss davon lediglich in den sehr frühen Arbeiten deutlich. So verbinden sich etwa in den Raumgestaltungen oder Gobelinentwürfen für das *Boudoir einer Dame*, 1929 – also noch in Studienzeiten Pallavicinis –, Entwürfe mit modernistisch-geometrisierenden Dekoren, allerdings mit dezidiertem Interesse in Materialwahl und Gestaltung an manueller, dekorativer Luxusgüterproduktion. Es sind Räume, weit entfernt von „International Style" oder gar konstruktivistischer Prägung. Das Vokabular bleibt auflockernde Dekoration im gesellschaftlichen Rahmen innerhalb der gegebenen sozialen Ordnung. Der Verhandlungsrahmen bleibt weiterhin das (Kunst-)Handwerk, nicht, wie etwa gleichzeitig am Bauhaus, die Industrie.

Die Arbeiten von Marianne My Ullmann (1905–95) und Elisabeth Karlinsky (1904–94) beispielsweise wurden, ebenso wie die von Berzeviczy-Pallavicini, erstmals 1929 mit der Ausstellung *60 Jahre Wiener Kunstgewerbeschule* in die öffentliche Wahrnehmung gerückt. Elisabeth Karlinsky studierte ab 1921 an der Wiener Kunstgewerbeschule und entwarf eine Reihe „flamboyanter" Kostüme, die in der Ausstellung zu sehen sind. Später betätigte sie sich als Illustratorin und gestaltete Auslagen für die Kaufhäuser Macy's und Gimbels in New York. Wie Elisabeth Karlinsky studierte auch Marianne My Ullmann in Franz Čižeks Abteilung für ornamentale Formenlehre, welche als Keimzelle des Wiener Kinetismus gilt. An Ullmanns Kostümentwürfen ihrer späten Studienjahre lässt sich zudem der Einfluss der im Herbst 1924 von Friedrich Kiesler organisierten *Internationalen Ausstellung neuer Theatertechnik* nachvollziehen, bei der unter anderem Oskar Schlemmers Figurinen des Bauhausballetts und russischen Revolutionsballetts vorgestellt wurden. Die gezeigten Kostümentwürfe fertigte Ullmann für die Ausstattung des Faschingsballs der Berliner Kunstgewerbeschule 1933 an. In der Ausstellung werden diese Themenfelder auch anhand anderer zeitgenössischer und aktueller Positionen umkreist.

Das Interesse der Künstlerin Ulrike Müller (*1971) gilt beispielsweise seit langem Positionen, die aus dem modernen Kanon verdrängt und als ornamental, folkloristisch oder dekorativ abgewertet wurden. Indem sie Materialien wie Emaille oder Textilien verwendet, knüpft sie zudem an Bereiche an, die im Kunstgewerbe speziell Frauen zugewiesen wurden. In der Ausstellung stellt sie ihre Emaille-Arbeiten einer Auswahl von Bonbonverpackungs-Entwürfen Berzeviczy-Pallavicinis gegenüber. Die buntbemalten aufgeklappten Grundrissformen changieren zwischen funktionaler Skizze und ungeklärter Form.

Auch die ausgestellte Prunkvase von Amelie von Wulffen und Nico Ihlein begibt sich in das provokative Spiel mit antimodernem, hier barockem Formenvokabular und damit ins Spannungsfeld zwischen angewandter und bildender Kunst. Amelie von Wulffen (*1966) arbeitet mit beißender Satire und analytischer Schärfe mit den Mitteln der Malerei an einer Auseinandersetzung mit dem gesellschaftlich Verdrängten. Nico Ihlein (*1972) wiederum arbeitet konzeptuell mit absurden, unzeitgemäßen Dekorelementen und Materialien. In seinen grotesken Arrangements aus Vasen, Tischchen, Wandbespannung und Bild, die an Displays erinnern, wie man sie aus Einrichtungshäusern kennt, schlägt das Verdrängte mit vulgärem Charme zurück.

In Werken von Min Yoon (*1986) spiegelt sich wiederum die florale Exzentrik Berzeviczy-Pallavicinis wider. Er stellt überdimensionale Blätter aus, die aus Leder genäht und mit künstlichen Rissen und Löchern versehen sind. Immer wieder greift er Techniken aus der „angewandten Kunst" auf und macht Werkzeuge der Kunstproduktion wie Bleistifte, Kugelschreiber, Farbtuben und Leinwandstoffe zum selbstreferenziellen Inhalt seiner Bilder. Min Yoon spielt mit Momenten von Trompe-l'Œil und Mimikry. Mit akribischer Handarbeit vollführt er eine Verausgabung, die das Absurde von Meisterschaft im Kunstkontext demonstriert.

Julian Göthe (*1966) bezieht sich in seinen Skulpturen und Zeichnungen bereits seit langem auf ein Formenrepertoire, das man aus Barock und Rokoko kennt. Unter seiner Hand verwandeln sich die Kandelaber, Obelisken und Kartuschen aber in monströse Gestalten. Sein Zugang erinnert damit an die *Capriccios* Giovanni Battista Piranesis (1720–78), der mit seinem spielerischen Gebrauch antiker Formenelemente launische Architekturfantasien schuf. Ebenso fantastisch muten Göthes Zeichnungen an. Sie zeigen surreale Collagen antimoderner Ornamentik, die sich in psychedelischer Weise gegenseitig verformen und durchdringen. Beeinflusst von den Filmsets legendärer Art-déco-Hollywood-Designer, erkundet er die Ränder der Kunst- und Designgeschichte. In einer von Göthe eigens für die Ausstellung entworfenen Vitrinenskulptur wird eine Auswahl der abstrakten Teppichentwürfe Berzeviczy-Pallavicinis gezeigt.

The painted installations by Scottish artist Lucy McKenzie (born 1977), meanwhile, often employ trompe-l'oeil effects. Her objects in the exhibition reference the Hungarian graphic designer and illustrator Kató Lukáts (1900–90), a contemporary and colleague of Berzeviczy-Pallavicini. While Berzeviczy-Pallavicini was designing for the confectioners Demel on Kohlmarkt, Lukáts was creating the packaging for nearby chocolatiers Altmann & Kühne on the Graben. Retaining their original size, Lucy McKenzie recreated these small, quirkily glamorous chocolate boxes, in which Neoclassical reinterpretations of anachronistic forms and motifs are combined with new materials and key ideas of Modernism. Like Pallavicini's work for Demel, Kató Lukáts's packaging and decorations were extremely successful and are still being made and used today.

Hans Hollein (1934–2014) was the architect of the Austrian Embassy in Berlin and as such had a strong influence on the setting of the Berlin exhibition. With his tongue-in-cheek, quote-laden references, he was a key protagonist of a Postmodernism inspired by James Stirling that stood in deliberate opposition to the "second postwar Modernism" prevailing in the 1960s. Also included in the exhibition were some of his designs for the Österreichisches Verkehrsbüro, a public-sector company set up to promote tourism and foreign travel for Austrians, for which Hollein designed several branches. His stage-like setting for the branch on Opernring in Vienna is particularly well known. The plethora of quotations he dipped into for its interior, which was destroyed in 1987, ranged from the postal savings bank building designed by Otto Wagner to direct references to exoticizing buildings (John Nash, Royal Kitchen, Brighton Pavilion, 1818) and even to colonial architecture (Ákos Moravánszky mentions the India Gate by Edwin Lutyens, 1921). It is a fantasy landscape, far removed from the cosmopolitan self-perception, which reveals distant flashes of Pallavicini's associated "exoticism."

Jack Smith (1932–89) is considered one of the central figures of the "other" New York. The exhibition featured the announcement he designed for Charles Ludlam's play *Big Hotel*, which was later restaged under the name *When Queens Collide* with the Ridiculous Theatre Company—so influential for the Greenwich Village gay and drag culture—and whose plot draws on advertising, Hollywood, pulp, and high literature. In a few Sharpie strokes, he indicates palms and camels, escalating the scene in his final poster design, in which he transforms this Orientalizing fantasy into a derailed orgiastic extravaganza with elephants and a burning palace, reminiscent of Flaubert's *Salammbô*. In his miniatures, Smith emerges as a protagonist of underground cinema, and works like *Flaming Creatures* (1961)—intensely promoted by Jonas "Uncle Fishhook" Mekas, and very soon a victim of censorship—exerted a decisive influence on artists like Andy Warhol and John Waters.

Artists Amy Lien (born 1987), Enzo Camacho (born 1985), and artist and photographer Ilya Lipkin (born 1983) are contemporary representatives of a global Bohemianism that operates in constantly changing networks. Their work shown at the exhibition was originally created as part of a photo series for *Starship* magazine, founded in Vienna but later relocated to Berlin. They discovered the five motifs in this work during a residency in Milan. Certain pictorial elements accentuate the local recognizability: An Ettorre Sottsass bookcase anchors the work in place and time. Combined with a Baroque chair, it conveys the grounded elegance of sophisticated flea-market Postmodernism, whole fish suggest a proximity to the sea or, at the very least, a Mediterranean decadence, and cables simulate the interconnectedness of a global *jeunesse dorée* (gilded youth). The surfaces of the milieu within which Berzeviczy-Pallavicini's designs and works still merged seamlessly have become faded signifiers, captured in an attempt to show indexical traces, but without offering any guarantees to the audience. No longer is there any certainty as to which social space one is shaping, and yet, however weak the signal, communication is continued.

In 1965, Yves Saint Laurent (1936–2008) designed his now iconic Mondrian costume; however, at around the same time, he also created similar costumes for Roland Petit's ballet *Notre Dame de Paris* (based on *The Hunchback of Notre Dame*, music: Maurice Jarre), which ran successfully at the Opéra Garnier for decades. Here Mondrian's influence is particularly evident in the designs for the costume of Captain Phoebus. Whereas the main costume design is heroic and statuesque, focusing on the effect of its colors—which YSL had conceived to echo the cathedral's stained glass—the variation shown in the exhibition, intended for the pas de deux with Esmeralda, is entirely designed to emphasize the now undressed figure, the desire that stands at the center of the framework plot, and its (fatal) eroticism. The rippling blue, planar cape, contrasting with the black lines, is abandoned in favor of the fetishistic design of a skin-tight costume, its belt-shaped lines forming a cross and thus subtly reflecting the story's context onto the performer's body.

Although this specifically European and post-aristocratic jet-set culture may now be a thing of the past, its cultural markers have not yet vanished ("social drag"). Today, these are mainly adopted by a homosexual subculture that inverts its insignia and opens them up to new spaces. Katharina Wulff (born 1968) describes one such space—which has also been addressed, since the early 1990s, by artists like Kai Althoff and Lukas Duwenhögger and their paintings—by inverting the apparatus of desire: décor, accessories, eccentric figuration, embodiment without subject. Her figurations are flanked by the subtle, sometimes surreal, codes that surround the sphere of painterly production.

In Berzeviczy-Pallavicinis malerischer Produktion kommt dem raumgreifenden Aspekt eine wichtige Stellung zu. Er entwickelte ungewöhnliche Paravents, Gobelins und Teppiche, die zwischen eigenständigem Bild und räumlichem funktionalem Element changieren. Auf umgekehrte Weise arbeitet Kamilla Bischof (*1986) mit ähnlichen Herangehensweisen in ihren Malereien, die sich eigenwillig auf den Umraum in Form von bühnenhaften Interieurs ausbreiten. In ihren Bildern vermischen sich feminine Wesen und Dekorobjekte zu Allegorien burlesker Erotik. In Zusammenarbeit von Kamilla Bischof und Laura Welker (*1985) entstand eine Puppenhausskulptur, die als Drehort für den Film *Victoria's Secret Subtenants* (2018) diente. Das Puppenhaus setzt sich aus aufwändig dekorierten Räumen zusammen, die von einer Überfülle trashiger Fundstücke und von hysterisch-pinken Farbtönen dominiert werden. Der Film zeigt zwei Hände, die, in Handschuhe gekleidet, lasziv und humorvoll interagieren, erotisch-esoterische Szenen durchspielen und schließlich Pizzateig in einer Badewanne zubereiten.

Als alternative Annäherung an einen bildhaft codierten (Gesellschafts-)Raum greift die Wiener Künstlerin Verena Dengler (*1981) Traditionen eines österreichischen Sozialismus immer wieder auf, etwa seine formalen Überreste in den Dingen des täglichen Gebrauchs. Aus dem *Phantastischen Realismus*, der sich in den 1950er-Jahren in Wien manifestierte, wird bei ihr ein „Fantastischer Sozialismus", ein andermal ziert ein Dekor der Gmundner Keramik Manufaktur die Oberfläche einen ihrer Raumteiler. Anders als bei Berzeviczy-Pallavicini soll bei Dengler die Verfasstheit der eigenen Biografie aber explizit als Marker funktionieren und anhand einer schwer als klassenlos zu lesenden Populärkultur zum lebenden Ornament verbaut werden. Die vorgefundenen kulturellen Bedingungen überführt sie in den Bereich des Sichtbaren, ohne den eigenen körperlichen Einsatz dabei auszusparen.

Die malerischen Installationen der schottischen Künstlerin Lucy McKenzie (*1977) wiederum arbeiten oft mit Trompe-l'Œil-Effekten. Die von ihr ausgestellten Objekte referenzieren auf das Schaffen der ungarischen Grafikdesignerin und Illustratorin Kató Lukáts (1900–90), einer Zeitgenossin und Kollegin Berzeviczy-Pallavicinis. Während er für die Konditorei Demel am Kohlmarkt entwarf, designte Lukáts die Verpackungen für die benachbarte Wiener Confiserie *Altmann und Kühne* am Graben. In diesen kleinen, in der Realität durchaus verschrobenglamourösen Gebrauchsgegenständen, in denen Pralinés aufbewahrt werden können und die Lucy McKenzie in Originalgröße nachstellt, verbanden sich neoklassizistische Reinterpretationen von anachronistischen Formen und Motiven mit neuen Materialien und zentralen Ideen der Moderne. Kató Lukáts Verpackungen und Dekore waren, wie jene Pallavicinis für Demel, äußerst erfolgreich und werden bis heute produziert und verwendet.

Hans Hollein (1934–2014), der mit seiner Architektursprache auch die Österreichische Botschaft in Berlin prägte und somit gleichsam den Rahmen der Berliner Ausstellung absteckt, ist mit seinem ironisierenden und zitatbeladenen Referenzprogramm zentraler Protagonist einer an James Stirling geschulten Postmoderne, die sich in Opposition zur „zweiten Nachkriegsmoderne" setzt. In der Ausstellung zusätzlich gezeigt wurden einige seiner Entwürfe für das Österreichische Verkehrsbüro, eine staatliche GmbH, die der Förderung des Tourismus und der Promotion von Auslandsreisen für Österreicher*innen gewidmet war und für die Hollein gleich mehrere Dependancen umsetzte. Besonders bekannt wurde sein bühnenartiges Setting für die Filiale am Opernring in Wien. Die Zitatpalette des 1987 zerstörten Interieurs reichte von Otto Wagners Postsparkasse bis hin zu direkten Bezügen zu exoti(sti)scher (John Nash, Royal Kitchens, Brighton, 1818) oder gar kolonialer Architektur (Ákos Moravánszky nennt hier das India Gate von Edwin Lutyens, 1921). Es ist eine Fantasielandschaft, weit der weltbürgerlichen Selbstverständlichkeit entrückt, in der auch die assoziierte „Exotik" Pallavicinis wie von ferne aufblitzt.

Jack Smith (1932–89) gilt als eine der zentralen Bezugsfiguren eines „anderen" New York. Gezeigt wird die von ihm gestaltete Ankündigung von Charles Ludlams Stück *Big Hotel*, das dieser mit der für die Gay und Drag Culture des Village äußerst einflussreiche Ridiculous Theatre Company unter dem Namen *When Queens Collide* wiederaufführte und dessen Plot sich bei Werbung, Hollywood, Pulp und High Literature bedient. In wenigen Sharpie-Strichen werden Palmen und Kamele angedeutet, die er im finalen Posterentwurf eskaliert, dabei die orientalisierende Fantasie in ein an Flauberts *Salammbô* erinnerndes entgleistes orgiastisches Fest mit Elefanten und brennendem Palast transformierend. In seinen Miniaturen scheint Smith auch als Protagonist des subkulturellen Films auf, dessen Arbeiten wie *Flaming Creatures* (1961) – massiv durch Jonas *Uncle Fishhook* Mekas promotet und alsbald Opfer der Zensur – einen prägenden Einfluss auf Andy Warhol oder John Waters ausübten.

Amy Lien (*1987), Enzo Camacho (*1985) und der mit Fotografie arbeitende Künstler Ilya Lipkin (*1983) wiederum sind zeitgenössische Repräsentant*innen einer globalen Bohème, die in wechselnden Netzwerken lebt und produziert. Ihr gezeigtes Werk entstand ursprünglich im Rahmen einer Bildstrecke für das in Wien gegründete und mittlerweile nach Berlin verlegte Starship Magazin. Gefunden wurden die fünf Motive der Arbeit während einer Residency in Mailand. Einzelne Bildelemente betonen die lokale Erkennbarkeit: Ein Sottsass-Regal markiert den Ort und die Zeit. In Kombination mit dem barocken Sessel verbreitet sich die solide Eleganz gehobener Flohmarkt-Postmoderne, ganze Fische suggerieren eine Nähe zum Meer oder zumindest zu mediterraner Dekadenz, Kabel simulieren die Vernetzung einer globalen Jeunesse dorée. Die

In his capacity as rector, Oswald Oberhuber (1931–2020) designed many pieces of furniture and everyday objects for the University of Applied Arts that are highly symbolic and evocative. Like all of Oberhuber's furniture, the lectern in the exhibition was made from solid oak. It vaguely echoes an architrave, lending an archaic gravitas to the speaker's words, thus forging a connection to the symbolic and temporal environment of Hollein's architecture at the Austrian Cultural Forum in Berlin. At the same time, the form of the two stylized columns frames the speaker's lower body. Oberhuber thus very subtly sexualizes the act of speaking, making it vulnerable while simultaneously defunctionalizing the furniture.

In conclusion it needs to be stated once again that the juxtapositions in the exhibition *Der Hausfreund* can be read as a subjectively organized model showing how it is possible, within the equally subjective and immersive design space of an artist like Berzeviczy-Pallavicini, to suggest (or feign) movements without succumbing to precipitated pigeonholing or a narrow perspective. Its positioning between monograph and commentary was to allow the exhibition's visitors to engage positively with the proliferating constellations of the works, to appreciate their effect and methodology, as well as their constitution as décor and everyday objects brimful with visual stimuli. At the same time, the aim was also to enable a necessary critical distance that would reveal the specific otherness of their aesthetic parameters and of the carrier objects, not only regarding their usage, but also in terms of their social context.

In this respect it was helpful that the exhibition was not shown in a museum context, but first in the grand, historical space of the Heiligenkreuzer Hof in Vienna—originally a religious place, which Oswald Oberhuber had adapted early on as an exhibition venue for the University of Applied Arts—and then in the embassy setting of the Austrian Cultural Forum in Berlin. In both environments, Berzeviczy's works, subtly tinged with nostalgia and retrospection, connect in a meaningful and uncontrived way with narratives that include the dominance of decorum and forms of institutionalized taste, bringing them to the fore through this interaction, while at the same time emphasizing their brittleness and, sometimes quite literal, fragility.

Pallavicini's fragile objects and creations, made in the simplest of materials—his polystyrene pieces sewn with glass beads or elaborately sequined, his window display backdrops with their delicate gold paper or gouache collages pinned to velvet—have something ephemeral and transient. This pictorial program, deeply rooted in another time and society, sometimes oozing nostalgia, casts reflections onto the audience, like flashes from a distant stage, thereby allowing them to observe in a well-disposed way this play with and from another time, which is remote yet simultaneously updated.

Oberflächen des Milieus, in denen Berzeviczy-Pallavicinis Entwürfe und Arbeiten noch nahtlos aufgingen, sind mittlerweile verblasste Signifikanten, festgehalten im Versuch, indexikalische Spuren vorzuführen, aber ohne Gewähr für die Zuschauer*innen. Es ist schon lange nicht mehr selbstverständlich, welchen sozialen Raum man eigentlich gestaltet, und trotzdem wird, sei das Signal noch so schwach, die Kommunikation weitergeführt.

1965 entwirft Yves Saint Laurent (1936–2008) sein mittlerweile ikonisches Mondrian-Kostüm, nahezu gleichzeitig aber auch die ganz ähnlichen Kostüme für Roland Petits jahrzehntelang erfolgreich an der Opéra Garnier laufendes Ballett *Notre Dame de Paris* (*Der Glöckner von Notre Dame*, Musik: Maurice Jarre). Besonders die Dessins für das Kostüm des Hauptmanns Phoebus zeigen den Einfluss Mondrians. Während der zentrale Entwurf für das Kostüm eher heroisch-statuarisch und ganz auf die Farbwirkung ausgelegt ist, die YSL an die Glasfenster der Kathedrale angelehnt wissen wollte, ist die in der Ausstellung gezeigte Variation für das Pas de deux mit Esmeralda ganz auf die Exposition der nun entkleideten Figur, auf das für die Rahmenhandlung zentrale Begehren und ihre (fatale) Erotik abgestellt. Das wallende blaue, mit den schwarzen Linien kontrastierende flächige Cape wird aufgegeben zugunsten einer fetischisierten Gestaltung des hautengen Kostüms, dessen gurtförmige Hauptlinien zudem ein Kreuz formen und damit subtil den Kontext der Handlung an den Körper des Handelnden zurückbinden.

Mittlerweile ist diese spezifisch postaristokratisch-europäisch geprägte Jetset-Kultur zwar vergangen, die kulturellen Marker der abgelegten Form sind aber nicht verschwunden. Übernommen werden sie heute vor allem durch eine homosexuelle Subkultur, die ihre Insignien umkehrt (Social Drag!) und für neue Räume öffnet. Katharina Wulff (*1968) beschreibt einen solchen Raum, der seit Beginn der 1990er-Jahre auch von Protagonisten wie Kai Althoff oder Lukas Duwenhögger in ihren Malereien umrissen wird, durch eine Verkehrung der Begehrensdispositive: Dekor, Accessoire, exzentrische Figuration, Verkörperung ohne Subjekt. Ihre Figurationen werden wiederum flankiert von den subtilen, bisweilen surrealen Codes, die sich um die malerische Produktionssphäre ranken.

Oswald Oberhuber (1931–2020) gestaltete in seiner Funktion als Rektor zahlreiche Möbel und Gebrauchsgegenstände für die Hochschule für angewandte Kunst, die ausgesprochen symbolisch und anspielungsreich sind. Das Stehpult, das in der Ausstellung gezeigt wird, wurde wie alle Möbel Oberhubers aus massiver Eiche gefertigt. Es zitiert vage einen Architrav, markiert damit eine archaische Bedeutungsebene des Gesprochenen und schlägt so eine Brücke zum symbolischen und zeitlichen Umraum der Architektur des Österreichischen Kulturforums in Berlin von Hollein. Zugleich wird durch die Form der beiden stilisierten Säulen der Unterleib der Redenden eingerahmt. Oberhuber sexualisiert so auf subtile Weise den Akt des Sprechens, macht ihn schutzlos und defunktionalisiert damit zugleich das Möbel.

Abschließend gilt es noch einmal festzuhalten, dass sich die in der Ausstellung *Der Hausfreund* organisierten Konstellationen als ein subjektiv organisiertes Modell lesen lassen, wie man im ebenso immersiv-subjektivierten Gestaltungsraum eines Künstlers wie Berzeviczy-Pallavicinis Bewegungen andeuten (oder antäuschen) kann, ohne einer vorschnellen Parteinahme oder eingehegten Perspektive anheimfallen zu müssen. Die Positionierung der Ausstellung zwischen Monografie und Kommentar sollte den Rezipient*innen ermöglichen, sich gegenüber den ausufernden Konstellationen der Arbeiten zunächst affirmativ verhalten zu können, um deren Wirksamkeit und Methodik, aber auch deren Verfasstheit als Dekor und Objekte des Gebrauchs mit ihren oft überbordenden visuellen Reizen einwirken zu lassen. Gleichzeitig war es aber auch das Ziel, eine notwendige, kritische Distanz zu erlauben, die die spezifische Andersartigkeit ihrer ästhetischen Parameter und der Trägerobjekte nicht nur in Bezug auf deren Gebrauch, sondern auch auf deren gesellschaftlichen Rahmen sichtbar machen sollte.

Dabei ist der Umstand, die Ausstellung nicht in einem musealen Kontext, sondern in historischen Räumen der Repräsentation (im Heiligenkreuzer Hof Wien, ein Ort sakralen Ursprungs, von Oswald Oberhuber früh für die Angewandte als Ausstellungsort adaptiert) und des Staates (die Österreichische Botschaft Berlin) zu präsentieren, durchaus hilfreich. In beiden Umgebungen verbinden sich die subtil von Nostalgie und Rückblick gefärbten Motive und Arbeiten Berzeviczys besonders sinnfällig und selbstverständlich mit den Narrativen einer Herrschaft der Sitten (decorum) und den Formen institutionalisierten Geschmacks, die diese im Zusammenspiel verstärkt sichtbar werden lässt, zum anderen aber auch deren Brüchigkeit und bisweilen buchstäbliche Fragilität betont.

Den fragilen und in einfachsten Materialien erzeugten Objekten und Kreationen Pallavicinis, die mit aufgenähten Glasperlen versehenen oder reich paillettierten Styroporobjekte, die Schaufensterhintergründe mit ihren zarten Goldfolien aus Papier oder ihren mit Nadeln angepinnten Gouachecollagen auf Samt haftet etwas Ephemeres, Vergängliches an. Dessen tief in einer anderen Zeit- und Gesellschaftsformation wucherndes und bisweilen Nostalgie verströmendes Bildprogramm wirft wie von einer fernen Bühne blitzende Spiegelungen auf die Zuschauer und erlaubt ihnen so, diesem Spiel in und aus einer anderen Zeit fern, aber gewogen und zugleich aktualisiert, entgegensehen zu können.

With Flair This Month

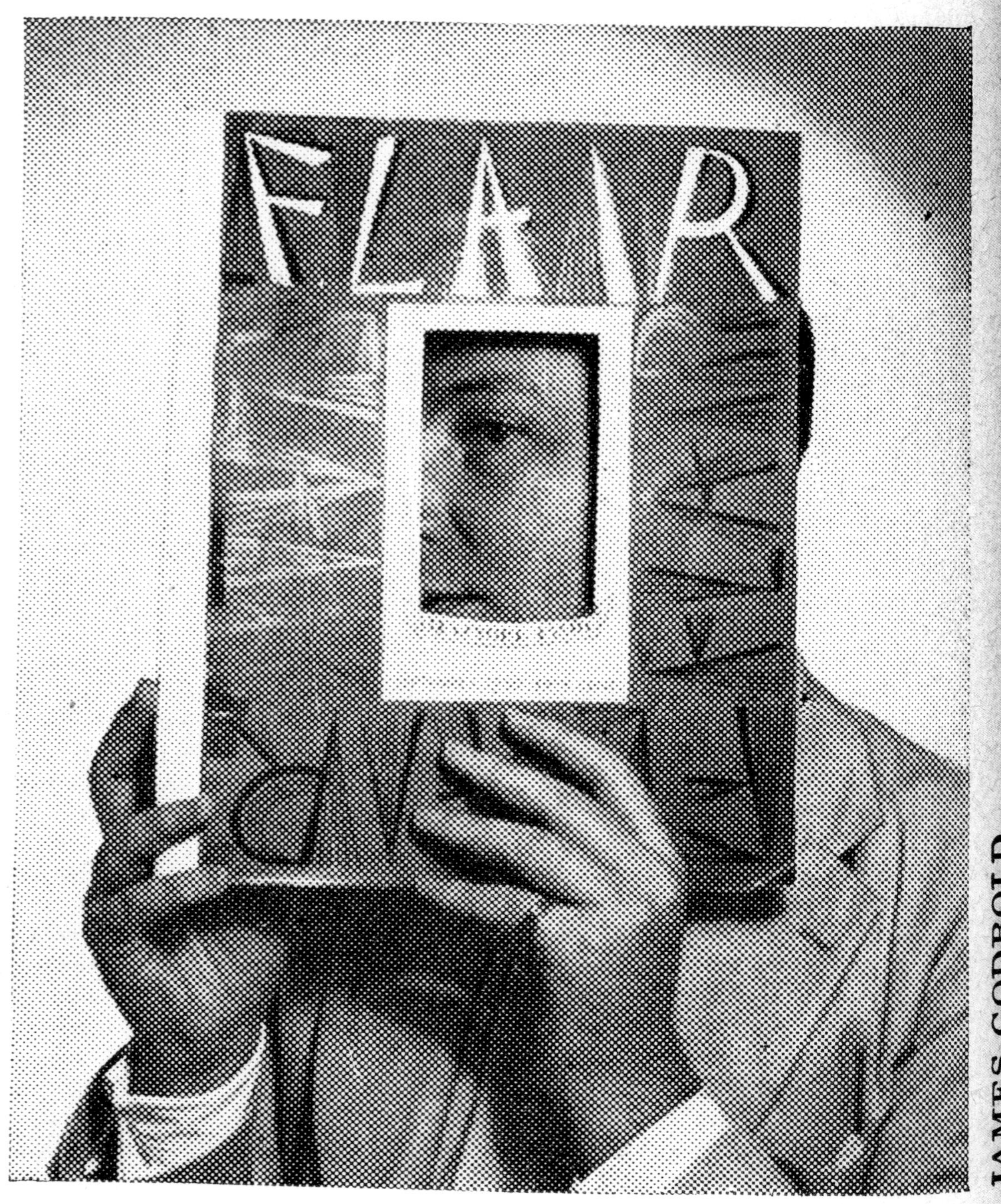

JAMES GODBOLD

Federico Pallavicini

ut, right behind the cover he designed, **Federico**
s his first crisp peek at New York, the U. S.
erican audience. The cosmopolitan Mr. Palla-

Die Kraft des Ephemeren

BRIGITTE FELDERER

Porträt von / Portrait of Friedrich von Berzeviczy-Pallavicini in: *Flair*, New York Issue, September 1950, S. / p. 8

Von seinem Erscheinen in den 1920ern bis heute präsentiert das Magazin *Architectural Digest* private Wohnungen und Häuser, die sich durch den außergewöhnlichen Geschmack der Menschen auszeichnen, die an diesen Orten leben. So ziert etwa das Cover der Maiausgabe im Jahr 1978 ein Blick in das New Yorker Apartment von Barbra Streisand. Die gezeigten Lebenswelten könnten kaum unterschiedlicher sein, die Bilder erlauben Einblicke in private Welten, ja, fast meint man, auf die Persönlichkeit eines Menschen schließen zu können. Vor diesen Kulissen spielt sich ein gesellschaftliches Leben ab, das real wie erträumt scheint. Das feine Magazin adelt gewissermaßen die aufwändigen Anstrengungen, stilbildend zu leben und zu konsumieren, und möchte dabei seine Leser*innen zu neuen Ideen anregen. Geschmack erscheint nicht als bloßes Privileg, sondern als erlernbare Differenzierung, für die das Magazin immer neue Ideen vorstellt. Und so werden in der erwähnten Ausgabe auch die beiden Wohnungen eines „European-born American artist" beschrieben, deren Interieurs an eine unwiderruflich verloren gegangene Gesellschaft – „hypercivilized and overprivileged"[1] – erinnern. Der Hausherr beider Apartments, eines davon in New York, das zweite in Paris, stellt jedoch gegenüber dem Autor des Artikels auch klar, dass er wohl *mit*, jedoch nicht *in* der Vergangenheit lebe. Ein abwechslungsreiches Leben lang – als das Heft erscheint, ist Federico Pallavicini nahezu 70 – hat sich dieser weltläufige Künstler nie mit rückwärtsgewandter Nostalgie aufgehalten. Die Eleganz seiner Wohnungen, weder luxuriös noch groß, entstand allein durch die souveräne Kombination aus Gegenständen und Möbelstücken, die aus unterschiedlichen Epochen und Orten stammen. Kein demonstrativer Konsum wird hier sichtbar, schon gar nicht das Werk eines beauftragten Designers. Wie in einer großen Residenz, die seit vielen Generationen bewohnt wird, schienen sich auch hier Dinge abgelagert zu haben, die an Personen, an Geschichte und Geschichten erinnern und die nichts von konfektionierter Massenware an sich haben, mochten es Erbstücke sein, vielleicht Geschenke oder sentimentale Souvenirs aus einer anderen Zeit, in jedem Fall aus nicht nur einem Leben.

Pallavicini verstand es, historischen Formen und Objekten eine zeitgenössische Lesart zu verleihen, indem er etwa eine Sammlung von Kupferstichen, gleichsam Massenmedien des 18. Jahrhunderts, dicht an dicht sowohl

1 Valentine Lawford, „Cosmopolitan Panache. Federico Pallavicini's New York and Paris Apartments", in: *Architectural Digest*, 4 (1978), S. 88–95, hier: S. 91.

The Force of the Ephemeral

BRIGITTE FELDERER

Since its first publication in the 1920s, the magazine *Architectural Digest* has been presenting private homes notable for the exceptional taste of their occupants. For example, the cover of the May 1978 issue showed Barbra Streisand's New York apartment. The lifestyles featured here could not be more varied, the images providing insights into individual worlds—which one might be tempted to read as a reflection of their occupants' personality. Here are backdrops for a social setting that, however real, seems like a dream. In a way, the exclusive magazine ennobles the extravagant efforts of these trendsetters' consumerist lifestyle, while aiming to inspire its readers with new ideas. Taste is presented not just as a privilege but as an acquirable mark of distinction, for which the magazine provides a constant supply of ideas. The same issue thus also featured the two homes of a "European-born American artist," whose interiors recall an irretrievably lost society, described as "hypercivilized and overprivileged."[1] However, the occupant of the two apartments, one in New York and the other in Paris, makes it quite clear to the author of the article that he is living *with* but not *in* the past. Throughout his long and eventful life—when the issue was published Federico Pallavicini was already approaching seventy—this cosmopolitan artist never indulged in backward-looking nostalgia. The elegance of his apartments, which were neither large nor luxurious, was created alone through the masterful combination of objects and furniture from different places and epochs. There is no conspicuous consumption on display here, nor are the apartments the work of a specially commissioned designer. Rather, as in a large residence inhabited for many generations, the things here appear to have been left behind, recalling people, history, and stories—like heirlooms, gifts perhaps, or sentimental souvenirs of another time—at all events not just from a single life, and certainly not mass-produced or off-the-shelf.

Pallavicini had the ability to give contemporary relevance to historical forms and objects, for example, by attaching a collection of copper engravings—effectively the mass media of the eighteenth century—tightly spaced on walls and ceiling. The prints on the ceiling were mounted behind plastic so as not to pose any danger should any of them fall. Biedermeier furniture was placed next to items from the time of Louis Philippe. The unusual mixture was

1 Valentine Lawford, "Cosmopolitan Panache: Federico Pallavicini's New York and Paris Apartments," in *Architectural Digest*, 4 (1978), pp. 88–95, here p. 91.

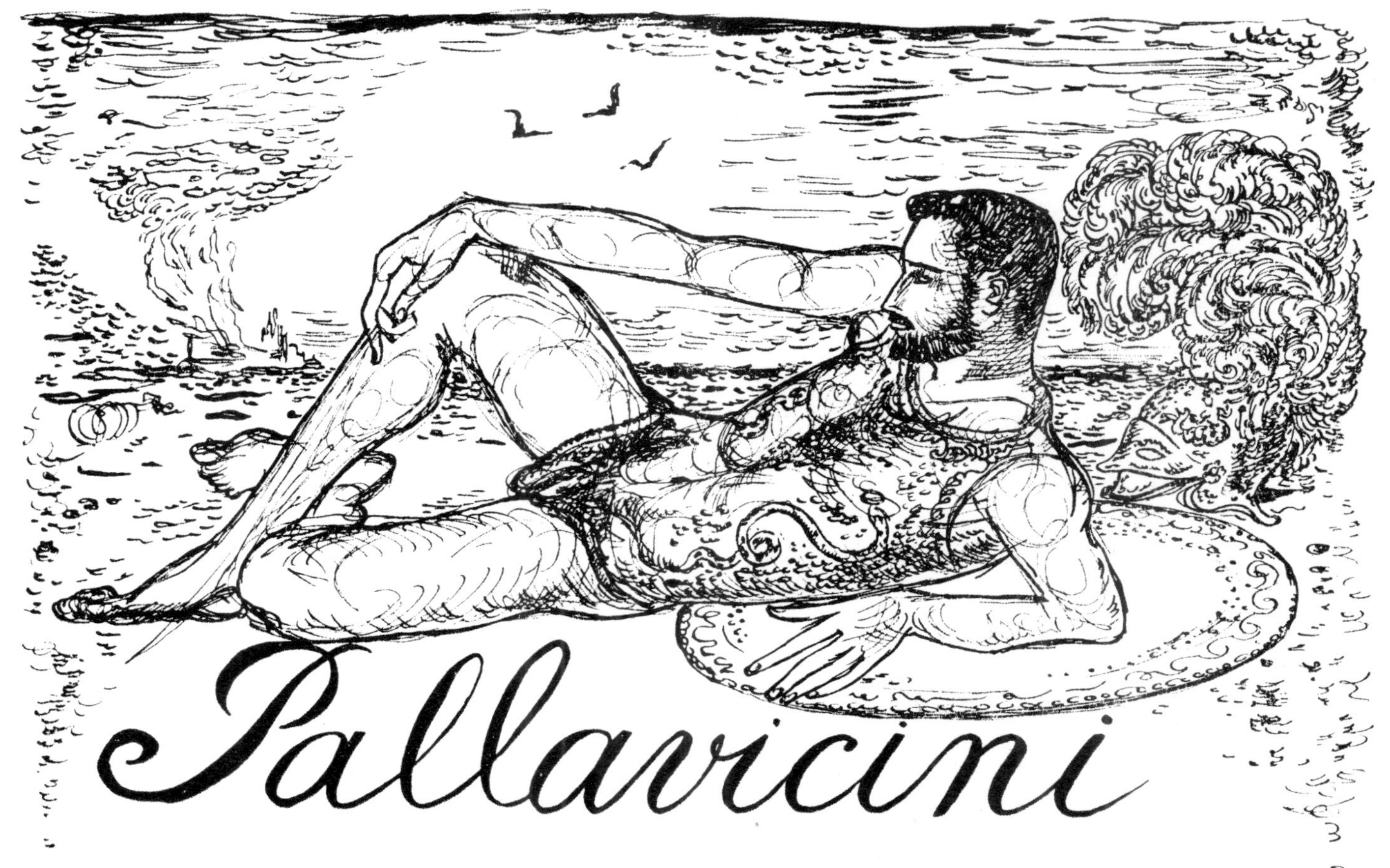

Hugo Gallery
26 East 55 Street
New York
April 23 to May 12 - 1951

Cover Einladungskarte / Invitation card,
Hugo Gallery New York, 1951

a product of Pallavicini's Vienna days, and their casual juxtaposition reflected the artist's contemporary nonchalance.

Born in 1909 as Friedrich Ludwig von Berzeviczy, Federico Pallavicini grew up in Switzerland and studied at the School of Applied Arts in Vienna. He married Klára Demel, heiress of the renowned former court-appointed Viennese confectioners, and left for Italy in response to the rise of Nazism in Austria, before settling in New York in the late 1940s, acquiring US citizenship in 1950. The artist's projects were both diverse and consistent in equal measure. Swiftly sketched, in a light and effortless manner, and with the *sprezzatura* of a sophisticated artist and cosmopolitan aristocrat, he created interiors ranging from the design of a "Boudoir for a Cosmopolitan Lady" [2] to wall paintings for a rustic "Bauernball" at the Austrian embassy in London.[3] Friedrich, or Fritz, von Berzeviczy (it was only during his time in fascist Italy that he took his mother's maiden name and Italianized his first name) always saw his own artistic output as applied art. Artistic ingenuity is needed to create social spaces, be they private or public, and to show them to be not necessarily expensive but rather tastefully nonchalant. Berzeviczy's art wanted to be experienced and enjoyed; it was entertaining and created a certain mood, an attitude to life, so that, even in 1937, an event like the "Bauernball in Alt-Salzburg" at the Austrian embassy in London could still be celebrated with pertinently ironic cheer.

The artist saw no contradiction between designing props for a ball, or even window displays for Elizabeth Arden or Helena Rubinstein in New York or Demel in Vienna, on the one hand, and exhibition projects for galleries on the other.[4] He did not consider the one as his bread-and-butter and the other as a noble expression of his art. Such artistic impartiality was not least a result of his formative years at the School of Applied Arts in Vienna. However, with the demise of the Wiener Werkstätte and the dramatic political upheavals, whose impact was felt not just after 1938 but already during the preceding years of Austrofascism, the city lost the clientele for such everyday refinements. Furthermore, many applied artists had been struggling to embrace the concept of luxury for the masses in 1920s Red Vienna and seemed somewhat out of touch with their time. An industrial aesthetic with political undertones was incompatible with the craftsmanship ethos of the exalted Viennese applied arts scene and its exclusive bespoke products. Embassy balls and exhibitions featuring elegant boudoirs, window displays for former purveyors to the court, and designs for the Augarten porcelain manufactory only served to emphasize the polarization of Austrian society in the interwar years. Friedrich von Berzeviczy's perception of historical reality was certainly not articulated as social criticism, but was rather reflected in an approach that saw taste and form as suitable vectors for individual freedom. Berzeviczy's disappearance from 1930s Vienna was no doubt owed above all to the restrictive conditions, and he eventually began to feel out of place in this city.[5] Like many of his colleagues, he found himself condemned to an enforced elitism that was met only with incomprehension or rejection, as it could not live up to the contemporary understanding of a democratic aesthetic and collided with a difficult economic reality in which refined elegance no longer offered any consolation.

The artist left Vienna for Capri, which was also a meeting place of international homosexual communities seeking to escape all-too-restrictive sexual norms.

Without means, but with the privileges afforded by his name, his education, networks, and upbringing, the artist was able to adapt to new places and surroundings without giving up his personal connections in Vienna. Federico Pallavicini may be thought of as a seismograph reacting sensitively to social changes, albeit without becoming an activist himself, but maintaining that even the ephemeral, the individual refinement of everyday life, could represent key themes for art, whose importance for the civilization of society should never be underestimated.

As an aristocrat without means, relying solely on his aesthetic sensibilities and personal relations, money was as elemental as it was ignored by him. When he died in New York in 1989, it emerged that he had never paid any taxes. The rent for his apartment there (he had long given up his Paris apartment) was twice the amount of his modest pension. And yet, as someone who during his diverse career had belonged to so many states, who was also seen as an "American artist," who, in Paris, Manhattan, and on his travels in general, had often lived from hand to mouth while at the same time representing a society governed by privilege and security, to whom could he feel obliged but above all the perpetuation of his own image?

The artist Federico Pallavicini, while never taking himself too seriously, epitomized a kind of studied superficiality, not in the sense of falseness, but in the importance of manners, of valuing refined form above unadorned truth—whether in art or in life. The special *art de vivre* of this citizen of the world was manifest in his great talent for the fleeting detail, the presentation of consumer worlds, in seeing the street always also as a place of everyday theater, a space for self-expression and for a mutual refining of individual taste. Everything he designed, décors for events and window displays, chocolate boxes, and sets for fashion shoots, even operas, was like a must-see

2 The "Boudoir for a Cosmopolitan Lady" was designed in 1929 for the 60th anniversary exhibition of the School of Applied Arts and was shown on the premises of the present-day Museum of Applied Arts, at the time Museum for Art and Industry.

3 "Bauernball in Alt-Salzburg: Vorbereitungen zum diesjährigen Ball der österreichischen Gesandtschaft in London," in *Die Bühne*, 461 (1937), pp. 32–35.

4 Such as an exhibition at Hugo Gallery in Manhattan in spring 1951. The gallery was co-founded by Elizabeth Arden and showed work, among others, by Frederick Kiesler, René Magritte, and also, in 1952, the first solo exhibition by Andy Warhol.

5 In one of his rare handwritten notes, Pallavicini stated in the 1980s that, because of the political situation and the war, his generation had not been able to "develop." "A real misfortune for our generation" (see autograph in 9834/AUT Friedrich von Berzeviczy-Pallavicini in the art collection and archive of the Vienna University of Applied Arts).

an den Wänden als auch am Plafond anbrachte. Die Drucke an der Decke waren hinter Kunststoff gerahmt, um das Risiko herabfallender Bilder zu vermeiden. Möbel aus dem Biedermeier fanden sich neben solchen aus der Zeit von Louis Philippe. Die ungewöhnliche Mischung verdankte sich den Wiener Zeiten Pallavicinis und vermittelte in ihrer unangestrengten Kombination die moderne Nonchalance des Künstlers.

Geboren 1909 als Friedrich Ludwig von Berzeviczy, war Federico Pallavicini nach seiner Kindheit in der Schweiz und einer Ausbildung an der Wiener Kunstgewerbeschule, seiner Ehe mit Klára Demel, Erbin der ehemaligen Wiener Hofzuckerbäckerei, zunächst als Reaktion auf den Nationalsozialismus in Österreich nach Italien gegangen, bevor er sich Ende der 1940er-Jahre in New York niederließ und schon 1950 die amerikanische Staatsbürgerschaft annehmen konnte. Die Projekte des Künstlers waren gleichermaßen vielfältig wie konsistent. Im schnellen Entwurf, in leichter und unangestrengter Manier, mit der *sprezzatura* des mondänen Aristokraten oder auch der des weltläufigen Künstlers entstanden Ausstattungen, die vom Entwurf für das *Boudoir einer mondänen Dame*[2] bis zu Wandgemälden für einen Bauernball in der österreichischen Botschaft in London[3] reichen mochten. Für Friedrich oder Fritz von Berzeviczy (erst während seiner Zeit im faschistischen Italien hatte er den Nachnamen seiner Mutter angenommen und seinen Vornamen italianisiert) war die eigene künstlerische Arbeit immer zugleich angewandt. Es braucht künstlerische Umsetzungen, um gesellschaftliche Räume, ob im Privaten oder auch für die Straße, zu eröffnen, die sich nicht zwingend in hohen Kosten, wohl aber in geschmackvoller Ungezwungenheit entfalten sollten. Die künstlerische Praxis Berzeviczys sollte erlebt und genossen werden, sie unterhielt und schuf eine Atmosphäre, ein Lebensgefühl, sodass sich selbst ein Fest wie der Londoner *Bauernball in Alt-Salzburg* noch 1937 in gebotener ironischer Leichtigkeit feiern ließ.

Die Ausstattung eines Fests oder auch die Gestaltung von Schaufenstern in Wien für Demel und in New York für Elizabeth Arden oder Helena Rubinstein standen für diesen Künstler nicht in Widerspruch zu Ausstellungsprojekten in Galerien.[4] Es war nicht das eine bloß Brotjob und das andere hehre Kunsterfüllung. Solch künstlerische Unvoreingenommenheit war auch dem Selbstverständnis der Wiener Kunstgewerbeschule geschuldet. Doch mit der Schließung der Wiener Werkstätte und den massiven politischen Veränderungen, die nicht erst 1938, sondern schon zuvor in den Jahren des Austrofaschismus wahrlich schlagend wurden, verlor die Stadt auch die Klientel für solche Alltagsverfeinerungen. Auch fanden Kunstgewerbler*innen in einem Roten Wien der 1920er-Jahre nicht unbedingt Anschluss an die Forderungen nach einem berechtigten Luxus für alle und erschienen mitunter aus der Zeit gefallen. Eine auch politisch zu verstehende Industrieästhetik entsprach nicht dem handwerklichen Ethos des edlen Wiener Kunstgewerbes und seinen exklusiven Maßanfertigungen. Botschaftsbälle und Ausstellungen zu schicken Boudoirs, Schaufenster für einstige Hoflieferanten oder Dessins für die Porzellanmanufaktur Augarten ließen die Gespaltenheit der Gesellschaften dieser Zeit zwischen den Kriegen nur umso deutlicher hervortreten. Friedrich von Berzeviczys Wahrnehmung der historischen Realität fand sich sicher nicht in einer gesellschaftskritisch formulierten Position wieder und wohl eher in einer Haltung, die in Geschmack und Form geeignete Medien für individuelle Freiheit fand. Wenn Berzeviczy also aus dem Wien der 1930er-Jahre verschwand, dann auch deswegen, weil sich die Verhältnisse verengt hatten, und letztlich gab es für ihn nichts mehr zu tun.[5] Er und viele seiner Kolleg*innen fanden sich vielleicht zu einem Elitarismus verdammt, der nur noch auf Unverständnis oder Ablehnung stieß, weil er zeitgemäßen Auffassungen einer demokratisch verstandenen Ästhetik nicht entsprechen konnte und auf eine Situation traf, die in wirtschaftlich schlechten Zeiten keinen Trost in einem verfeinerten Alltag fand.

Der Künstler verließ Wien und ging nach Capri, auch Anziehungspunkt internationaler homosexueller Communitys, die allzu beengten normativen Geschlechterordnungen zu entkommen trachteten.

Mittellos, aber privilegiert durch seinen Namen wie seine Erziehung, durch Netzwerke und Manieren war der Künstler in der Lage, sich auf neue Orte und neue Umgebungen einzustellen, ohne seine persönlichen Verbindungen in Wien aufzugeben. Man mag sich Federico Pallavicini als einen Seismografen vorstellen, der empfindlich auf gesellschaftliche Veränderungen reagierte, zwar keinen Aktivismus entfaltete, doch daran festhielt, dass gerade auch Flüchtiges die individuelle Verfeinerung jeden Alltags auch zentrale künstlerische Themen darstellen konnten, deren Bedeutung für die Zivilisiertheit einer Gesellschaft nie zu unterschätzen ist.

Als mittelloser Aristokrat, der allein auf seinen Geschmack und seine persönlichen Beziehungen setzen konnte, fand er Geld so bedeutend wie gleichgültig. Als er 1989 in New York verstarb, sollte sich herausstellen, dass er nie Steuern bezahlt hatte. Die Miete für seine Wohnung (das Pariser Apartment hatte er längst aufgegeben) hatte seine kleine Pension um das Doppelte überstiegen. Doch wem

2 Der Entwurf für das *Boudoir einer mondänen Dame* entstand 1929 anlässlich der Jubiläumsausstellung der Kunstgewerbeschule zu ihrem 60-jährigen Bestehen und wurde in den Räumen des heutigen Museums für angewandte Kunst, damals k. k. Österreichisches Museum für Kunst und Industrie, gezeigt.

3 „Bauernball in Alt-Salzburg. Vorbereitungen zum diesjährigen Ball der österreichischen Gesandtschaft in London", in: *Die Bühne*, 461 (1937), S. 32–35.

4 Wie etwa eine Ausstellung in der Hugo Gallery in Manhattan im Frühling 1951. Die Galerie war von Elizabeth Arden mitbegründet worden und zeigte u. a. Arbeiten von Friedrich Kiesler, René Magritte oder auch 1952 die erste Soloausstellung von Andy Warhol.

5 In einer seiner seltenen handschriftlichen Notizen hält Pallavicini in den 1980er-Jahren fest, dass sich seine Generation aufgrund der politischen Verhältnisse und des Krieges „nicht entwickeln" konnte. „Für unsere Generation ein wahres Unglück", so seine Worte (siehe Autograf IN 9834/AUT Friedrich von Berzeviczy-Pallavicini in Kunstsammlung und Archiv der Universität für angewandte Kunst Wien).

theater performance. In an interview in 1988,[6] Pallavicini expressed regret that, to him, Vienna had become like a spa resort, a place that was too tranquil, too quiet, especially for someone coming from New York or Paris and already about to return there.

The artist applied an aesthetic that was notable for its lightness, whose elegance was communicated not least by his ability to employ his knowledge of historical models while at the same time detaching himself from them and reigniting them with wit and irony. He was not a dogmatic Modernist but created a public persona as a cosmopolitan aristocrat, "baptized in champagne," as Fleur Cowles, publisher of the New York lifestyle magazine *Flair*, which Pallavicini also worked for, once put it. It was no doubt thanks to her that the artist was so readily embraced by New York society and obtained his US citizenship so swiftly. People were eager for his expertise, the kind that could not be easily learned or taught, for his talent for surviving with elegance, for existing as someone who was convinced that, if necessary, even something as simple as a candy wrapper could open up a world, or, indeed, close it again.

He was no supporter of the modern concept of efficiency, even in fast-paced New York. He must have known only too well that his uniqueness lay in his ability to communicate his ideas with casual self-assurance and without elaborate means. His success is difficult to measure in financial terms; much rather, he presented himself and his particular lifestyle, a combination of privilege and want, cosmopolitan spirit and a contemporary form of courtesy, which may once have been more aptly described as "urbanity."[7] No longer was this determined by the court but by the urban environment and its inhabitants. Pallavicini used his art to contribute to the distinctive features of a city, be it through Demel in Vienna or through his work for new cosmetics companies such as Elizabeth Arden or Helena Rubinstein, who had transformed make-up into a new product for modern women.

This artist still appears fresh and distinctive today on account of his understanding of luxury as a lifestyle manifesting itself equally in personal manners as in the presentation of a skin cream or fine pastry in a store window, as precious components of an urban world whose density and freedom are informed as much by dreams and possibilities as by real conditions. Because Pallavicini did not equate products with their price, and exhibited candies exactly as he would jewelry, he also conveyed the important message (even if it was never his intention to convey messages) that luxury has nothing to do with conspicuous consumption.

His importance as an applied artist does not need to be emphasized. The attention this artist attracts today—perhaps more than ever—may be partly due to the fact that he never pursued a career, never served a market; he ultimately relied on a network of friends and his own independence, maintaining the ironic lightness in his work and countering the seriousness of life with the full force of the ephemeral.

The artist was not afforded an honorary grave in Vienna. A well-founded request for one was made but was turned down. His oeuvre was not designed for eternity. In our precarious times, so preoccupied with the yearning for security, he thus occupies a radical position—namely that of ephemeral lightness. He had little to lose. Pallavicini remained entirely committed to the moment.

Fürst Rehrücken, Originalentwurf für das Buch / Original design for the publication *Die K. u. K. Hofzuckerbäckerei Demel. Ein Wiener Märchen.* / *The Imperial and Royal Confectioners Demel: A Viennese Fairytale*, 1975

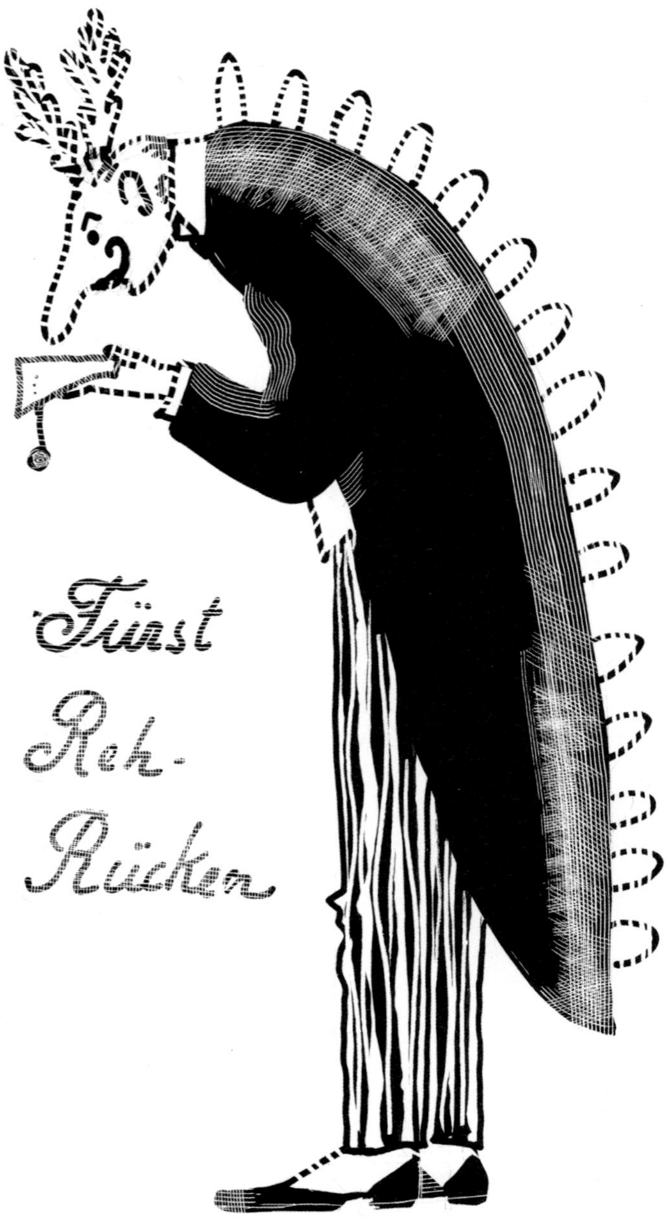

6 In 1988, the University for Applied Arts in Vienna showed an exhibition of Pallavacini's work at Heiligenkreuzer Hof, now the University Gallery. The *Kronen Zeitung* featured an extensive review of the event, in which the artist is quoted as follows: "I used to feel the heartbeat of a world city on Kärntnerstrasse, now it seems as though I am in a spa resort." (*Kronen Zeitung*, April 25, 1988, p. 14).
7 See the entry on "Höflichkeit" in *Das Deutsche Wörterbuch* by Jacob und Wilhelm Grimm.

sollte sich jemand, der auf seinen diversen Umlaufbahnen vielen Staaten angehört hatte, der auch als ein „American artist“ galt, in Paris, Manhattan und letztendlich auf Reisen wohl nicht selten von der Hand in den Mund lebte und doch für eine Gesellschaft stand, die von Privilegien und Sicherheiten bestimmt war, verpflichtet fühlen als vor allem der eigenen Inszenierung?

Mit der Künstlerfigur des Federico Pallavicini, der sich dabei aber nie allzu wichtig nahm, sei einer geschulten Oberflächlichkeit das Wort geredet, die nicht Falschheit meint, sondern die Bedeutung der Manieren, die höfliche Formen über unfeine Wahrhaftigkeit stellt – ob in Kunst oder Leben. Die Lebenskunst dieses Weltbürgers materialisierte sich in seiner hohen Kompetenz für das flüchtige Detail, bei der Inszenierung von Konsumwelten, die immer auch die Straße als Ort eines Alltagstheaters meinte, als Raum für Selbstdarstellung und eine wechselseitige Schärfung individuellen Geschmacks. Wie eine Theateraufführung, die man eben auch selbst gesehen haben musste, gestaltete er Festdekorationen und Auslagen, Bonbonnieren genauso wie die Sets für Modefotografien oder sogar Opern. In einem Interview 1988[6] bedauerte Pallavicini einmal, dass sich Wien für ihn zu einer Kurstadt verändert hätte, zu beschaulich, zu ruhig war es ihm hier geworden, aus New York oder Paris kommend oder schon wieder im Aufbruch dorthin.

Der Künstler wandte eine Ästhetik an, die sich durch Leichtigkeit auszeichnet, deren Eleganz sich auch deswegen vermittelte, weil sie sich bei aller Kenntnis der historischen Vorbilder zugleich von diesen löste und diese mit Witz und Ironie aufgriff. Er verfolgte keine dogmatische Moderne und schuf eine *public persona* des weltläufigen Adeligen, „getauft in Champagner“, wie es die Herausgeberin des in New York erscheinenden Lifestyle-Magazins *Flair* einmal formulierte, für das der Künstler aktiv war. Pallavicini verdankte Fleur Cowles wohl auch seine unkomplizierte Aufnahme in die New Yorker Gesellschaft und seine schnelle Einbürgerung. Man war begierig nach dieser Art von Wissen, das sich nicht so ohne Weiteres lernen und lehren ließ, seinen Kenntnissen zu einem Überleben in Eleganz, zu existieren als jemand, der davon überzeugt war, dass sich auch mit einem Zuckerlpapier eine Welt eröffnen oder eben schließen mochte.

Ein moderner Effizienzgedanke blieb ihm auch im schnellen New York fremd. Zu gut dürfte er gewusst haben, dass seine unnachahmliche Besonderheit darin lang, seine Ideen in lässiger Selbstverständlichkeit und ohne aufwändige Mittel umzusetzen. Sein Erfolg war kaum ökonomisch zu bemessen, vielmehr bot er sich selbst, seinen persönlichen Lebensstil dar, der sich einer Kombination aus Privileg und Mangel verdankte, aus Weltläufigkeit und einer zeitgemäßen Form von Höflichkeit, die man einst wohl treffender als *urbanitas*[7] beschrieben hätte. Kein Hof war für ihn mehr stilgebend, sondern die Metropole und ihre Bewohner*innen. Pallavicini verwendete seine künstlerische Arbeit dazu, zur Eigenart einer Stadt beizutragen, mochte das mit Demel in Wien oder aber mit seiner Arbeit für neue Kosmetikfirmen wie Elizabeth Arden oder Rubinstein sein, die Make-up in ein neues Produkt für moderne Frauen verwandelt hatten.

Was diesen Künstler auch heute frisch und exemplarisch erscheinen lässt, ist sein Verständnis für Luxus, verstanden als Lebensform, die sich in persönlichen Manieren genauso manifestiert wie in dem Anspruch, eine neue Hautcreme oder feines Konfekt in einer Auslage zu inszenieren, als kostbare Versatzstücke einer städtischen Welt, deren Dichte und Freiheit sich genauso aus Träumen und Möglichkeiten speist wie aus realen Bedingungen. Weil Pallavicini Produkte und ihre Preise nicht gleichsetzte, Bonbons wie Juwelen ausstellte, vermittelte er auch die wichtige Botschaft (und wollte doch bestimmt nie Botschaften verkünden), dass sich Luxus und demonstrativer Konsum nie gleichsetzen lassen und ließen.

Seine Bedeutung als angewandter Künstler muss nicht speziell hervorgehoben werden. Was heute noch und vielleicht sogar mehr denn je die Aufmerksamkeit für diesen Künstler wachhält, ist vielleicht auch, dass er keine Karriere verfolgte, keinen Markt bediente, sich letztendlich auf ein Netzwerk von Freund*innen und seine eigene Unabhängigkeit zurückzog, seine ironische Leichtigkeit auch in der Arbeit bewahrte und dem Ernst des Lebens die ganze Kraft des Ephemeren entgegensetzte.

Ehrengrab wurde dem Künstler in Wien keines zuteil. Wohl gab es eine ernsthafte Anfrage, doch wurde diese abschlägig beschieden. Sein Lebenswerk war nicht auf Ewigkeit ausgerichtet. Darin vertritt er, in einer prekären Gegenwart, die sich so sehr dem Begehren nach Sicherheit verschrieben hat, einen radikalen Standpunkt – in flüchtiger Leichtigkeit. Er hatte wenig zu verlieren. Pallavicini blieb ganz dem Moment verpflichtet.

6 1988 zeigt die damals noch Hochschule für angewandte Kunst eine Ausstellung zum Werk Pallavicinis im Heiligenkreuzer Hof, die heutige Universitätsgalerie der Angewandten. Aus diesem Anlass erschien in der *Kronen Zeitung* eine ausführliche Rezension. Darin wird der Künstler mit folgenden Worten zitiert: „Früher spürte ich in der Kärntnerstraße die Weltstadt, heute glaube ich, in einen Kurort geraten zu sein“ (*Kronen Zeitung*, 25.04.1988, S. 14).

7 Vgl. etwa den Eintrag zu „Höflichkeit“ in *Das Deutsche Wörterbuch* von Jacob und Wilhelm Grimm.

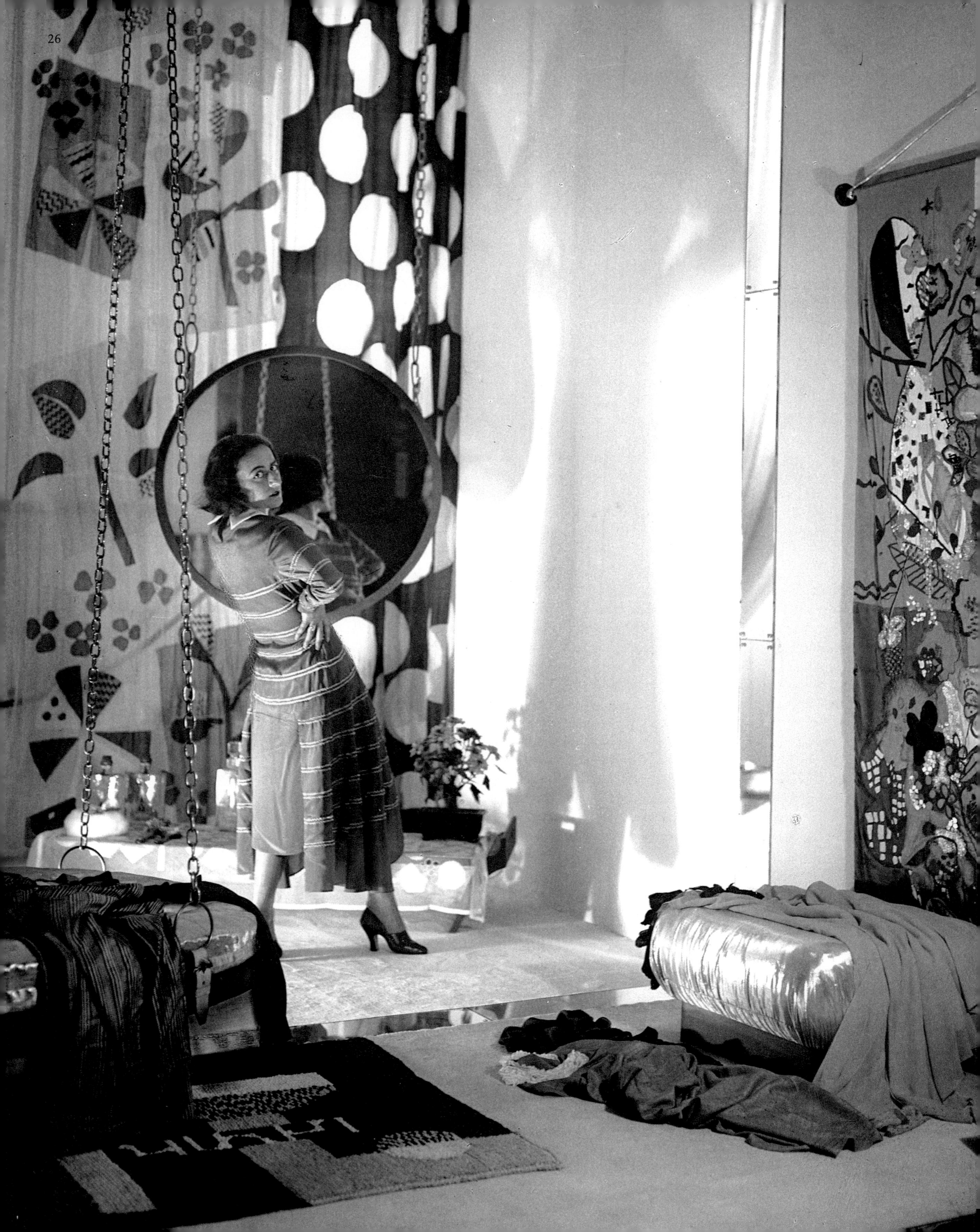

WIE IM CHAMPAGNERGLAS

Berzeviczy-Pallavicinis Raumgestaltungen

ANNE-KATRIN ROSSBERG

(1) Modefotografie in *Boudoir einer mondänen Dame* / Fashion photograph in *Boudoir for a Cosmopolitan Lady*, Gestaltung / design: Friedrich von Berzeviczy-Pallavicini, ausgestellt im Kunstgewerbemuseum Wien / exhibited at the Museum of Applied Arts Vienna, 1929

Im Sommer 1929 präsentierte der gerade 20-jährige Kunstgewerbeschüler Friedrich Ludwig Berzeviczy sein erstes Interieur auf der Ausstellung zum 60-Jahr-Jubiläum der Schule.[1] Als Student in der von Eduard Wimmer-Wisgrill geleiteten Werkstätte für Mode und Textilarbeiten kreierte er das *Boudoir einer mondänen Dame*, welches medial besondere Aufmerksamkeit erregte. Der Kritiker der *Neuen Freien Presse* zeigte sich begeistert vom „faszinierende[n] Einfall des blutjungen Berzeviczy: Hängeruhebett an Ketten, Spiegel im Fußboden, Rundspiegel an der Wand über der märchenhaft niedrigen Frisiertoilette mit überlebensgroßen Parfümflaschen und Puderquasten. Dominierende Farben: Silberlamé, Zinnoberrot und Schwarz." Er verlässt dabei kurz den Telegrammstil, der den gesamten Artikel prägt, und gibt sich seinen Assoziationen hin: „Die schöne Dame sitzt wie in einem Champagnerglas, und die witzigen bizarren Einfälle, die ihrer Schönheit huldigen, umwogen sie wie Schaumperlen […]."[2]

1 Die Ausstellung fand im k. k. Österreichisches Museum für Kunst und Industrie (heute MAK) statt. An dieser Stelle danke ich Lara Steinhäußer, MAK-Kustodin der Sammlung Textilien und Teppiche, für wertvolle Hinweise im Zuge der Recherchearbeiten zu diesem Text.

2 W. D., „Die Jubiläumsausstellung der Kunstgewerbeschule", in: *Neue Freie Presse*, 24.05.1929, S. 14.

Tatsächlich folgte Berzeviczy den klassischen Vorstellungen einer Boudoir-Einrichtung mit den üblichen Versatzstücken (Ruhebett, Toilettetisch) in extravagantem Stil und tradierte damit den im Rokoko entwickelten Raumtypus. Als „Schmollwinkel" (*bouder* ist der französische Begriff für „schmollen") diente das Boudoir anfänglich beiden Geschlechtern, wurde jedoch im Laufe des 19. Jahrhunderts zu einem weiblich bestimmten Raum, der „weibliche Eigenschaften" durch seine Funktion, Form und Ausstattung auszudrücken vermochte. Berzeviczy erhöhte die Wirkung des Boudoirs, das er in seiner Erinnerung für eine „feenhafte, nicht existente Dame" vorgesehen hatte, durch eine spezielle Inszenierung: „Ich dachte mir aus, daß das Publikum durch einen schwarzen Gang gehen sollte, und sich der Raum rot, rosa, blaßrosa und zuletzt weiß bis zum Fenster erstrecken sollte, immer von Spiegelstreifen eingegrenzt. Je nach den Farben auch Boden, Wände, Plafond."[3] Aus dem Dunkel des „Zuschauerraums" tat sich also gleichsam eine Bühne auf, deren Bühnenbild sich schrittweise ins gleißende Nichts auflöste

3 Friedrich von Berzeviczy-Pallavicini, „Erinnerungen", in: *Friedrich von Berzeviczy-Pallavicini. Poesie der Inszenierung*, Ausst.-Kat. Hochschule für angewandte Kunst, Wien, Wien 1988, S. 19 f.

AS IF IN A CHAMPAGNE GLASS

Berzeviczy-Pallavicini's Interior Designs

ANNE-KATRIN ROSSBERG

(2) *Boudoir einer mondänen Dame / Boudoir for a Cosmopolitan Lady*, ausgestellt im Kunstgewerbemuseum Wien / exhibited at the Museum of Applied Arts Vienna, 1929

In summer 1929, at the age of just twenty, Friedrich Berzeviczy presented his first interior design at an exhibition to commemorate the sixtieth anniversary of the School of Applied Arts.[1] As a student in the fashion and textile workshop taught by Eduard Wimmer-Wisgrill, he created a "boudoir for a cosmopolitan lady," which attracted considerable media attention. The *Neue Freie Presse* reviewer enthused about the "fascinating idea by the young Berzeviczy: daybed suspended on chains, mirror in the floor, round mirror on the wall above the fabulously low dressing table with oversize perfume flasks and powder puffs. Dominating colors: silver lamé, vermilion, and black." He then briefly abandoned the telegram style that pervades the article as a whole and indulged his imagination: "The elegant lady sits, as if in a champagne glass, and the quirky ideas paying homage to her beauty swirl around her like bubbles […]."[2]

1 The exhibition took place in the Austrian Museum for Art and Industry (now the MAK). I am grateful to Lara Steinhäusser, MAK custodian of the Textiles and Carpets Collection, for her valuable assistance during the preparation of this essay.

2 W. D., "Die Jubiläumsausstellung der Kunstgewerbeschule," in *Neue Freie Presse*, May 24, 1929, p. 14.

In fact, Berzeviczy's design was in keeping with the classic idea of a boudoir, with its typical, extravagantly styled accoutrements (daybed, dressing table), and was thus a continuation of the Rococo tradition. The boudoir as a "pouting place" (*bouder* in French means "to pout") was originally intended for both men and women, but during the nineteenth century it became primarily associated with women, and its function, form, and design expressed "female characteristics." Berzeviczy enhanced the effect of the boudoir, which he recalled as being intended for an "ethereal, non-existent lady," through a dramatic *mise-en-scène*: "I imagined that the visitors would first pass through a black passage, from which the room would open out in red, pink, pale pink, and finally white, all the way to the window, and always framed by the mirror strips: on the floor, walls, and ceiling, in line with the colors."[3] From the darkness of the "auditorium," a stage would effectively reveal itself, with the scenery gradually disappearing into a glaring nothingness, endowing the room with an element of the fantastic. One of the surviving illustrations shows

3 Friedrich von Berzeviczy-Pallavicini, "Erinnerungen," in *Friedrich von Berzeviczy-Pallavicini: Poesie der Inszenierung*, exh. cat., University of Applied Arts (Vienna, 1988), pp. 19–20.

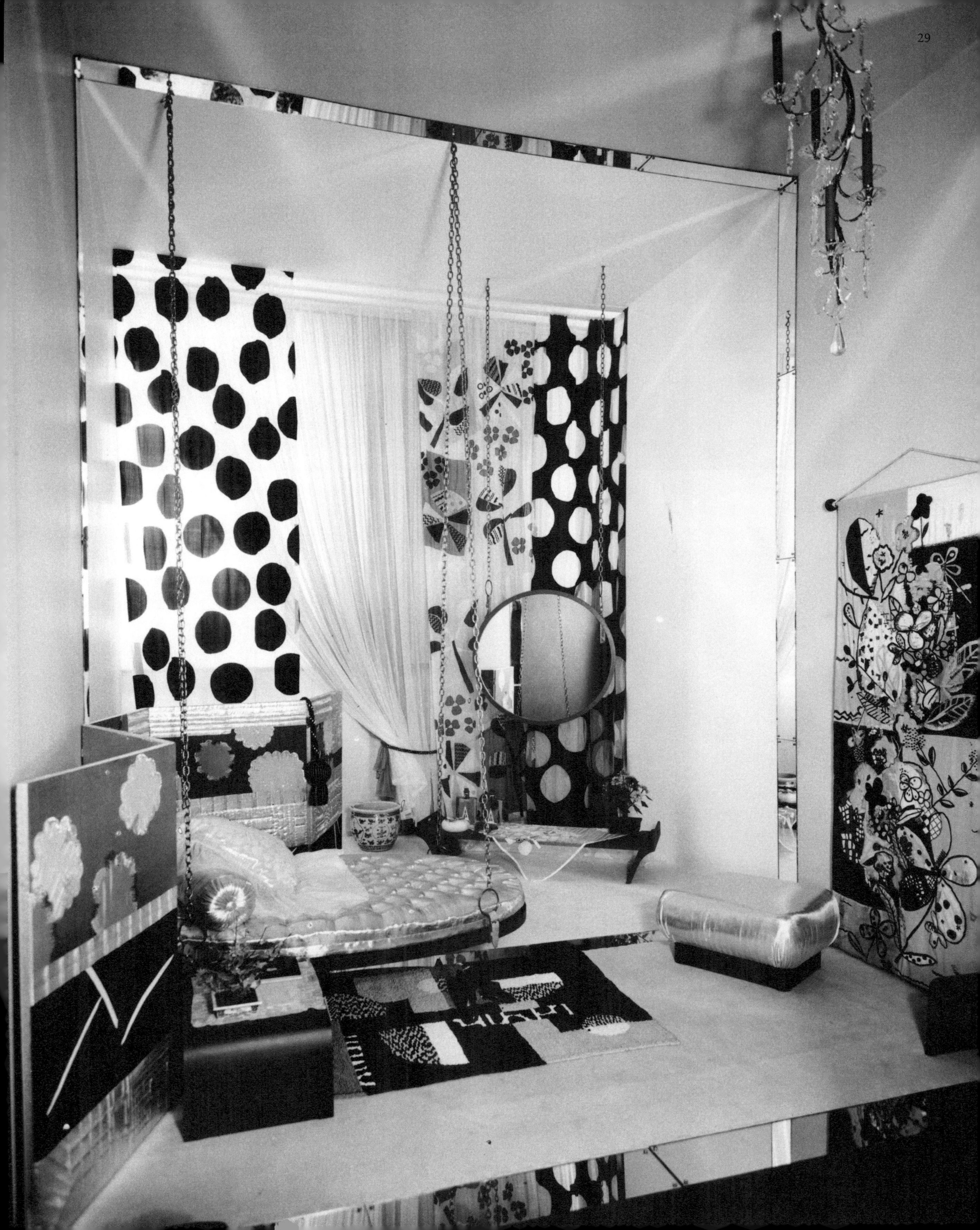

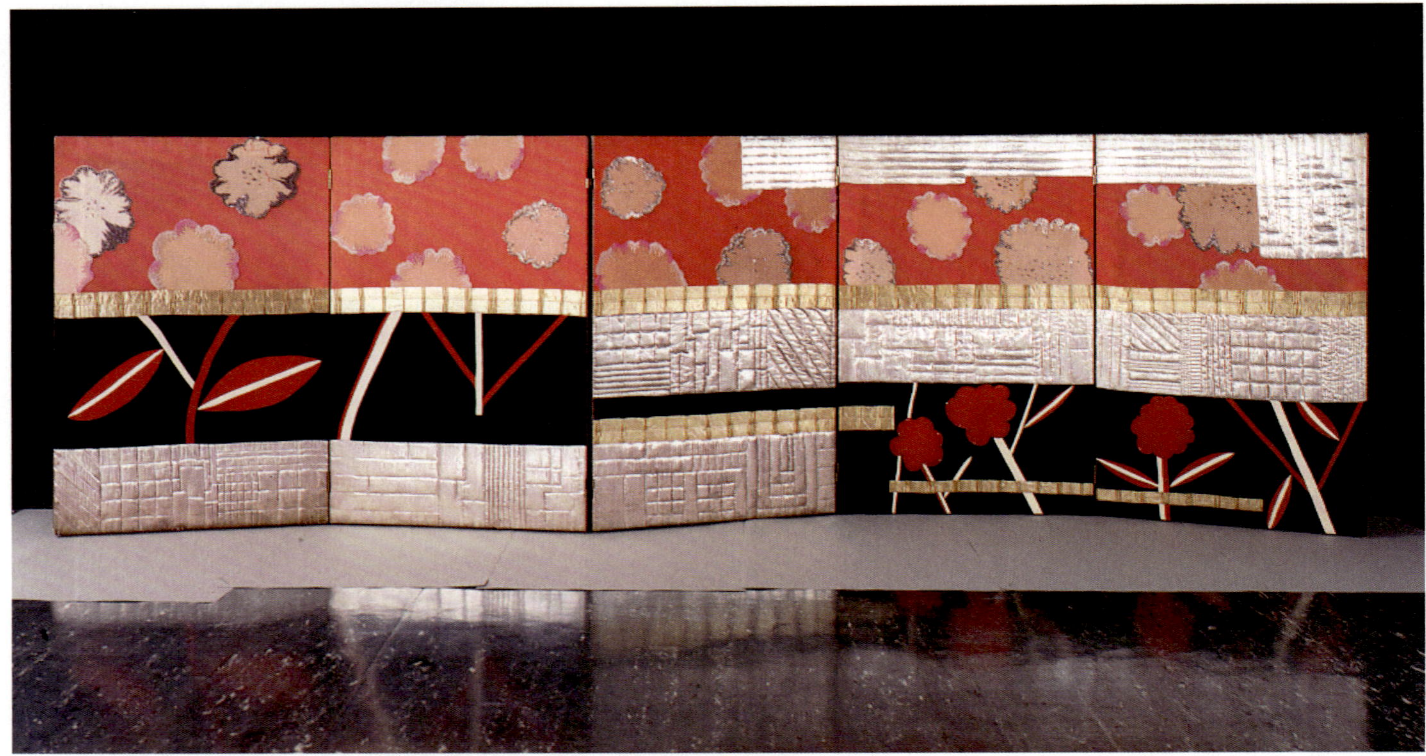

(3) Paravent für / Folding screen for *Boudoir einer mondänen Dame / Boudoir for a Cosmopolitan Lady*, 1929

(4) Rechts / right: Bodenteppich für / Rug for *Boudoir einer mondänen Dame / Boudoir for a Cosmopolitan Lady*, 1929

the boudoir under floodlights, multiplied in the mirrors and causing the materials—crystal chandelier and silver lamé—to sparkle (fig. 2). This glamorous setting made the room an ideal background for fashion photographs (fig. 1).

In order to present the artistic skills and craftsmanship of the textile class "without appearing boring,"[4] Berzeviczy created a pleasing ambiance reflecting the rich use of fabrics and soft upholstered furniture associated with boudoirs since their inception. This tradition was respected with large-patterned curtains, a folding screen, a wall hanging with appliqué embroidery, metal threads, and glass beads, a rep-weave rug, and voluminous upholstery (figs. 3-5). Mirrors had always been a key feature in these usually small, intimate rooms for resting, reading, or amorous activities. Berzeviczy used mirror strips to structure the room, partially disguising its basic components—wall, floor, and ceiling. This confounding game culminated in the oval swing bed, covered in silver wallpaper and suspended from the ceiling by long chains, which, together with a similarly suspended mirror, further emphasized the delicacy of the interior.

4 Ibid., p. 19.

This piece of furniture once again evoked the eighteenth century, when swings were a popular motif in the depictions of rural courtly pleasures. Jean-Honoré Fragonard's renowned painting *The Swing* (1767) transformed the swing's significance from an innocent prop into an erotically charged metaphor: the subject of the painting had explicitly requested to be shown as a voyeur looking up at his lover on the swing.[5] In the early twentieth century, swings featured in boudoir interiors in the form of extravagant seats or divans. As a metaphor for a carefree, idle, and luxuriant lifestyle, Otto Lendecke made it a focus of his illustrations, which appeared in *Simplicissimus* as critical commentaries, while serving in the women's magazine *Damenwelt* to reflect its readers' yearnings. In *Preis Nebensache* (*Price is No Object*) (fig. 6) the swing becomes a gondola, while *Der Tag bricht an* (*Daybreak*) (fig. 7) has a wicker bed with elaborate drapes, a circular mattress, and a mirror mounted directly by the bedside, a reference to the *lit en bateau* or *lit corbeille* furniture of the late eighteenth century. Both designs—the latter of which was actually

5 Hans Wentzel, "Jean-Honoré Fragonards 'Schaukel': Bemerkungen zur Ikonografie der Schaukel in der bildenden Kunst," in *Wallraf-Richartz-Jahrbuch*, 26 (1964), pp. 187–218, here p. 207.

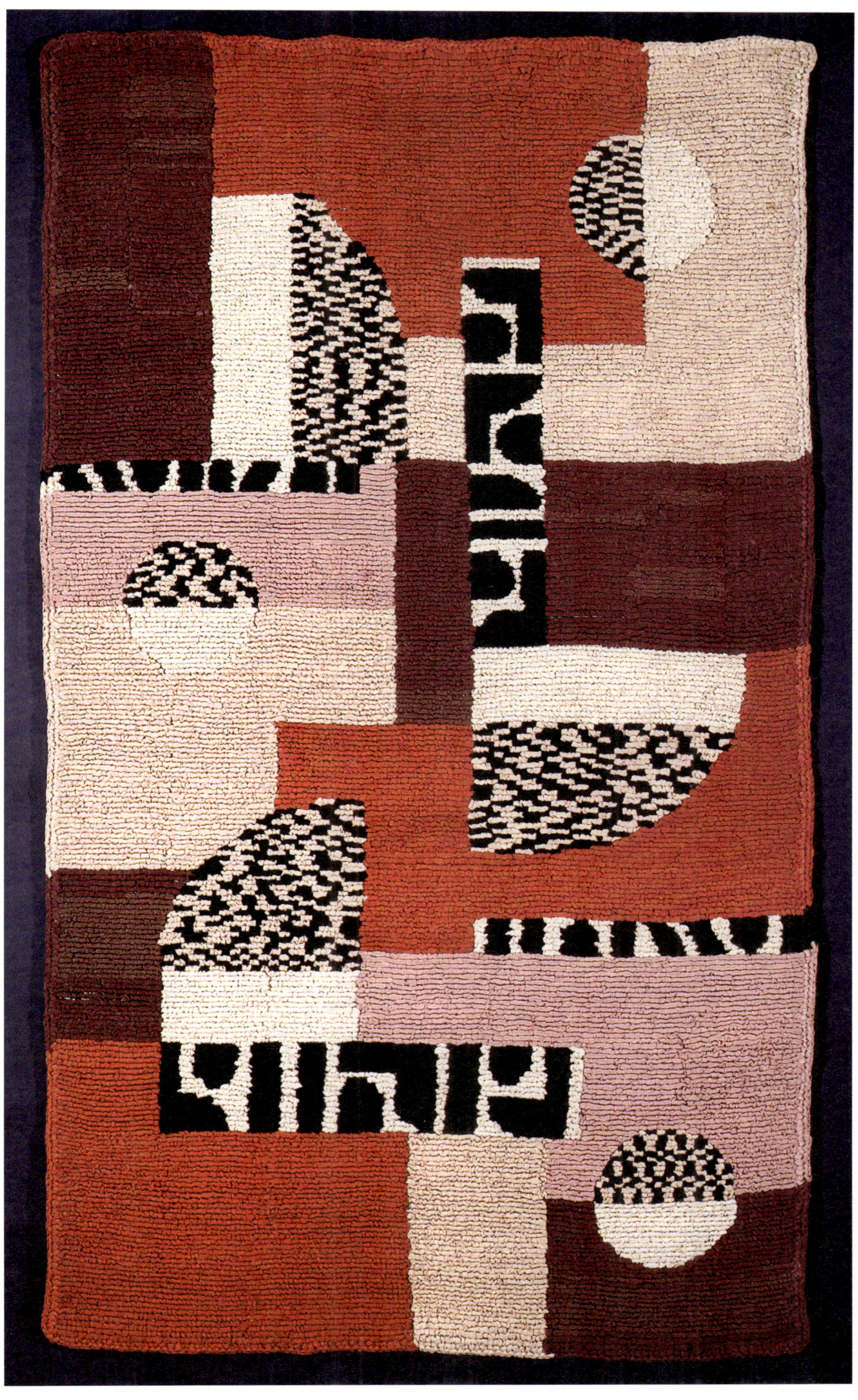

Der Hausfreund, Anne-Katrin Rossberg

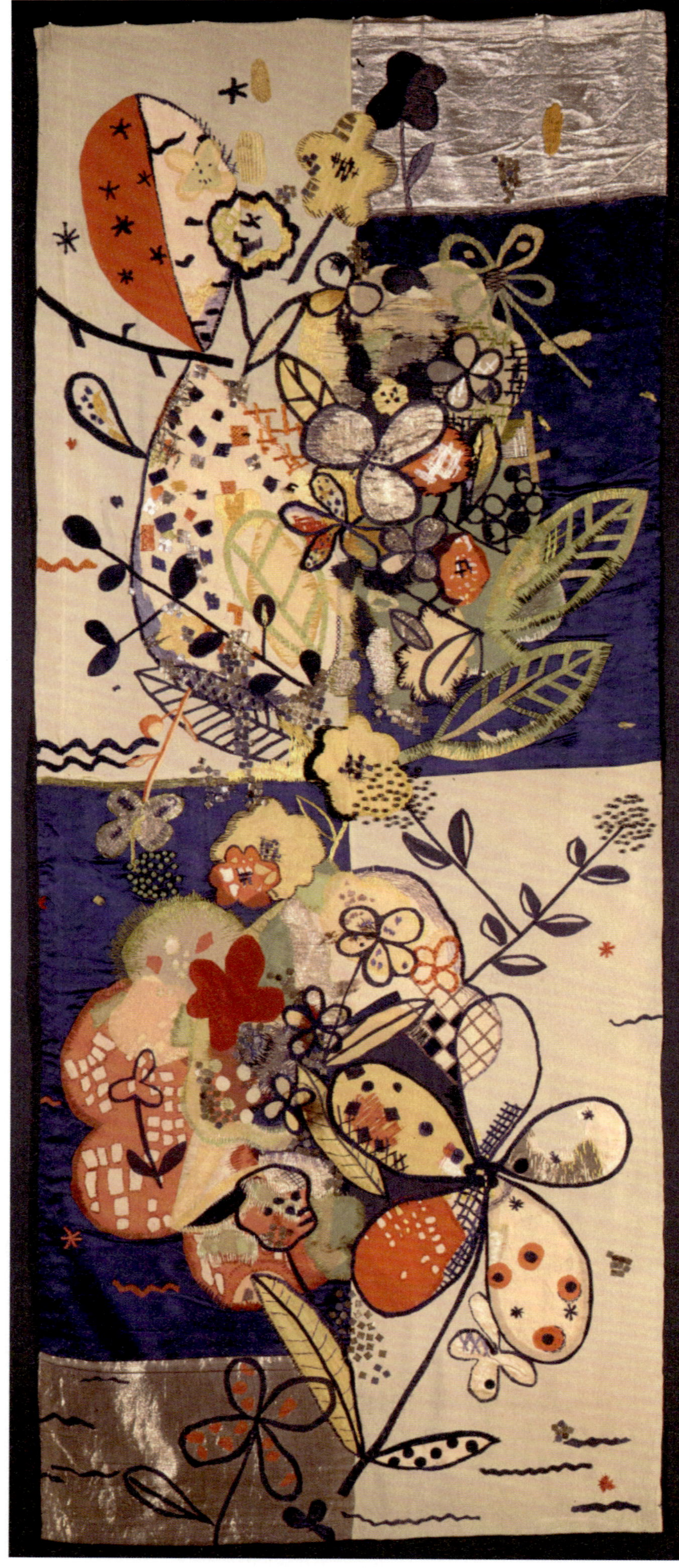

(5) Wandbehang für / Tapestry for
Boudoir einer mondänen Dame / Boudoir for a Cosmopolitan Lady, 1929

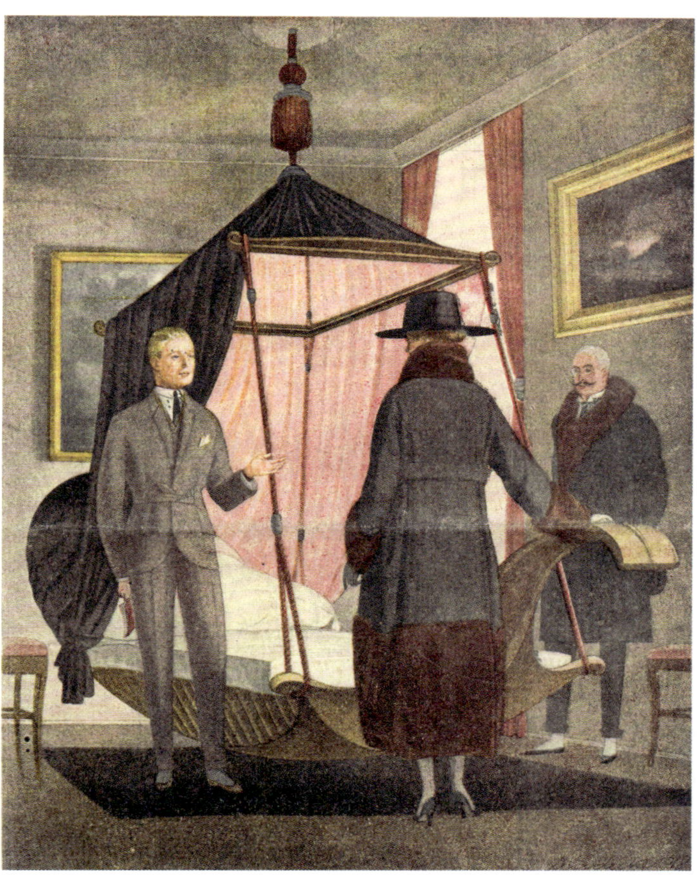

(6) Otto Lendecke, *Preis Nebensache* / *Price is No Object*, 1918

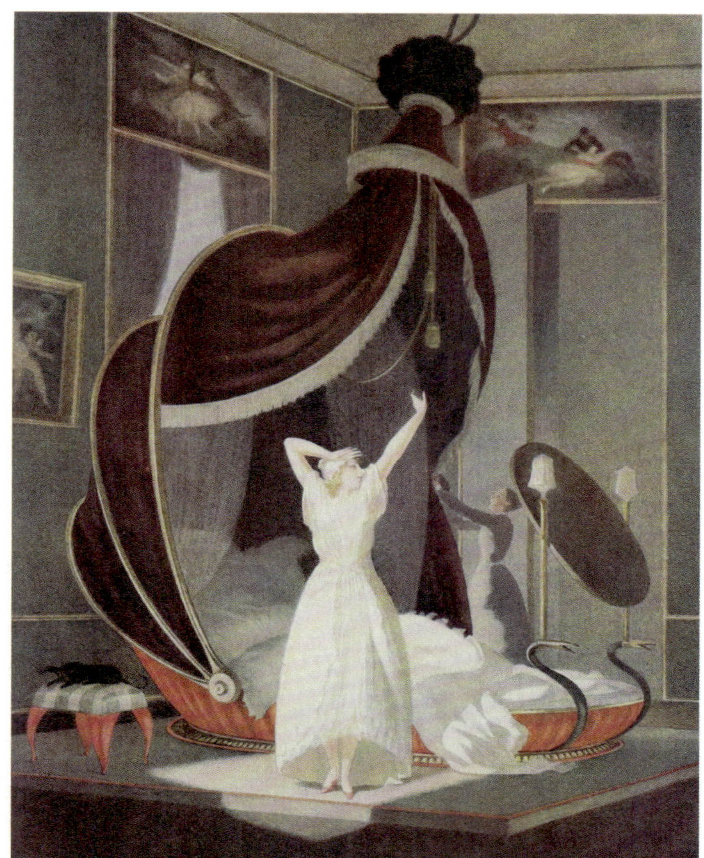

(7) Otto Lendecke, *Der Tag bricht an* / *Daybreak*, 1917

und damit dem Raum eine fantastische Komponente verlieh. Eine der erhaltenen Abbildungen zeigt das Boudoir im Scheinwerferlicht, dessen Strahlen sich durch die Spiegelelemente vervielfältigen und die Materialien – Lusterkristalle und Silberstoff – zum Funkeln bringen (Abb. 2). Mit diesen Glamour-Faktoren stellte der Raum das ideale Setting für Modeaufnahmen dar (Abb. 1).

Um die künstlerischen und handwerklichen Fertigkeiten der Textilklasse zu präsentieren, „ohne langweilig zu wirken",[4] schuf Berzeviczy ein kongeniales Ambiente, war doch das Boudoir seit seiner Entstehung durch die reichliche Verwendung von Stoffen sowie weichgepolsterte Sitz- und Liegemöbel charakterisiert. Mit großgemusterten Vorhängen, einem Paravent und einem Wandbehang mit Applikationsstickerei, Metallfäden und Glasperlen, einem Ripsteppich sowie voluminösen Polsterarbeiten wurde dem hier Rechnung getragen (Abb. 3–5). Ebenso hatten Spiegel zur Ausstattung jenes meist kleinen, intimen Raumes gehört, der als Rückzugsort dem Körper, der Lektüre, dem Eros gewidmet war. Berzeviczy setzte Spiegelstreifen zur Gliederung des Raumes ein, löste damit aber auch dessen konstruktive Teile – Wand, Boden und Decke – partiell auf. Dieses Spiel mit Irritationen fand seinen Höhepunkt im silbern tapezierten ovalen Schaukelbett, das an langen Ketten vom Plafond hing und mit dem ebenso montierten Spiegel die Fragilität des Interieurs noch einmal steigerte.

Dieses Möbel führt erneut ins 18. Jahrhundert zurück, als die Schaukel ein beliebtes Motiv in den Darstellungen ländlicher Vergnügungen der höfischen Gesellschaft war. Mit Jean-Honoré Fragonards bekanntem Gemälde *Die Schaukel* (1767) wandelte sich seine Bedeutung von einem harmlosen Erwachsenenspielzeug zu einer erotisch aufgeladenen Metapher: Der Auftraggeber wünschte dezidiert als Voyeur unter seiner schaukelnden Geliebten dargestellt zu werden.[5] In Form eines extravaganten Sitz- oder Liegemöbels fand die Schaukel Eingang in die Damen-Interieurs des frühen 20. Jahrhunderts. Als Sinnbild für Sorglosigkeit, Müßiggang und Luxus stellte es Otto Lendecke in den Mittelpunkt seiner Illustrationen, die im *Simplicissimus* als kritischer Kommentar erschienen,

4 Ebd., S. 19.

5 Hans Wentzel, „Jean-Honoré Fragonards ‚Schaukel'. Bemerkungen zur Ikonografie der Schaukel in der bildenden Kunst", in: *Wallraf-Richartz-Jahrbuch*, 26 (1964), S. 187–218, hier S. 207.

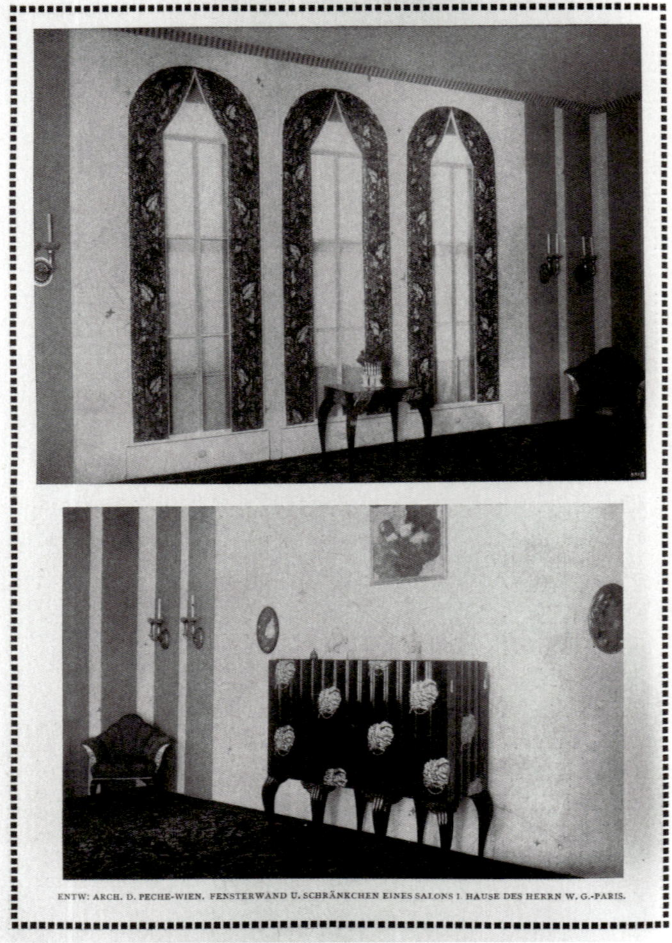

(8) Dagobert Peche, Salon in der 45. Ausstellung der Wiener Secession / Salon in the 45th exhibition of the Wiener Secession, 1913

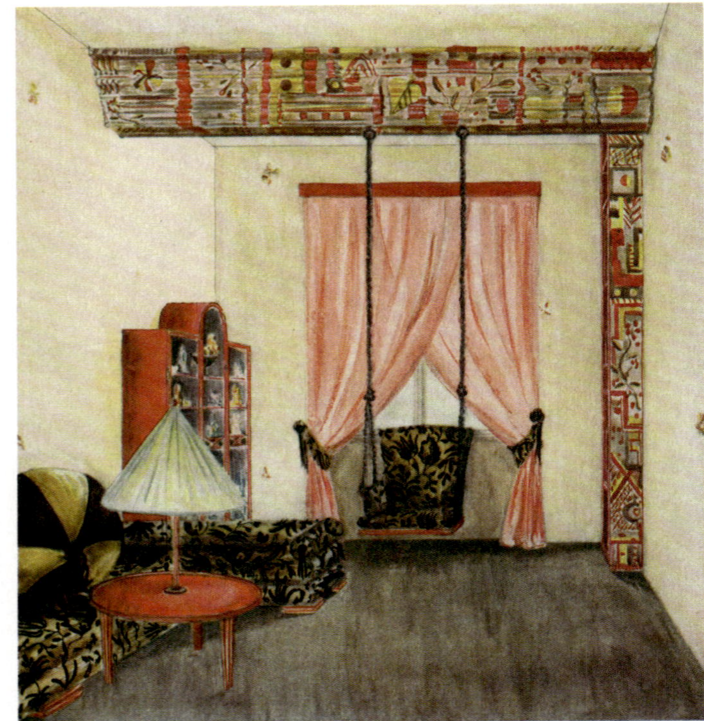

(9) Christa Ehrlich, *Ecke in einem Damensalon / Corner of a Lady's Salon*, 1927

(10) Rechts / right: Speisezimmer in der Ausstellung / Dining room in the exhibition *Raum und Mode*, k. k. Österreichisches Museum für Kunst und Industrie / Austrian Museum for Art and Industry, Wien / Vienna, 1932

made[6]—feature red, the color of love, in various shades, as well as white, the color of innocence. The same color palette is to be found in a design for a lady's room with swing by Christa Ehrlich, one of Josef Hoffmann's students (fig. 9), and again in Berzeviczy's boudoir.[7]

His interior is typical of the Art Déco style of the 1920s, which in Vienna had already been anticipated by Josef Hoffmann and, above all, by Dagobert Peche in the years before the war. The 45th Secession exhibition in 1913 included a design by Peche for a lady's salon, in which the furniture combined Rococo and Neoclassical elements in such a way that the two styles neutralized and at the same time liberated each other (fig. 8). The salon cabinet—which still exists—a large cube on eight delicate legs, combines further contrasts: light and dark, surface and volume, lightness and heaviness.[8] This kind of design reveals a greater interest in drama and surprise than in function and practicality—an attitude that met with an increasing lack of understanding in the interwar years.

Criticism regarding the anachronistic display of splendor in interior design was levied, for example, against the 1932 exhibition *Raum und Mode* at the Austrian Museum for Art and Industry (now MAK). Initiated by the Chamber of Commerce Institute for the Promotion of Trade and Industry (Gewerbeförderungsinstitut), it was intended to draw attention to the products of the passementerie industry, as well as to other decorative arts products such as wallpaper, embroidery, and linen—interpreted in a modern style through designs from the School of Applied Arts. Together with Josef Hoffmann and Oswald Haerdtl, Eduard Wimmer-Wisgrill conceived the exhibition in the form of a house "For Two" (for a well-off couple), with its various rooms—from bridge room to private chapel—providing the setting for the exhibition displays. In the foreword to the catalogue, Wimmer-Wisgrill justified his concept, explaining that, "in spite of the current difficulties," by presenting exquisite items, he hoped to stimulate interest and attract the attention of wealthy customers

6 Lady's bedroom in Palais Stourdza, Baden-Baden, after a design by Otto Lendecke, completed by Friedmann & Weber, Berlin; reproduced in *Deutsche Kunst und Dekoration*, 46 (1920), p. 244.
7 The reference to Christa Ehrlich's design is in Waltraud Kaufmann, "Eine andere Welt: Friedrich von Berzeviczy-Pallavicini—Sein Wiener Frühwerk der Zwischenkriegszeit," diss. (Vienna, 2010), p. 45.
8 The salon cabinet is in the Furniture and Woodwork Collection of the MAK - Museum of Applied Arts (H 2814) and is on permanent display in the *Vienna 1900* section.

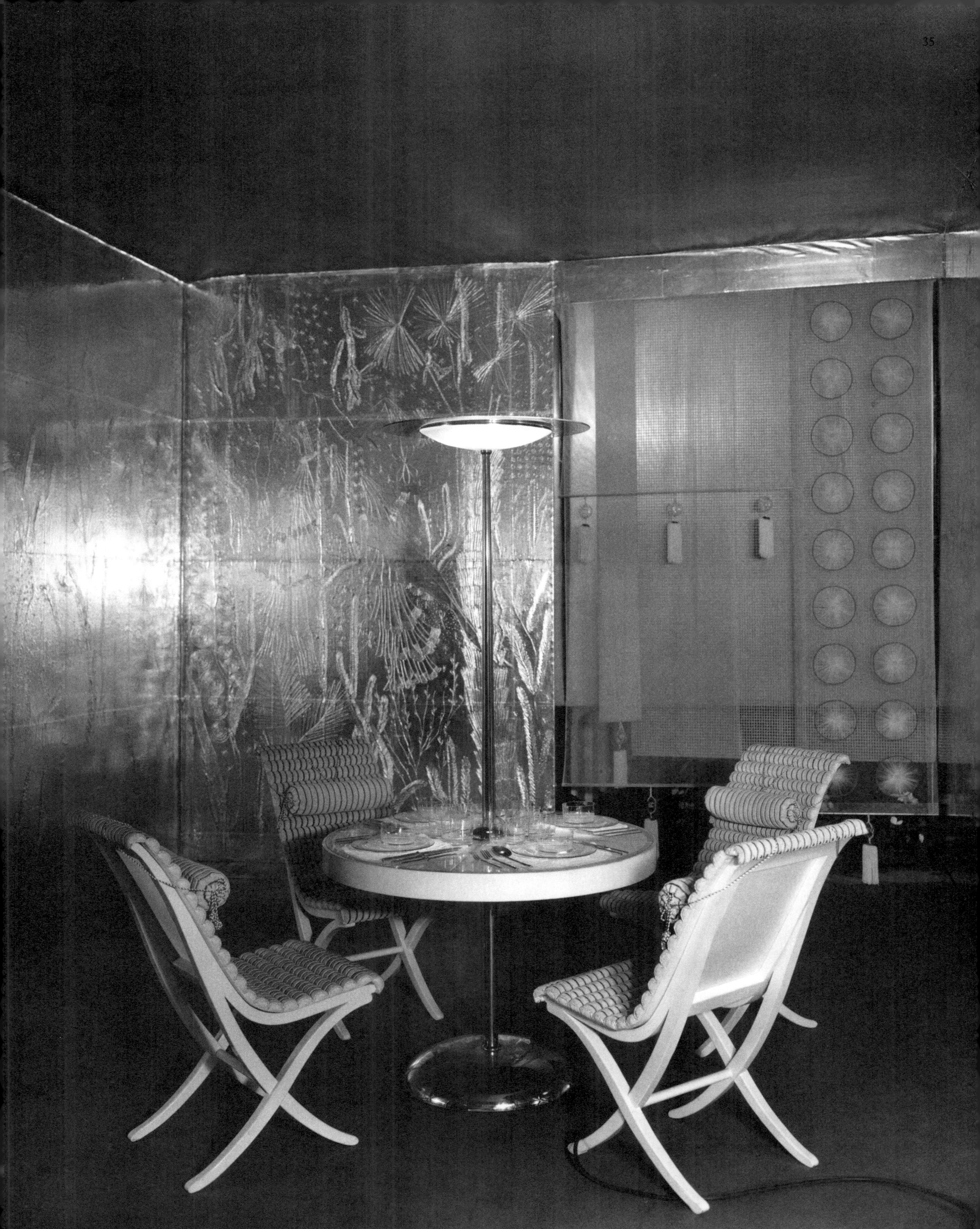

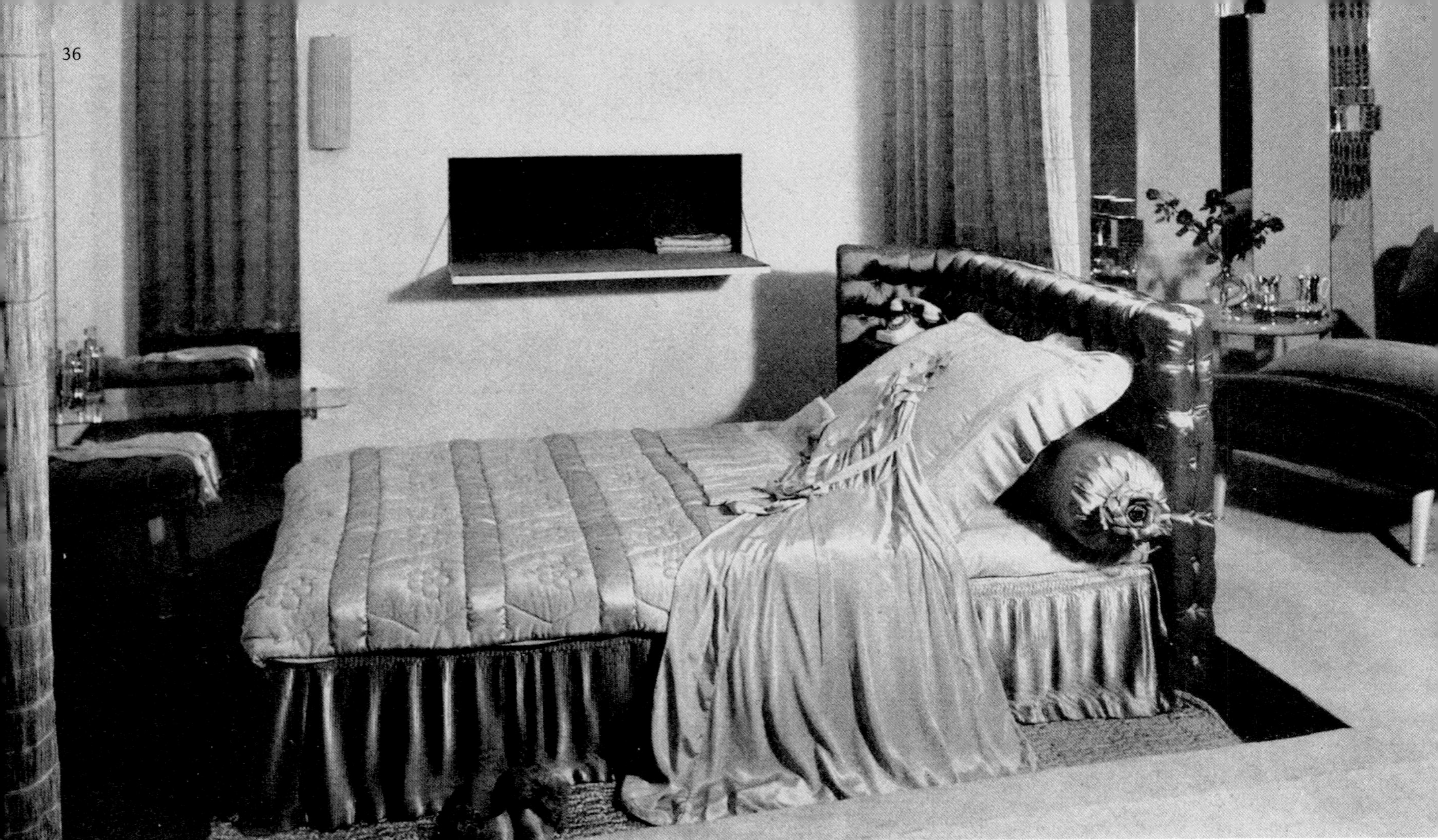

(11) Damenzimmer in der Ausstellung / Lady's bedroom in the exhibition *Raum und Mode*, k. k. Österreichisches Museum für Kunst und Industrie / Austrian Museum for Art and Industry, Wien / Vienna, 1932

from other countries.[9] Nine months after the demise of the Wiener Werkstätte, it was thought that a new start could be made by exporting Viennese taste and exclusive handicrafts to the New World.

"It's like being in a Hollywood film studio: part fairy tale, part ghostly cinematic vision," wrote one newspaper reviewer.[10] This association is not far off the mark, given the "key to the entire exhibition," as another reviewer put it, referring to the lady's bedroom designed by Berzeviczy: "a symphony in blue and white."[11] This time, Wimmer-Wisgrill had entrusted his student with two interiors. For the dining room, Berzeviczy used silver foil wallpaper "and while the wallpaper was still wet, I quickly sketched plants on it. Prof. Hoffmann said about me at the time: 'He is the last romantic and has the entire world of botany in his head'" (fig. 10).[12] His lady's bedroom was arranged across two levels. One step led down to the bed and another up to the adjacent room (figs. 11, 12). The sleeping area could be completely closed off by means of tulle drapes, and a fine mesh of passementerie concealed the circular opening to the "gymnasium." With accessories like shiny satin and velour fabrics, mirror strips to structure the wall, and a sophisticated lighting system, it included all the familiar hallmarks of a traditional boudoir, but its 1929 version was styled as an elegant film set fit for a major star. At the same time, the design was more pragmatic and the color palette cooler. A star-shaped lamp hung above the bed, and a moon gate—"like in China," as Berzeviczy described the circular opening[13]—connected the two rooms. A hand-drawn sketch shows in great detail the glittering universe of the gymnasium, which Wimmer-Wisgrill slightly modified in the final version (fig. 13).[14]

The precious interiors that no one could afford reflected fairy-tale ideals of women that no one had ever met:

9 *Raum und Mode: Ausstellung gezeigt vom Wiener Gewerbe: Genossenschaften der Posamentierer, Tapezierer, Wäschewarenerzeuger und Sticker, sowie der Modegewerbe und der Wiener Kunstgewerbeschule*, exh. cat., Austrian Museum for Art and Industry, (Vienna, 1932), n.p.
10 *Das Kleine Blatt*, December 18, 1932, p. 15.
11 *Reichspost*, December 4, 1932, pp. 21–22, here p. 22.
12 Berzeviczy-Pallavicini, "Erinnerungen" (see note 3), p. 20.
13 Ibid.
14 The catalogue deliberately omitted the designers' names so as to draw attention to the craftsmen and -women carrying out the work. The designers' names were nevertheless known, since contemporary reports mention Wimmer-Wisgrill as the gymnasium designer; see *Innendekoration*, 44 (1933), p. 41; *Die Bühne*, 343 (1933), p. 26.

in der Zeitschrift *Damenwelt* hingegen die Sehnsüchte der Leserinnen bedienen sollten. In *Preis Nebensache* (Abb. 6) ist die Schaukel zu einer Gondel avanciert, *Der Tag bricht an* (Abb. 7) stellt ein Körbchenbett mit aufwändiger Draperie vor runder Matratze und einem direkt am Bett montierten Spiegel vor; sie tradieren die Möbeltypen *lit en bateau* bzw. *lit corbeille* des späten 18. Jahrhunderts. Beide Entwürfe – wovon letzterer auch umgesetzt wurde[6] – zeigen die Liebesfarbe Rot in verschiedenen Nuancen und die Unschuldsfarbe Weiß. Es ist die Farbpalette, die wenig später einen Damenzimmer-Entwurf mit Schaukelsitz von Christa Ehrlich, einer Studentin Josef Hoffmanns, charakterisiert (Abb. 9) und schließlich auch Berzeviczys Boudoir.[7]

Sein Interieur repräsentierte den aktuellen Art-déco-Stil der 1920er-Jahre, welcher in Wien schon in der Vorkriegszeit von Josef Hoffmann, vor allem aber Dagobert Peche antizipiert wurde. Auf der 45. Secessionsausstellung 1913 war ein Damensalon nach Peches Entwurf zu sehen, dessen Mobiliar Rokoko- und klassizistische Elemente so miteinander verschmolz, dass der eine Stil den anderen bändigte bzw. befreite (Abb. 8). Der erhaltene Salonschrank, ein großer Kubus auf acht zierlichen Füßen, vereint darüber hinaus weitere Gegensätze: hell und dunkel, Fläche und Volumen, Leichtigkeit und Schwere.[8] Diese Art der Gestaltung zeugt von einem größeren Interesse an Inszenierung und Verblüffung als an Funktion und Zweckmäßigkeit – eine Haltung, die in der Zwischenkriegszeit auf vermehrtes Unverständnis stieß.

Kritik an der anachronistischen Prachtentfaltung im Innenraum musste sich etwa die Ausstellung *Raum und Mode* gefallen lassen, die 1932 im k. k. Österreichischen Museum für Kunst und Industrie (heute MAK) stattfand. Initiiert vom Gewerbeförderungsinstitut der Handelskammer, sollte sie die Aufmerksamkeit auf die Produkte der Posamentierer, Tapezierer, Stickereien und Wäscheerzeuger lenken – modern interpretiert durch Entwürfe aus der Kunstgewerbeschule. Gemeinsam mit Josef Hoffmann und Oswald Haerdtl ersann Eduard Wimmer-Wisgrill ein Haus *For Two* (für ein begütertes Ehepaar), dessen Räumlichkeiten (vom Bridgezimmer bis zur Hauskapelle) das Ausstellungsdisplay boten. Im Vorwort des Katalogs rechtfertigt Wimmer-Wisgrill dieses Konzept damit, „trotz der schweren Gegenwart“ durch hochwertige Erzeugnisse stärker anregen und Kundschaft aus dem finanziell besser gestellten Ausland gewinnen zu können.[9] Ein Dreivierteljahr nach der Liquidation der Wiener Werkstätte meinte man, hier wieder ansetzen zu können: an der Wiener Geschmackskultur und erlesenen Handwerkskunst als Exportartikel für die Neue Welt.

„Man glaubt sich in ein Hollywooder Filmatelier versetzt. Halb Märchen, halb Kinospuk“, so eine Zeitungskritik.[10] Diese Assoziation ist nicht unberechtigt, besonders in Hinblick auf den „Clou der ganzen Ausstellung“, wie es in einer anderen Rezension heißt. Damit war das von Berzeviczy entworfene Damenzimmer gemeint, „eine Sinfonie in Blau und Weiß“.[11] Wimmer-Wisgrill hatte seinem Schüler diesmal gleich zwei Interieurs überantwortet. Das Speisezimmer ließ Berzeviczy mit Silberstanniolpapier tapezieren, „und solange die Tapete noch naß war, zeichnete ich rasch Pflanzen hinein. Prof. Hoffmann sagte damals über mich: ‚Er ist der letzte Romantiker, er hat eine ganze Botanik im Kopf!‘“[12] (Abb. 10). Das Damenzimmer legte Berzeviczy auf zwei Ebenen an: Zum Bett führte eine Stufe hinunter, zum anschließenden Raum eine Stufe hinauf (Abb. 11, 12). Tüllvorhänge konnten die Schlafstätte gänzlich verhüllen, vor die runde Öffnung zum *Gymnasium* zog sich ein feines Posamentrie-Gespinst. Glänzende Satin- und Velourstoffe, Spiegelstreifen als Wandgliederung und eine ausgeklügelte Beleuchtung – die Versatzstücke sind bekannt, doch die Boudoir-Bühne von 1929 hat sich nun zum eleganten Filmset gesteigert, zur Inszenierung eines großen Stars. Dabei hat sich die Gestaltung versachlicht, die Farbstellung ist kühl geworden. Eine Sternampel wacht über der Bettstatt, ein Mondtor – „wie in China“, so Berzeviczy über die runde Öffnung[13] – verbindet die Räumlichkeiten. Ein Entwurf von seiner Hand skizziert detailreich die Idee vom glitzernden Universum des Gymnasiums, welche für die Ausführung von Wimmer-Wisgrill modifiziert wurde[14] (Abb. 13).

Die kostbaren Interieurs, die sich niemand leisten kann, spiegeln märchenhafte Frauenbilder wider, denen niemand entspricht: die entrückte Fee oder der unerreichbare Stern. Dabei machen die Stereotypen auch vor den Interieurs der Gestalterinnen nicht halt. Gabi Lagus-Möschl kreierte 1929 für die Ausstellung *Das Bild im Raum* – veranstaltet von der Vereinigung *Wiener Frauenkunst* – ein Damenzimmer mit erhöhter, dick gepolsterter Liegestatt und zarten Wandmalereien (Abb. 15). Es vermittelte damit die im 19. Jahrhundert etablierten Rollendefinitionen für die versorgte Ehefrau: demonstrativer Müßiggang, Repräsentation im Haus, Verfügbarkeit. Oder sollte es exklusiver Ausdruck der modernen, selbstständigen Frau sein, deren Leben (wie in den Malereien angedeutet) Sport und

6 Damen-Schlafzimmer im Palais Stourdza, Baden-Baden, nach einem Entwurf von Otto Lendecke, ausgeführt von Friedmann & Weber, Berlin, Abb. in: *Deutsche Kunst und Dekoration*, 46 (1920), S. 244.

7 Der Hinweis auf den Entwurf von Christa Ehrlich findet sich in: Waltraud Kaufmann, *Eine andere Welt: Friedrich von Berzeviczy-Pallavicini. Sein Wiener Frühwerk der Zwischenkriegszeit*, Dipl.-Arb., Wien 2010, S. 45.

8 Der Salonschrank befindet sich in der Sammlung für Möbel und Holzarbeiten des MAK – Museum für angewandte Kunst Wien (H 2814) und wird in der Schausammlung *Wien 1900* gezeigt.

9 *Raum und Mode. Ausstellung gezeigt vom Wiener Gewerbe: Genossenschaften der Posamentierer, Tapezierer, Wäschewarenerzeuger und Sticker, sowie der Modegewerbe und der Wiener Kunstgewerbeschule*, Ausst.-Kat. k. k. Österreichisches Museum für Kunst und Industrie, Wien, Wien 1932, o. S.

10 *Das Kleine Blatt*, 18.12.1932, S. 15.

11 *Reichspost*, 04.12.1932, S. 21 f., hier: S. 22.

12 Berzeviczy-Pallavicini, „Erinnerungen“ (s. Anm. 3), S. 20.

13 Ebd.

14 Der Katalog nennt bewusst nicht die Entwerfer der Interieurs, um das Augenmerk auf die ausführenden Handwerker*innen und Firmen zu richten. Ihre Namen wurden aber offensichtlich kommuniziert, da die zeitgenössische Berichterstattung Wimmer-Wisgrill als Entwerfer des Gymnasiums ausweist. Vgl. *Innendekoration*, 44 (1933), S. 41; *Die Bühne*, 343 (1933), S. 26.

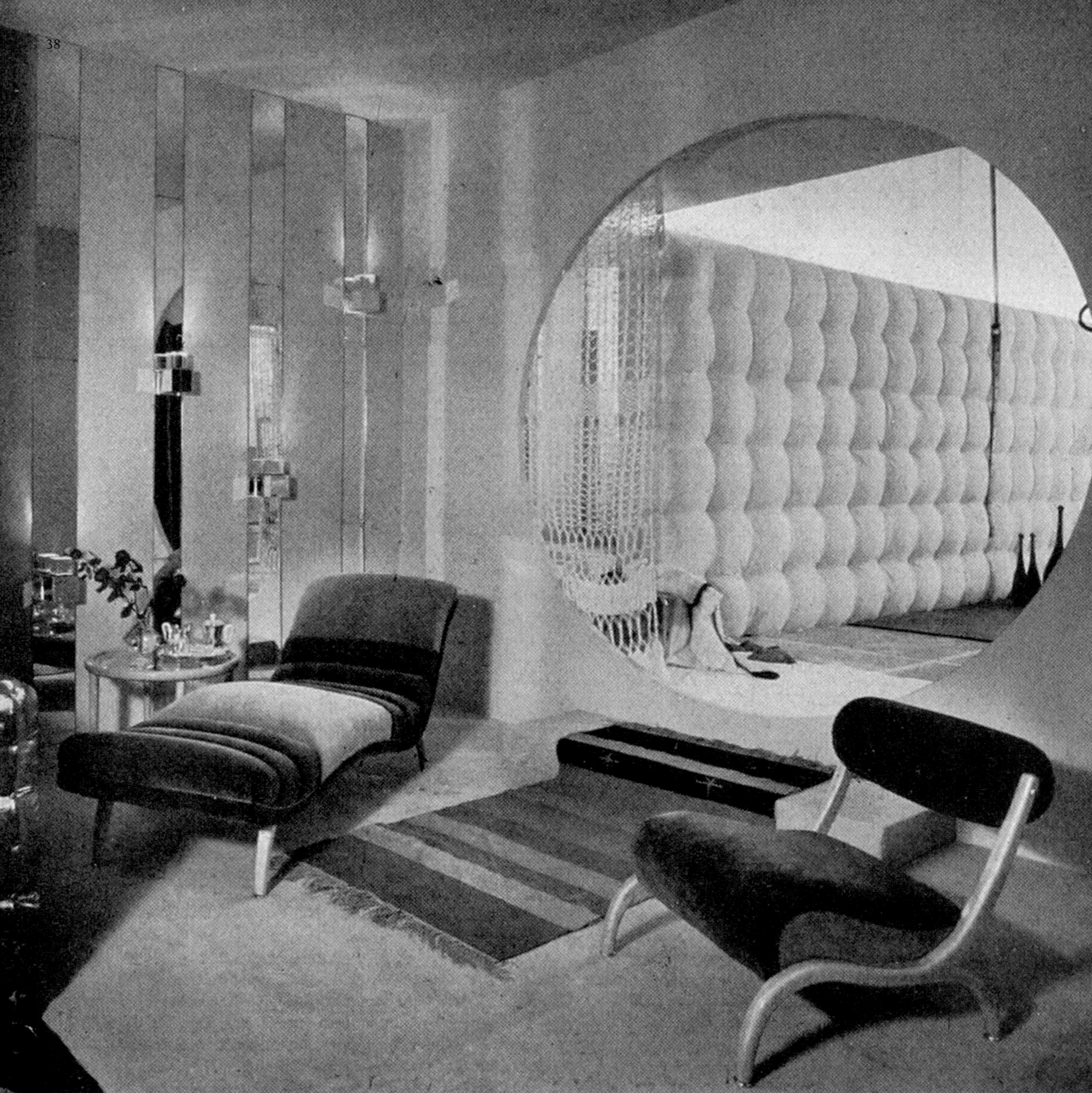

(12) Damenzimmer in der Ausstellung / Lady's bedroom in the exhibition *Raum und Mode*, k. k. Österreichisches Museum für Kunst und Industrie / Austrian Museum for Art and Industry, Wien / Vienna, 1932

(13) Rechts / right: Entwurf Gymnasium der Dame / Design for a lady's gymnasium (*Raum und Mode*), 1932

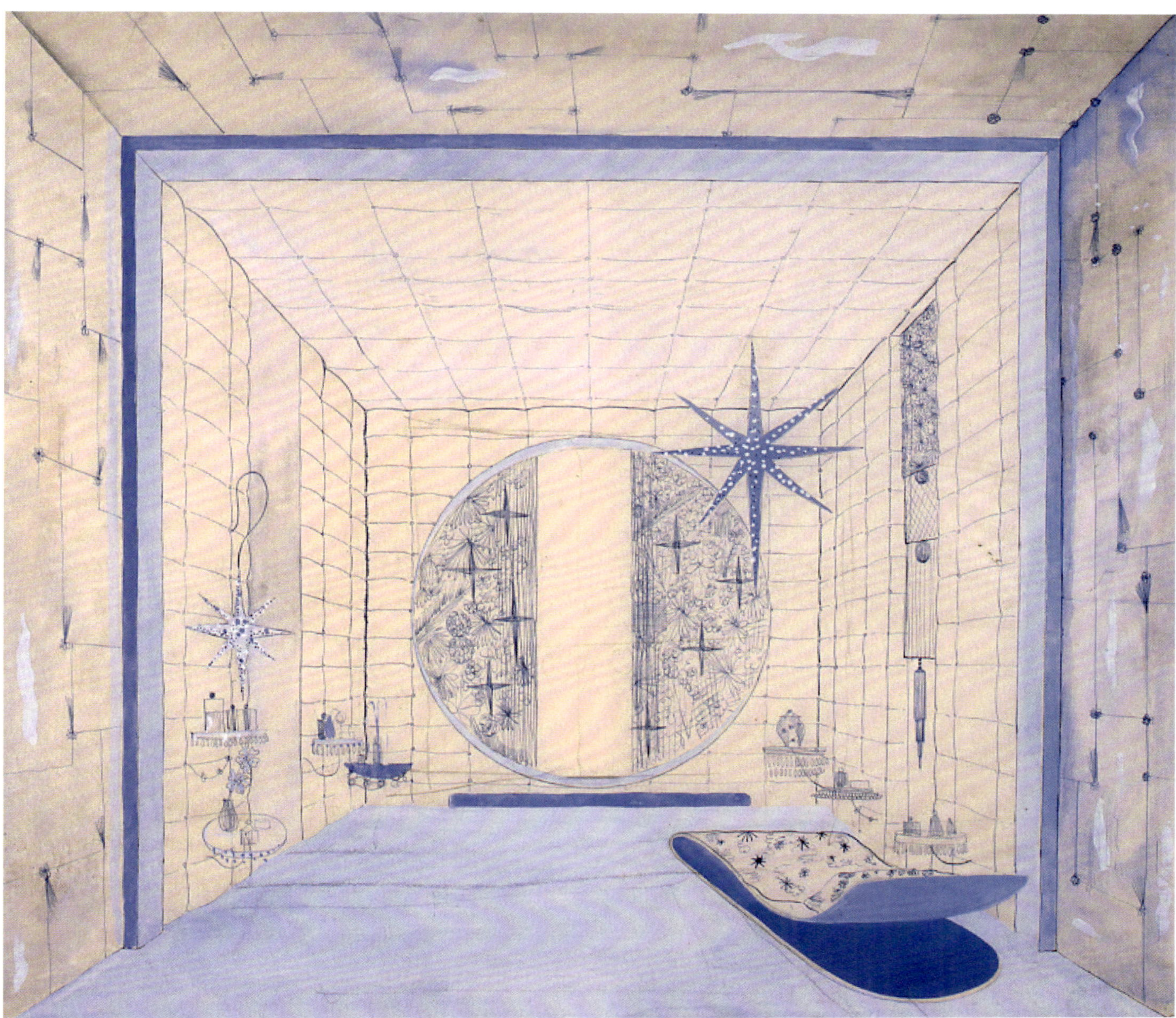

Reisen erlaubt? Auch Berzeviczys bzw. Wimmer-Wisgrills *Gymnasium* reflektierte den neuen Stellenwert von Körpertraining und -pflege mit Turngeräten und Planschbecken zwischen gummigepolsterten Wänden. Diese Entwicklung enthielt emanzipatorisches Potenzial und folgte zugleich einem neuen Zwang: dem androgynen Figurenideal zu entsprechen.

War das Ambiente von Gabi Lagus-Möschl vergleichsweise nüchtern geraten, wurde der „Champagnerstil" in Josef Hoffmanns Beitrag zur Weltausstellung in Paris 1937 noch einmal aufwändig zelebriert. In seinem *Boudoir d'une grande vedette* huldigte er einem großen Star mit der Gestaltung eines goldenen Käfigs – oder vielmehr silbernen: Sämtliche Wände sowie die Decke waren silbern tapeziert, die Möbel silbern gefasst; der Boden war mit Spiegeln ausgelegt, die Tischplatte der Sitzgruppe bestand aus Spiegelglas, den Toilettetisch integrierte eine bis zum Plafond reichende Spiegelnische (Abb. 14). Was Berzeviczy an Gestaltungselementen für ein luxuriöses Art-déco-Interieur vorgegeben hatte (erinnert sei auch an die Stanniolwände im Speisezimmer 1932), führte Hoffmann zu einem letzten Höhepunkt vor dem Zweiten Weltkrieg. Das Schatzkästchen schloss dann nicht nur den Starkult, sondern auch die Wiener Geschmackskultur, im Sinne einheitlicher Durchgestaltung, vorläufig ein.

Sein eigenes Appartement in New York, 1978 publiziert, wies Berzeviczy auch später noch als extravaganten Innenarchitekten aus.[15] Der Living Room überrascht mit der Einbeziehung der Decke als Hängefläche für Grafiken (Abb. 16). Die Gleichbehandlung von Wand und Decke charakterisierte jedoch bereits 1929 das Boudoir mit seinen über den gesamten Raum gezogenen Spiegelstreifen. Auch eine konkrete Anregung könnte noch aus dieser Ausstellung stammen: Die von Bertold Löffler geleitete Grafik-Fachklasse führte damals das sogenannte Plafondplakat erstmalig vor. Berzeviczy mag sich daran in New York erinnert haben.

15 Valentine Lawford, „Cosmopolitan Panache. Federico Pallavicini's New York and Paris Apartments", in: *Architectural Digest*, Mai 1978, S. 89–95.

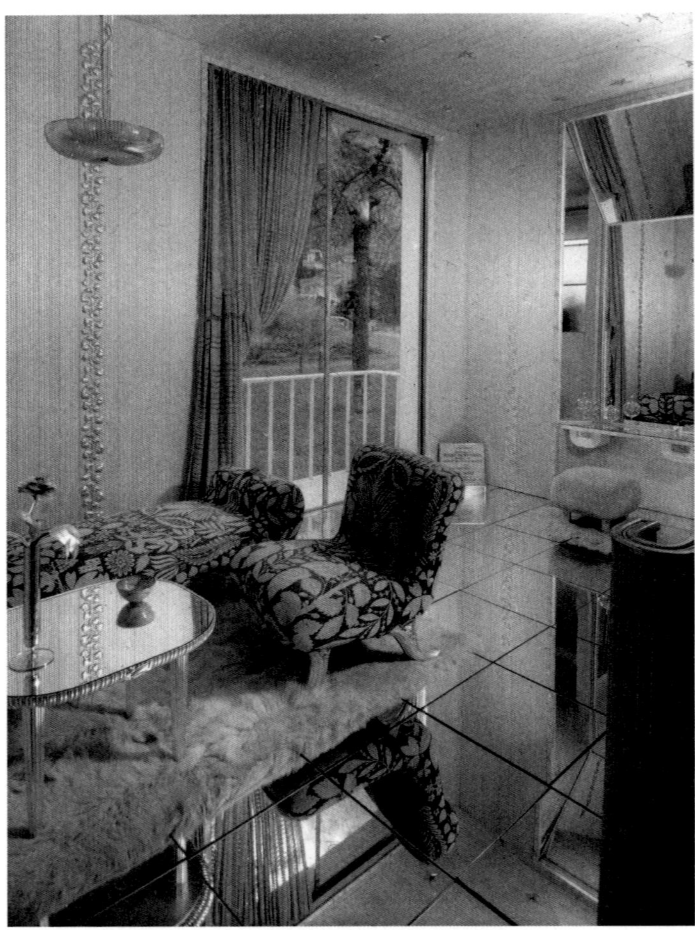

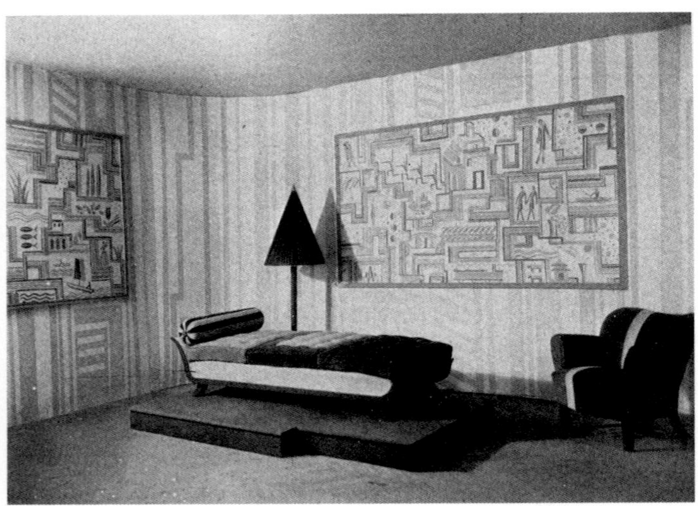

(15) Gabi Lagus-Möschl, Damenzimmer in der Ausstellung / Lady's bedroom in the exhibition *Das Bild im Raum*, k. k. Österreichisches Museum für Kunst und Industrie / Austrian Museum for Art and Industry, Wien / Vienna, 1929

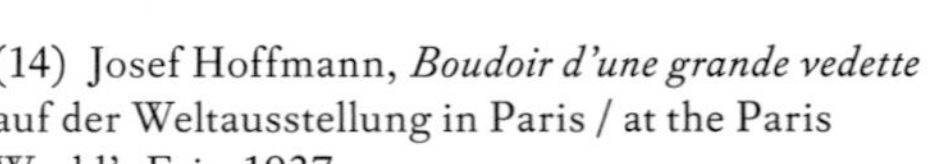

(14) Josef Hoffmann, *Boudoir d'une grande vedette* auf der Weltausstellung in Paris / at the Paris World's Fair, 1937

(16) Rechts / right: Foto von / Photo of Friedrich von Berzeviczy-Pallavicinis Wohnung / apartment in New York, abgebildet / depicted in: *Architectural Digest*, Mai / May 1978

ethereal sylphs or unapproachable stars. And such stereotypes were not confined to the work of male designers. In 1929, Gabi Lagus-Möschl created a lady's room for the exhibition *Das Bild im Raum*, organized by the Wiener Frauenkunst artists' association, with an elevated, thickly upholstered divan and dainty wall paintings (fig. 15). It communicated the nineteenth-century role definitions of the contented housewife: demonstrative idleness, home entertaining, availability. Or was it meant to be an exclusive expression of the modern, independent woman, whose life enabled her to travel and play sports (as suggested in the paintings)? Berzeviczy and Wimmer-Wisgrill's gymnasium, too, reflected the new popularity of physical exercise and body care, with gymnastic apparatus and a wading basin flanked by rubber-padded walls. This development echoed the new-found emancipation, yet also implied a new obligation to live up to the ideal of an androgynous figure.

While the mood in Gabi Lagus-Möschl's design was relatively restrained, the "champagne style" was elaborately celebrated one more time in Josef Hoffmann's contribution to the 1937 World's Fair in Paris. In his *Boudoir d'une grande vedette*, he paid tribute to a major star with the design of a gilded cage—albeit silver in this instance: walls and ceiling were covered in silver wallpaper and the furniture silver-trimmed; the floor was tiled with mirrors, the tabletop made of mirrored glass, and the dressing table was integrated in a ceiling-high mirrored niche (fig. 14). All the design elements Berzeviczy had introduced for a luxurious Art Déco interior (such as the silver foil walls in his 1932 dining room) Hoffmann took to a new level just before World War II. His design arsenal now included not only the film star cult but also the famous Viennese style, in particular its penchant for unified design.

Berzeviczy's own apartment in New York, depicted in a photograph in 1978, showed him to have lost none of his extravagance as an interior designer.[15] Unusually, the living room incorporated the ceiling as a hanging surface for prints (fig. 16). The equal treatment of walls and ceiling was also a feature in his 1929 boudoir, with its mirrored strips covering the entire room. And this exhibition may also have provided the inspiration in one specific detail: it was there that the graphic design class taught by Bertold Löffler introduced the concept of the ceiling poster. Berzeviczy may well have been thinking of this when he decorated his New York apartment.

15 Valentine Lawford, "Cosmopolitan Panache: Federico Pallavicini's New York and Paris Apartments," in *Architectural Digest*, May 1978, pp. 89–95.

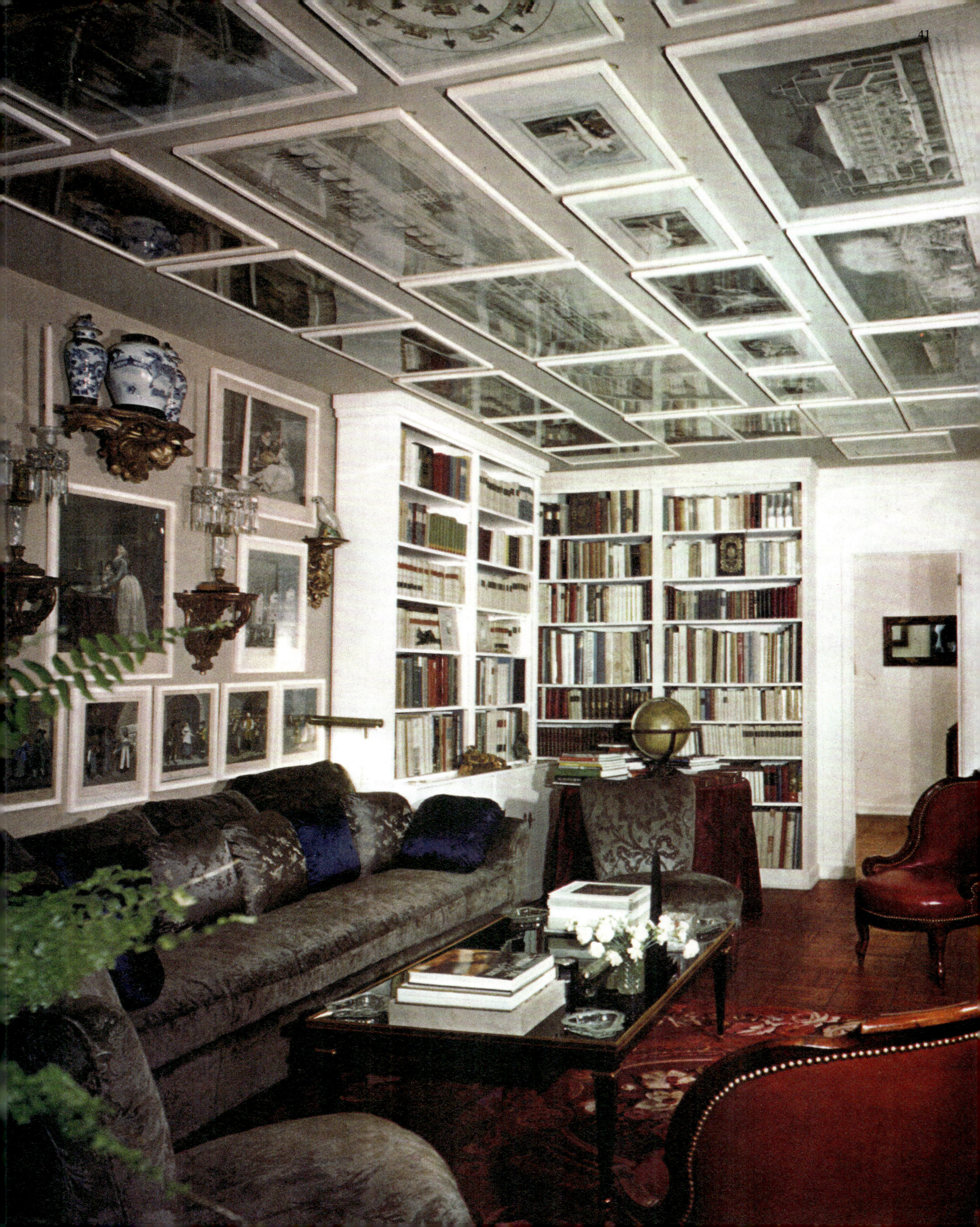

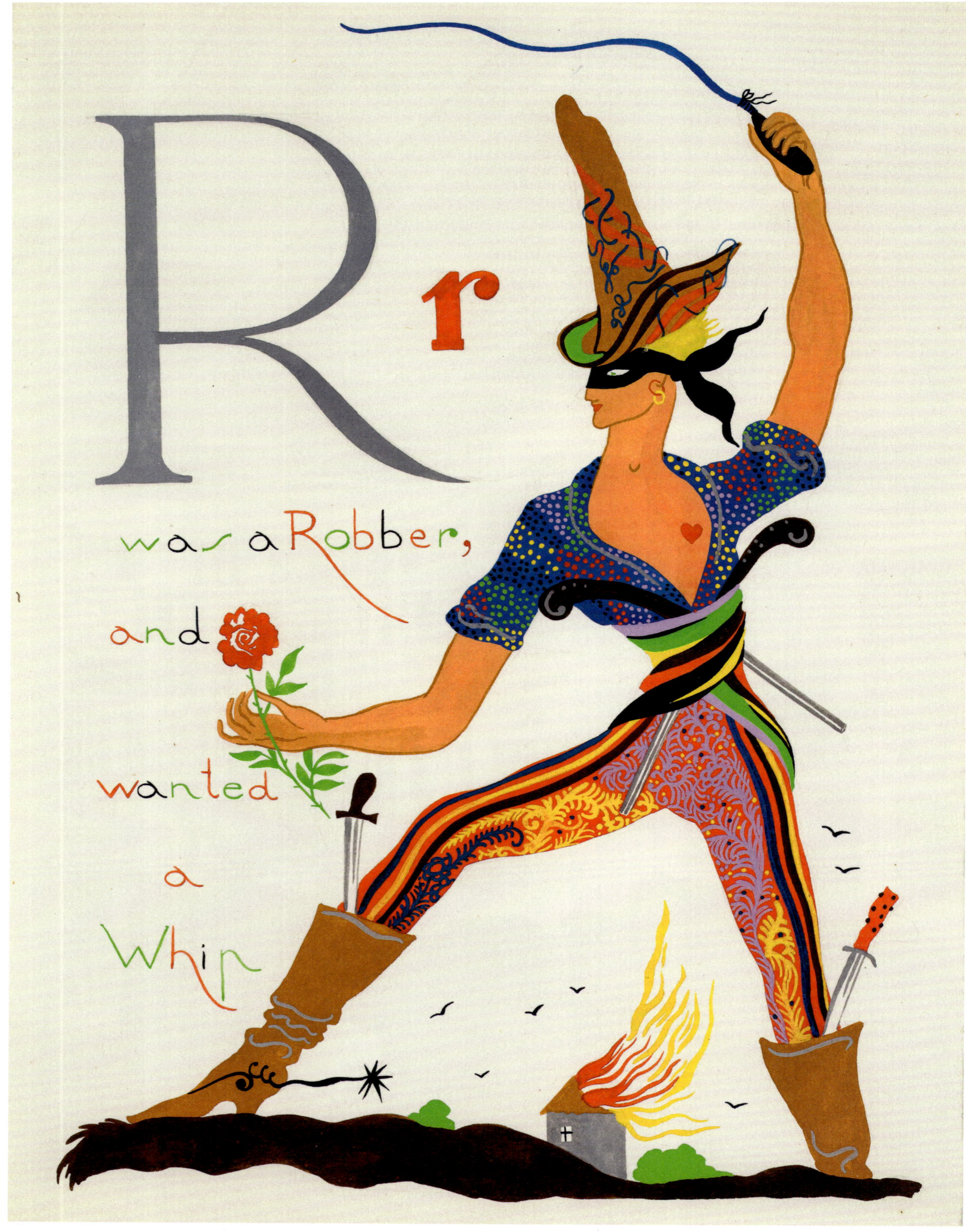

Maquette for the Alphabet Book,
Buchstabe / letter R, undatiert / undated

ABCs IM KLASSENKAMPF

Was die „Dekorateure" Federico Pallavicini und Andy Warhol verbindet (und was sie trennt)

MANUELA AMMER

1949 siedelten sich zwei Kreative in New York an, deren weitere Karrieren nicht unterschiedlicher verlaufen hätten können. Der eine, Andy Warhol, sollte als einflussreichster Künstler des 20. Jahrhunderts in die Geschichte eingehen, der andere, Friedrich von Berzeviczy-Pallavicini (oder Federico Pallavicini, wie er sich damals nannte), weitgehend in Vergessenheit geraten. Dass die Wege der beiden sich kreuzten, belegt ein auf Tonband aufgezeichnetes Interview von 1982, in dem Pallavicini sich ausführlich zu Warhol äußert (von dem 20 Jahre jüngeren Warhol sind keine Aussagen über Pallavicini bekannt):

> „Den [Warhol] kann ich überhaupt nicht ausstehen. Ich habe ihn vom ersten Moment [an gekannt], ich bin der Erste, der ihn kennengelernt hat. Das ist eine Mache, das ist ein Bluff. Er verkauft sich sehr gut. Und er ist ein guter Zeichner, aber kein wunderbarer. [...] Sein großer Trick ist, dass er immer, immer, immer, immer seinen Namen überall hingibt. In den tiefsten Provinzen, im Ausland, durch die Zeitungen ist er dann [präsent], glauben die Leute, dass er was ist, er ist gar nichts. [...]
>
> Ich war dabei, wir haben beide denselben Mann gehabt, der Weihnachtskarten gemacht hat. Das war auch so Siebdruck. Einmal hat er eine Weihnachtskarte gemacht mit einer Fotografie von der Marilyn Monroe [...]. Bevor man die Siebdrucke macht, macht man Probedrucke, und diese ganzen Sachen werden schief, und die Formen gehen übereinander. So ein Papier am Boden wurde aufgehoben, wie es war, und er hat es dann als große Kunst gezeichnet. [...] Abfall, wirklich wahr, ich war dabei.
>
> Er ist penetrant in seiner Publizität, penetrant, für Jahre hatte ich Zeichnungen von ihm bekommen, aber ich hab' sie alle in den Papierkorb geworfen. Noch vor zwei Jahren, eine Menge, die sind bestimmt sehr wertvoll, glaub' ich, ich hab' sie alle weggeworfen."[1]

Ohne diese Tonbandaufnahme gäbe es kaum Grund, sich über das Verhältnis von Pallavicini und Warhol Gedanken zu machen. Auf den ersten Blick verbindet die beiden wenig; sie gehören unterschiedlichen Generationen an und stehen für – wie auch Pallavicinis Aussage dokumentiert – gänzlich unterschiedliche künstlerische Auffassungen, Lebens- und Arbeitsstile. Die Intensität allerdings, mit der Pallavicini über Warhol spricht, sowie seine Behauptung, der „Erste" zu sein, „der ihn kennengelernt hat", geben Anlass, ihre frühen Jahre in New York genauer in den Blick zu nehmen.

Im Unterschied zu seinen Anfängen in Wien, wo Pallavicini im Umfeld der Kunstgewerbeschule (heute Universität für angewandte Kunst) und für die Konditorei Demel tätig war, haben wir von seiner Zeit in den USA nur oberflächliche Kenntnisse.[2] Was wir wissen, speist sich aus wenigen – teils leicht widersprüchlichen – Quellen, die sich primär auf Angaben des Künstlers stützen und sein Leben als märchenhafte Verkettung unwahrscheinlicher Ereignisse schildern.[3] Der Ruf nach New York erfolgte aufgrund von Pallavicinis Tätigkeit als Gestalter und Illustrator für diverse italienische Magazine. Der „ebenso extravagante [...] wie feinfühlige [...] und sensible [...]" Künstler war 1938, nach dem Einmarsch Hitlers in Österreichs nach Italien emigriert, wo er über ein weitreichendes Netzwerk von Verwandten und Freund*innen verfügte.[4] Seine Frau Klára, zukünftige Demel-Erbin, mit der der homosexuelle Pallavicini seit 1936 eine arrangierte Ehe führte, blieb in Wien zurück. Es war das Lifestyle-Magazin *Aria d'Italia* (1939–41), welches Pallavicini gemeinsam mit Daria Guarnati kreierte, das internationale Aufmerksamkeit erregte. Auf Recherchereise in Mailand entdeckte die Publizistin, Autorin und Society-Lady Fleur Cowles die opulent gestaltete Zeitschrift und überzeugte ihren Mann, den amerikanischen Verleger Gardner „Mike" Cowles Jr., Herausgeber von *Look*, die amerikanischen Rechte zu kaufen und die beiden Verantwortlichen nach New York zu holen.[5] Dort schrieb man einmal mehr Grafikdesigngeschichte: Unter der Schirmherrschaft von Fleur Cowles wurde *Flair* aus der Taufe gehoben, ein Magazin, dessen anspruchsvoller Mix aus Mode, Kunst und Kultur sich an eine exklusive Leser*innenschaft richtete und dessen extravagantes Erscheinungsbild Pallavicini

1 Pallavicini in einem Audiointerview mit Erika Patka, Lutz Musner und Oswald Oberhuber an der Hochschule für angewandte Kunst Wien, 17.05.1982.

2 Zu Pallavicinis Wirken in Wien siehe beispielsweise Waltraud Kaufmann, *Eine andere Welt. Friedrich von Berzeviczy-Pallavicini – sein Wiener Frühwerk der Zwischenkriegszeit*, Diplomarbeit Universität Wien, 2010, und Gabriele Koller, „Die Auflösung der Dinge", in: *Friedrich von Berzeviczy-Pallavicini. Poesie der Inszenierung*, Wien 1988, S. 51–61.

3 Nennenswert sind hier der Text von Gotthard Böhm für die Publikation *Federico von Berzeviczy-Pallavicini. Die K. u. K. Hofzuckerbäckerei Demel. Ein Wiener Märchen* (1976) und die von Erika Patka verfasste Biografie in der Begleitpublikation zur Ausstellung *Friedrich von Berzeviczy-Pallavicini. Poesie der Inszenierung* (1988). Pallavicinis Memoiren, von denen ein Auszug in *Poesie der Inszenierung* abgedruckt ist, wurden nie publiziert und sind auch in Manuskriptform nicht überliefert.

4 Gotthard Böhm, „Ein Wiener Märchen", in: Christian Brandstätter (Hg.), *Federico von Berzeviczy-Pallavicini. Die K. u. K. Hofzuckerbäckerei Demel. Ein Wiener Märchen*, Wien u. a. 1976, S. 7–145, hier: S. 126.

5 Im Unterschied zu Pallavicini kehrte Daria Guarnati New York bald wieder den Rücken, um nach Italien zurückzugehen.

ABCs AND CLASS STRUGGLE

What Connects the Two "Decorative Artists" Federico Pallavicini and Andy Warhol (and What Separates Them)

MANUELA AMMER

In 1949, two creatives settled in New York, whose careers could not have taken a more different course. One of them, Andy Warhol, would enter history as one of the most influential artists of the twentieth century, while the other, Friedrich von Berzeviczy-Pallavicini (or Federico Pallavicini, as he was then known), largely faded into obscurity. That the two artists crossed paths is documented in a tape-recorded interview from 1982, in which Pallavicini talks at length about Warhol (Warhol, who was twenty years his junior, is not on record as having spoken about Pallavicini):

> "I cannot stand him [Warhol]. I have known him from the very beginning; I was the first person to meet him. It's all a show, a bluff. He sells himself very well. And he's a good draftsman, but by no means outstanding. [...] His big trick is that he gets his name out there, always, everywhere, without fail. In the deepest provinces, overseas, in the papers: then, because he has a presence, people think he is something. He is nothing. [...]
> I was there, we both used the same man who made Christmas cards. It was a kind of silk-screen print. He once made a Christmas card with a photograph of Marilyn Monroe [...]. Before you make the silk-screen prints, you make test prints, and these end up wonky and the forms overlap. One of these test sheets was picked up off the floor, just as it was, and he then fobbed it off as great art. [...] Trash. Really. I was there.
> He is very persistent in his publicity, very persistent. For years he sent me drawings, but I threw them all in the bin. Even two years ago still, he sent me a whole lot, they were probably worth a lot of money, I think. I threw them all away."[1]

Without this audio recording, there would hardly be a reason to write about the relationship between Pallavicini and Warhol. At first glance there is little connection between the two; they belong to different generations and, as Pallavicini's statement documents, represent completely different approaches to art, lifestyle, and ways of working. However, the intensity with which Pallavicini speaks about Warhol, along with his assertion that he was "the first person to meet him," gives reason to explore their early years in New York in greater detail.

In contrast to his early years in Vienna, where Pallavicini was involved with the School of Applied Arts and the Demel confectionery store, our knowledge about his time in the USA is sketchy.[2] What we do know has been gathered from a small number of—at times somewhat contradictory—sources, based largely on the artist's own statements, which chart his life as a fantastical chain of unlikely events.[3] The call to New York arose from Pallavicini's work as a designer and illustrator for various Italian magazines. In 1938, after Hitler's invasion of Austria, the "extravagant [...] yet subtle [...] and sensitive [...]" artist had emigrated to Italy, where he had an extensive network of relatives and friends.[4] His wife Klára, the future heiress of Demel, with whom the homosexual Pallavicini had been in a marriage of convenience since 1936, stayed in Vienna. It was the lifestyle magazine *Aria d'Italia* (1939–41), created by Pallavicini together with Daria Guarnati, which attracted international attention. On a research trip to Milan, the publicist, author, and society lady Fleur Cowles discovered the opulently designed magazine and persuaded her husband, the American publisher of *Look*, Gardner "Mike" Cowles Jr., to purchase the American rights and summon the pair to New York.[5] Once there, they went about making graphic design history. Under the patronage of Fleur Cowles, *Flair* was launched, a magazine offering a sophisticated combination of fashion, art, and culture aimed at an exclusive readership, and whose extravagant design was significantly shaped by Pallavicini. Although *Flair* only ran for twelve issues (following a pilot issue in September 1949), the magazine remains legendary to this day. Assorted papers (some of them perfumed), die-cut covers, bound booklets, fold-out pages, etc.—the very same exceptional (and exceptionally expensive) design features that provoked warnings about the "femininity and effeminity" of the magazine also consolidated its cult status among fans.[6]

1 Pallavicini in an audio interview with Erika Patka, Lutz Musner, and Oswald Oberhuber at the University of Applied Arts Vienna, May 17, 1982.

2 For more on Pallavicini's activities in Vienna, see, for example, Waltraud Kaufmann, *Eine andere Welt: Friedrich von Berzeviczy-Pallavicini – sein Wiener Frühwerk der Zwischenkriegszeit*, master's thesis, University of Vienna, 2010, and Gabriele Koller, "Die Auflösung der Dinge," in *Friedrich von Berzeviczy-Pallavicini: Poesie der Inszenierung* (Vienna, 1988), pp. 51–61.

3 Worth mentioning here is the text by Gotthard Böhm published in *Federico von Berzeviczy-Pallavicini: Die K. u. K. Hofzuckerbäckerei Demel. Ein Wiener Märchen* (1976) and the biography written by Erika Patka for the book accompanying the exhibition *Friedrich von Berzeviczy-Pallavicini: Poesie der Inszenierung* (1988). Pallavicini's memoirs, of which *Poesie der Inszenierung* includes an excerpt, were never published and the whereabouts of the manuscript is unknown.

4 Gotthard Böhm, "Ein Wiener Märchen," in *Federico von Berzeviczy-Pallavicini: Die K. u. K. Hofzuckerbäckerei Demel. Ein Wiener Märchen*, ed. Christian Brandstätter (Vienna et al, 1976), pp. 7–145, here: p. 126.

5 Unlike Pallavicini, Daria Guarnati soon turned her back on New York and returned to Italy.

6 *Space & Time*, an advertising industry newsletter, warned customers "allergic to femininity and effeminity" against placing ads in *Flair.*

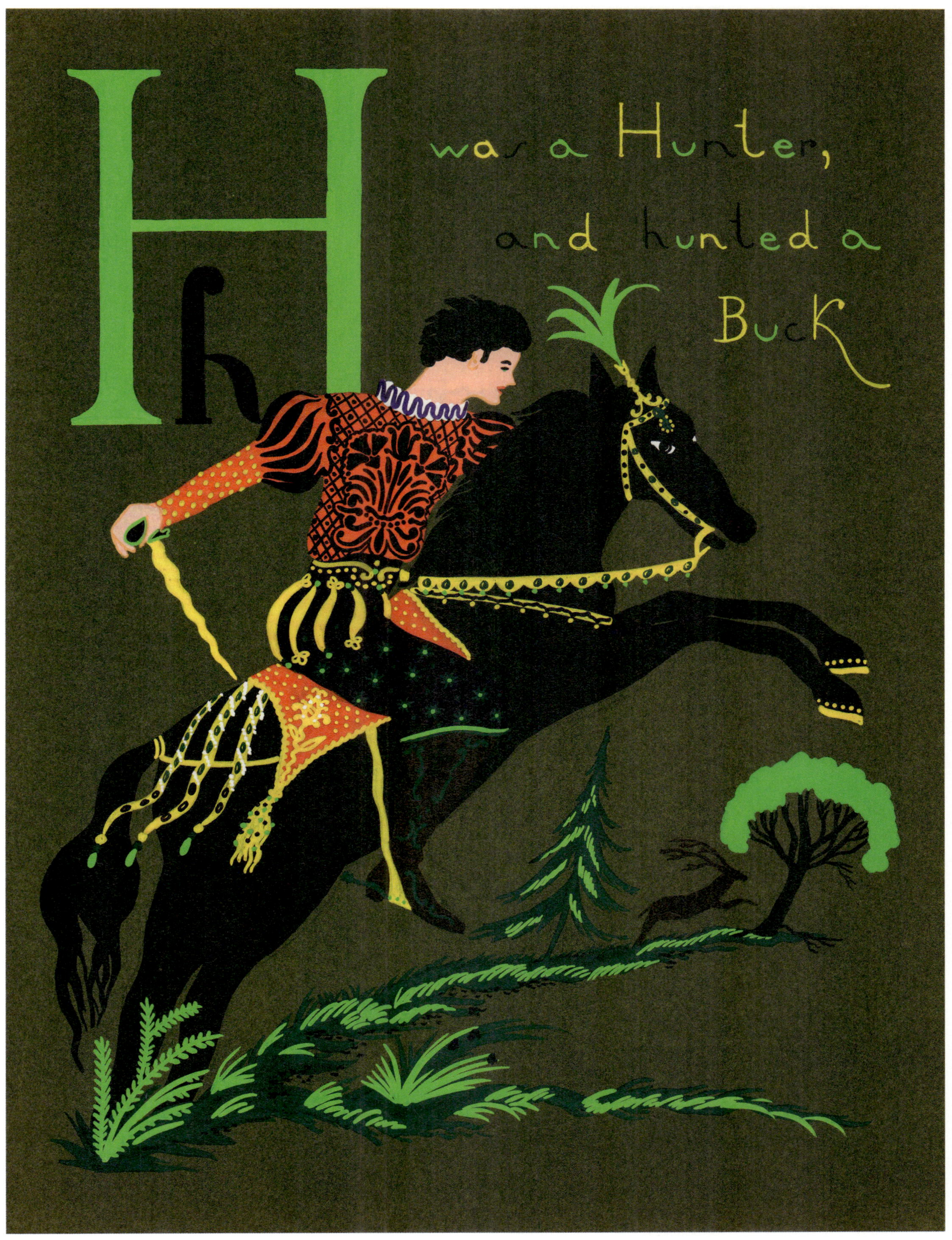

Maquette for the Alphabet Book,
Buchstabe / letter H, undatiert / undated

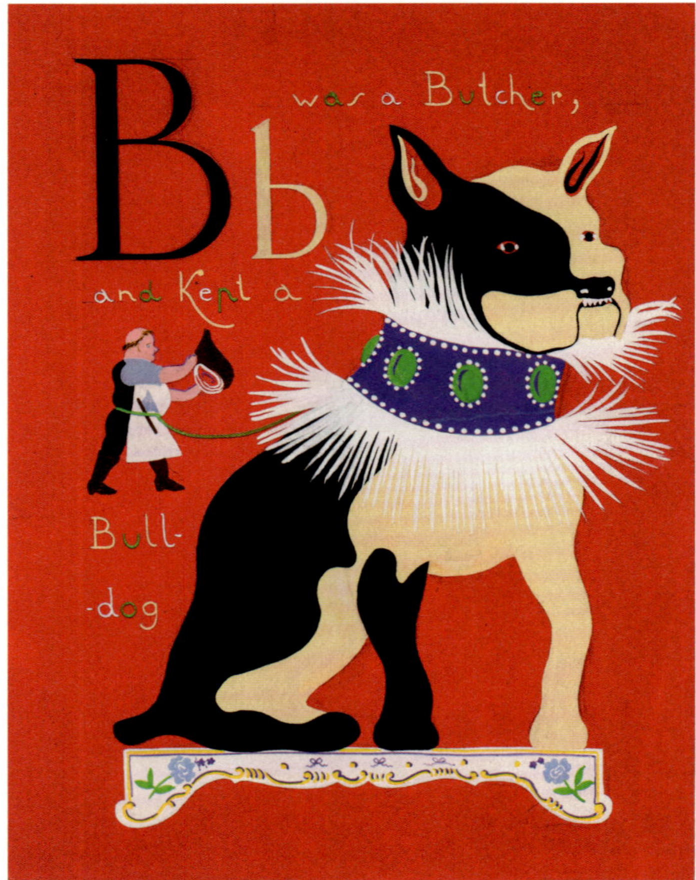

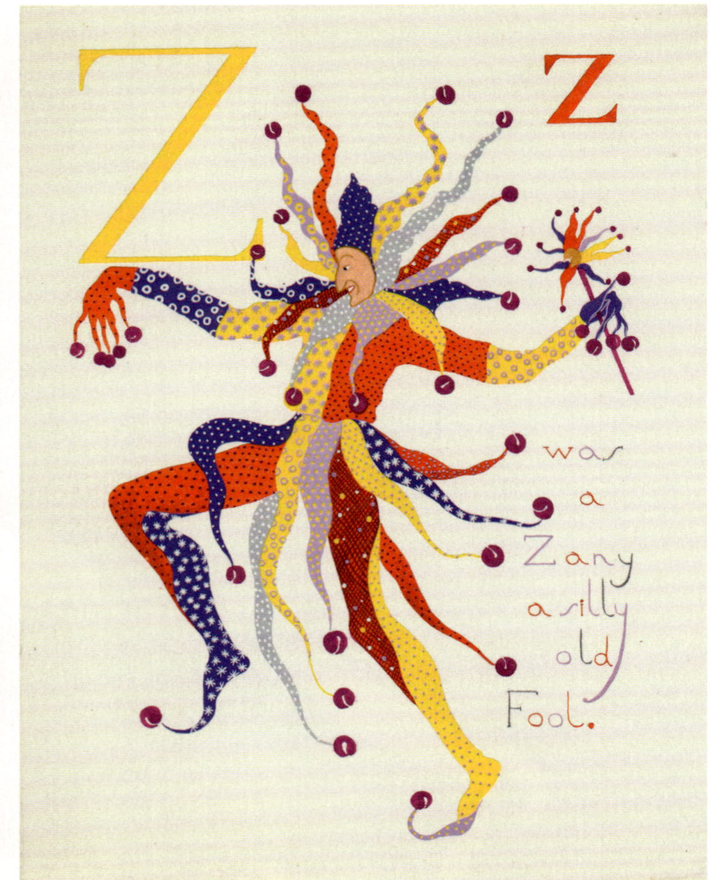

Maquette for the Alphabet Book,
Buchstaben / letters B, Z, Y, T, undatiert / undated

For Pallavicini, working with Fleur Cowles offered a fast track into the New York creative scene, both professionally and socially. With the magazine's staff sometimes exceeding one hundred, led by chief editor George Davis (the "discoverer" of Truman Capote), *Flair* provided a network of illustrious—"multilingual, pan-generational, omnisexual"[7]—personalities from fashion, lifestyle, photography, art, and advertising, which would benefit Pallavicini for years to come. Within this context, he himself cultivated the habitus of an "Old World" eccentric and entertained staff with his "aristocratic manners, ebullience, and spicy gossip," as a member of the editorial team recalled.[8] Financially, *Flair* was a disaster, and in December 1950—Pallavicini had obtained his American citizenship by then—the *Look* publishing house announced the discontinuation of the magazine. In time for the Christmas season of 1952, however, Fleur Cowles staged a return to the market with the *Flair Annual 1953*, which brought together unpublished articles from previous issues. This version of *Flair* (which was intended to continue) involved not one hundred, but three people, including Cowles. Pallavicini had sole responsibility for the design of the 230-page publication, which once again featured fold-out pages and bound booklets. After the end of *Flair*, Pallavicini continued to work as a stylist for *Look*—a photo from August 1953, for example, shows him with Jackson Pollock, Lee Krasner, and *Look*'s art director Charlotte Willards on a visit to Pollock's studio in East Hampton.[9] He also had the opportunity to resume the kind of work familiar to him from his time in Vienna and at Demel: in 1955, Elizabeth Arden commissioned him as art director to design, among other things, the displays at her salons; in 1956, he moved to Arden's competitor Helena Rubinstein, with whom he remained friends until her death in 1965. He decorated her private residences, stores and window displays, and designed packaging for her cosmetics products.[10]

Cf. Amy Fine Collins, "A *Flair* for Living," *Vanity Fair* (October, 1996). Online at: www.vanityfair.com/magazine/1996/10/fleur-cowles199610 [accessed on December 31, 2019].
7 Ibid.
8 Ibid.

9 The photo was taken by Tony Vaccaro, who had been commissioned by Fleur Cowles (who also continued to work as editor for *Look*) to document Long Island's emerging art scene together with Charlotte Willards.
10 As an entrepreneur, Rubinstein had already been skillfully

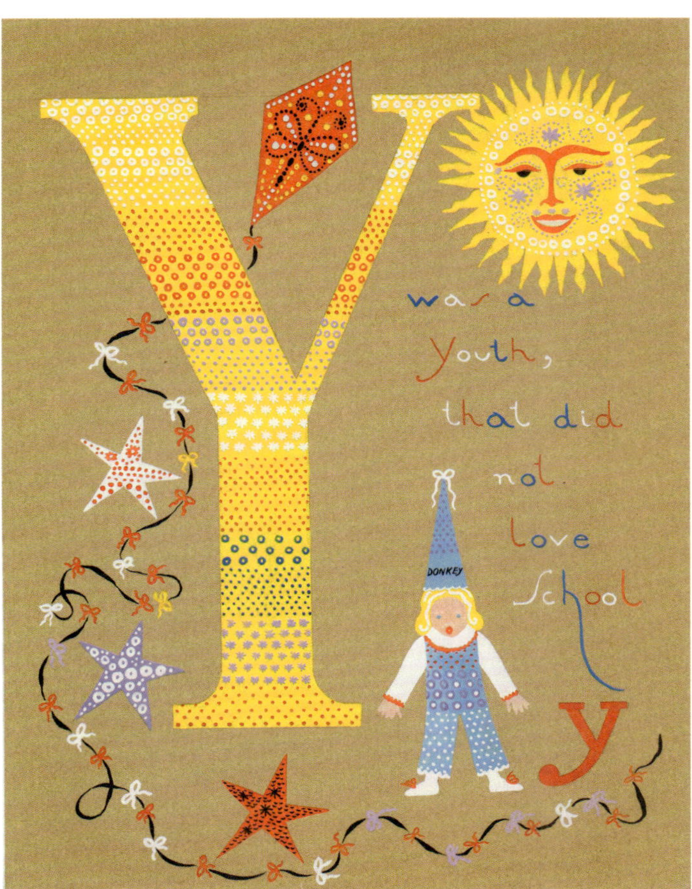

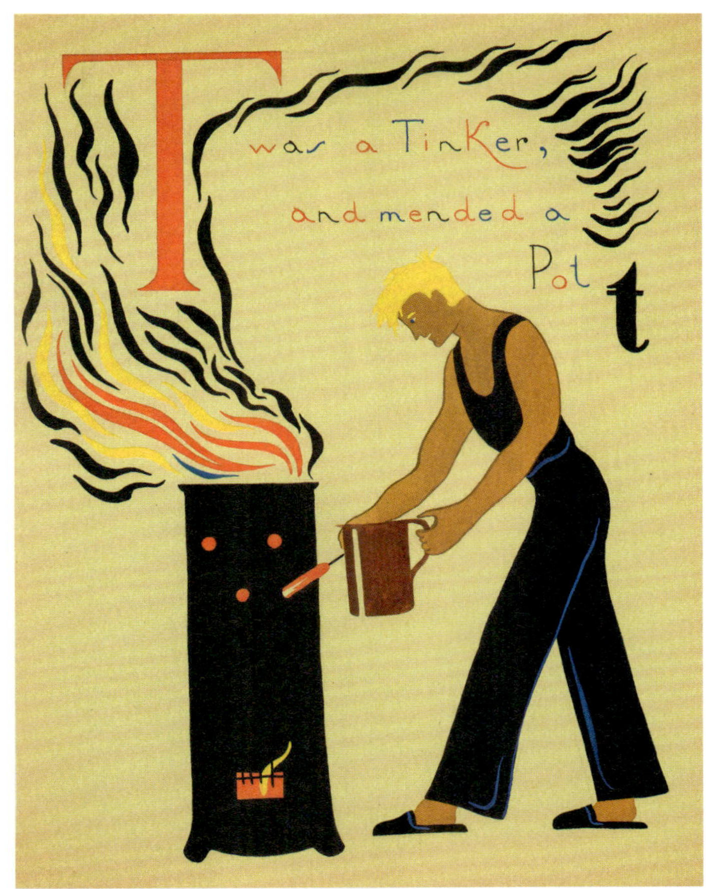

wesentlich mitprägte. Obwohl *Flair* (nach einer Probenummer im September 1949) nur zwölf Ausgaben erleben sollte, gilt die Zeitschrift bis heute als legendär: Der Einsatz von verschiedenen (auch parfümierten) Papieren, gestanzten Covers, eingebundenen Booklets, ausklappbaren Seiten usw. – alle jene außergewöhnlichen (und außergewöhnlich kostspieligen) Gestaltungsmittel, die in professionellen Kreisen zu Warnungen vor der „Feminität und Effeminität" der Zeitschrift führten – begründete unter Liebhaber*innen ihren Kultstatus.[6]

Für Pallavicini bedeutete die Arbeit mit Fleur Cowles beruflich wie sozial einen „fast track" in die New Yorker Kreativszene. Mit einer teils mehr als 100-köpfigen Belegschaft unter der Leitung von Chefredakteur George Davis („Entdecker" von Truman Capote) stellte *Flair* ein Netzwerk illustrer – „multilingual, pan-generational, omnisexual"[7] – Persönlichkeiten aus den Bereichen Mode, Lifestyle, Fotografie, Kunst und Werbung bereit, von dem Pallavicini wohl auch in den Folgejahren profitierte. Er selbst kultivierte in diesem Kontext den Habitus eines Exzentrikers aus der „Alten Welt" und unterhielt die Belegschaft mit seinen „aristokratischen Manieren, seinem überschäumenden Wesen und pikantem Klatsch", wie sich einer der Redakteure erinnert.[8] Finanziell war *Flair* ein Debakel, und der *Look*-Konzern besiegelte im Dezember 1950 – Pallavicini hatte in der Zwischenzeit die amerikanische Staatsbürgerschaft erworben – das Ende der Zeitschrift. Rechtzeitig zur Weihnachtssaison 1952 allerdings brachte Fleur Cowles noch ein Dacapo auf den Markt, das *Flair Annual 1953*, das in den Heftausgaben nicht publizierte Beiträge in der Form eines Jahrbuchs versammelte. An dieser (zur Fortsetzung geplanten) Version von *Flair* waren nicht 100, sondern inklusive Cowles drei Personen beteiligt: Pallavicini zeichnete alleine für das Design der 230 Seiten starken Publikation verantwortlich, die einmal mehr aus- und aufklappbare Seiten sowie eingebundene Heftchen enthielt. Nach dem Ende von *Flair* arbeitete Pallavicini weiter als Stylist für *Look* – ein Foto vom

6 *Space & Time*, ein Newsletter der Werbebranche, warnte Kunden „allergic to femininity and effeminity" vor Inseraten in *Flair*. Vgl. Amy Fine Collins, „A *Flair* for Living", in: *Vanity Fair*, Oktober 1996. Online unter: www.vanityfair.com/magazine/1996/10/fleur-cowles 199610 [Stand 31.12.2019].
7 Ebd.

8 Ebd.

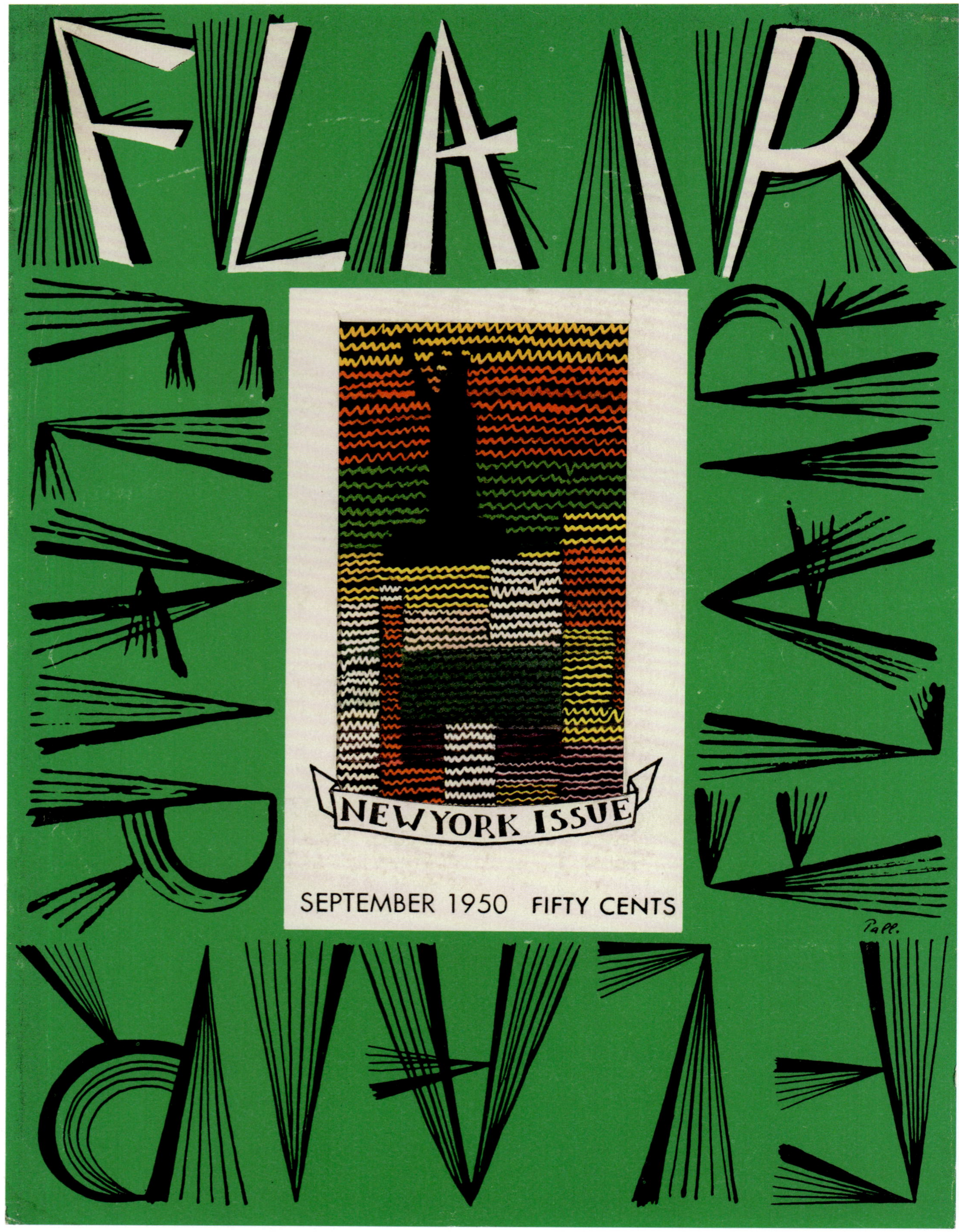

Cover *Flair*, Ausgabe / issue September 1950
Cowles Magazine Inc., New York, 1950

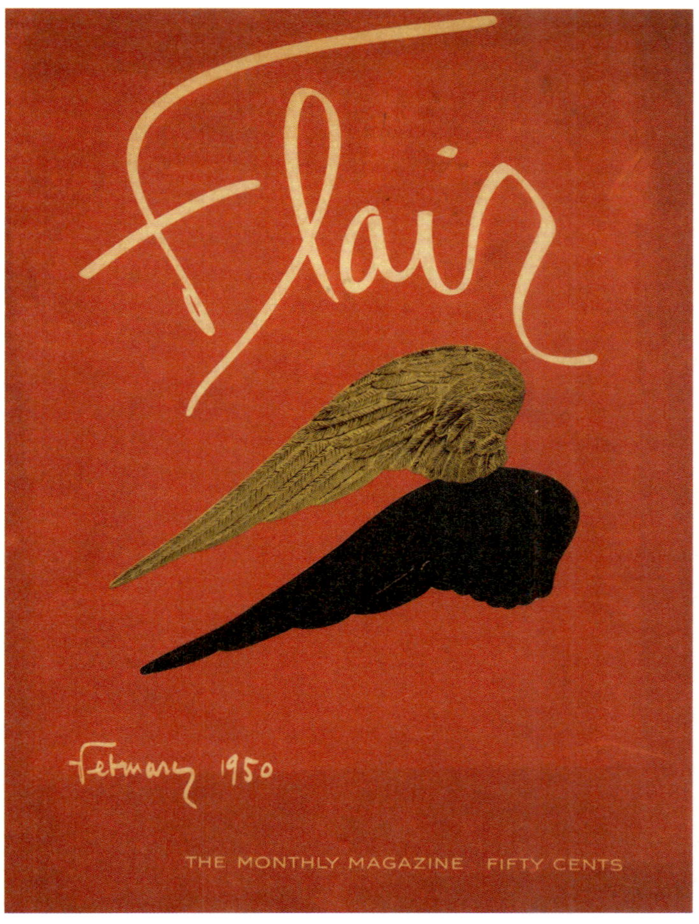

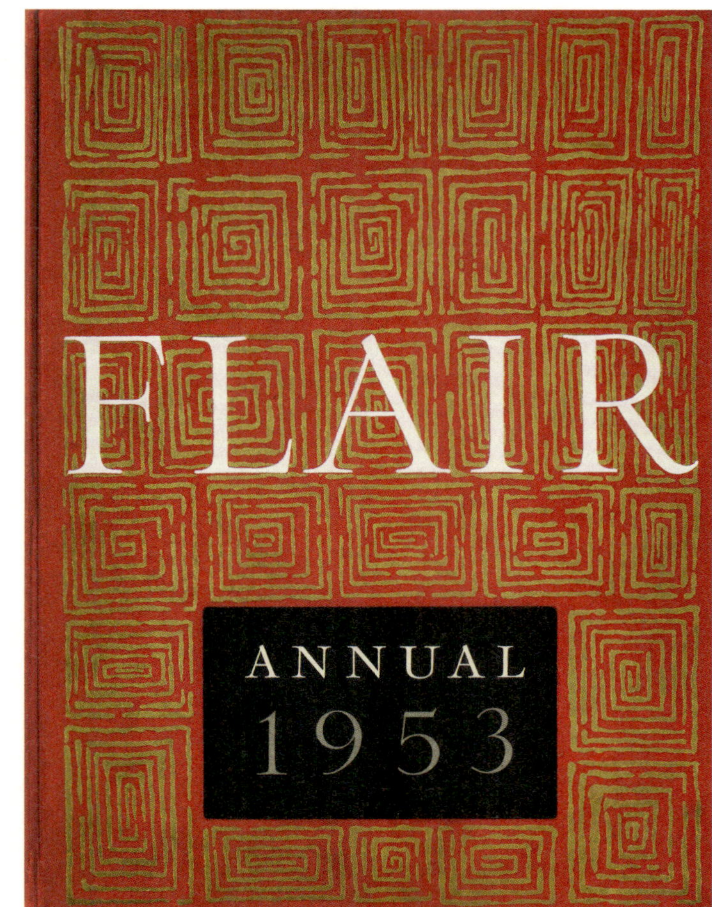

Links / left: Cover *Flair*, Ausgabe / issue Februar / February 1950, Cowles Magazine Inc., New York, 1950

Rechts / right: Cover *Flair Annual 1953*, Cowles Magazine Inc., New York, 1953

August 1953 zeigt ihn beispielsweise mit Jackson Pollock, Lee Krasner und *Look*-Art-Director Charlotte Willards beim Besuch von Pollocks Atelier in East Hampton.[9] Und er erhielt die Gelegenheit, an Tätigkeiten anzuknüpfen, die ihm aus seiner Zeit in Wien und am Demel wohlvertraut waren: 1955 wurde er von Elizabeth Arden als Art Director engagiert und gestaltete unter anderem die Auslagen der Salons des Kosmetikkonzerns; 1956 wechselte er zu Ardens Konkurrentin Helena Rubinstein, der er bis zu ihrem Tod 1965 verbunden blieb. Er dekorierte ihre privaten Domizile ebenso wie die Geschäftslokale und Schaufenster des Unternehmens und entwarf Verpackungen für die Kosmetikprodukte.[10]

Während sich Pallavicinis Engagements als Grafiker, Stylist und Gestalter über seine Assoziation mit prominenten Namen zumindest teilweise gut nachvollziehen lassen, ist die Quellenlage zu seinen künstlerischen Aktivitäten in New York deutlich dünner. Ausgestellt hatte Pallavicini bereits in Italien, darunter in der für das Nachkriegs-Rom so wichtigen Galerie L'Obelisco (1946–78), die etablierte Künstler wie Giorgio de Chirico oder Salvador Dalí, aber auch neue Talente wie Alberto Burri oder Lucio Fontana sowie Keramiken und Schmuck zeigte. Das Gründerpaar der Galerie, Irene Brin und Gaspero del Corso, hatte Pallavicini über seine Arbeit für die Zeitschrift *Bellezza* kennengelernt, wo Brin als Modejournalistin tätig war.[11] Über del Corso und Brin lässt sich auch ein Link nach New York und zu Pallavicinis wohl einflussreichstem Galeristen, Alexander Iolas, herstellen: Bereits 1945, als die beiden noch Ausstellungen im Antiquariat und

9 Das Foto stammt von Tony Vaccaro, der von Fleur Cowles (die ebenfalls weiterhin als Redakteurin für *Look* arbeitete) den Auftrag erhalten hatte, gemeinsam mit Willards die neu entstehende Kunstszene auf Long Island zu dokumentieren.

10 Als Unternehmerin wusste Rubinstein die Einrichtung ihrer Schönheitssalons schon Jahrzehnte vor ihrer Begegnung mit Pallavicini gekonnt mit Vorstellungen „moderner Weiblichkeit" zu verknüpfen. Vgl. beispielsweise Marie J. Clifford, „Helena Rubinstein's Beauty Salons, Fashion and Modernist Display", in: *Winterthur Portfolio*, 2/3 (2003), S. 83–108.

11 Pallavicinis erste Ausstellung bei L'Obelisco mit dem Titel *Ipocrisie* (*Heucheleien*) zeigte Gouachen und Zeichnungen und fand im April 1948 statt; seine zweite im April 1959. Siehe Ilaria Schiaffini, „Between Fashion, Art and Photography: Irene Brin and the Early Activities of the Galleria L'Obelisco", in: Giovanna Motta, Antonello Biagini (Hg.), *Fashion through History. Costumes, Symbols, Communication (Volume II)*, Newcastle upon Tyne 2017, S. 591–602.

While Pallavicini's work as illustrator, stylist, and designer can at least partly be traced from his connections with well-known names, his activities as an artist in New York are less well documented. Pallavicini had already been exhibiting in Italy, including at the L'Obelisco gallery (1946–78), an important location in postwar Rome, which showcased established artists such as Giorgio de Chirico or Salvador Dalí alongside new talents like Alberto Burri or Lucio Fontana, as well as ceramics and jewelry. The couple who founded the gallery, Irene Brin and Gaspero del Corso, had met Pallavicini through his work for the magazine *Bellezza*, for which Brin worked as a fashion journalist.[11] Via Del Corso and Brin, a link can be established to New York and to what was probably Pallavicini's most influential gallerist, Alexander Iolas. As early as 1945, when the two were still organizing exhibitions at the antiquarian bookshop and anti-fascist meeting point La Margherita in Rome, Iolas contacted Brin and Del Corso and expressed an interest in their program, especially in the work of the Italian Surrealists.[12] From 1952, Brin also acted as the first Italian correspondent for *Harper's Bazaar*, and the pair played an important role in the promotion of contemporary Italian art in the USA (with the support of Helena Rubinstein, among others).[13]

In Alexander Iolas, Pallavicini once more encountered a personality who was at least as eccentric as the art he promoted. The Alexandrian native and son of a wealthy Greek family had been a ballet dancer in Paris, where he developed a taste for Surrealist art. After his dancing career came to an end, in November 1945, he opened the Hugo Gallery with the help of Elizabeth Arden, the banker's son Robert Rothschild, and Maria Ruspoli, a former dance partner and Italian aristocrat married to a great-grandson of the author Victor Hugo. The gallery was to become an important platform for European (exile) art; opulently clad in purple velvet by the Russian painter and theater designer Pavel Tchelitchew, its rooms hosted not only solo exhibitions by Joseph Cornell, René Magritte, and Max Ernst, but also the Surrealist group exhibition *Blood Flames* (1947), whose legendary display was designed by Frederick Kiesler. Following his involvement with the Hugo Gallery, Iolas, who was openly gay—"as they used to say in the 50s, he was 'camp as a row of tents'"[14]—established the first gallery in his own name at around 1952/53, which he subsequently grew into an international empire.[15] Alongside European artists, the Iolas Gallery also provided a home for American individualists such as William N. Copley, who, like Iolas and Pallavicini, resisted the trend to total abstraction and instead embraced an eclectic blend of the figurative and the decorative in his paintings.

Pallavicini's first collaboration with Iolas still took place at the Hugo Gallery, as documented by a folded invitation card. Under the simple headline *Pallavicini*, the card invites the recipient—by way of an ornate inscription framed by an opulent wreath—to an exhibition of "decorative drawings and paintings" in April 1951. We also learn that the exhibition was dedicated to "Amor, Venus, and Mars," and the latter indeed seems to be the figure chosen by Pallavicini for the title page. In this drawing, the god of war has cast aside his helmet and shield (and most other items of clothing) and is reclining on the ground in a lascivious pose—apparently placated by the goddess of love—while flames lick at the sky in the background. Evidence of another exhibition with Iolas in 1952, as mentioned in the literature on Pallavicini, could not be found.[16] There is, however, a photo which, according to the caption, was published in *Look* and shows the artist in 1953 in front of one of his folding screens at the "A. Iolas Gallery."[17] What exactly was on display at these early New York exhibitions remains speculation. What we do know is that the early 1950s were a particularly prolific period for Pallavicini as a painter. The collection of the University of Applied Arts in Vienna includes a range of images with decorative, planar floral arrangements in front of atmospheric

integrating notions of "modern 'feminine' space" in the designs of her beauty salons, decades before meeting Pallavicini. Cf. as an example Marie J. Clifford, "Helena Rubinstein's Beauty Salons, Fashion and Modernist Display," *Winterthur Portfolio*, 2/3 (2003), pp. 83–108.

11 Pallavicini's first exhibition at L'Obelisco titled *Ipocrisie* (Hypocrisies) was held in April 1948 and showed gouaches and drawings; his second was in April 1959. See Ilaria Schiaffini, "Between Fashion, Art and Photography: Irene Brin and the Early Activities of the Galleria L'Obelisco," in *Fashion through History: Costumes, Symbols, Communication (Volume II)*, eds. Giovanna Motta and Antonello Biagini (Newcastle upon Tyne, 2017), pp. 591–602.

12 "A telegram arrived from a man named Iolas, a Greek man, announcing the opening of the Hugo gallery, directed by the duchess of Gromont, previously married to Mister Gromont and now with Jean Hugo, surrealist and descendant of Victor. Iolas asked me about works by Leonor Fini, Filippo De Pisis, Stanislao Lepri, and other Italian surrealists." Diary of Gaspero del Corso, 1945, quoted from Giulia Tulino, "Alberto Savinio, Critic and Artist: A New Reading of Fantastic and Post-Metafisica Art in Relation to Surrealism between Rome and New York (1943–46)," *Italian Modern Art: Alberto Savinio*, 2 (2019). Online at: www.italianmodernart.org/journal/articles/alberto-savinio-critic-and-artist-a-new-reading-of-fantastic-and-post-metafisica-art-in-relation-to-surrealism-between-rome-and-new-york-1943-46 [accessed on December 31, 2019].

13 Brin and Del Corso were able to convince Rubinstein to commission works from young artists supported by the gallery, which were shown in 1953 under the title *Twenty Imaginary Views of the American Scene by Twenty Young Italian Artists* as part of Rubinstein's collection, first at L'Obelisco and eventually, after several stops in Europe, at the Brooklyn Museum in New York.

14 Interview with Sir John Richardson by Adrian Dannatt in *Alexander the Great: The Iolas Gallery 1955–1987* (New York, 2014), p. 82.

15 I have been unable to establish when exactly the Iolas Gallery in New York was founded. References in the literature and in interviews with contemporaries vary greatly, and invitations or catalogues from those years are rare (a more thorough research would require the consultation of relevant archives and libraries in the USA). What is certain is that in February 1953 an exhibition by Kurt Seligmann was held at the Alexander Iolas Gallery at 46 East 57th Street. (The Hugo Gallery had its premises at 26 East 55th Street.) There are also references to earlier exhibitions at the Alexander Iolas Gallery, but these lack an address, making it impossible to determine whether the Hugo Gallery operated under Iolas's name from a certain point onward, was simply identified with him, or whether perhaps two galleries existed in parallel for a brief period.

16 Erika Patka, "Friedrich von Berzeviczy-Pallavicini," in *Friedrich von Berzeviczy-Pallavicini: Poesie der Inszenierung* (see note 2), pp. 6–17, here p. 13.

17 See ibid., p. 14.

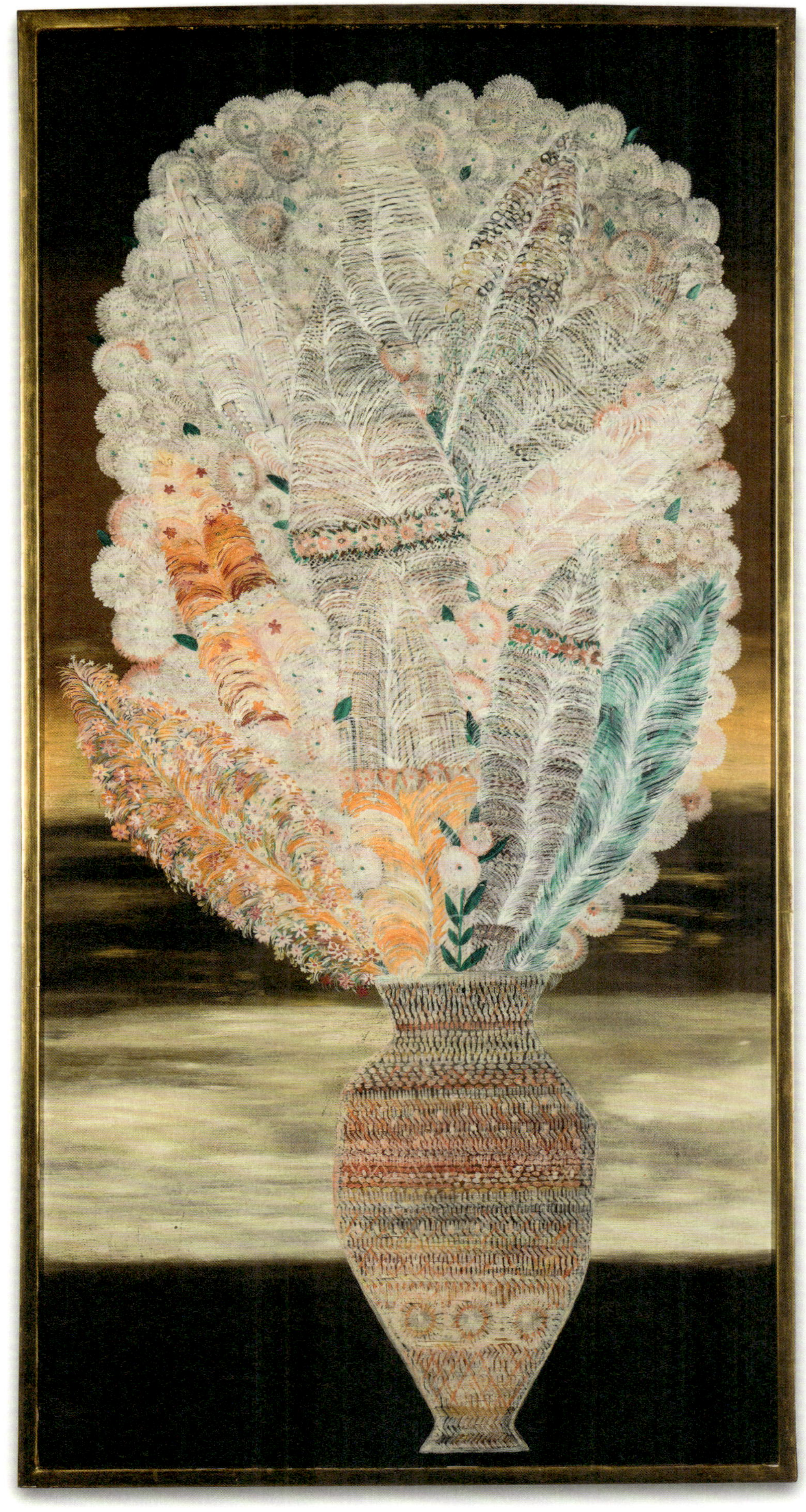

ohne Titel / Untitled, Vase mit Blättern und Federn / vase with leaves and feathers, um / c. 1950

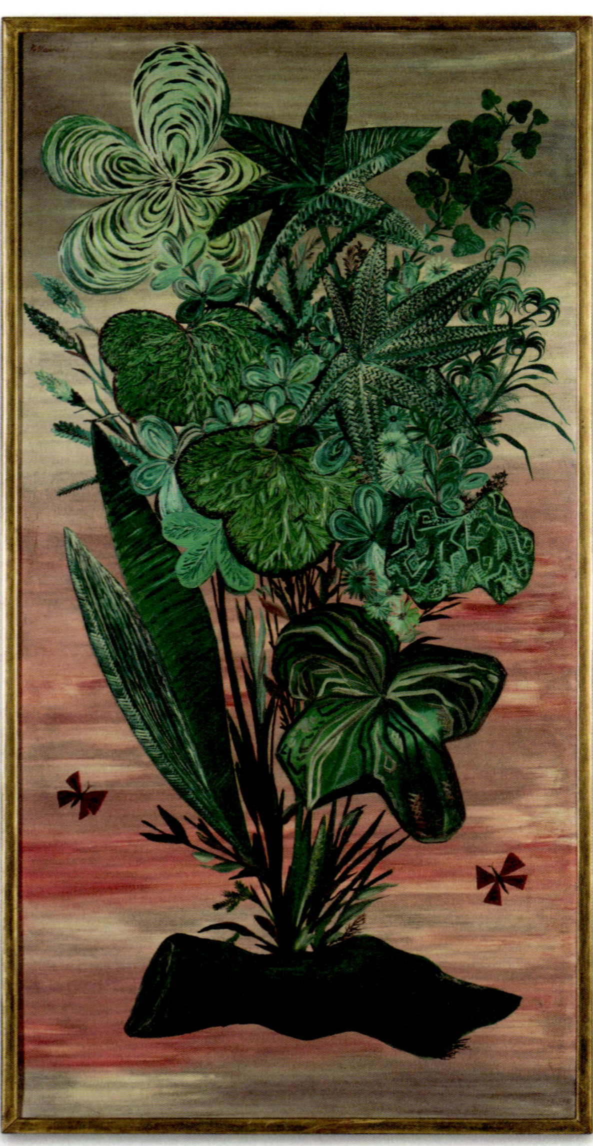

ohne Titel / Untitled,
Fantastische Blumen / fantasy flowers,
1952

backgrounds, some of which, albeit slightly less spectral, are reminiscent of still lifes by Jean Fautrier, who exhibited at the Hugo Gallery in 1952. Pallavicini is also thought to have designed the ceilings of the gallery, as well as the gallerist's living room and his sister's dining room.[18] Another project with Iolas from a slightly later date can be reconstructed in more detail. "Alexander Iolas and Arthur Stifel cordially invite you to come to the opening of the Zodiac Gallery and see the 12 signs painted especially for it by Federico Pallavicini," an invitation card reads, listing the exhibition dates as December 1956 to January 1957. In 1956, Iolas and his gallery moved to another building a few streets away. Descriptions suggest that the main room of the gallery was on the first floor, while the so-called "Zodiac Room" was in a back room on the ground floor.[19] The industrialist Arthur Stifel, who, together with Iolas, is mentioned as host of the opening of this room, was married to Iolas's sister Niki and was, presumably, also an occasional sponsor of the gallery.[20]

The twelve star signs painted by Pallavicini for the Zodiac Gallery all follow the same principle: in the center of a portrait-format panel, below the English name for each sign, is its symbol, and it would seem that the artist chose a style of depiction that matched each respective motif. The delicately rendered Virgo, for instance, could almost be from a Botticelli painting, while Taurus, and especially Leo, have been set down in rough, gestural brush strokes. Gold paint and tiny glass beads, scattered on like glitter, embellish the figures and create a tactile surface. Also notable is Pallavicini's treatment of the backgrounds, to which he—in the manner of a true "decorator"—devoted at least as much attention as to the star signs themselves. In colors that complement the motif, he

18 "As a painter he found a home at the New York gallery of Alexander Iolas, for which he designed the ceilings; it was said that Max Ernst was so impressed with the dining room that [Pallavicini] had painted for Alexander Iolas's sister that he added a flower and his signature to the design." Böhm, "Ein Wiener Märchen" (see note 4), p. 133. See also Kaufmann, *Eine andere Welt* (see note 2), p. 64.

19 Jules Olitski, "Clement Greenberg in My Studio," *American Art*, 3/4 (1994), pp. 125–29, here p. 125.

20 In an interview in *Vogue* from 1965, Iolas said: "Fortunately, I have a brother-in-law, a marvelous man, who has a great deal of confidence in me. I ask him for millions of dollars, and he gives them to me, just like that." "Iolas: The Art Dealer of the Moment Shares His Secrets with Maurice Rheims," reprinted in *Alexander the Great* (see note 14), pp. 34–42, here p. 36.

antifaschistischen Treffpunkt La Margharita in Rom organisierten, nahm Iolas Kontakt auf und äußerte Interesse an ihrem Programm, insbesondere am Werk der italienischen Surrealisten.[12] Ab 1952 fungierte Brin zudem als erste Italien-Korrespondentin für *Harper's Bazaar* und das Paar nahm eine wichtige Rolle in der Beförderung zeitgenössischer italienischer Kunst in den USA ein (unter anderem mit Unterstützung von Helena Rubinstein).[13]

Mit Alexander Iolas geriet Pallavicini einmal mehr an eine Persönlichkeit, die mindestens so exzentrisch war wie die Kunst, die er propagierte. Der in Alexandria geborene Sohn einer wohlhabenden griechischen Familie hatte als Balletttänzer in Paris einen Geschmack für surrealistische Kunst entwickelt. Nach dem Ende seiner Tanzkarriere in New York eröffnete er im November 1945 mit Unterstützung von Maria Ruspoli, einer ehemaligen Tanzpartnerin und italienischen Adeligen, die einen Urenkel des Schriftstellers Victor Hugo geehelicht hatte, dem Bankierssohn Robert Rothschild und Elizabeth Arden die Galerie Hugo, die zu einem wichtigen Umschlagplatz europäischer (Exil-) Kunst werden sollte. In den vom russischen Maler, Bühnen- und Kostümbildner Pawel Tschelitschew mit violetten Samtwänden opulent ausgestatteten Räumlichkeiten fanden nicht nur Einzelausstellungen von Joseph Cornell, René Magritte oder Max Ernst statt, sondern etwa auch die surrealistische Gruppenausstellung *Blood Flames* (1947), deren legendäres Display Friedrich Kiesler verantwortete. Auf sein Engagement in der Galerie Hugo folgte bald die Selbstständigkeit: Vermutlich um 1952/53 gründete der offen homosexuelle Iolas – „as they used to say in the 50s, he was ‚camp as a row of tents'"[14] – die erste Galerie unter eigenem Namen und baute sie in der Folge zu einem internationalen Imperium aus.[15] In der Galerie Alexander Iolas fanden neben europäischen Positionen auch amerikanische Individualisten wie William N. Copley eine Heimstatt, der sich – wie Iolas und Pallavicini – dem Trend zur totalen Abstraktion konsequent verweigerte und in seiner Malerei stattdessen eine eklektische Verschränkung des Figurativen mit dem Dekorativen praktizierte.

Pallavicinis erste Zusammenarbeit mit Iolas fand noch in den Räumlichkeiten der Galerie Hugo statt, wie eine aufklappbare Einladungskarte dokumentiert. Schlicht *Pallavicini* tituliert, wird im Inneren der Karte – im Stile einer opulent umkränzten Inschrift – zu einer Ausstellung von „decorative drawings and paintings" im April 1951 eingeladen. Dass diese Ausstellung „Amor, Venus and Mars" gewidmet sei, ist dort ebenfalls zu lesen, und Mars ist wohl auch die Figur, die Pallavicini auf dem Titelblatt darstellt: In seiner Zeichnung hat der Kriegsgott Schild und Helm (und die meisten anderen Kleidungsstücke) abgelegt und ruht – durch die Göttin der Liebe gezähmt – in lasziver Pose auf der Erde, während im Hintergrund Flammen gen Himmel züngeln. Belege für eine weitere Ausstellung mit Iolas 1952, wie die Pallavicini-Literatur angibt, ließen sich nicht finden.[16] Es existiert allerdings ein Foto, das – laut Bildlegende – in *Look* veröffentlicht wurde und den Künstler 1953 vor einem seiner Paravents in der „A. Iolas Gallery" zeigt.[17] Was es in diesen ersten New Yorker Ausstellungen genau zu sehen gab, muss Spekulation bleiben; sicher ist, dass Pallavicini in den frühen 1950er-Jahren als Maler recht produktiv war. Die Sammlung der Universität für angewandte Kunst in Wien verfügt über eine Reihe von Bildern mit dekorativ flächig gehaltenen Blumenarrangements vor atmosphärischen Hintergründen, von denen einige – wenn auch weniger gespenstisch – an Stillleben von Jean Fautrier denken lassen, der 1952 in der Galerie Hugo ausstellte. Auch soll Pallavicini die Plafonds der Galerie gestaltet haben sowie das Wohnzimmer des Galeristen und das Speisezimmer von dessen Schwester.[18] Ein etwas später mit Iolas realisiertes Projekt lässt sich genauer rekonstruieren: „Alexander Iolas and Arthur Stifel cordially invite you to come to the opening of the Zodiac Gallery and see the 12 signs painted especially for it by Federico Pallavicini" heißt es auf einer Karte, die als Ausstellungszeitraum Dezember 1956/Jänner 1957 nennt. 1956 zog Iolas mit seiner Galerie in ein anderes Gebäude wenige Straßen weiter um. Beschreibungen zufolge

12 „A telegram arrived from a man named Iolas, a Greek man, announcing the opening of the Hugo gallery, directed by the duchess of Gromont, previously married to Mister Gromont and now with Jean Hugo, surrealist and descendant of Victor. Iolas asked me about works by Leonor Fini, Filippo De Pisis, Stanislao Lepri, and other Italien surrealists." Tagebuch von Gaspero del Corso, 1945, zit. nach Giulia Tulino, „Alberto Savinio, Critic and Artist: A New Reading of Fantastic and Post-Metafisica Art in Relation to Surrealism between Rome and New York (1943–46)", in: *Italian Modern Art. Alberto Savinio*, 2 (2019). Online unter: www.italianmodernart.org/journal/articles/alberto-savinio-critic-and-artist-a-new-reading-of-fantastic-and-post-metafisica-art-in-relation-to-surrealism-between-rome-and-new-york-1943-46 [Stand 31.12.2019].

13 Brin und del Corso konnten Rubinstein dafür gewinnen, bei jungen Künstlern der Galerie Arbeiten in Auftrag zu geben, die 1953 – als Teil von Rubinsteins Sammlung – unter dem Titel *Twenty Imaginary Views of the American Scene by Twenty Young Italian Artists* zuerst bei L'Obelisco und nach weiteren Stationen in Europa schließlich in den USA mit Endstation im Brooklyn Museum in New York gezeigt wurden.

14 Interview mit Sir John Richardson von Adrian Dannatt, in: *Alexander the Great. The Iolas Gallery 1955–1987*, New York 2014, S. 82.

15 Es war mir nicht möglich, den exakten Zeitpunkt der Gründung der Galerie Alexander Iolas in New York zu eruieren. Die in der Literatur und in Interviews mit Zeitzeugen zu findenden Angaben divergieren stark, und Einladungskarten oder Kataloge aus jenen Jahren sind spärlich (für eine substanziellere Recherche wäre die Durchsicht von Archiven und Bibliotheken in den USA erforderlich). Sicher ist, dass im Februar 1953 eine Ausstellung von Kurt Seligmann in der Galerie Alexander Iolas stattfand, und zwar in der 46 East 57th Street. (Die Galerie Hugo hatte ihre Räumlichkeiten in der 26 East 55th Street.) Es finden sich auch Hinweise auf frühere Ausstellungen in der Galerie Alexander Iolas, allerdings ohne Adressangabe, sodass sich nicht eruieren ließ, ob die Galerie Hugo ab einem bestimmten Zeitpunkt unter Iolas' Namen geführt, schlicht mit ihm identifiziert wurde oder sogar kurzzeitig zwei Galerien parallel existierten.

16 Erika Patka, „Friedrich von Berzeviczy-Pallavicini", in: *Friedrich von Berzeviczy-Pallavicini. Poesie der Inszenierung* (wie Anm. 2), S. 6–17, hier: S. 13.

17 Siehe ebd., S. 14.

18 „Als Maler fand er eine Heimstätte in der New Yorker Galerie Alexander Iolas, deren Plafonds er gestaltete, und schnell sprach sich herum, daß Max Ernst das von ihm gemalte Speisezimmer von Alexander Iolas' Schwester so gut gefiel, daß er ein Blümchen dazupinselte und es signierte." Böhm, *Ein Wiener Märchen* (s. Anm. 4), S. 133. Siehe auch Kaufmann, *Eine andere Welt* (s. Anm. 2), S. 64.

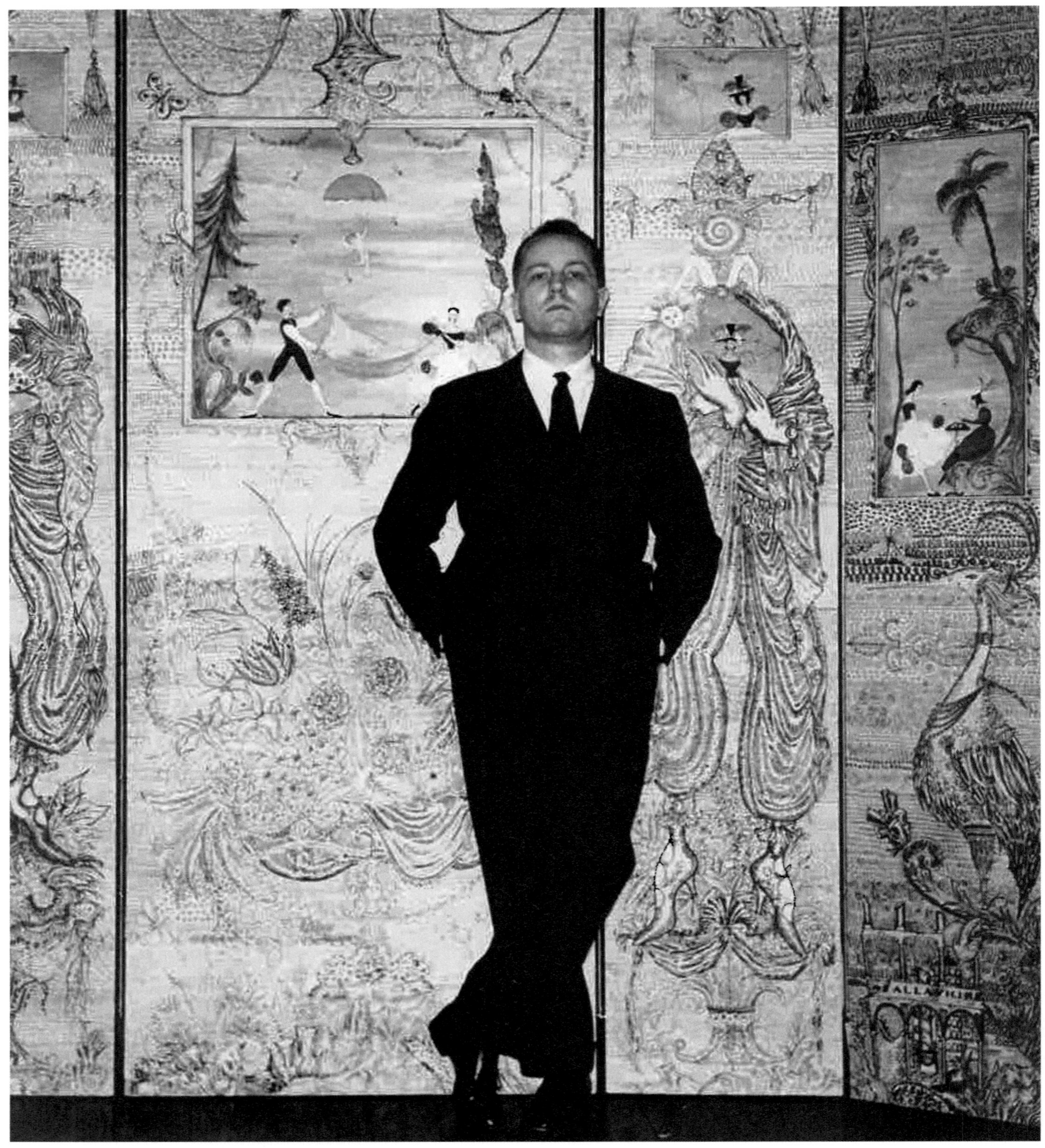

Porträt von / Portrait of Federico Pallavicini
vor einem Paravent / in front of a folding screen,
Iolas Gallery, New York, 1953

ALEXANDER IOLAS AND ARTHUR STIFEL
CORDIALLY INVITE YOU TO COME TO THE OPENING
OF THE

ZODIAC GALLERY

AND SEE THE 12 SIGNS PAINTED ESPECIALLY FOR IT
By FEDERICO PALLAVICINI

DECEMBER 14, 1956—JANUARY 1957
ZODIAC GALLERY 123 E. 55 • PL 5-6778

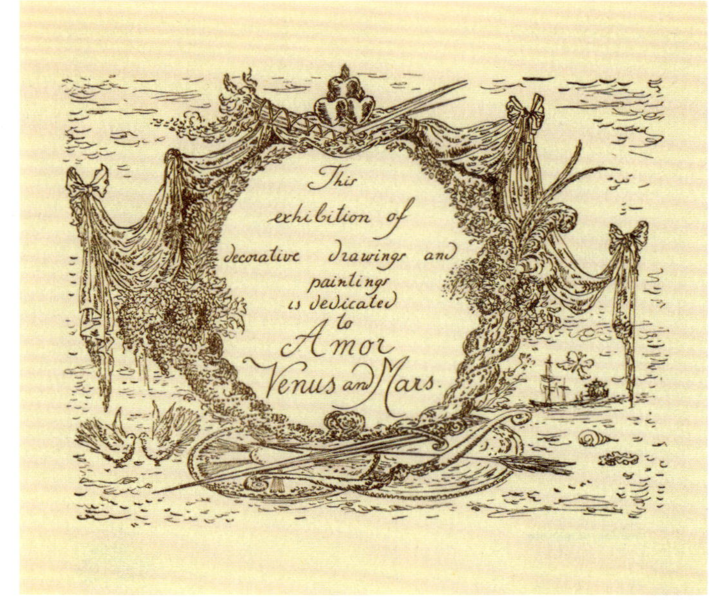

Einladungskarte zur Ausstellung von / Invitation card for the exhibition by Federico Pallavicini in der / at Zodiac Gallery, New York, 1956

Innenseite der Einladungskarte / inside of the Invitation card, Hugo Gallery, New York, 1951

befand sich der Hauptraum der Galerie im ersten Stock und in einem Hinterzimmer im Erdgeschoss der sogenannte Zodiac Room.[19] Der Industrielle Arthur Stifel, der hier gemeinsam mit Iolas zur Eröffnung dieses Raumes einlädt, war mit Iolas' Schwester Niki verheiratet und gelegentlich wohl auch Geldgeber der Galerie.[20]

Die zwölf Sternzeichen, die Pallavicini für die Zodiac Gallery malte, sind alle nach demselben Prinzip aufgebaut: Im Zentrum der hochformatigen Tafeln findet sich unter der englischen Bezeichnung des Sternzeichens jeweils sein Symbol, wobei der Künstler den Stil der Darstellung an das jeweilige Motiv angepasst zu haben scheint. Die mit feinen Linien wiedergegebene Jungfrau könnte einem Bild von Botticelli entsprungen sein, während der Stier und insbesondere der Löwe mit groben, gestischen Pinselstrichen ins Bild gesetzt wurden. Goldfarbe und winzige, wie Glitter aufgestreute Glasperlen „veredeln" die Figuren und sorgen für haptische Oberflächeneffekte. Ebenso bemerkenswert ist Pallavicinis Behandlung der Hintergründe, denen er – in bester Manier eines „Dekorateurs" – mindestens so viel gestalterische Aufmerksamkeit zuteil werden lässt wie den Sternzeichen selbst. In farblicher Abstimmung mit dem jeweiligen Motiv macht er sich die Maserung des hölzernen Bildträgers zunutze, um fantastisch-apokalyptische Landschaften (Jungfrau), erdig-steinernen Boden (Skorpion) oder auch ein an Tapeten und bedruckte Stoffe erinnerndes geometrisches Muster (Zwillinge) entstehen zu lassen. Ob der Zodiac Room seinen Namen dieser ersten Ausstellungsidee verdankt, ob Pallavicini sich den Namen zum Programm machte oder ob die Sternzeichen-Bilder gar eine Auftragsarbeit waren, ist nicht bekannt. In jedem Fall demonstriert der Zyklus beispielhaft, dass Pallavicini sich auch im Kontext der bildenden Kunst der 1950er-Jahre primär als Gestalter, Illustrator und Ausstatter verstand, dessen Interesse nicht der Autonomie des Werks galt, sondern seinen dekorativen und funktionalen Aspekten.

Der Versuch, Pallavicinis Aktivitäten in New York nachzuvollziehen, umreißt eine Figur, die oftmals als

19 Jules Olitski, „Clement Greenberg in My Studio", in: *American Art*, 3/4 (1994), S. 125–129, hier: S. 125.
20 In einem Interview in der *Vogue* 1965 erzählte Iolas: „Fortunately, I have a brother-in-law, a marvelous man, who has a great deal of confidence in me. I ask him for millions of dollars, and he gives them to me, just like that." „Iolas: The Art Dealer of the Moment Shares His Secrets with Maurice Rheims", wiederabgedruckt in: *Alexander the Great* (s. Anm. 14), S. 34–42, hier: S. 36.

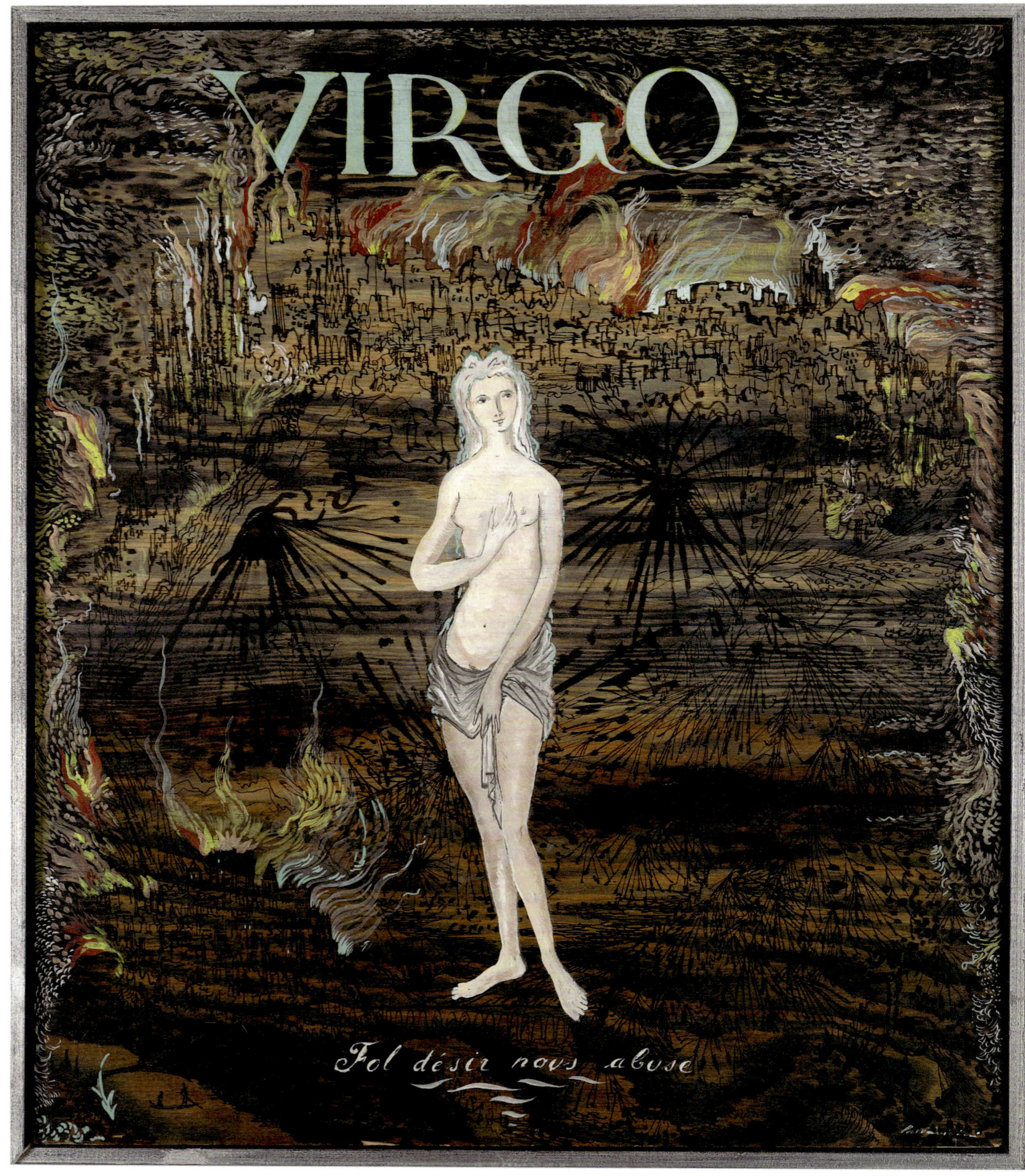

Die 12 Sternzeichen / The 12 Signs of the Zodiac,
Virgo, um / c. 1956

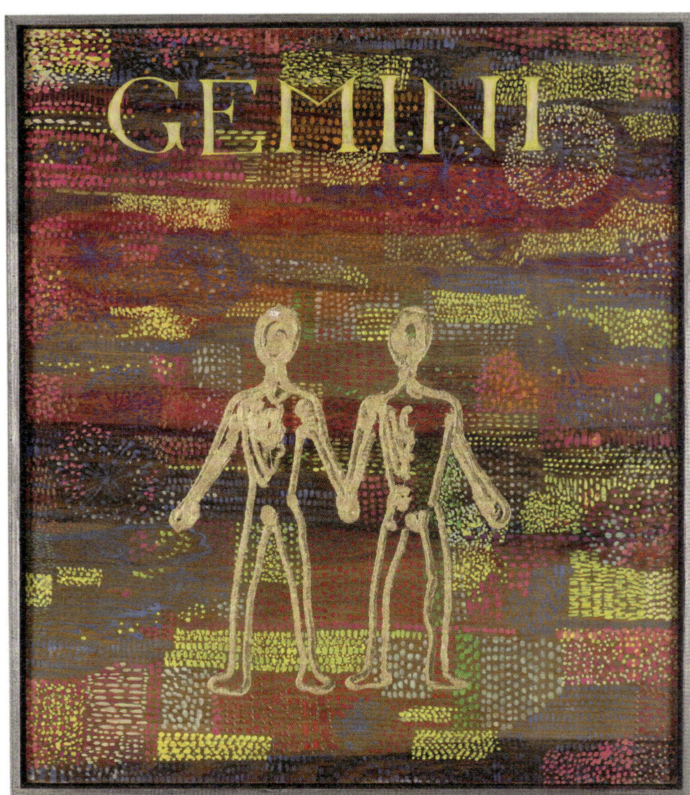

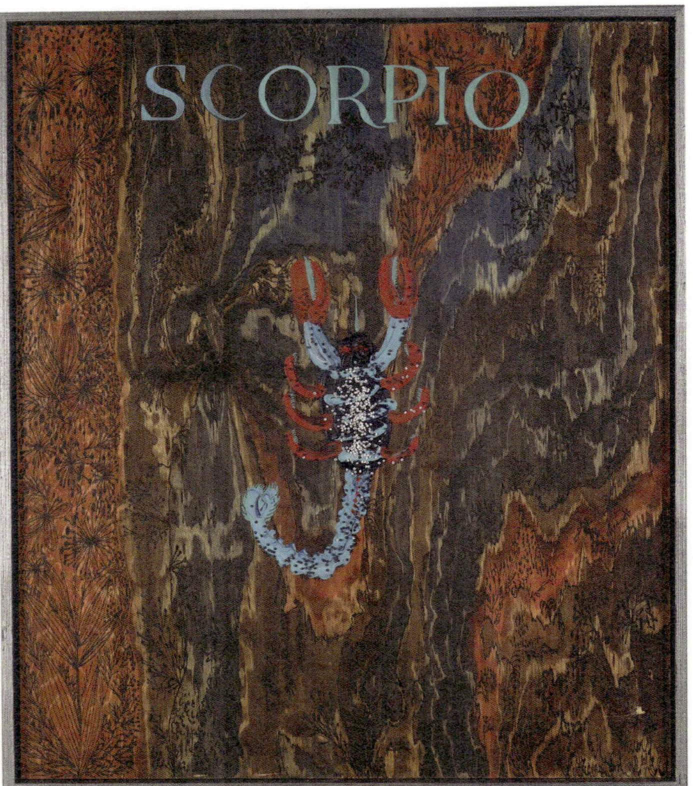

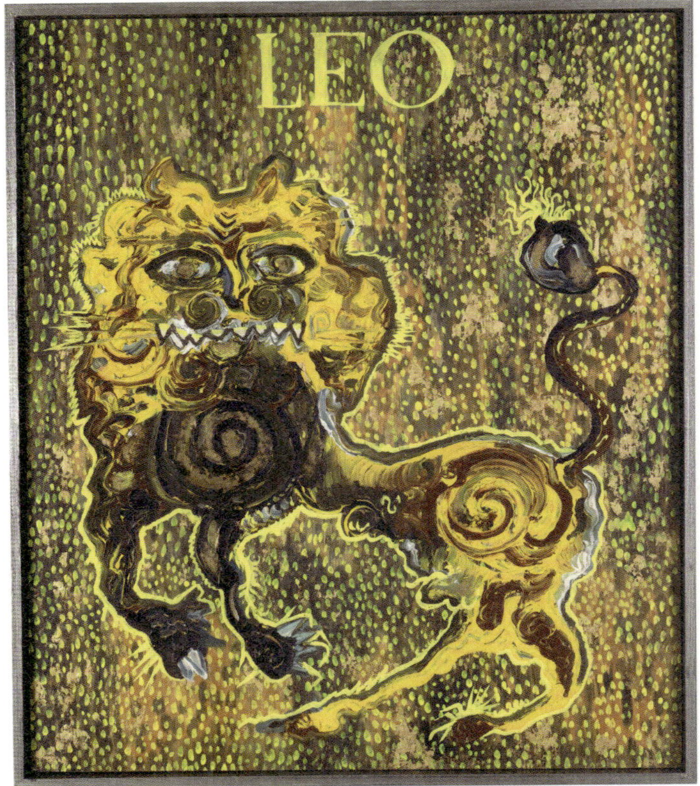

Die 12 Sternzeichen / The 12 Signs of the Zodiac,
Gemini, Scorpio, Leo, um / c. 1956

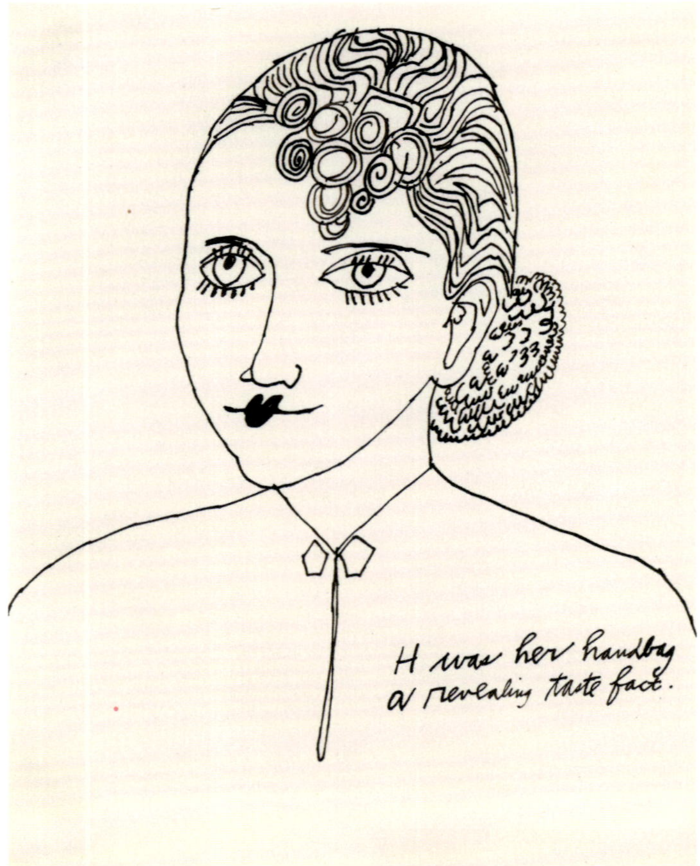

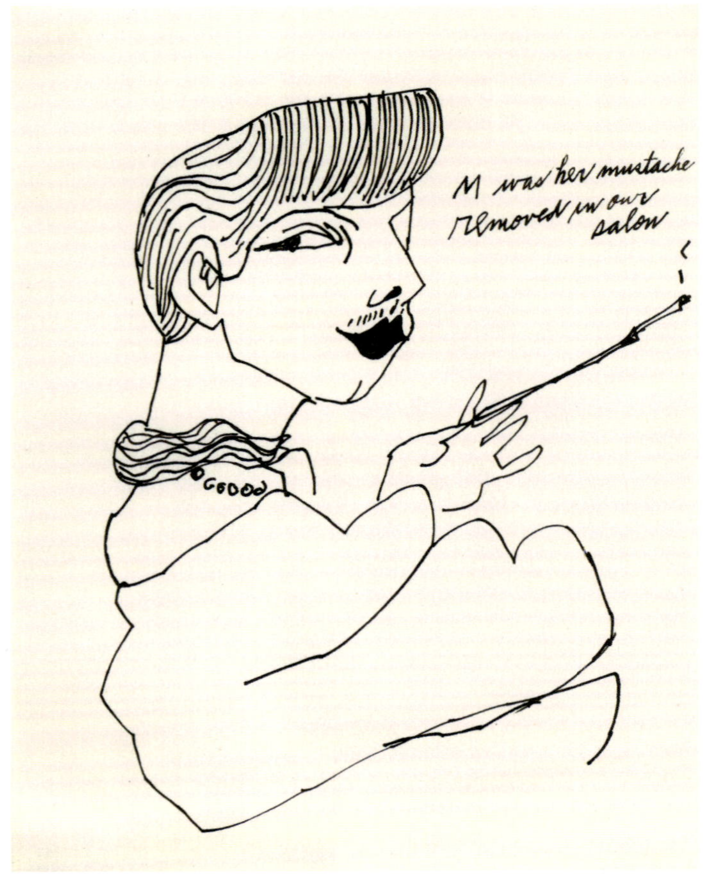

Andy Warhol, Ralph Thomas Ward, *H was her handbag a revealing taste fact*, um / c. 1953

Andy Warhol, Ralph Thomas Ward, *M was her mustache removed in our salon*, um / c. 1953

took inspiration from the grain of the wooden picture supports to create fantastical, apocalyptic landscapes (Virgo), earthy stone grounds (Scorpio), or a geometric pattern reminiscent of wallpapers or printed fabrics (Gemini). Whether the "Zodiac Room" was named after this initial exhibition, whether the name came first and Pallavicini took this as prompt for his artworks, or whether the zodiac pictures were even commissioned, remains unknown. In any event, this series vividly demonstrates that, even in the context of the visual arts of the 1950s, Pallavicini saw himself primarily as a designer, illustrator, and outfitter, whose main interest was not the autonomy of the work, but its decorative and functional aspects.

Efforts at tracing Pallavicini's activities in New York reveal a figure who appears frequently as a supporting character in the biographies of personalities whose lives seem at least as "fairytale-like" as his own—and who, in interviews and memoirs, were only too happy to contribute to the construction of their myth. Protagonists such as Iolas, Cowles, or Rubinstein remind us of just how closely intertwined the fine arts and the decorative and applied arts—the world of fashion, style, beauty; in short: of luxury—were in those years, even if this relationship has been largely ignored by art history. The "fairytale" elements of those biographies, the happy coincidences and unlikely twists that seem to define them, are—this also becomes clear—not least the result of relationships and networks that opened doors across national borders for individuals with a certain social background. Although his economic circumstances were precarious, Pallavicini undoubtedly benefited from such contacts and, in the USA in particular, from his aristocratic roots, which he shrewdly emphasized with anecdotes from the "elegant world." As late as 1972, the American author and journalist Leo Lerman noted in his journals (published in 2007) that Federico's stories were "the best" and highlights the influence of this "feminine world" of luxury on his comportment: "Federico has layers and layers of mannerisms derived from great ladies, whole families he knew when he was a child—a history of *Die Elegante Welt*—the continental world of luxe—Vienna, Rome, Paris, Budapest, Berlin, St. Petersburg—the gestures of that female world preserved in Federico's body language […]."[21]

21 Leo Lerman, "Opening Night Every Day," in *The Grand Surprise. The Journals of Leo Lerman*, ed. Stephen Pascal (New York, 2007), pp. 324–406, here: p. 376.

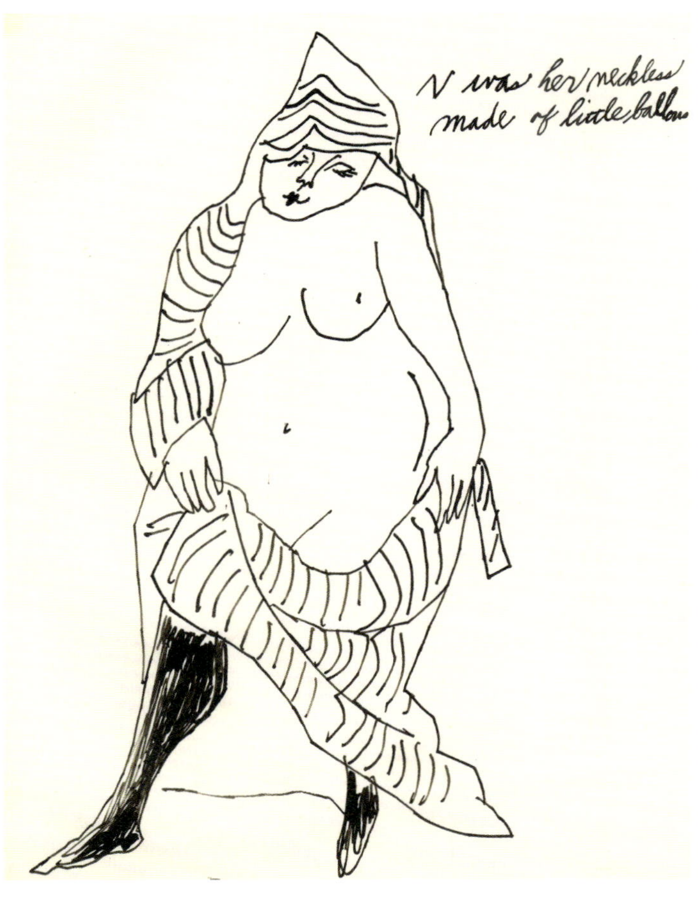

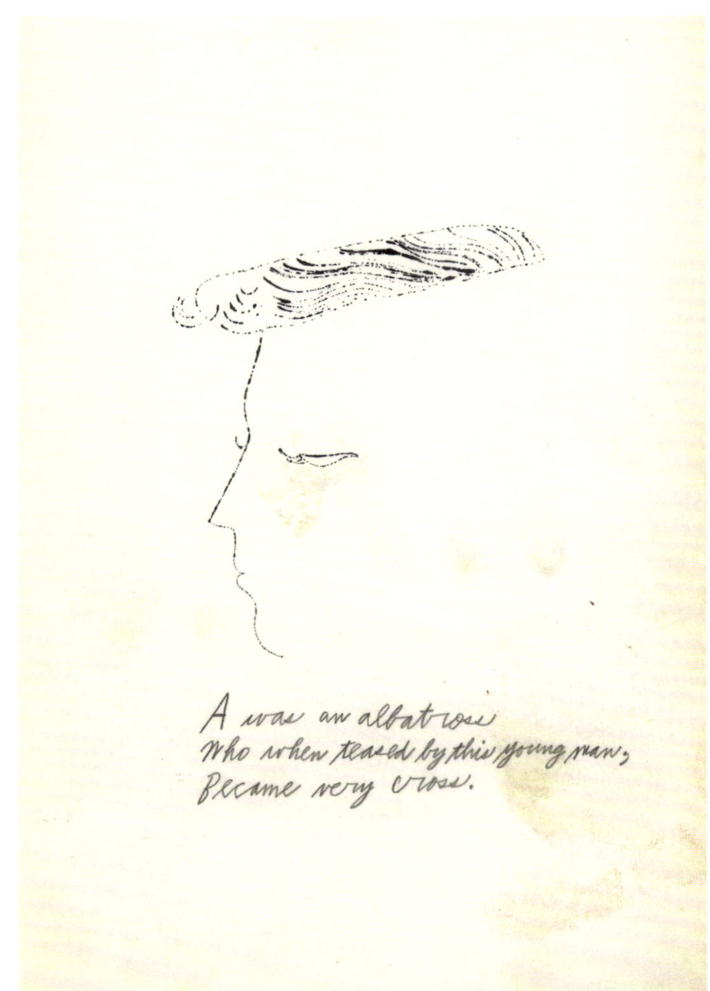

Andy Warhol, Ralph Thomas Ward, *N was her neckless made of little balloons*, um / c. 1953

Andy Warhol, Ralph Thomas Ward, *A was an albatross...*, 1953

Nebendarsteller in den Biografien von Persönlichkeiten auftritt, deren Leben mindestens so „märchenhaft" erscheint wie sein eigenes – und die in Interviews und Memoiren bereitwillig zur Mythenbildung beitrugen. Protagonist*innen wie Iolas, Cowles oder Rubinstein bringen in Erinnerung, wie eng die bildende Kunst in jenen Jahren mit den dekorativen und angewandten Künsten – der Welt der Mode, des Styles, der Schönheit, kurz: des Luxus – verquickt war, auch wenn die Kunstgeschichtsschreibung dies weitgehend ignoriert hat. Das „Märchenhafte" an jenen Biografien, die glücklichen Fügungen und unwahrscheinlichen Wendungen, die sie zu bestimmen scheinen, sind – auch das wird offenkundig – nicht zuletzt das Resultat von Beziehungen und Netzwerken, die Individuen mit bestimmten gesellschaftlichen Voraussetzungen über nationale Grenzen hinweg Türen öffneten. Wenngleich aus ökonomisch prekären Verhältnissen, hat Pallavicini zweifelsohne von solchen Kontakten profitiert und insbesondere in den USA wohl auch von seiner adligen Abstammung, die er mit Anekdoten aus der „eleganten Welt" zu illustrieren wusste. Noch 1972 hält der amerikanische Autor und Journalist Leo Lerman in seinen später veröffentlichten Tagebüchern fest, dass Federicos Geschichten „die besten" seien, und betont den Einfluss dieser „weiblichen Welt" des Luxus auf seinen Habitus: „Federico has layers and layers of mannerisms derived from great ladies, whole families he knew when he was a child – a history of *Die Elegante Welt* – the continental world of luxe – Vienna, Rome, Paris, Budapest, Berlin, St. Petersburg – the gestures of that female world preserved in Federico's body language [...]."[21]

2019 tauchte ein bis dato unbekanntes Werk des Künstlers auf, das mutmaßlich ebenfalls im New York jener Jahre entstanden ist: ein illustriertes Alphabet, in dem Fragen der gesellschaftlichen Ordnung und des Status des Dekorativen thematisch werden.[22] Auch bringt dieses Alphabet Andy Warhol wieder ins Spiel, der unsere Wege

21 Leo Lerman, „Opening Night Every Day", in: Stephen Pascal (Hg.), *The Grand Surprise. The Journals of Leo Lerman*, New York 2007, S. 324–406, hier: S. 376.

22 Bis vor kurzem befand sich das Alphabet im Besitz des New Yorker Antiquars Michael Weintraub, der es gemeinsam mit Pallavicinis umfangreicher Bibliothek erworben hatte, als die Stadt New York einen Teil des Nachlasses des Künstlers versteigerte. Anlässlich der Ausstellung *Der Hausfreund* nahmen die Organisator*innen des Projekts, vermittelt durch Christian Witt-Dörring und Janis Staggs von der Neuen Galerie New York, mit Weintraub Kontakt auf und erfuhren von der Existenz des Alphabets, das sich nun in der Sammlung der Universität für angewandte Kunst in Wien befindet (IN 19.027/Ma).

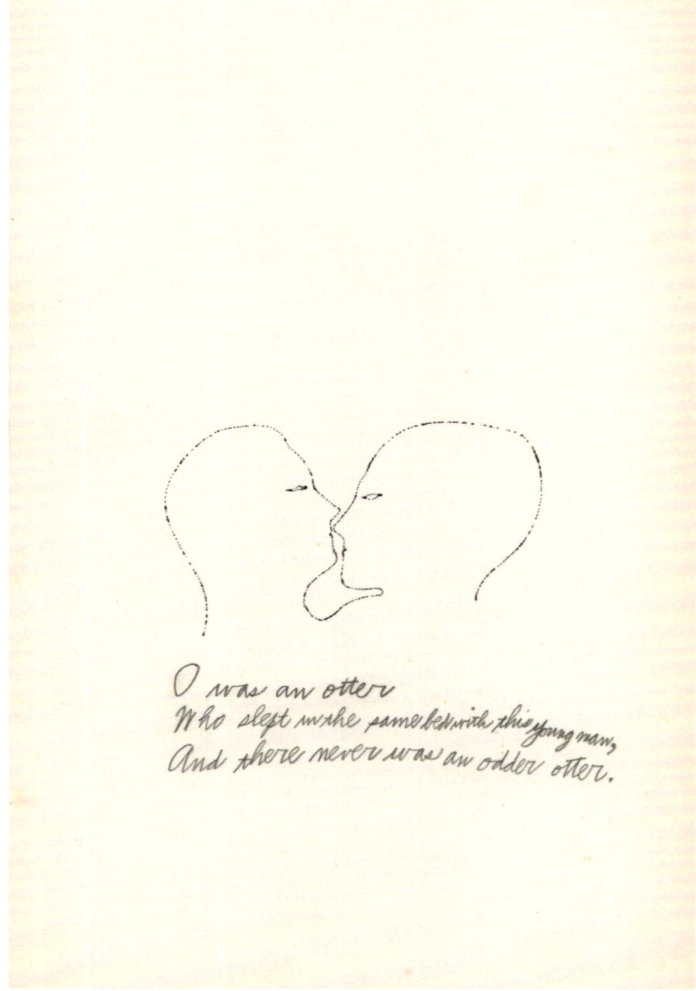

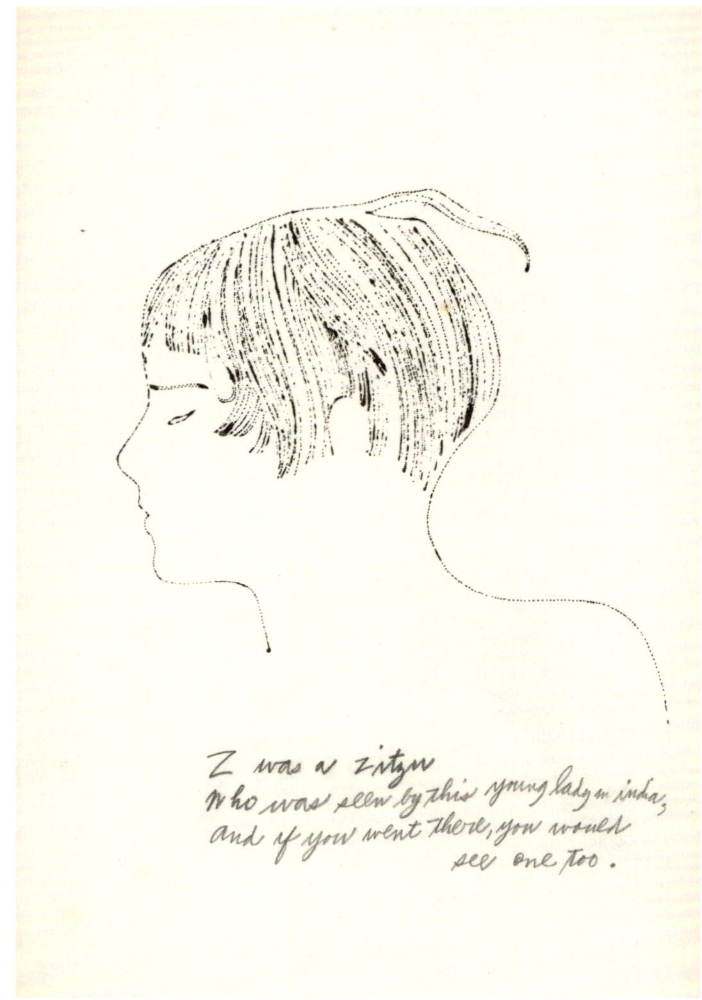

Andy Warhol, Ralph Thomas Ward, *O was an otter…*, 1953

Andy Warhol, Ralph Thomas Ward, *Z was an zitzen…*, 1953

In 2019, a hitherto unknown work by the artist was discovered, which may arguably also have been produced in New York during those years: an illustrated alphabet that picks up themes of social order and the status of the decorative.[22] With this alphabet, Andy Warhol—who has already silently crossed our path several times—once again enters the frame, returning us to our opening question about the connection between the "last romantic" Pallavicini and Pop Art's poster boy, beyond their simultaneous arrival in New York.[23] Said alphabet comprises a total of twenty-six sheets, each combining a capital and lower case letter, usually placed in the top left corner and marking the start of a verse, with an illustration. Two of the sheets—the A and the N—are in landscape format, measuring 59 by 29 centimeters; the rest are in portrait format and half the size. Also preserved are twenty-four calligraphic compositions with only the capital and lower case letters, rendered in elegant, sweeping lines. For the alphabet's theme Pallavicini used an old children's rhyme:

A was an Archer, and shot at a frog,
B was a Butcher, and kept a bulldog.
C was a Captain, all covered with lace,
D was a Drunkhard [sic], and had a red face.
E was an Esquire, with insolent brow,
F was a Farmer, and followed the plow.
G was a Gamester, who had but ill luck,
H was a Hunter, and hunted a buck.
I was an Innkeeper, who lowed [sic] to bouse,
J was a Joiner, and built up a house.
K was King William, once governed this land,
L was a Lady, who had a white hand.
M was a Miser, and hoarded up gold,
N was a Nobleman, gallant and bold.
O was an Oyster-wench, and went about town,
P was a Parson, and wore a black gown.
Q was a Queen, who was fond of good flip,

22 Until recently, the alphabet was in the possession of New York antiquarian Michael Weintraub, who had acquired it along with Pallavicini's extensive library when the City of New York auctioned off parts of the artist's estate. For the exhibition *Der Hausfreund*, the organizers contacted Weintraub with the help of Christian Witt-Dörring and Janis Staggs of the Neue Galerie in New York and learned about the existence of the alphabet, which is now in the collection of the University of Applied Arts in Vienna (IN 19.027/Ma).
23 Pallavicini's classification as the "last romantic" is ascribed to Josef Hoffmann. Böhm, "Ein Wiener Märchen" (see note 4), p. 122.

unausgesprochen bereits mehrere Male gekreuzt hat, und führt uns damit zur Eingangsüberlegung zurück, was den „letzten Romantiker" Pallavicini und den prominentesten Vertreter der Pop Art über ihre gleichzeitige Ankunft in New York hinaus verbindet.[23] Besagtes Alphabet besteht aus insgesamt 26 Blättern, in denen jeweils ein zumeist links oben platzierter Klein- und Großbuchstabe, die den Anfang eines Verses markieren, mit einer Illustration kombiniert sind. Zwei der Blätter – das „A" und das „N" – sind Querformate mit den Maßen 59 mal 29 Zentimeter; die restlichen, hochformatigen Blätter sind halb so groß dimensioniert. Ebenfalls erhalten sind 24 kalligrafische Kompositionen, die in eleganten Schwüngen jeweils nur die Groß- und Kleinbuchstaben wiedergeben. Für das Programm des Alphabets bediente sich Pallavicini eines Kinderreimes:

A was an Archer, and shot at a frog,
B was a Butcher, and kept a bulldog.
C was a Captain, all covered with lace,
D was a Drunkhard [sic], and had a red face.
E was an Esquire, with insolent brow,
F was a Farmer, and followed the plow.
G was a Gamester, who had but ill luck,
H was a Hunter, and hunted a buck.
I was an Innkeeper, who lowed [sic] to bouse,
J was a Joiner, and built up a house.
K was King William, once governed this land,
L was a Lady, who had a white hand.
M was a Miser, and hoarded up gold,
N was a Nobleman, gallant and bold.
O was an Oyster-wench, and went about town,
P was a Parson, and wore a black gown.
Q was a Queen, who was fond of good flip,
R was a Robber, and wanted a whip.
S was a Sailor, and spent all he got,
T was a Tinker, and mended a pot.
U was a Usurer, a miseble [sic] elf,
V was a Vintner, who drank all himself.
W was a Watchman, and guarded the door,
X was Expensive, and so became poor.
Y was a Youth, that did not love school,
Z was a Zany, a silly old fool.

Versionen dieses Reims sind als *Tom Thumb's Alphabet* bekannt und tauchen in gedruckter Form erstmals im 18. Jahrhundert im Kontext von Erziehungsbüchern für Kinder auf.[24] Bemerkenswert an diesem frühen narrativen Alphabet ist, dass es auf Tropen aus Volkserzählungen und -märchen rekurriert und eine bestimmte Gesellschaftsordnung zugleich vermittelt und parodiert. Die Verse präsentieren eine „republic of ABCs whose citizen-letters are identified and categorized according to trade (‚B was a Butcher'), state (‚D was a Drunkard', ‚X was expensive'), or station (‚K was a King', ‚N was a Nobleman')".[25] Dass eine solche Textvorlage Pallavicinis Interesse weckte, ist keine Überraschung: Die Versammlung von Typen und Rollen, die einem Katalog für Karnevalskostüme entnommen sein könnte, entsprach sowohl seinem Sinn für das Theatrale, wie es sich etwa in seinen Modeentwürfen und Schaufensterdekorationen manifestiert, als auch seiner Neigung zu klischeehaften Motiven, die traditionell Gegenstand des Dekorativen sind.

In diesem Sinne „konventionell" sind auch Pallavicinis Illustrationen von *Tom Thumb's Alphabet* angelegt: Ein farbenfrohes Ensemble von stilisierten, größtenteils historisch gewandeten Protagonist*innen – Pallavicini besaß eine große Sammlung von aus Druckwerken ausgeschnittenen Ornamenten, Zierbuchstaben und Figuren[26] – bringt das in den Versen Beschriebene zur Darstellung. Text und Bild gehen widerspruchsfrei Hand in Hand. Der Bogenschütze visiert einen Frosch an, der Bauer folgt dem Pflug und der Pfarrer trägt bei der Bibellektüre sein schwarzes Gewand. Bei allem Respekt für überlieferte Formen und erzählerische Kohärenz sind Pallavicinis Bilder allerdings von einer außergewöhnlichen Raffinesse, sowohl was die Komposition der einzelnen Blätter betrifft als auch ihre detailverliebte Ausstattung. So sitzt der Frosch beispielsweise im Hohlraum des „A", der rotwangige Betrunkene stützt sich am „D" ab, das blaue „S" erscheint als Teil eines Schwarms Seevögel am Himmel, das rote „T" umzüngeln Flammen und Ruß aus dem Ofen, und am „V" ranken sich Weinreben entlang. Das als einziger Buchstabe beinahe das ganze Bildfeld ausfüllende „Y" lässt den beigestellten „Jüngling" – hier eher ein verschrecktes Kleinkind, dem eine Eselskappe aufgesetzt wurde – noch kleiner erscheinen, als er tatsächlich ist, und hebt hervor, dass der Vers vom lernunwilligen Kind, das (noch) nicht über ein Handwerk, einen Zustand oder sozialen Rang definiert ist, sich direkt an die zu alphabetisierende (sozialisierende) junge Leser*innenschaft richtet. Nicht zufällig folgt darauf der „alberne, alte Narr", der sich aus der Commedia dell'Arte ableitet und in dessen schellenbesetztem Flattergewand Pallavicini die das „Y" umspielende, mit Schleifen und Sternen geschmückte Drachenschnur nachklingen lässt.

Während das Mittelalter die Bildwelt eindeutig dominiert – und hier gilt die Faustregel: Je bunter und enger, desto höher der Stand –, offenbart ein zweiter Blick größere Diversität. Trägt der männliche Adel durchgängig knappe Hosen und körperbetonte Röcke, greift Pallavicini für die wenigen weiblichen Figuren auf Renaissance- und Biedermeieraufmachungen zurück. Das arbeitende Volk schließlich – der Metzger, Schreiner oder Kesselflicker – tritt in durchgängig schlichterer Kleidung auf, die ob ihrer

23 Die Kategorisierung Pallavicinis als „letzter Romantiker" wird Josef Hoffmann zugeschrieben. Böhm, *Ein Wiener Märchen* (s. Anm. 4), S. 122.

24 Zur Geschichte der zum Zwecke der Alphabetisierung eingesetzten ABCs siehe Patricia Crain, *The Story of A. The Alphabetization of America from the* New England Primer *to the* The Scarlet Letter, Standford/CA 2000, insbesondere das Kapitel „The Republic of ABC: Alphabetizing Americans, 1750 to 1850", S. 55–101.

25 Ebd., S. 68.

26 Auskunft Michael Weintraub in einem E-Mail an die Autorin vom 29.08.2019.

R was a Robber, and wanted a whip.
S was a Sailor, and spent all he got,
T was a Tinker, and mended a pot.
U was a Usurer, a miseble [sic] elf,
V was a Vintner, who drank all himself.
W was a Watchman, and guarded the door,
X was Expensive, and so became poor.
Y was a Youth, that did not love school,
Z was a Zany, a silly old fool.

Versions of this rhyme are known as *Tom Thumb's Alphabet* and first appear in printed form in the eighteenth century in the context of educational books for children.[24] A notable feature of this early narrative alphabet are its references to traditional folktale tropes and the way it simultaneously introduces and parodies a clear social order. The verses present a "republic of ABCs whose citizen-letters are identified and categorized according to trade ('B was a Butcher'), state ('D was a Drunkard,' 'X was expensive'), or station ('K was a King,' 'N was a Nobleman')."[25] That such a text would pique Pallavicini's interest comes as no surprise: the assemblage of roles and characters, which could have been drawn from a catalogue of carnival costumes, corresponded with his sense of the theatrical—as manifested, for instance, in his fashion designs and window displays—as well as his penchant for clichéd motifs, the traditional subject of the decorative.

And in this sense Pallavicini's illustrations for *Tom Thumb's Alphabet* are also "conventional." A colorful ensemble of stylized protagonists, mostly in historical costumes—Pallavicini owned a large collection of ornaments, decorative letters, and figures cut out from printed works[26]—illustrates what is described in the verses. Text and image reliably go hand in hand. The archer takes aim at a frog, the farmer follows the plow, and the priest studies the bible clothed in black. Yet, while he respects traditional forms and narrative coherence, Pallavicini's pictures are nevertheless exceptionally sophisticated, both in terms of the composition of each individual sheet and in small narrative details like, for example, the frog sitting inside the space of the A, the red-cheeked drunkard who props himself up against the D, the blue S which appears as one of a flock of seabirds in the sky, soot and flames leaping up from the stove below the fiery red T, or the V entwined by vine tendrils. The Y, as the only letter to fill practically the entire frame, makes the associated youth—who looks more like a frightened toddler wearing a dunce's cap—appear even smaller than he actually is, thus drawing attention to the fact that this verse about the child that is unwilling to learn and is (as yet) undefined by a craft, by status or social rank, is aimed directly at the young readership to be alphabetized (i.e. socialized). It is no coincidence that what follows next is the "silly old fool" from the Commedia dell'Arte, whose costume with bells and streamers is echoed in the bows and stars of the kite string that is wrapped around the Y.

While medieval garments clearly dominate the imagery—the general rule here is: the tighter and the more colorful, the higher the status—a second glance reveals greater diversity. While the noblemen generally wear close-fitting trousers and figure-hugging coats, for the alphabet's few female figures Pallavicini resorted to outfits from the Renaissance and the Biedermeier period. Finally, the working classes—the butcher, joiner, and tinker—are generally clothed in simpler garb, which, due to its functionality, seems at times almost contemporary. In the decoration of backgrounds and surfaces Pallavicini yet again excels: be it clothing, props, or scenery—there is hardly a sheet that doesn't feature flowering tendrils, dancing stars, fluttering butterflies, curling Arabesques, or swirls of dots—and always with an unerring sense for the coloring of these compositions, which also incorporate the sometimes colored backing paper. In one point, however, Pallavicini notably deviates from the original children's rhyme template: embedded within this hierarchical society are unmistakably homoerotic undertones, which, along with the hunky aristocrats' figure-hugging outfits, include the bared chest of the flamboyant robber, coquettishly adorned by Pallavicini with a small red heart. The illustration for the letter B—arguably the most unusual sheet in this whole alphabet—banishes the very "butch" butcher into the background of the composition, while the foreground is filled with a bulldog perched on an ornamental pedestal. Its feathery, jewel-encrusted collar seems designed not so much to keep the animal in check but the miniaturized figure of the butcher, who is hanging off the other end of the leash like an accessory.

Despite being undated, there are reasons to place this alphabet in the early 1950s. Pallavicini had already designed a Christmas alphabet while still working for Demel in Vienna—the letters in this case being formed of star-covered candles and fir branches in various combinations—and in New York he found himself confronted with the theme once more.[27] The first part of the *Flair Annual 1953*, which he designed, is dedicated to communication ("Flair for Communication") and, alongside articles on the Tower of Babel and translating poems by Rilke, also contains a section on alphabets.[28] This features illustrations on sign language and calligraphic alphabets, as well as a "musical alphabet" for children, its score extending over four pages. Captioned as "souvenir of a less sophisticated day in child education," the score combines melody, rhythm, and images—"A for an Apple, an Archer, and Arrow, B for a Bull, a Bear & a Barrow" and so on—to assist learning,

24 For the history of ABCs used for alphabetization, see Patricia Crain, *The Story of A: The Alphabetization of America from the* New England Primer *to the* Scarlet Letter (Standford, CA, 2000), especially the chapter "The Republic of ABC: Alphabetizing Americans, 1750 to 1850," pp. 55–101.
25 Ibid., p. 68.
26 Information from Michael Weintraub in an email to the author dated August 29, 2019.
27 The alphabet, together with other Christmas illustrations, is in the collection of the publisher Christian Brandstätter.
28 *Flair Annual 1953* (New York, 1952), pp. 7–36.

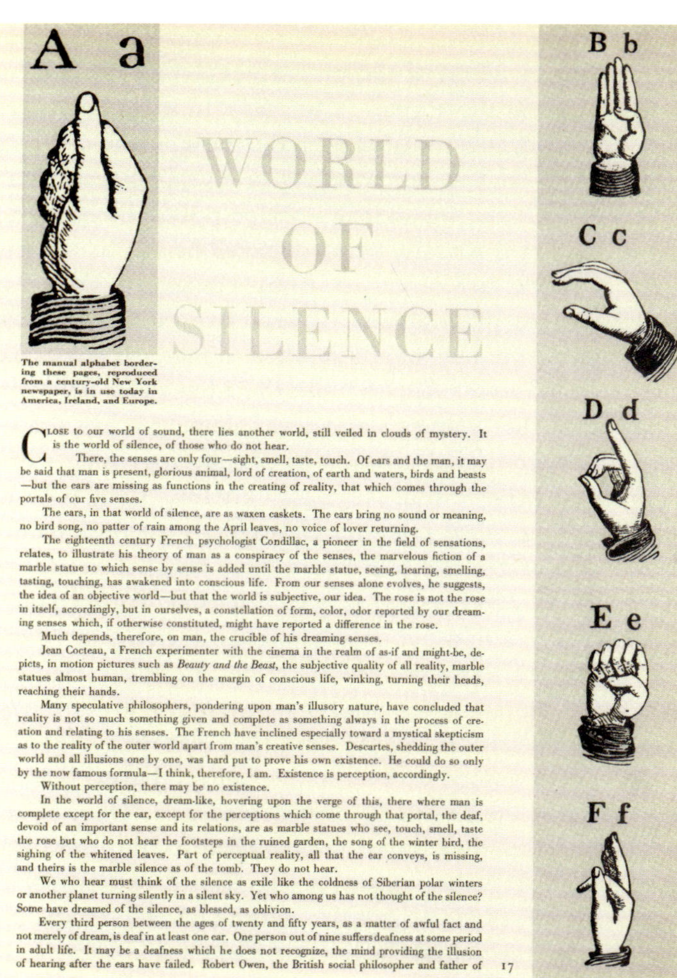

A a

WORLD OF SILENCE

The manual alphabet bordering these pages, reproduced from a century-old New York newspaper, is in use today in America, Ireland, and Europe.

Close to our world of sound, there lies another world, still veiled in clouds of mystery. It is the world of silence, of those who do not hear.

There, the senses are only four—sight, smell, taste, touch. Of ears and the man, it may be said that man is present, glorious animal, lord of creation, of earth and waters, birds and beasts—but the ears are missing as functions in the creating of reality, that which comes through the portals of our five senses.

The ears, in that world of silence, are as waxen caskets. The ears bring no sound or meaning, no bird song, no patter of rain among the April leaves, no voice of lover returning.

The eighteenth century French psychologist Condillac, a pioneer in the field of sensations, relates, to illustrate his theory of man as a conspiracy of the senses, the marvelous fiction of a marble statue to which sense by sense is added until the marble statue, seeing, hearing, smelling, tasting, touching, has awakened into conscious life. From our senses alone evolves, he suggests, the idea of an objective world—but that the world is subjective, our idea. The rose is not the rose in itself, accordingly, but in ourselves, a constellation of form, color, odor reported by our dreaming senses which, if otherwise constituted, might have reported a difference in the rose.

Much depends, therefore, on man, the crucible of his dreaming senses.

Jean Cocteau, a French experimenter with the cinema in the realm of as-if and might-be, depicts, in motion pictures such as *Beauty and the Beast*, the subjective quality of all reality, marble statues almost human, trembling on the margin of conscious life, winking, turning their heads, reaching their hands.

Many speculative philosophers, pondering upon man's illusory nature, have concluded that reality is not so much something given and complete as something always in the process of creation and relating to his senses. The French have inclined especially toward a mystical skepticism as to the reality of the outer world apart from man's creative senses. Descartes, shedding the outer world and all illusions one by one, was hard put to prove his own existence. He could do so only by the now famous formula—I think, therefore, I am. Existence is perception, accordingly.

Without perception, there may be no existence.

In the world of silence, dream-like, hovering upon the verge of this, there where man is complete except for the ear, except for the perceptions which come through that portal, the deaf, devoid of an important sense and its relations, are as marble statues who see, touch, smell, taste the rose but who do not hear the footsteps in the ruined garden, the song of the winter bird, the sighing of the whitened leaves. Part of perceptual reality, all that the ear conveys, is missing, and theirs is the marble silence as of the tomb. They do not hear.

We who hear must think of the silence as exile like the coldness of Siberian polar winters or another planet turning silently in a silent sky. Yet who among us has not thought of the silence? Some have dreamed of the silence, as blessed, as oblivion.

Every third person between the ages of twenty and fifty years, as a matter of awful fact and not merely of dream, is deaf in at least one ear. One person out of nine suffers deafness at some period in adult life. It may be a deafness which he does not recognize, the mind providing the illusion of hearing after the ears have failed. Robert Owen, the British social philosopher and father of

B b

C c

D d

E e

F f

17

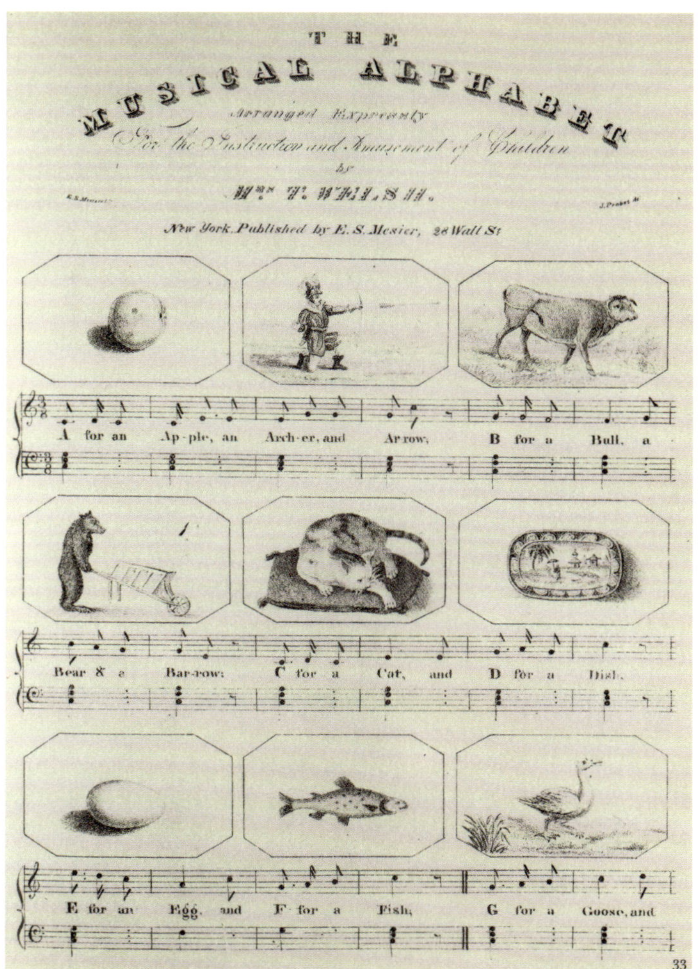

Illustration eines Fingeralphabets / Illustration of a finger alphabet in: *Flair Annual*, S. 17, Cowles Magazine Inc., 1953

"The Musical Alphabet" in: *Flair Annual*, S. 33, Cowles Magazine Inc., 1953

Funktionalität an manchen Stellen fast zeitgenössisch anmutet. Beim Dekorieren von Hintergründen und Oberflächen tut sich Pallavicini einmal mehr besonders hervor: Seien es die Gewänder, die Requisiten oder die Settings – es gibt kaum ein Blatt, auf dem nicht Blumen ranken, Sterne tanzen, Schmetterlinge flattern, Arabesken wuchern oder Punkte wirbeln, und dies stets mit einem untrüglichen Sinn für die Farbigkeit der Kompositionen, der die teils bunten Trägerpapiere miteinbezieht. In einem Punkt weicht Pallavicini dezidiert von der Vorlage des Kinderreims ab: Eingebettet in die Ständegesellschaft finden sich unübersehbar homoerotische Anspielungen, die neben den körperbetonten Aufmachungen der adligen Recken etwa auch die entblößte Brust des flamboyanten Räubers umfassen, die Pallavicini kokett mit einem roten Herzchen ziert. Die Illustration zum Buchstaben „B" – das wohl ungewöhnlichste Blatt des Alphabets – verbannt den sehr *butchen* „Butcher" in den Hintergrund der Komposition, während im Vordergrund auf einem schnörkeligen Podest bildfüllend die Bulldogge thront. Ihr juwelenbesetzter und mit Federn geschmückter Choker scheint weniger das Tier zu gängeln denn den Metzger, der miniaturhaft und einem Accessoire gleich am anderen Ende der Leine hängt.

Auch wenn das Alphabet keine Datierung aufweist, gibt es Gründe, seine Entstehung in den frühen 1950er-Jahren anzusiedeln. Hatte Pallavicini bereits im Rahmen seiner Arbeit für den Demel ein weihnachtliches Alphabet gestaltet – die Buchstaben bestehen aus jeweils unterschiedlichen Kombinationen von sternenbesetzten, brennenden Kerzen und Tannenzweigen –, sah er sich in New York noch einmal mit dem Thema konfrontiert.[27] Der erste Abschnitt in dem von ihm gestalteten *Flair Annual 1953* ist der „Kommunikation" gewidmet (*Flair for Communication*) und enthält neben Beiträgen zum Turmbau zu Babel und der Übersetzung von Rilke-Gedichten auch eine Sektion zu Alphabeten.[28] Darin enthalten sind Abbildungen zur Gebärdensprache und zu kalligrafischen Alphabeten sowie ein „musikalisches Alphabet" für Kinder, dessen Partitur sich über vier Seiten erstreckt. In der Bildunterschrift als „souvenir of a less sophisticated day in child education" ausgewiesen, verknüpft die Partitur Melodie, Rhythmus und Bilder – „A for an Apple, an Archer, and Arrow, B for a Bull, a Bear & a Barrow" usw. – zum Zwecke des leichteren

27 Das Alphabet befindet sich gemeinsam mit weiteren weihnachtlichen Illustrationen in der Sammlung des Verlegers Christian Brandstätter.
28 *Flair Annual 1953*, New York 1952, S. 7–36.

thus locating it in the same tradition of children's rhymes that also inspired Pallavicini's alphabet. What prompted the artist to make these illustrations—whether they were a commission and/or intended for publication—is difficult to determine. Although smaller than the zodiac signs, the sheets are impressive enough to be shown in an exhibition context. The landscape formats of the A and N divide the alphabet into two equal groups, suggesting an arrangement in two rows or columns. However, if various possibilities are simulated, inconsistencies emerge: While all the letters from A to M are placed in the left-hand corner of each sheet, Pallavicini allows the letters in the second group to jump from left to right, creating an ungainly rhythm, whether arranged horizontally or in columns (a pair of letters at a time below the N), which could not have been the intention of a designer like Pallavicini. Indeed, the alphabet seems most consistent when all the letters are arranged individually below the two landscape formats. Although not feasible for an exhibition wall, it might have been intended for a double-sided, portrait-format leporello with fold-out A and N title pages. While children cannot be ruled out as a potential target audience for these illustrations, the homoerotic undertones definitely point to another audience as well.

In the early 1950s, Pallavicini was not alone in his interest in illustrated alphabets. In 1953, Andy Warhol—who subtitled his 1975 autobiography *From A to B and Back Again*—also devoted attention to this theme in the form of two drawing series. Pallavicini was undoubtedly familiar with one of them, *A Is an Alphabet*. The other, the unfinished *Ladies' Alphabet*, remained unpublished during Warhol's lifetime, but can serve as proof that Warhol likewise knew Pallavicini's work.[29] *Ladies' Alphabet* was a collaboration with the poet Ralph Thomas "Corkie" Ward, who was responsible for the rhymes and with whom Warhol frequently collaborated in those years (including on a range of manuscripts for children's books). Each sheet combines a posing "lady" with a rhyme in the style of a child's ABC verse, based on an item of clothing, an accessory, or cosmetics—in other words: an article from the consumer world of the magazines for which Warhol worked during those years. Curiously, in some drawings the very product associated with the initial is the one that is missing—"H was her handbag, a revealing taste fact" makes do without a handbag—which poses the question what it is that is actually being depicted here. The models for the "ladies" are revealing in this context: to the most part they are photographs of actresses, which Warhol had copied from magazines he liked to read, such as *Life*, *Vogue*, and *Harper's Bazaar*.[30] But there are also a few men "hiding" in the "women's alphabet," namely in the drawings made from photos taken by the photographer Otto Fenn at his private drag sessions.[31] Finally, "Lady N," the only drawing based not on a photograph but on a painting, has its origin in a publication very familiar to us: the *Flair Annual 1953*, a copy of which was in Warhol's possession.[32] On a fold-out double page in the section "Flair for Americana" is a color reproduction of a beach scene by the American painter George O'Brien, which is unusually liberal for the late nineteenth century in featuring naked or scantily clad women bathing in the Hudson River. Warhol appropriated the painting's central figure as "Lady N." If he studied this illustration, he would also have noticed, as some of the ladies' gestures suggest, the alphabets in *Flair Annual 1953*—a possible source of inspiration for Pallavicini.[33] Although little more than speculation, it is tempting to assume the same point of departure for both of these artists' ABCs.

Unlike the unpublished *Ladies' Alphabet*, *A is an Alphabet*—Warhol's second alphabet—was circulated precisely within the professional circles to which Pallavicini also belonged. Between 1952 and 1960, Warhol produced an annual "promotional book," a self-published volume, printed using an inexpensive offset process, which he distributed as a gift to friends, colleagues, and potential clients, such as art directors at magazines. Possibly as an

29 The scarcity of sources on Pallavicini stands in contrast to the overwhelming volume of literature on Warhol—increasingly also focusing on his pre-Pop years. The following publications were consulted for this essay: Rainer Crone, *Andy Warhol: Das zeichnerische Werk 1942–1975* (Stuttgart, 1976); Jesse Kornbluth, *Pre-Pop Warhol* (Munich, 1989); Donna De Salvo, ed., *"Success is a Job in New York..." The Early Art and Business of Andy Warhol* (New York, 1989), especially the essays "Learning the Ropes: Some Notes about the Early Work of Andy Warhol" by Donna De Salvo (pp. 1–25) and "Tomorrow's Man" by Trevor Fairbrother (pp. 55–74); The Andy Warhol Museum Pittsburgh, ed., *Andy Warhol: Zeichnungen 1942–1987*, (Pittsburgh et al, 1998), particularly the essay "Andy Warhols Zeichnungen nach der Photonatur" by Dieter Koepplin; Nina Schleif, ed., *Reading Andy Warhol* (Ostfildern, 2013), especially the essays "Sorgfältig ungeplant: Bücher im Werk von Andy Warhol" (pp. 10–77) and "Clevere Frivolität *in Excelsis*" (pp. 78–133) by Nina Schleif, "A was a Lady: Warhols Alphabet der Frauen" by Nina Rühl (pp. 146–55), "Gesellschaftsanalyse in Gestalt eines Kochbuchs: Warhols *Wild Raspberries*" by Susan M. Rossi-Wilcox, and "Ich bin O.K. – Du bist O.K.: Andy Warhol, Transaktionsanalyse und Bücher" by Reva Wolf; and—in first place—Nina Schleif, *Drag & Draw: Andy Warhol, The Unknown Fifties* (Munich, 2018). Thanks to Marianne Dobner for her help in identifying the relevant literature on Warhol.

30 For more on the photo models, see Schleif, *Drag & Draw* (see note 29), pp. 52–54. Warhol also owned several vintage alphabet books for children, as well as artists' ABCs, including Charles Henri Ford's *ABC's* (1940) with a cover by Joseph Cornell, and Man Ray's *Alphabet for Adults* (1948). Ford's alphabet—the American poet lived together with Pavel Tchelitchew—is full of homoerotic undertones. At which point in time Warhol acquired these books is not recorded, unfortunately. Also part of his library was the famous fashion alphabet by the French artist and fashion designer Erté, which was started in 1927, but only exhibited for the first time in 1967 (ibid., p. 41–42).

31 Ibid., p. 50. Characters such as Fenn, Bill Cecil (a set designer), or the window dresser Gene Moore were hugely important to the young Warhol, as they helped him gain access to a gay "upper class"—which Pallavicini was undoubtedly also part of—which would otherwise have remained closed to Warhol, with his immigrant, working-class background, sloppy appearance, and lack of manners.

32 Ibid., p. 37 and p. 52–53. Schleif is the only author to mention the *Flair Annual 1953* and Pallavicini's role as designer, and offers a brief commentary on what may have prompted Warhol's interest in this publication. According to Neil Printz, editor of *The Andy Warhol Catalogue Raisonné*, Warhol included several individual issues of *Flair* from 1950 in his *Time Capsules*, although the name Pallavicini does not appear in them (email to the author dated July 12, 2019).

33 Schleif hints plausibly at the similarities between the gestures of several "ladies" and the images in the sign language alphabet. Ibid. p. 42.

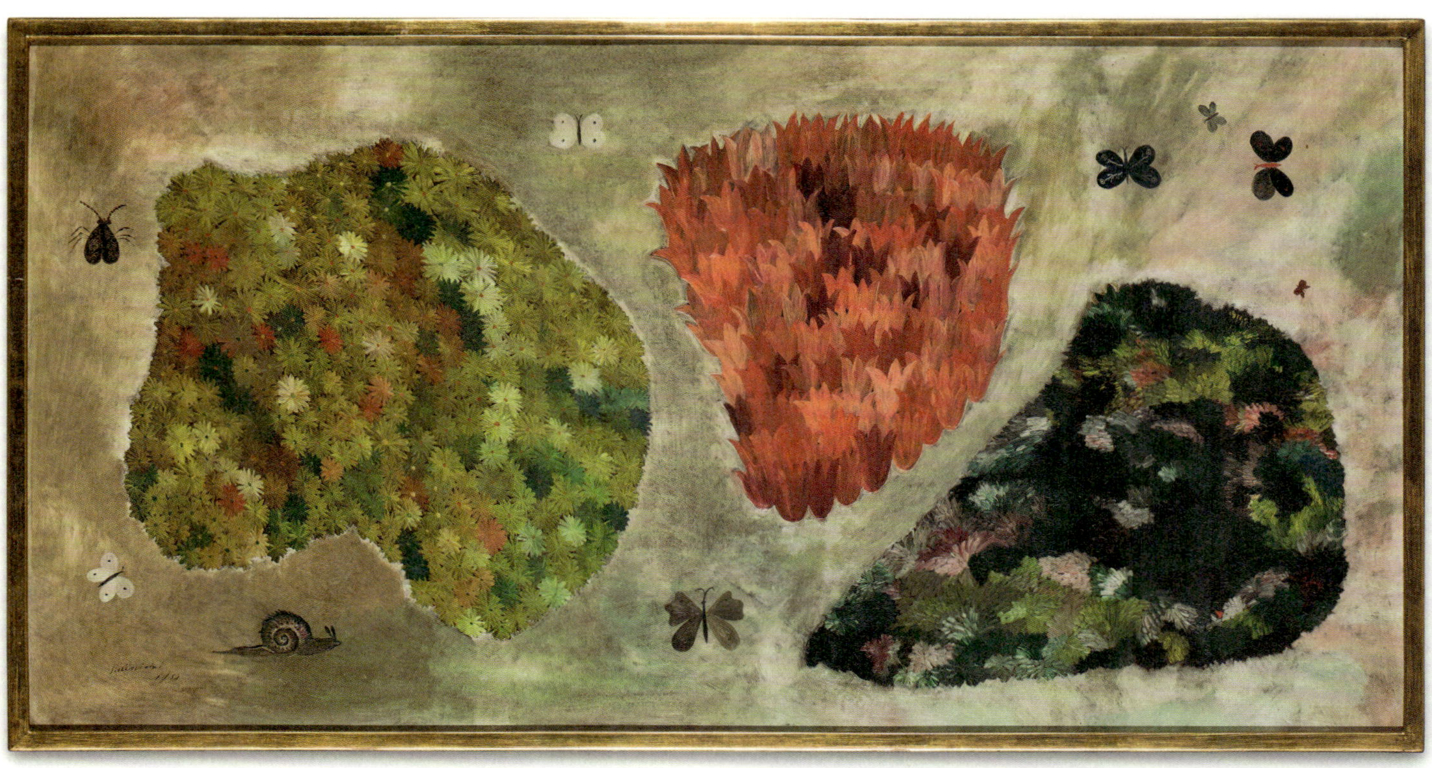

ohne Titel / Untitled, Blumen-Parterre / floral parterre, 1952

Erlernens der Buchstaben und zählt damit zu jener Tradition von Kinderreimen, die auch Pallavicinis Alphabet inspiriert hat. Wofür der Künstler seine Illustrationen angefertigt hat, ob sie ein Auftragswerk waren und/oder zur Publikation gedacht waren, ist schwer zu bestimmen. Zwar kleiner als die Sternzeichen, sind die Blätter repräsentativ genug, um in einem Ausstellungskontext gezeigt werden zu können. Die Querformate des „A" und „N" teilen das Alphabet in zwei gleich große Gruppen, was die Ordnung in zwei Reihen oder Spalten nahelegt. Simuliert man allerdings unterschiedliche Anordnungen, tun sich Inkohärenzen auf: Während alle Buchstaben von „A" bis „M" links platziert sind, lässt Pallavicini die Buchstaben der zweiten Gruppe wechselnd von links nach rechts springen, was sowohl bei einer horizontalen Anordnung als auch bei einer Anordnung in Spalten (jeweils ein Buchstabenpaar unterhalb des „N") zu einem unschönen Rhythmus führt, der nicht im Sinne eines Gestalters wie Pallavicini gewesen sein kann. Am stimmigsten mutet das Alphabet tatsächlich an, wenn alle Buchstaben einzeln unterhalb der beiden Querformate angeordnet sind. Für eine Ausstellungswand ist dies nicht vorstellbar, aber vielleicht für eine Art beidseitig bedrucktes, hochformatiges Leporello, dessen Titelblätter „A" und „N" sich falten oder ausklappen ließen. Dass Kinder das Zielpublikum dieser Grafiken waren, ist nicht ausgeschlossen, die homoerotischen Anspielungen haben aber definitiv auch ein anderes Publikum im Blick.

Mit seinem Interesse an illustrierten Alphabeten war Pallavicini in den frühen 1950er-Jahren nicht allein. Auch Andy Warhol, der seine 1975 publizierte Autobiografie bekanntermaßen *From A to B and Back Again* untertitelte, schenkte dem Thema 1953 in Form von zwei Grafikserien seine Aufmerksamkeit. Mit der einen – *A is an Alphabet* – war Pallavicini zweifelsohne vertraut; die andere – das unvollendete *Ladies' Alphabet* – wurde zu Lebzeiten Warhols nicht publiziert, belegt jedoch, dass diesem wiederum Pallavicinis Arbeit ein Begriff war.[29] *Ladies' Alphabet* entstand

29 Der dünnen Quellenlage bei Pallavicini steht eine fast unermessliche und zunehmend auch die Prä-Pop-Jahre in den Fokus nehmende Anzahl von Texten zum Werk Warhols gegenüber. Für diesen Text hilfreich waren folgende Publikationen: Rainer Crone, *Andy Warhol. Das zeichnerische Werk 1942–1975*, Stuttgart 1976; Jesse Kornbluth, *Pre-Pop Warhol*, München 1989; Donna De Salvo (Hg.), *„Success is a Job in New York…". The Early Art and Business of Andy Warhol*, New York 1989, insbesondere die Essays „Learning the Ropes: Some Notes about the Early Work of Andy Warhol" von Donna De Salvo (S. 1–25) und „Tomorrow's Man" von Trevor Fairbrother (S. 55–74); The Andy Warhol Museum Pittsburgh (Hg.), *Andy Warhol. Zeichnungen 1942–1987*, Pittsburgh u. a. 1998,

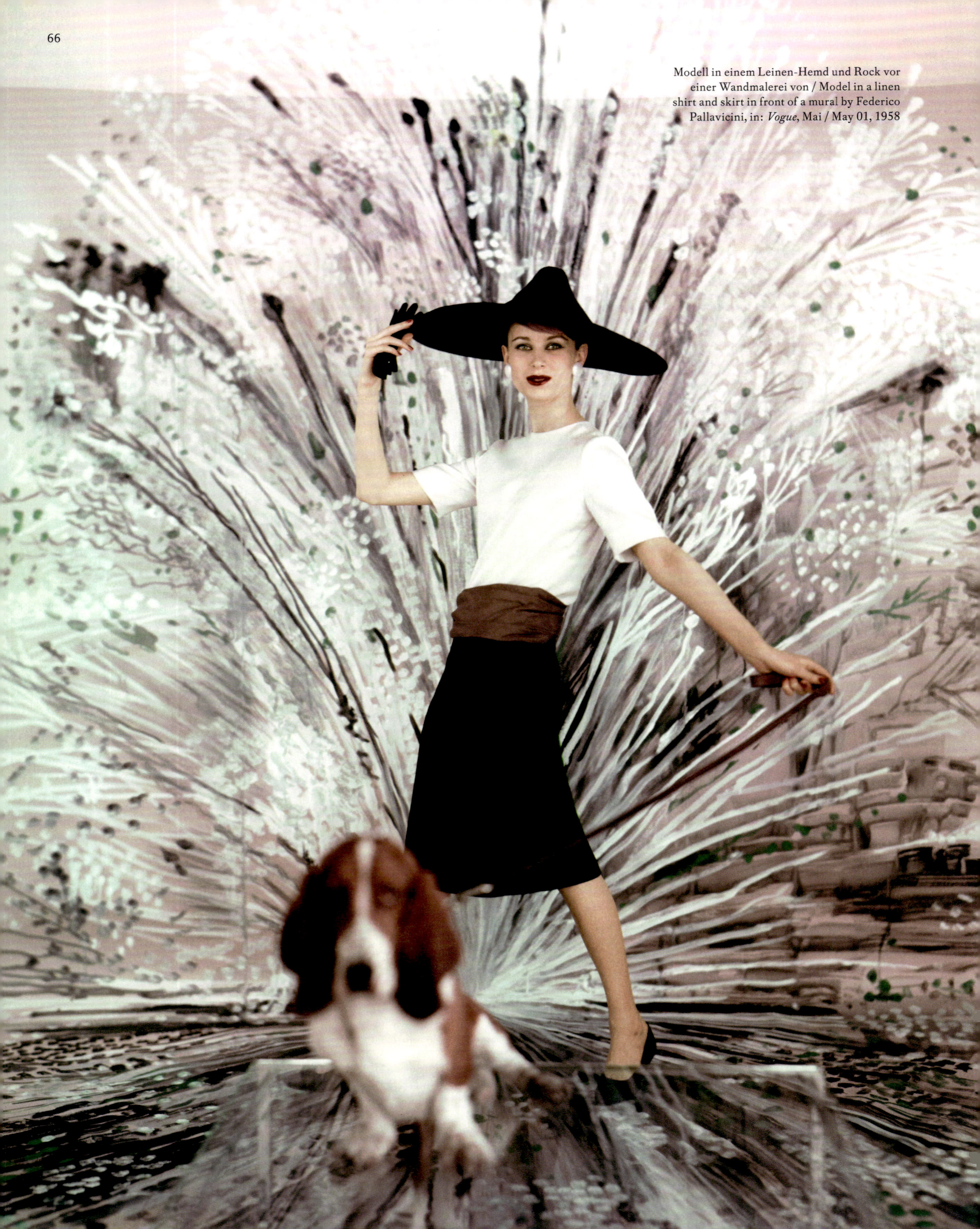

Modell in einem Leinen-Hemd und Rock vor einer Wandmalerei von / Model in a linen shirt and skirt in front of a mural by Federico Pallavicini, in: *Vogue*, Mai / May 01, 1958

in Zusammenarbeit mit dem Dichter Ralph Thomas „Corkie" Ward, der für die Reime verantwortlich zeichnet und mit dem Warhol in jenen Jahren mehrmals kollaborierte (unter anderem für eine Reihe von Kinderbuch-Manuskripten). Die Blätter kombinieren jeweils eine posierende „Lady" mit einem Reim nach dem Schema der ABC-Kinderverse, der von einem Kleidungsstück, Accessoire oder Kosmetik handelt, kurz: von der Warenwelt der Magazine, für die Warhol in jenen Jahren tätig war. Auffällig ist, dass in manchen Zeichnungen gerade die mit dem Initial bezeichnete Ware fehlt – „H was her handbag, a revealing taste fact" kommt ohne Handtasche aus –, und so stellt sich die Frage, was hier eigentlich gezeigt wird. Die Vorlagen für die „Ladies" sind in dem Zusammenhang aufschlussreich: Größtenteils handelt es sich dabei um Fotografien von Schauspielerinnen, welche Warhol Zeitschriften entnahm, die er gerne las, darunter *Life*, *Vogue* oder *Harper's Bazaar.*[30] Aber es „verstecken" sich auch einige Männer in dem „Frauen-Alphabet", und zwar in jenen Zeichnungen, die nach Aufnahmen aus privaten Drag-Sessions des Fotografen Otto Fenn entstanden.[31] „Lady N" schließlich, die einzige Zeichnung, die nicht auf einer Fotografie, sondern auf einer Malerei basiert, hat ihren Ursprung in einer Publikation, die uns wohlvertraut ist: dem *Flair Annual 1953*, von dem Warhol ein Exemplar besaß.[32] Als Teil der Sektion *Flair for Americana* findet sich auf einer ausklappbaren Doppelseite die Farbabbildung einer ob ihrer Freizügigkeit für das späte 19. Jahrhundert ungewöhnlichen Strandszene des amerikanischen Malers George O'Brien, die nackte oder spärlich bekleidete Frauen beim Bad im Hudson River zeigt. Die zentrale Figur in dem Gemälde appropriiert Warhol als „Lady N". Studierte er diese Abbildung, so sind ihm auch die in *Flair Annual 1953* enthaltenen Alphabete nicht entgangen, die möglicherweise Pallavicini als Anreiz dienten – manche Gesten der „Ladies" legen dies nahe.[33] Obgleich reine Spekulation, ist es reizvoll, für die ABC-Projekte beider Künstler denselben Ausgangspunkt anzunehmen.

Anders als das unveröffentlicht gebliebene *Ladies' Alphabet* zirkulierte *A is an Alphabet*, Warhols zweites ABC, in genau dem Umfeld, in dem auch Pallavicini professionell verkehrte. Zwischen 1952 und 1960 produzierte Warhol jährlich ein sogenanntes „promotional book", eine selbst verlegte Publikation im billigen Offsetdruck, die er als kleines (Werbe-)Geschenk an Freund*innen, Kolleg*innen und potenzielle Auftraggeber*innen, etwa die Art Directors von Zeitschriften, verteilte. Möglicherweise Ersatz für das erste, abgebrochene Projekt, ist *A is an Alphabet* nach demselben Prinzip aufgebaut: Jedem Buchstaben ist eine Seite gewidmet, auf der eine Zeichnung von Warhol mit einem Reim von Ward kombiniert wird. Hier sind es Tiere, die durch das ABC führen und die auf einen „young man" oder eine „young lady" treffen, der die entsprechende Illustration gewidmet ist. Wards Verse folgen dabei einem Schema, das uns bereits aus Pallavicinis Alphabet bekannt ist: „A was an albatross / who when teased by this young man, / became very cross." In den Zeichnungen, die einmal mehr auf fotografischen Vorlagen aus Magazinen basieren, verzichtet Warhol zur Gänze auf einen direkten Textbezug, die Darstellung der Tiere oder der geschilderten Interaktion. Seine Bilder beschränken sich auf stark vereinfachte Silhouetten der menschlichen Gegenüber von „albatross", „bat" oder „cricket" in der für ihn typischen „Blotted line"-Technik.[34] Auch in *A is an Alphabet* gibt es unzweideutig homoerotische Anspielungen: Im Blatt zum Buchstaben „O" heißt es beispielsweise: „O was an otter / who slept in the same bed with this young man / and there never was an odder otter", während das zugehörige Bild die mit einer Linie gezeichneten Umrisse zweier Männerköpfe zeigt, die nahe genug beieinander sind, um als Küssende gelesen zu werden.

Nimmt man die beiden Alphabete zum Anlass, auch Warhols Anfänge in New York genauer zu betrachten, so stellt sich ein seltsamer Effekt der Koinzidenzen und Parallelen ein: Wie Pallavicini arbeitete Warhol nach seiner Ankunft in der Stadt im Sommer 1949 zuerst als Grafiker für Modemagazine und Bücher. Wie Pallavicini bediente er sich dazu Vorlagen aus unterschiedlichsten Quellen, hatte ein Faible für klischeehafte Bilder (Herzen, Blumen, Schmetterlinge) und Kitsch (Gold!) und keinerlei Skrupel, eine Idee mehrmals zu verwerten. Beide dekorierten Schaufenster von Luxuskaufhäusern (Warhol für

insbesondere der Essay „Andy Warhols Zeichnungen nach der Photonatur" von Dieter Koepplin; Nina Schleif (Hg.), *Reading Andy Warhol*, Ostfildern 2013, insbesondere die Essays „Sorgfältig ungeplant: Die Bücher im Werk von Andy Warhol" (S. 10–77) und „Clevere Frivolität *in Excelsis*" (S. 78–133) von Nina Schleif, „A was a Lady: Warhols Alphabet der Frauen" von Nina Rühl (S. 146–155), „Gesellschaftsanalyse in Gestalt eines Kochbuchs: Warhols *Wild Raspberries*" von Susan M. Rossi-Wilcox und „Ich bin O.K. – Du bist O.K.: Andy Warhol, Transaktionsanalyse und Bücher" von Reva Wolf; und – an erster Stelle – Nina Schleif, *Drag & Draw. Andy Warhol. The Unknown Fifties*, München 2018. Ich danke Marianne Dobner für ihre Unterstützung bei der Identifikation der für meine Zwecke relevanten Warhol-Literatur.

30 Zu den fotografischen Vorlagen siehe Schleif, *Drag & Draw* (s. Anm. 29), S. 52–54. Warhol besaß auch einige klassische Alphabet-Bücher für Kinder, ebenso wie Künstler-ABCs, darunter Charles Henri Fords *ABC's* (1940) mit einem Cover von Joseph Cornell und Man Rays *Alphabet for Adults* (1948). Fords Alphabet – der amerikanische Dichter lebte mit Pawel Tschelitschew zusammen – ist voller homoerotischer Anspielungen. Wann Warhol diese Bücher erwarb, ist leider nicht belegt. Ebenfalls Teil seiner Bibliothek war das berühmte Mode-Alphabet des französischen Künstlers und Modeschöpfers Erté, das 1927 begonnen, aber erst 1967 erstmals ausgestellt wurde (ebd., S. 41 f.).

31 Ebd., S. 50. Personen wie Fenn, der Designer Bill Cecil oder der Schaufensterdekorateur Gene Moore waren für den jungen Warhol von immenser Bedeutung, da sie ihm Zutritt zu einer schwulen „Upper Class" verschafften – der Pallavicini zweifelsohne angehörte –, die dem Künstler mit migrantischem Arbeiterklassenhintergrund, schlampigem Auftreten und mangelnden Umgangsformen sonst wohl verschlossen geblieben wäre.

32 Ebd., S. 37 und S. 52 f. Schleif ist die einzige Autorin, die auf das *Flair Annual 1953* sowie auf Pallavicinis Rolle als Gestalter verweist und kurze Überlegungen dazu anstellt, was Warhol an der Publikation fasziniert haben könnte. Laut Neil Printz, Herausgeber von *The Andy Warhol Catalogue Raisonné*, finden sich auch einige Einzelausgaben von *Flair* von 1950 in Warhols *Time Capsules*; der Name Pallavicini taucht darin allerdings nicht auf (E-Mail an die Autorin vom 12.07.2019).

33 Schleif verweist plausibel auf die Nähe der Gesten einiger „Ladies" zu den Darstellungen des Gehörlosenalphabets. Ebd., S. 42.

34 Eine Abklatschtechnik, mit der Warhol bereits als Student experimentierte und der sich die delikaten gebrochenen Linien seiner Grafiken jener Jahre verdanken.

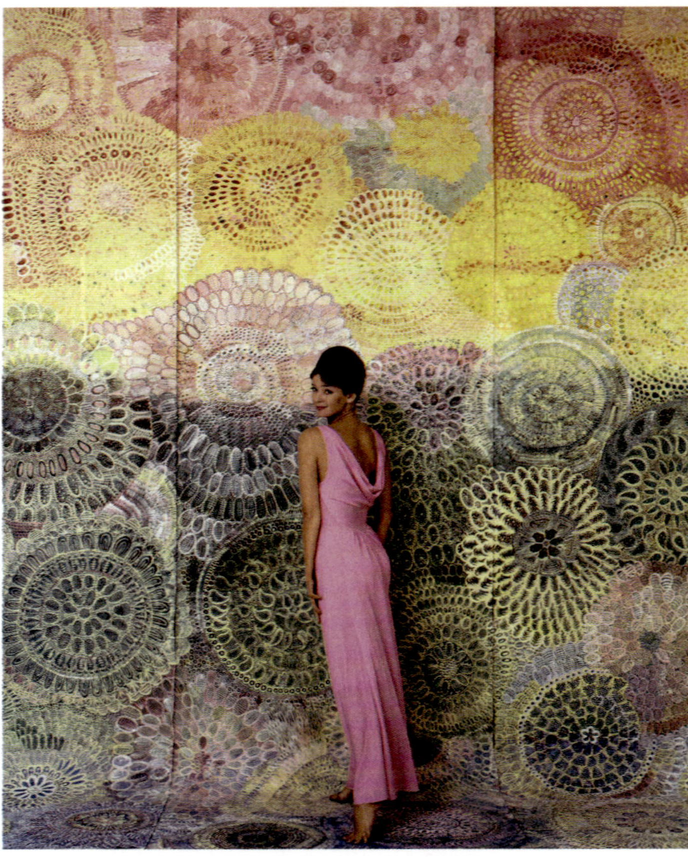

Modell in einem Rogers-Abendkleid vor einer Wandmalerei von / Model in a Rogers evening dress in front of a mural by Federico Pallavicini in: *Vogue*, November 01, 1959

Stilleben von / Still life by Federico Pallavicini, *Katze und Tassen / Cat and Cups*, 1957

alternative to his abandoned first project, *A is an Alphabet* follows the same principle: each letter has one page devoted to it, featuring a drawing by Warhol combined with a rhyme by Ward. Leading through this ABC are animals encountering the respective "young man" or "young lady" to whom each illustration is dedicated. Ward's verses follow a pattern already familiar to us from Pallavicini's alphabet: "A was an albatross / who when teased by this young man, / became very cross." In the drawings, which are again based on photographs from magazines, Warhol does entirely without any direct reference to the text, representation of the animals, or of the interactions described. His pictures are restricted to heavily simplified silhouettes of the human counterpart to the "albatross," "bat," or "cricket," rendered in his characteristic blotted line technique.[34] *A is an Alphabet* also contains clear homoerotic undertones. The sheet for the letter O, for instance, reads: "O was an otter / who slept in the same bed with this young man / and there never was an odder otter," while the accompanying picture, rendered in a single uninterrupted line, shows the outlines of two male heads that are close enough together to suggest a kiss.

34 A copying technique with which Warhol had already experimented as a student and to which the delicate broken lines of his drawings from those years are owed.

Taking the two alphabets as an opportunity to also examine Warhol's early years in New York more closely, a peculiar pattern of coincidences and parallels is revealed. Like Pallavicini, following his arrival in the city in the summer of 1949, Warhol worked initially as an illustrator for fashion magazines and books. Like Pallavicini, he took inspiration from a wide variety of sources, was partial to clichés (hearts, flowers, butterflies) and kitsch (gold!), and had no qualms about revisiting the same idea multiple times. Both artists decorated windows for luxury department stores (Warhol for the chief window dresser Gene Moore at Bonwit Teller; Pallavicini for Lord & Taylor) and produced backgrounds for fashion features (Warhol for photo sessions by Otto Fenn; Pallavicini for *Vogue*). This—and details such as the existence of numerous decorative Christmas tree illustrations by both artists—may be owed to the circumstances surrounding commissions for graphic artists in the 1950s. But the points of convergence are also present when no commercial clients were involved: Pallavicini was not the only one to celebrate his New York exhibition debut at the Hugo Gallery in 1951;

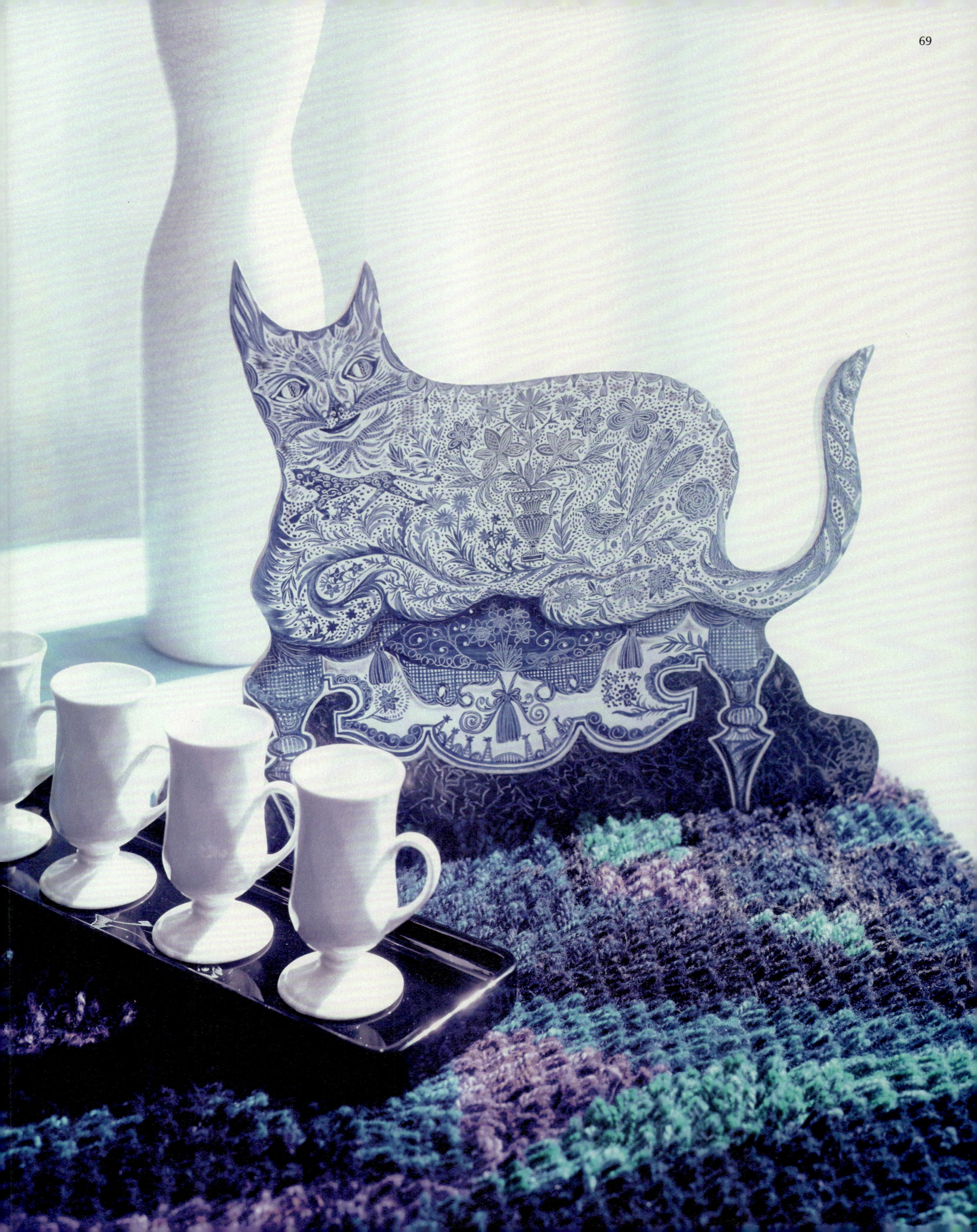

in the following year, Warhol, too, had his first ever exhibition there (with drawings based on stories by Truman Capote, America's openly homosexual star author and Warhol's great idol).[35] And, while Pallavicini dedicated his first exhibition to the mythological lovers Mars and Venus, the theme of what is possibly Warhol's very first "promotional book," *Love is a Pink Cake* (1952) is—yes, indeed—romantic love.[36] Illustrations of putti and figures in historical costume are accompanied by Ward's rhapsodies to legendary (and legendarily tragic) lovers such as Romeo and Juliet, Antony and Cleopatra, or Daphne and Apollo (as well as Oscar Wilde and André Gide). Pallavicini and Warhol then both went on to exhibit their works at the Bodley Gallery, which, after the closure of the Hugo Gallery, was run by Iolas's former assistant David Mann.[37] When, in December 1956, Warhol exhibited his drawings of women's legs and shoes embellished with gold leaf and punched gold decorations—including a feathered slipper dedicated to "Mme. Helena Rubinstein The Princess Gourielli"—a short walk away, at Iolas's gallery, Pallavicini's glass-bead-studded zodiac signs were on display. It should not go unmentioned that Warhol also took on the subject of the zodiac in his manuscript *Horoscopes for the Coc(k)tail Hour* (1959), in which each page features a star sign and a cocktail recipe. Again, located just a few blocks away from the Bodley Gallery was the café and restaurant Serendipity 3, which, shortly after its opening in 1954, became a hotspot for the (gay) advertising, fashion, and creative scene. Although not quite the same as Demel—on the menu were desserts from the American South—Serendipity 3 was as important to Warhol's social life and career as the famous café in Vienna had been for Pallavicini. At Serendipity 3, the "promotional books" were hand-colored as part of "coloring-in parties" with assistants and friends (whereby Warhol readily accepted "mistakes" and inaccuracies), and drawings by the artist were a regular feature on the walls—shoes, for example, or cats—and were available for sale, as were his books. On the subject of cats, again, Warhol shared this affinity with Pallavicini. For the former, the "promotional book" *25 Cats Name [sic!] Sam and One Blue Pussy* (1954) can be cited as an example, while a remarkable one for Pallavicini are the richly decorated "cat stands," which made it into the 1957 issue of *Vogue* as a Christmas gift suggestion.[38] The jewel- and lace-covered "domestic cat" would be ideal for the boudoir, the Delft Blue version for the breakfast table.[39]

The list could go on. But what to do with these points of convergence? Given Pallavicini's unflattering appraisal of Warhol, should we assume a state of competition? A lack of understanding on the part of the older generation toward the young upstart, who, despite his poor manners, "sloppy" work (uneven application of paint, errors in titles), and penchant for cheap materials and methods (*Flair* versus the "promotional books"), enjoyed success—thanks to his "persistent publicity"? Who, although, like Pallavicini, he too has a weakness for celebrity and gossip, has no sense of "noblesse oblige"? Who, while clearly familiar with style, tradition, and etiquette, prefers to employ them as a source of amusement? (Warhol's interest in social norms is evident from his contribution of illustrations for Amy Vanderbilt's classic *Complete Book of Etiquette* [1952]. His own "promotional book" *Wild Raspberries* [1959] is designed as a parody of the French gourmet recipe books used by American "epicures" attempting to imitate a refined European lifestyle.) And who, not least, also like Pallavicini, tends to include allusions to his sexual orientation in his work, but frequently overshoots the target and breaches the boundaries of "good taste"? (With the best will in the world, Warhol's "boy drawings," exhibited at the Bodley Gallery in 1956, can no longer be described as coded.) And, finally, whereabouts in this field are the alphabets to be located, which, although seemingly intertwined in many ways, are particularly different in style, compared to other works by the two artists?

"Children's fiction," writes Jacqueline Rose, "emerges, therefore, out of a conception [...] which places the innocence of the child and the primary state of language and/or culture in a close and mutually dependent relation."[40] With this in mind, working with ABC rhymes means engaging with the fiction of origins—of a primary state of language (before the construction of words and meaning) and a primary state of being human (before sexuality). It also means confronting didactic tools that are used to shape subjectivity, as well as working with a serial system that asserts differences in what is essentially the same. ABC rhymes are among the most rigid formats in children's literature; their fascination thus always lay in pushing their narrow constraints. Pallavicini embraces this tradition. Using the popular text in its original, unadapted form, he assumes the role of illustrator, whose pictures match the rhymes—he does not depict individuals, but types, which are identified by their clothing and attributes. Neither the subtle modernisms nor the homoerotic undertones fundamentally call into question the hierarchical structure of the

35 One of the things that "Iolas artists" seem to have in common is the folding screen. A familiar design object for Pallavicini, Warhol attempted one in 1956, featuring an angel surrounded by opulent floral vegetation. William N. Copley made his first folding screen for his premiere at Iolas's gallery in 1958.

36 According to Schleif, *Love is a Pink Cake* may have already been printed in 1952; other authors date the publication to 1953. Schleif "Clevere Frivolität in Excelsis" (see note 29), p. 81.

37 A poster (IN 7169/PI) in the collection of the University of Applied Arts, advertising an exhibition by Pallavicini at the Bodley Gallery, is unfortunately undated. An oil painting (IN 6313/B) in the collection, which bears strong similarities to the card design, is marked "Bodley Gallery Dec. 61 N.Y" on the back. However, it is also entirely possible that this was not Pallavicini's first exhibition at the Bodley Gallery. Warhol's premiere at Bodley took place in February 1956, with *Studies for a Boy Book*, his most unapologetically homoerotic exhibition of the 1950s.

38 "Vogue's Fashions in Living," *Vogue*, November 15, 1957, pp. 161–69.

39 Pallavicini's placement of the animals on cushions and pedestals in these works, published in 1957, whereby the blue cat's pedestal vaguely resembles that of the bulldog in his ABC, could be a further indication that the alphabet was produced in the 1950s.

40 Jacqueline Rose, *The Case of Peter Pan or the Impossibility of Children's Fiction* (London/Basingstoke, 1984), p. 9.

Chefdekorateur Gene Moore bei Bonwit Teller; Pallavicini für Lord & Taylor) und fertigten Hintergründe für Modestrecken an (Warhol für Fotosessions von Otto Fenn; Pallavicini für die *Vogue*). Dies – und Details wie die Existenz zahlreicher dekorativer Weihnachtsbaumillustrationen beider Künstler – mag der Auftragslage für Grafiker*innen in den 1950er-Jahren geschuldet sein. Aber die Konvergenzen lassen sich auch dort finden, wo keine kommerziellen Auftraggeber*innen im Spiel waren: So feierte nicht nur Pallavicini 1951 in der Galerie Hugo sein New Yorker Ausstellungsdebut, auch Warhol hatte dort im Jahr darauf seine erste Ausstellung überhaupt (mit Zeichnungen nach Erzählungen von Truman Capote, Amerikas offen homosexuellem Starautor und Warhols großem Idol).[35] Und während Pallavicini diese erste Ausstellung dem mythologischen Liebespaar Mars und Venus widmete, ist das Thema von Warhols vermutlich allererstem „promotional book" *Love is a Pink Cake* (1952) – ja, genau – ebenfalls die romantische Liebe:[36] Zu Illustrationen von Putten und Figuren in historischen Kostümen besingt Ward in Reimen legendäre (und legendär tragische) Liebespaare wie Romeo und Julia, Antonius und Kleopatra oder Daphne und Apollo (aber auch Oscar Wilde und André Gide). Weiterhin präsentierten sowohl Pallavicini als auch Warhol ihre Arbeiten in der Galerie Bodley, die nach der Schließung der Galerie Hugo von Iolas' ehemaligem Assistenten David Mann geleitet wurde.[37] Als Warhol dort im Dezember 1956 seine mit Goldfolie und gestanztem Golddekor verzierten Zeichnungen von Damenbeinen und Schuhen zeigte – darunter einen der „MMe. Helena Rubinstein The Princess Gourielli" gewidmeten federbesetzten Pantoffel –, waren einen kurzen Fußmarsch entfernt bei Iolas Pallavicinis mit Glasperlen veredelte Sternzeichen-Bilder zu sehen. (Nicht unerwähnt bleiben soll, dass sich auch Warhol der Sternzeichen annahm, und zwar im Manuskript *Horoscopes for the Coc(k)tail Hour* (1959), in dem sich je ein Sternzeichen und ein Cocktailrezept das Blatt teilen.) Wiederum nur wenige Häuserblöcke von der Galerie Bodley entfernt lag das Café-Restaurant Serendipity 3, das sich unmittelbar nach seiner Eröffnung 1954 zu einem Hotspot der (schwulen) Werbe-, Mode- und Kreativszene entwickelte. Wenn auch kein Demel – man servierte Süßes aus dem amerikanischen Süden –, so war das Serendipity 3 für Warhols Sozialleben und Karriere ähnlich wichtig wie das Wiener Traditionshaus für Pallavicini. Im Serendipity 3 wurden die „promotional books" in Ausmalpartys mit Assistenten und Freunden koloriert (wobei Warhol „Fehler" und Ungenauigkeiten bereitwillig akzeptierte); und es hingen dort immer wieder Zeichnungen des Künstlers an der Wand – Schuhe etwa oder Katzen –, die man ebenso wie seine Bücher käuflich erwerben konnte. Apropos Katzen: Auch diese Affinität teilte Warhol mit Pallavicini. Für Ersteren lässt sich hier exemplarisch das „promotional book" *25 Cats Name [sic!] Sam and One Blue Pussy* (1954) anführen. Ein schönes Beispiel von Pallavicini sind die reich dekorierten „Katzenaufsteller", die es als weihnachtlicher Geschenkvorschlag 1957 bis in die *Vogue* schafften.[38] Die spitzen- und juwelenbesetzte „Hauskatze" empfiehlt sich fürs Boudoir, die in Delfter Blau gehaltene für den Frühstückstisch.[39]

Die Liste ließe sich fortsetzen. Was aber tun mit diesen Konvergenzen? Muss man, gestützt auf Pallavicinis unvorteilhafte Schilderung Warhols, ein Konkurrenzverhältnis annehmen? Unverständnis der älteren Generation gegenüber dem jungen Emporkömmling, der trotz mangelnder Umgangsformen, „schlampiger" Arbeit (ungleicher Farbauftrag, fehlerhafte Titel) und einem Hang zu billigen Materialien und Mitteln (*Flair* versus die „promotional books") Erfolge feiert – seiner „penetranten Publizität" sei Dank? Der zwar, wie man selbst, ein Faible hat für Berühmtheiten und Klatsch, aber keinen Sinn für „noblesse oblige"? Dem Tradition, Stil und Etikette offenkundig nicht fremd sind, jedoch bevorzugt als Anlass zur Belustigung dienen? Warhols Interesse an gesellschaftlichen Verhaltensnormen lässt sich beispielsweise daran festmachen, dass er Illustrationen zu Amy Vanderbilts Benimmklassiker *Complete Book of Etiquette* (1952) beisteuerte. Sein eigenes „promotional book" *Wild Raspberries* (1959) ist als Persiflage auf jene französischen Gourmetkochbücher angelegt, mit denen amerikanische „Feinschmecker" einen gepflegten europäischen Lebensstil zu imitieren suchten. Und der nicht zuletzt, wie man selbst, Anspielungen auf seine sexuelle Orientierung in seine Arbeit zu integrieren weiß, dabei aber immer wieder übers Ziel hinausschießt und die Grenzen des „guten Geschmacks" überschreitet? (Warhols 1956 in der Galerie Bodley ausgestellte *Boy Drawings* lassen sich beim besten Willen nicht mehr als codiert bezeichnen.) Wo in diesem Feld schließlich lassen sich die Alphabete verorten, die – wiewohl sie vielfach verschränkt scheinen – im Unterschied zu anderen Arbeiten der beiden Künstler stilistisch besonders stark divergieren?

„Children's fiction", schreibt Jacqueline Rose, „emerges, therefore, out of a conception […] which places the innocence of the child and the primary state of language and/or culture in a close and mutually dependent relation."[40] Sich

35 Was „Iolas-Künstler" unter anderem zu verbinden scheint, ist der Paravent. Für Pallavicini war er ein vertrautes Gestaltungsobjekt, Warhol versuchte sich 1956 an einem ersten Exemplar, das einen Engel inmitten opulenter Blumenvegetation zeigt. William N. Copley fertigte für seine Premiere bei Iolas 1958 ebenfalls seinen ersten Paravent an.

36 Nach Schleif könnte *Love is a Pink Cake* bereits 1952 gedruckt worden sein, andere Autor*innen datieren das Büchlein auf 1953. Schleif „Clevere Frivolität in Excelsis" (s. Anm. 29), S. 81.

37 Ein Plakat (IN 7169/PI) zu einer Ausstellung Pallavicinis in der Galerie Bodley, das sich in der Sammlung der Universität für angewandte Kunst befindet, weist leider keine Jahreszahl auf. Ein Ölbild (IN 6313/B) in der Sammlung, das dem Kartenmotiv stark ähnelt, trägt auf der Rückseite den Vermerk „Bodley Gallery Dec. 61 N.Y". Es ist allerdings durchaus möglich, dass es sich dabei nicht um Pallavicinis erste Ausstellung in der Galerie Bodley handelt. Warhols Bodley-Premiere fand im Februar 1956 mit *Studies for a Boy Book* statt, seine wohl unverblümteste homoerotische Ausstellung in den 1950er-Jahren.

38 „Vogue's Fashions in Living", in: *Vogue*, 15.11.1957, S. 161–169.

39 Dass Pallavicini in diesen 1957 publizierten Arbeiten Tiere auf Pölstern und Podesten platziert, von denen das der blauen Katze vage an das Podest der Bulldogge erinnert, könnte ein weiteres Indiz dafür sein, dass das Alphabet in den 1950er-Jahren entstanden ist.

40 Jacqueline Rose, *The Case of Peter Pan or the Impossibility of Children's Fiction*, London, Basingstoke 1984, S. 9.

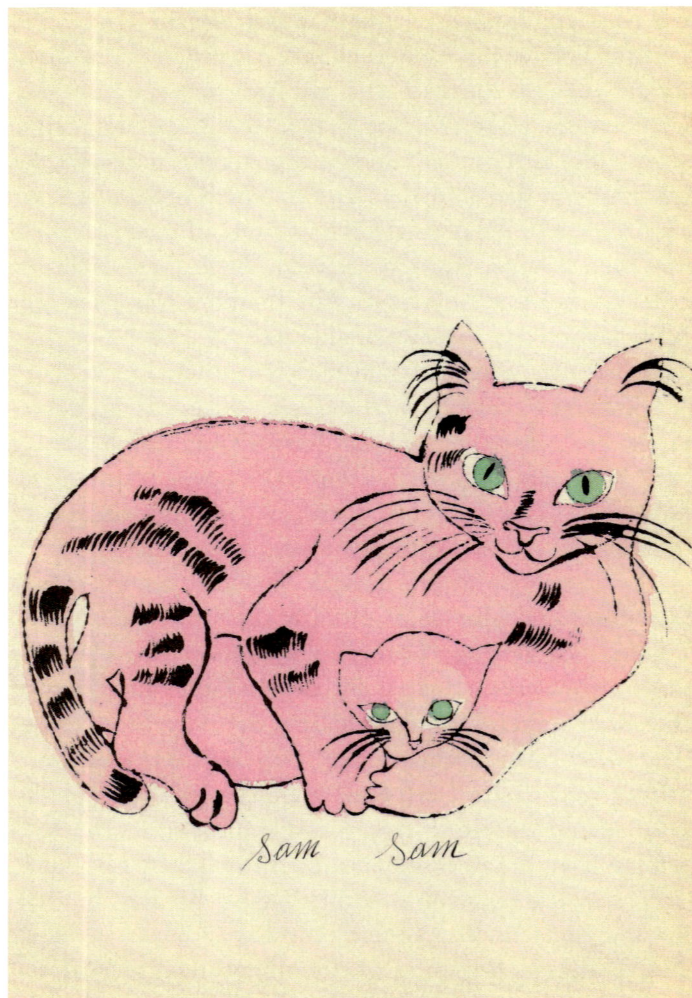

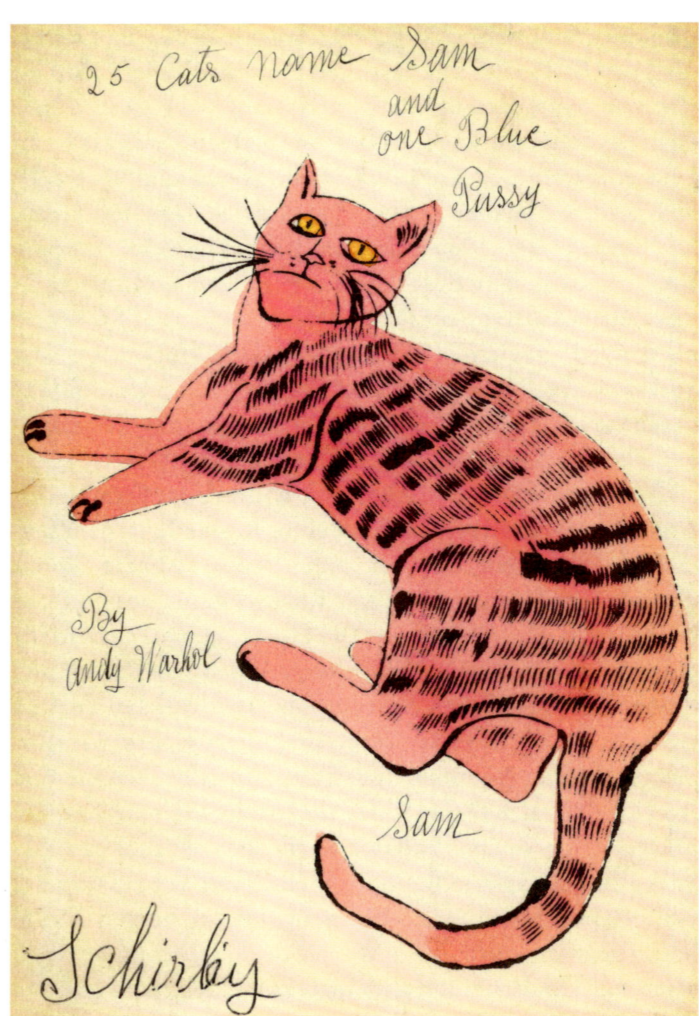

Andy Warhol, *25 Cats Name [sic!] Sam and One Blue Pussy*, 1954, Künstlerbuch, Abbildung und Titelblatt / artist's book, one sheet and cover page

"class society." Warhol's alphabets, meanwhile, although still echoing the tradition of the ABC rhyme, already at the text level depart from any differentiation by class or status. The protagonists of the *Ladies' Alphabet* are, without exception, presented as style-conscious consumers, irrespective of their identity as actresses or men in drag. Moreover, since the accessories named in the rhymes—the décor of the body—are partly missing, "personality" and gender are the only attributes on display for the purpose of alphabetization. *A is an Alphabet* loses all decorative adornments entirely, as well as the parodistic tinge that characterizes the *Ladies' Alphabet.* In a sense, the pictures address us "off-book," i.e. unofficially, exposing the arbitrary relationship between sign and signified, which to mask is normally the purpose of this kind of ABC. This corresponds with the sketchily outlined protagonists, who are anonymous and yet individualized at the same time. *A is an Alphabet* takes us from the theater stage to the stage of the everyday, where everyone is both the same and different, depending on the situation.

One way of approaching the differences between Pallavicini's and Warhol's alphabets is to locate them within a contemporary spectrum of "camp." A sentimental view of the past, a penchant for the decorative, artificiality, stylization, aestheticization, life as theater, irony, corruption of the "innocent," etc.—criteria which Susan Sontag lists in her essay "Notes on 'Camp'" (1964) as characteristic of a "camp" sensitivity—can also be found to varying degrees in the work of both artists.[41] Another key might be in what is possibly the earliest attempt at a definition of "camp," which Sontag also references: Christopher Isherwood's 1954 novel *The World in the Evening*, which makes the distinction between "high camp" and "low camp." Charles, the gay protagonist of the novel, describes "low camp" as a vulgar, effeminate form, "a swishy little boy with peroxided hair, dressed in a picture hat and feather boa, pretending to be Marlene Dietrich."[42] "High camp," on the other hand, runs deeper and forms the "emotional basis" of ballet and Baroque art—an earnest examination with high aesthetic and philosophical standards, while being cloaked in humor and irony.[43] Pallavicini's alphabet and Warhol's

41 Susan Sontag, "Notes on 'Camp,'" in *Against Interpretation and Other Essays* (New York, 2001), pp. 275–92.
42 Christopher Isherwood, *The World in the Evening* (New York, 1954), p. 110.
43 Ibid.

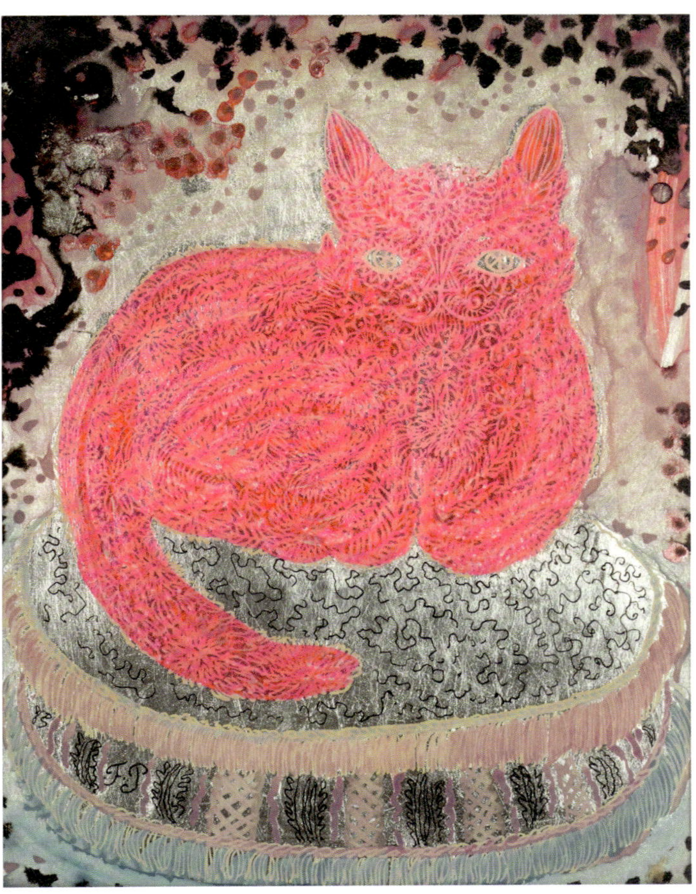

Chat I, undatiert / undated

mit ABC-Reimen zu beschäftigen, bedeutet demgemäß, sich auf die Fiktion von Ursprüngen einzulassen – von einem Primärzustand von Sprache (vor der Konstruktion von Wörtern und Bedeutung) und von einem Primärzustand des Menschseins (vor der Sexualität). Es bedeutet auch, sich mit didaktischen Werkzeugen zu konfrontieren, die eingesetzt werden, um Subjektivität zu formen, und mit einem seriellen System, das Differenzen im wesentlich Gleichen behauptet. ABC-Reime gehören zu den rigidesten Formen der Kinderliteratur; ihr Unterhaltungswert lag deshalb schon immer im Ausloten ihrer eng gesteckten Grenzen. Pallavicini stellt sich in diese Tradition. Er übernimmt den populären Vorlagentext unverändert und erfüllt die Rolle des Illustrators, dessen Bilder den Reimen entsprechen – er stellt Typen dar, die über ihre Kleidung und Attribute identifiziert werden, keine Individuen. Weder die subtilen Modernismen noch die homoerotischen Anspielungen stellen die hierarchische Struktur des „Ständestaats" grundlegend infrage. In Warhols Alphabeten wiederum klingt zwar die Tradition der ABC-Reime nach, bereits auf der Textebene allerdings wird eine Differenzierung über Klasse oder Stand verabschiedet. Die Protagonist*innen des *Ladies' Alphabet* werden allesamt als stilbewusste Konsument*innen vorgestellt, ungeachtet ihrer Identität als Schauspielerinnen oder Männer in Drag. Fehlen darüber hinaus die in den Reimen genannten Accessoires – das Dekor der Körper –, sind „personality" und Geschlecht die einzigen Attribute, die zum Zwecke der Alphabetisierung zur Aufführung gebracht werden. *A is an Alphabet* verzichtet gänzlich auf schmückende Beigaben und auch auf die parodistische Note, die das *Ladies' Alphabet* auszeichnet. Die Bilder adressieren uns gewissermaßen „off-book", also inoffiziell, was das arbiträre Verhältnis von Zeichen und Bezeichnetem exponiert, das zu maskieren eigentlich die Aufgabe dieser Art von ABC ist. Dem entsprechen die umrisshaften Protagonist*innen, die anonym und individualisiert zugleich sind. *A is an Alphabet* bringt uns von der Showbühne auf die Bühne des Alltags, wo alle gleich und zugleich situativ verschieden sind.

Eine Möglichkeit, sich den Unterschieden zwischen Pallavicinis und Warhols Alphabeten anzunähern, ist, sie innerhalb eines zeitgenössischen Camp-Spektrums zu verorten. Der sentimentale Blick auf die Vergangenheit, der Hang zum Dekorativen, Artifizialität, Stilisierung, Ästhetisierung, das Leben als Theater, Ironie, Korruption des „Unschuldigen" usw. – all jene Kriterien, die Susan Sontag in ihren „Notes on ‚Camp'" (1964) als charakteristisch für

Ladies' Alphabet can easily fit in such dichotomies, as does the older artist's irritation at the younger. The (pre-Pop) Warhol would thus correspond with Sontag's "dandy in the age of mass culture," and Pallavicini with the "old-style dandy," who hates the vulgar and has nothing but disdain for the mass-produced.[44] While there may be a grain of truth in it, the judgmental ascription of "conservative" (bad) and "progressive" (good) seems to fall short. The more interesting hypothesis is that, with their ABC works, both artists intended to create an alphabet that could also be read as a social commentary. The differences between the alphabets would therefore be programmatic, not least regarding the function of the decorative, a field explored by both Pallavicini and Warhol in those years.

In her essay about Matisse's late work (he died in 1954), Amy Goldin asserts that the development of a differentiation between the decorative and the pictorial found a parallel in the historic separation of prose and poetry: "Decoration and poetry are older and more basic."[45] Following Goldin, the decorative thus is also endowed with the fiction of an originality, which—as with the rhyme (or the alphabet)—focuses not on the singular author, but on the notion of repetition and tradition through a collective. Since decorative art is not about individual expression or introspection, its subject is the banal, the clichéd, the stereotypical (Goldin cites the zodiac signs as an example)—objects and events whose function is primarily social.[46] "Your job," Goldin tells the decorative artist, "is to clarify and heighten the impact of objects and occasions that already exist, that already have meaning."[47] I would like to suggest that, from their preoccupation with the decorative, this "older" and "more fundamental" form of creativity, Pallavicini and Warhol drew opposite conclusions for their work in and on the present—conclusions that are not only reflected in their alphabets, but also in their later artistic careers, and that touch on the question of the function of art in society. For Pallavicini, the decorative was in service to a quasi-mythological order that travels through time as an anachronistic formula and merely changes its guise. The cyclical moment that defines the decorative, to him, has a stabilizing, preserving effect, creating an aesthetic distance to the present. Warhol, on the other hand, identified a dynamic element in the meaning-enhancing function of the decorative, that could be mobilized according to the logic of his present. The cyclical moment finds its contemporary application in serial (re)production, which aims not to cement differences but, ultimately, to liquidate them.

"In Europe the royalty and aristocracy used to eat a lot better than the peasants—they weren't eating the same things at all. It was either partridge or porridge, and each class stuck to its own food. But when Queen Elizabeth came here and President Eisenhower bought her a hot dog I'm sure he felt confident that she couldn't have had delivered to Buckingham Palace a better hot dog than that one he bought her for maybe twenty cents at the ballpark. Because there *is* no better hot dog than a ballpark hot dog. Not for a dollar, not for ten dollars, not for a hundred thousand dollars could she get a better hot dog. She could get one for twenty cents and so could anybody else."[48]

"When Hitler drove by, he was like ivory."[49]

Today, almost seventy years later, the differences in status between Warhol and Pallavicini could not be greater. As such, both approaches, the ever-reproducing formula that exerts pressure on the present and the reproducing present that exerts pressure on the formula, appear to have been overtaken by reality. Solely in their dismissal of the emphatic concept of subject, both Pallavicini and Warhol have demonstrated prophetic qualities.

44 Sontag, "Notes on 'Camp'" (see note 41), pp. 288–89.
45 Amy Goldin, "Matisse and Decoration: The Late Cut-Outs," in *Amy Goldin: Art in a Hairshirt*, ed. Robert Kushner (Stockbridge/MA, 2011), pp. 144–61, here p. 160. First published in *Art in America*, July–August 1975.
46 Ibid., p. 146.
47 Amy Goldin, transcript of a lecture on Middle Eastern art, cited after Michael Duncan, "Amy Goldin: Public Life, the Intellect, and the Low Pleasures of Decoration," in *Amy Goldin: Art in a Hairshirt* (see note 45), pp. 140–43, here p. 141.
48 Andy Warhol, *The Philosophy of Andy Warhol (From A to B and Back Again)* (New York, 1975), p. 101.
49 Friedrich Ludwig Berzeviczy-Pallavicini, "Die besten jungen Leute waren plötzlich alle Nazis," in *Nachrichten aus dem 4. Reich: Gespräche mit österreichischen Emigranten*, ed. Gerhard Jelinek (Salzburg, 2008), pp. 41–43, here p. 42.

eine Camp-Sensibilität auflistet, lassen sich in verschiedenen Graden auch in den Arbeiten der beiden Künstler finden.[41] Einen Schlüssel könnte auch der wohl früheste Definitionsversuch von Camp bergen, auf den Sontag ebenfalls verweist: Christopher Isherwoods Roman *The World in the Evening* von 1954, wo zwischen „high camp" und „low camp" unterschieden wird. Charles, der queere Protagonist des Romans, beschreibt „low camp" als vulgäre, verweiblichte Form, „a swishy little boy with peroxided hair, dressed in a picture hat and feather boa, pretending to be Marlene Dietrich".[42] „High camp" wiederum geht tiefer, sei die „emotionale Basis" etwa des Balletts und von Barockkunst, eine in Humor und Ironie gekleidete, ernsthafte Auseinandersetzung mit ästhetischem und philosophischem Anspruch.[43] Pallavicinis Alphabet und Warhols *Ladies' Alphabet* ließen sich ohne Schwierigkeiten in solchen Dichotomien erklären, ebenso wie die Irritation des älteren durch den jüngeren Künstler. Der (Prä-Pop-) Warhol entspräche dann Sontags „dandy in the age of mass culture" und Pallavicini dem „old-style dandy", der das Vulgäre hasst und für das Massenproduzierte nur Verachtung übrig hat.[44] Mag darin auch ein Funken Wahrheit stecken, erscheint die wertende Zuschreibung von „konservativ" (schlecht) und „progressiv" (gut) zu kurz gegriffen. Die interessantere Hypothese ist, dass beide Künstler mit ihren ABC-Arbeiten den Anspruch verfolgten, ein Alphabet zu generieren, das auch als gesellschaftlicher Kommentar zu lesen ist. Die Unterschiede zwischen den Alphabeten wären demnach programmatisch, nicht zuletzt in Hinblick auf die Funktion des Dekorativen – jenes Feld, das sowohl Pallavicini als auch Warhol in jenen Jahren bespielten.

In ihrem Text über das Spätwerk von Matisse (er verstarb 1954) hält Amy Goldin fest, dass die Entwicklung einer Unterscheidung zwischen dem Dekorativen und der bildenden Kunst eine Parallele in der historischen Trennung von Prosa und Lyrik hätte: „Decoration and poetry are older and more basic."[45] Folgt man Goldin, haftet also auch dem Dekorativen die Fiktion einer Ursprünglichkeit an, in der – wie beim Reim (oder beim Alphabet) – nicht der/die singuläre Autor*in im Mittelpunkt steht, sondern die Idee der Wiederholung und Überlieferung durch ein Kollektiv. Weil es in der dekorativen Kunst nicht um individuellen Ausdruck oder Introspektion geht, ist ihr Gegenstand das Banale, Klischeehafte, Stereotype (Goldin nennt die Sternzeichen als Beispiel) – Dinge und Anlässe, deren Funktion primär eine soziale ist.[46] „Your job", adressiert Goldin die dekorative Künstlerin/den dekorativen Künstler, „is to clarify and heighten the impact of objects and occasions that already exist, that already have meaning."[47] Ich möchte behaupten, dass Pallavicini und Warhol aus ihrer Beschäftigung mit dem Dekorativen, dieser „älteren" und „grundlegenderen" Form gestalterischer Tätigkeit, entgegengesetzte Schlüsse für ihre Arbeit in und an der Gegenwart zogen – Schlüsse, die sich nicht nur in ihren Alphabeten abbilden, sondern auch in ihren weiteren künstlerischen Laufbahnen und die an die Frage der Funktion der Kunst in der Gesellschaft rühren. Für Pallavicini steht das Dekorative im Dienst einer quasimythologischen Ordnung, die als anachronistische Formel durch die Zeit reist und bloß ihr Gewand ändert. Das zyklische Moment, das dem Dekorativen eigen ist, hat für ihn eine stabilisierende und konservierende Wirkung, die ästhetische Distanz zur Gegenwart schafft. Warhol wiederum identifiziert in der bedeutungsverstärkenden Funktion des Dekorativen einen dynamischen Faktor, der entsprechend der Logik seiner Gegenwart mobilisiert werden kann. In der seriellen (Re-)Produktion hat das zyklische Moment seine zeitgenössische Applikation gefunden, und ihr Ziel ist nicht die Solidifizierung von Differenzen, sondern – letztlich – deren Liquidation.

> „In Europe the royalty and aristocracy used to eat a lot better than the peasants – they weren't eating the same things at all. It was either partridge or porridge, and each class stuck to its own food. But when Queen Elizabeth came here and President Eisenhower bought her a hot dog I'm sure he felt confident that she couldn't have had delivered to Buckingham Palace a better hot dog than that one he bought her for maybe twenty cents at the ballpark. Because there *is* no better hot dog than a ballpark hot dog. Not for a dollar, not for ten dollars, not for a hundred thousand dollars could she get a better hot dog. She could get one for twenty cents and so could anybody else."[48]

> „Als Hitler vorbeigefahren ist, war er ganz wie aus Elfenbein."[49]

Heute, knapp 70 Jahre später, da die Statusunterschiede zwischen Warhol und Pallavicini nicht größer sein könnten, scheinen beider Ansätze von der Realität überholt: die sich reproduzierende Formel, die Druck auf die Gegenwart ausübt, und die sich reproduzierende Gegenwart, die Druck auf die Formel ausübt. Allein mit der Verabschiedung des emphatischen Subjektbegriffs haben sowohl Pallavicini als auch Warhol prophetische Qualitäten bewiesen.

41 Susan Sontag, „Notes on ‚Camp'", in: *Against Interpretation and Other Essays*, New York 2001, S. 275–292.
42 Christopher Isherwood, *The World in the Evening*, New York 1954, S. 110.
43 Ebd.
44 Sontag, „Notes on ‚Camp'" (s. Anm. 41), S. 288 f.
45 Amy Goldin, „Matisse and Decoration: The Late Cut-Outs", in: Robert Kushner (Hg.), *Amy Goldin. Art in a Hairshirt*, Stockbridge/MA 2011, S. 144–161, hier: S. 160. Erstmals publiziert in: *Art in America*, Juli / August 1975.
46 Ebd., S. 146.
47 Amy Goldin, Abschrift eines Vortrags zur Kunst aus dem Nahen Osten, zit. nach Michael Duncan, „Amy Goldin: Public Life, the Intellect, and the Low Pleasures of Decoration", in: *Amy Goldin. Art in a Hairshirt* (s. Anm. 45), S. 140–143, hier: S. 141.
48 Andy Warhol, *The Philosophy of Andy Warhol (From A to B and Back Again)*, New York 1975, S. 101.
49 Friedrich Ludwig Berzeviczy-Pallavicini, „„Die besten jungen Leute waren plötzlich alle Nazis."", in: Gerhard Jelinek (Hg.), *Nachrichten aus dem 4. Reich. Gespräche mit österreichischen Emigranten*, Salzburg 2008, S. 41–43, hier: S. 42.

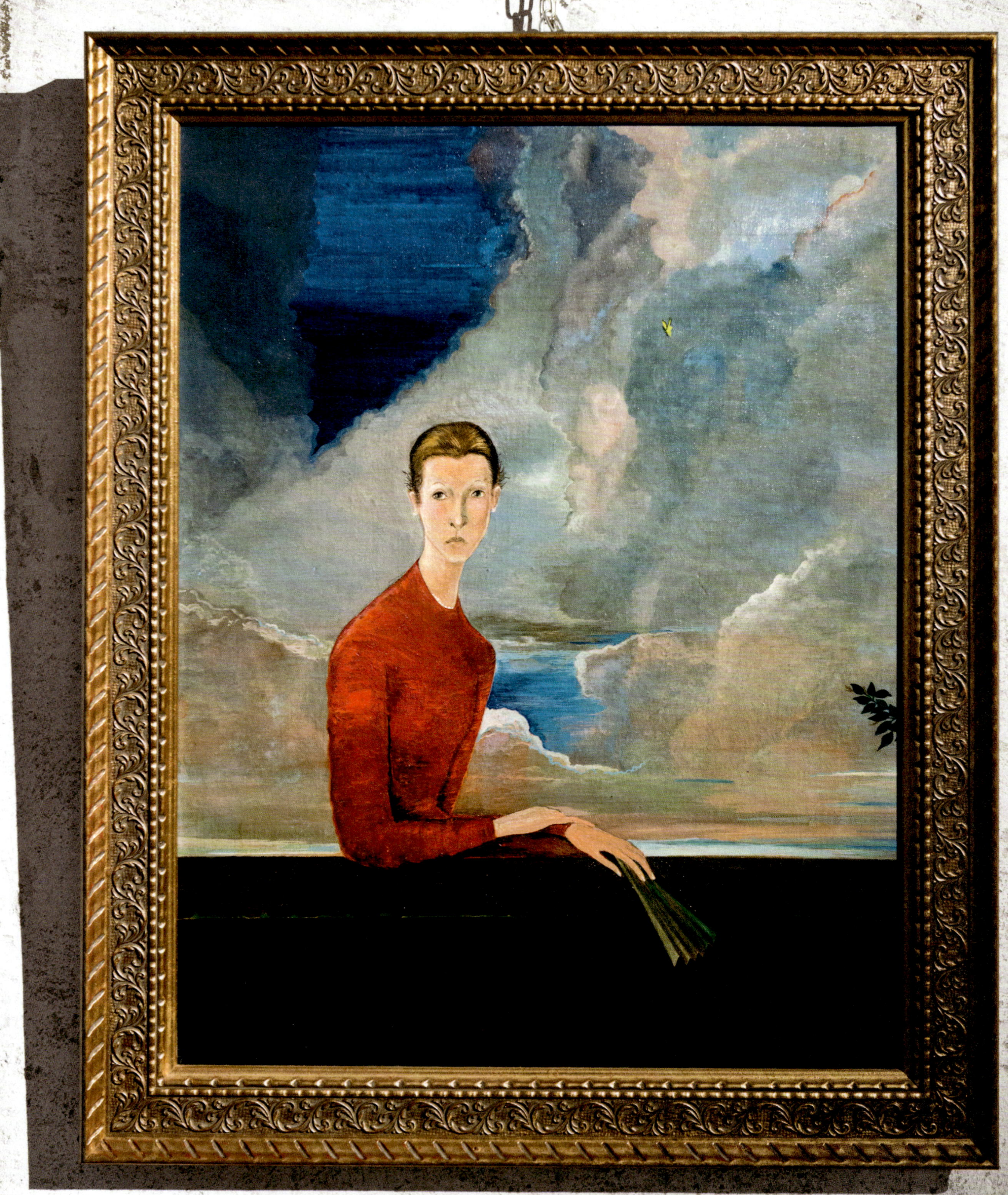

Bildnis einer jungen Dame / Portrait of a Young Woman, undatiert / undated

Ausstellungsansichten / Exhibiton Views, Universistätsgalerie Heiligenkreuzer Hof Wien / Vienna
2. Mai bis 1. Juni 2019 / May 2 to June 1, 2019

DER HAUSFREUND

Eine Wiederentdeckung des exzentrischen Werks von
A Rediscovery of the Eccentric Work of
FRIEDRICH VON BERZEVICZY-PALLAVICINI

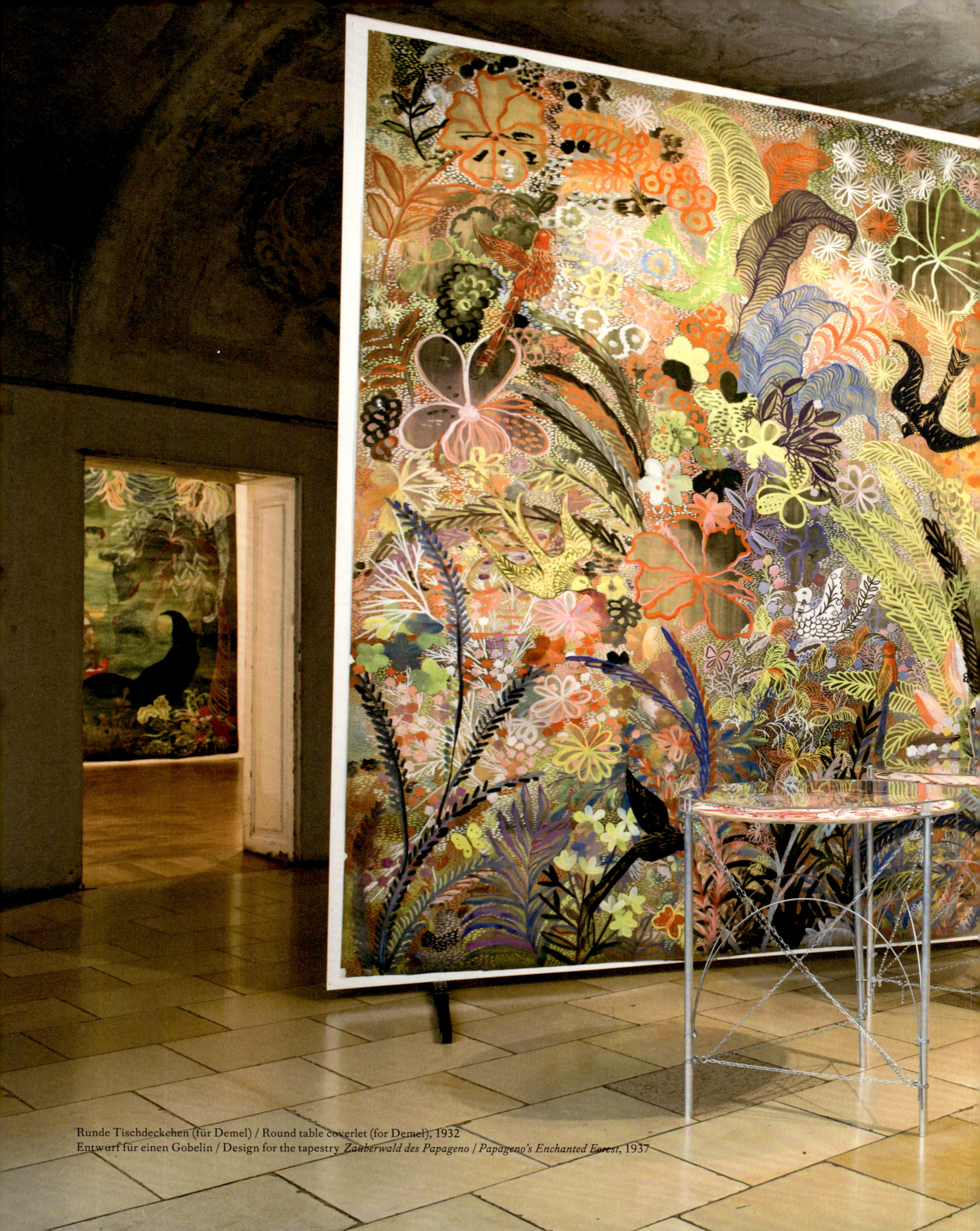

Runde Tischdeckchen (für Demel) / Round table coverlet (for Demel), 1932
Entwurf für einen Gobelin / Design for the tapestry *Zauberwald des Papageno / Papageno's Enchanted Forest*, 1937

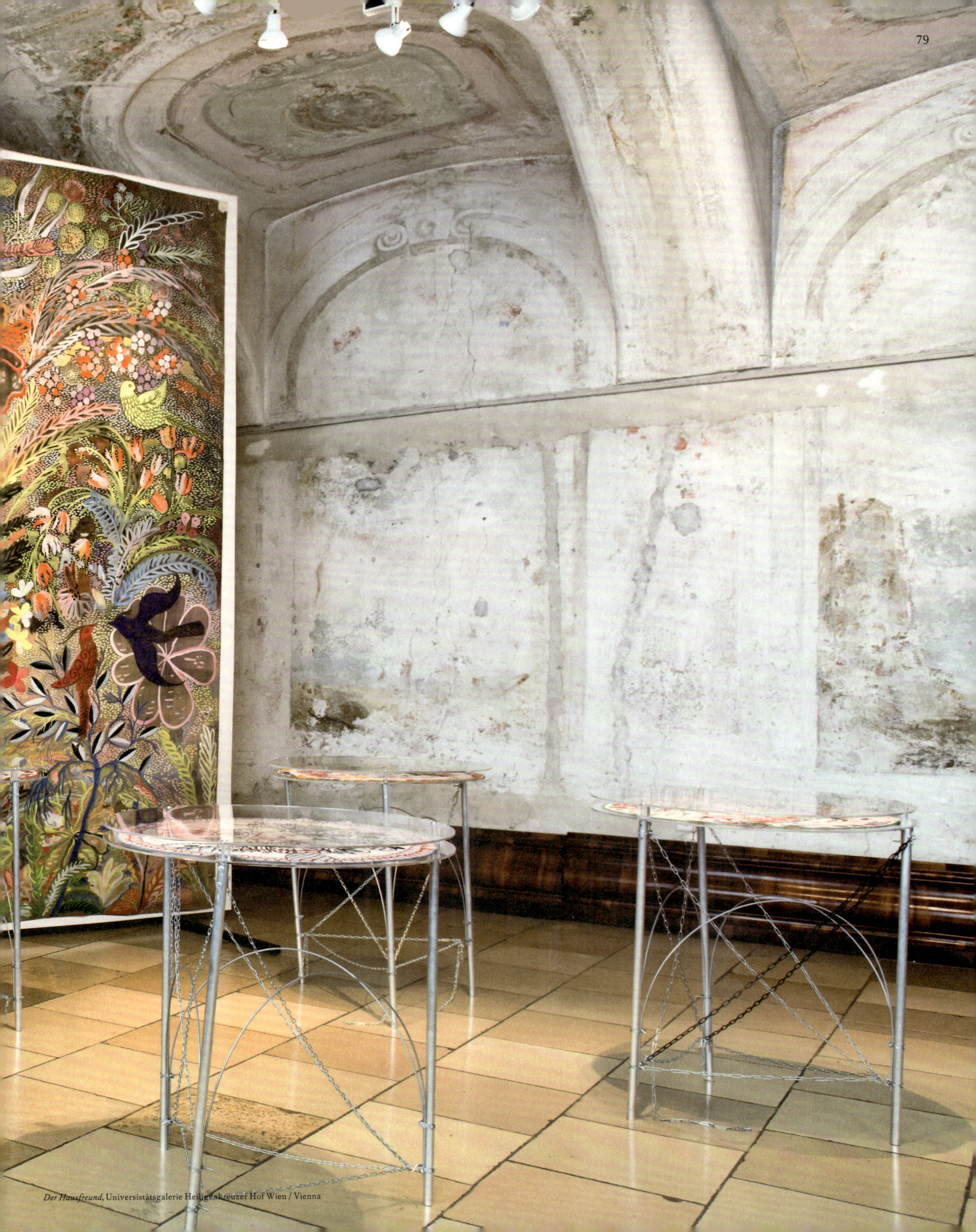

Der Hausfreund, Universitätsgalerie Heiligenkreuzer Hof Wien / Vienna

Entwurf für einen Gobelin / Design for the tapestry *Die Vier Jahreszeiten / The Four Seasons*, 1937
Josef Frank, Stoffmuster / Fabric pattern *Primavera*, undatiert / undated,
Ulrike Müller, *Others*, 2017
Hafen (Wolgalandschaft) / Harbor (Volga Landscape), 1932
Flair, 1950–51

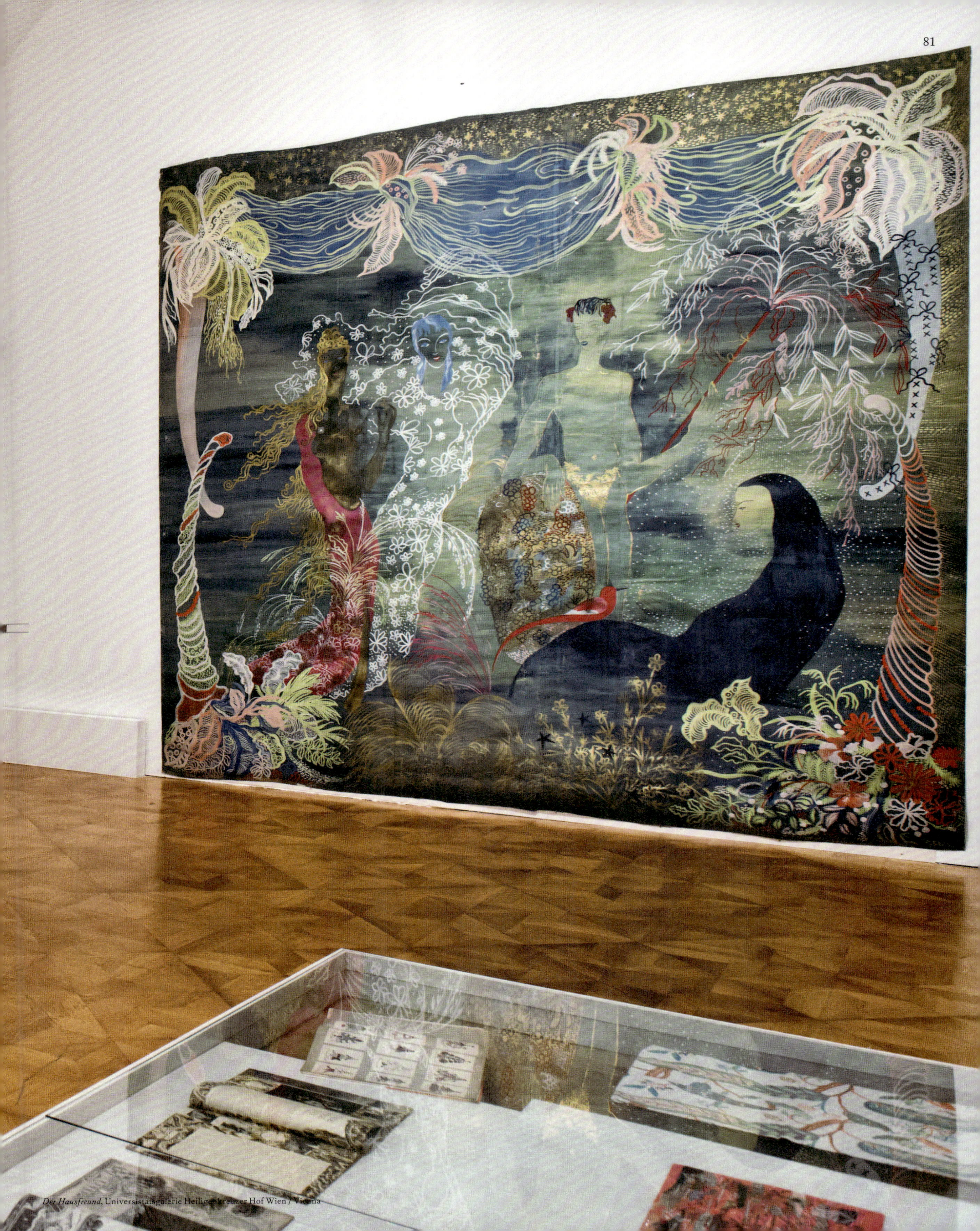

Der Hausfreund, Universistätsgalerie Heiligenkreuzer Hof Wien / Vienna

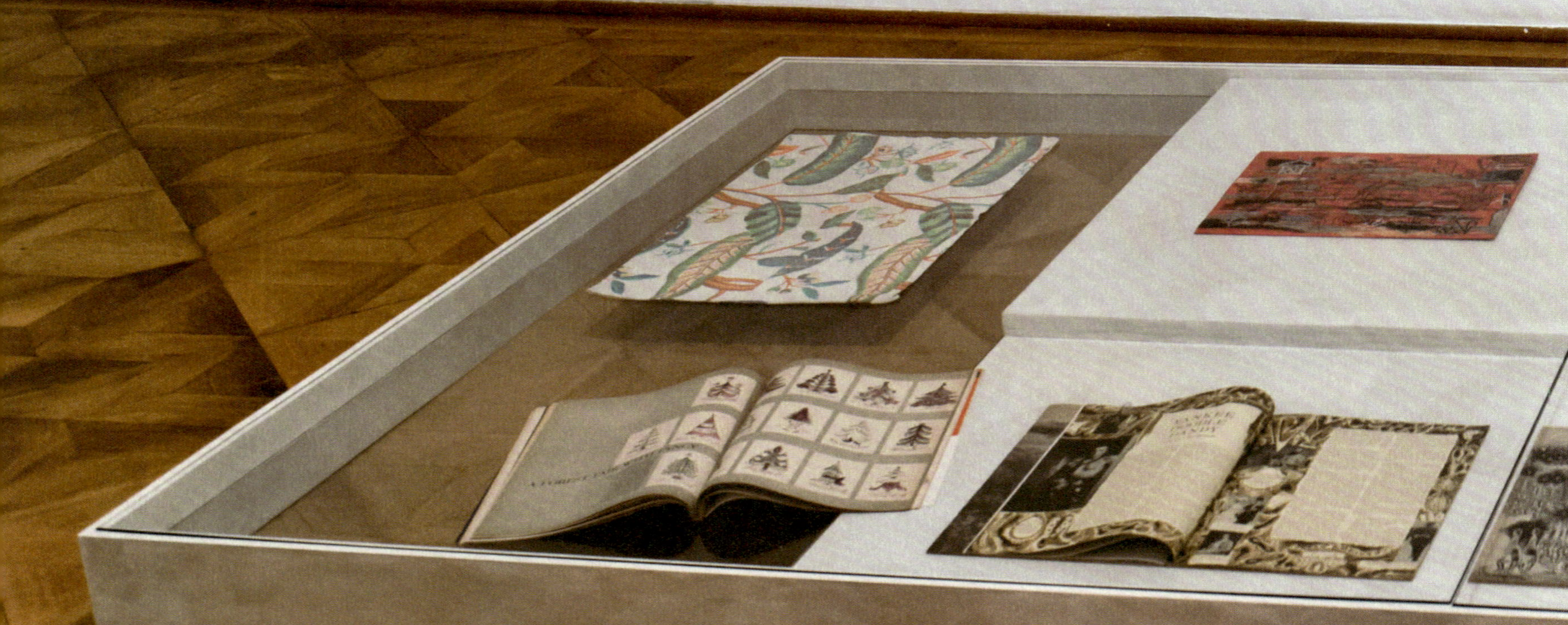

Modezeichnung für die Zeitschrift / Fashion drawing for the magazine *Bellezza*, 1943
Vitrine: Josef Frank, Stoffmuster / Fabric pattern, *Kirschzweige / Cherry Branches*, 1925–30
Hafen (Wolgalandschaft) / Harbor (Volga Landscape), 1932
Josef Frank, Stoffmuster / Fabric pattern *Primavera*, undatiert / undated
Flair, 1950–51

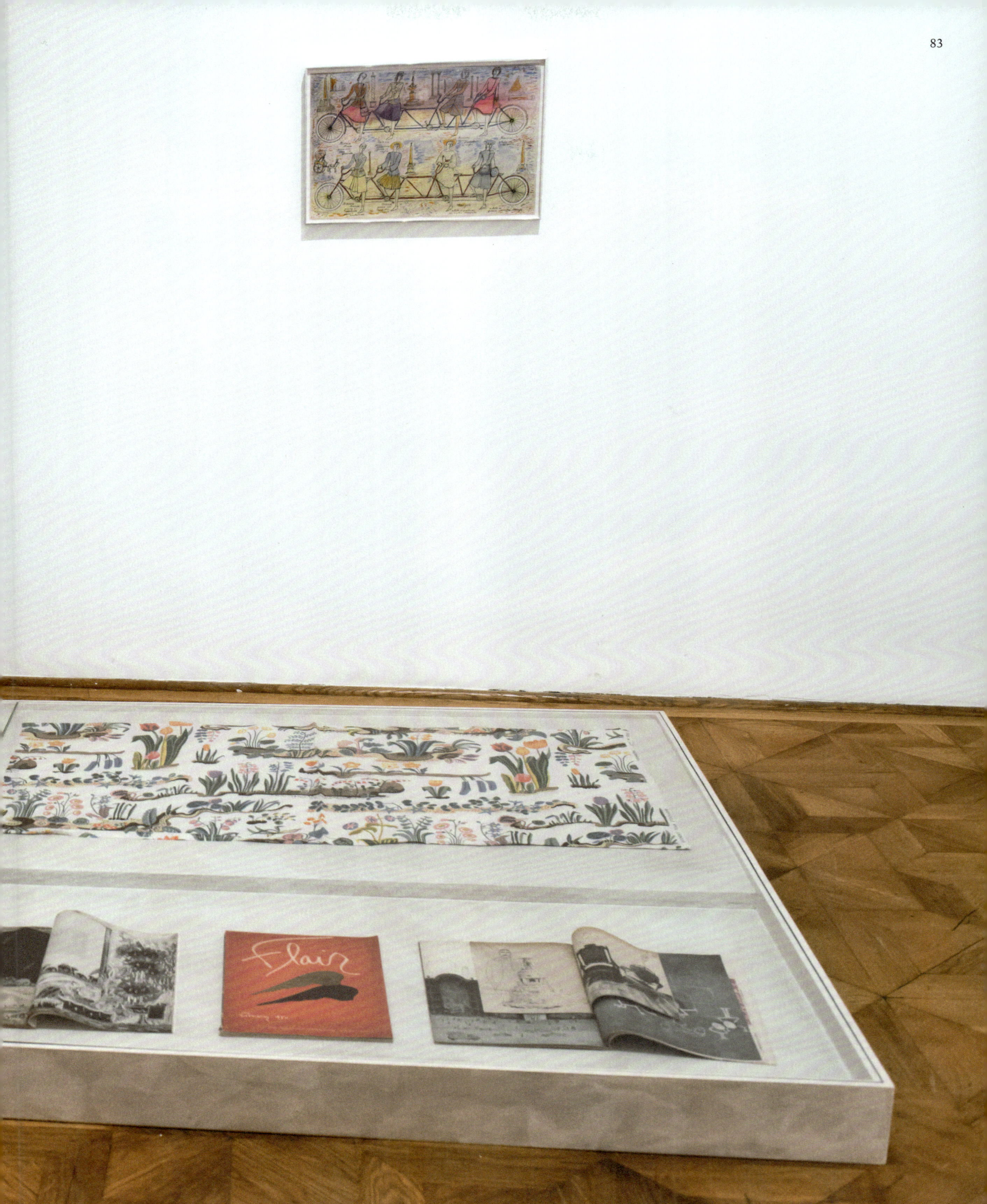

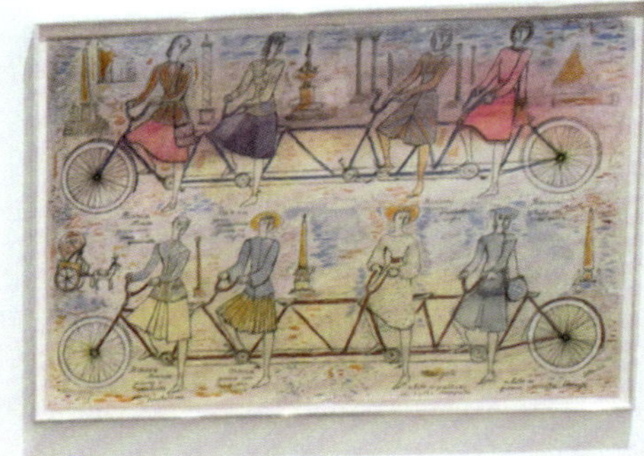

Der Hausfreund, Universitätsgalerie Heiligenkreuzer Hof Wien / Vienna

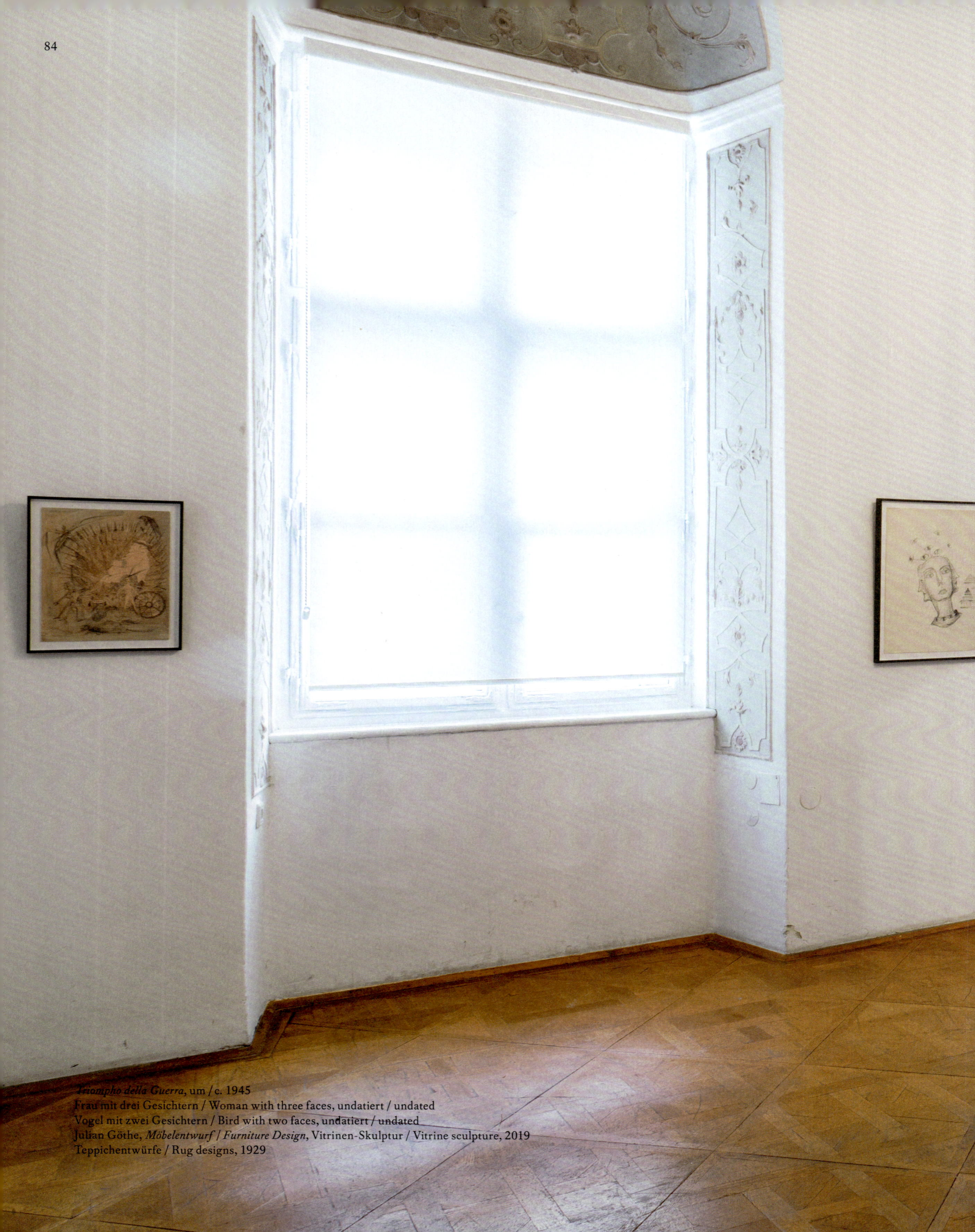

Triompho della Guerra, um / c. 1945
Frau mit drei Gesichtern / Woman with three faces, undatiert / undated
Vogel mit zwei Gesichtern / Bird with two faces, undatiert / undated
Julian Göthe, *Möbelentwurf / Furniture Design*, Vitrinen-Skulptur / Vitrine sculpture, 2019
Teppichentwürfe / Rug designs, 1929

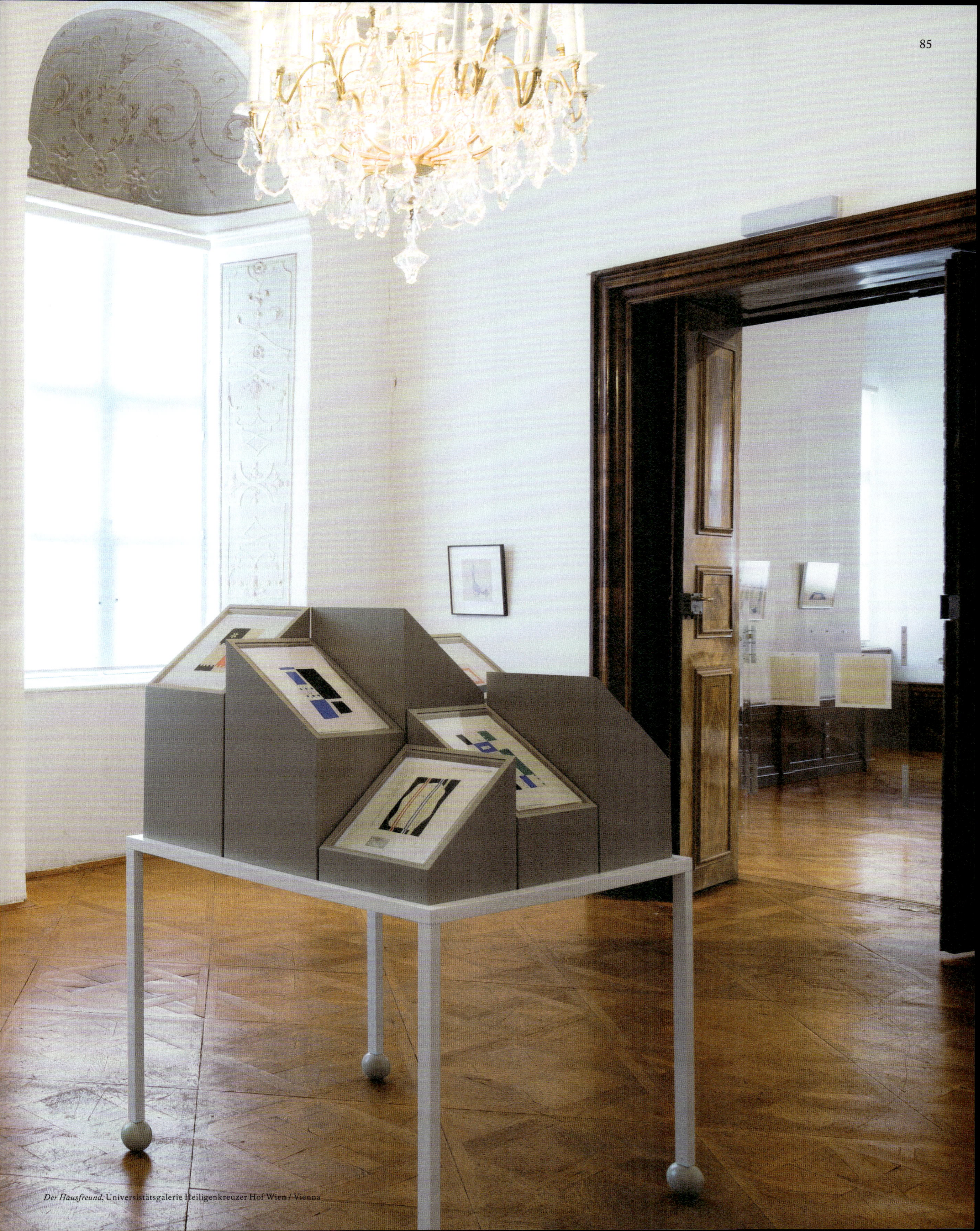

Der Hausfreund, Universistätsgalerie Heiligenkreuzer Hof Wien / Vienna

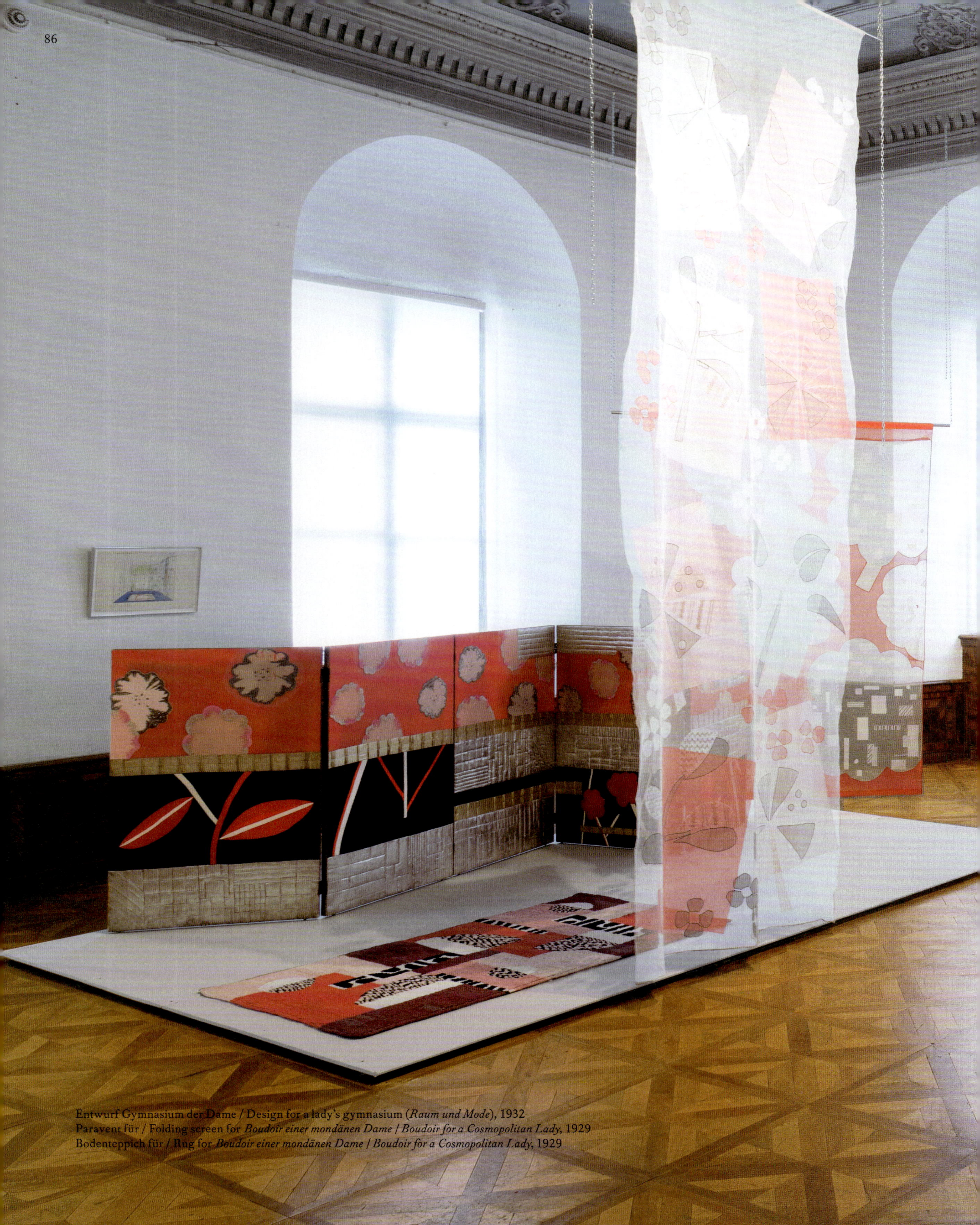

Entwurf Gymnasium der Dame / Design for a lady's gymnasium (*Raum und Mode*), 1932
Paravent für / Folding screen for *Boudoir einer mondänen Dame / Boudoir for a Cosmopolitan Lady*, 1929
Bodenteppich für / Rug for *Boudoir einer mondänen Dame / Boudoir for a Cosmopolitan Lady*, 1929

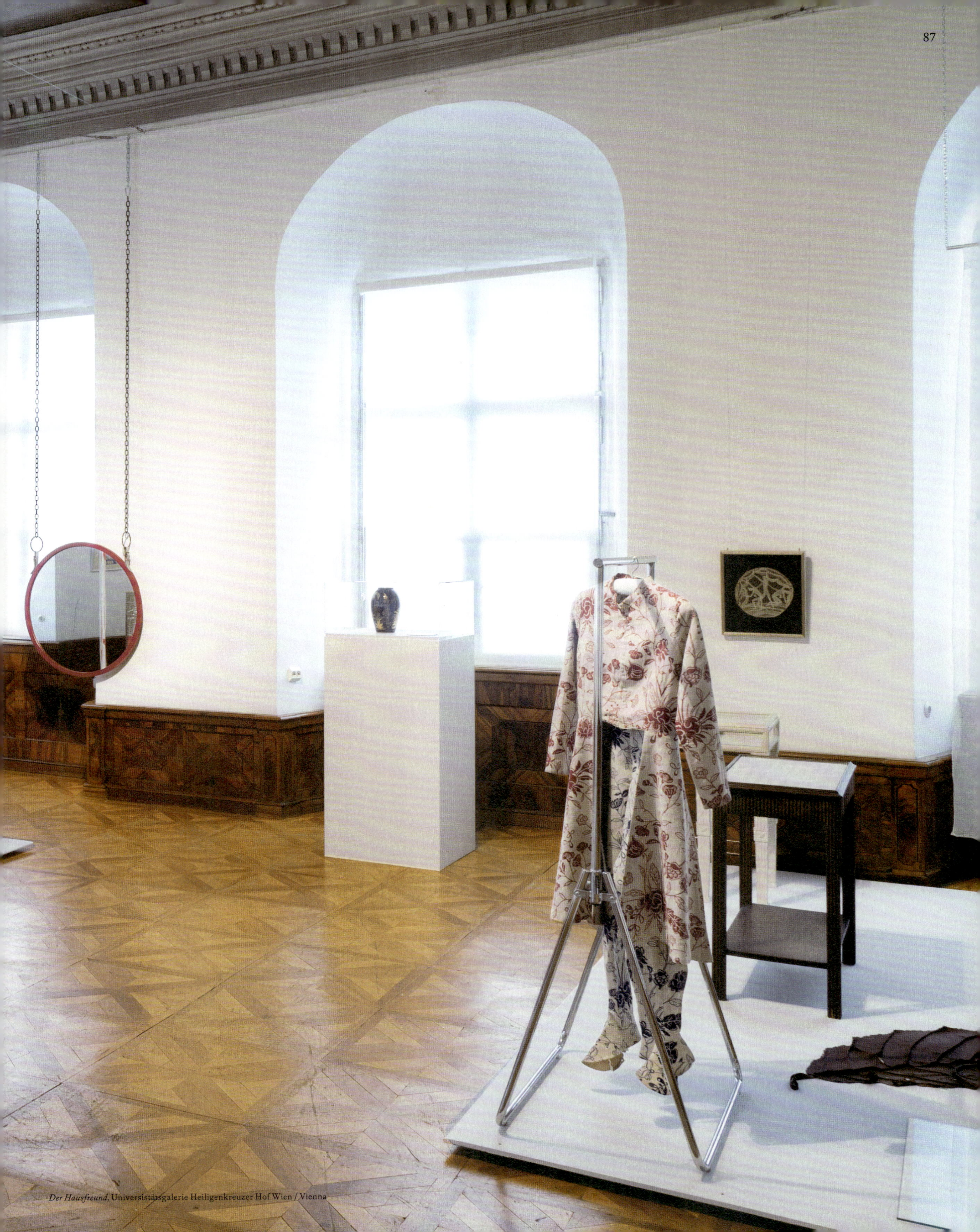

Der Hausfreund, Universitätsgalerie Heiligenkreuzer Hof Wien / Vienna

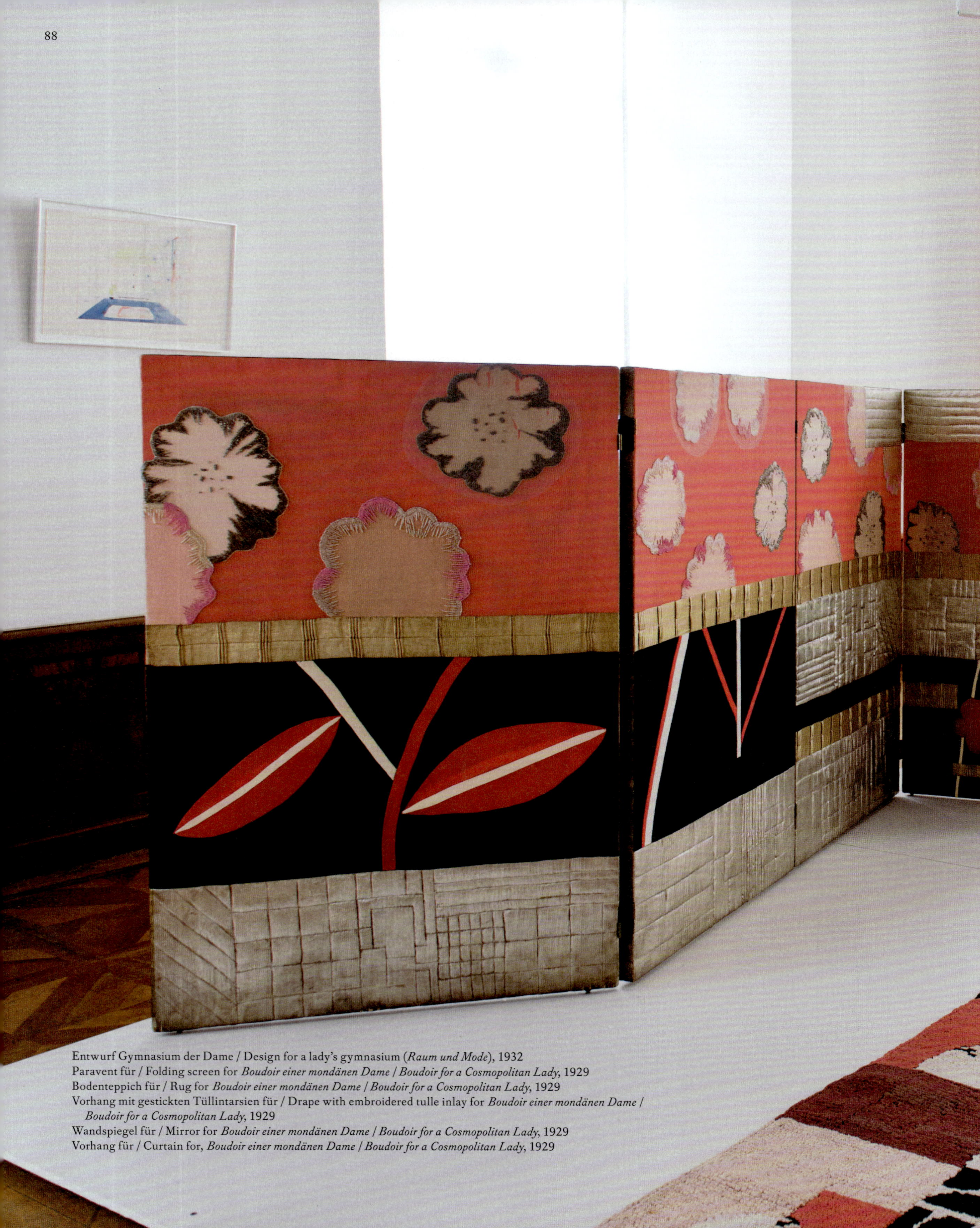

Entwurf Gymnasium der Dame / Design for a lady's gymnasium (*Raum und Mode*), 1932
Paravent für / Folding screen for *Boudoir einer mondänen Dame / Boudoir for a Cosmopolitan Lady*, 1929
Bodenteppich für / Rug for *Boudoir einer mondänen Dame / Boudoir for a Cosmopolitan Lady*, 1929
Vorhang mit gestickten Tüllintarsien für / Drape with embroidered tulle inlay for *Boudoir einer mondänen Dame / Boudoir for a Cosmopolitan Lady*, 1929
Wandspiegel für / Mirror for *Boudoir einer mondänen Dame / Boudoir for a Cosmopolitan Lady*, 1929
Vorhang für / Curtain for, *Boudoir einer mondänen Dame / Boudoir for a Cosmopolitan Lady*, 1929

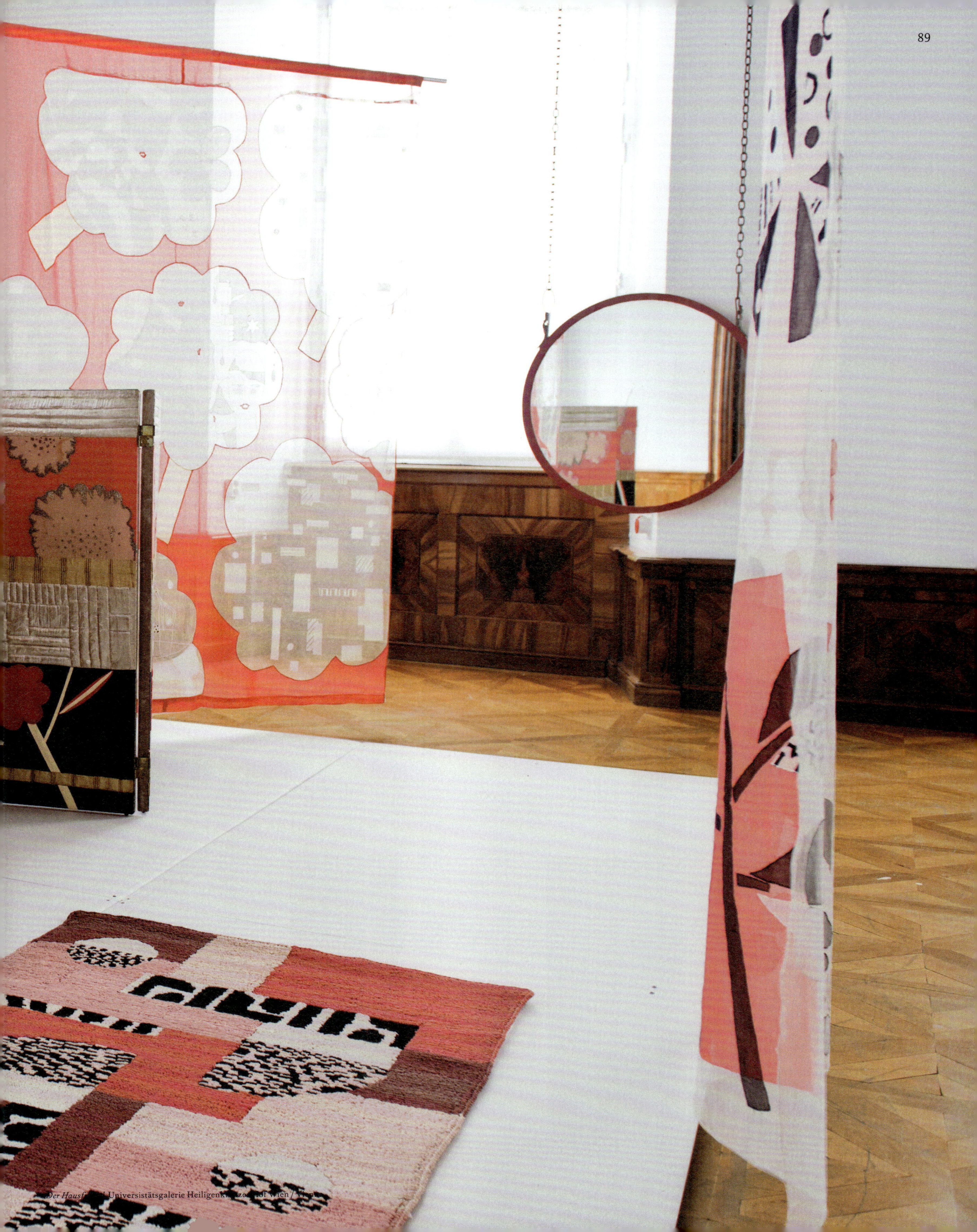

Der Hausf[illegible] | Universitätsgalerie Heiligenk[illegible]ze[illegible]of Wien / Vien[illegible]

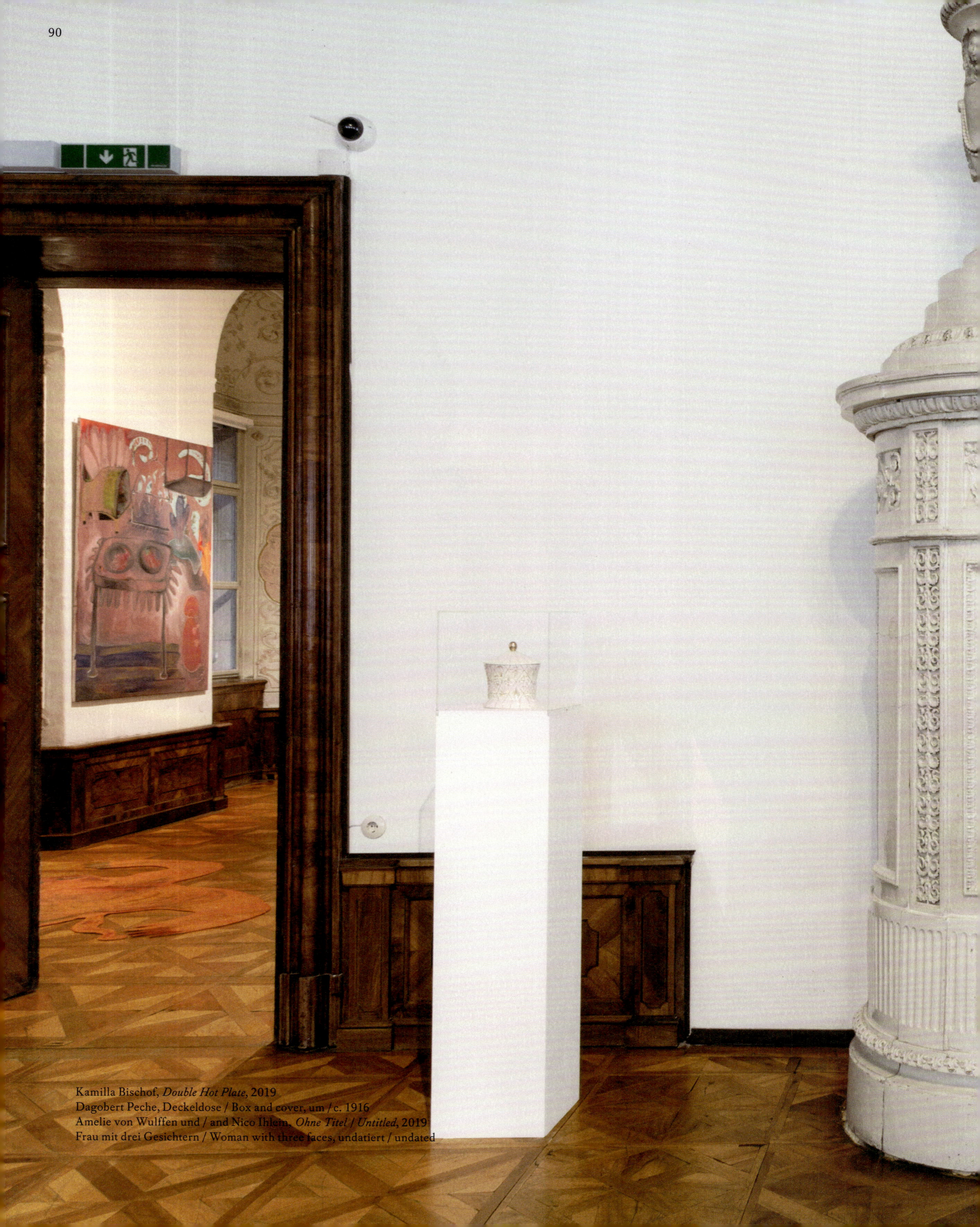

Kamilla Bischof, *Double Hot Plate*, 2019
Dagobert Peche, Deckeldose / Box and cover, um / c. 1916
Amelie von Wulffen und / and Nico Ihlein, *Ohne Titel / Untitled*, 2019
Frau mit drei Gesichtern / Woman with three faces, undatiert / undated

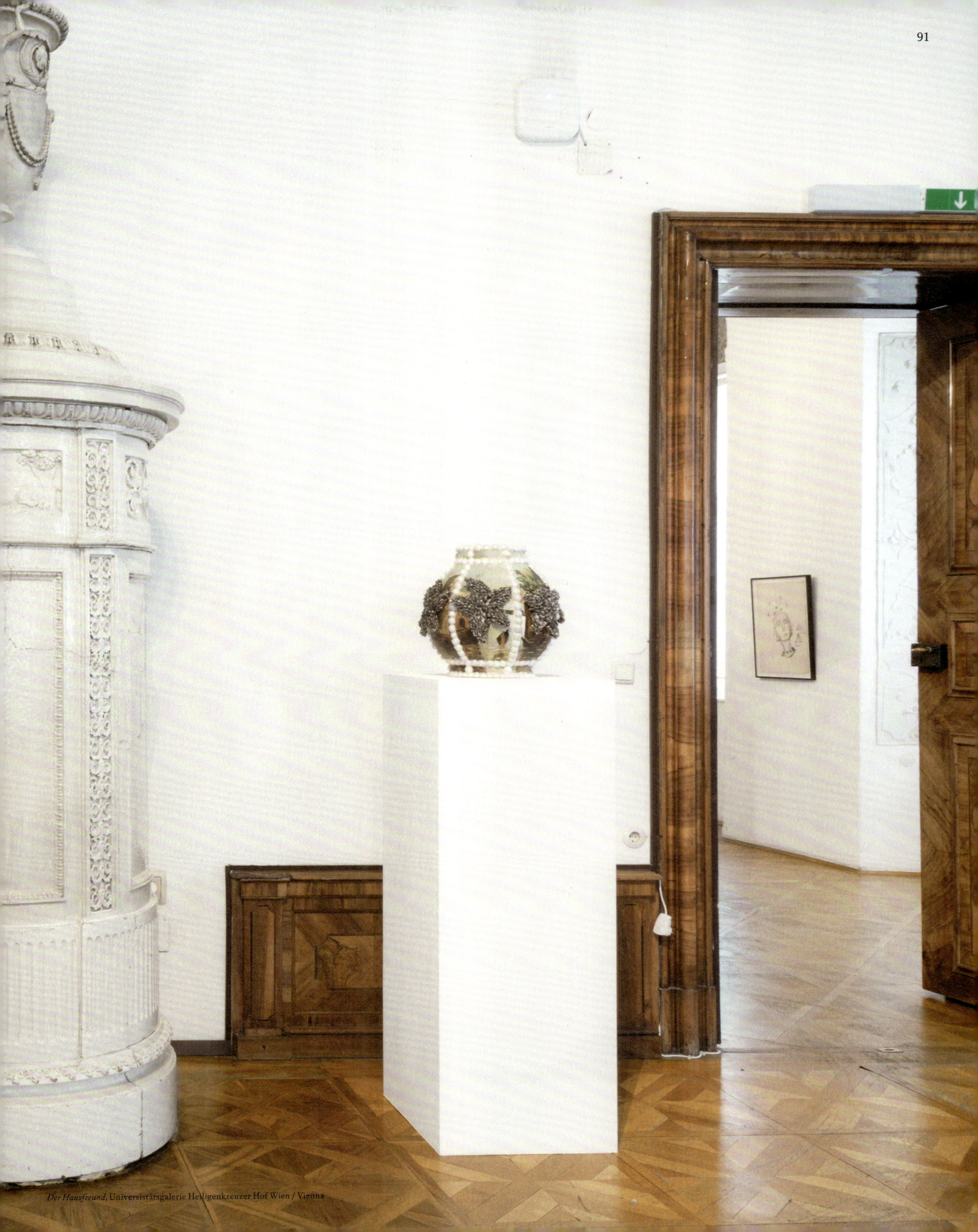

Der Hausfreund, Universistätsgalerie Heiligenkreuzer Hof Wien / Vienna

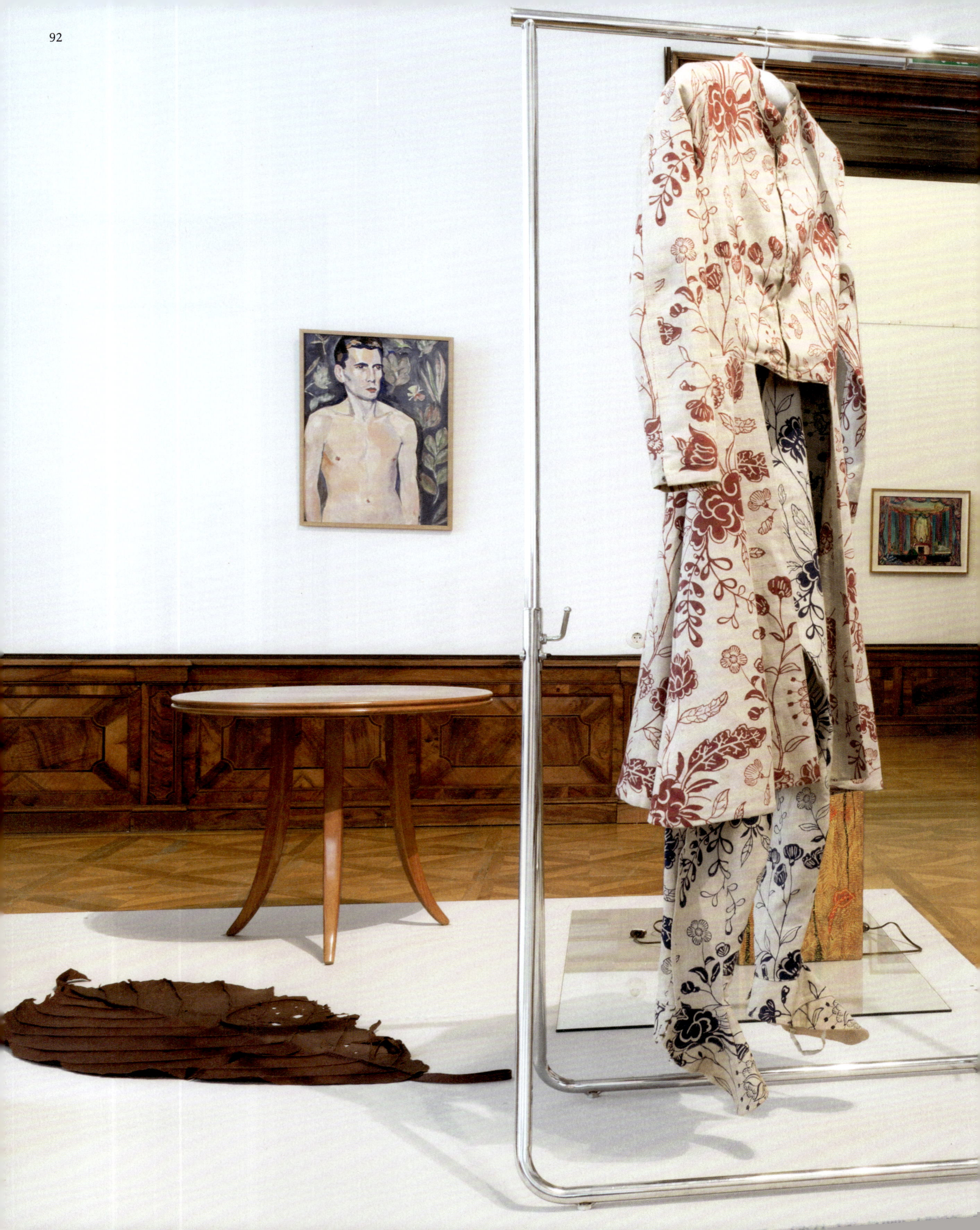

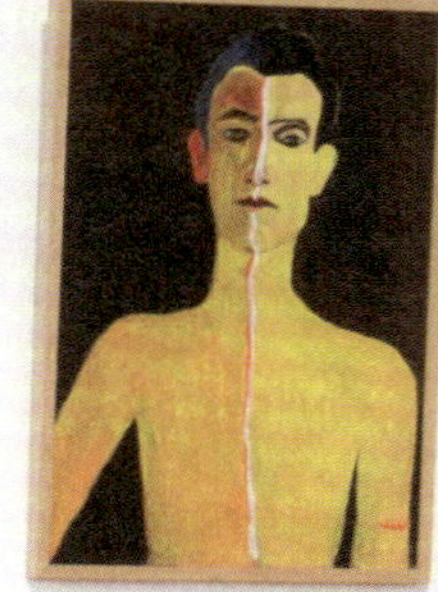

Min Yoon, *Ohne Titel / Untitled*, 2019
Josef Frank, Couchtisch / Coffee table, um / c. 1925
Eduard Wimmer-Wisgrill, *Ohne Titel (Stehender männlicher Halbakt) / Untitled (Standing Male Semi-Nude)*, um / c. 1955
Maskenkostüm (Jacke mit Hose) / Fancy dress costume (jacket and trousers), 1937
Entwurf für ein Bühnenbild im Akademietheater / Design for a stage set at the Akademietheater *Aimée*, 1937–38
Eduard Wimmer-Wisgrill, Oswald Oberhuber, *Ohne Titel (Männlicher Halbakt in Gelb) / Untitled (Male Semi-Nude in Yellow)*, um / c. 1938, um / c. 1980

Der Hausfreund, Universistätsgalerie Heiligenkreuzer Hof Wien / Vienna

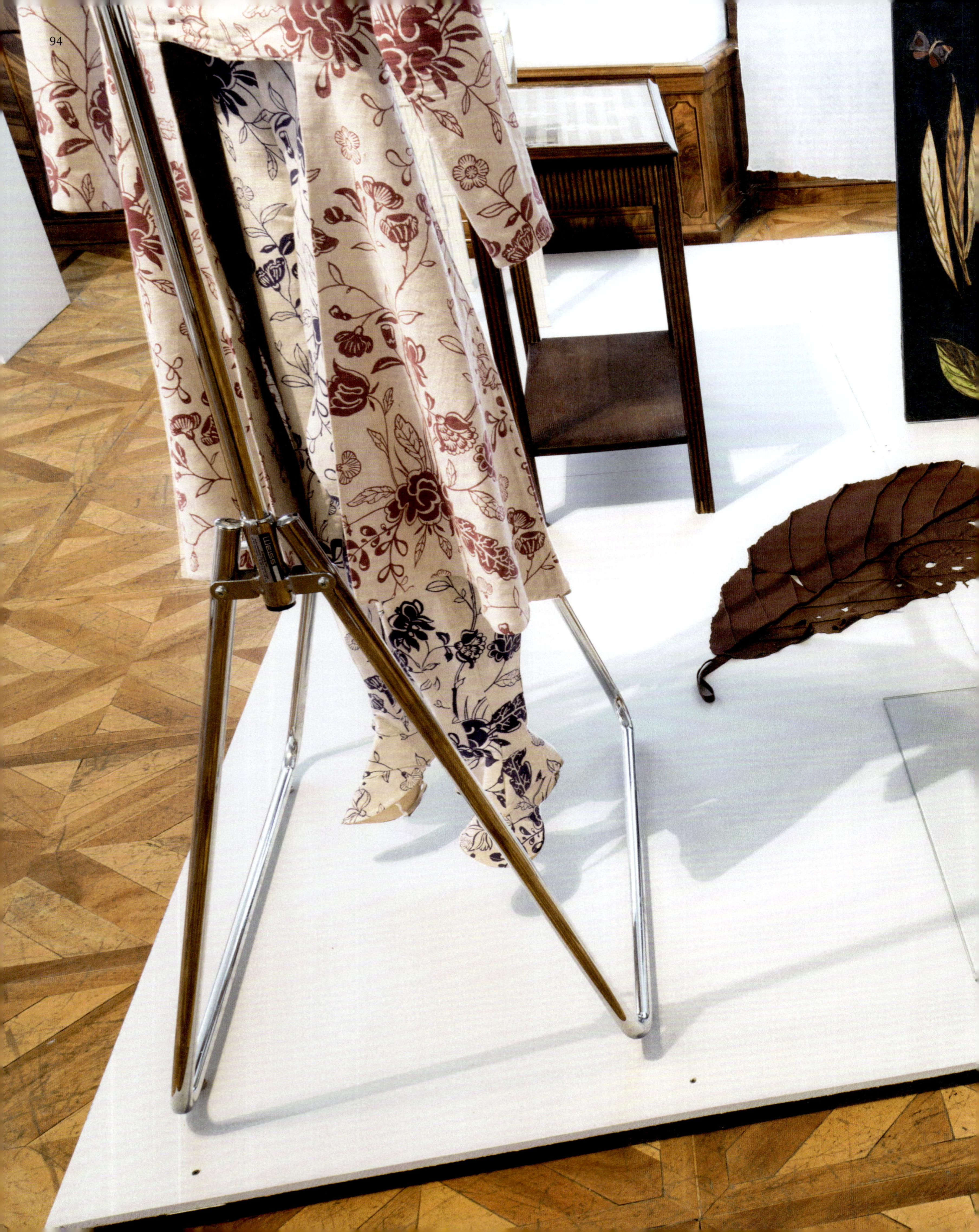

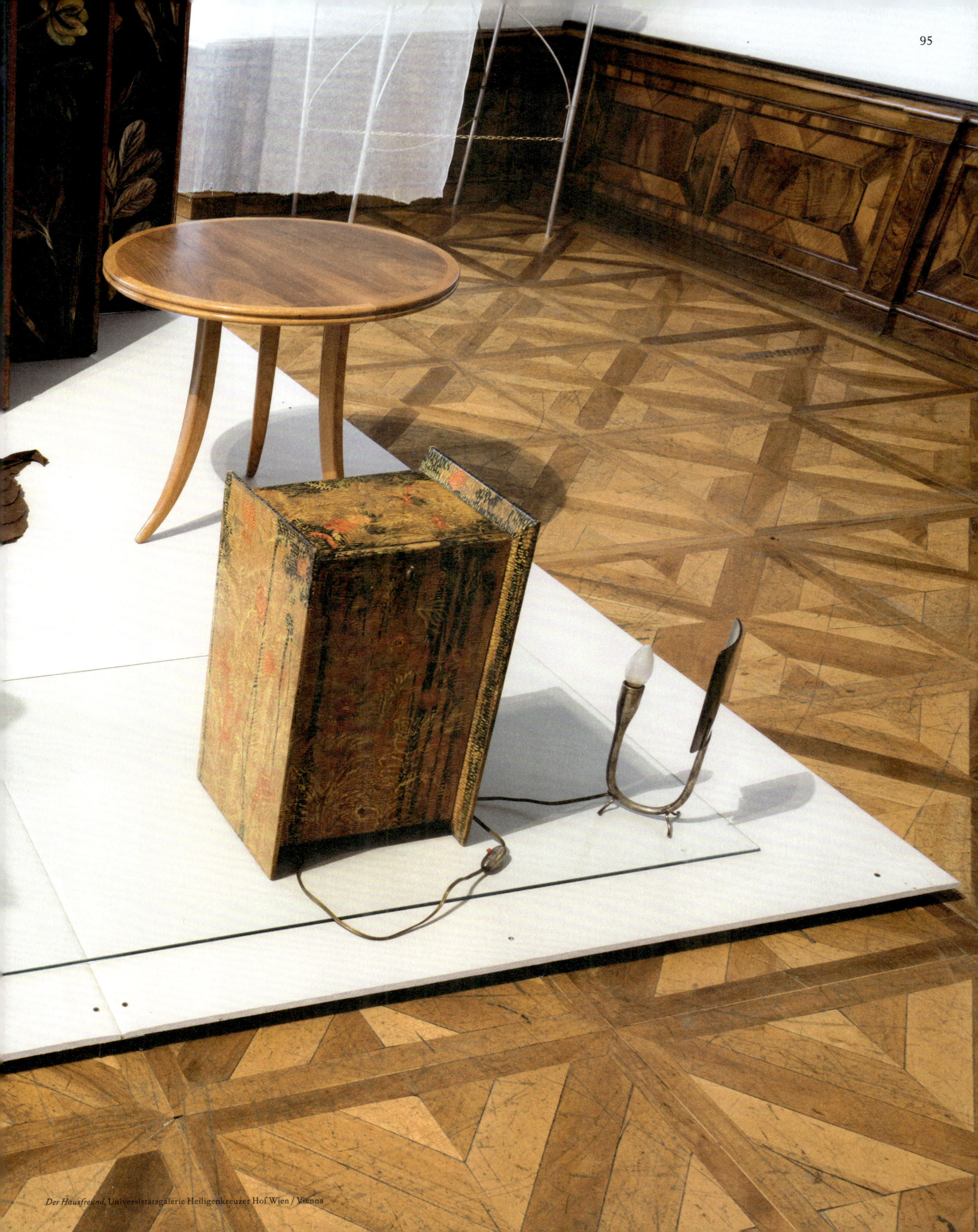

Der Hausfreund, Universitätsgalerie Heiligenkreuzer Hof Wien / Vienna

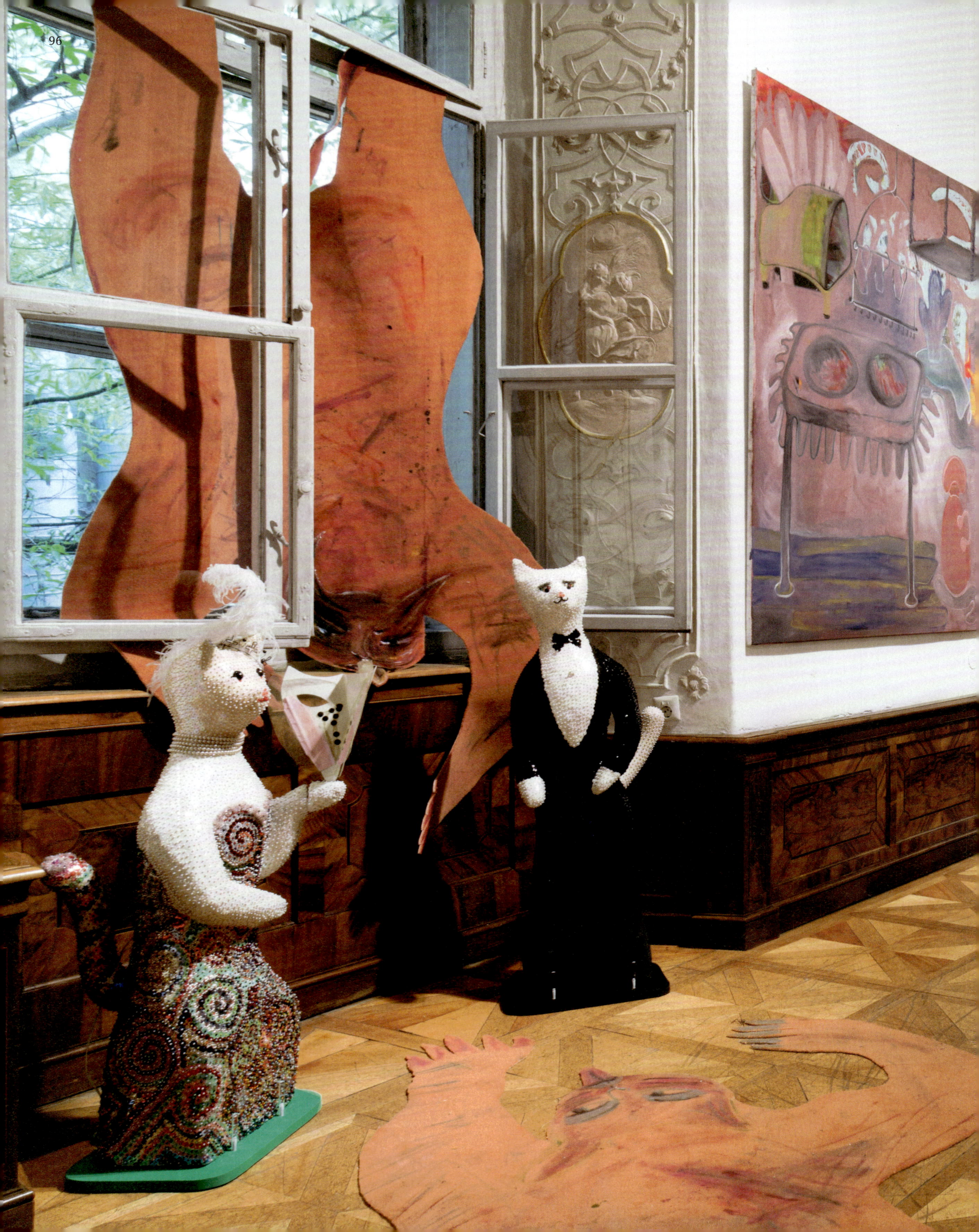

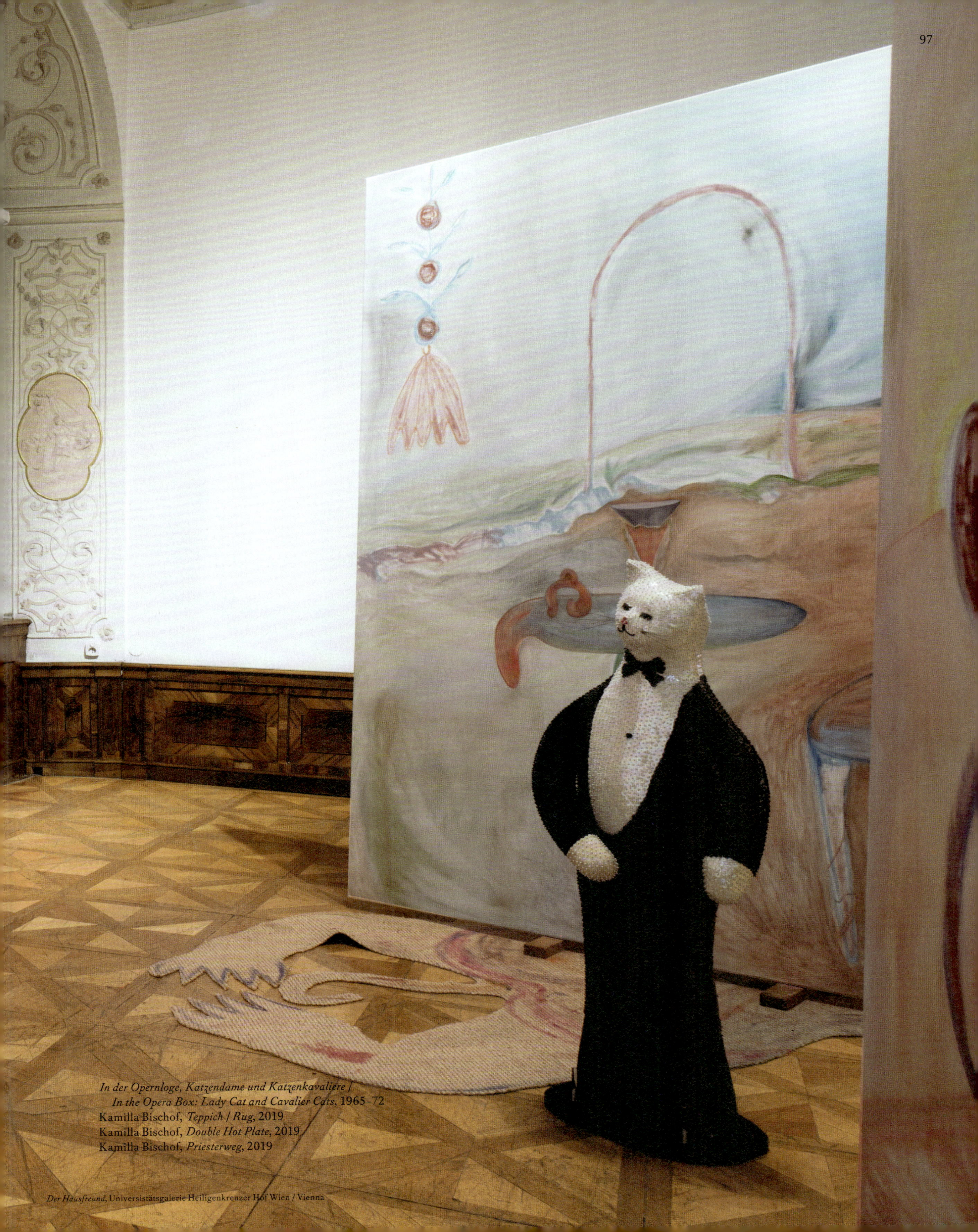

In der Opernloge, Katzendame und Katzenkavaliere / In the Opera Box: Lady Cat and Cavalier Cats, 1965–72
Kamilla Bischof, *Teppich / Rug*, 2019
Kamilla Bischof, *Double Hot Plate*, 2019
Kamilla Bischof, *Priesterweg*, 2019

Der Hausfreund, Universitätsgalerie Heiligenkreuzer Hof Wien / Vienna

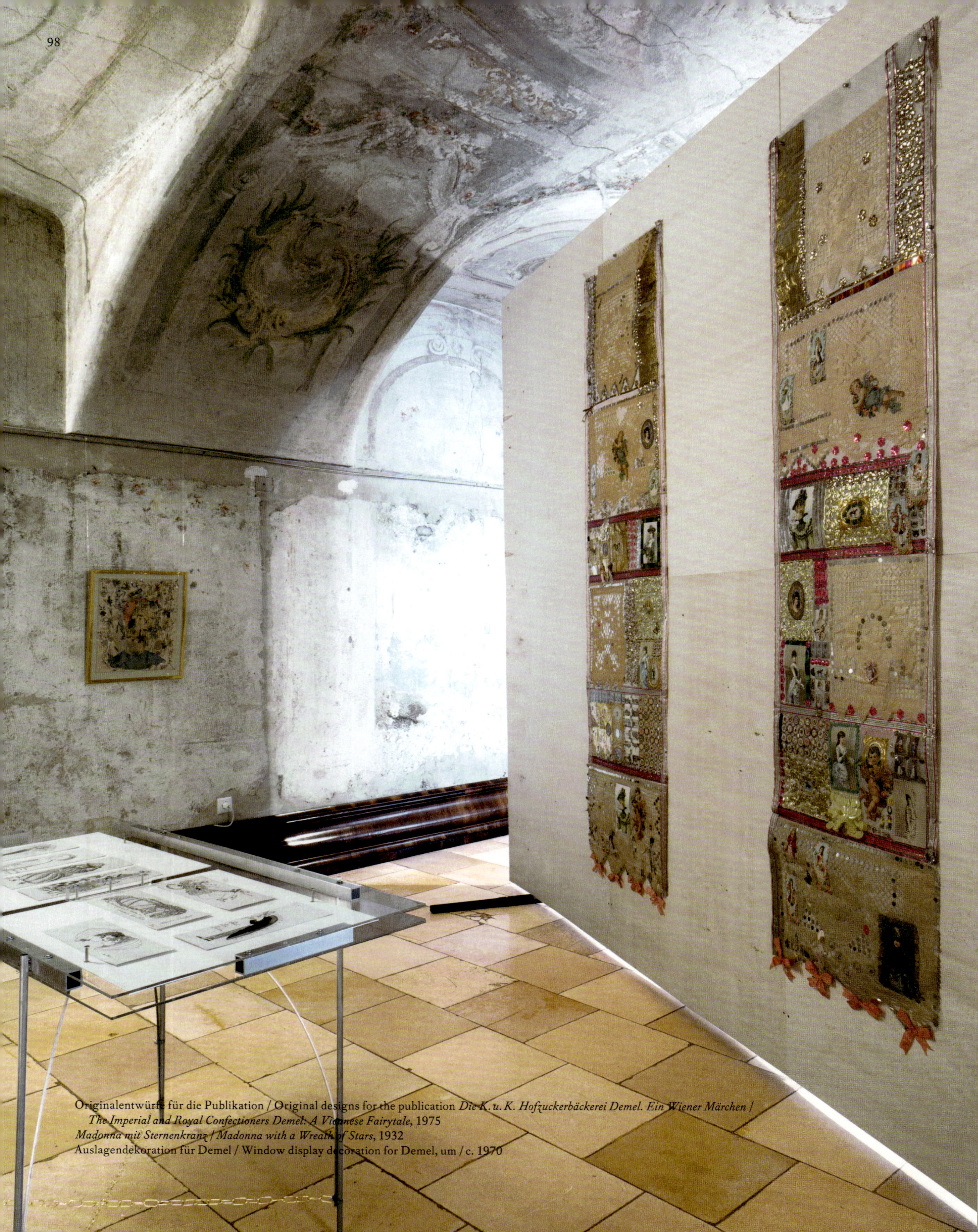

Originalentwürfe für die Publikation / Original designs for the publication *Die K. u. K. Hofzuckerbäckerei Demel. Ein Wiener Märchen / The Imperial and Royal Confectioners Demel: A Viennese Fairytale*, 1975
Madonna mit Sternenkranz / Madonna with a Wreath of Stars, 1932
Auslagendekoration für Demel / Window display decoration for Demel, um / c. 1970

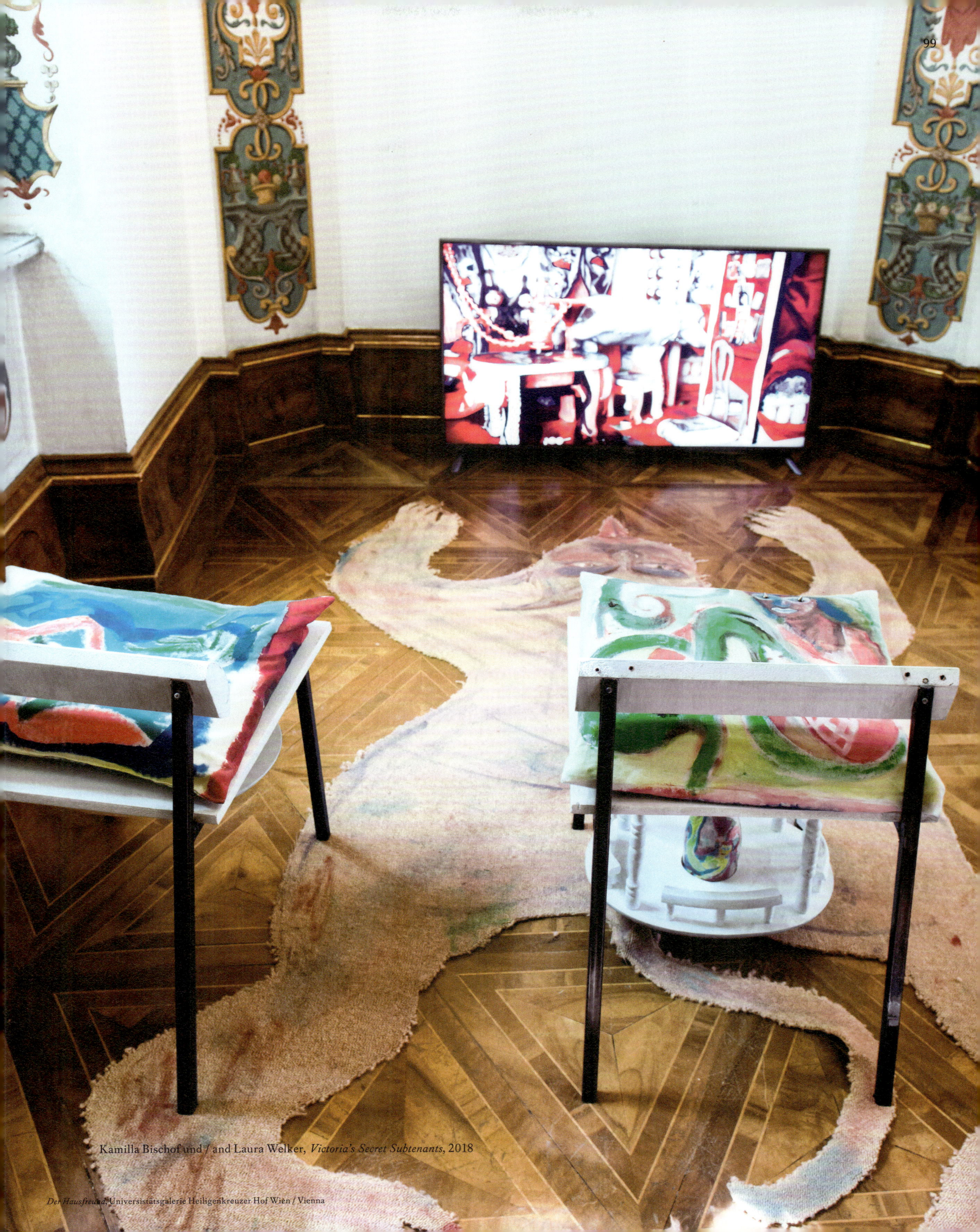

Kamilla Bischof und / and Laura Welker, *Victoria's Secret Subtenants*, 2018

Der Hausfreund, Universistätsgalerie Heiligenkreuzer Hof Wien / Vienna

ciphers of regression

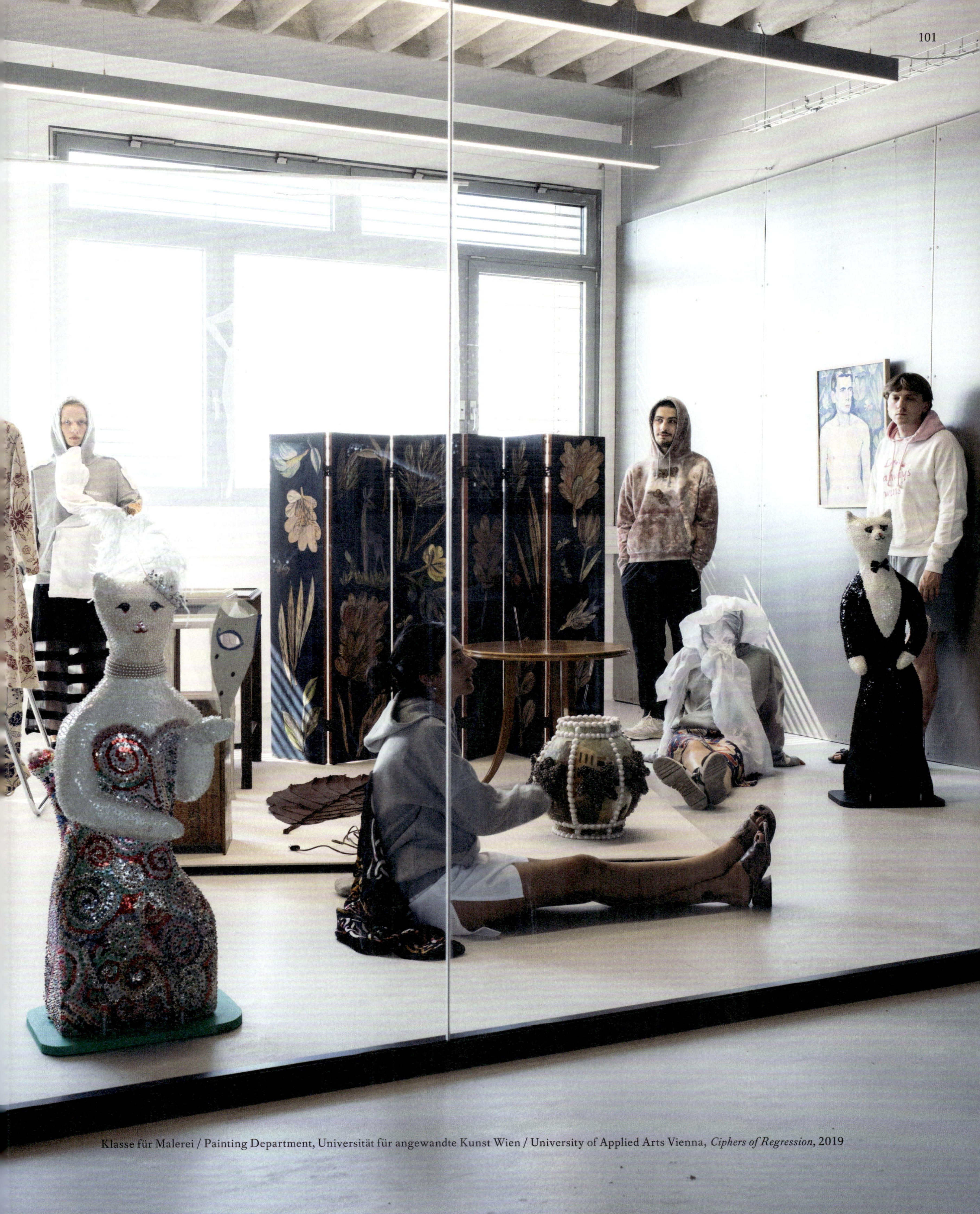

Klasse für Malerei / Painting Department, Universität für angewandte Kunst Wien / University of Applied Arts Vienna, *Ciphers of Regression*, 2019

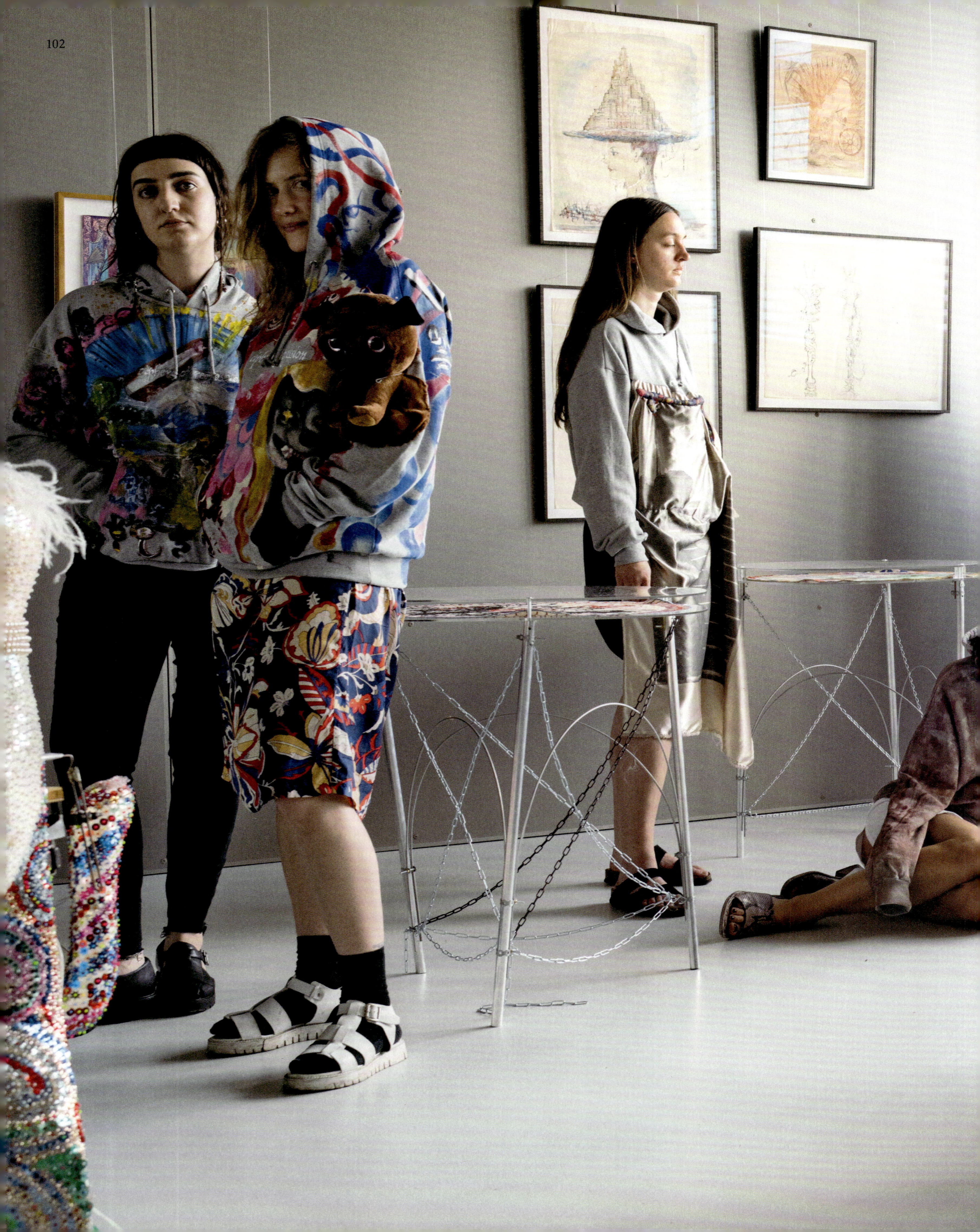

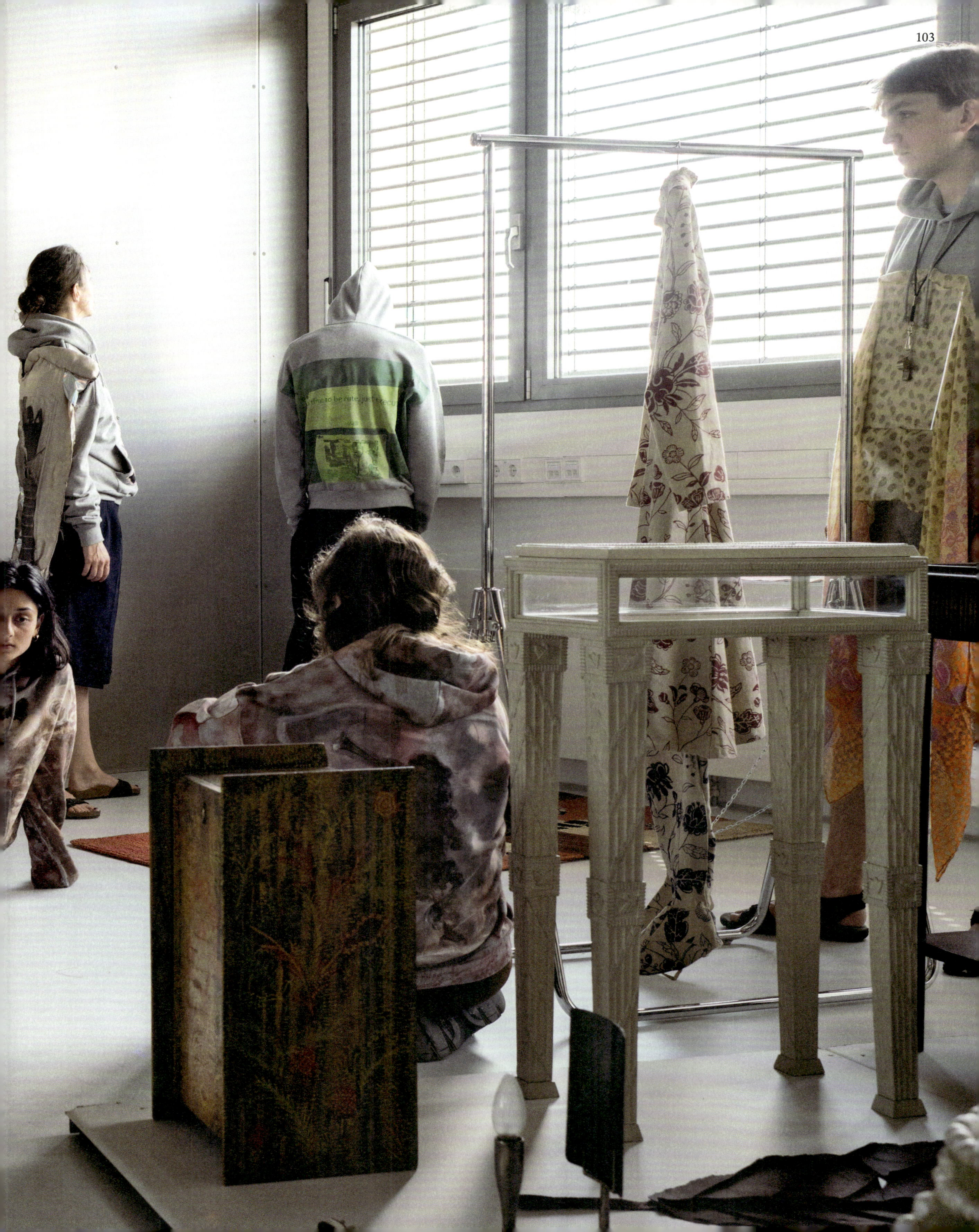

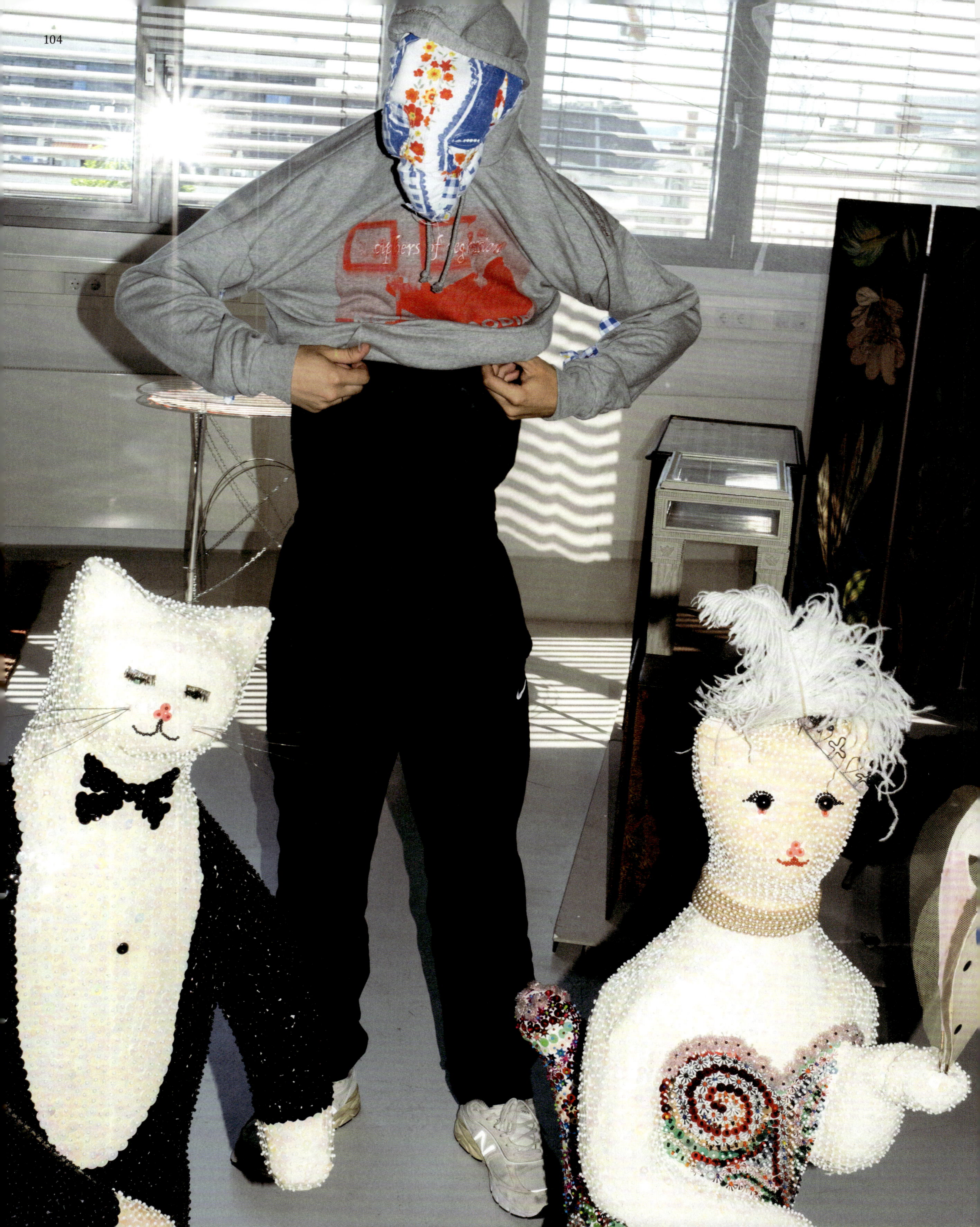

Ciphers of Regression (25. bis 28. Juni 2019) war ein Projekt der Klasse für Malerei in Zusammenarbeit mit Kunstsammlung und Archiv der Universität für angewandte Kunst Wien. Das Projekt bestand aus einer Auktion (25. Juni 2019), moderiert von Marei Buhmann und Sofie Fatouretchi; musikalischen Einlagen von Jutta Maris & Reena King, Angst, Die Süsen Mäuse und In My Talons; einer Adaption der Ausstellung *Der Hausfreund*, zuvor zu sehen im Heiligenkreuzerhof (2. Mai bis 1. Juni 2019) und einer Ausstellung mit paarweise umgearbeiteten Kapuzenpullovern. Teilnehmer*innen an der Auktion erwarben einen Pullover, das Gegenstück wurde an die Kostüm- und Modesammlung der Universität gespendet.
Ciphers of Regression (June 25 to 28, 2019) was a project by the Painting Department in collaboration with the Collection of the University of Applied Arts Vienna. It consisted of an auction (June 25, 2019) conducted by Marei Buhmann and Sofie Fatouretchi; musical interludes by Jutta Maris & Reena King, Angst, Die Süsen Mäuse, and In My Talons; an adaption of the exhibition *Der Hausfreund*, previously on view at Heiligenkreuzer Hof (May 2 to June 1, 2019); and an exhibition of hoodies. Pairs of hoodies were reworked, of which auction attendees acquired one. The counterpart was donated to the university's collection.

Mitwirkende / Contributors: Henning Bohl, Wolfgang Breuer, Marei Buhmann, Pit Christ, Daisy, Viktoria Dopler, Amanda Du, Sofie Fatouretchi, Christian Gailer, Ana Gurashvili, Luna-Mae Heflin, Suzuka Hisamatsu, Demian Kern, Martina Lajczak, Yoon A Lee, Hannes Loichinger, Alex Macedo, Sebastian Mittl, David Peschka, Florian Pfaffenberger, Leonie Plattner, Vika Prokopaviciute, Kathrin Isabell Rhomberg, Milena-Marie Rohde, Ulla Rossek, Vanessa Schmidt, Niclas Schöler, Pol Summer, Sebastian Supanz, Till Weinhold, Kathrin Wojtowicz, Moka Sheung Yan, Takeshi Yoshida, Malte Zander

Organisation / Organization: Alex Macedo, Vanessa Schmidt, Marielena Stark, Malte Zander

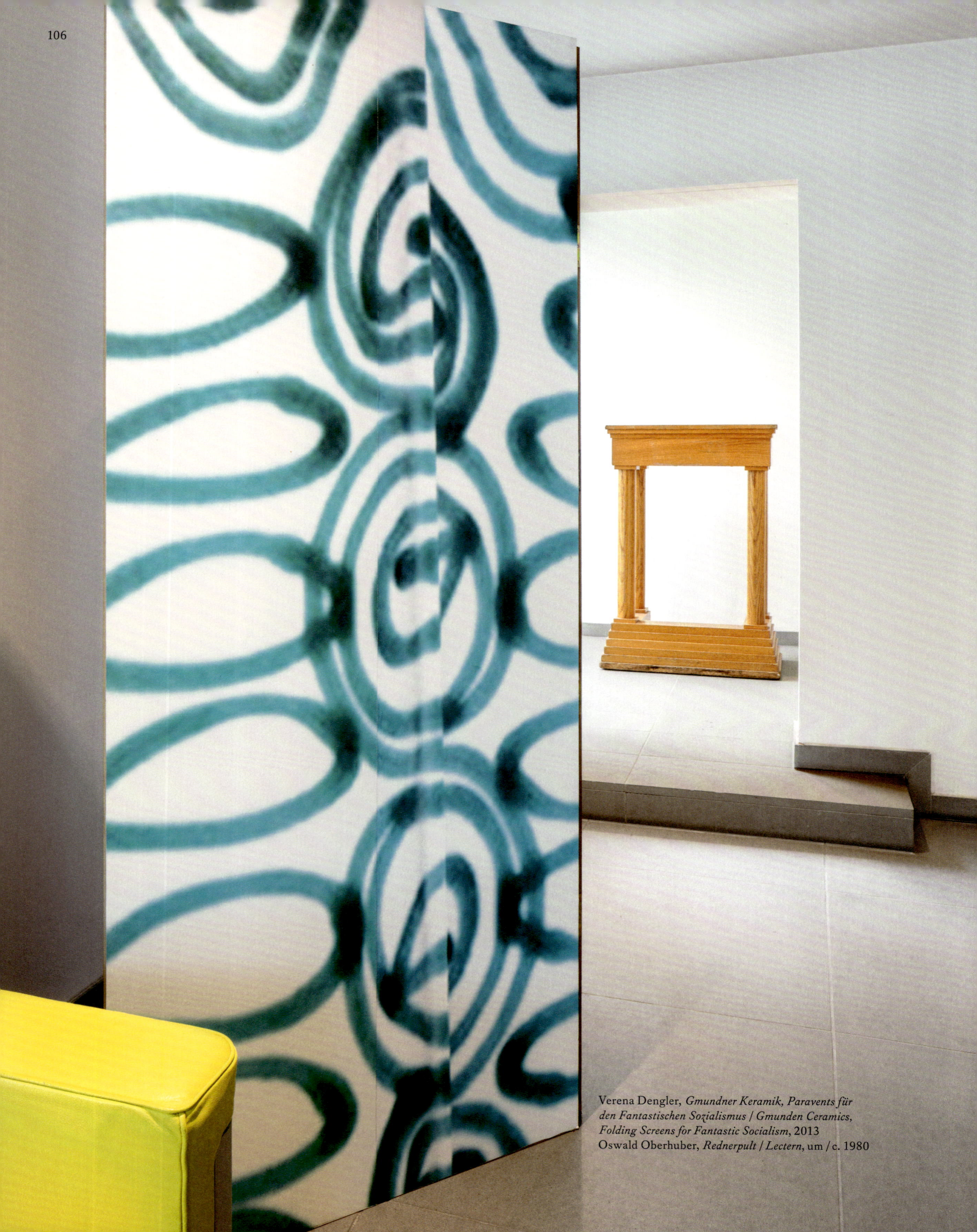

Verena Dengler, *Gmundner Keramik, Paravents für den Fantastischen Sozialismus / Gmunden Ceramics, Folding Screens for Fantastic Socialism*, 2013
Oswald Oberhuber, *Rednerpult / Lectern*, um / c. 1980

Ausstellungsansichten / Exhibiton views, Österreichisches Kulturforum / Austrian Cultural Forum, Berlin
13. September bis 25. Oktober 2019 / September 13 to October 25, 2019

DER HAUSFREUND

Eine Wiederentdeckung des exzentrischen Werks von
A Rediscovery of the Eccentric Work of
FRIEDRICH VON BERZEVICZY-PALLAVICINI

Der Hausfreund, Österreichisches Kulturforum / Austrian Cultural Forum, Berlin

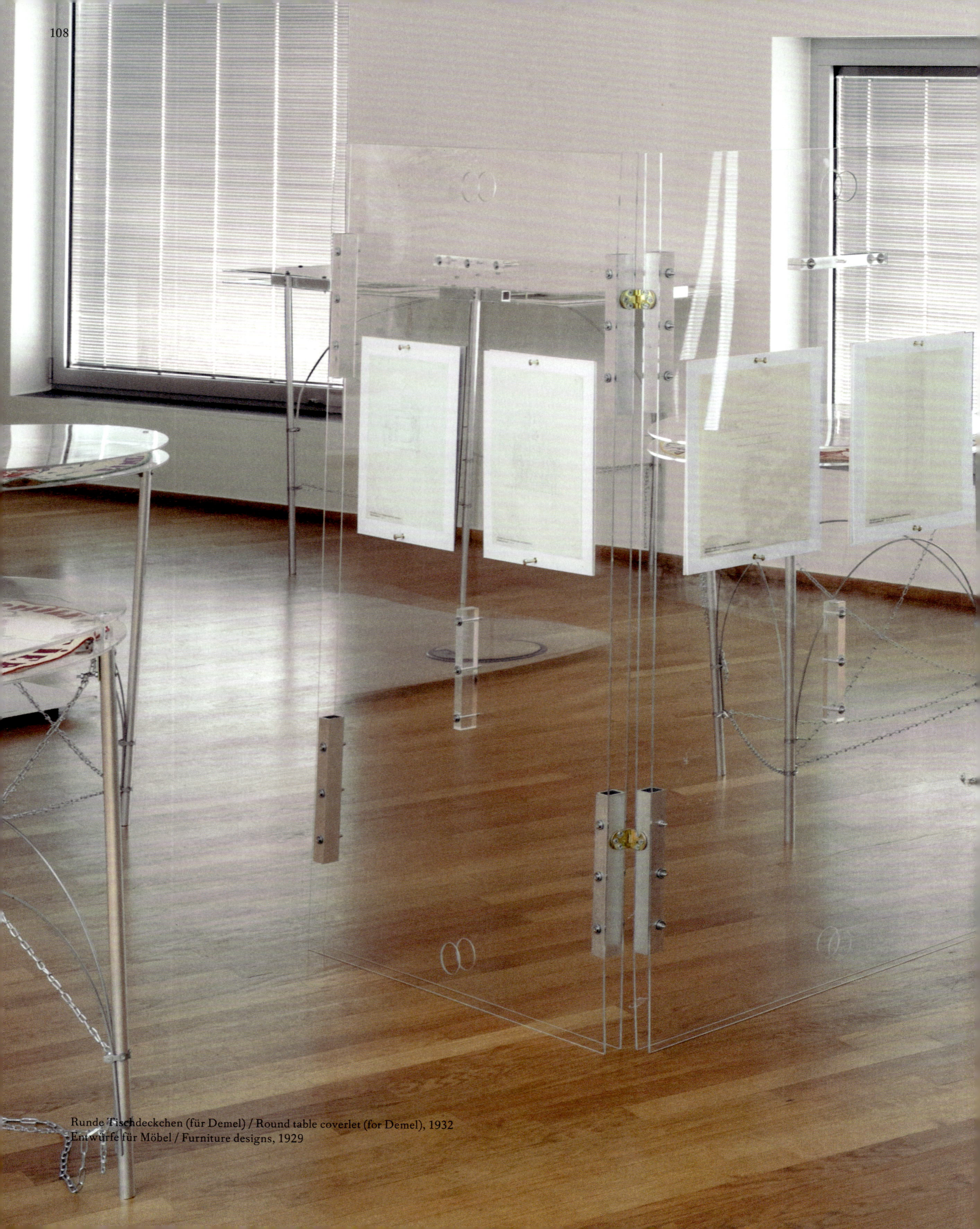

Runde Tischdeckchen (für Demel) / Round table coverlet (for Demel), 1932
Entwürfe für Möbel / Furniture designs, 1929

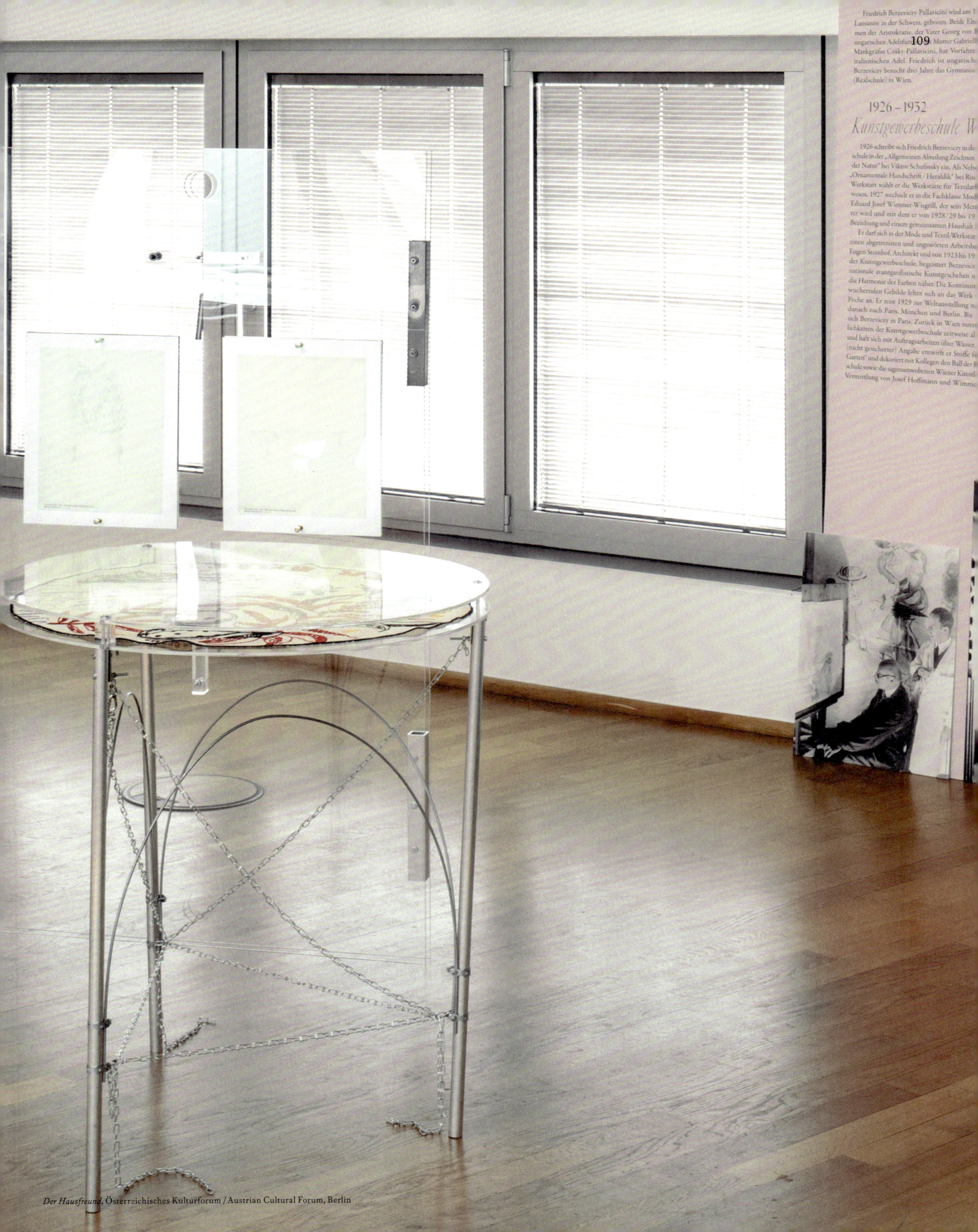

Der Hausfreund, Österreichisches Kulturforum / Austrian Cultural Forum, Berlin

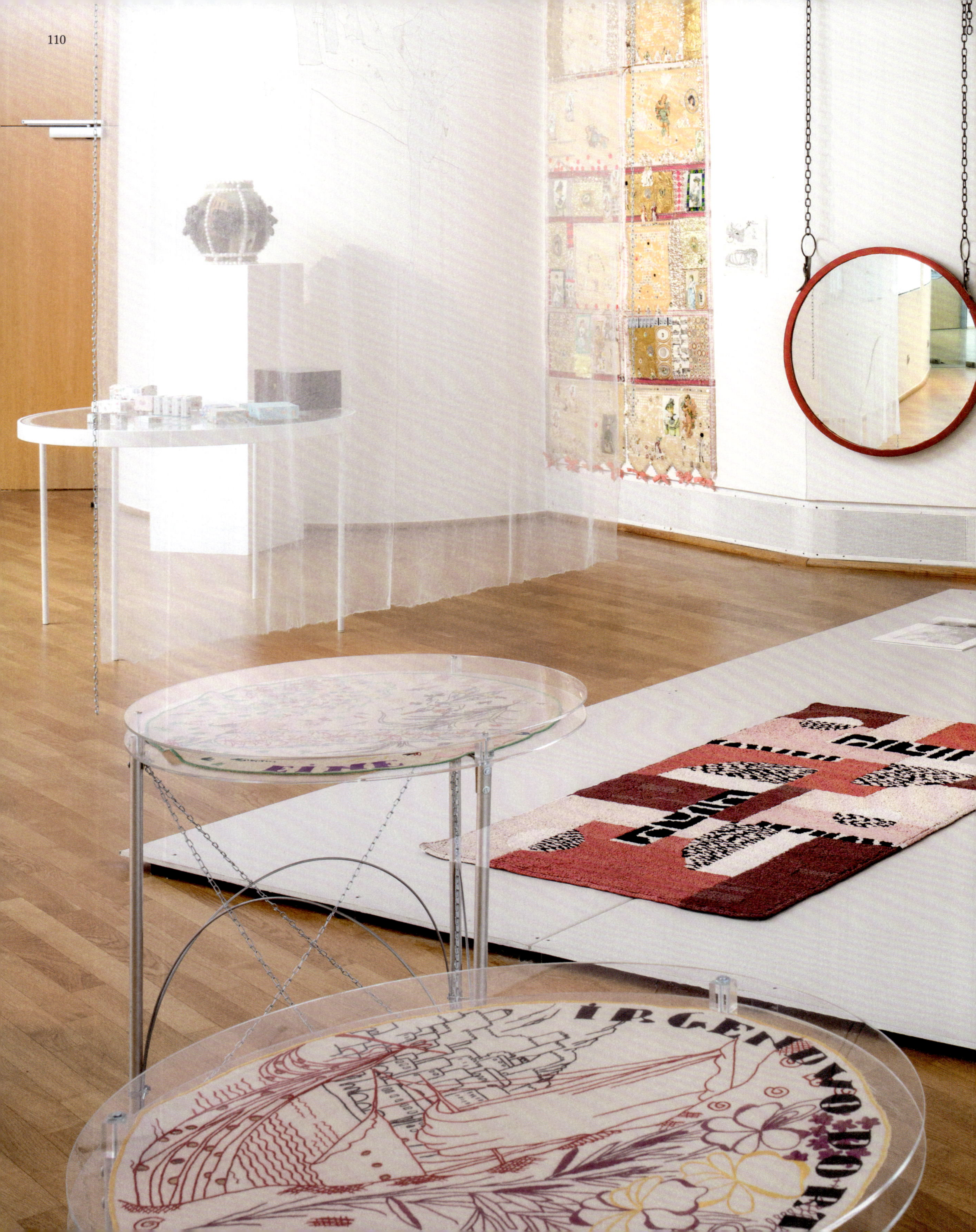

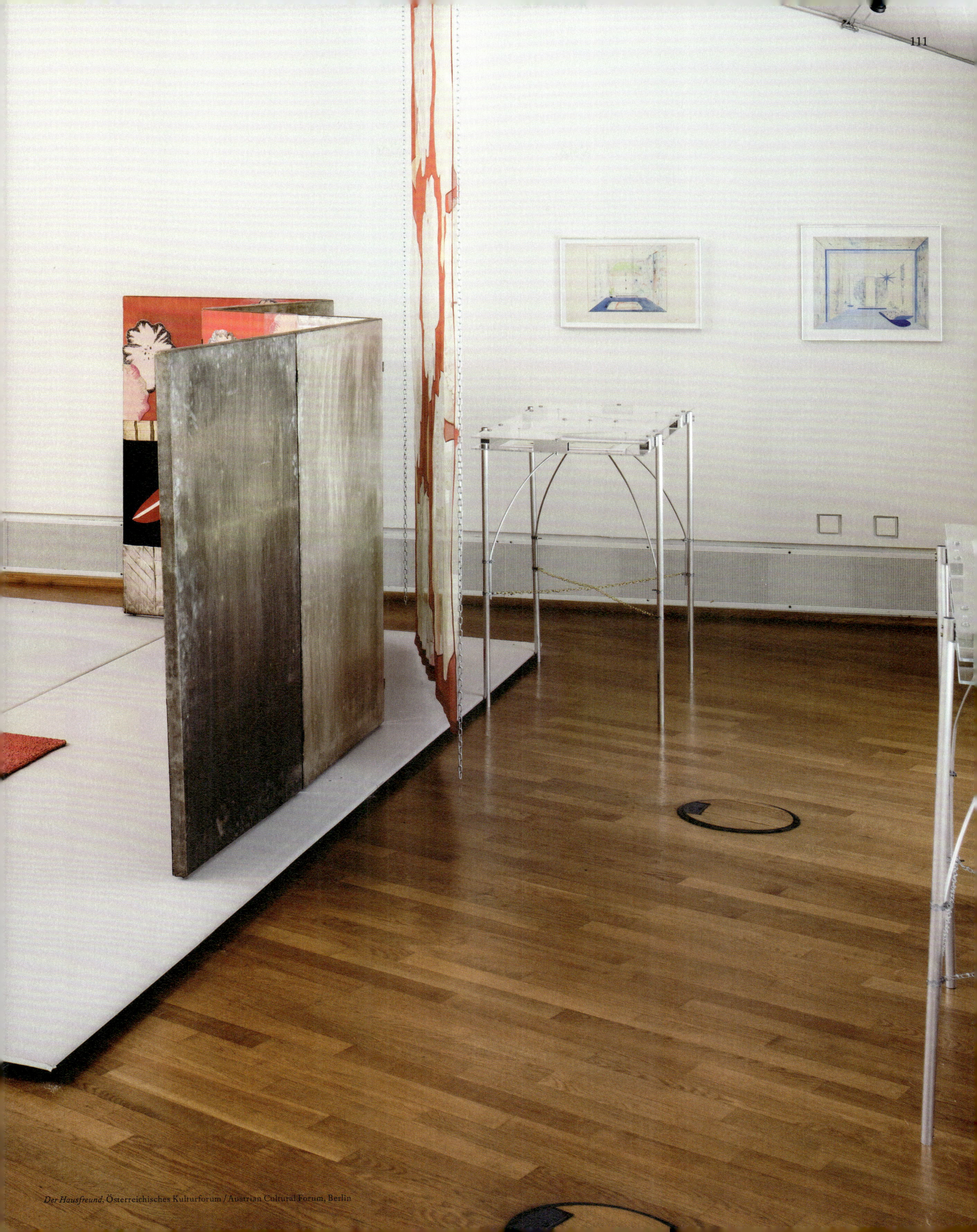

Der Hausfreund, Österreichisches Kulturforum / Austrian Cultural Forum, Berlin

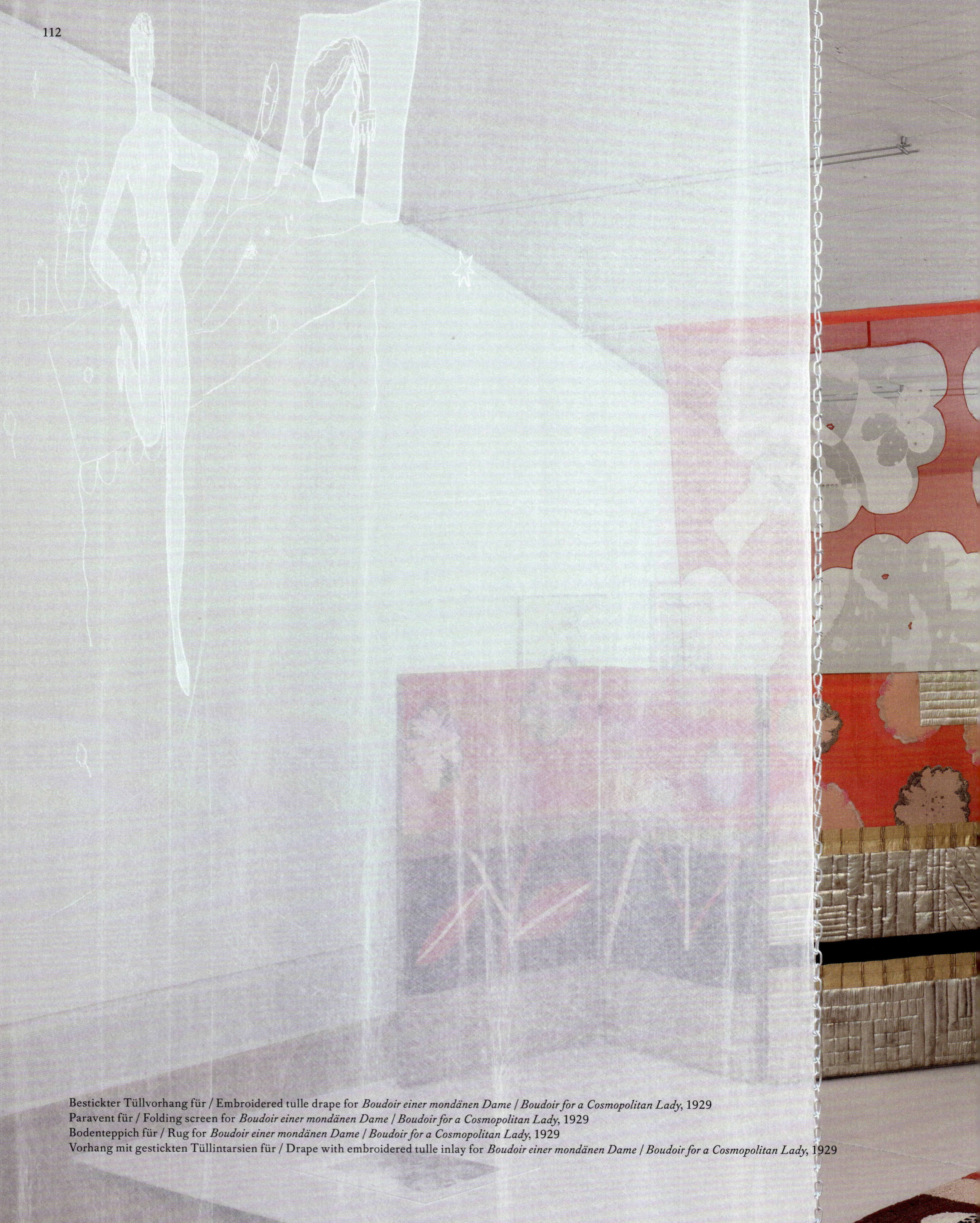

Bestickter Tüllvorhang für / Embroidered tulle drape for *Boudoir einer mondänen Dame / Boudoir for a Cosmopolitan Lady*, 1929
Paravent für / Folding screen for *Boudoir einer mondänen Dame / Boudoir for a Cosmopolitan Lady*, 1929
Bodenteppich für / Rug for *Boudoir einer mondänen Dame / Boudoir for a Cosmopolitan Lady*, 1929
Vorhang mit gestickten Tüllintarsien für / Drape with embroidered tulle inlay for *Boudoir einer mondänen Dame / Boudoir for a Cosmopolitan Lady*, 1929

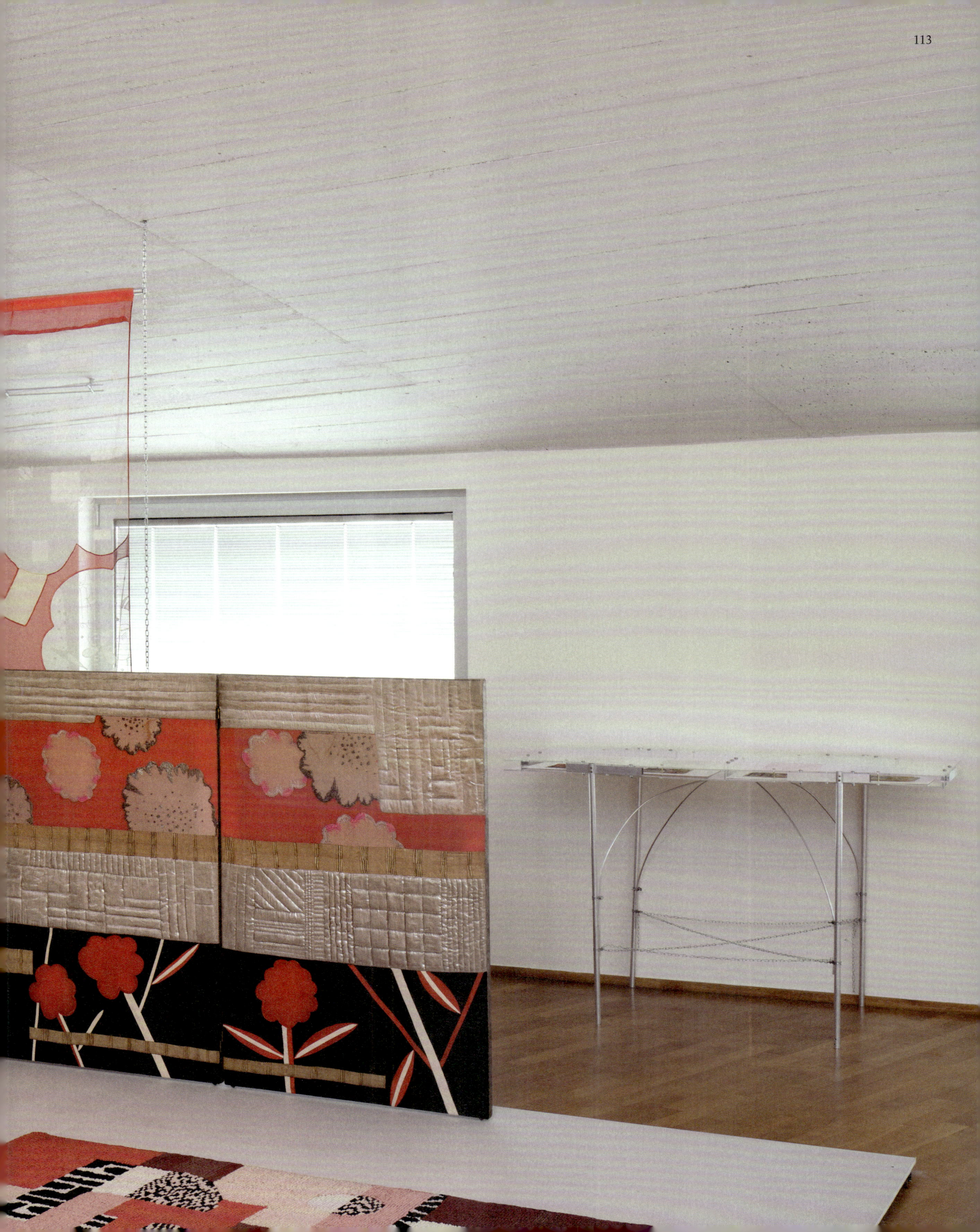

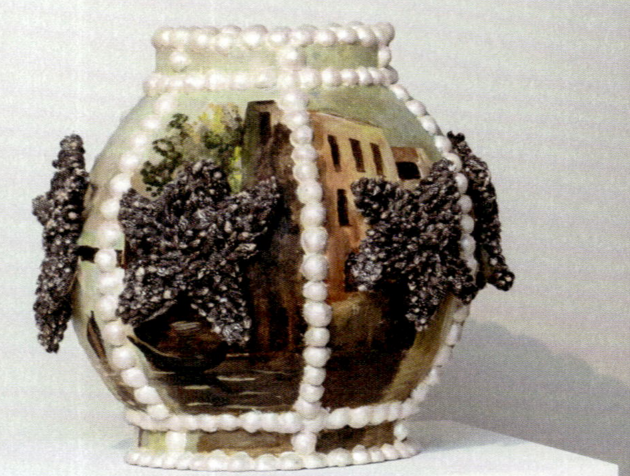

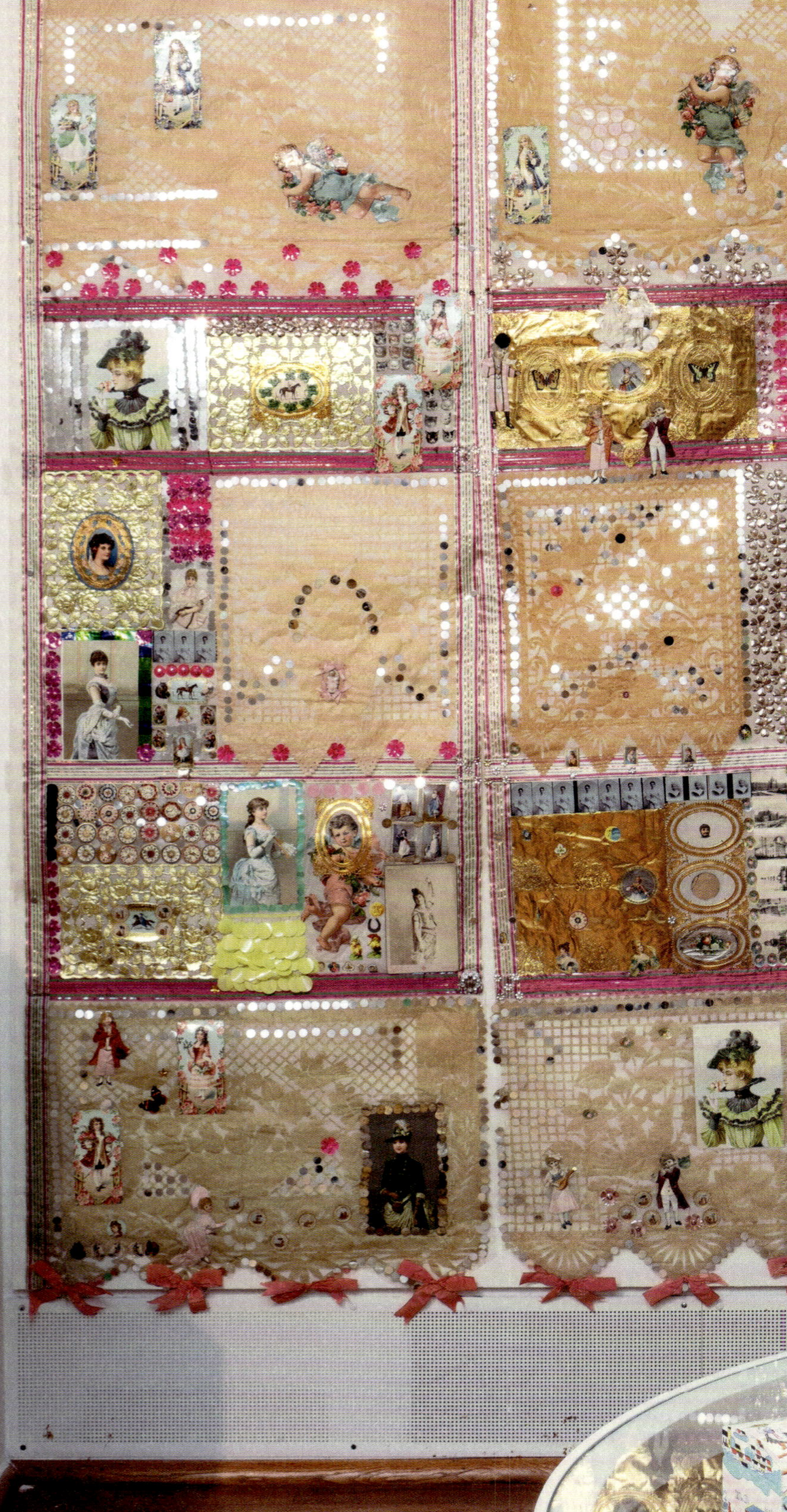

Amelie von Wulffen und / and Nico Ihlein, *Ohne Titel / Untitled*, 2019
Auslagendekoration für Demel / Window display decoration for Demel, um / c. 1970
Originalentwürfe für die Publikation / Original designs for the publication *Die K. u. K. Hofzuckerbäckerei Demel. Ein Wiener Märchen / The Imperial and Royal Confectioners Demel: A Viennese Fairytale*, 1975
Wandspiegel für / Mirror for *Boudoir einer mondänen Dame / Boudoir for a Cosmopolitan Lady*, 1929
Lucy McKenzie, *Painted boxes, Table III*, 2017

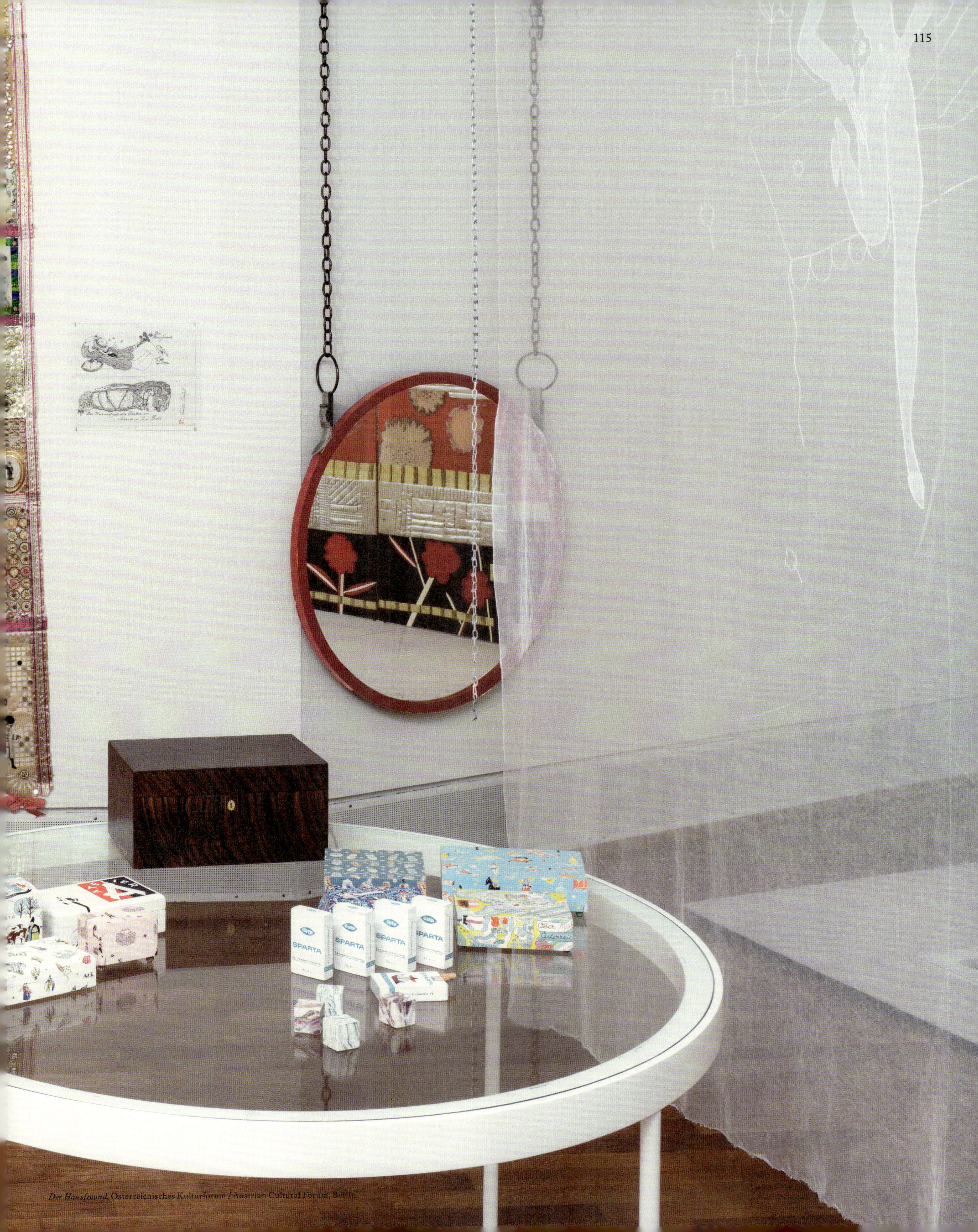

Der Hausfreund, Österreichisches Kulturforum / Austrian Cultural Forum, Berlin

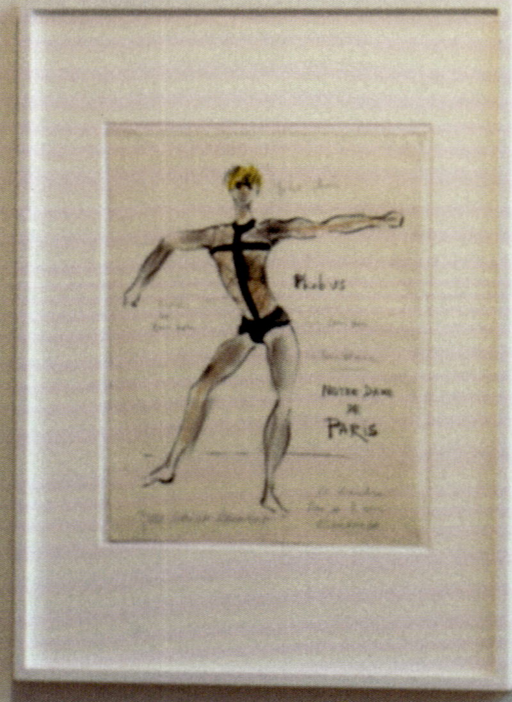

Yves Saint Laurent, *Untitled*, 1965
Dagobert Peche, Deckeldose / Box and cover, um / c. 1916
Vase *Bogenschütze und Falknerin* / *Archer and Falconer*, 1937
Fliese mit dem Motiv / Tile with the motif *Kniende, in den Spiegel schauende Dame, Brieftaube* / *Kneeling Woman Looking in the Mirror, Carrier Pigeon*, um / c. 1936
[illegible] Nina Ihlein, *Ohne Titel* / *Untitled*, 2019
Auslagendekor[illegible]

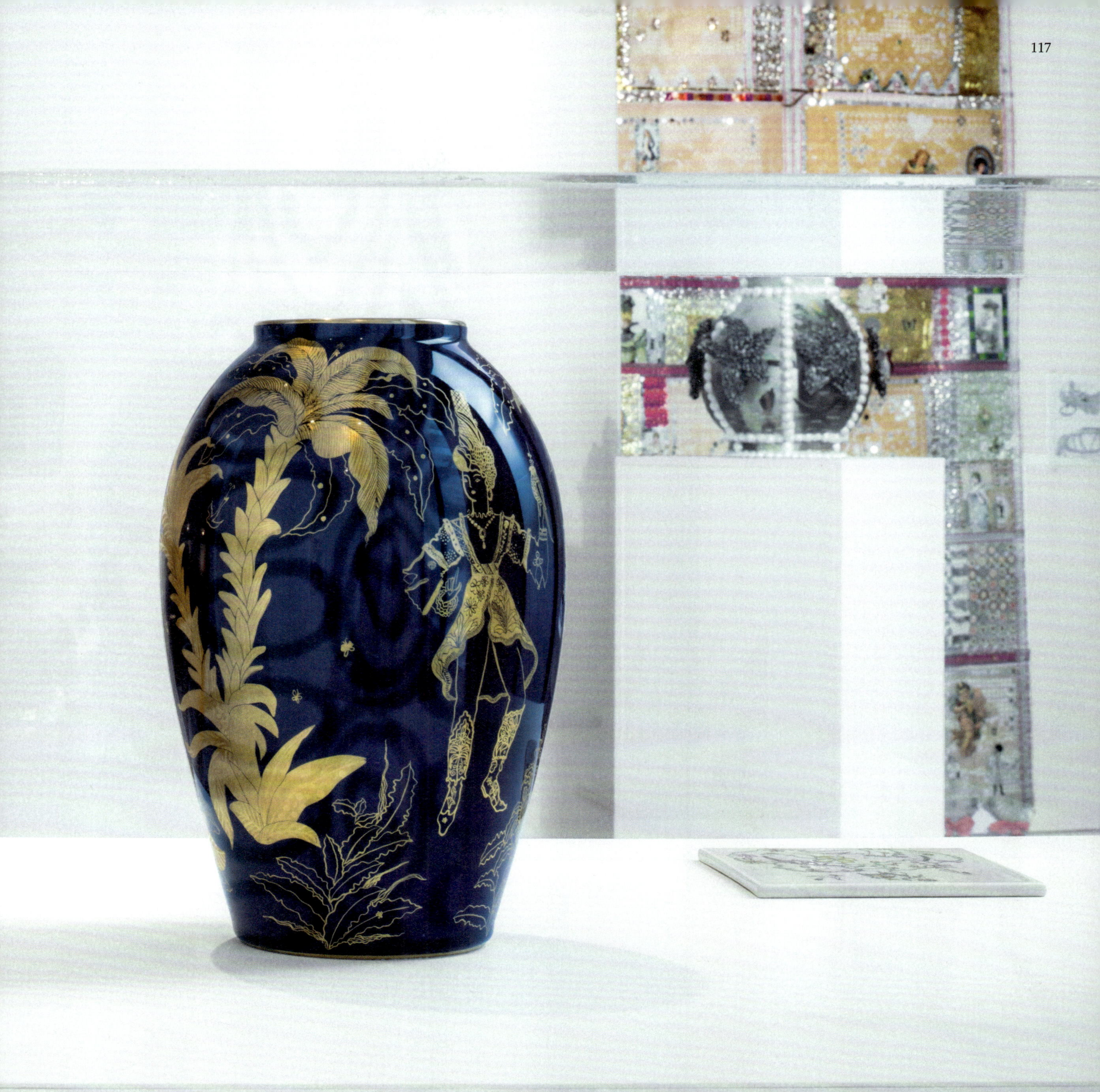

Der Hausfreund, Österreichisches Kulturforum / Austrian Cultural Forum, Berlin

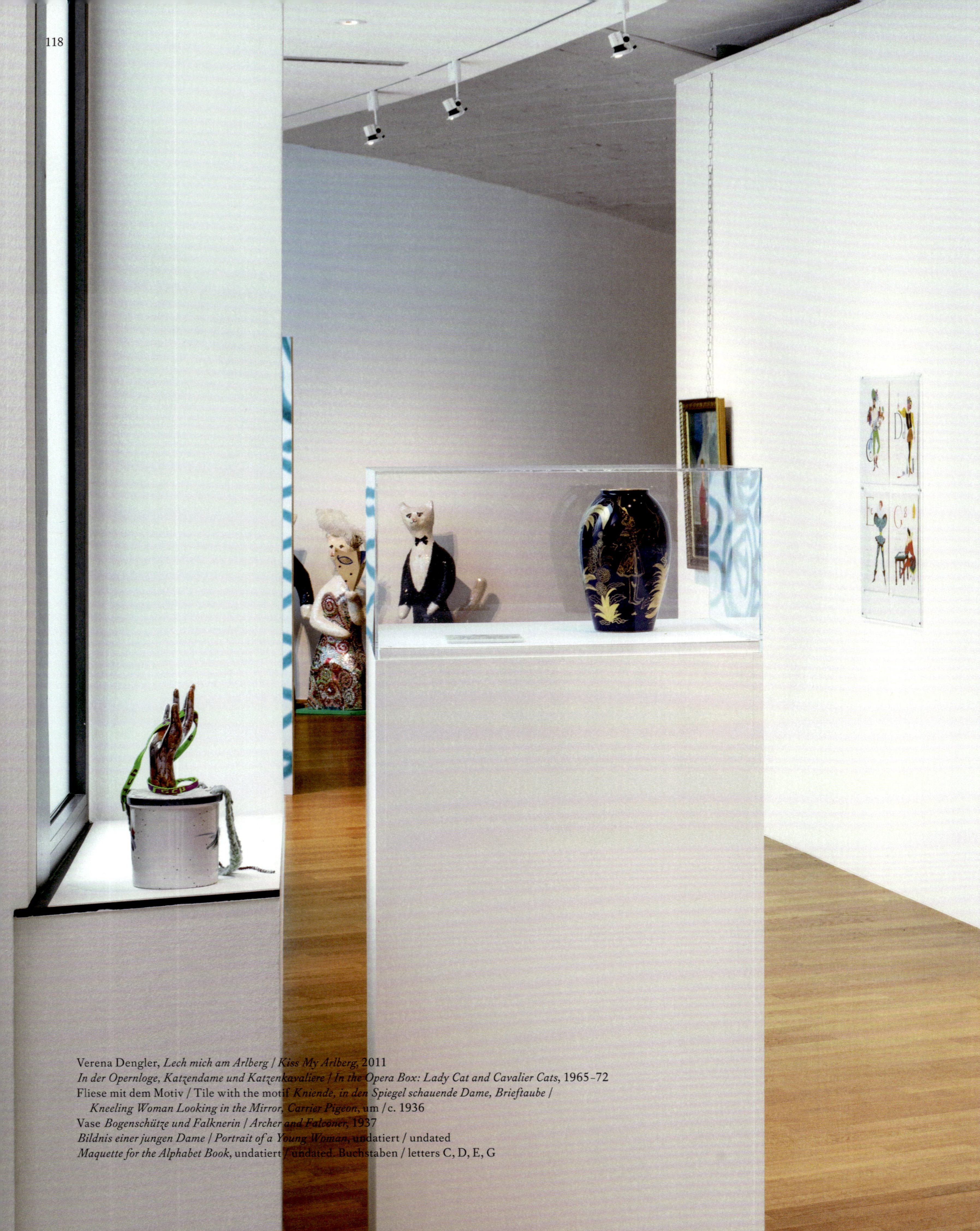

Verena Dengler, *Lech mich am Arlberg / Kiss My Arlberg*, 2011
In der Opernloge, Katzendame und Katzenkavaliere / In the Opera Box: Lady Cat and Cavalier Cats, 1965–72
Fliese mit dem Motiv / Tile with the motif *Kniende, in den Spiegel schauende Dame, Brieftaube / Kneeling Woman Looking in the Mirror, Carrier Pigeon*, um / c. 1936
Vase *Bogenschütze und Falknerin / Archer and Falconer*, 1937
Bildnis einer jungen Dame / Portrait of a Young Woman, undatiert / undated
Maquette for the Alphabet Book, undatiert / undated. Buchstaben / letters C, D, E, G

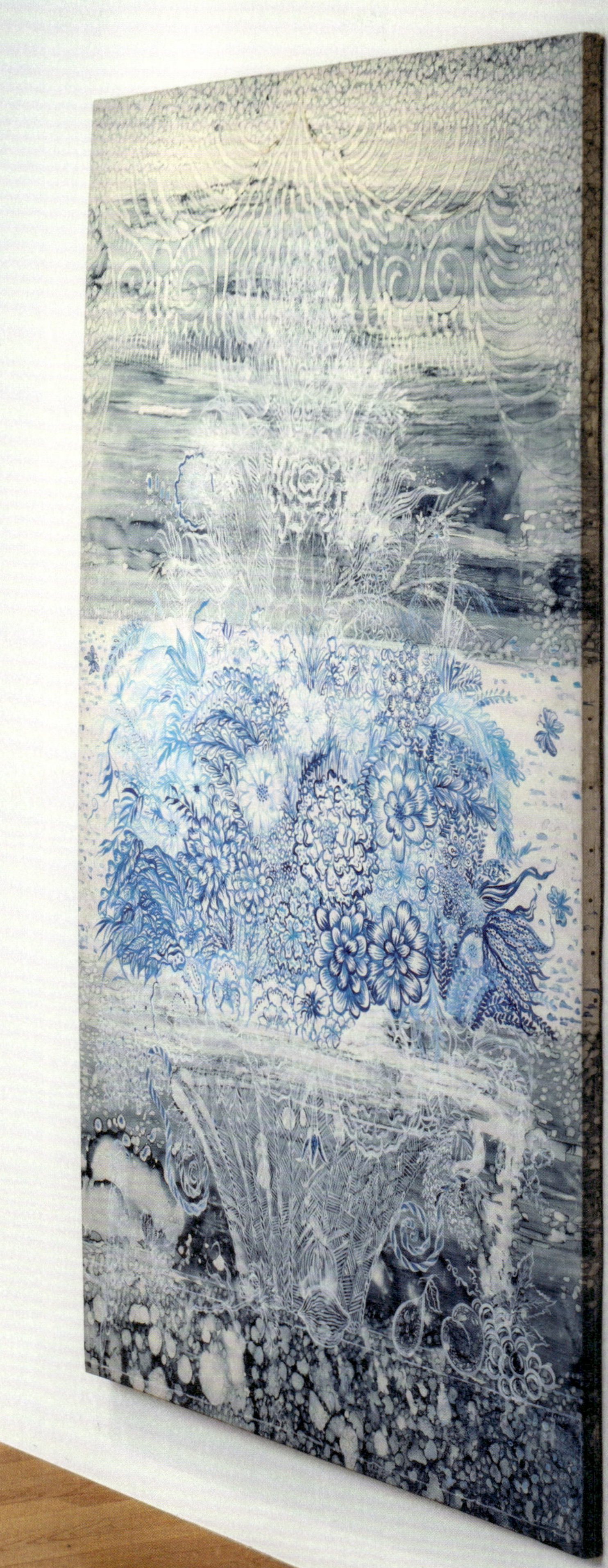

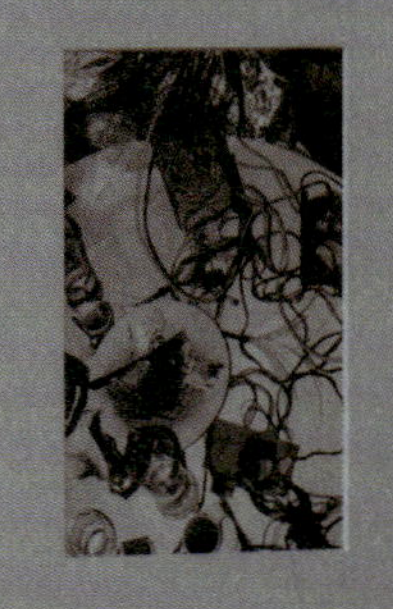

Der Hausfreund, Österreichisches Kulturforum / Austrian Cultural Forum, Berlin

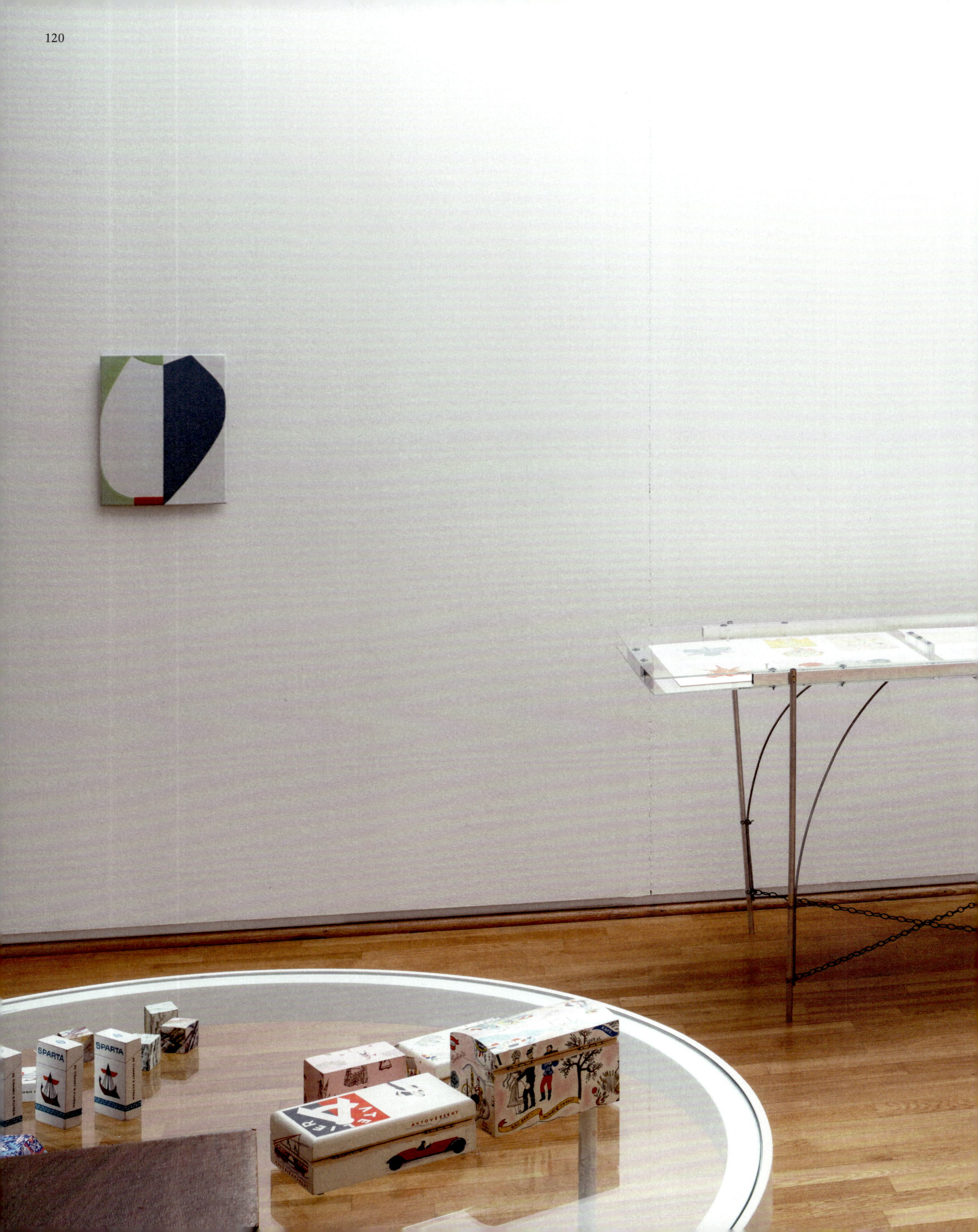

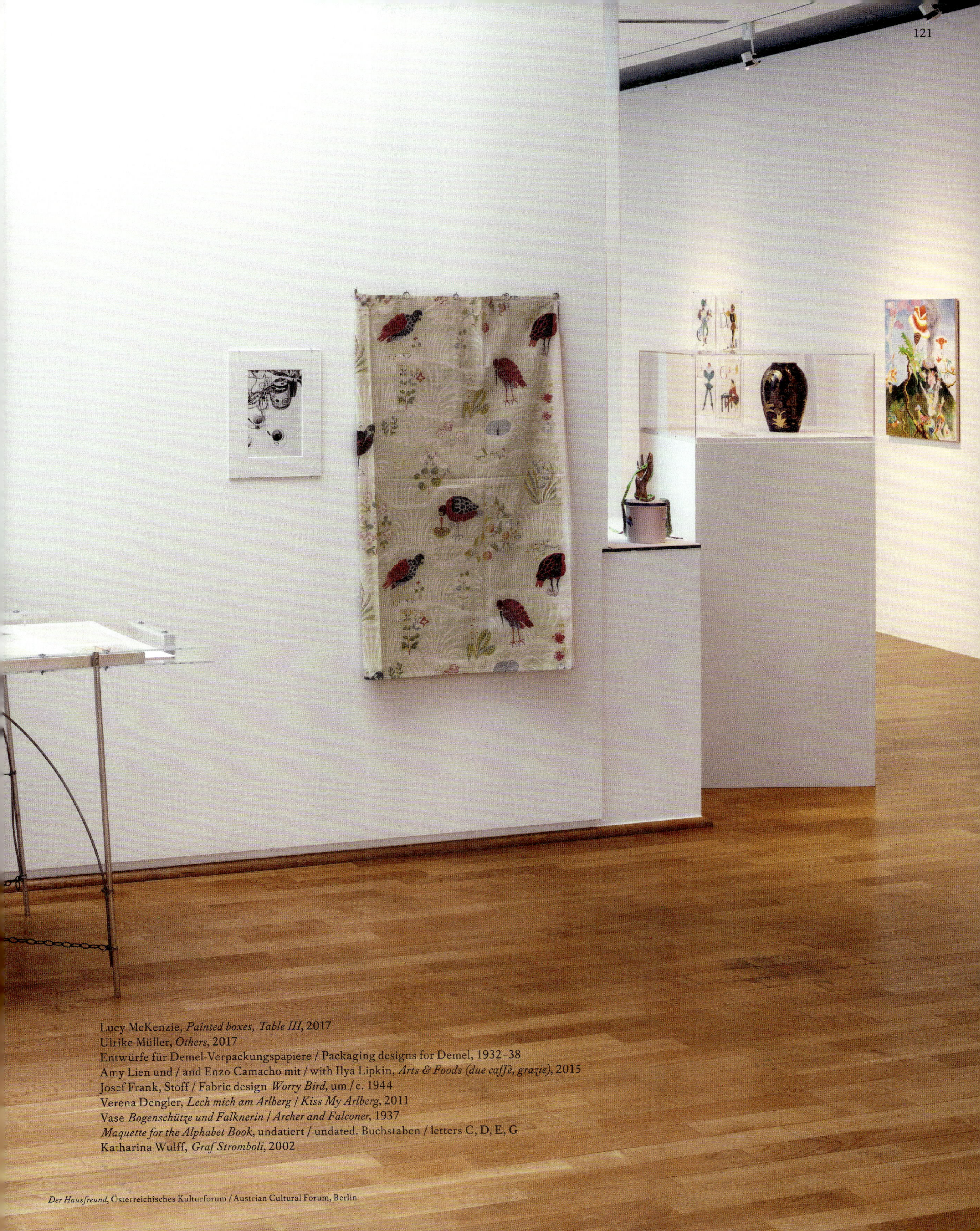

Lucy McKenzie, *Painted boxes, Table III*, 2017
Ulrike Müller, *Others*, 2017
Entwürfe für Demel-Verpackungspapiere / Packaging designs for Demel, 1932–38
Amy Lien und / and Enzo Camacho mit / with Ilya Lipkin, *Arts & Foods (due caffè, grazie)*, 2015
Josef Frank, Stoff / Fabric design *Worry Bird*, um / c. 1944
Verena Dengler, *Lech mich am Arlberg / Kiss My Arlberg*, 2011
Vase *Bogenschütze und Falknerin / Archer and Falconer*, 1937
Maquette for the Alphabet Book, undatiert / undated. Buchstaben / letters C, D, E, G
Katharina Wulff, *Graf Stromboli*, 2002

Der Hausfreund, Österreichisches Kulturforum / Austrian Cultural Forum, Berlin

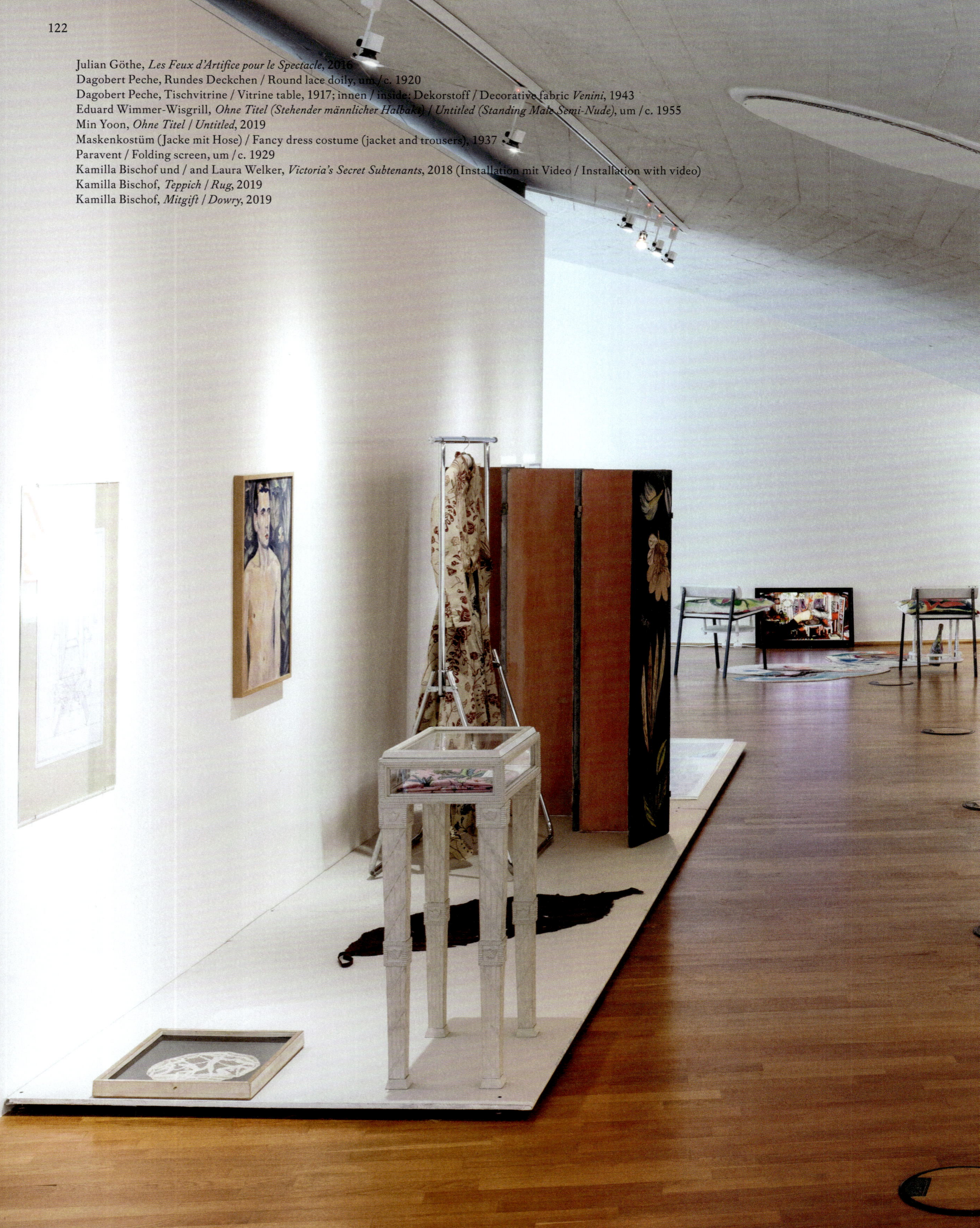

Julian Göthe, *Les Feux d'Artifice pour le Spectacle*, 2016
Dagobert Peche, Rundes Deckchen / Round lace doily, um / c. 1920
Dagobert Peche, Tischvitrine / Vitrine table, 1917; innen / inside: Dekorstoff / Decorative fabric *Venini*, 1943
Eduard Wimmer-Wisgrill, *Ohne Titel (Stehender männlicher Halbakt) / Untitled (Standing Male Semi-Nude)*, um / c. 1955
Min Yoon, *Ohne Titel / Untitled*, 2019
Maskenkostüm (Jacke mit Hose) / Fancy dress costume (jacket and trousers), 1937
Paravent / Folding screen, um / c. 1929
Kamilla Bischof und / and Laura Welker, *Victoria's Secret Subtenants*, 2018 (Installation mit Video / Installation with video)
Kamilla Bischof, *Teppich / Rug*, 2019
Kamilla Bischof, *Mitgift / Dowry*, 2019

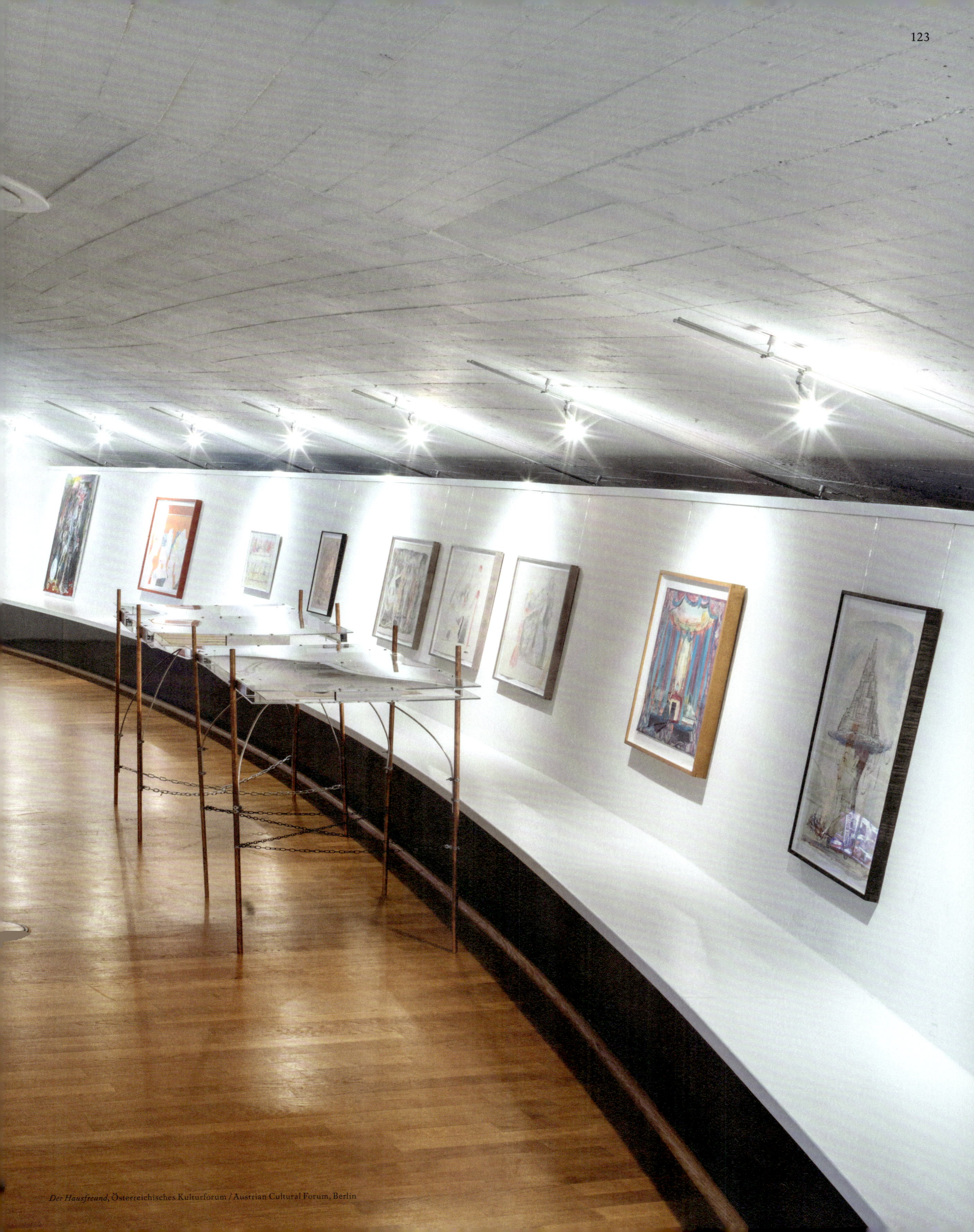

Der Hausfreund, Österreichisches Kulturforum / Austrian Cultural Forum, Berlin

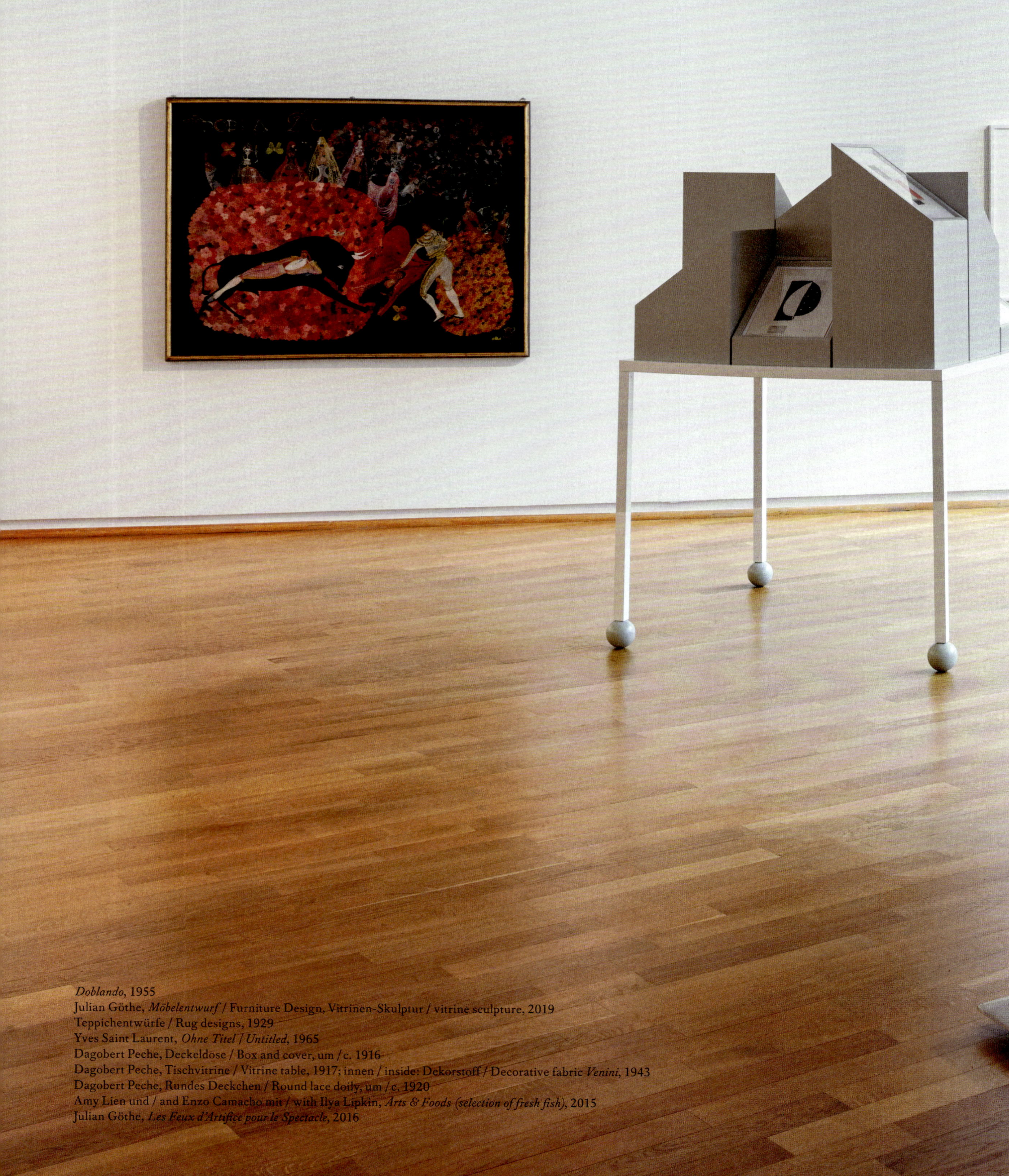

Doblando, 1955
Julian Göthe, *Möbelentwurf* / Furniture Design, Vitrinen-Skulptur / vitrine sculpture, 2019
Teppichentwürfe / Rug designs, 1929
Yves Saint Laurent, *Ohne Titel* / *Untitled*, 1965
Dagobert Peche, Deckeldose / Box and cover, um / c. 1916
Dagobert Peche, Tischvitrine / Vitrine table, 1917; innen / inside: Dekorstoff / Decorative fabric *Venini*, 1943
Dagobert Peche, Rundes Deckchen / Round lace doily, um / c. 1920
Amy Lien und / and Enzo Camacho mit / with Ilya Lipkin, *Arts & Foods (selection of fresh fish)*, 2015
Julian Göthe, *Les Feux d'Artifice pour le Spectacle*, 2016

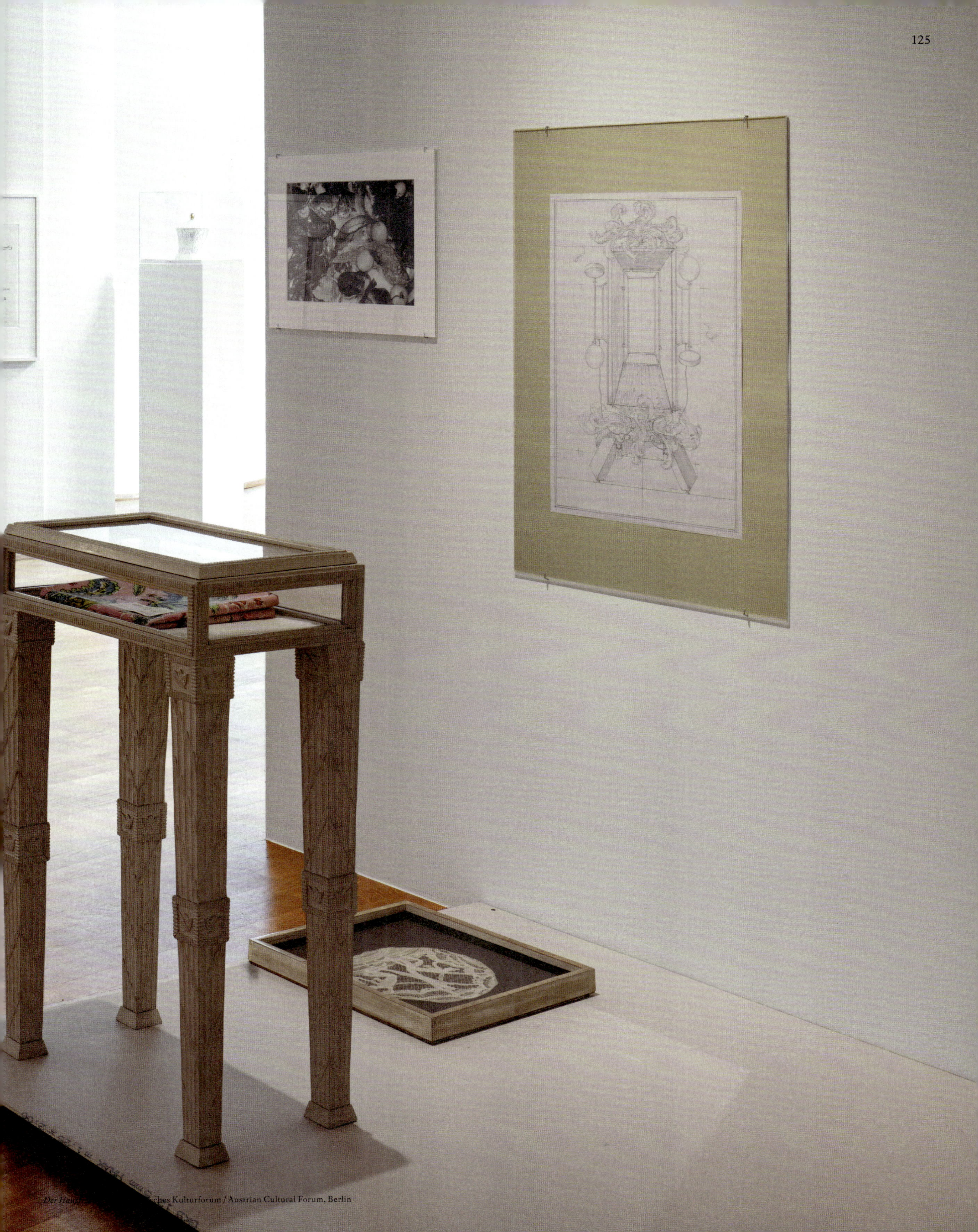

Der Haus[illegible] [illegible]ches Kulturforum / Austrian Cultural Forum, Berlin

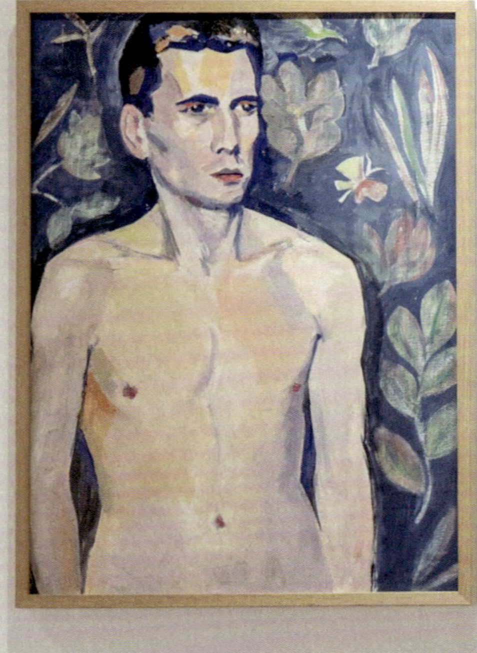

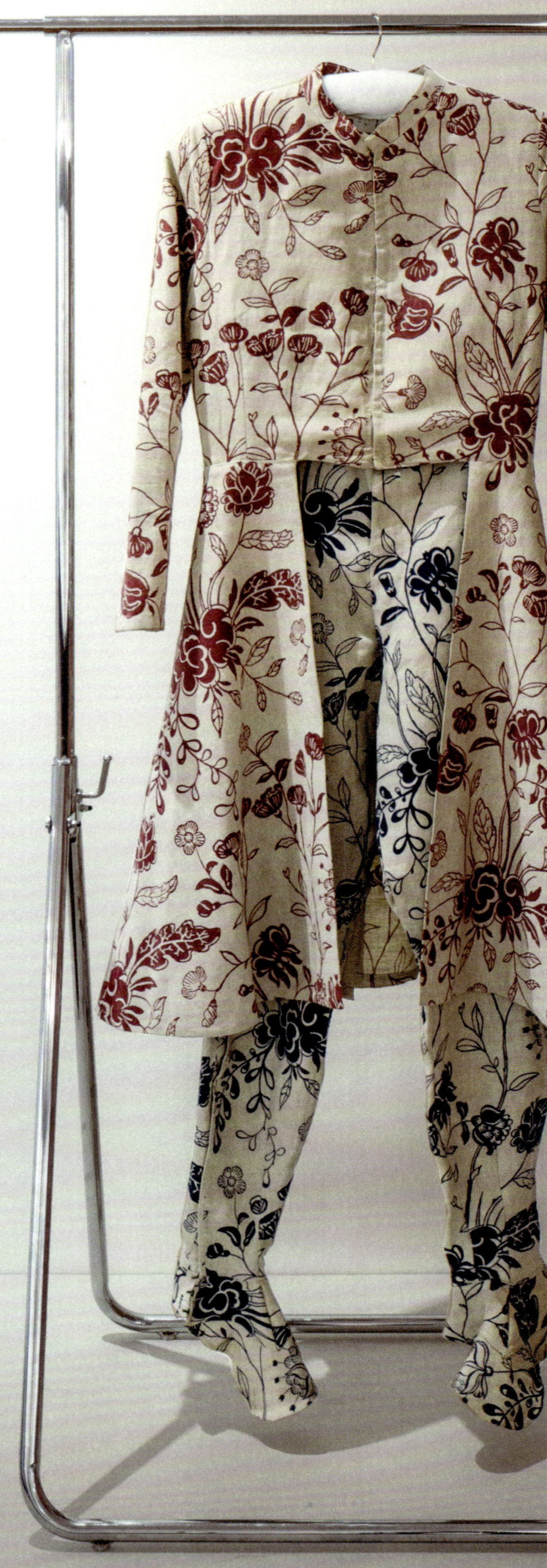

Min Yoon, *Ohne Titel / Untitled*, 2019
Eduard Wimmer-Wisgrill, *Ohne Titel (Stehender männlicher Halbakt) / Untitled (Standing Male Semi-Nude)*, um / c. 1955
Maskenkostüm (Jacke mit Hose) / Fancy dress costume (jacket and trousers), 1937
Paravent / Folding screen, um / c. 1929
Eduard Wimmer-Wisgrill, Oswald Oberhuber, *Ohne Titel (Männlicher Halbakt in Gelb) / Untitled (Male Semi-Nude in Yellow)*, um / c. 1938, um / c. 1980
Josef Frank, verschiedene Stoffmuster / various fabric designs *Mirakel*, *Primavera*, *Mistral*, *Semiramis*, 1925–40

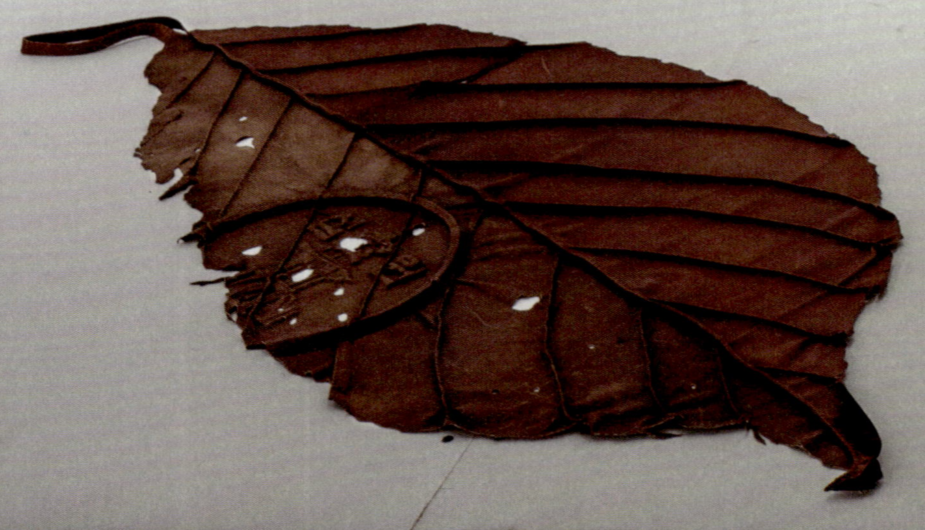

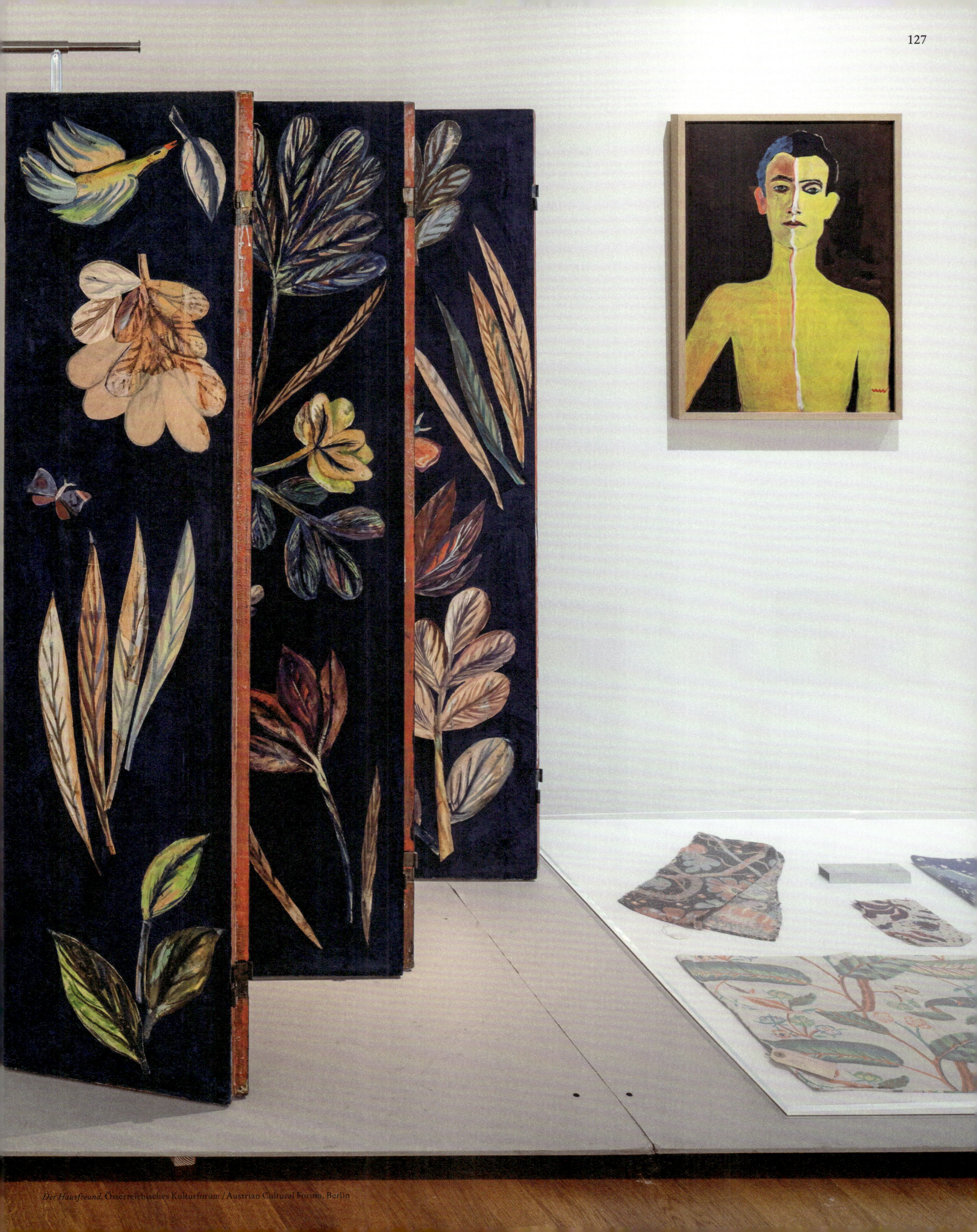

Der Hausfreund, Österreichisches Kulturforum / Austrian Cultural Forum, Berlin

Doblando, 1955
Julian Göthe, *Möbelentwurf* / Furniture Design, Vitrinen-Skulptur / vitrine sculpture, 2019
Teppichentwürfe / Rug designs, 1929
Dagobert Peche, Tischvitrine / Vitrine table, 1917; innen / inside: Dekorstoff / Decorative fabric *Venini*, 1943
Min Yoon, *Ohne Titel* / *Untitled*, 2019
Paravent / Folding screen, um / c. 1929
Eduard Wimmer-Wisgrill, Oswald Oberhuber, *ohne Titel (Männlicher Halbakt in Gelb)* / *Untitled (Male Semi-Nude in Yellow)*, um / c. 1938, um / c. 1980
Thee und Kaffee / *Tea and Coffee*, 1943
Jack Smith, *Untitled, Big Hotel*, 1968
Jack Smith, *Untitled*, 1968
Amy Lien und / and Enzo Camacho mit / with Ilya Lipkin, *Arts & Foods (bookshelf)*, 2015
Verena Dengler, *Gmundner Keramik, Paravents für den Fantastischen Sozialismus* / *Gmunden Ceramics, Folding Screens for Fantastic Socialism*, 2013
Hans Hollein, Österreichisches Verkehrsbüro, 1976–78

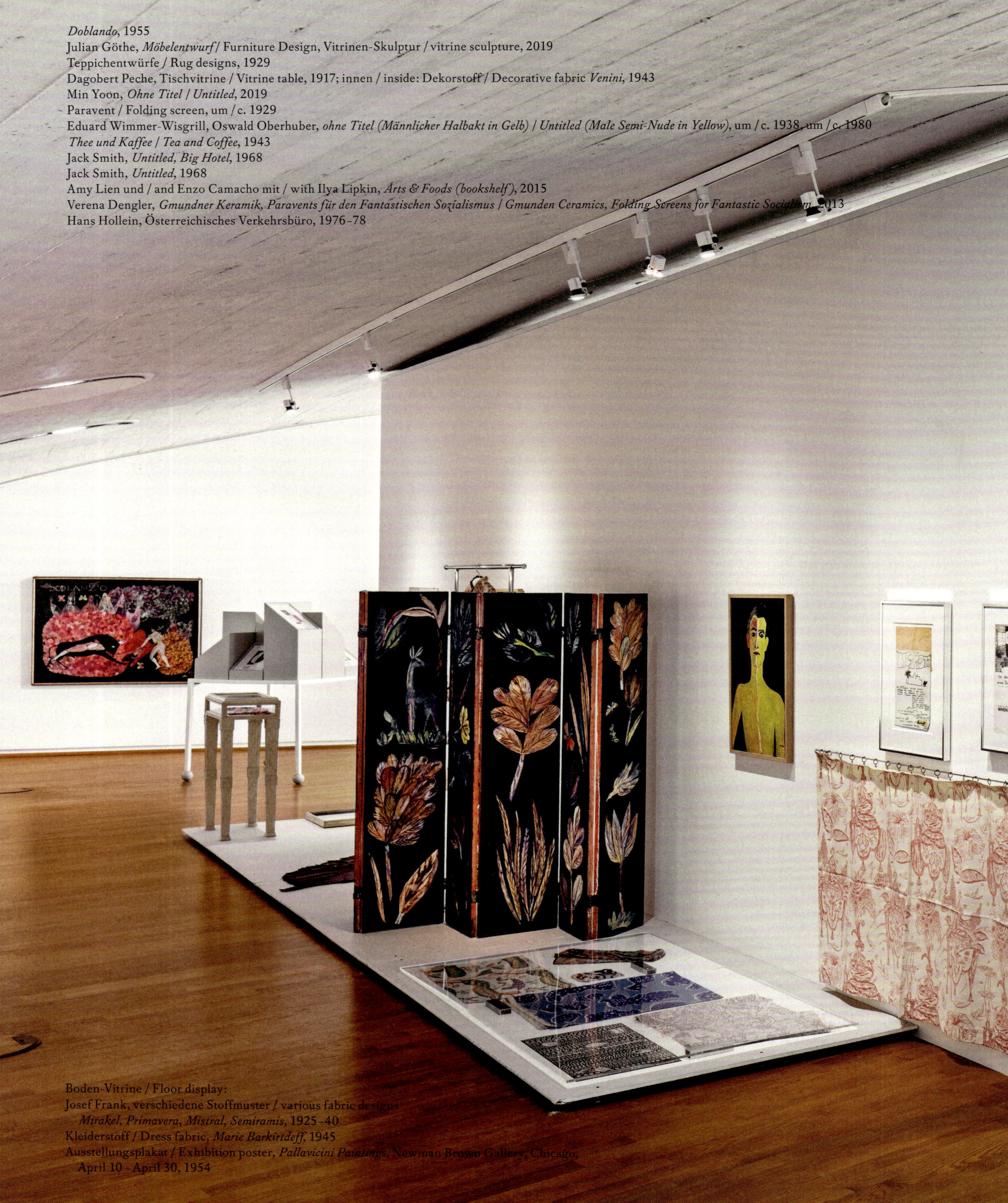

Boden-Vitrine / Floor display:
Josef Frank, verschiedene Stoffmuster / various fabric designs
Mirakel, *Primavera*, *Mistral*, *Semiramis*, 1925–40
Kleiderstoff / Dress fabric, *Marie Barkirtdeff*, 1945
Ausstellungsplakat / Exhibition poster, *Pallavicini Paintings*, Newman Brown Gallery, Chicago, April 10 – April 30, 1954

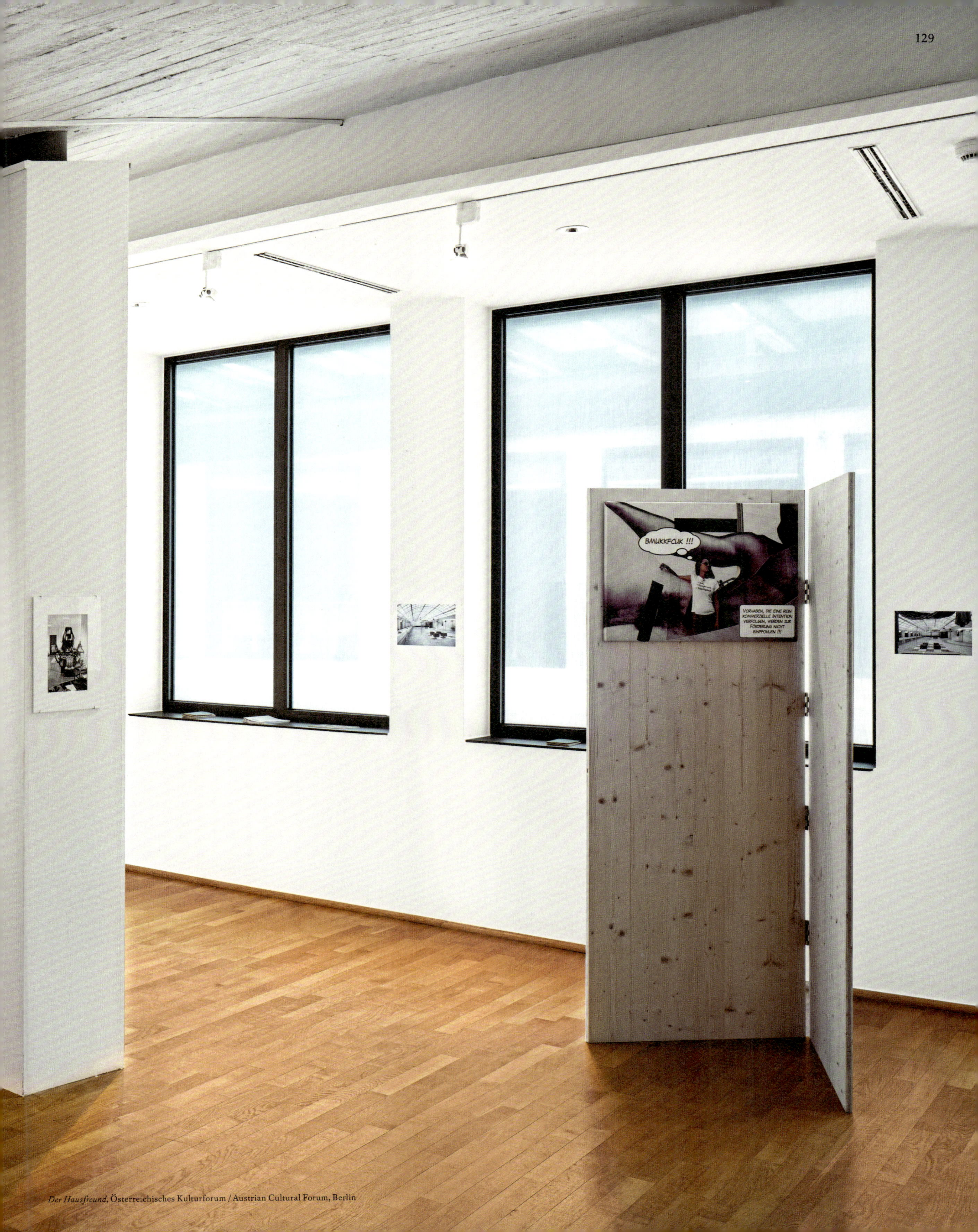

Der Hausfreund, Österreichisches Kulturforum / Austrian Cultural Forum, Berlin

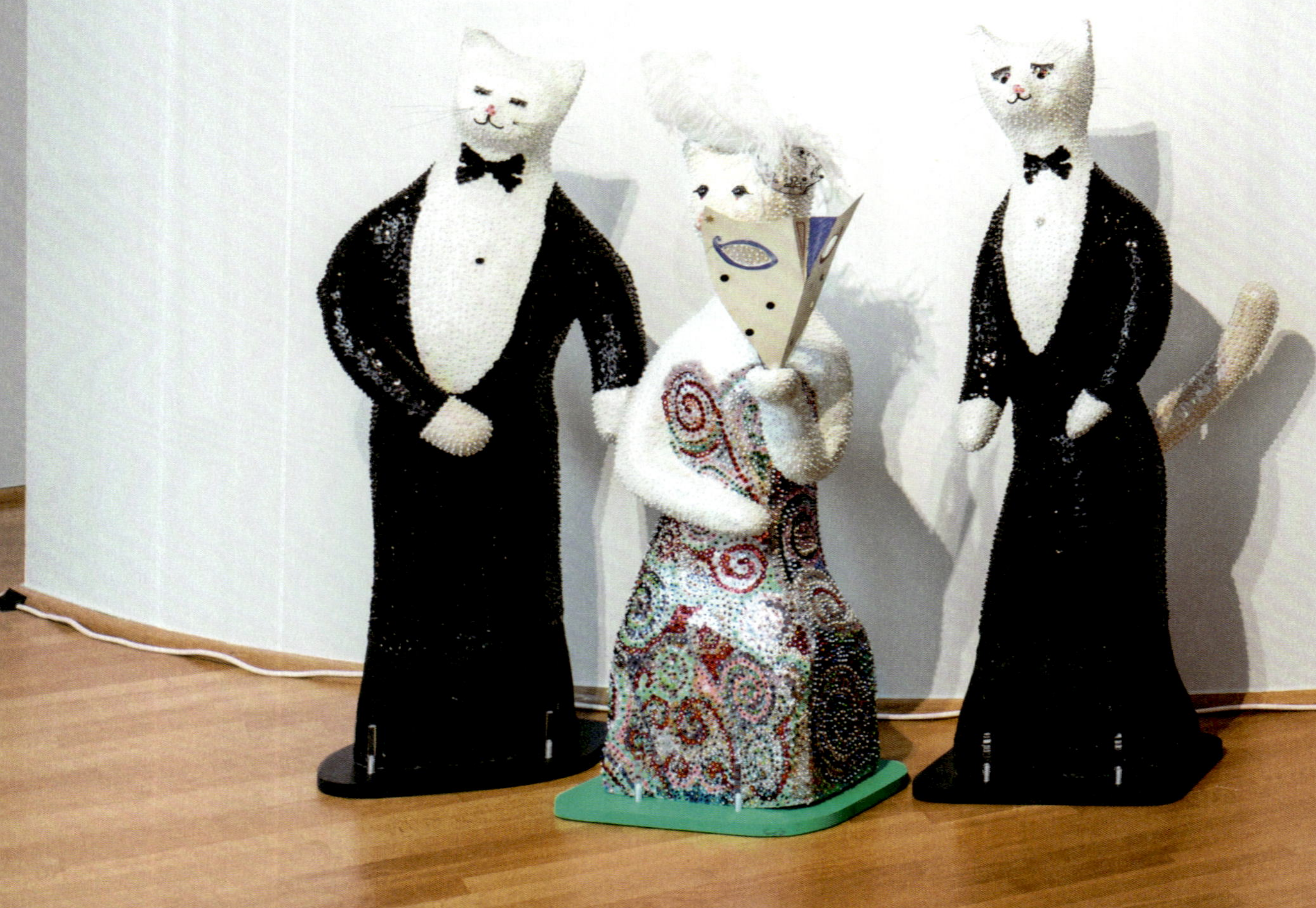

In der Opernloge, Katzendame und Katzenkavaliere / In the Opera Box: Lady Cat and Cavalier Cats, 1965–72
Kamilla Bischof und / and Laura Welker, *Victoria's Secret Subtenants*, 2018 (Installation mit Video / Installation with video)
Kamilla Bischof, *Mitgift / Dowry*, 2019

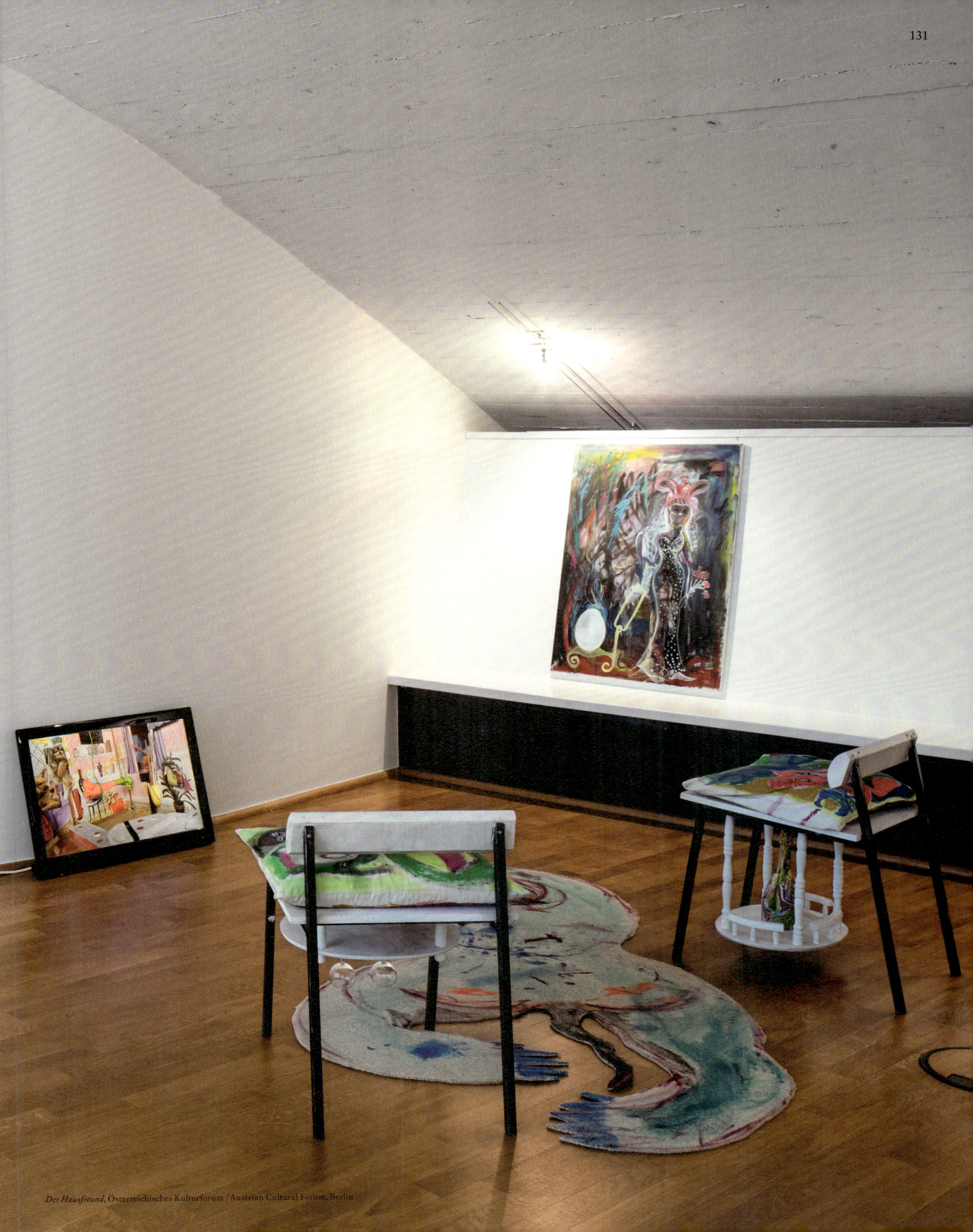

Der Hausfreund, Österreichisches Kulturforum / Austrian Cultural Forum, Berlin

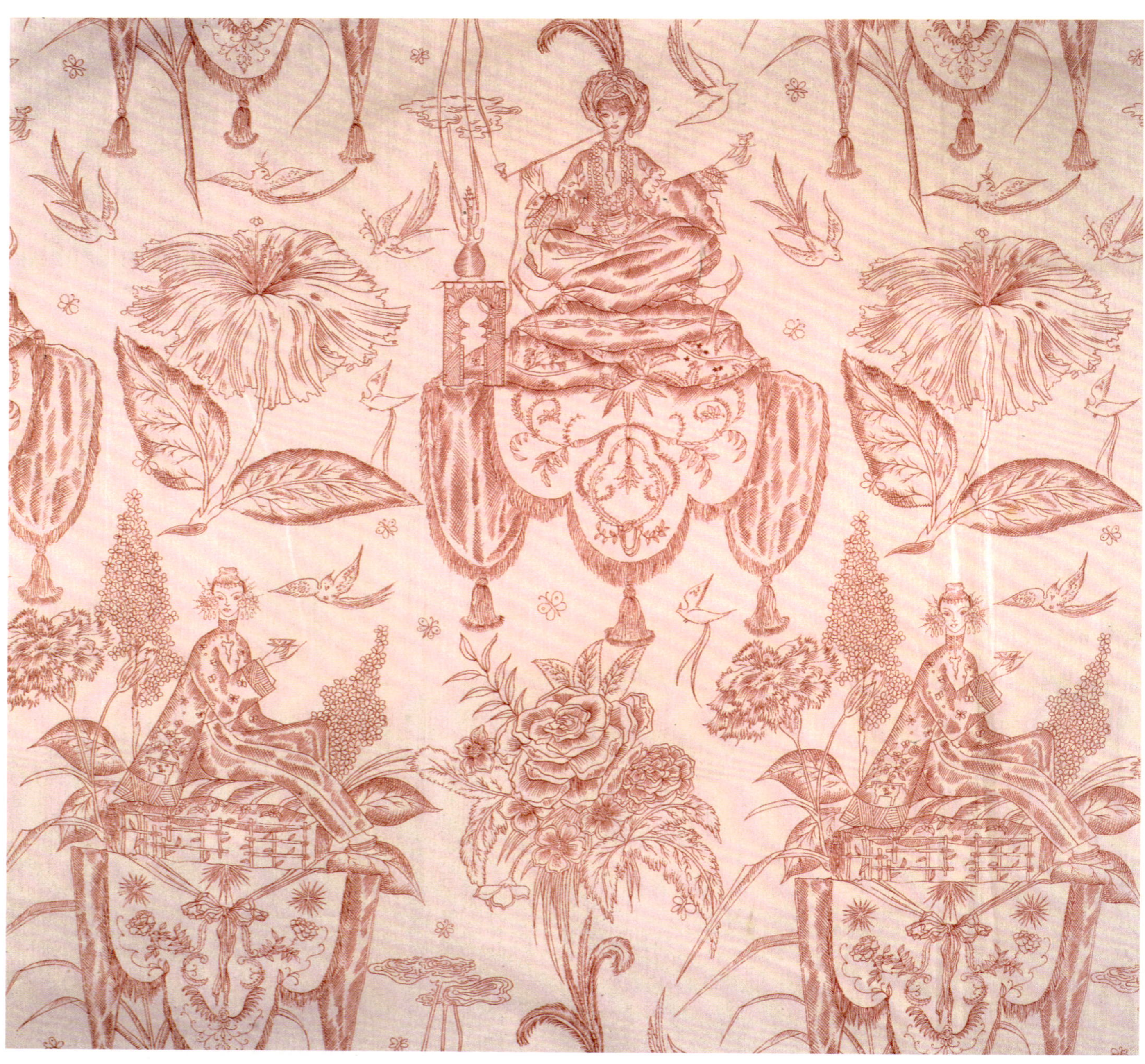

Thee und Kaffee / *Tea and Coffee*, 1943
Dekorstoff Ausführung für Manufaktur Campisotta /
Decorative fabric for Campisotta

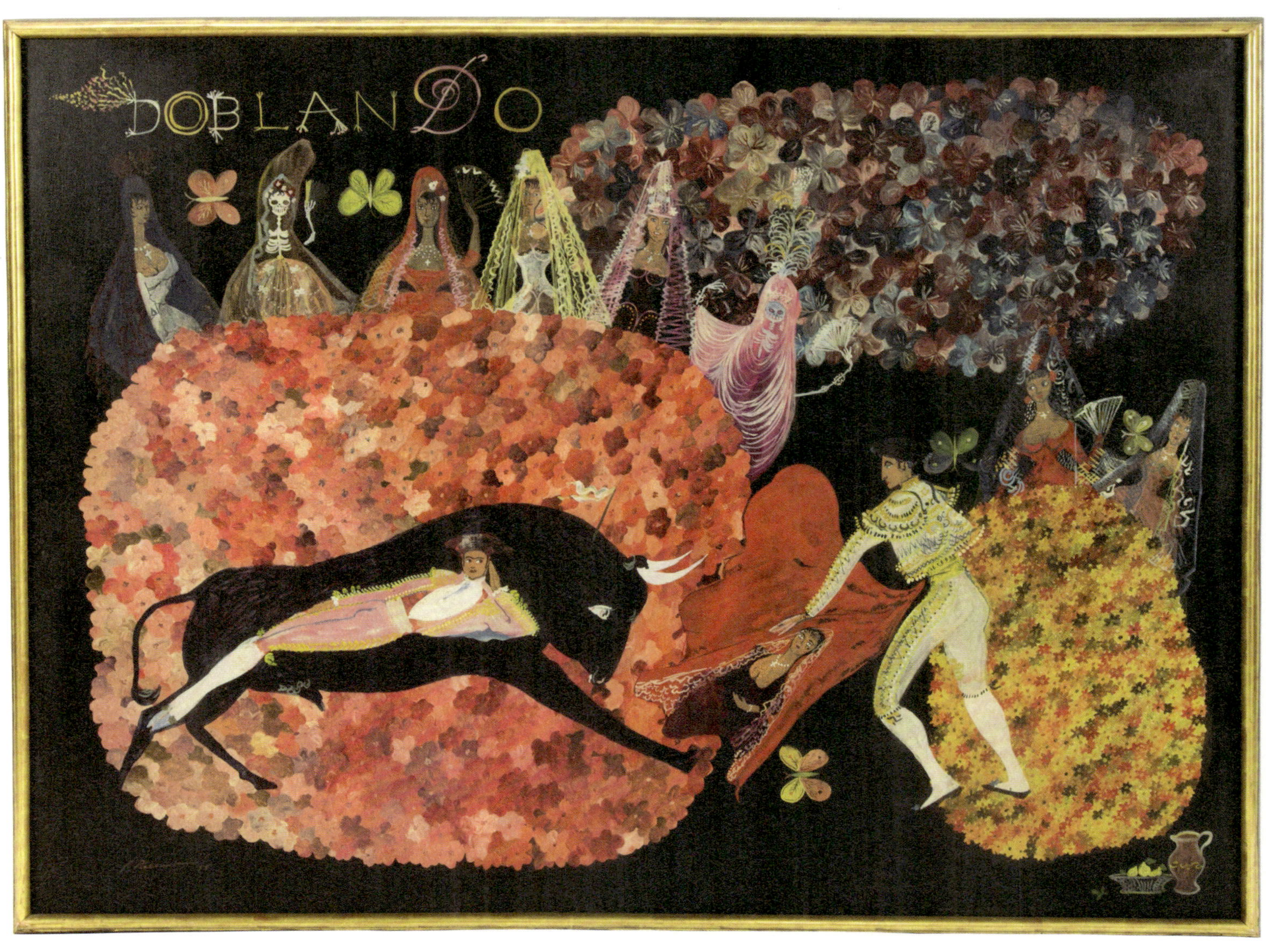

Doblando, 1955

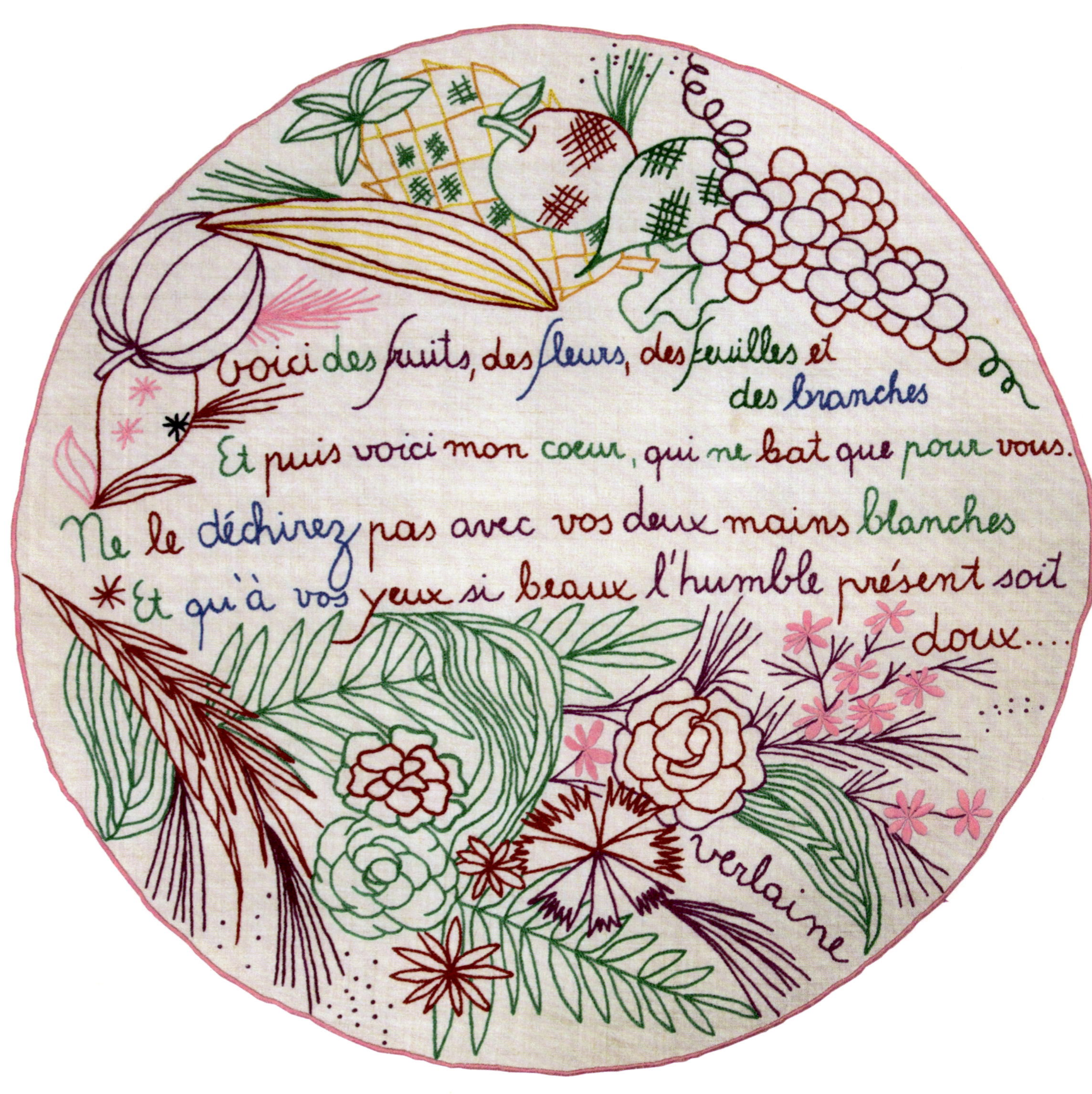

Rundes Tischdeckchen (für Demel) /
Round table coverlet (for Demel), 1932

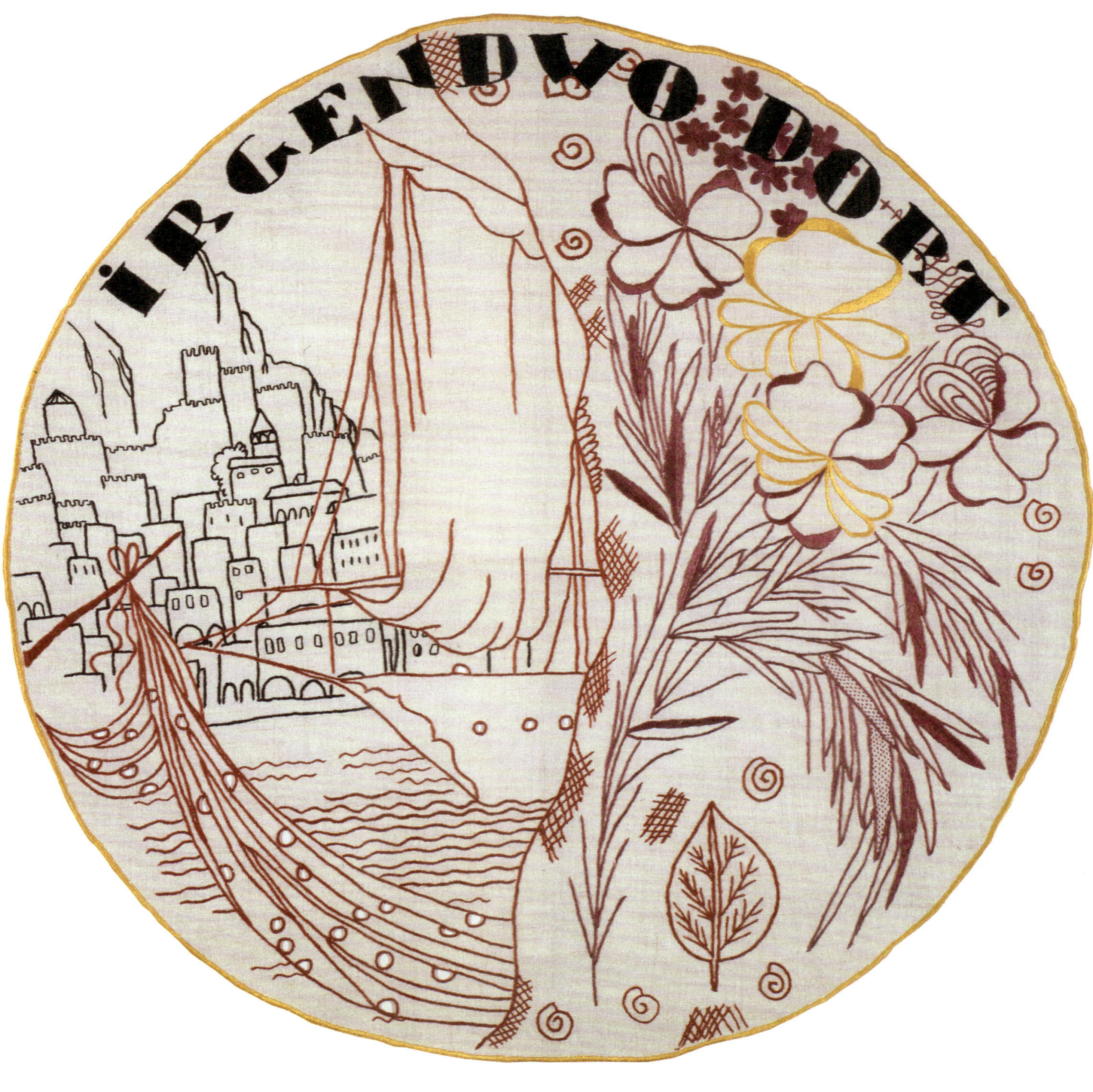

Rundes Tischdeckchen (für Demel) /
Round table coverlet (for Demel), 1932

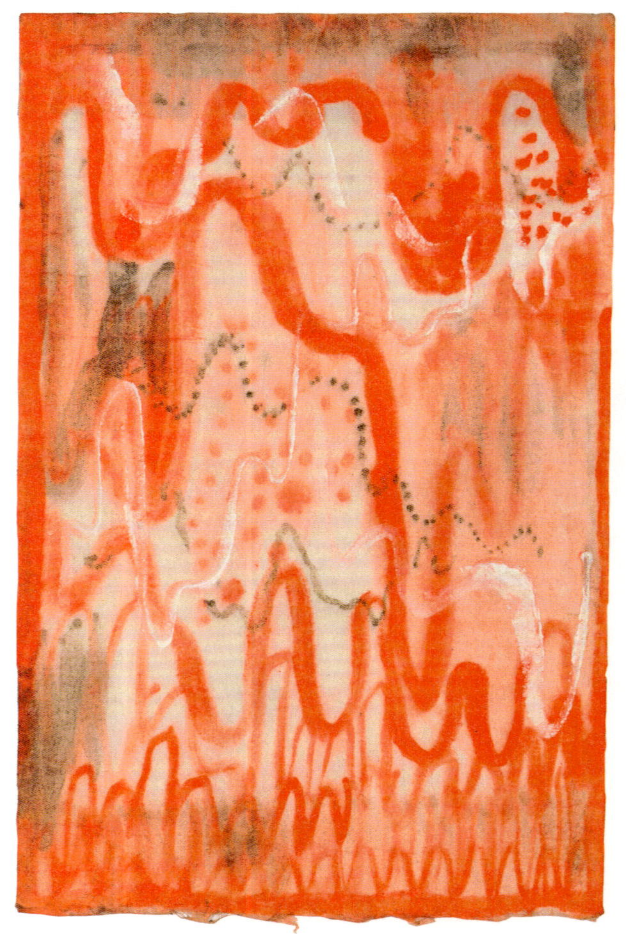

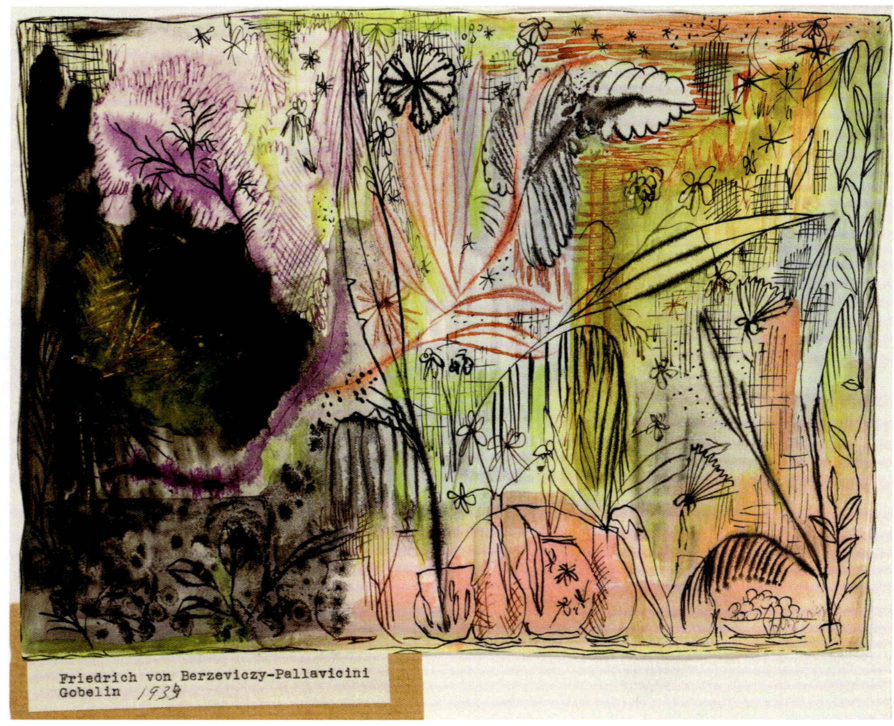

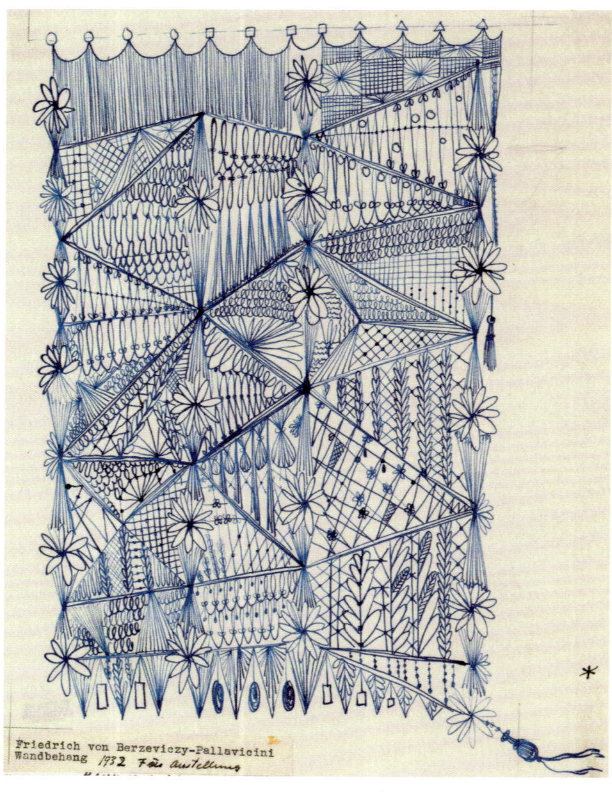

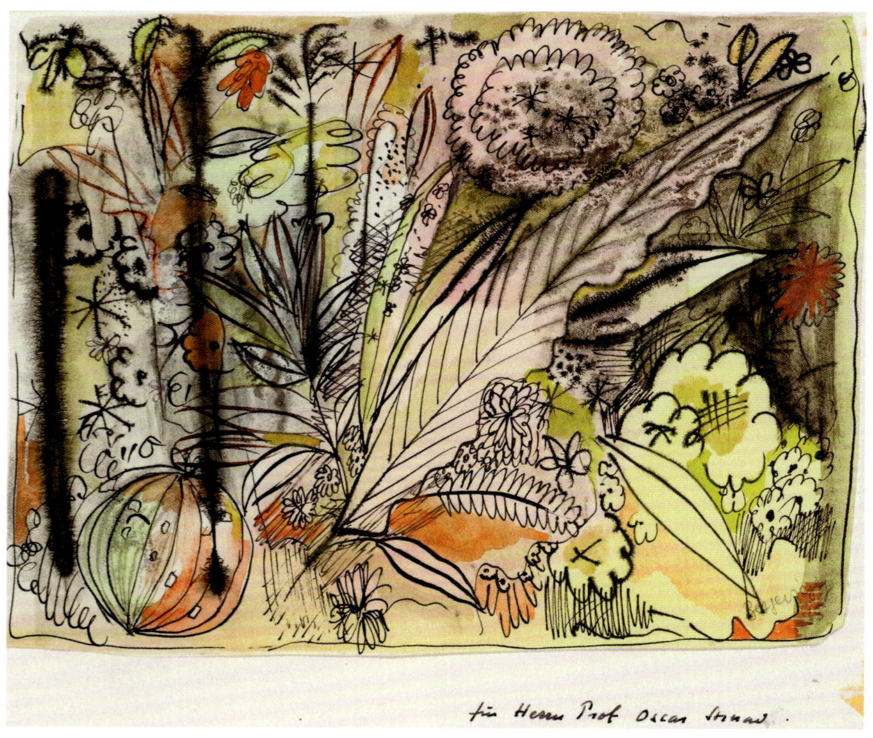

Entwurf für einen Wandbehang / Design for a wall hanging, 1933
Entwurf für einen Gobelin / Design for a tapestry, 1934
Entwurf für einen Gobelin / Design for a tapestry, 1935
Entwurf für einen Wandbehang / Design for a wall hanging, 1932

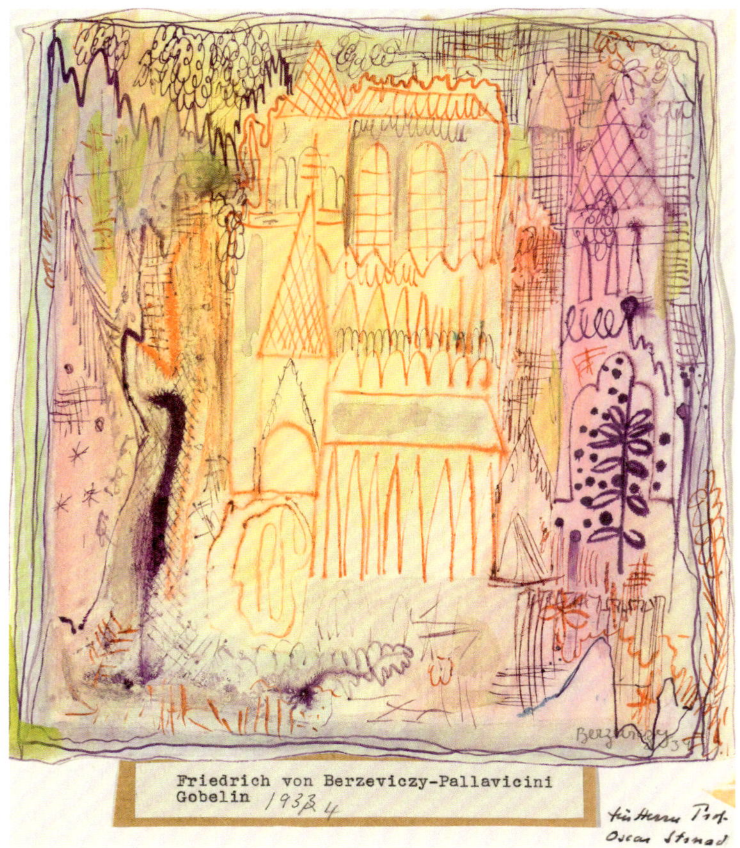

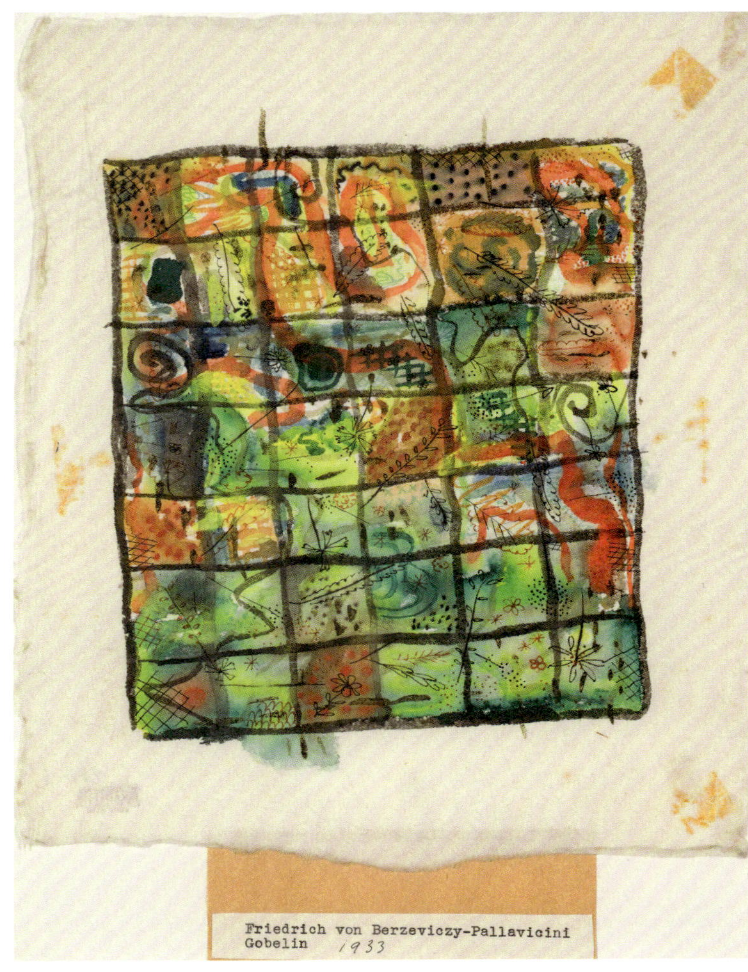

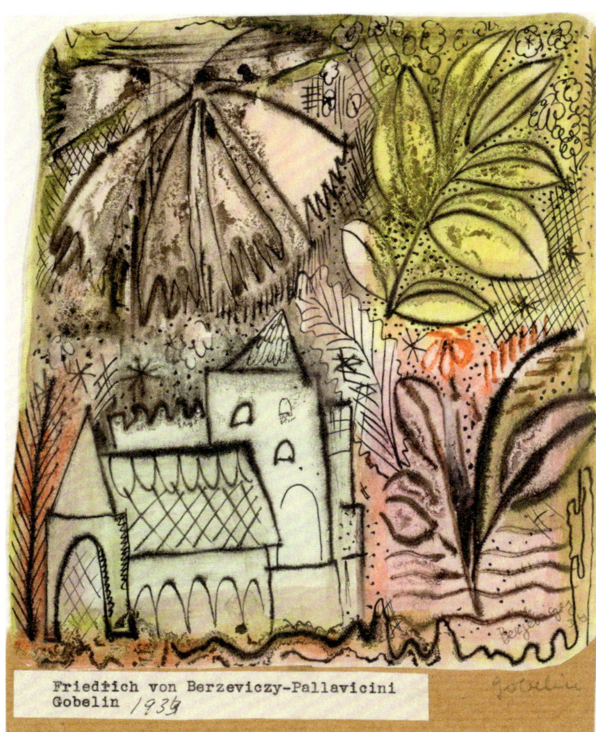

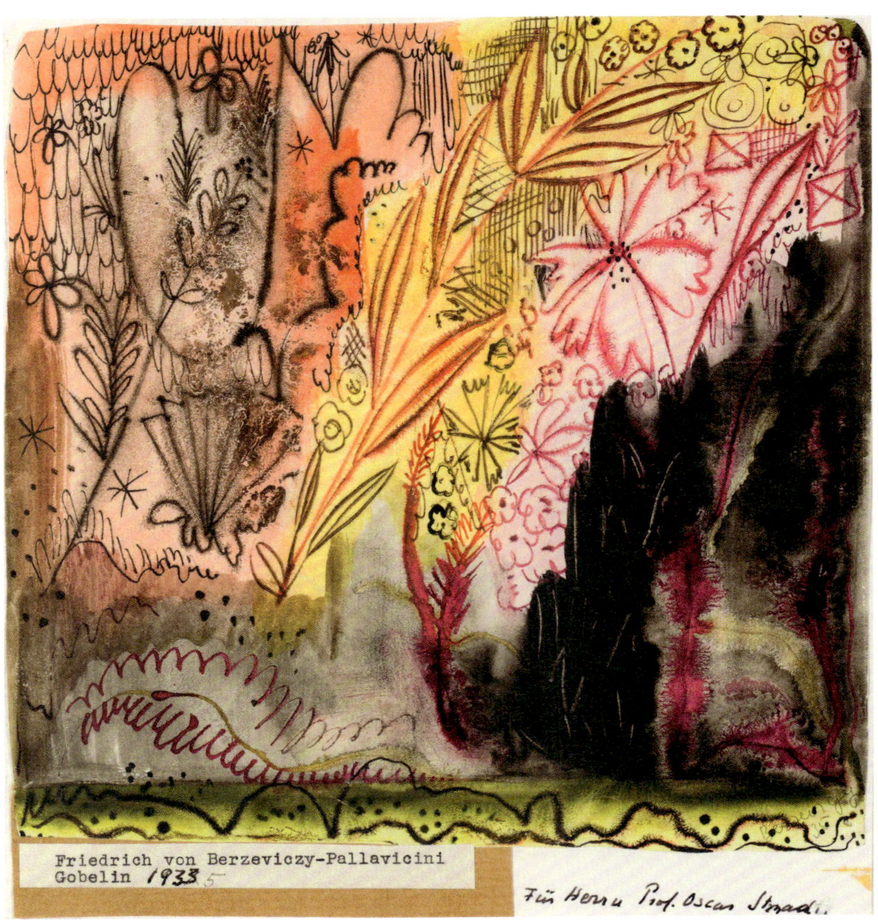

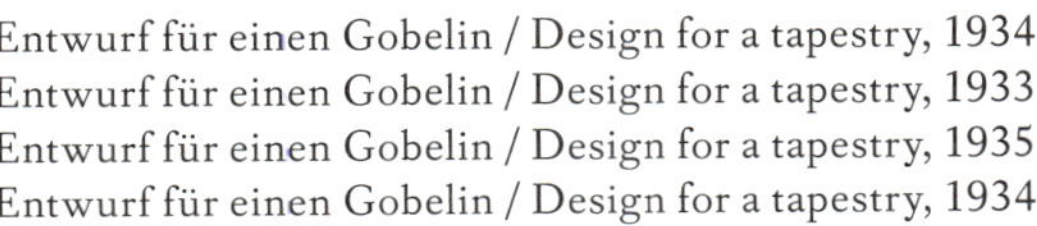
Entwurf für einen Gobelin / Design for a tapestry, 1934
Entwurf für einen Gobelin / Design for a tapestry, 1933
Entwurf für einen Gobelin / Design for a tapestry, 1935
Entwurf für einen Gobelin / Design for a tapestry, 1934

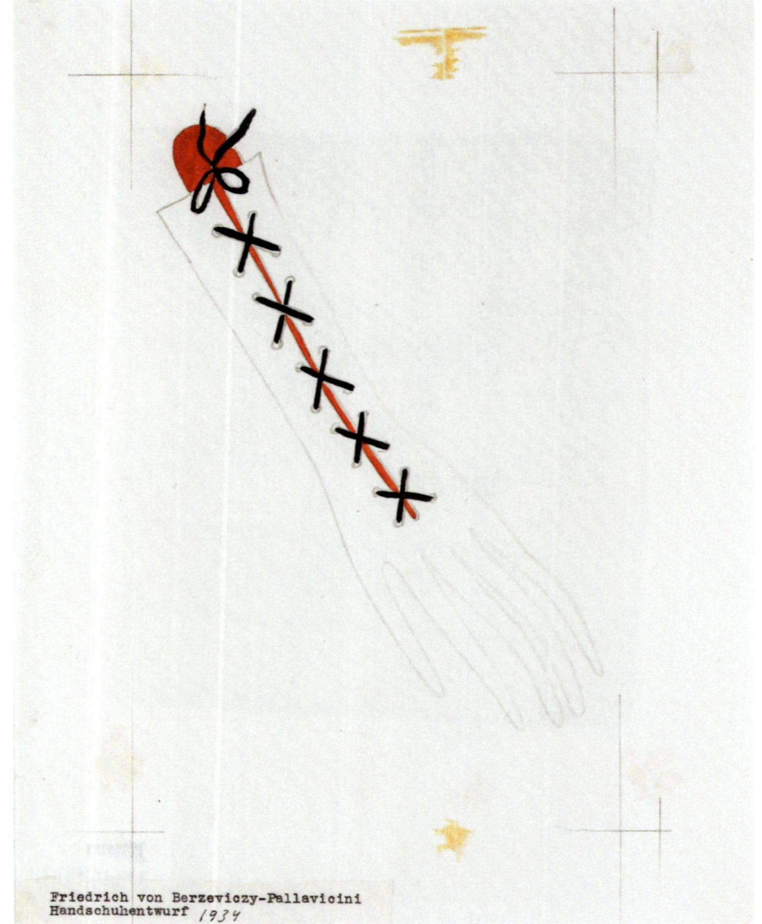

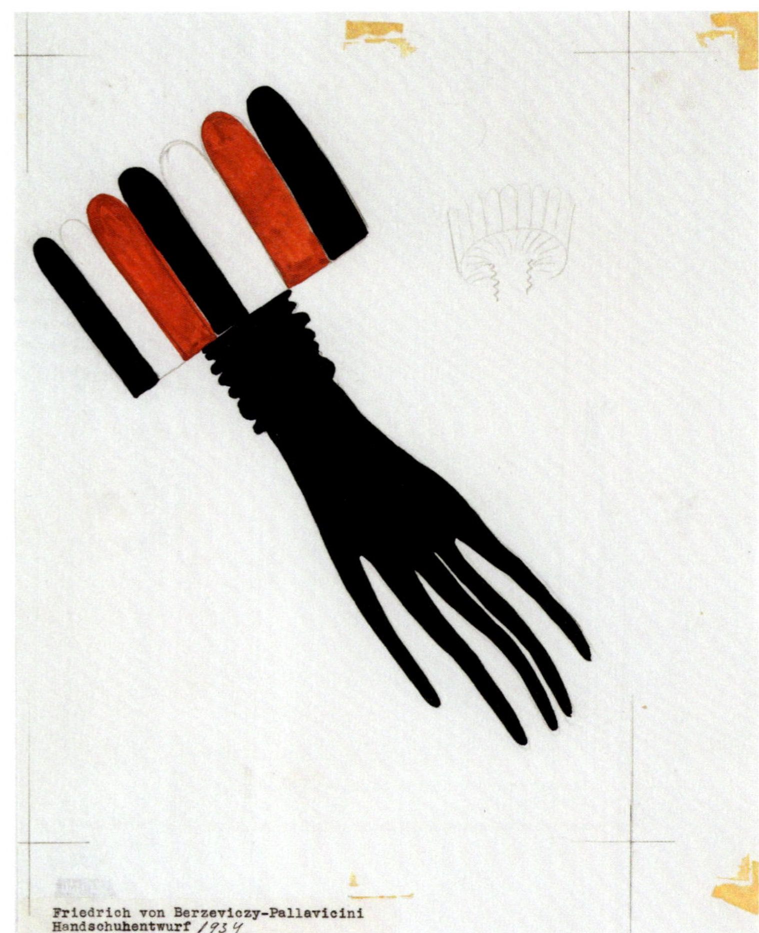

Entwürfe für Handschuhe / Designs for gloves, ohne Datierung / undated

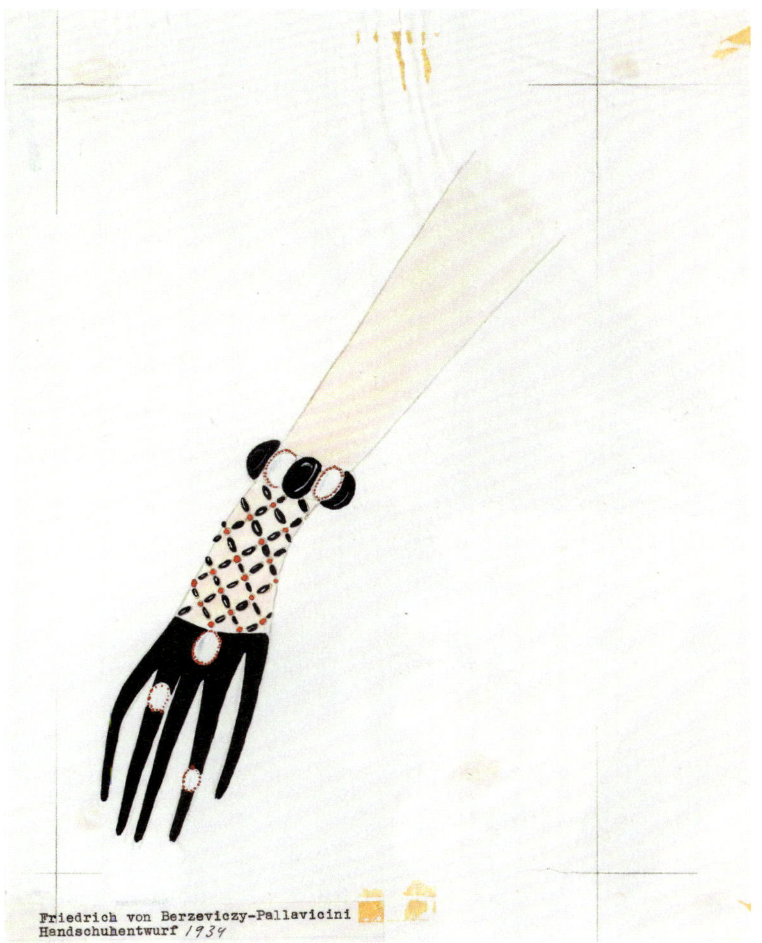
Friedrich von Berzeviczy-Pallavicini
Handschuhentwurf 1934

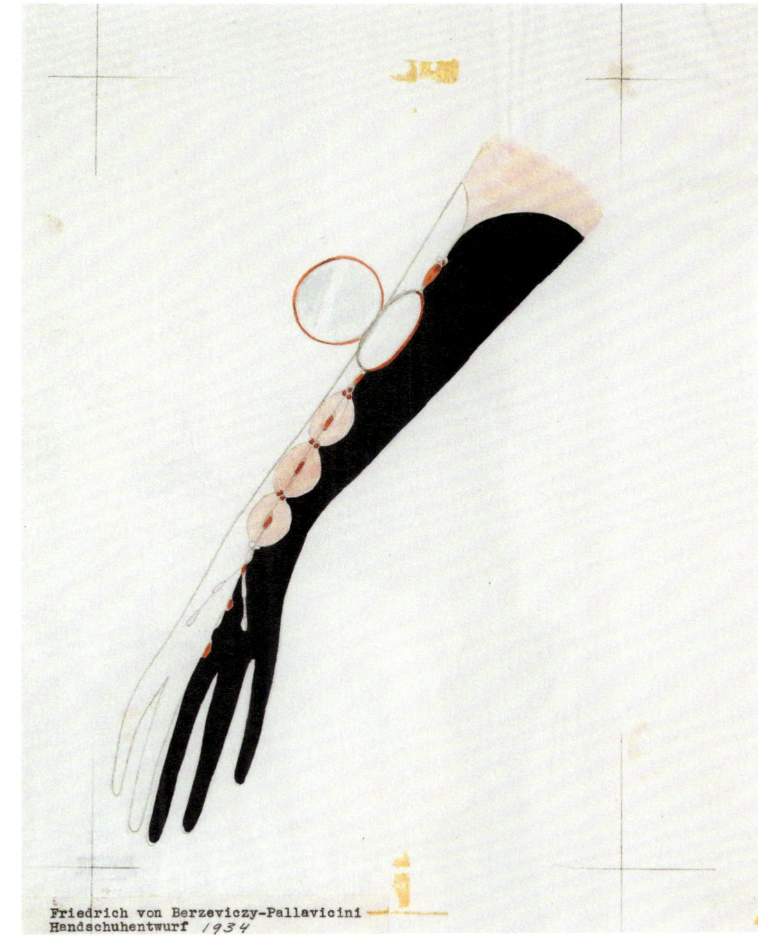
Friedrich von Berzeviczy-Pallavicini
Handschuhentwurf 1934

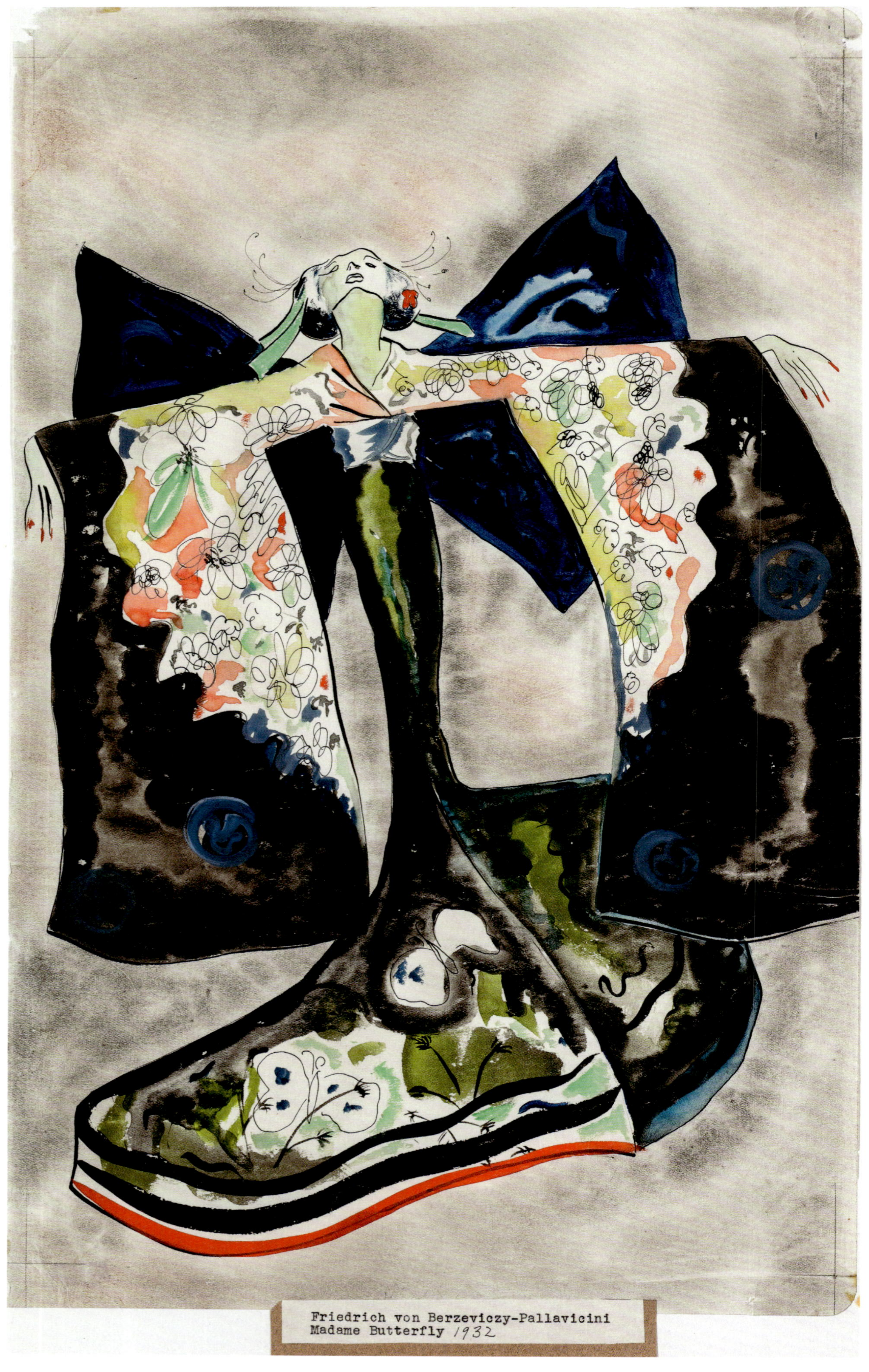
Friedrich von Berzeviczy-Pallavicini
Madame Butterfly 1932

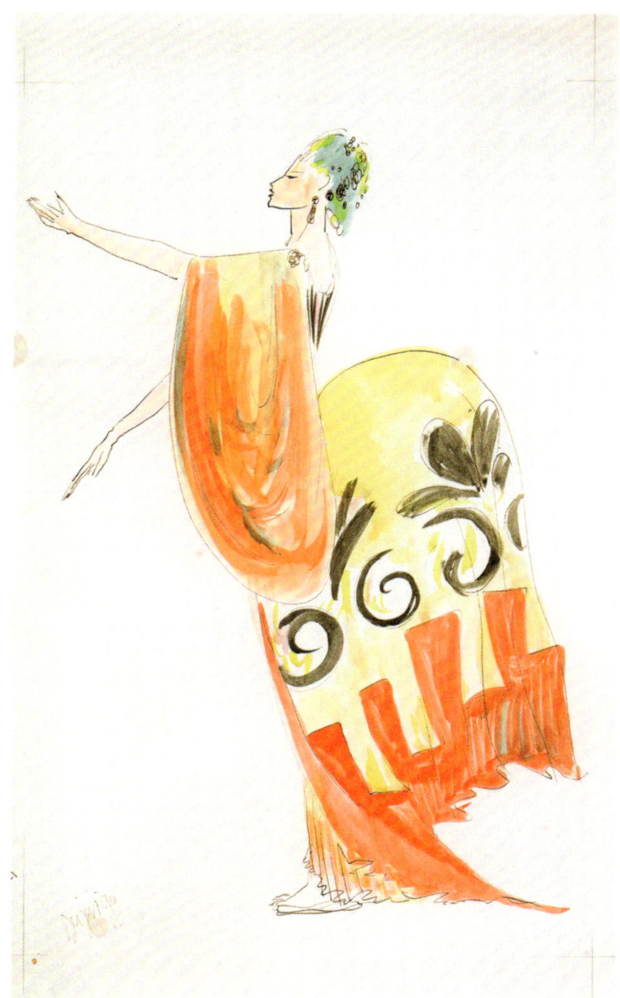

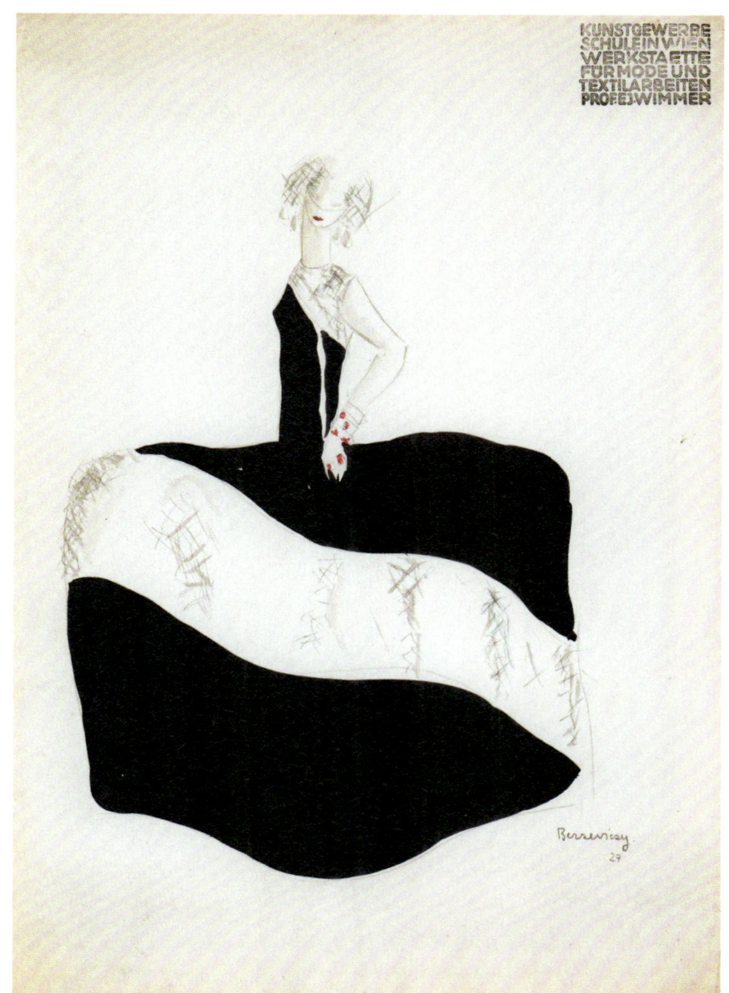

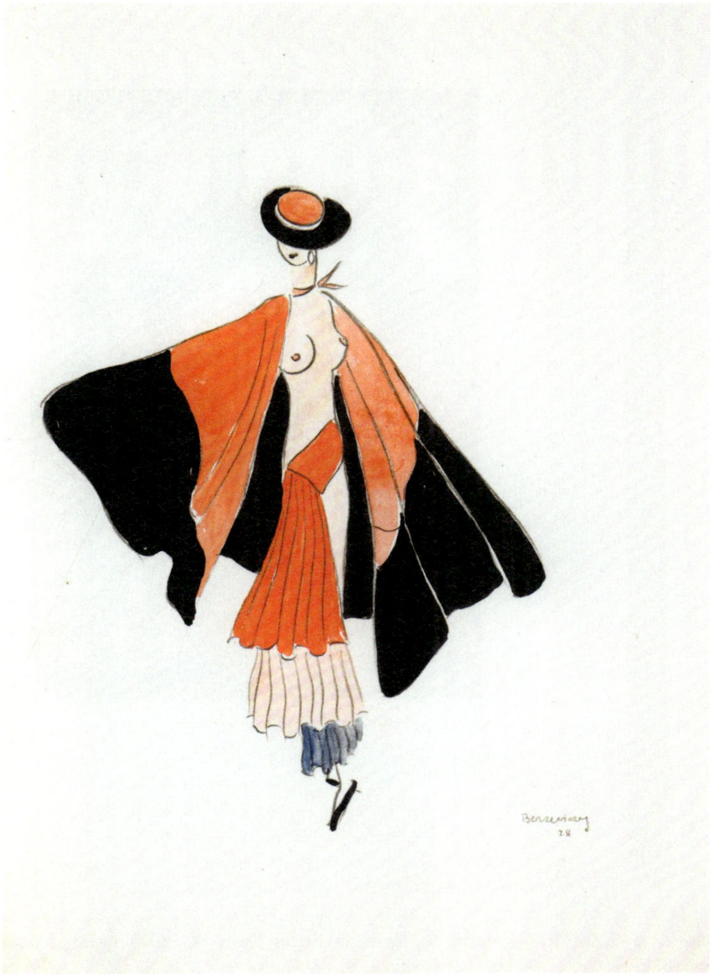

Links / Left: Entwurf für ein Bühnenkostüm zu / Design for a costume for *Madama Butterfly*, 1932
Entwurf für ein Bühnenkostüm zu / Design for a costume for Jean Giraudoux' *La Guerre de Troie n'aura pas lieu*, 1932
Entwurf für ein Krinolinenkleid in Schwarz und Weiß / Design for a crinoline dress in black and white, 1927
Entwurf für ein Kostüm mit Lendenschurz und rot-schwarzem Cape / Design for a costume with loincloth and red-and-black cape, 1928

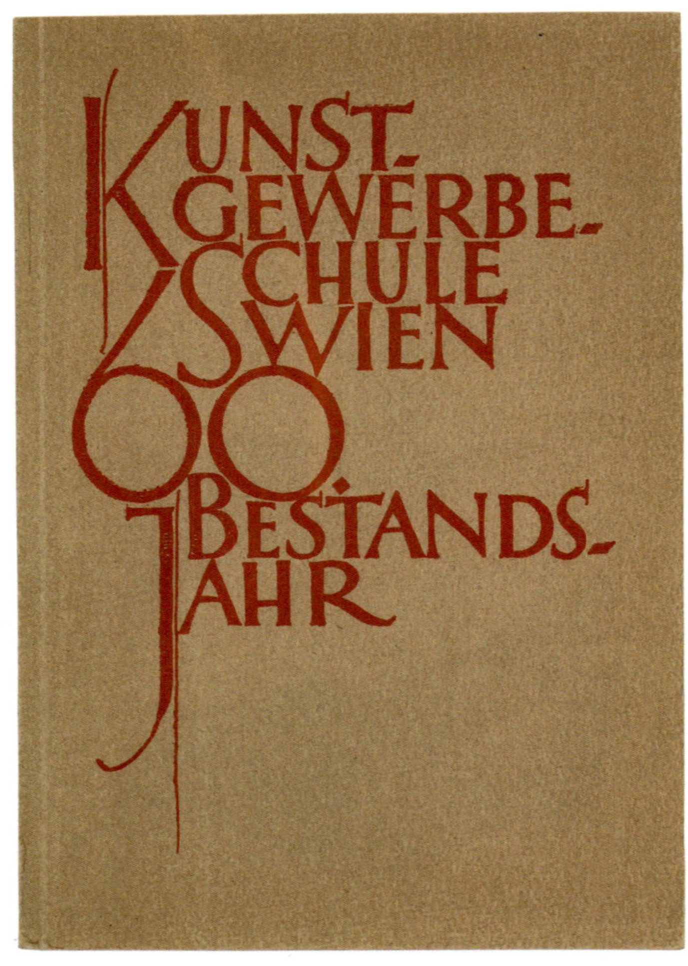

RAUM 1

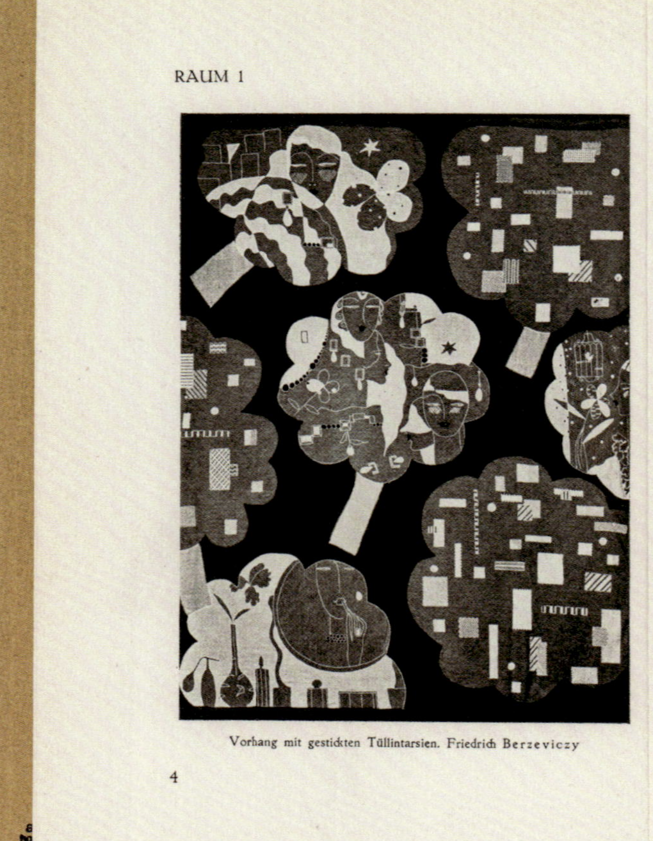

Vorhang mit gestickten Tüllintarsien. Friedrich Berzeviczy

4

RAUM 1

WERKSTÄTTE FÜR KERAMIK

Regierungsrat Professor Michael Powolny

Hilfslehrer Stephan Erdös

12 Schüler, davon 10 weiblich

30 Wochenstunden. Ausbildung zu selbständig schaffenden Keramikern, Modelleuren und keramischen Malern. Arbeiten in der Topfkeramik, im Modellieren, Schneiden und Formen von Originalkeramiken und im Entwerfen und Ausführen von Ofen- und Gartenkeramik sowie im Glasieren, Bemalen und Brennen dieser Arbeiten.

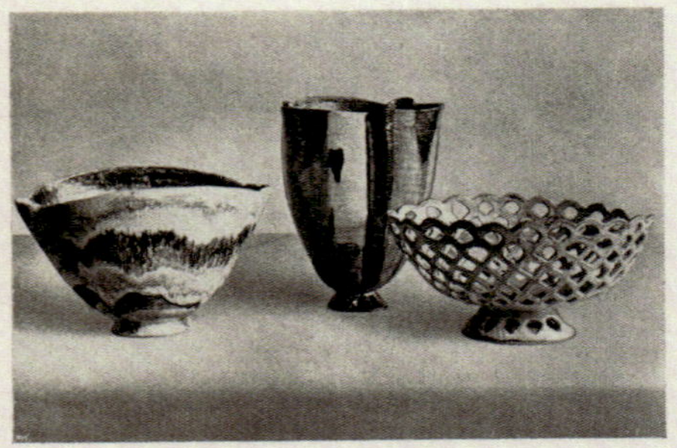

Gefäße in Majolika. Luzie Gomperz

5

Ausstellungskatalog / Exhibition catalogue, Kunstgewerbeschule Wien 60. Bestandsjahr / School of Applied Arts Vienna, 60th anniversary, 1937

RAUM 3

ALLGEMEINE ABTEILUNG
ALLGEMEINE FORMENLEHRE
Regierungsrat Professor Franz Cizek
Hilfslehrer Otto Wagner
54 Schüler, davon 34 weiblich

24 Wochenstunden. Der Unterricht bezweckt Gewinnung der geistigen und materiellen Grundlagen des rhythmischen Schaffens sowie Erkenntnis des Ornamentalen als äußere Notwendigkeit innerlich waltender Gesetze. Er erweckt somit bei den Schülern Verständnis und Empfinden für die werkgerechte Form handwerklicher Schöpfungen, schult Geist, Auge und Hand für die Hervorbringung solcher werkgerechter Formen und erzieht die Schüler zu sachlich denkenden, gediegenen Arbeitskräften.

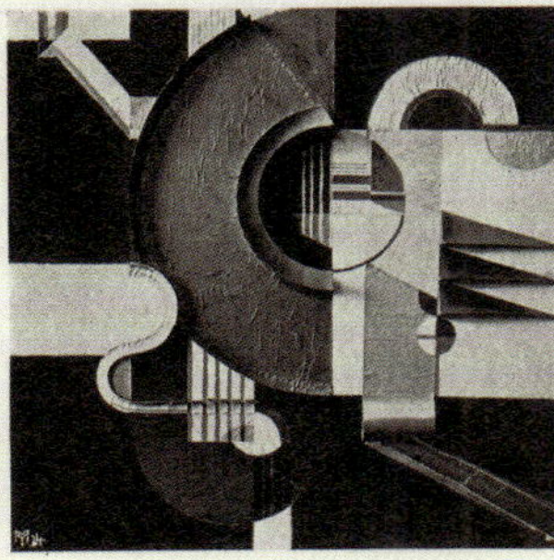

Konstruktion. Marie Ullmann

20

RAUM 3

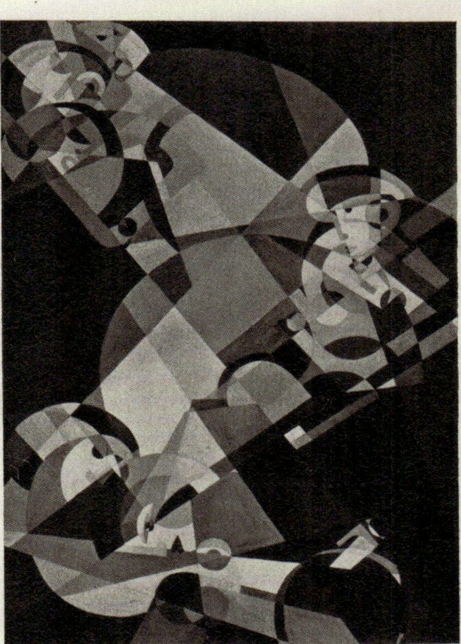

Bau des Bildraumes. Gertrude Tomaschek

21

RAUM 11

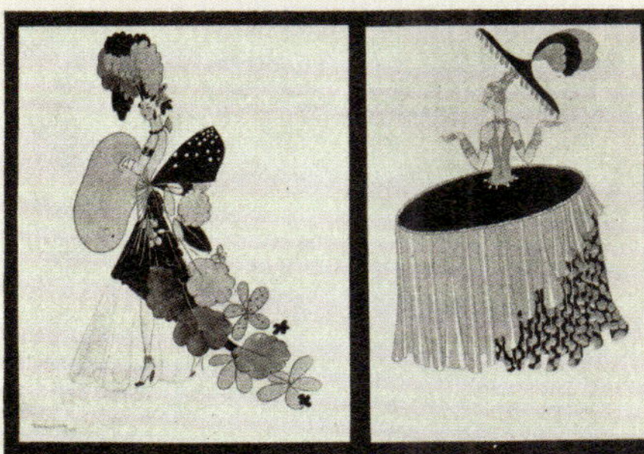

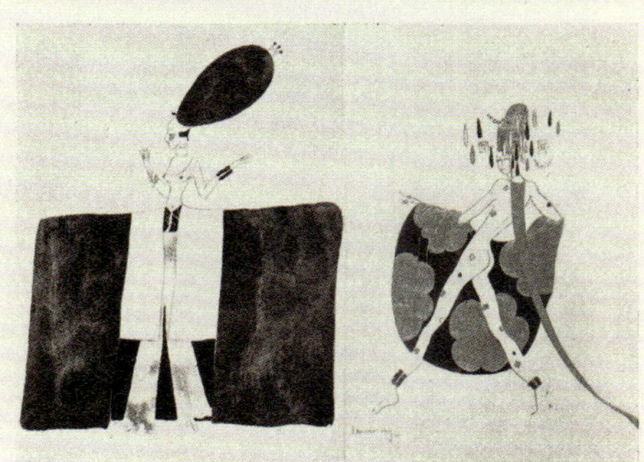

Entwürfe für Revuekostüme. Friedrich Berzeviczy

44

RAUM 12

FACHKLASSE FÜR MALEREI
Professor Wilhelm Müller Hofmann
13 Schüler, davon 5 weiblich

30 Wochenstunden. Auffassung der Fläche als ein rhythmisch zu gliederndes und farbig zu einer Harmonie zusammenzufassendes Ganzes. Arbeitsgebiet sind alle Aufgaben der angewandten Malerei und Graphik.

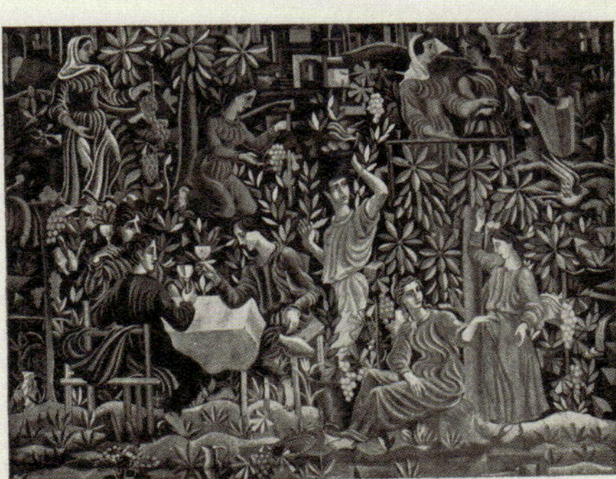

Gobelin-Entwurf. Grete Reinhold und Engelbert Karasek

45

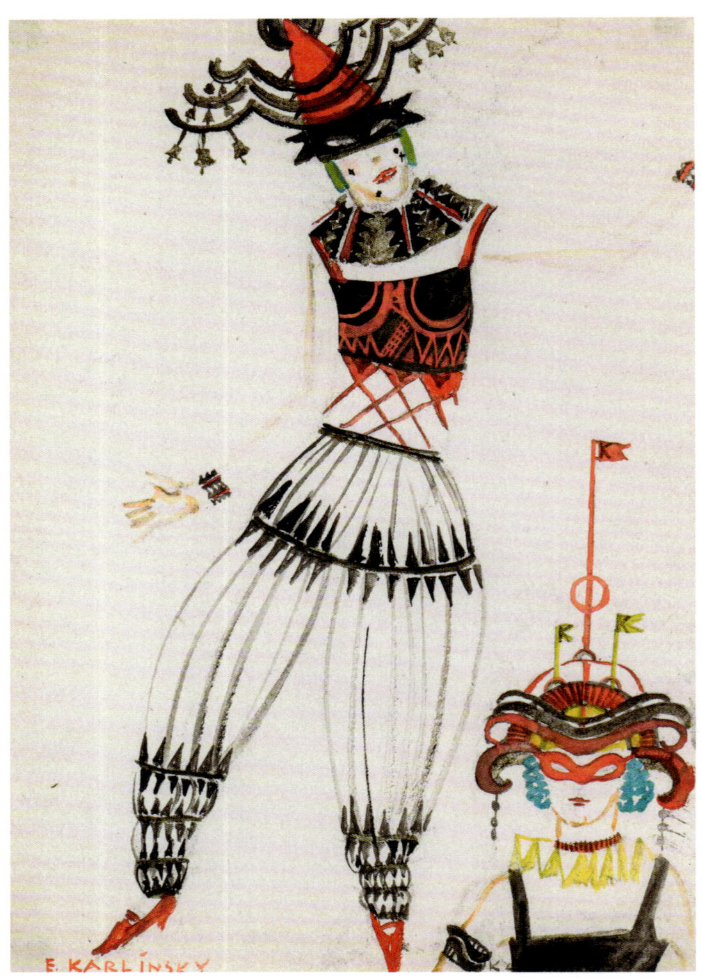

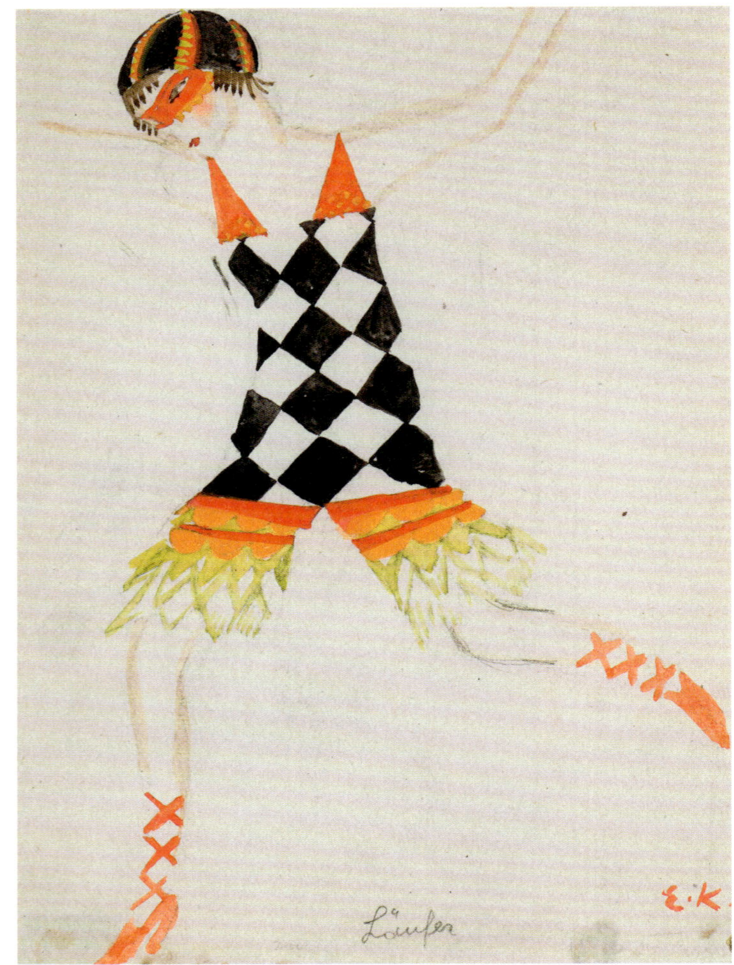

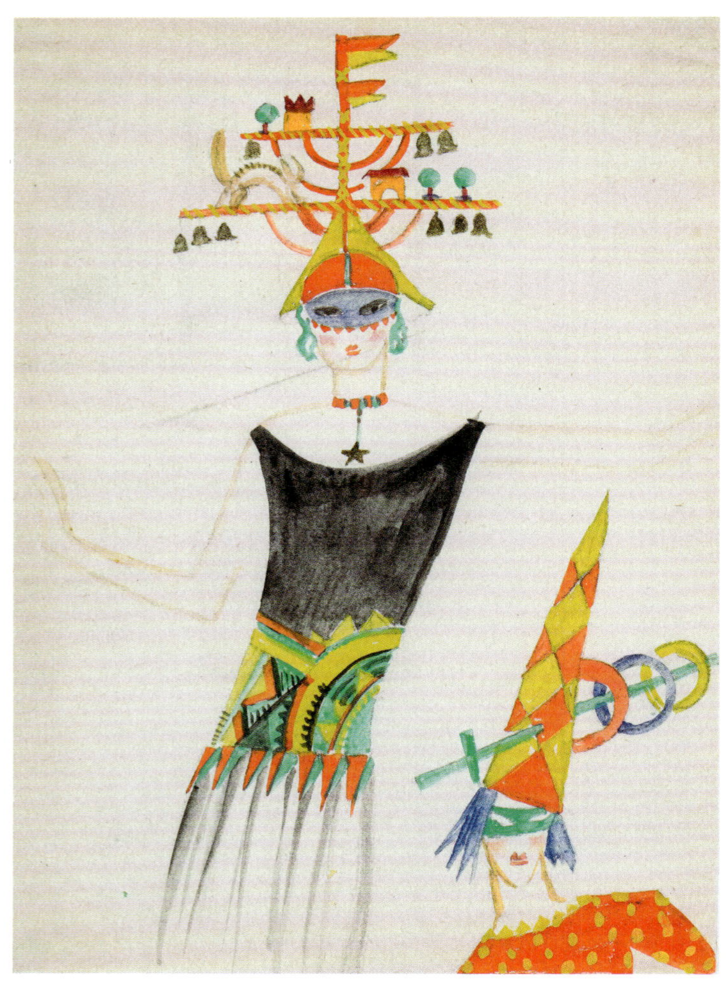

Elisabeth Karlinsky, Kostümentwurf / Costume design, 1923–24
Elisabeth Karlinsky, Kostümentwurf / Costume design *Läufer / Runner*, 1923–24
Elisabeth Karlinsky, Kostümentwurf / Costume design, 1923–24

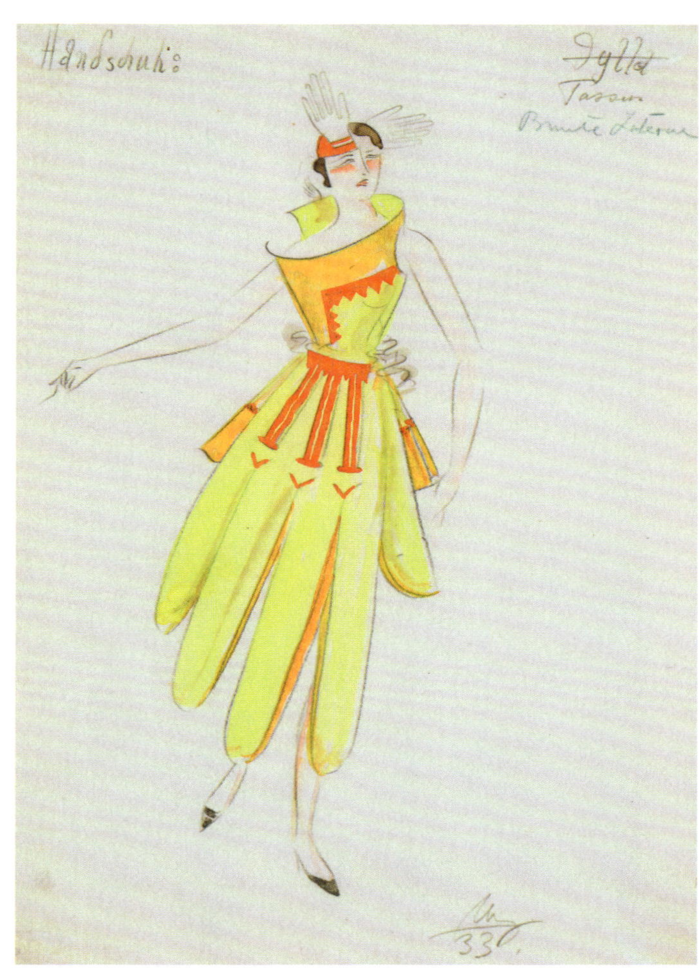

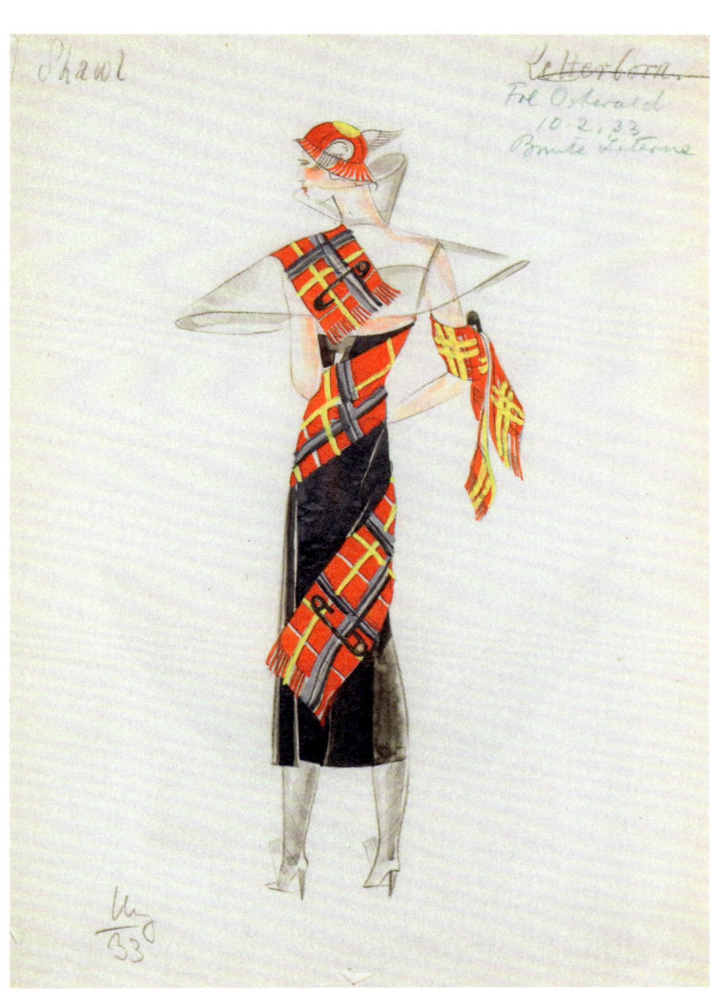

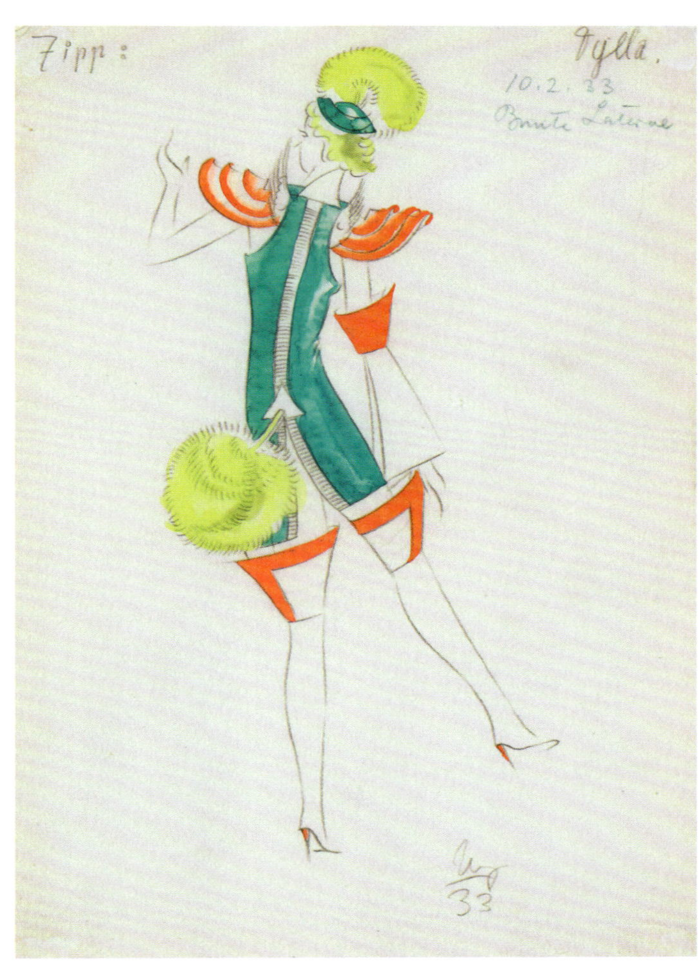

Marianne My Ullmann, Kostümentwurf für / Costume design for the *Bunte Laterne* carnival ball, *Shawl*, 1933
Marianne My Ullmann, Kostümentwurf für einen Handschuh / Costume design for a glove, 1933
Marianne My Ullmann, Kostümentwurf / Costume design *Zipp*, 1933

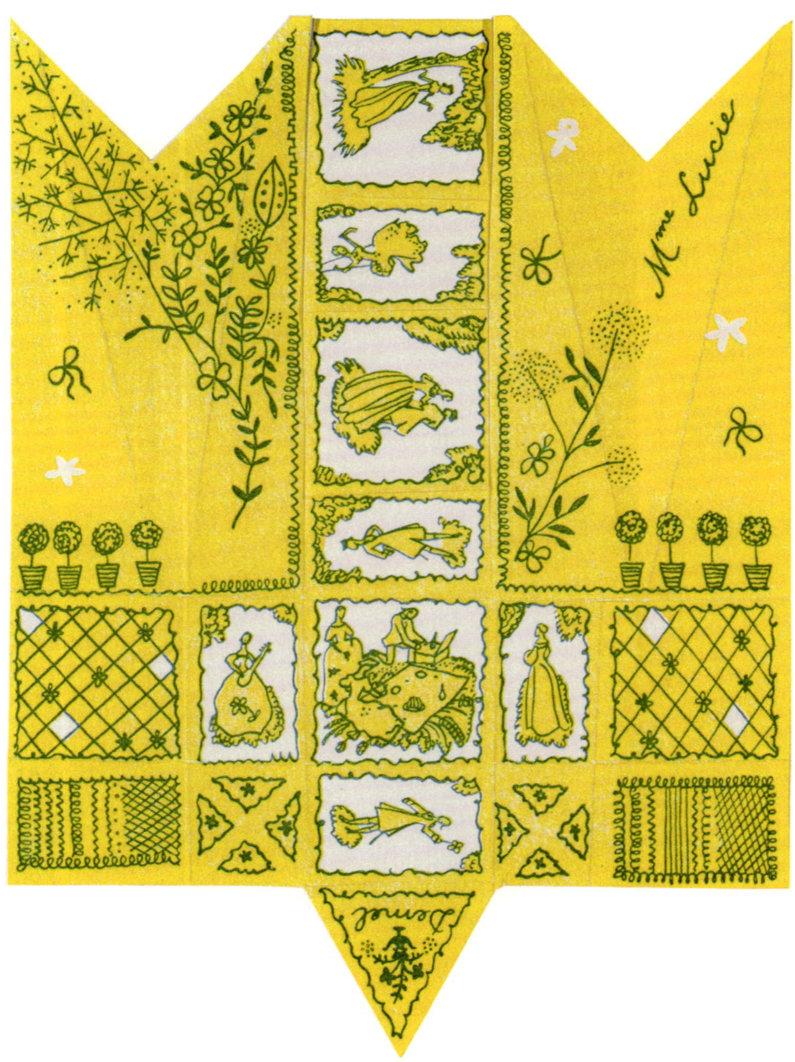

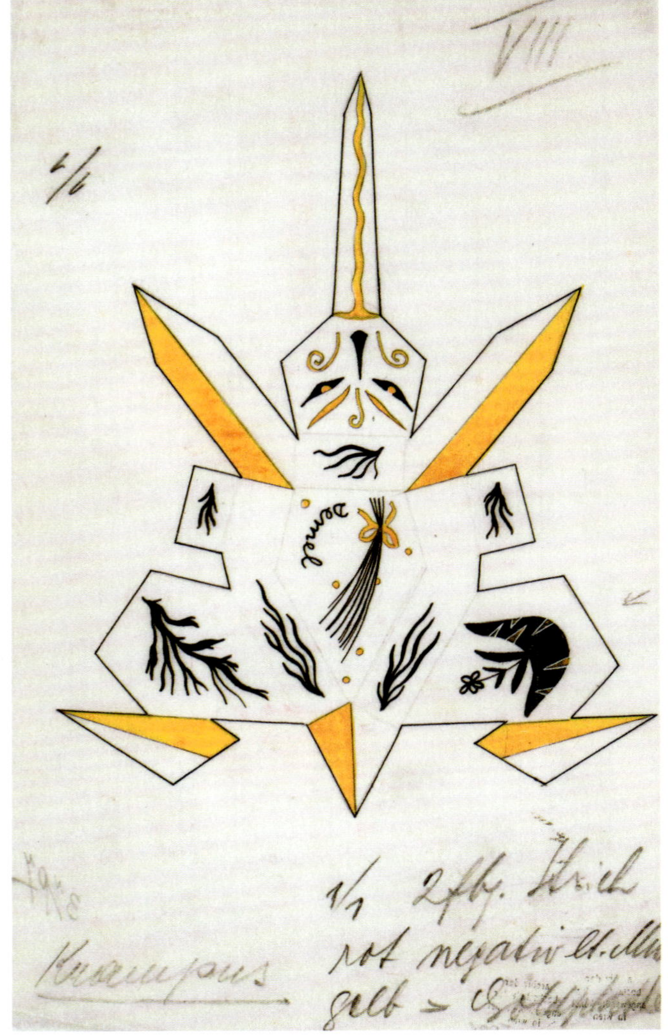

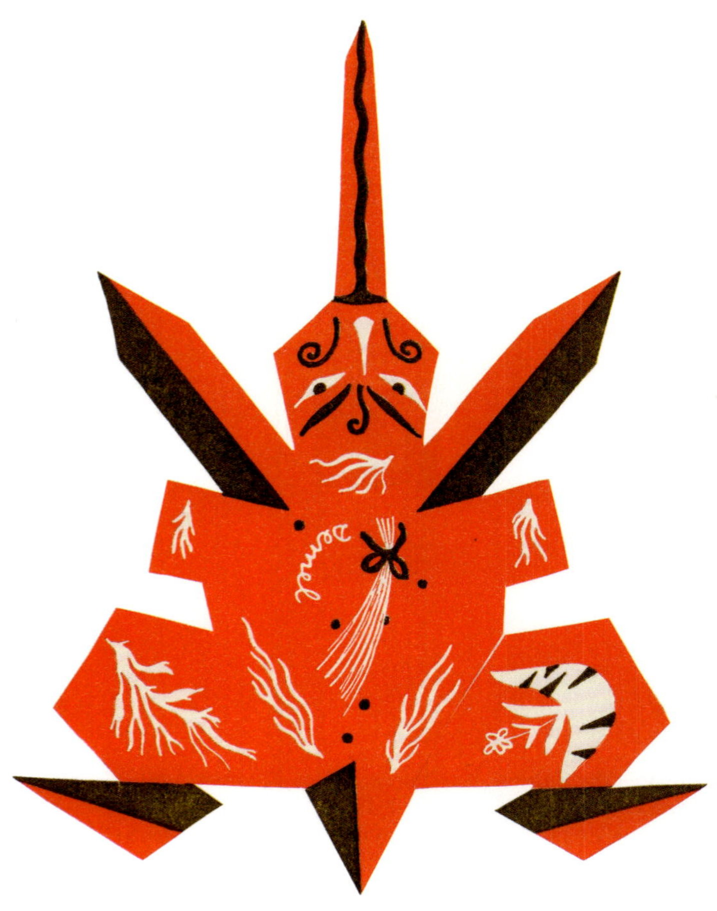

Entwürfe für Demel-Verpackungspapiere /
Packaging designs for Demel, 1932–38

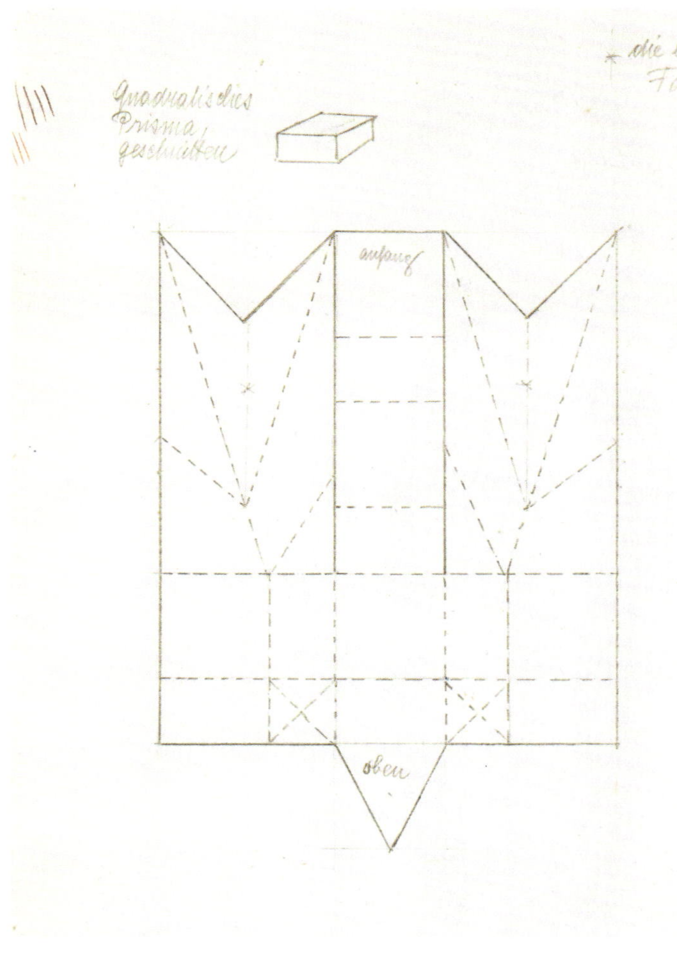
die letzte Falte
anfang
oben

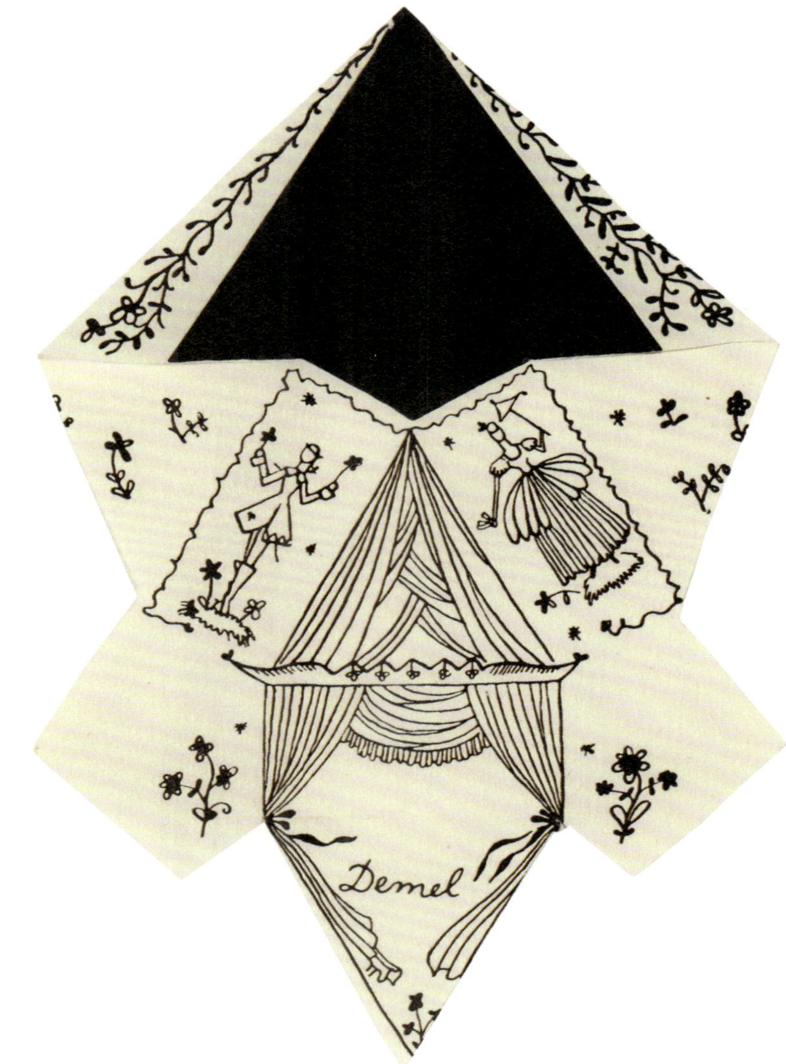
Demel

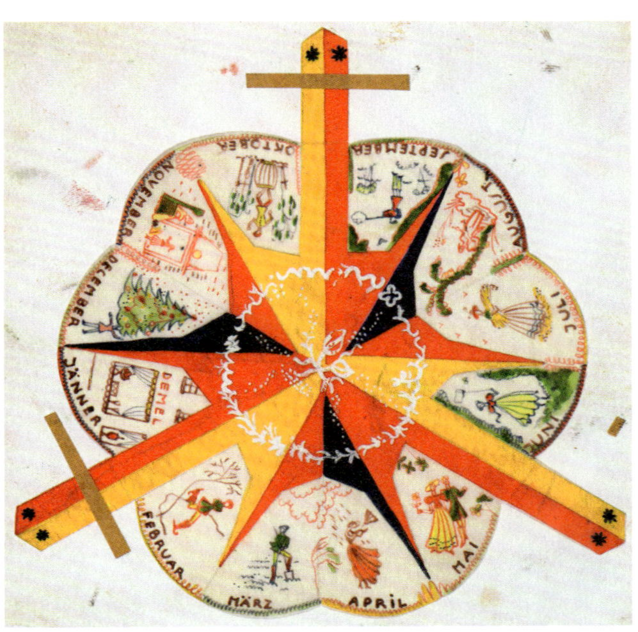
OKTOBER
JULI
DEMEL
MAI
APRIL
MÄRZ

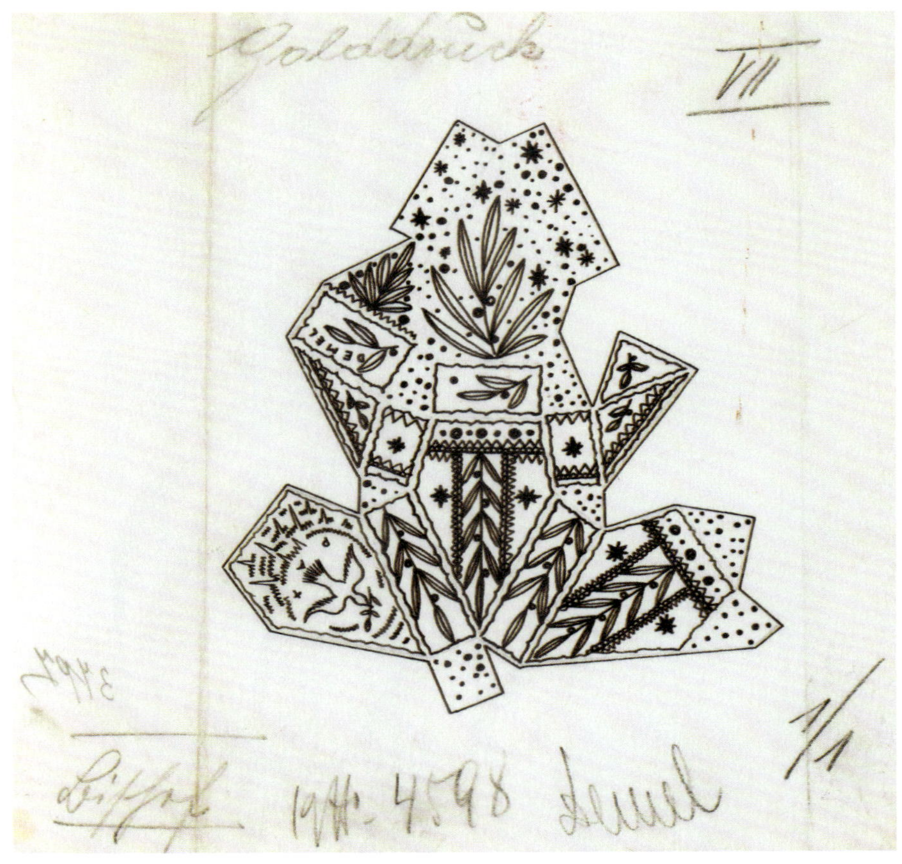
Golddruck
VII
DEMEL
1/1
4598
Demel

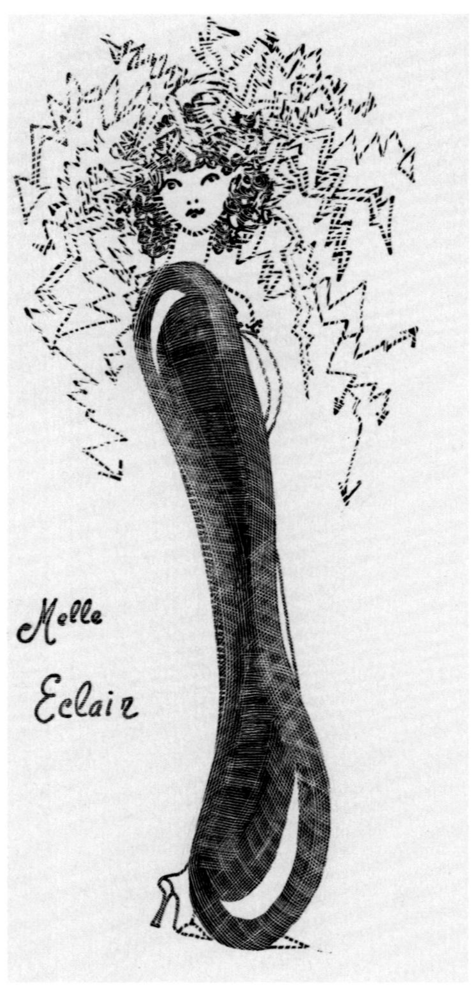
Melle
Eclair

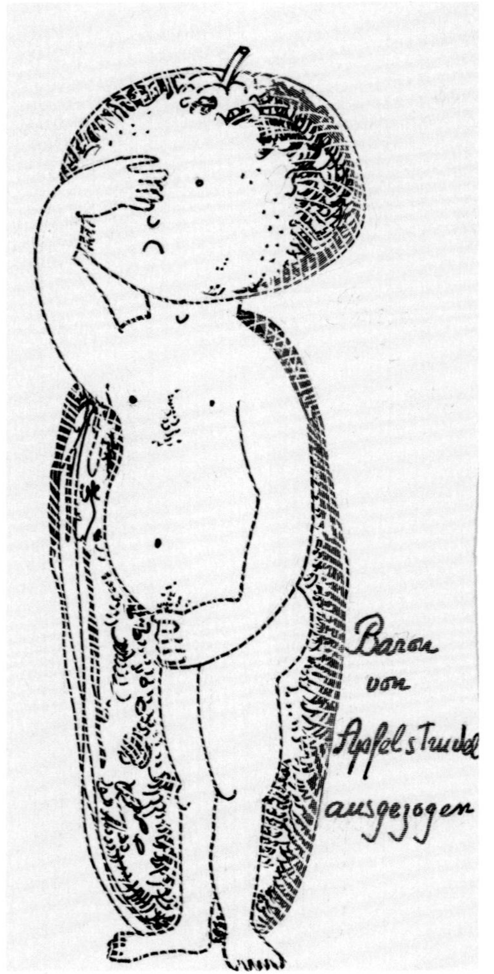
Baron
von
Apfelstrudel
ausgezogen

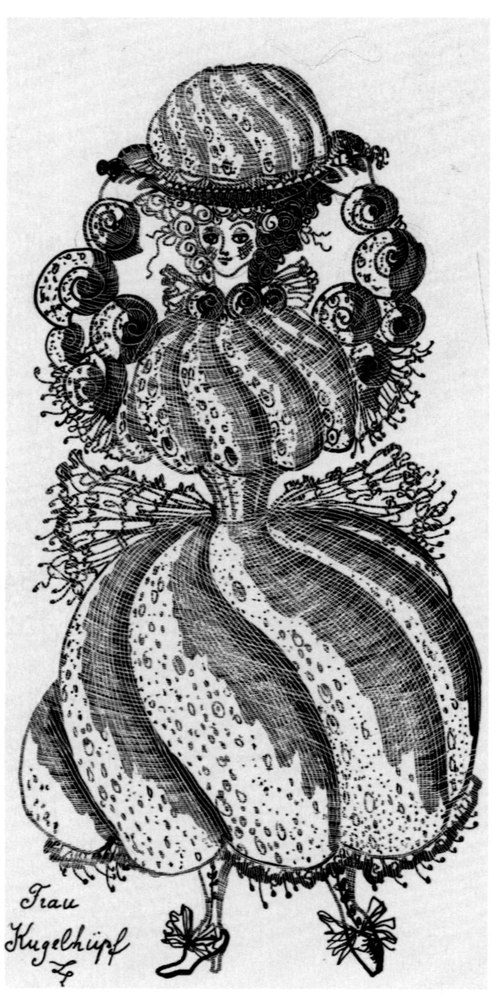
Frau
Kugelhüpf

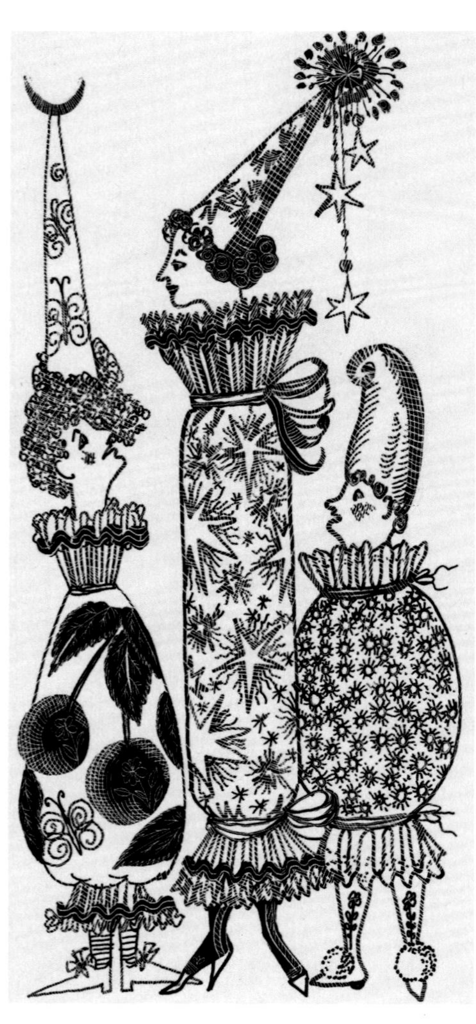

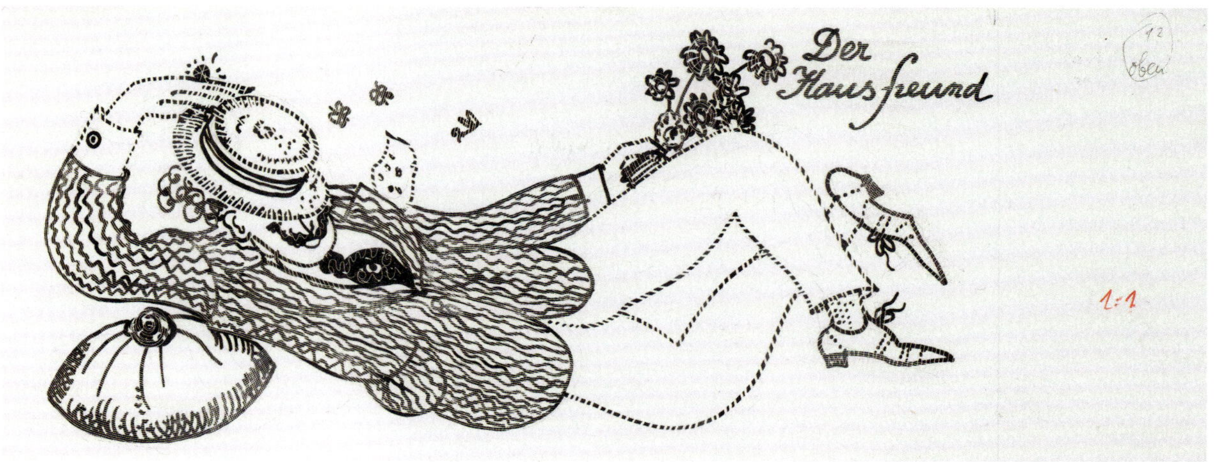

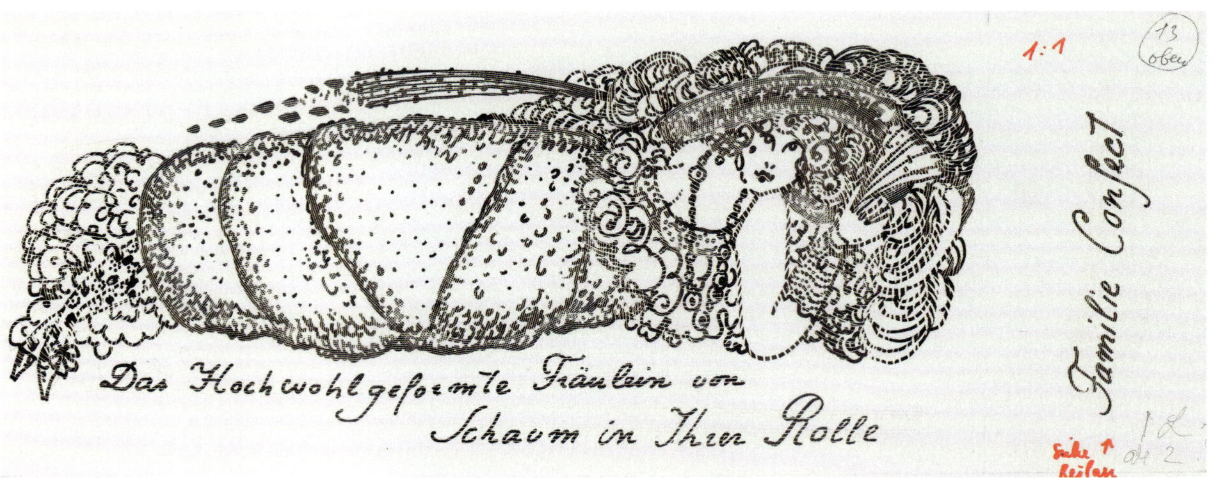

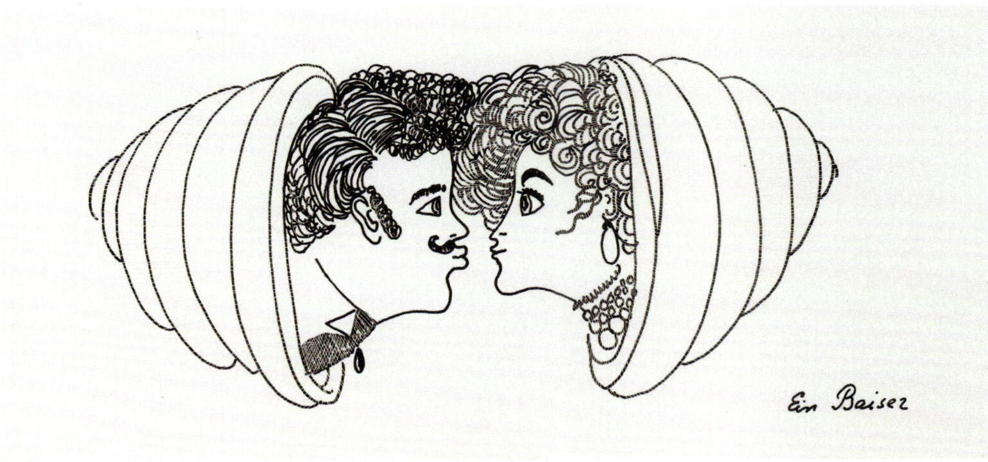

Originalentwürfe für die Publikation / Original designs for the publication
Die K. u. K. Hofzuckerbäckerei Demel. Ein Wiener Märchen / The Imperial and Royal Confectioners Demel: A Viennese Fairytale, 1975

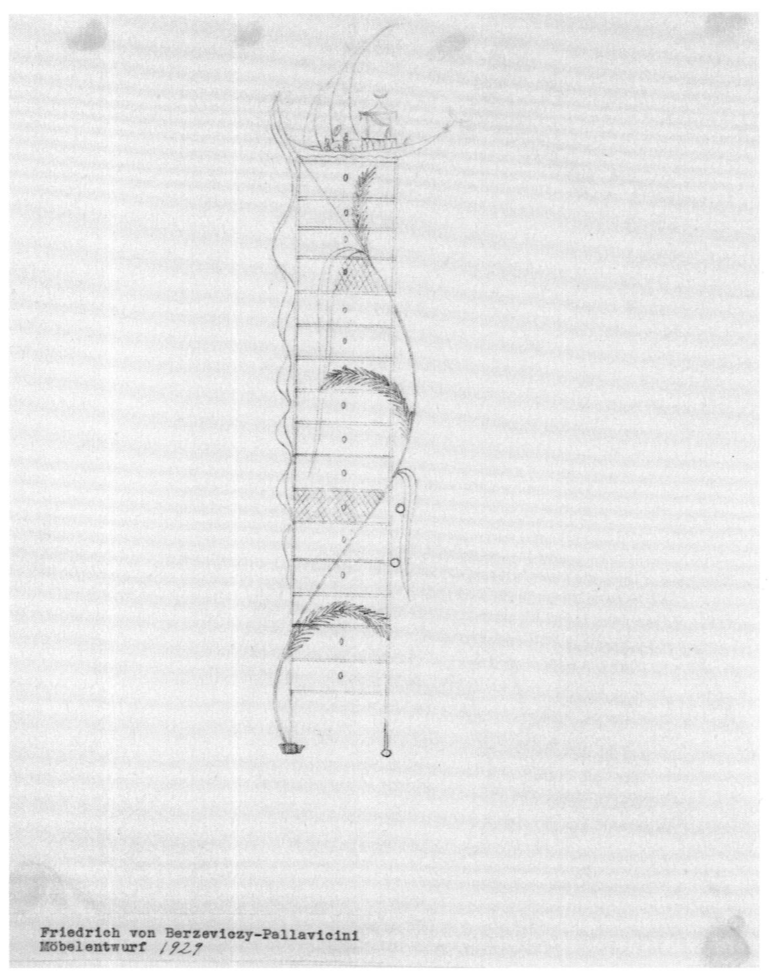

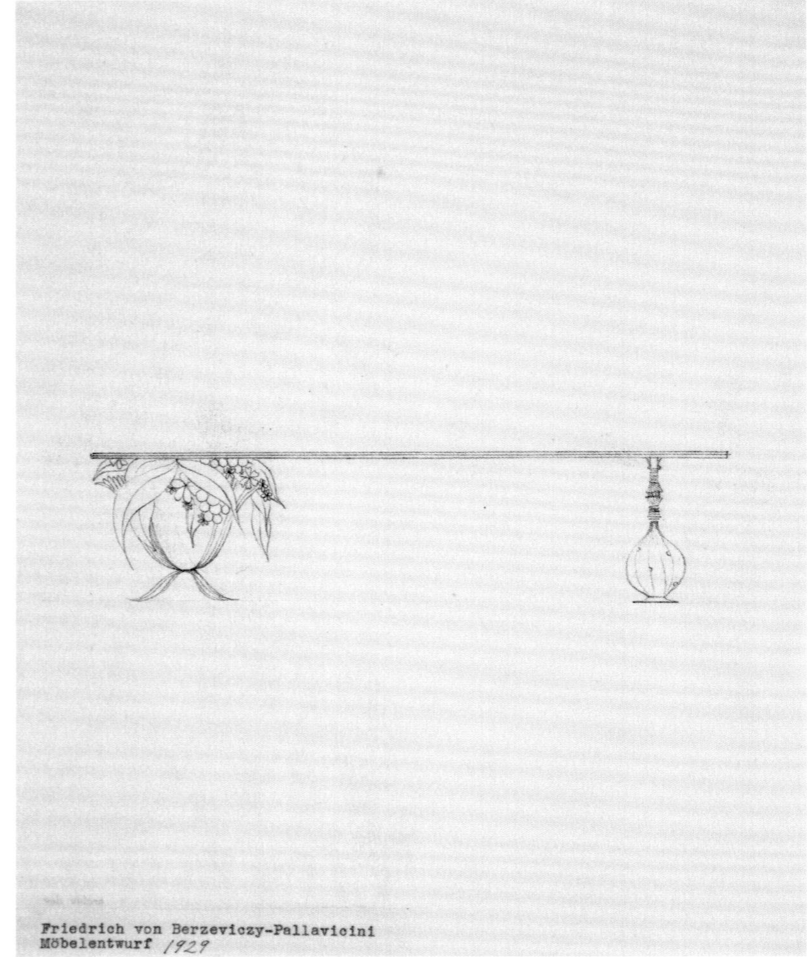

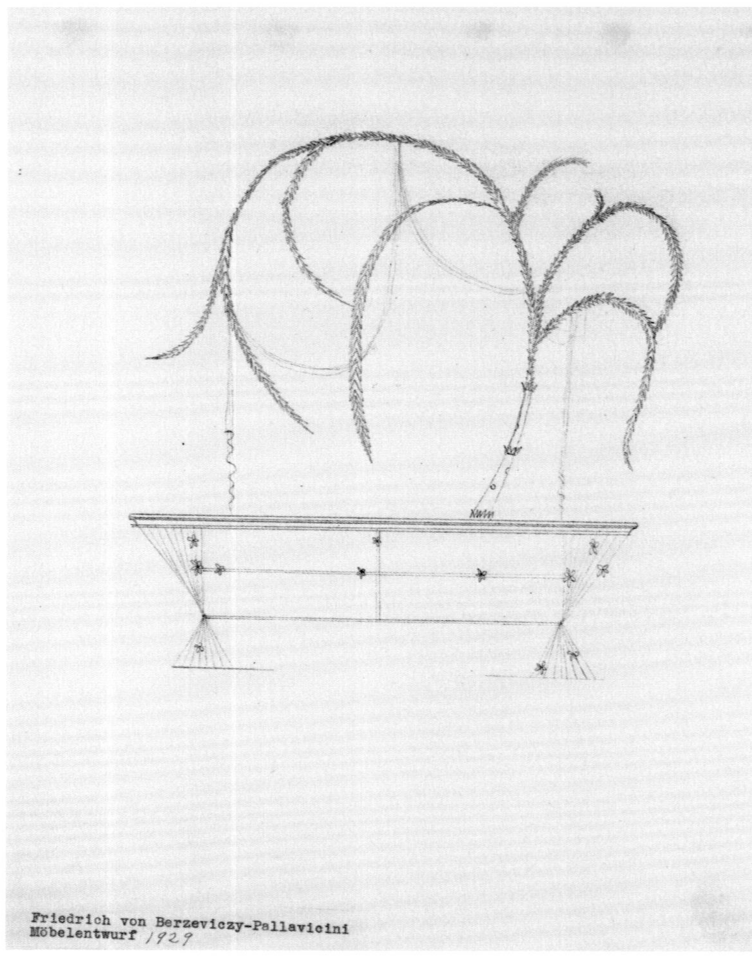

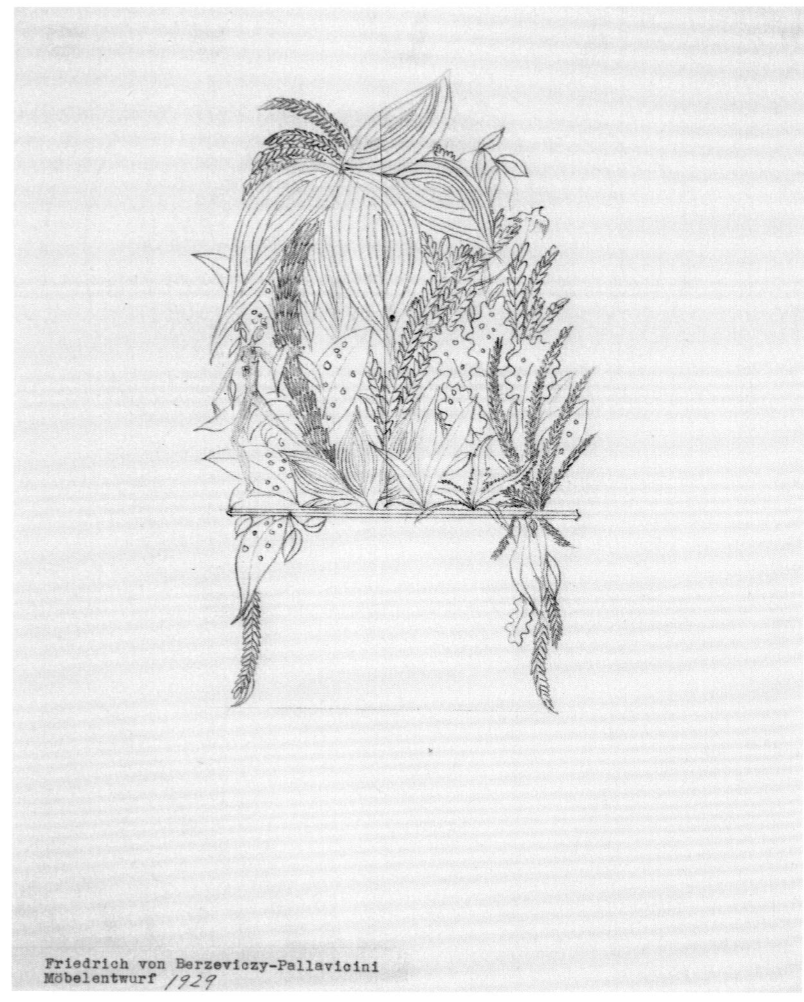

Entwürfe für Möbel / Furniture designs, 1929

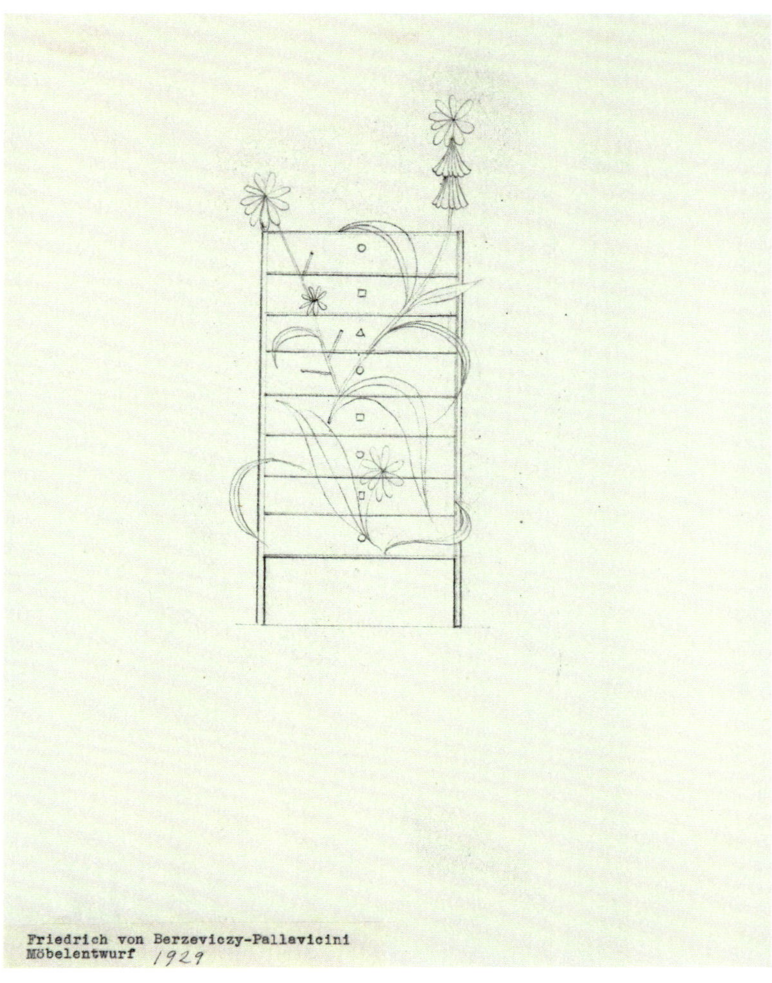
Friedrich von Berzeviczy-Pallavicini
Möbelentwurf 1929

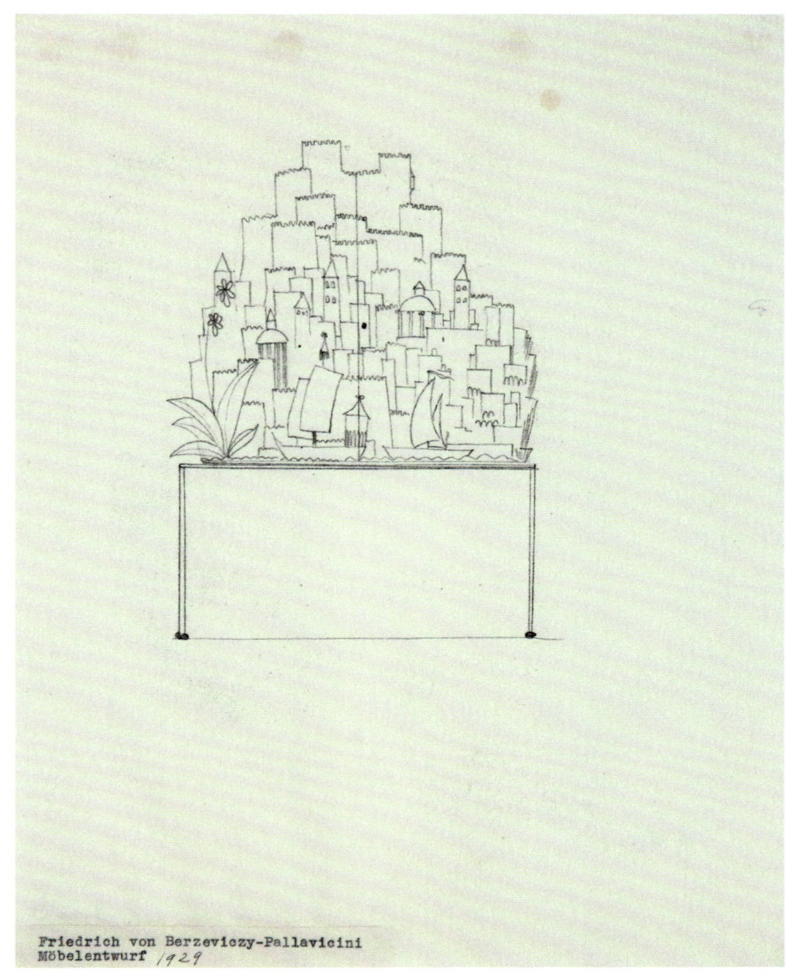
Friedrich von Berzeviczy-Pallavicini
Möbelentwurf 1929

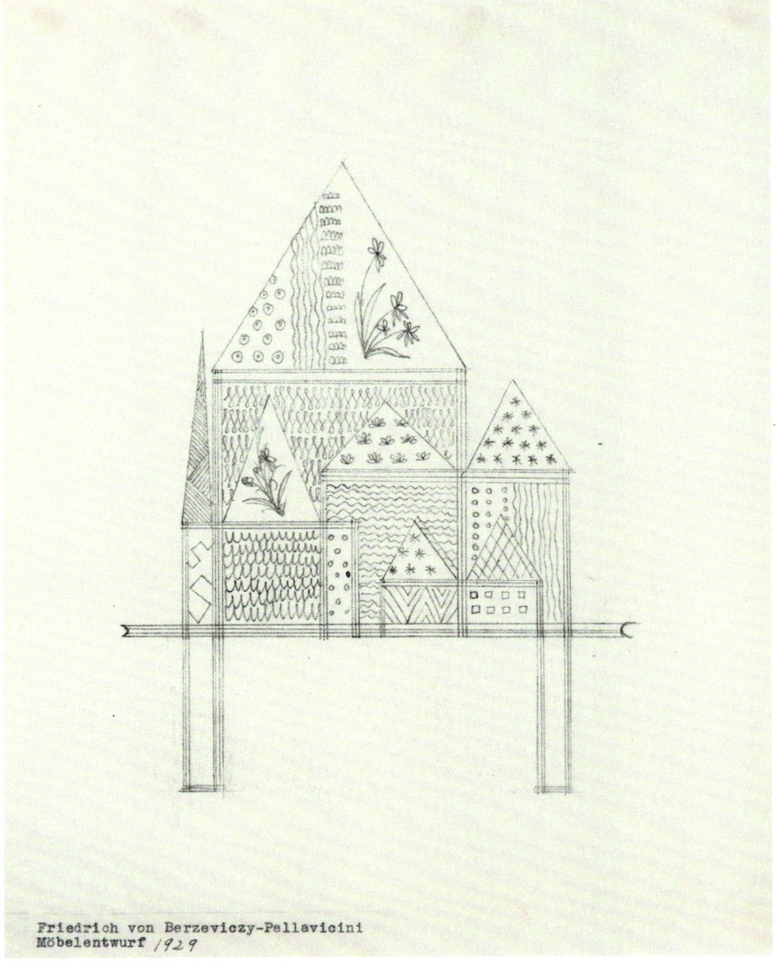
Friedrich von Berzeviczy-Pallavicini
Möbelentwurf 1929

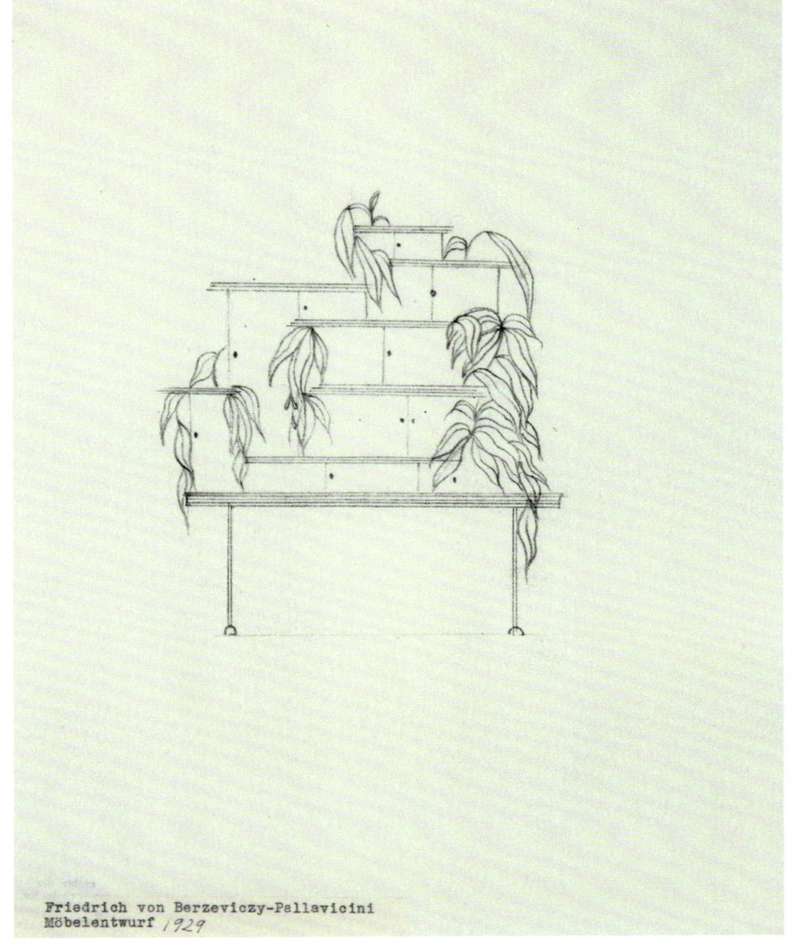
Friedrich von Berzeviczy-Pallavicini
Möbelentwurf 1929

Künstler*innen der Ausstellungen / Artists at the Exhibitions

Kamilla Bischof und / and Laura Welker
Amy Lien und / and Enzo Camacho mit / with Ilya Lipkin
Verena Dengler
Julian Göthe
Lucy McKenzie
Ulrike Müller
Katharina Wulff
Amelie von Wulffen und / and Nico Ihlein
Min Yoon

Auf einem Kissen ist eine sitzende Frau dargestellt, auf die man sich setzen kann. Der Stuhl, vielleicht ein Toilettenstuhl, hat anstelle eines Auffangbehältnisses unter dem Sitz zwei umgedrehte Weingläser. Die dazugehörige Champagnerflasche befindet sich unter einem zweiten Stuhl. Die sitzende Frau hat außerdem eine grüne Schlange zwischen den Beinen. Vielleicht frisst die Schlange auch ein Bein und bildet zugleich einen Stiefel für die Dame und an anderer Stelle ein Kissen. Das ist nicht so genau auseinanderzuhalten. Wie in vielen Arbeiten von Kamilla Bischof gibt es ein stetiges Zirkulieren, Umdeuten und Changieren zwischen Figur und Grund, von einer Form und einer Funktion in eine andere. Der Kreis schließt sich jedoch nie. In diesem Fall, weil die Figur keinen Sekt trinkt, die Gläser nichts auffangen und man sich wahrscheinlich nicht auf das Kissen setzen würde, weil man, trotz aller Abgeklärtheit, das Dargestellte doch für wahr nimmt und sich nicht auf das Gesicht einer Frau setzen würde, nicht im Museum, und schon gar nicht auf eine Schlange. Die Hemmschwelle, ein Bild zu betreten, wird niedriger, wenn es sich um das Bild einer Katze auf einem Teppich handelt, der wie eine Jagdtrophäe ausgeschnitten ist. Die Künstlerin macht die Betrachter*innen zu Kompliz*innen, indem sie sie in diesem Spiel von Auf- und Abwertung mitentscheiden lässt.

Man könnte meinen, ihre Arbeiten seien raumgreifend, weil sich ihre Malerei auf allen möglichen Oberflächen und an unüblichen Stellen wiederfindet, an der Decke, am Boden, auf Möbeln. Doch dieser erste Eindruck trügt. Tatsächlich erzeugen ihre kulissenhaften Kompositionen kaum die Illusion räumlicher Tiefe. Bischof imaginiert sich nicht in andere Welten, selbst wenn durch ihre Arbeiten überraschend kreative Energien fließen. Viel zu durchlässig sind ihre Darstellungen für Realitäts- und Gegenwartspartikel. Häufig verwendet sie Material, das sie in ihrer Umgebung findet, Motive wie Objekte, z. B. Möbel oder andere Reste von Sperrmüll. Ihre Produktion erstreckt sich von der Leinwand weg auf Alltagsgegenstände. Trotzdem handelt es sich nicht um ein Gesamtkunstwerk wie etwa bei Vanessa Bell (der Schwester von Virginia Woolf) und ihren Freunden, die ihre Umgebung komplett neu gestalteten und bemalten und einen für ihre Zeit extrem freizügigen, antibürgerlichen Lebensstil pflegten.

In Bischofs Bildern wie in ihren Texten verlaufen die Trennlinien nicht zwischen ihr selbst und der Gesellschaft, sondern zwischen ihr und ihren Figuren, die immer neue Abspaltungen generieren: hochhackige Amazonen, mondäne Ladys, Katzen. In einem dieser Texte liegt eine kapriziöse Künstlerin mit ihrer Intuition in eifersüchtigem Clinch. Bischofs Erfindungen könnten einer trashigen Serie entsprungen sein. Es bleibt immer im Bewusstsein, dass es sich bei ihren eleganten Bildinszenierungen um eine Art Cabaret handelt. Oder um ein Puppenspiel? Mit Laura Welker – mit ihr gemeinsam hat sie auch die oben beschriebenen Stühle gemacht – hat sie eine Puppenstube mit gebastelten Mädchenträumen ausgestattet, als Setdesign für den Film *Victoria's Secret Subtenants*, in dem behandschuhte Hände erotische Spiele aufführen, um anschließend Pizza zu backen. Den kreativen Strom ihrer virtuos-lässigen Verschiebungen bezieht Bischof nicht aus der Steckdose, sondern aus der Travestie. Dort wo Lee Lozano an die Stelle des *Ursprungs der Welt* eine Steckdose für einen Toaster platziert, setzt Kamilla Bischof die Filmszene zweier cocktailtrinkender Girls in eine Muschi bzw. Mandorla. *Themenpark* ist der Titel des Bildes. Kamilla Bischof beschwört keine alternativen Lebensentwürfe, nicht nur starke Frauenbilder, sondern viele verschiedene, bisweilen auch altmodische, schräge Vorstellungen von Weiblichkeit. Die besondere Freiheit liegt im freien Flow der Sujets.

A cushion shows a picture of a seated woman, on which you can sit. The chair, a night stool or commode perhaps, contains two upturned wine glasses below the seat in place of a chamber pot. The concomitant champagne bottle stands under a second chair. The seated woman furthermore has a green snake between her legs. Or maybe the snake is devouring one of the woman's legs, while doubling up as a boot and, elsewhere, also as a pillow. It is difficult to make out clearly. As in many of Kamilla Bischof's works, there is a constant circulation, reinterpretation, and oscillation between figure and background, from one form and function to another. But it never comes full circle. In this case, because the figure is not drinking the champagne, the glasses are not collecting anything, and it is unlikely we would actually want to sit on the pillow, because, despite all dispassion, we still see the depiction as real and would not feel comfortable to sit on a woman's face, not in a museum, and certainly not on a snake. The inhibition threshold to step onto an image is lower if it is a picture of a cat painted on a rug cut to the shape of a hunting trophy. The artist turns viewers into her accomplices by giving them a say in this game of evaluation and devaluation.

One might think of her works as spatially expansive because her paintings emerge on various surfaces and in unusual places—on the ceiling, the floor, and on the furniture. But this first impression is deceptive. In fact, her stage-set-like compositions barely create the illusion of spatial depth. Bischof does not imagine herself in alternate universes, even though surprisingly creative energies flow through her works. She allows far too much reality and presence to permeate her depictions. Quite often she uses materials found in her surroundings, in the form of motifs or objects, like furniture or left-over debris from house clearances. Her production reaches away from the canvas to encompass everyday objects. And yet, it is not a gesamtkunstwerk, like the works of Vanessa Bell (Virginia Woolf's sister) and her friends, who completely rearranged and painted their surroundings, and cultivated a highly libertine, anti-bourgeois lifestyle.

In Bischof's paintings and texts, the dividing lines do not run between herself and society, but between herself and her characters, who constantly generate new sub-divisions: high-heeled Amazons, sophisticated ladies, cats. In one of these texts, a capricious artist is embroiled in a jealous clinch with her intuition. Bischof's inventions could have sprung from a trashy TV series. One always remains aware that her elegant pictorial stagings are a kind of cabaret. Or perhaps a puppet show? Together with Laura Welker—with whom she also made the aforementioned chairs—she fitted out a doll's house with a hand-made girl's dream, as a film set for *Victoria's Secret Subtenants*, in which gloved hands perform erotic games before making pizza. The creative juice for Bischof's virtuoso, nonchalant displacements does not come from the power socket, but from travesty. Where Lee Lozano turns Courbet's *Origin of the World* into a toaster socket, Kamilla Bischof places the film scene of two cocktail-drinking girls inside a vagina, i.e., a mandorla. *Theme Park* is the title of the piece. Kamilla Bischof does not conjure up alternative designs for life, and not only powerful female images, but a wide range, including weird and old-fashioned notions of femininity. The extraordinary freedom lies in the free flow of the subjects.

—Anette Freudenberger

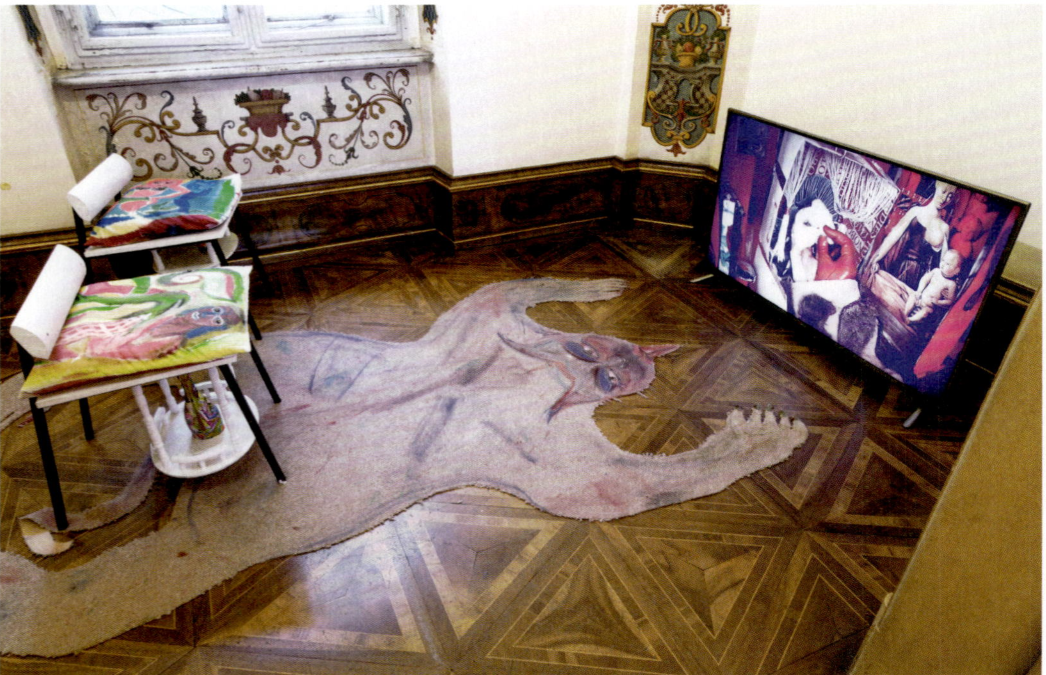

Kamilla Bischof und / and Laura Welker, *Victoria's Secret Subtenants*, 2018

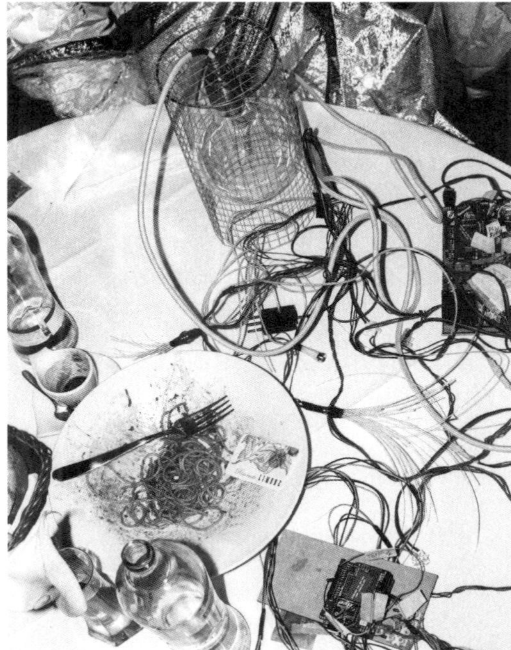

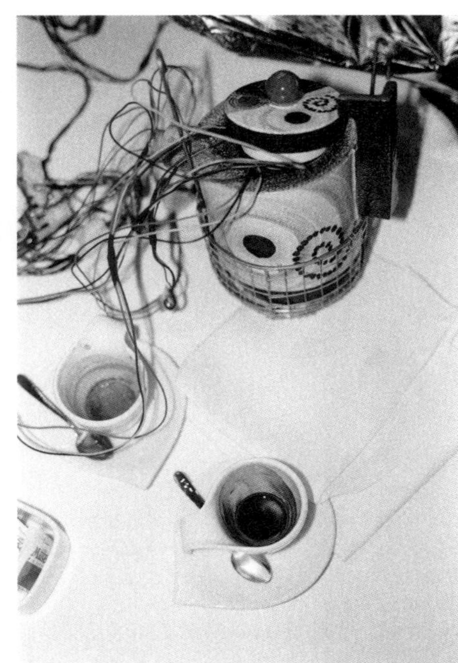

Amy Lien und / and Enzo Camacho mit / with Ilya Lipkin, *Arts & Foods (spaghetti al pomodoro)* und / and *Arts & Foods (due caffè, grazie)*, 2015

Die Arbeiten von Amy Lien, Enzo Camacho und Ilya Lipkin entstanden 2015 im Rahmen der Künstler*innen-Residenz Gluck50 in Mailand. Diese wurde von Mario Nuciforo ins Leben gerufen, selbst Sammler, Koch und aller Wahrscheinlichkeit nach auch Restaurantbesitzer. „Gregarious" ist ein Adjektiv, mit dem die Künstler*innen ihren Gastgeber beschrieben haben. Dieses Wort, im Deutschen etwa mit „gesellig" übersetzt, leitet sich ab von „gregär", wiederum ein naturkundlicher Begriff für Arten, die – je nachdem ob es sich um Flora oder Fauna handelt – in Büscheln zusammenwachsen oder sich herdenartig organisieren. Der grundlegende Aufbau der Serie *Arts & Foods* in Form eines üppig gedeckten Tischs ist auch als Hommage an Nuciforo zu verstehen.

Lien und Camacho nutzten ihren Aufenthalt in Mailand, um in den Räumen vor Ort eine Ausstellung zu realisieren, zu der verschiedene Künstler*innen eingeladen wurden. Im Anschluss daran erschien ein Katalog, der nicht nur die Residenz und die Zusammenarbeit an besagter Ausstellung, sondern auch die Mailänder Kunst- und Galerienszene dokumentierte und reflektierte. Die Serie *Arts & Foods*, die von Ilya Lipkin fotografiert und mitkonzipiert wurde und deren Aufnahmen hier als umfangreiche Barytedition vorliegen, taucht ebenfalls im Katalog auf.

Die Form der künstlerischen Forschung, von der dieses Projekt im weitesten Sinne informiert wird, lässt sich als Mikrostruktur auf die Bildstrecke übertragen. Längst jenseits einer Selbstverständlichkeit in der ästhetischen „Oberflächenbehandlung" des eigenen Milieus verortet, in der beispielsweise Berzeviczy-Pallavicinis Entwürfe und Arbeiten noch nahtlos aufgingen, wird hier nach Bildern gesucht, welche die formal und inhaltlich möglichst zahlreichen losen Fäden der Narration gleichzeitig in der Mitte zusammen- und an den Rändern offenhalten können. Das sind mitunter ganz buchstäblich Kabel, die die einzelnen Elemente der von Camacho und Lien handgefertigten *cyber ceramics* verbinden und dabei diverse Inputsignale in als Lichtmuster codierten Output umwandeln, oder auch Spaghetti. Zusammen mit dem abgebildeten Interieur der Arbeitsräume, in denen Ettore Sottsass Reproduktion in Kombination mit einem barocken Sessel die solide Eleganz gehobener Flohmarkt-Postmoderne vorführt, bieten die Fotografien tatsächlich einen reichgedeckten Tisch generischer Repräsentation einer globalen Boheme. Dass das Ganze in Italien stattfindet, wird erkennbar höchstens daran, dass die Zitronen noch Stiele und Blätter haben und die barocke Üppigkeit und Auswahl der ausgestellten Fische einen kurzen Weg zum Mittelmeer vermuten lassen.

Jede vermeintlich zufällig zusammengefügte Konstellation von Gegenständen verwandelt sich unter diesem Blick in eine zeitgenössische Installation, deren Indexikalität jedoch ohne Gewähr ist. Die ästhetischen Funktionen der einzelnen Objekte und die ökonomischen Funktionen der Protagonisten, ihre persönlichen Eigenarten lassen sich weder einfach zuordnen noch als Einheit beschreiben. Es ist schon lange nicht mehr klar, welchen sozialen Raum man eigentlich gestaltet, wird die Kommunikation und Erzählung weiter fortgeführt. Alles vermittelt hier Information über Vernetzung. Diese fragile Disposition teilen die Betrachtenden mit den Produzent*innen, die als Akteur*innen ebenfalls im Bild anwesend sind.

The works by Enzo Camacho, Amy Lien, and Ilya Lipkin originated during the Gluck50 artist residency in Milan in 2015. The residency was founded by Mario Nuciforo, who was a collector, cook, and—most probably—restaurant owner, too. "Gregarious" is the word the artists used to describe their host. In zoology, the term refers to species of flora or fauna that grow together in clusters or organize themselves in herds. The core concept of the *Arts & Foods* series, expressed in the form of a sumptuously laid table, is simultaneously a tribute to Nuciforo himself.

Lien and Camacho used their time in Milan to create an exhibition on site, inviting various artists to participate. This culminated in a catalogue documenting the residency and collaborative exhibition, as well as reflecting on the Milan art and gallery scene. The catalogue also featured the *Arts & Foods* series, which was co-created and photographed by Ilya Lipkin and produced as a comprehensive Baryta edition.

The photo series is structured as a microcosm of the artistic research underpinning this project in the broadest sense. Always located, beyond question, in the aesthetic "surface treatment" of one's own milieu—in which, for example, Berzeviczy-Pallavicini's designs and works still merged seamlessly—the artists here are searching for images that can hold the many formal and narrative threads, simultaneously keeping them together in the center and open around the edges. And sometimes even literally: with cables that connect the individual elements of Camacho and Lien's handmade *cyber ceramics*, converting various input signals into output coded as light patterns—or simply a tangled mess of spaghetti.

With interior shots of the studios, in which an Ettore Sottsass reproduction combined with a baroque armchair demonstrates the sound elegance of sophisticated flea-market Postmodernism, the photographs offer a rich feast of generic representation of a global bohemia. The fact that the whole thing is set in Italy can only be ascertained by details such as the lemons, which still have leaves and stems attached, while the baroque opulence and choice of the fish platters also suggests a proximity to the Mediterranean.

From this viewpoint, every supposedly incidental constellation of objects is transformed into a contemporary installation, whose indexicality, however, is without guarantee. The aesthetic functions of the individual objects and the economic functions of the protagonists, their personal idiosyncrasies, can neither be easily assigned nor described as a unit.

And even though it has long since become unclear which social space is actually being designed, the communication and narrative continues, everything conveys information about interconnectedness. The viewers share this fragile disposition with the work's producers, who are also present in the pictures as protagonists.

—Inka Meißner

Verena Dengler ist in letzter Zeit zu einer Art Chronistin der österreichischen politischen Verhältnisse geworden, die deutschsprachige Kunst- und Tageszeitungen immer wieder gerne nach ihrer Sicht auf die aktuelle Lage fragen. Auch die hier gezeigten Arbeiten sind direkt aus politischen, ökonomischen und ästhetischen Realitäten geschöpft, die ihr die Stadt Wien, in der sie lebt, sowie Österreich insgesamt bieten.

Ihre Verbindung zu Friedrich von Berzeviczy-Pallavicini ist damit eine doppelte: Nicht nur gestaltet sie, wie er es tat, direkt an einer auch über Wien hinausreichenden Öffentlichkeit mit (ob auf Facebook oder in der *FAZ*), sie positioniert sich zudem mit ihrer schon länger andauernden Beschäftigung mit Dekor und „Radical Chic" selbst in der Nähe von Gestalter*innen und Künstler*innen, die Künstler*innenmythen und letztlich auch die Unterscheidung von Skill und Genie bearbeiten.

Gmundner Keramik, Paravents für den Fantastischen Sozialismus aus dem Jahr 2013 zitieren in der Form der Inneneinrichtung mit Handwerksdekor und im Titel ein klassisches Vorhaben linker Bewegungen des frühen 20. Jahrhunderts, nämlich die Kunst in der Gestaltung des Alltags aufzulösen. Ein Selbstporträt auf der Innenseite spielt auf die augenscheinliche Ablehnung eines Förderansuchens an, so als hätte ihr das damals bmukk genannte Ministerium eine Absage wegen einer allzu großen Nähe zur Kommerzialität erteilt. Ob Dengler tatsächlich Keramik herstellen wollte, und dies möglichst finanziell unterstützt durch das Kulturförderungsprogramm des Landes Österreich, sei hier egal (dessen Förderungskatalog umfasst schließlich auch Programme für Designer*innen, Start-ups und Galerien). Wichtig ist, dass Dengler damit die Grenze markiert, an der Verkäuflichkeit scheinbar zum Gegenteil von Kunst wird. Die einfarbigen Schlingen auf den Paravents sind inspiriert von eben jener Gmundner Keramik, die mittels Fototapete mit dem für die Stadt und ihre Manufakturen typischen Muster auf Spanplatten übertragen wurde.

Die zweite Arbeit greift Keramik und Dekor in einer ironischen Wendung wieder auf, in einem wohl ubiquitären Keramikmuster der 1990er-Jahre (ich erinnere mich deutlich an Schalen im Haus meiner Eltern, andere Besucher*innen, mit denen ich darüber sprach, ebenso). Die kleine Assemblage *Lech mich am Arlberg* (2011) weitet zudem das Österreich-Spektrum aus. Eine Hand reckt sich aus dem Blumentopf mit blauem Rand und mehrfarbigem, fast abstraktem Landschaftsmotiv. Sie ist umwickelt mit einem Fundstück selbstironischen Merchandisings des Urlaubsortes, einem Schnürsenkel, in den der titelgebende Spruch gewebt ist; vielleicht eine Referenz an die ästhetischen Prägungen, ein Nutzen und Umnutzen des Alltäglichen, um es zu einer dramatischen kleinen Szene zusammenzubringen, eine wie spontan wirkende Anmerkung zu den kaufbaren und massenproduzierten Dingen und dazu, was man mit ihnen tun kann, um wieder in und mit ihnen leben zu können.

Verena Dengler has recently become something of a chronicler of the Austrian political situation. It is to her that German-language arts and news publications turn for opinions on the current state of affairs. The works presented here, too, are drawn directly from political, socio-economic, and aesthetic realities offered to her by the city of Vienna, where she lives, and Austria as a whole.

Her connection to Friedrich Berzeviczy-Pallavicini is thus twofold: she operates, as he did, in a public realm that extends beyond Vienna (whether on Facebook or in the *Frankfurter Allgemeine Zeitung*) and, secondly, through her long-standing preoccupation with décor and "radical chic" she also places herself in proximity to artists and designers who engage with the myth of the artist and, ultimately, also with the distinction between skill and genius.

With handicraft-decorated furnishings as well as through its title, her 2013 work *Gmundner Keramik Paravents für den Fantastischen Sozialismus (Gmunden Ceramics Paravents for Fantastic Socialism)* invokes a classic objective of early-twentieth-century leftist movements, namely to dissolve the arts within everyday design. A self-portrait on the inside alludes to the apparent rejection of an application for funding, as if the Austrian arts ministry, then called the bmukk, had rejected it because it was too close to commercialism.

Whether Dengler really wished to produce ceramics, and do so with the financial support of the Austrian arts and culture funding body (whose funding program also includes support for designers, start-ups, and galleries) is irrelevant. The point is that she highlights the threshold at which salability apparently becomes antithetical to art. The monochromatic loops on the folding screens are inspired by original Gmunden ceramics, with patterns in the manufacturer's characteristic style printed on photographic wallpaper and pasted onto chipboard.

The second work also picks up on ceramics and décor, but adds an ironic twist, using what was apparently a ubiquitous ceramic pattern in the 1990s (I have clear memories of bowls at my parents' house, as do other exhibition visitors I spoke to). The small assemblage *Lech mich am Arlberg* (2011) also expands on the Austrian theme. A hand stretches out of a flowerpot with a blue rim and a colorful, almost abstract landscape motif.

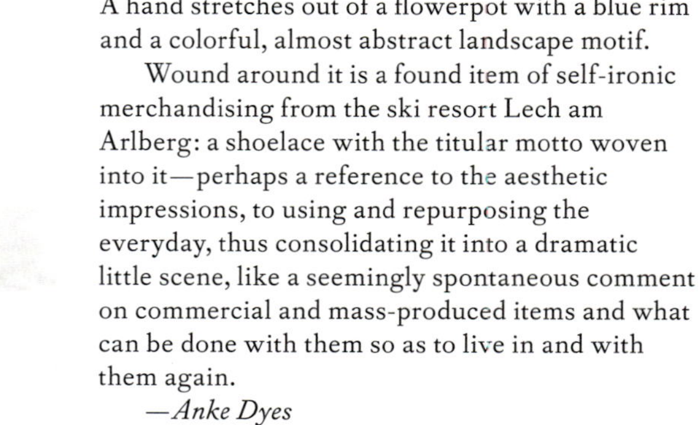

Wound around it is a found item of self-ironic merchandising from the ski resort Lech am Arlberg: a shoelace with the titular motto woven into it—perhaps a reference to the aesthetic impressions, to using and repurposing the everyday, thus consolidating it into a dramatic little scene, like a seemingly spontaneous comment on commercial and mass-produced items and what can be done with them so as to live in and with them again.

—*Anke Dyes*

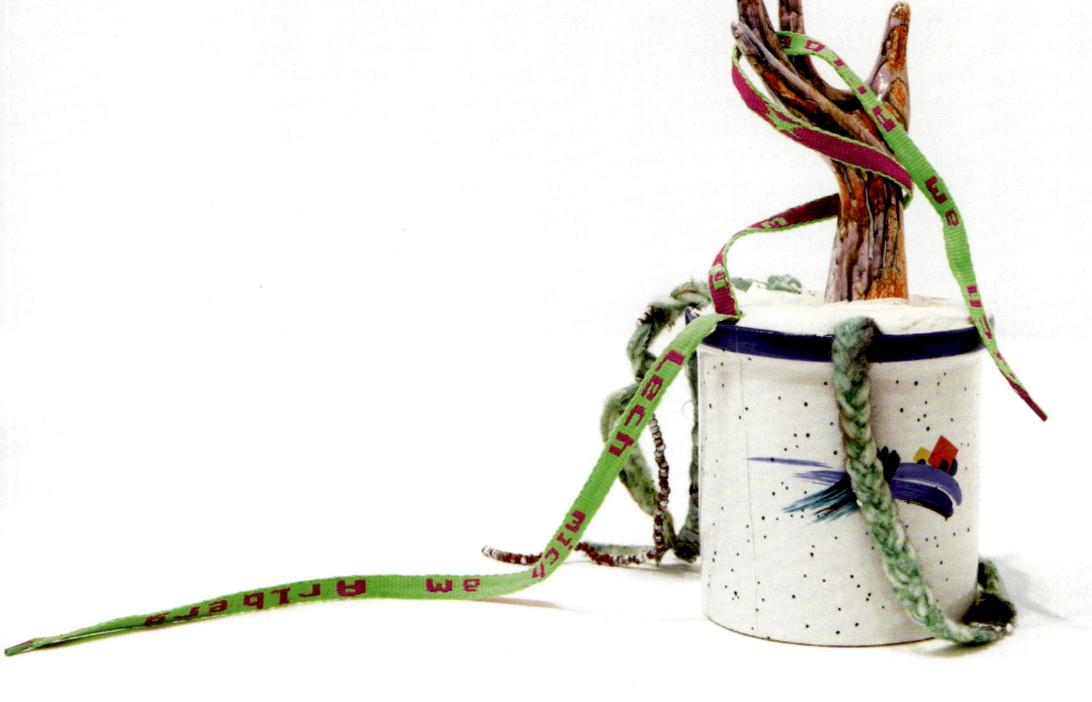

Verena Dengler, *Lech mich am Arlberg / Kiss my Arlberg*, 2011

Lilies that fester smell far worse than weeds[1]

Beim Betreten von Julian Göthes Büro in den Bildhauerateliers der Akademie der bildenden Künste Wien wird man empfangen von einer Gruppe möbelartiger „Persönlichkeiten".[2] Das Ensemble verweist auf den fortwährenden Dialog, den der Künstler mit den ihn zum einen alltäglich umgebenden, zum anderen zufällig entdeckten Gegenständen führt. „At the moment one comes into the presence of something beautiful, it greets you"[3], schreibt Elaine Scarry in ihrem Aufsatz *On Beauty* (1999). Was genau dieses „Schöne" ist, das uns willkommen heißt, ist eine Frage, deren Antwort man durch Göthes monumental-theatralische Skulpturen, detailreiche Zeichnungen und raumgreifende Installationen ein wenig näherkommen kann. Ihre Formensprache speist sich aus Bereichen des Produktdesigns, der Film- und Raumausstattung sowie des Dekors und Ornaments – aus Gebieten also, die bis vor nicht allzu langer Zeit in der Rangordnung der künstlerischen Felder dem der bildenden Kunst untergeordnet waren. Die von einem Objekt ausgehende Anziehung liegt für Göthe dabei vor allem in dessen Charakter, einer ihm eingeschriebenen Besonderheit und nicht in seiner „Schönheit" im Sinne von „Reinheit" oder gutem Geschmack. Das uns Begrüßende ist demnach das unsere Sinne Ansprechende, das, was „sinnlich" ist (und auch chaotisch, dialektisch, unheimlich sein kann). Ebenso stößt man sich an und tritt zugleich in Kontakt zu seinen hybriden Objekten, die zum einen kantig-autoritär wirken und meist makellos glänzende Oberflächen besitzen, zum anderen aber grotesk, humorvoll und etwas hilflos scheinen. Die Erfahrung der „Schönheit" wird hier wie in einer fortwährenden Zellteilung weitergeführt: Sie schwappt aus seinen Arbeiten heraus und in den Besucher*innenraum hinein. In Bezugnahme auf Wittgenstein beschreibt Scarry dieses „Überschwappen von Schönheit" auch mit dem Fokus auf körperliche Bewegungen und Musik: „[…] whenever Augustine touches something smooth, he begins to think of music and of God."[4] Die so unmittelbare Begegnung zwischen Gegenstand und Person wird möglich durch einen veränderten Blick auf die uns umgebenden Objekte als Subjekte. Göthes Arbeiten weigern sich, Teil kanonischer Kunstgeschichte zu werden und weisen auf eine mögliche Zukunft, die sich kategorischen Ordnungssystemen entzieht. Sie bewirken eine Unterbrechung einer linearen (und heteronormativen) Vorstellung von Entwicklung und Reproduktion, gesellschaftlichen Normen sowie Hierarchien von Repräsentation innerhalb und außerhalb künstlerischer Produktion. Statt einer fortdauernden Dekonstruktion repräsentativer Formen, die schnell Gefahr läuft, sich immer wieder in einem selbstreferenziellen Kreis von Bedeutungssplittern zu drehen, liegt Göthes Versuch nicht nur darin, bestehende Setzungen des Kanons zu verwirren, sondern Einordnungs- und Interpretationszwängen generell zu entkommen. Das Ziel ist dabei nicht nur, die Zuschreibung von „Sinn" gänzlich aufzugeben, sondern die symbolische Ordnung durch Strategien wie Parodie und den Stil als Technik zu durchbrechen und durch queere Hybridität andere Wertesysteme einzufordern.

1 William Shakespeare, *Sonnet 94: They that have power to hurt and will do none*, 1609.
2 Die Einrichtungsgegenstände des Büros wurden von Studierenden der Akademie angefertigt.
3 Elaine Scarry, *On Beauty*, Princeton 2001, S. 25.
4 Ebd., S. 4; Tom Holert beschreibt Göthes Interesse an Musik vor allem als ein Interesse an den sozialen Effekten ästhetischer Handlung. Ähnlich wie beim Hören von Musik können durch seine Arbeiten Handlungen, Affekte, Erinnerungen ausgelöst werden. Tom Holert, *Soziale Hochspannungsmasten und andere Techniken zur Steigerung des Als-ob*, in: Julian Göthe, *You are living in a world of magic*, Köln 2011, S. 10–40.

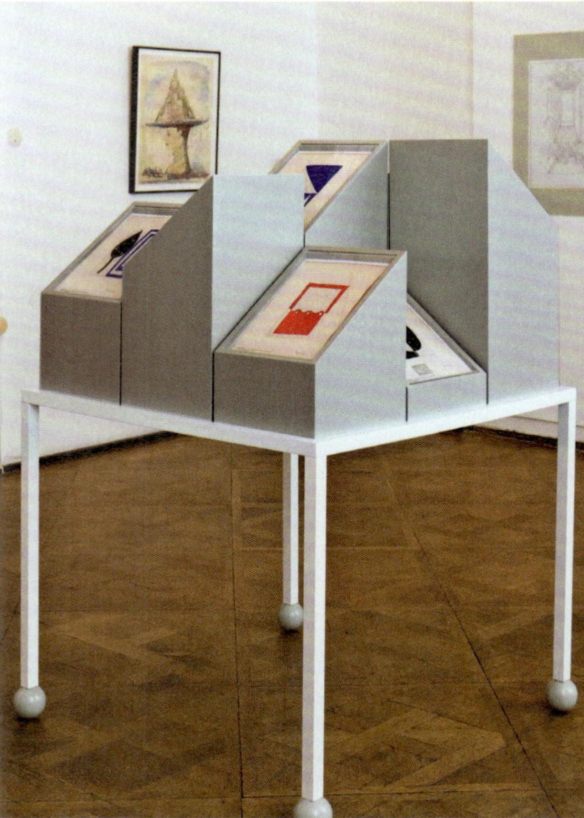

Julian Göthe, *Möbelentwurf / Furniture Design*, Vitrinen-Skulptur / vitrine sculpture, 2019

Lilies that fester smell far worse than weeds[1]

Upon entering Julian Göthe's office in the sculpture department of the Academy of Applied Arts Vienna, one is met with a group of furnituresque "personalities."[2] The ensemble references the artist's ongoing dialogue with the objects that surround him on an everyday basis, as well as those discovered by chance. "At the moment one comes into the presence of something beautiful, it greets you,"[3] Elaine Scarry writes in her essay *On Beauty and Being Just* (1999). The nature of this welcoming "beauty" becomes clearer through Göthe's monumentally theatrical sculptures, detailed drawings, and expansive installations. Their formal language takes from fields such as film, product and interior design, décor, and ornamentation—domains that until recently were subordinate to fine art in the hierarchy of artistic fields. To Göthe, an object's inherent attraction lies primarily in its character, in its peculiarity, rather than some kind of "beauty" in the sense of "purity" or good taste. So what welcomes us is that which appeals to our senses, the sensual (as well as the chaotic, dialectical, or eerie). Likewise, one bumps into and at the same time establishes contact with his hybrid objects, which on the one hand have something angular-authoritarian about them with their oft impeccably shiny surfaces, but on the other hand also seem grotesque, droll, and a little forlorn. The experience of "beauty" proceeds as though in a continuous cell division: spilling out of his works and into the viewer's internal world. Referencing Wittgenstein, Scarry also describes this "spillover of beauty" with a focus on physical movements and music: "[…] whenever Augustine touches something smooth, he begins to think of music and of God."[4]

A direct encounter between object and person can occur by shifting our view of the objects surrounding us to subjects. Göthe's works refuse to submit to canonical art history, pointing to a possible future that eludes categorical classification systems. They interrupt a linear (and heteronormative) assumption of development and reproduction, social norms and hierarchies of representation, both within and outside of artistic production. Rather than a continuous deconstruction of representative forms, which quickly runs the risk of spiraling into self-referential cycles of fragments of meaning, Göthe attempts to disrupt the prevailing configurations of the canon, and to escape the constraints of classification and interpretation in general. The aim here is not just to abandon the attribution of "meaning" completely, but to break through the symbolic order, applying strategies such as parody and style as techniques, and queer hybridity, to demand different value systems."

1 William Shakespeare, *Sonnet 94: They that have power to hurt and will do none*, 1609.
2 The office furnishings were made by students of the Academy.
3 Elaine Scarry, *On Beauty and Being Just*, Princeton 2001, p. 25.
4 ibid., p. 4; Tom Holert describes Göthe's interest in music primarily as an interest in the social effects of aesthetic acts. Like listening to music, his works trigger actions, emotions, and memories. Tom Holert, "Soziale Hochspannungsmasten und andere Techniken zur Steigerung des Als-ob," in: Julian Göthe, *You are Living in a World of Magic*, Cologne 2011, p. 10–40.

—Inga Charlotte Thiele

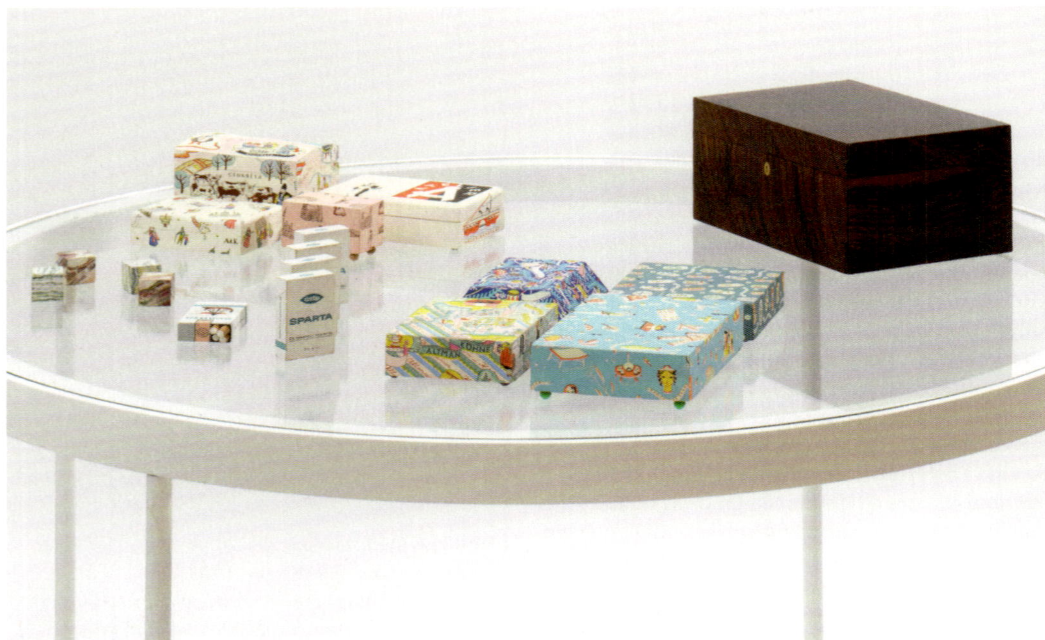

Lucy McKenzie, *Painted boxes, Table III*, 2017

Lucy McKenzie (*1977) wurde der Öffentlichkeit in erster Linie als Malerin bekannt – ihre künstlerische Praxis beschränkt sich jedoch nicht auf ein Medium oder eine Technik. Sie ist unter anderem Autorin, Kuratorin, Designerin und Mitbegründerin eines Mode- und eines Plattenlabels.

Charakteristisch für McKenzies künstlerische Arbeitsweise ist die systematische Aneignung von Stilen und Designs aus unterschiedlichen Bereichen. Ihr Vorgehen ist dabei prozessual und in seiner Präzision beinahe mechanisch, zugleich aber immer genau auf den jeweiligen Kontext und Anlass ausgerichtet. Ausgangspunkt ihrer bekanntesten Arbeiten ist die illusionistische Nachahmung konkreter Vorlagen aus Architektur, Interieur, Werbung oder Grafik mittels malerischer Trompe-l'Œil-Effekte – so griff sie zum Beispiel Designs von Charles Rennie Mackintosh und Adolf Loos auf und bezog sich direkt auf Entwürfe und Patterns aus der Zeit des Artnouveau.

Objekte aus Holz oder Metall, deren Oberflächen täuschend echt mit den jeweiligen Motiven bemalt sind oder auch nur spezifische Oberflächen wie Marmor oder Papier nachahmen – bisweilen in ihrer übersteigerten Künstlichkeit Renderings in 3D-Software vergleichbar – werden in Ausstellungen zu Installationen arrangiert, die in ihrer konzeptuellen Verfasstheit an ästhetische Ansätze des Gesamtkunstwerks denken lassen und dabei oft weit über einfache mimetische Effekte hinausgehen. In einem changierenden Modus der Ambialenz stellen sie einerseits ihre „Gemachtheit", ihre Künstlichkeit offensiv aus, vermögen es aber zugleich trotzdem, spezifische Atmosphären zu erzeugen bzw. zu simulieren und so Stile und Gestaltungskonventionen nicht nur nostalgisch in Erinnerung zu rufen, sondern den Blick auf dahinterstehende soziokulturelle Konventionen und Utopien zu lenken – mit dem paradoxen Ergebnis, die Dingen gerade durch ihre Wiederholung in einer scheinbar exakten Nachbildung zu verfremden. Ihr dabei permanent präsenter Doppelcharakter – zwischen Skulptur und Malerei, Design und Kunst, Modell und Unikat, Originalität und Aneignung – lässt die so behandelten Objekte geradezu unheimlich werden, trägt zur Auflösung von Hierarchien bei und stellt Zusammenhänge und gewohnte Sichtweisen infrage.

Die bemalten Objekte, aus denen *Painted boxes, Table III* besteht, sind direkte Aneignungen von bekannten Arbeiten der ungarischen Grafikdesignerin und Illustratorin Kató Lukáts (1900–90), einer Zeitgenossin Berzeviczy-Pallavicinis. Die von McKenzie in Originalgröße nachgebildeten Verpackungen für Confiseriewaren, Zigaretten und Alltagsdinge, gefertigt unter anderem für *Altmann & Kühne* in Wien (und mit den Dekoren der Gestalterin bis heute im Verkauf) wurden von Lukáts im neoklassizistischen Duktus der Zeit entworfen. Dabei interpretierte sie traditionelle Motive neu und ließ zentrale Fragestellungen der Moderne in ihre Umsetzungen einfließen. Bereits bei Lukáts spielte die Auseinandersetzung mit dem Spannungsfeld von künstlerischer Freiheit und kommerzieller Anwendung eine zentrale Rolle. Durch McKenzies Neubearbeitung werden dieser Konflikt und der souveräne Umgang der Gestalterin mit ihm erneut sichtbar gemacht.

Lucy McKenzie (born 1977) is known primarily as a painter—her artistic practice, however, extends beyond a single medium or technique. She is, among other things, an author, curator, designer, and co-founder of a fashion and record label.

A characteristic feature of McKenzie's artistic approach is her systematic appropriation of styles and designs from various fields. Her method is process-based and almost mechanical in its precision, while at the same time always carefully aligned to the respective context and occasion. Her most famous works originate from her illusionary imitation of specific examples of architecture, interior design, advertising, or graphics, using painterly trompe-l'oeil effects. Examples include her use of designs by Charles Rennie Mackintosh and Adolf Loos, and direct reference to concepts and patterns from the Art Nouveau era.

She paints the surfaces of wooden or metal objects with textures such as marble or paper to a deceptively realistic effect—their exaggerated artificiality perhaps calling to mind digital 3D renderings. In her exhibitions she arranges the objects into installations whose conceptual nature brings to mind aesthetic approaches to the gesamtkunstwerk, often extending far beyond simple mimetic effects. In a mercurial mode of ambivalence, they aggressively display their "fabrication," their artificiality, while still managing to create or simulate specific atmospheres that not only recall nostalgic styles and design traditions, but also draw attention to the underlying socio-cultural conventions and utopias—with the paradoxical result of alienating things precisely *because of* their repetition in a seemingly exact replica. Their permanently dual character—between sculpture and painting, art and design, archetype and unique specimen, originality and appropriation—gives the objects treated thus a somewhat eerie quality, and contributes to dissolving hierarchies and raising questions about relationships and habitual perspectives.

The painted objects that make up *Painted boxes, Table III* are direct appropriations of renowned works by Hungarian graphic designer and illustrator Kató Lukáts (1900–90), a contemporary of Berzeviczy-Pallavicini. Reproduced by McKenzie in their original scale, the packaging for confectionery, cigarettes, and everyday items were manufactured in Vienna for Altmann & Kühne among others. They are still sold today with the original packaging designed by Lukáts in the Neoclassical style of the time. Reinterpreting traditional motifs and incorporating central questions of Modernism into her designs, Lukáts was already engaged in confronting the conflicted zone between artistic freedom and commercial application. McKenzie's reworking brings this friction and the designer's confident handling of it into the foreground once again.

—*Michael Franz*

In den 1920er- und 1930er-Jahren sprach sich Sōetsu Yanagi, ein japanischer Philosoph im Bereich der Ästhetik und Gründer der „Mingei"-(Volkskunst-)Bewegung, für die Rückkehr zu alltäglichen Gebrauchsgegenständen aus, die von anonymen Handwerkern auf dem Land gefertigt wurden. Er argumentierte, dass die Formen dieser bescheidenen, über Jahrhunderte hinweg entwickelten Artefakte in ihrer Reinheit und Funktionalität den authentischsten Ausdruck des Menschen verkörperten.

Dies wurde jedoch durch massengefertigte Waren bedroht, und Yanagi rief zeitgenössische Künstler und Designer auf, von diesen „Volkskünstlern" zu lernen, um das ästhetische Verständnis der Nation zu revolutionieren. Den Hintergrund dieser einflussreichen Kunstbewegung bilden die rasante Modernisierung und Urbanisierung Japans und die daraus resultierende radikale Neuorganisation seiner sozialen und wirtschaftlichen Ordnungen. Ein Jahrhundert später befindet sich die Welt vor einer ebenso radikalen Umstrukturierung. Besonders in den Industrieländern beschleunigt sich die Automatisierung der einst manuellen Fertigung und ihre sozialen und kulturellen Aspekte verschwinden rasant. In einer Situation wie dieser, so könnte man argumentieren, steht die Kultur rund um industrielle Produktion und die Artefakte ihrer Blütezeit mitsamt ihrer Formgebung an genau derselben Stelle, an der sich das Volkshandwerk auf dem Höhepunkt der Industrialisierung befand, und dass hierin eine kunsthistorische Logik für das Interesse von zeitgenössischen Künstler*innen an einer solchen abnehmenden Kultur begründet wäre. Ulrike Müllers Arbeit stellt diese Evaluierung der industriellen Ästhetik dar.

Ihre Arbeiten, am prominentesten die Bilder in Emaille auf Stahl, erinnern an den beliebten und einst spektakulär verbreiteten Modernismus der Nachkriegskunst. Mit ihren kräftigen Farben, dem ungezwungenen Wechselspiel zwischen Abstraktion und hochreduzierten figurativen Motiven und ihrer heiteren Anordnung erinnern Werke wie aus den Serien *Some* (2017) oder *Others* (ab 2015) an Poster und Buchcover der 1950er- und 1960er-Jahre. Diese zu ihrer Zeit allgegenwärtigen grafischen Werke, die oftmals von nicht namentlich genannten Designer*innen kreiert wurden, zählen zu den am weitesten verbreiteten Ausdrücken des industriellen Zeitalters. Mit ihren glatten metallenen Oberflächen, ohne jegliche Spur eines Pinselstrichs, betont Müller diese ihrer Technik anhaftende Anonymität. Zudem rufen die scheinbar makellose Vollendung und der kurvenreiche „Stil" die glorreichen Tage der industriellen Produktion in Erinnerung, etwa die Stromlinienform von Automobilen. Die bescheidene Größe der Arbeiten, die immer 39,4 mal 30,5 cm beträgt, reflektiert dabei jedoch eine gewisse Distanz zum Optimismus dieser Ära. Bei näherer Betrachtung fallen mit den leicht ausgefransten Rändern subtile, aber eindeutige Unvollkommenheiten ins Auge. Diese zurückhaltenden und durchdachten Fehlerstellen zeugen vom Abstand, den Müller davon nimmt, die industrielle Produktion zu romantisieren. Stattdessen nähert sie sich in ihrer bildlichen Sprache dem Gegenstand durch kritisch informierte Neugierde an.

Auch die Textilarbeiten von Müller, darunter *Rug (con tacónes)* (2018), demonstrieren ihr genaues Beobachtungsvermögen kultureller Begebenheiten. Obwohl ihre Kompositionen immer noch die visuelle Sprache der Mitte des 20. Jahrhunderts aufgreifen, sind sie in einer Werkstatt in Mexiko handgewebt.

Somit synthetisiert die Künstlerin die bildnerische Sensibilität des industriellen Zeitalters, das momentan ersetzt wird, mit handwerklichen Prozessen, die es einst verdrängte; zwei historische Momente von radikaler sozialer Umwälzung treffen in einem Werk aufeinander.

Diese Neubewertung der unmittelbaren Vergangenheit ist ein Akt, der ein tieferes Verständnis für die eigene Zeit zu vermitteln sucht. So sind die Arbeiten von Müller trotz ihrer selbstbewussten Eleganz als klares Abbild unserer turbulenten und wechselhaften Zeit zu lesen. Im Gegensatz zu ihrem historischen Gegenpart zu Beginn des 20. Jahrhunderts in Japan verfolgt sie kein romantisches Streben, nach verlorener Authentizität. Stattdessen ist ihre Arbeit unaufgeregt und frei von jeglicher Sentimentalität gegenüber der schwindenden Industrie, als ob man behaupte, dass die gefasste Auseinandersetzung mit dem Niedergang kultureller Phänomene die beste ästhetische Vorbereitung für die bevorstehenden Veränderungen ist.

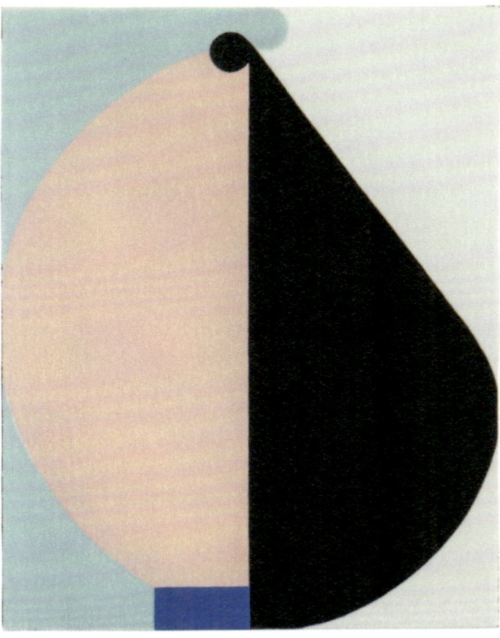

Ulrike Müller, *Others*, 2017

In the 1920s and 1930s, Yanagi Sōetsu, the aesthetic philosopher and founder of the Japanese folk art movement known as *Mingei*, advocated the return to everyday utensils, hand-crafted by anonymous rural artisans. The forms of such humble artifacts, he reasoned, were developed over centuries to attain their purity and functionality, and were therefore the most authentic expression of the people. It was threatened, however, by mass-produced goods, and he urged contemporary artists and designers to learn from these folk artisans in order to revolutionize the nation's sensitivity to beauty.

The background to this highly influential art movement was Japan's rapid modernization and urbanization, and the associated radical reorganization of its social and economic order. Fast-forward one century and the world as a whole is facing an equally radical restructuring. At least in developed countries, automation of manufacturing is accelerating and its social and cultural aspects are disappearing fast. In such circumstances one might argue that the culture of industrial production, including the artifacts from its heydays and their aesthetic, is now exactly where the folk crafts were at the height of industrialization, and, from an art history perspective, there is a logic to contemporary artists' interest in such a waning culture. Ulrike Müller's practice embodies such a reappraisal of industrial aesthetics.

Her works, most prominently her paintings in enamel on steel, strongly evoke the popular Modernism once so widespread in postwar applied arts. With their bright colors, cheerful disposition, and effortless shifting between abstraction and highly reduced figurative depictions, works such as her *Some* (2017) and *Others* (as of 2015) series call to mind posters and book covers from the 1950s and 1960s. These, at the time ubiquitous, graphic works, often created by anonymous designers, count among the most prominent popular expressions of the industrial age. Müller's works, with their impeccable metallic surfaces and no visible traces of brush strokes, exaggerate this sense of anonymity in the techniques employed. Moreover, their apparently smooth finish and curvilinear style evokes images of streamlined cars and thus recalls the glory days of manufacturing.

The pictures' modest size, always measuring 39.4 cm by 30.5 cm, however, implies the vast distance from the optimism of that era. And, upon closer inspection, one notices subtle yet definite imperfections, such as ever so slightly frayed edges. These small, deliberate flaws demonstrate Müller's refusal to romanticize industrial production and instead to approach its pictorial vocabulary through critical inquisitiveness.

Müller's textile works, such as *Rug (con tacónes)* (2018), further illustrate her acute sense of cultural history. Although their composition still invokes the mid-twentieth-century visual language, they are hand-woven at a workshop in Mexico. Thus, she synthesizes the pictorial sensibilities of the industrial era currently being replaced with the manual crafts it once destroyed, collapsing the two historical moments of radical social transformation into one body of work.

A re-evaluation of the immediate past often intends to gain a deeper understanding of one's own time, and Müller's works are clearly of our turbulent and shifting time, despite their confident elegance. However, unlike her historical counterpart in early-twentieth-century Japan, she does not harbor a romantic ambition to return to authenticity. Instead, her practice is calm and free of any sentimentality toward the declining industry, as if to say that a composed examination of a vanishing culture is the best aesthetic preparation for the changes to come.

—Yuki Higashino

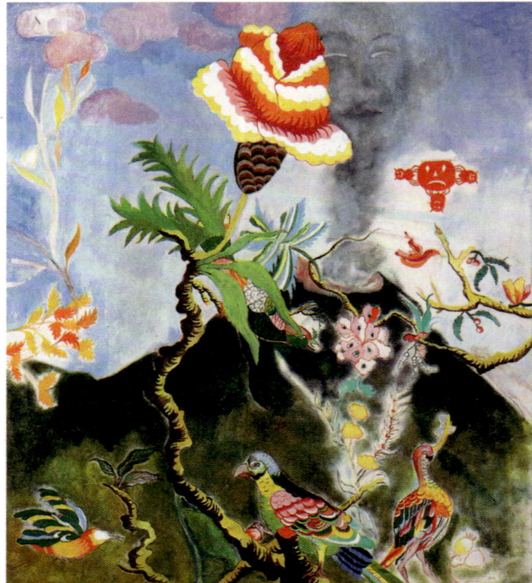

Katharina Wulff, *Graf Stromboli*, 2002

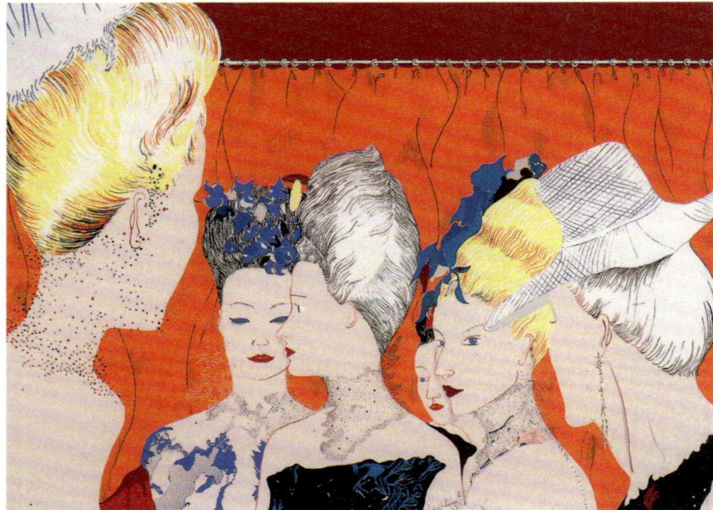

Katharina Wulff, *Dr. Ruppel*, 2001

Ende der 1990er-Jahre international bekannt geworden, entwickelte Katharina Wulff eine distinkte Bildsprache, deren Figuration, vage und ungenau im erweiterten Feld einer Generation von Künstler*innen wie Elizabeth Peyton, Kai Althoff und Lukas Duwenhögger angesiedelt, sich dennoch klar absetzt. Ihr Aufwachsen im sozialistischen Deutschland, ihre Ausbildungen im Tanz und im Frisörhandwerk und die Aufnahme des Kunststudiums erst nach der Flucht nach Westberlin, diese biografischen Daten beschreiben einen speziellen Weg und eine spezielle Definition ihres Berufs. Dieses Berufsbild, jenes der Künstlerin, und wie sie dorthin gekommen ist, das verleiht ihrer Malerei einen eigenen Duktus, eine Abwendung vom Konzept, eine Hinwendung zum Handwerk, und oft eine geschärfte, durch den Sozialismus und die proletarische Erfahrung herangebildete Beobachtungsgabe.

Ausgehend von klassischen Sujets wie Porträt, Landschaft oder Genreszene entstehen Bilder, die auf den ersten Blick oft seltsam außerzeitlich wirken, jedoch bei näherer Betrachtung zeigen, dass sie stets von der Gegenwart informiert sind. Dabei werden unter anderem ornamental-formale, surreale, romantische – immer aber hochartifizielle – Elemente in theatralischen Arrangements wie auf einer Bühne vereint. Dekors, Stile und Moden spielen nicht nur auf malerisch-technischer Ebene eine hervorgehobene Rolle, auch bei den Bildinhalten erzeugen sie Verschiebungen und Brüche.

Referenzen auf zeitgenössische Ästhetiken, historische Stilelemente und der souveräne, oft nicht einmal besonders augenfällige Wechsel zwischen formalen und inhaltlichen Registern ergeben ein dichtes Gewebe, in dem nichts angestrengt oder gewollt wirkt und trotzdem alles gemacht und ausgestellt ist. In genau und bewusst kalkulierten, nur scheinbar traumverlorenen, mitunter symbolbeladen Szenerien bilden Figuren, die zwischen Ent-Indiviualisierung und Intimität changieren, komplexe Tableaus: mal dandyhaft und exzentrisch, mal beinahe wahnhaft entrückt, mal an Puppen erinnernd. Anhand ihrer Oberflächen werden Stilfragen, Kleidungs- oder Frisurprobleme erörtert. Trotzdem wirkt die Personnage, die Wulffs Malereien bevölkert, seltsam vertraut. Daran ändert auch ihre Stilisiertheit nichts, die sich bisweilen auf der Ebene der sehr bewusst formulierten Titel fortsetzt.

Im Zusammenspiel mit der Art der Ausführung entsteht ein komplexes Gefüge, in dem scheinbar einfache Gesten, die weder naiv noch simplifizierend oder platt mystifizierend eingesetzt werden, eine Eigendynamik entwickeln und die Betrachter unmittelbar involvieren. Zugleich wird – wie in den traditionellen darstellenden Künsten – stets eine gewisse Distanz aufrechterhalten. So können Wulffs Bilder vielleicht als Abstraktionen der psychologischen oder gar „spirituellen" Dimension des Daseins gelesen werden.

In den letzten Jahren hat die Künstlerin ihre Arrangements mitunter auch in den physischen Ausstellungsraum erweitert. Zusammen mit Kunsthandwerkern aus Marrakesch, wo sie zeitweise lebt, fertigte Wulff filigrane, ornamentale Wandelemente und Türdurchgänge aus Holz an, in denen sie traditionelle Designs aus dem arabischen Raum aufgreift, aber durch Bemalung und Applikationen individuell verfremdet. Diese Displays wirken wie die Bestandteile von Wulffs Malereien völlig artifiziell und bleiben trotz ihrer Präsenz auf jene Weise entrückt, die tatsächlich einen neuen Möglichkeitsraum für die Wahrnehmung eröffnet.

Emerging internationally in the late 1990s, Wulff developed a very distinct pictorial language whose figuration maintains remote ties with the broader field of artists of her generation, such as Elizabeth Peyton, Kai Althoff, and Lukas Duwenhögger, while also clearly differentiating itself from them. Katharina Wulff grew up in socialist East Germany, trained in dance and hairdressing, and began to study art only after fleeing to West Berlin. These biographical details describe a particular path and thus give a specific definition to her profession. The artist's career arc, and how she got there, affords her work its own characteristic style, marked by a departure from the conceptual and a turn towards craftsmanship, along with a gift for observation honed by her experience of socialism and proletarian life.

Starting with classical subjects such as portraits, landscapes, or genre scenes, she produces images that at first glance appear strangely extra-temporal, but on closer inspection reveal that they are always informed by the present. Elements that include the ornamental-formal, the surreal, and the romantic—but are always highly artificial—are combined in theatrical compositions as if on a stage. Décors, styles, and fashions play a prominent role on a technical, painterly level, but also create shifts and breaks in the visual content of the images. References to contemporary aesthetics and historical style elements, and the confident, often inconspicuous transition between formal and content-related registers, result in a dense web in which nothing comes across as strained or deliberate and yet everything is produced and on display.

In seemingly dreamy but carefully calculated, often symbolically laden scenes, figures oscillating between de-individualization and apparent intimacy form complex tableaux: at times dandyish and eccentric, at other times almost delusional, or reminiscent of mannequins whose surfaces the artist employs to explore issues of style, clothing, or hairstyle. Nevertheless, the personages populating Wulff's paintings appear strangely familiar, even with their stylization, which sometimes extends to the level of the cleverly formulated titles.

Augmented by the method of execution, a complex structure emerges, in which seemingly basic gestures, neither naive nor simplifying nor flatly mystifying, develop their own dynamics and directly involve the viewer. At the same time—as in the traditional performing arts—a certain distance is always maintained. Thus one could perhaps read Wulff's imagery as abstractions of the psychological or even "spiritual" dimension of existence.

In recent years, the artist has also expanded her compositions into the physical exhibition space. Together with artisans from Marrakech, where she occasionally lives, Wulff creates delicate, ornamental wall elements and wooden doorways that incorporate traditional designs from the Arabic region, which she individually modifies through painting and applications. Like the components of Wulff's paintings, these displays come across as completely artificial and, despite their presence, remain ethereal in a way that effectively opens up new realms of perception.

Alfred Hitchcock nutzte die surrealen Häuser und Straßen in der Malerei Giorgio de Chiricos zur Szenografie und Ausstattung seiner Horrorfilme, bevor die Gemälde zum Kalendermotiv wurden. Die beinahe menschenleeren Stadtansichten mit langen Schatten und unklaren Distanzen boten ihm ein Vokabular, um das Unbewusste, Unheimliche und Bedrohliche des Verdrängten im Filmstudio darzustellen. Diese Effekte schwingen im kollaborativen Objekt von Nico Ihlein und Amelie von Wulffen nach. Die Keramikvase mit ihren mediterran anmutenden und ebenfalls menschenleeren Stadtansichten, Muscheln und der Perlmutt-Effektfarbe wirkt aber wenig bedrohlich im Sinne eines uns grundsätzlich fremden Unbewussten. Sie ist unheimlich als Einrichtungsgegenstand, gerade weil uns alle ihre Elemente vertraut sind.

Die Vase stammt von Nico Ihlein. Vasenförmige Keramiken sind zentrale Protagonistinnen in den inszenierten Interieurs seines Werks. Diese fein, aber nicht zu fein produzierten Objekte changieren zwischen abstrakter Form, Ornament und Schmuck. Sie stehen auf gebauten Sockeln oder gefundenen und bearbeiteten Möbeln im Dialog mit Vorhängen, Zeichnungen, Malereien und Abfall. Sie sind Verkörperungen verworfener, verdrängter und wiederauftauchender Ästhetiken - Einrichtungen des Lebens, gemischt aus Selbstgemachtem, Kaputtem, aus der Mode Geratenem und wieder Aktuellem, wie sie beispielsweise in Gebrauchtwarenhäusern zu finden sind.

Amelie von Wulffen inszeniert in ihrer Malerei in filmisch oder bühnenhaft anmutenden Arrangements Fragen der Biografie und des Ausdrucks als Genre alltäglicher Krisen. Sie nutzt dafür Monster, Comicfiguren, Filmstills, Paraphrasen von Gemälden der Kunstgeschichte und der Hobbymalerei. Neben Leinwänden und Holztafeln bemalt sie auch Möbel wie gefundene Stühle oder gebaute Liegen - dienende Objekte. Aber auch Schränke, Betten und Truhen werden ihr zum Bildträger: Möbel, die fast klischeehaft mit Geheimnissen und Verdrängtem assoziiert werden. Das Dekor der gemeinsamen Vase stammt von ihr.

Das Gefäß ohne Titel umgibt eine humorvolle Schwere. Erinnerung an einen unheilvollen Urlaub. Volkshochschulkurs. Urne. Es ist lächerlich, in der Menge der vulgär dicken, schimmernden falschen Perlen, in den dunklen Fensteröffnungen der gemalten Häuser und den von der Künstlerin gemeinsam mit kindlicher Gewalt knubbelig verklebten leeren Wohnhäusern verstorbener Mollusken ein Bild der eigenen Misere und der eigenen Träume zu sehen. Die Vase konkretisiert das Latente, buchstabiert es aus wie in einem Horrorfilm. Wir gucken in die Öffnung der Vase und uns blickt ein Formalismus des Dekors um einen Hohlraum entgegen. Wir lachen. Befragt nach dem existenziellen Anspruch der Kunst antwortet das Gefäß mit der Gegenfrage: Hast du schon *House of Cards* gesehen?

Alfred Hitchcock adopted the surreal buildings and street scenes of Giorgio de Chirico's paintings for the sets and scenography of his horror films long before the images became calendar motifs. The mostly deserted cityscapes with their elongated shadows and ambiguous perspectives offered him a vocabulary for cinematically depicting the unconscious, the sinister, the threat of the repressed. And these effects also resonate in Nico Ihlein and Amelie von Wulffen's collaborative project. The weirdness of the ceramic vase with its Mediterranesque, equally desolate city scenes, sea shells, and pearlescent-effect paint is not so much threatening in the sense of a fundamentally alien subconscious, it seems uncanny as a decorative item precisely because of the familiarity of its elements.

The vase is a piece by Nico Ihlein. Vase-shaped ceramics feature prominently in the staged interiors that are his work. These finely—yet not too finely—produced objects oscillate between abstract forms, ornaments, and jewelry. They sit on customized pedestals or readymade and modified furniture, in dialogue with curtains, drawings, paintings, and rubbish. They embody discarded, suppressed, and re-emergent aesthetics—the accoutrements of life, a mixture of homemade, broken, outdated and then again relevant items, like things you would find in a second-hand store.

The dramatic, cinematic arrangements of Amelie von Wulffens' paintings raise questions about biography as a genre and expression of everyday crises. For this she employs monsters, cartoon figures, film stills and paraphrases from art history and hobby painting. Besides using canvases and wooden panels, she paints on furniture such as found chairs or customized loungers—supportive objects. But cupboards, beds, and coffers also act as canvases: furniture that has clichéd associations with secrets and the repressed. She is also responsible for the vase's decor.

There is a humorous gravity to the untitled vessel: memories of an ill-fated vacation, evening classes, an urn. It would be ridiculous to project a vision of personal desires and suffering into the vulgarly thick varnish of shimmering fake pearl, the shadowy windows of the painted houses, and the vacant homes of deceased mollusks jaggedly glued on with puerile violence by von Wulffen. The vase substantiates that which lies latent, spells it out like a horror film. We peek into the opening of the vase and formal decoration around a cavity looks back at us. We laugh. When asked about art's existential demands, the vessel counters by asking: "Have you seen *House of Cards* yet?"

—*Tonio Kröner*

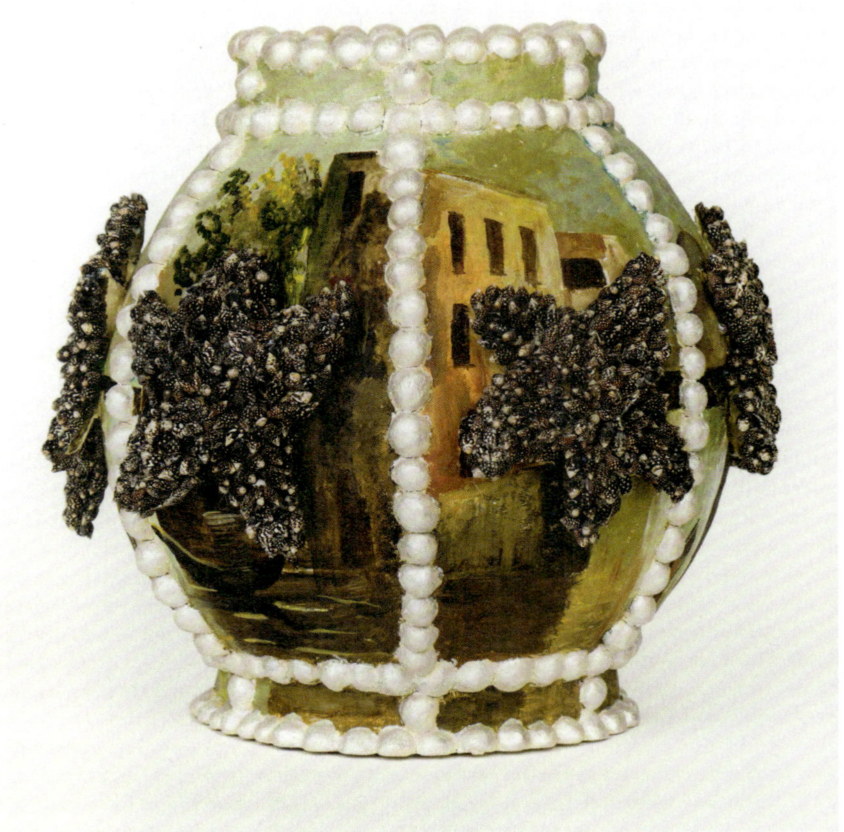

Amelie von Wulffen und / and Nico Ihlein, *Ohne Titel / Untitled*, 2019

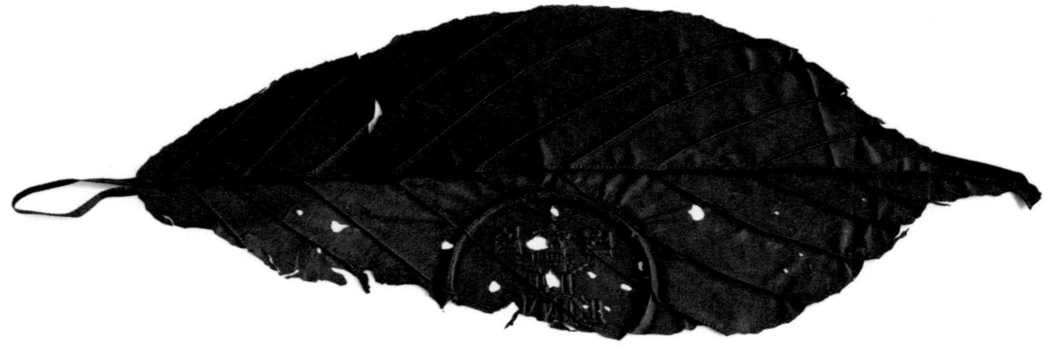

Min Yoon, *Ohne Titel / Untitled*, 2019

Herabfallendes Laub hat die Eigenschaft, auf dem Boden liegen zu bleiben. Das erhöht zwar das Risiko, zertreten und damit beschädigt zu werden - exponiert insofern die Fragilität des Materials -, markiert aber auch den Moment, in dem die Blätter anfangen, den Raum einzunehmen, der in unseren Kontexten Wert generiert. Von hier aus okkupieren sie reale Fläche, werden zu ihrem eigenen Real Estate, und mit zunehmender Nässe beginnt der „rutschige Teil" ihrer Ökonomisierung.

Wenn Josef Hoffmann etwa Friedrich Ludwig Berzeviczy-Pallavicinis florale Exzesse als Ausdruck einer Romantik konnotiert, die ihr Objekt des Begehrens in der Botanik findet, ließe sich die Parallele oder Überschneidung zu Min Yoons Arbeit jenseits der aufgeblühten Form suchen, also dann, wenn Veränderungen der Farbe, der Haptik oder des Geruchs die infrastrukturellen Kreisläufe hinter der frischen Oberfläche des vormals noch am Zweig haftenden Blattes zu offenbaren beginnen. Aber das ist nur eine Seite der (buchstäblich einseitigen) Münze. Einige dieser Blätter, die Yoon seit Jahren kontinuierlich seinem Werk hinzufügt, haben den Abdruck eines koreanischen Geldstücks eingeprägt, das dem Maßstab des ohnehin vergrößerten Objekts entspricht. Der Logik dieser Skalierung folgend, wird das Blatt zu einem Trompe-l'Œil fürs Schaufenster, das unsere eigene Verfasstheit maßstäblich proportional miniaturisiert.

Yoons Begehren hat weniger mit Botanik zu tun als vielmehr mit einer Partizipation im Feld der Kunst. Dabei wird neben dem Kunstobjekt die Analyse gleich mitgeliefert, wenn auch chiffriert im poetischen Potenzial der von ihm ausgewählten Motive. Die eigenen Möglichkeiten und Bedürfnisse sind relativ komplex verschlüsselt in jede einzelne seiner Arbeiten inkorporiert. Während narrative Spuren Rückschlüsse auf einen spezifischen kulturellen Kontext und dessen Jargon zulassen, bleiben sie am Ende so intim wie Traumerzählungen, denen die Pointe fehlt. Sie spielen mit dem nahezu banalen Geheimnis, dass „schöne Dinge" als Motivation für fast alles fast immer schon ausreichen - mitunter auch für die Erneuerung von ästhetischen Begrifflichkeiten, denen im Prozess der Übersetzung genau die richtige Fixierung abhandenkommen kann.

Das Blatt, welches Min Yoon für die Ausstellung *Der Hausfreund* produzierte, wurde aus dünnem, eingefärbtem Schweineleder gefertigt. Handgenäht, verfügt es neben präzise komponierten Rissen und Löchern über kleine, beinahe unsichtbare mechanische Vorrichtungen, die helfen, einen verhältnismäßig realistischen Effekt zu simulieren, z. B. das Einrollen der Kanten. Die Nähe zu angewandten und spezifisch in der Mode zu findenden Techniken ist dabei kein Zufall. Die Verknüpfung von Münze und Blatt, beides präsente Leitmotive europäischer Folklore mit einer auf Invention und Offenheit ausgerichteten Fashiontradition zeigt einmal mehr, wie Yoon mystische mit kapitalistischen Ritualen zu verweben weiß und diese zugleich als pragmatische Einschätzung unserer Gegenwart funktionalisiert.

One of the properties of fallen leaves is that they remain on the ground. This increases the risk of being trodden on and damaged, exposing the fragility of their makeup, but it is here that the leaves take on their value-generating role in our environment. It is here that they occupy real space, become their own *real estate*, and with increasing dampness the "slippery part" of their reorganization begins. Josef Hoffmann's implication that Friedrich Ludwig Berzeviczy-Pallavicini's floral excesses express a romanticism that seeks its object of desire in botany could find a parallel or overlap with Min Yoon's work. Only, in Yoon's case, it goes beyond the blossoming form, when alterations in color, structure, and odor have already commenced, revealing the organic cycles behind the fresh surface of the leaf when it was still attached to the branch.

But this is only one side of the (literally one-sided) coin. Some of these leaves, which Yoon has been producing for years as an ongoing part of his work, have been embossed with the image of a Korean piece of money that corresponds to the scale of the enlarged leaf. Following the logic of this scaling, it brings to mind a trompe-l'oeil window display which miniaturizes our own stature proportionally.

Yoon's desire has less to do with botany than with engagement in the art field. This analysis is delivered instantly, albeit masked behind the poetic potential of the motifs Yoon selects to manifest as objects or paintings. How, and the extent to which, one can modify this desire according to one's own goals and resources is encoded with relative complexity and incorporated into each of his pieces. While narrative traces may enable us to draw conclusions about specific cultural contexts and their vernacular, they ultimately remain as intimate as dream narratives without a punch line. They play with the banal secret that "beautiful things" will almost always suffice as a motivation for almost anything—including updating terminology that can lose some of its fixed definition in the translation process.

The leaf Min Yoon produced for the *Der Hausfreund* exhibition is made of fine, dyed pighide. Sewn by hand, there are precisely composed tears and holes as well as tiny, barely visible devices that help simulate a rather realistic effect, such as rolling in at the edges.

The proximity to applied art and, particularly, fashion-related techniques is no coincidence. Linking the coin and the leaf—both two of the most present leitmotifs of European folklore—with a tailoring art oriented towards invention and candor, once again testifies to the skill with which Yoon interweaves both mystical and capitalist rituals, and functionalizes them to pragmatically evaluate the contemporary moment.

—*Inka Meißner*

1909–89

A Chronology

SOFIE MATHOI

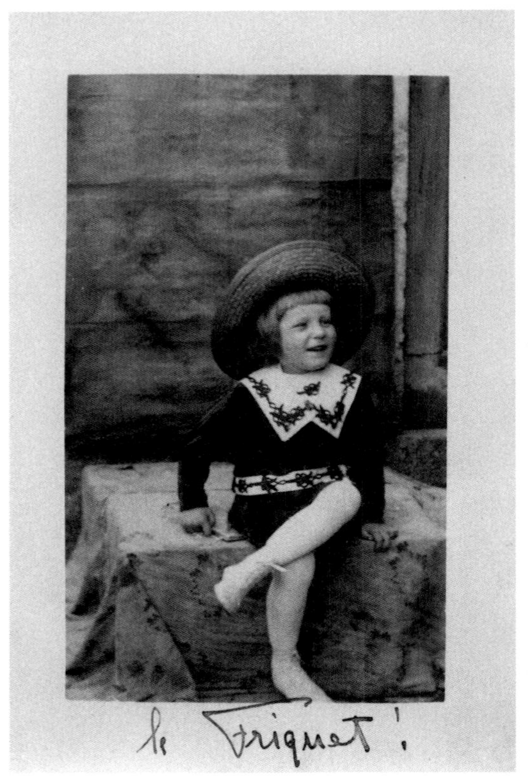

Friedrich Berzeviczy im Alter von vier Jahren / at the age of four, 1913

1909–26

Childhood and youth

Friedrich von Berzeviczy is born on April 12, 1909, in Lausanne, Switzerland. Both his parents are of aristocratic descent. His father, Georg von Berzeviczy, comes from a Hungarian noble family, while his mother, Margravine Gabrielle Csáky-Pallavicini, has Hungarian-Italian ancestry. Friedrich is born as a Hungarian national. The fall of the monarchy after the First World War, combined with his father's penchant for gambling, cost the family its fortune. Berzeviczy attends the Theresianum secondary school in Vienna for three years. In 1925, at his uncle's suggestion, he enrolls at the School of Applied Arts in Vienna; however, he attends no classes and is removed from the school's attendance list on February 15, 1926.

1925

The architects Josef Frank and Oskar Wlach establish the Haus & Garten furniture store in Vienna. With a broad portfolio covering interior design and furnishing of houses and apartments, as well as the design of furniture, textile patterns, and home accessories, the company emerges as a competitor to the Wiener Werkstätte (1903–32). After Josef Frank's emigration to Sweden in 1938, the lighting manufacturer Julius Kalmar takes over the business. On November 1, 1925, after several years in America, Eduard Wimmer-Wisgrill takes over the workshop for textile work and tapestry weaving at the School of Applied Arts in Vienna, which until then had been run by Rosalia Rothansl. In 1926, he changes its remit and it is henceforth known as "workshop for textiles and fashion."

1926

In December, the Bauhaus school of art, architecture, and design opens its new building in Dessau, designed by Walter Gropius. Most of the furniture has been designed at the Bauhaus workshops and produced in collaboration with manufacturers (tubular steel furniture by Marcel Breuer, lamps by Marianne Brandt, fabrics for furniture and curtains from the weaving mill run by Gunta Stölzl.)

1927

On April 20, Adolf Loos delivers the lecture "The Viennese Woe (The Wiener Werkstätte): A Settlement of Accounts. With Photographs from the Paris Exhibition." Loos launches a vehement attack on Josef Hoffmann and the Wiener Werkstätte, emphasizing the following: "Of all of my theories, the most important to posterity will be the one stating that there is no connection whatsoever between art and craft." A media debate ensues between the Wiener Werkstätte and Adolf Loos and his followers.

1909–89

Eine Chronologie

SOFIE MATHOI

1909–26
Kindheit und Jugend

Friedrich von Berzeviczy wird am 12. April 1909 in Lausanne in der Schweiz geboren. Beide Elternteile entstammen der Aristokratie, der Vater Georg von Berzeviczy einer ungarischen Adelsfamilie, die Mutter Gabrielle, eine geborene Markgräfin Csáky-Pallavicini, hat Vorfahren im ungarisch-italienischen Adel. Friedrich ist ungarischer Nationalität.
Der Fall der Monarchie nach dem Ersten Weltkrieg und die Spielleidenschaft des Vaters bringen die Familie um ihr Vermögen. Berzeviczy besucht drei Jahre das Gymnasium Theresianum (Realschule) in Wien. 1925 schreibt er sich auf Anraten eines Onkels in der Kunstgewerbeschule in Wien ein, erscheint jedoch nicht zum Unterricht und wird mit 15. Februar 1926 gestrichen.

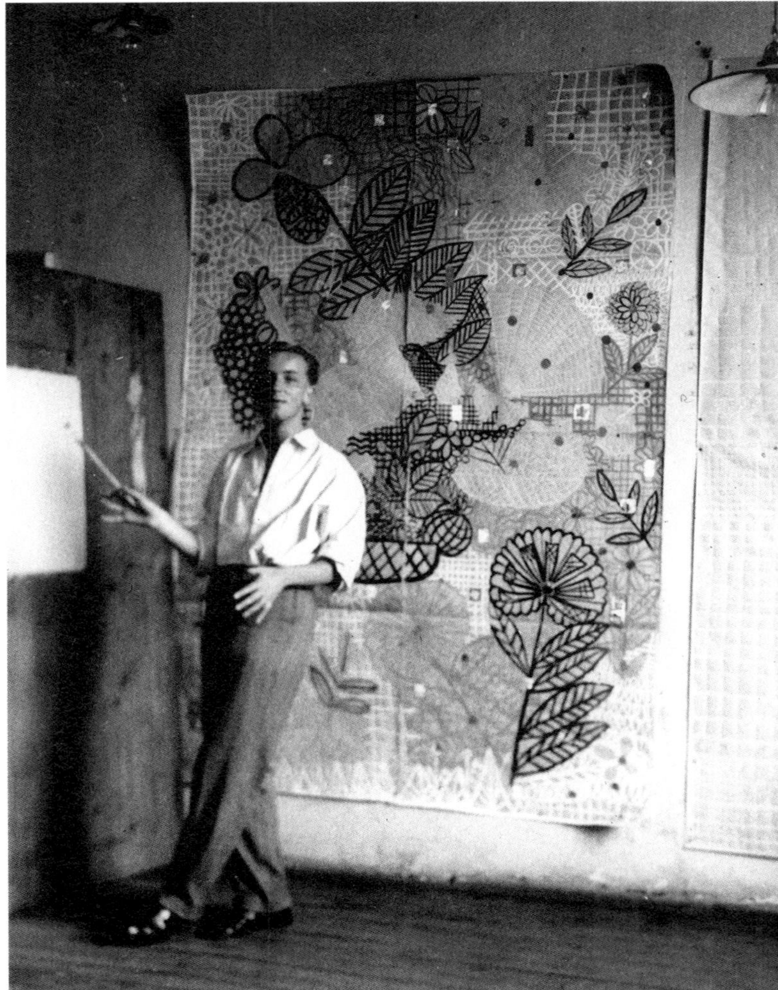

Friedrich Berzeviczy vor seinen Arbeiten an der Kunstgewerbeschule / in front of his work at the School of Applied Arts, 1933–34

1925

Die Architekten Josef Frank und Oskar Wlach gründen in Wien das Einrichtungsgeschäft *Haus & Garten.* Mit einem breitgefächerten Angebot für die Planung und Einrichtung von Häusern und Wohnungen und der Gestaltung von Möbeln, Stoffmustern und Wohnaccessoires ist das Unternehmen eine Konkurrenz zur Wiener Werkstätte (1903–32). Nach der Emigration Josef Franks nach Schweden im Jahr 1938 übernimmt der Lampenfabrikant Julius Kalmar das Geschäft.
Eduard Wimmer-Wisgrill übernimmt am 1. November 1925, nach einem mehrjährigen Aufenthalt in Amerika, die Werkstätte für Textilarbeiten und Gobelinweberei an der Kunstgewerbeschule Wien, die bis dahin von Rosalia Rothansl geleitet wurde. 1926 ändert er den Betrieb der Werkstatt; sie heißt nun *Werkstatt für Textil und Mode.*

1926

Das von Walter Gropius entworfene Gebäude für die Kunst-, Design- und Architekturschule Bauhaus wird im Dezember in Dessau eröffnet. Der Großteil der Einrichtung wird von den Bauhaus-Werkstätten entworfen und in Zusammenarbeit mit Firmen ausgeführt

1928

In January, the first issue of *Domus* is published, an architecture magazine founded in Italy by the architect Gio Ponti and the Barnabite priest Giovanni Semeria. The first issue, subtitled "Architecture and décor of the modern home in the city and in the country," focuses on new architecture, interior design, and decorative art in Italy.

1929

Mies van der Rohe designs the German pavilion at the World's Fair in Barcelona. In New York the Museum of Modern Art opens, the world's first museum explicitly dedicated to modern art. The School of Applied Arts Vienna celebrates its sixtieth anniversary.

1926–32

School of Applied Arts Vienna

In 1926, Friedrich Berzeviczy enrolls once again at the School of Applied Arts, now attending the department for "drawing and sculpting from nature" under Viktor Schufinsky. As a minor subject he studies ornamental handwriting and heraldry under Rudolf Larisch and chooses the workshop for textiles and fashion. In 1927, he transfers to the fashion and textile class run by Wimmer-Wisgrill, who becomes his mentor and patron and with whom he enters a relationship and shares a home from 1928/29 to 1932/33.

Using folding screens (*paravents*), Berzeviczy creates a separate space within the workshop, where he is able to work undisturbed. Eugen Steinhof, architect and director of the School of Applied Arts from 1923 to 1930, ignites his interest in the art of the international avant-garde and introduces him to the concepts of color harmony. The continuity of his sprawling floral imagery is inspired by the work of Dagobert Peche. In 1929, Berzeviczy travels to the World's Fair in Barcelona and on to Paris, Munich, and Berlin. He then lives in Paris until 1931. When he becomes seriously ill, Wimmer-Wisgrill takes him back to Vienna, where he uses the rooms of the School of Applied Arts as a temporary live-in studio and works on commissions to make ends meet. By his own (unconfirmed) account, he designs fabrics for Haus & Garten and joins his colleagues in creating decorations for the ball at the School of Applied Arts and the legendary *Wiener Künstlerfeste*. The school offers a regular luncheon table to Berzeviczy and two of his fellow students, which is funded by proceeds from the ball. He also finds a patron: the Klimt collector Serena Lederer supports the young talent by commissioning him to create an album of Venice panoramas, as she can no longer manage the journey herself. Josef Hoffmann and Wimmer-Wisgrill recommend Berzeviczy to the Demel confectionery store, Purveyor to the Imperial and Royal Court, and from 1932 he is responsible for the company's interior and graphic design. He creates a new, contemporary image for the traditional business, with redesigned stores, striking displays, and sophisticated folded packaging.

1929

Boudoir for a Cosmopolitan Lady

In 1929, the School of Applied Arts celebrates its sixtieth anniversary with an exhibition at the Austrian Museum for Art and Industry. The young Berzeviczy contributes a most remarkable interior design: his *Boudoir for a Cosmopolitan Lady* features an oval bed, which is suspended from the ceiling on chains, combined with a profusion of round forms and delicate fabrics with appliqué patterns. The extravagant formal language, coloration, and materials make a lasting impression on the Viennese public.

Through the international connections of his mentors Josef Hoffmann and Wimmer-Wisgrill, Berzeviczy is kept abreast of the latest fashion trends from Paris and New York and interprets these accordingly in his interior designs. For Berzeviczy, Wimmer-Wisgrill has "a great nose for discovering the new, the elegant, the artistic, and the fashionable in everything." The exhibition makes

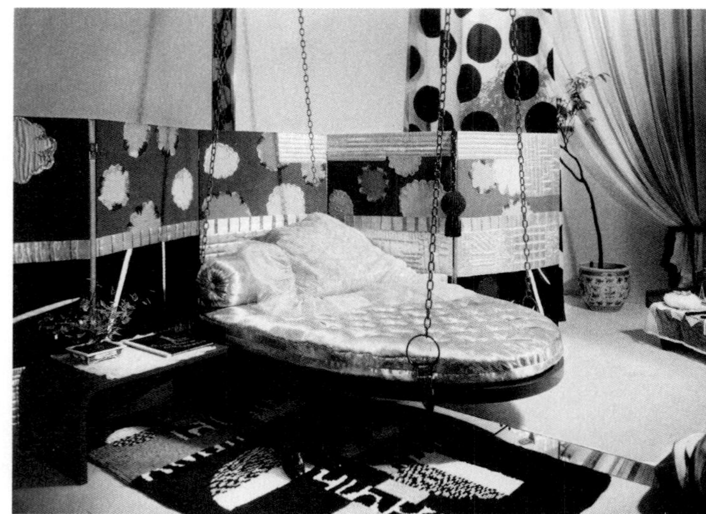

Boudoir einer mondänen Dame / Boudoir for a Cosmopolitan Lady, 1929

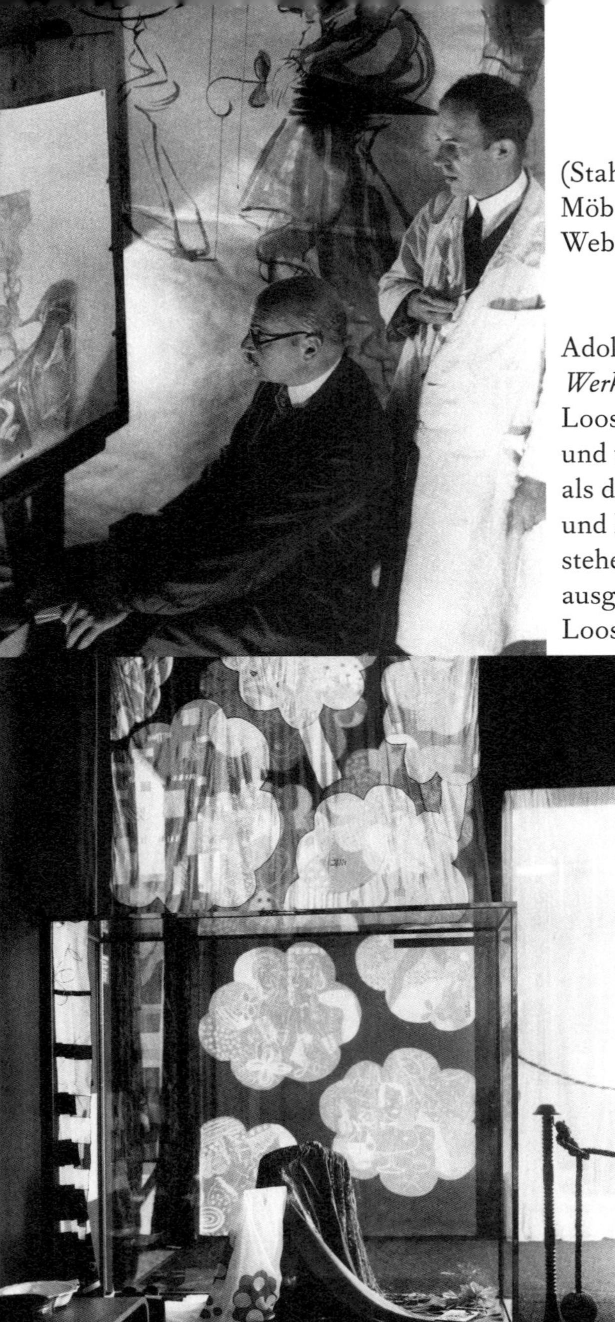

Oben / Above: Eduard Wimmer-Wisgrill mit / with Friedrich Berzeviczy in der Kunstgewerbeschule / at the School of Applied Arts, um / c. 1935
Unten / Below: *Boudoir einer mondänen Dame / Boudoir for a Cosmopolitan Lady*, 1929

(Stahlrohrmöbel von Marcel Breuer, Lampen von Marianne Brandt, Möbel- und Vorhangstoffe aus der von Gunta Stölzl geleiteten Weberei).

1927

Adolf Loos hält am 20. April den Vortrag *Das Wiener Weh (Wiener Werkstätte). Eine Abrechnung! Mit Lichtbildern der Pariser Ausstellung.* Loos greift die Wiener Werkstätte und Josef Hoffmann vehement an und unterstreicht Folgendes: „Von allen meinen Thesen wird diejenige als die wichtigste auf die Nachwelt kommen, die besagt, daß Kunst und Handwerk in keinem wie immer gearteten Zusammenhang stehen.“ Daraufhin entspinnt sich ein über Medien öffentlich ausgetragener Diskurs zwischen der Wiener Werkstätte und Adolf Loos sowie seinen Anhänger*innen.

1928

Im Jänner erscheint die erste Ausgabe der Architekturzeitschrift *Domus*, die vom Architekten Gio Ponti gemeinsam mit dem Barnabitenpater Giovanni Semeria in Italien gegründet worden ist. Die erste Ausgabe mit dem Untertitel *Architektur und Innenarchitektur der modernen Wohnung in der Stadt und auf dem Land* beschäftigt sich mit neuer Architektur, Raumgestaltung und dekorativer Kunst in Italien.

1929

Mies van der Rohe gestaltet auf der Weltausstellung in Barcelona den deutschen Pavillon. In New York wird das Museum of Modern Art, das weltweit erste Museum für moderne Kunst, eröffnet.
Die Kunstgewerbeschule Wien feiert ihr 60-jähriges Bestehen.

1926–32

Kunstgewerbeschule Wien

1926 schreibt sich Friedrich Berzeviczy erneut an der Kunstgewerbeschule in der „Allgemeinen Abteilung Zeichnen & Formen nach der Natur“ bei Viktor Schufinsky ein. Als Nebenfach belegt er „Ornamentale Handschrift/Heraldik“ bei Rudolf Larisch und wählt die Werkstätte für Textilarbeit und Modewesen. 1927 wechselt er in die Mode- und Textilfachklasse Wimmer-Wisgrills, der sein Mentor und Förderer wird und mit dem er von 1928/29 bis 1932/33 in einer Beziehung und im gemeinsamen Haushalt lebt. Berzeviczy darf sich in der Werkstatt mit Paravents einen abgetrennten und ungestörten Arbeitsbereich schaffen. Eugen Steinhof, Architekt und von 1923 bis 1930 Direktor der Kunstgewerbeschule, begeistert ihn für das internationale avantgardistische Kunstgeschehen und bringt ihm die Harmonie der Farben näher. Die Kontinuität seiner floral wuchernden Gebilde lehnt sich an das Werk Dagobert Peches an. Er reist 1929 zur Weltausstellung nach Barcelona, danach nach Paris, München und Berlin. Bis 1931 hält sich Berzeviczy in Paris auf. Da er schwer erkrankt, wird Berzeviczy von Wimmer-Wisgrill nach Wien geholt. Zurück in Wien, nutzt er die Räumlichkeiten der Kunstgewerbeschule zeitweise als Wohnatelier und hält sich mit Auftragsarbeiten über Wasser. Nach eigener (nicht gesicherter) Angabe entwirft er Stoffe für *Haus & Garten* und dekoriert mit Kollegen den Ball der Kunstgewerbeschule sowie die legendären Wiener Künstlerfeste. Die Schule richtet für Berzeviczy und zwei seiner Kommilitonen einen Mittagstisch ein, der aus dem Erlös des Balls finanziert wird. Er findet auch eine Mäzenin;

Berzeviczy, despite his young age, a recognized name on the Viennese art scene.

1932
Raum und Mode
At *Raum und Mode* (November 29, 1932 to February 15, 1933), an exhibition organized by the Chamber of Commerce Institute for the Promotion of Trade and Industry, Berzeviczy is represented with two works. The show's theme is the ideal living space for the modern couple and its aim is to breathe new life into the traditional Viennese luxury industry. Its artistic director is Wimmer-Wisgrill; other contributors include Josef Hoffmann and Oswald Haerdtl. The interiors by the twenty-four-year-old Berzeviczy are imaginative designs with effectively employed materials. He is responsible for the dining room and the lady's bedroom in the "House for Two." The dining room is furnished with an up-lit frosted-glass dining table and the walls are decorated with silver foil wallpaper with embossed plant ornaments. This is contrasted with ceilings and floors in dark blue. The lady's bedroom is defined by a cool color scheme in a range of blue tones. The furniture, covered with soft fabrics, the mirror, and the sheer curtains imply a passive female stereotype that was already outdated at the time.

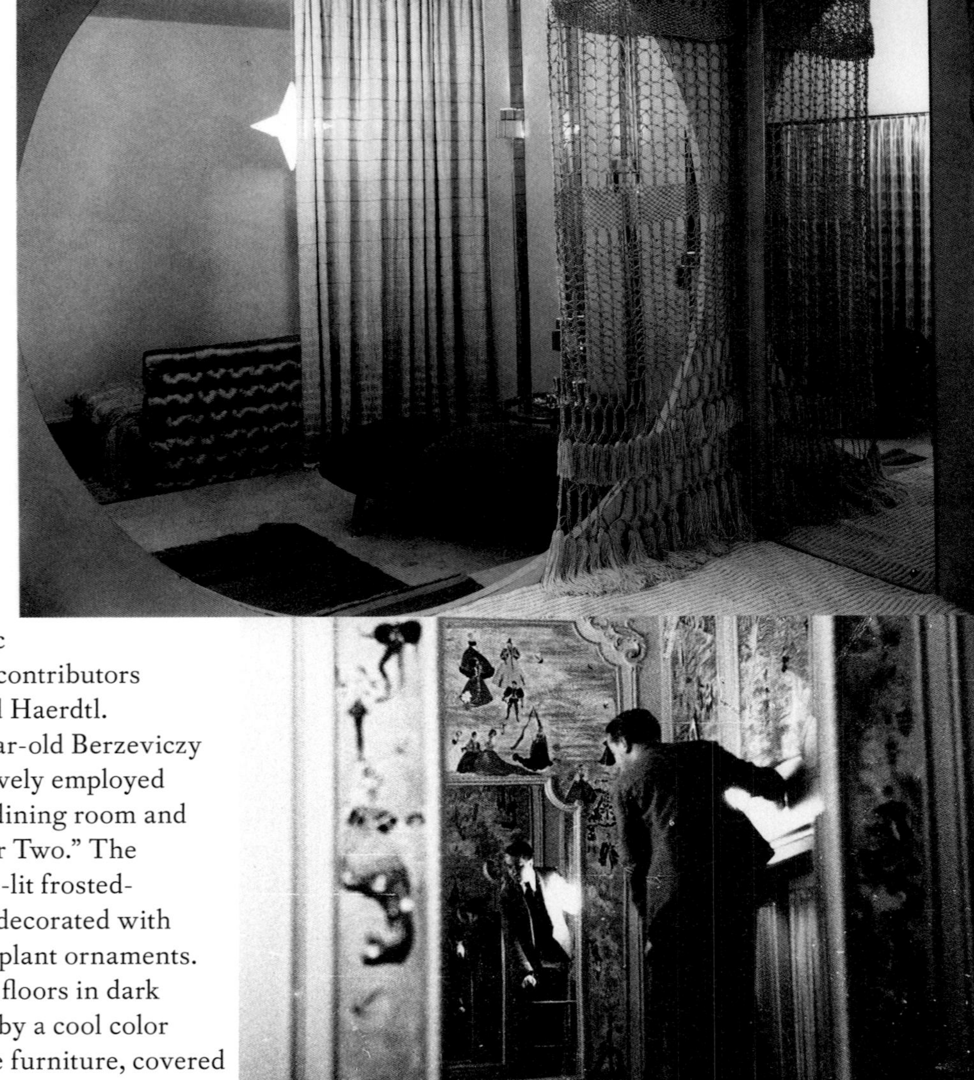

Oben / Above: Ausstellungsansicht / Exhibition view *Raum und Mode*, Zimmer der Dame / lady's bedroom, 1932
Unten / Below: Berzeviczy bei der Montage im Demel / installing wall paintings at Demel, 1935

1932
The Wiener Werkstätte ceases operation. In September its remaining warehouse stock is auctioned off at the Vienna auction house Glückselig. Vienna's Werkbundsiedlung, developed under the leadership of Josef Frank, is completed. Thirty-one architects took part, designing seventy homes with gardens. The houses are furnished by Haus & Garten.

1936
The photographer and enthusiastic gardener Edward Steichen exhibits his larkspur varieties at MoMA in New York. It is the first and only show devoted to flowers. The exhibition runs for just one week under the title *Edward Steichen's Delphiniums*. The presentation elevates the cultivation of plants to an art form.

1933–37
Demel – Augarten – World's Fair – London
In the years around 1933, Berzeviczy creates a number of designs for wall hangings and a series of abstract compositions. In 1935, he participates in an exhibition at Galerie Würthle in Vienna with two stage set designs for Grillparzer's play *A Dream Is Life*. In winter 1935/36, he starts designing décors for the Augarten porcelain manufactory, characterized by their extravagance and radiant colors. Some of the pieces he designs are shown at the World's Fair in Paris in 1937.
In 1936, Berzeviczy marries Klára Demel, the niece and heiress of Anna Demel, proprietress of the Demel confectionery business. This is primarily a marriage of convenience.

die Klimt-Sammlerin Serena Lederer beauftragt ihn, ein Album mit Venedig-Ansichten anzufertigen, da ihr das Reisen bereits zu beschwerlich sei, und unterstützt so das junge Talent. Durch Vermittlung von Josef Hoffmann und Wimmer-Wisgrill ist Berzeviczy ab 1932 für die grafische Gestaltung und Innenausstattung der Hofzuckerbäckerei Demel Wien zuständig. Er verhilft dem traditionellen Unternehmen zu einem zeitgemäßen, neuen Auftreten, indem er raffiniert gefaltete Verpackungen gestaltet, die Salons neu dekoriert und die Auslagen inszeniert.

1929

Boudoir einer mondänen Dame

Die Kunstgewerbeschule feiert 1929 ihr 60-jähriges Bestehen in einer Ausstellung im k. k. Österreichischen Museum für Kunst und Industrie. Der junge Berzeviczy beteiligt sich mit einem überaus auffallenden Beitrag: *Boudoir einer mondänen Dame* besticht durch ein an Ketten von der Decke abgehängtes ovales Bett und dominante runde Formen sowie leichte Stoffe mit applizierten Mustern. Die extravagante Formensprache sowie Farbgebung und Material hinterlassen beim Wiener Publikum einen bleibenden Eindruck. Durch seine international gut vernetzten Mentoren Josef Hoffmann und Eduard Wimmer-Wisgrill erfährt Berzeviczy von den aktuellen Modetrends aus Paris und New York und interpretiert diese dementsprechend in seiner Raumgestaltung. Für Berzeviczy hat Wimmer-Wisgrill „einen großartigen Spürsinn, das Neue, das Elegante, Künstlerische, Modische in allem herauszufinden". Durch die Ausstellung avanciert Berzeviczy bereits in jungen Jahren zu einer anerkannten Persönlichkeit der Wiener Kunstszene.

1932

Raum und Mode

Bei der 1932 vom Gewerbeförderungsinstitut der Handelskammer Wien ausgerichteten Ausstellung *Raum und Mode* (29. November 1932 bis 15. Februar 1933) ist Berzeviczy mit zwei Beiträgen vertreten. Die Thematik der Ausstellung dreht sich um den idealen Wohnraum für moderne Ehepaare und will die traditionellen Wiener Luxusgewerbe neu beleben. Der künstlerische Leiter ist Wimmer-Wisgrill, weitere Beteiligte sind Josef Hoffmann und Oswald Haerdtl.

Die Interieurs des 24-jährigen Berzeviczy sind fantasievolle Gestaltungen mit effektvoll eingesetzten Materialien. Er zeichnet für das Speisezimmer und das Zimmer der Dame im Haus *For Two* verantwortlich. Das Speisezimmer ist mit einem von unten beleuchteten Esstisch aus Mattglas und einer die Wände überziehenden Silberfolientapete ausgestattet, die mit Pflanzenornamentprägungen verziert ist. Im Kontrast dazu stehen Zimmerdecke und Fußboden, jeweils in Dunkelblau gehalten. Das *Zimmer der Dame* bestimmt eine kühle Farbgebung in verschiedenen Blautönen. Die mit weichen Stoffen bezogenen Möbel, der Spiegel und die durchlässigen Vorhänge implizieren einen schon seinerzeit wenig progressiven, passiven Frauentyp.

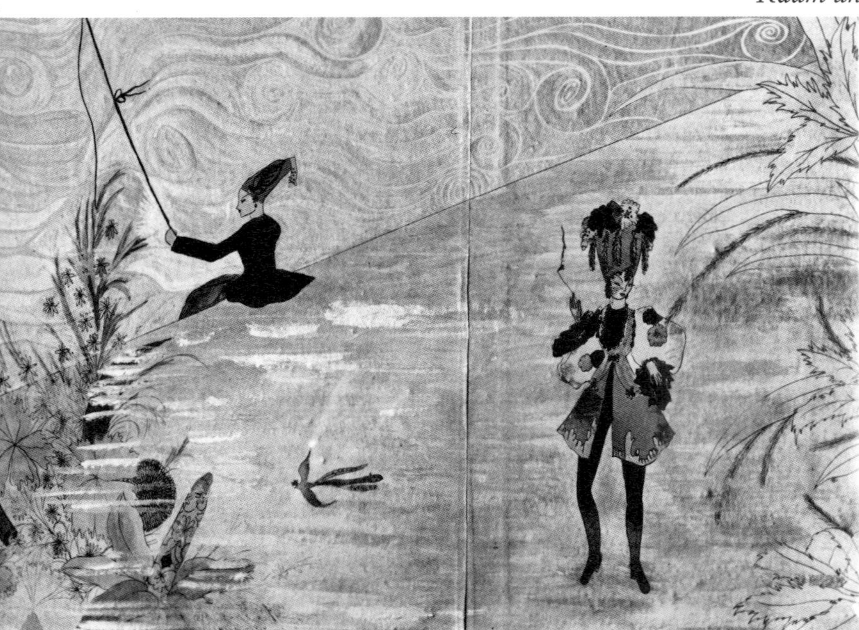

Detail, Innenräume der Zuckerbäckerei Demel Wandmalerei / Interior of the Demel confectionery store, wall painting, 1935

1932

Die Wiener Werkstätte wird geschlossen. Im September werden die Restbestände aus dem Warenlager im Wiener Auktionshaus Glückselig versteigert.

Die Wiener Werkbundsiedlung, entstanden unter der Leitung von Josef Frank, wird fertiggestellt. 31 Architekt*innen verantworten die Planung der 70 Eigenheime mit Garten. Die Einrichtung der Häuser übernimmt *Haus & Garten.*

In 1937, Berzeviczy creates tapestry designs for Oskar Strnad, to be shown at the World's Fair in Paris (May 25 – November 25, 1937); however, the pieces are never made. One of these designs, *Papageno's Enchanted Forest*, is used as decoration for the "Bauernball in Alt Salzburg," which takes place at the Austrian embassy in London on December 9, 1937. Berzeviczy and the artist Franz Taussig design the decorations for this event in the style of Vienna's famous *Künstlerfeste*. They are made during the classes of Paul Kirnig and Wimmer-Wisgrill at the School of Applied Arts and transported to London in special freight carriages.
Between 1934 and 1937, Berzeviczy designs a number of stage sets and costumes for the Theater für 49 in Vienna, one of the city's first cabarets, which is located in the basement of the Hotel de France on Maria-Theresien-Strasse near the Schottentor and primarily shows contemporary avant-garde plays. In 1937, the theater moves to Lothringerstrasse 14 in Vienna's 3rd district. Berzeviczy is in charge of the interior design of the foyer and auditorium of the now renamed "Modernes Theater am Schwarzenbergplatz." He is also thought to have created designs for the Jüdisches Kulturtheater.
Berzeviczy is commissioned by the Akademietheater to design stage sets and costumes for the play *Aimée*. However, the play is never staged, as the Nazis remove it from the repertoire in 1938.

1937

After the bombing of the Basque town of Guernica on April 26, 1937, Pablo Picasso paints the picture *Guernica* for the World's Fair in Paris. The mood at this World's Fair oscillates between dictatorship and democracy, between avant-garde and reactionary, Neoclassical architecture. Its theme "Art and Technology in Modern Life" seeks to establish a consensus. Oswald Haerdtl designs the Austrian pavilion, a monumental showcase of large-scale transport projects, including the Grossglockner High Alpine Road, and a gigantic Alpine panorama by Robert Haas. The *Reichsausstellung Schaffendes Volk* takes place in Düsseldorf. Alongside "new German art," there are displays of "new German housing" and "new German industry." The exhibition creates an entire new district in the city.

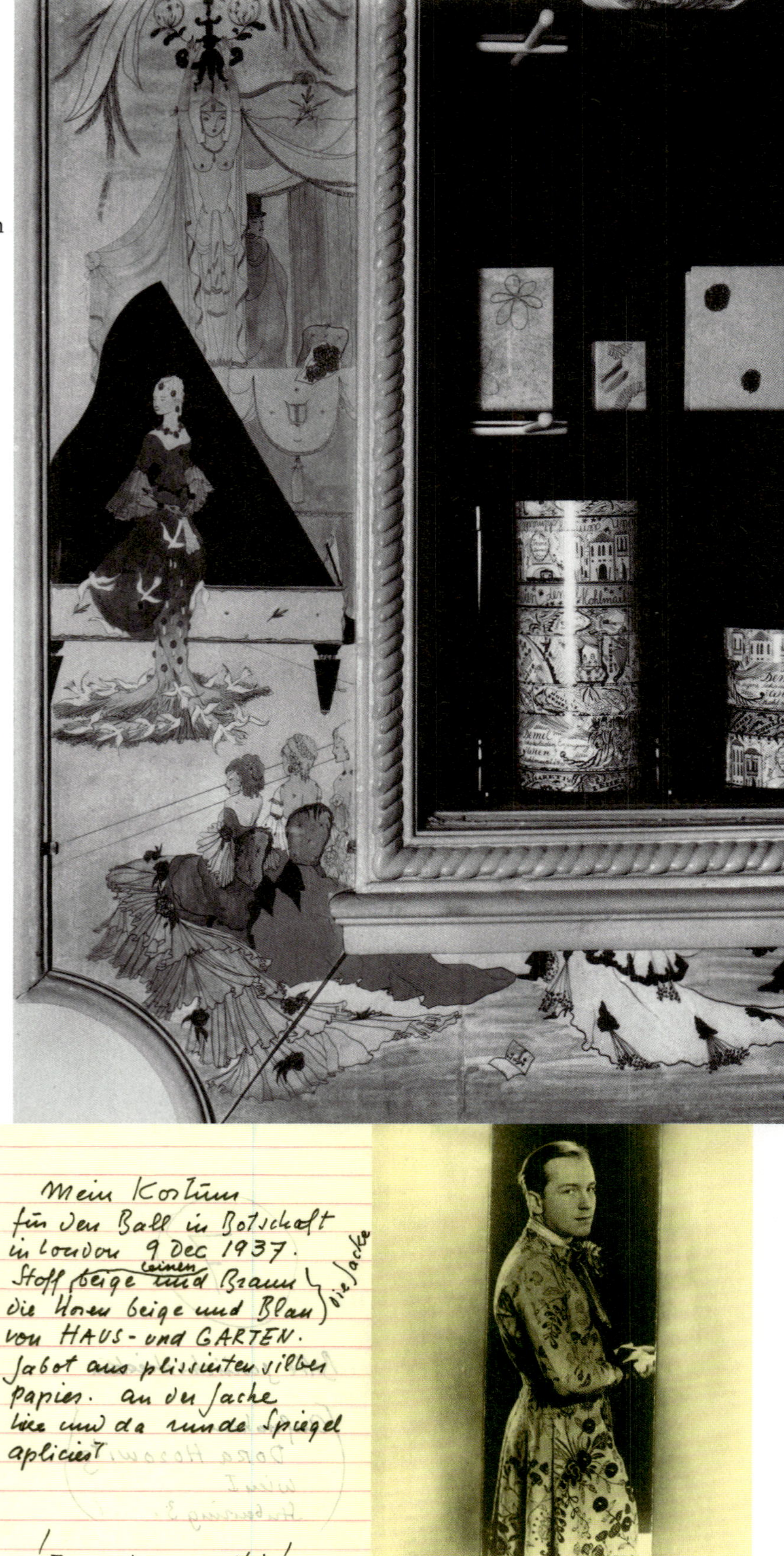

Oben / Above: Detail, Innenräume der Zuckerbäckerei Demel, Wandmalerei und Vitrine mit Bonbonieren / Interior of the Demel confectionery store, wall painting and display case with bonbonnières, 1935
Unten / Below: Friedrich Berzeviczy im Kostüm für den *Bauernball in Alt Salzburg* / in costume for the "Bauernball in Alt Salzburg" in London, 1937

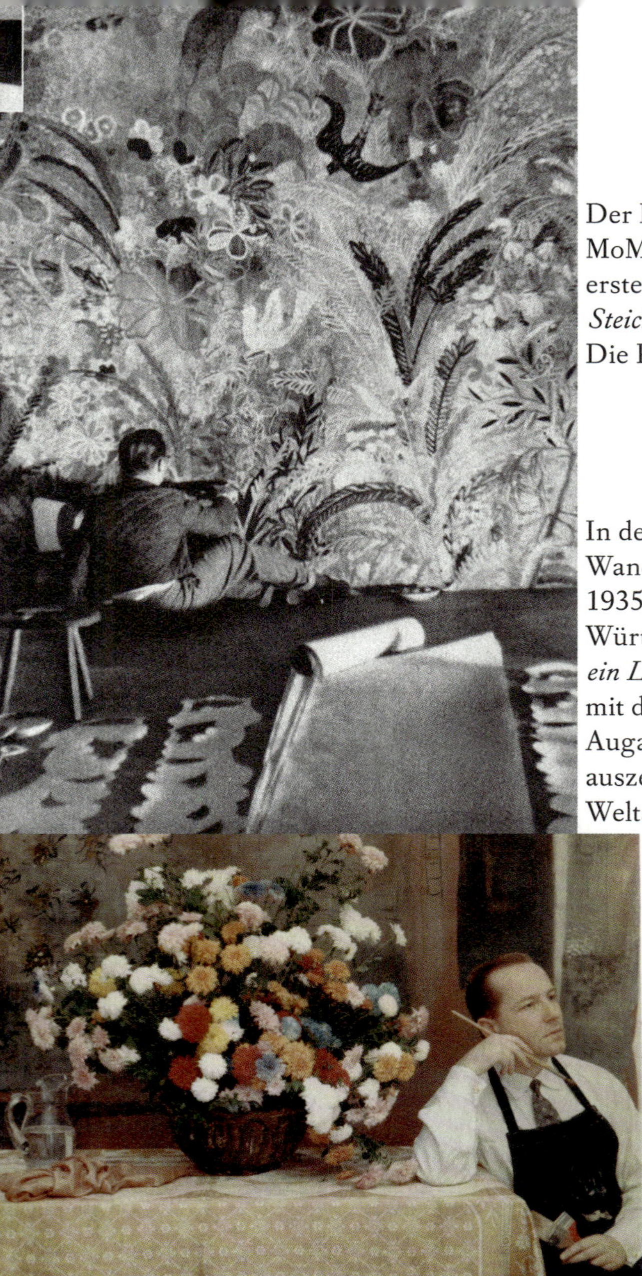

Oben / Above: Friedrich Berzeviczy-Pallavicini beim Malen von *Zauberwald des Papageno* / while painting *Papageno's Enchanted Forest*, 1937
Unten / Below: Porträt von / Portrait of Friedrich von Berzeviczy-Pallavicini, undatiert / undated

1936

Der Fotograf und begeisterte Gärtner Edward Steichen stellt im MoMA in New York seine Ritterspornzüchtungen aus. Es ist die erste und einzige Blumen gewidmete Schau. Unter dem Titel *Edward Steichen's Delphiniums* ist die Ausstellung nur eine Woche zu sehen. Die Präsentation erhebt die Züchtung von Pflanzen zur Kunst.

1933–37
Demel – Augarten –
Weltausstellung – London

In den Jahren um 1933 entstehen zahlreiche Entwürfe für Wandbehänge sowie eine Serie von abstrakten Kompositionen. 1935 nimmt Berzeviczy an einer Ausstellung in der Wiener Galerie Würthle mit zwei Bühnenbildentwürfen für das Stück *Der Traum ein Leben* von Grillparzer teil. Im Winter 1935/36 beginnt er mit der Arbeit an Dekorentwürfen für die Porzellanmanufaktur Augarten, die sich durch ihre intensive Farbgebung und Extravaganz auszeichnen. Einige von ihm entworfene Stücke werden auf der Weltausstellung 1937 in Paris gezeigt.
Berzeviczy heiratet im Jahr 1936 Klára Demel, die Nichte und Erbin der Demel-Inhaberin Anna Demel. Es handelt sich primär um eine Zweckehe.
Für die in Paris stattfindende Weltausstellung (25. Mai bis 25. November 1937) entwirft Berzeviczy 1937 für Oskar Strnad Gobelins, die jedoch nicht ausgeführt werden. Einer dieser Entwürfe, *Zauberwald des Papageno*, wird u. a. auf dem Fest *Bauernball in Alt Salzburg*, das am 9. Dezember 1937 in der österreichischen Botschaft in London stattfindet, als Dekoration verwendet. Berzeviczy gestaltet die Dekoration des Festes gemeinsam mit dem Künstler Franz Taussig im Stil der Wiener Künstlerfeste. Die Dekorationen werden an der Kunstgewerbeschule in den Klassen von Paul Kirnig und Eduard Wimmer-Wisgrill vorbereitet und mittels eigener Waggons nach London transportiert.
Zwischen 1934 und 1937 entwirft Berzeviczy einige Bühnenbilder und Kostüme für das *Theater für 49* in Wien, eine der ersten Kleinkunstbühnen der Stadt im Souterrain des Hotel de France in der Maria-Theresien-Straße beim Schottentor, wo primär zeitgenössische, avantgardistische Stücke aufgeführt werden. 1937 übersiedelt das Theater in die Lothringerstraße 14 im 3. Wiener Gemeindebezirk. Berzeviczy übernimmt die Innenraumgestaltung von Foyer und Zuschauerraum des nunmehrigen *Modernen Theaters am Schwarzenbergplatz*. Es wird auch vermutet, dass Berzeviczy einige Entwürfe für das *Jüdische Kulturtheater* gefertigt hat.
Berzeviczy erhält vom Akademietheater den Auftrag, Bühnenbilder und Kostüme für das Stück *Aimée* zu gestalten. Das Stück wird jedoch nicht realisiert, da es die Nationalsozialisten 1938 vom Spielplan streichen.

1937

Nach dem Luftangriff auf die baskische Stadt Guernica am 26. April 1937 malt Pablo Picasso für die Weltausstellung in Paris das Bild *Guernica*. Die Weltausstellung beherrscht ein zwischen Diktatur und Demokratie, aber auch zwischen Avantgarde und reaktionärer, klassizistischer Architektur schwankendes Klima. Durch das Thema *Die Künste und Technik im modernen Leben* versucht man, einen Konsens herzustellen. Oswald Haerdtl entwirft den österreichischen Pavillon, ein monumentales Schaufenster, in dem u. a. verkehrstechnische Großprojekte wie die Großglockner Hochalpenstraße und ein gigantisches Alpenpanorama von Robert Haas präsentiert werden.

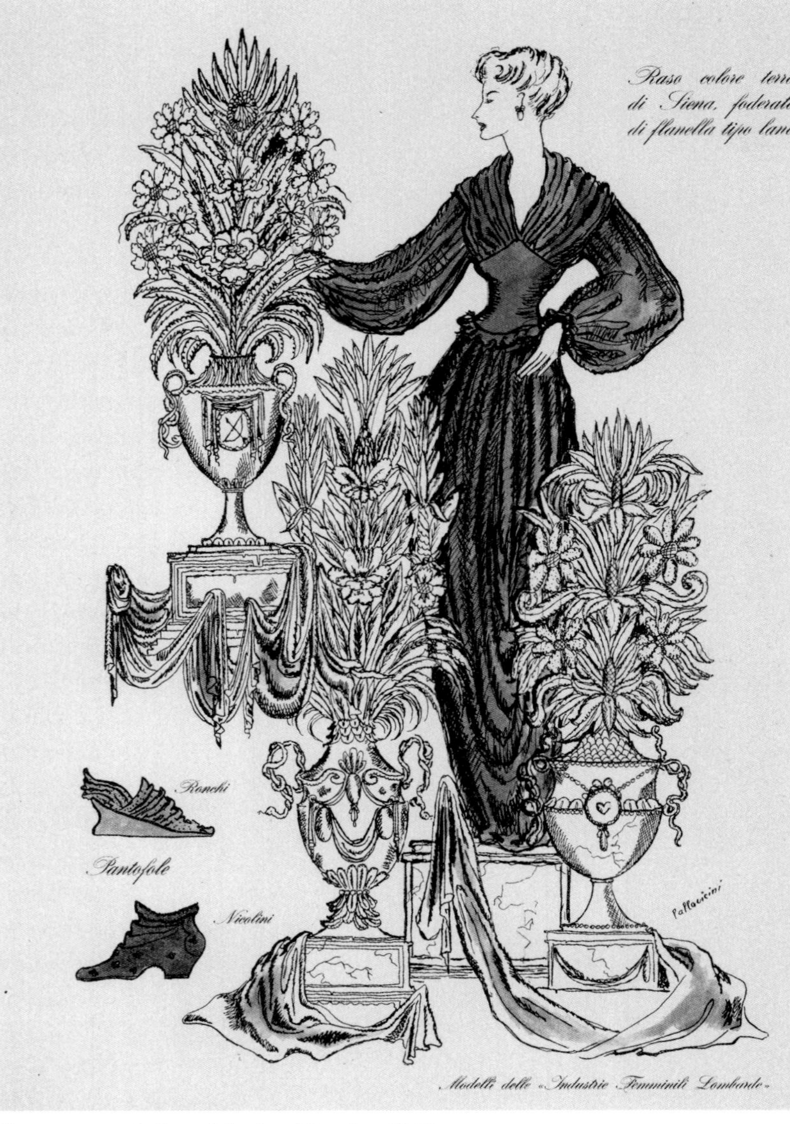

Illustration in *Bellezza*, Oktober / October 1942

1938

In March, Austria is annexed to the German Reich.
André Breton and Paul Éluard organize the *Exposition Internationale du Surréalisme* at the Galerie Beaux-Arts in Paris.
In New York City, the legendary Café Society jazz club opens in Greenwich Village. It is the first club in a white neighborhood that is open to all ethnic and social groups, despite strict social segregation.

1938–49
Italy

Due to the political developments in Austria, Berzeviczy leaves Vienna in 1938, traveling first to Capri and then to Milan. His wife Klára stays in Vienna. Berzeviczy describes himself as a pacifist with no interest in politics. As a Hungarian citizen, he considers himself a guest in Austria and therefore feels no responsibility to make a stand against the Nazis. Berzeviczy embodies the romantic dreamer who does not see social criticism as part of his role and lives primarily in his own little world of decorative art.
He is well connected in Italy. His university friend Camela Haerdtl (née Prati) recommends him to the Italian architect and designer Gio Ponti.
To help with obtaining a work permit and for practical reasons, he assumes his maternal name, Pallavicini, and is known from that point on as Federico Pallavicini.
In Capri he designs fabric patterns that he sells to Milan. Gio Ponti introduces him to the Milanese cultural scene. He works for Ponti's architecture magazine *Domus* as a graphic designer and illustrator. When Mussolini founds the magazine *Bellezza*,[1] Pallavicini contributes the fashion illustrations. The project was originally connected with the *Domus* editorial team from 1941 to 1943: Together with Daria Guarnati, Pallavicini designs the Italian style magazine *Aria d'Italia*. He illustrates books and magazines, creates fabric collections, accessories, and theater costumes. From 1946, his pictures are exhibited at renowned galleries in Florence, Rome, and Milan.

1949
Fleur Cowles and *Flair*

In Italy, Pallavicini meets Fleur Cowles, an American author, artist, and publisher, who is traveling around Europe to research printing techniques for her new magazine *Flair.* Cowles is inspired by *Aria d'Italia* and persuades Pallavicini and Daria Guarnati to join her at *Flair.*
Being well connected, Fleur Cowles enables for Federico to travel to New York and start working for her.
"I found and brought with me Prince Pallavicini, a gifted artist-designer escapee from Hungary whom I found in Milan, and for whom I arranged a stateless person's passport." (Fleur Cowles)

1 Friedrich von Berzeviczy-Pallavicini, recollections in Erika Patka, ed., *Friedrich von Berzeviczy-Pallavicini: Poesie der Inszenierung* (Vienna, 1988).

In Düsseldorf findet die *Reichsausstellung Schaffendes Volk* statt. Darin werden neben „neuer deutscher Kunst“ auch „neues deutsches Wohnen“ und „neues deutsches Arbeiten“ vorgeführt. Mit der Ausstellung entsteht in Düsseldorf ein völlig neuer Stadtteil.

1938

Im März findet der „Anschluss“ Österreichs an das Deutsche Reich statt.
André Breton und Paul Éluard organisieren in der Pariser Galerie Beaux-Arts von Georges Wildenstein die *Exposition Internationale du Surréalisme.*
In New York City eröffnet der legendäre Jazzclub *Café Society* im Stadtteil Greenwich Village. Es ist der erste Club in einer weißen Wohngegend, der sich allen – sonst voneinander gesellschaftlich streng getrennten – ethnischen und sozialen Gruppen gegenüber öffnet.

1938–49
Italien

Aufgrund der politischen Entwicklung in Österreich verlässt Berzeviczy im Jahr 1938 Wien und geht zuerst nach Capri und später nach Mailand. Seine Frau Klára bleibt unterdessen in Wien. Nach eigener Aussage ist Berzeviczy Pazifist und interessiert sich nicht für Politik. Als ungarischer Staatsbürger sieht er sich als Gast in Österreich und fühlt sich daher nicht verantwortlich, gegen die Nationalsozialisten zu rebellieren. Berzeviczy verkörpert einen romantischen Träumer, der soziale Kritik nicht als seine Aufgabe versteht und primär in der heilen Welt seiner dekorativen Kunst existiert.
In Italien ist er gut vernetzt. Seine Freundin und Studienkollegin Camela Haerdtl (geb. Prati) empfiehlt ihn an den italienischen Architekten Gio Ponti.
Für die Arbeitsbewilligung und aus praktischen Gründen nimmt er den Namen der Mutter, Pallavicini, an und nennt sich ab nun Federico Pallavicini.
Auf Capri entwirft er Stoffmuster, die er nach Mailand verkauft. Gio Ponti führt ihn in die Kulturszene Mailands ein. Als grafischer Gestalter und Illustrator arbeitet er für dessen Architekturzeitschrift *Domus.* Als Mussolini das Magazin *Bellezza* gründet[1], zeichnet Pallavicini die Modeillustrationen. Das Projekt war ursprünglich von 1941 bis 1943 mit der Gruppe der Mitarbeiter von *Domus* verbunden. Mit Daria Guarnati entwirft er das italienische Stylemagazin *Aria d'Italia.* Er illustriert Bücher und Zeitschriften, kreiert Stoffkollektionen, Accessoires und Bühnenkostüme. Seine Bilder werden ab 1946 in namhaften Galerien in Florenz, Rom und Mailand ausgestellt.

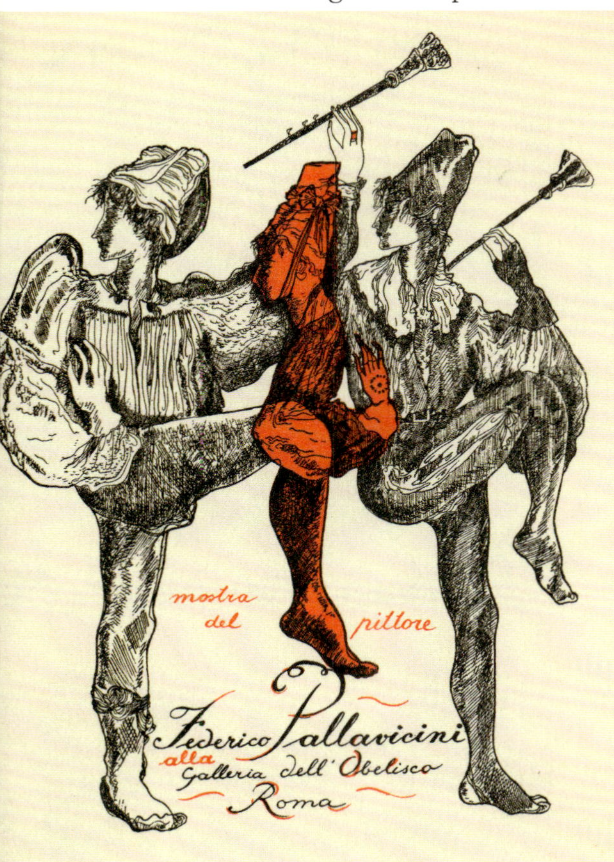

Einladung / Invitation, Galleria dell Obelisco, Rom / Rome, 1948

1949
Fleur Cowles und *Flair*

1949 trifft Pallavicini in Italien auf Fleur Cowles, eine amerikanische Schriftstellerin, Künstlerin und Herausgeberin. Sie befindet sich auf einer Reise durch Europa, um sich über die gängigen Drucktechniken für ihr neues Magazin *Flair* zu informieren. Cowles ist von *Aria d'Italia* begeistert und kann Pallavicini und Daria Guarnati für *Flair* gewinnen. Aufgrund ihrer guten Beziehungen ermöglicht Fleur Cowles Federico die Einreise nach New York, um für sie zu arbeiten. „I found and brought with me Prince Pallavicini, a gifted artist-designer escapee from Hungary whom I found in Milan, and for whom I arranged a stateless person's passport.“ (Fleur Cowles)

1 Friedrich von Berzeviczy-Pallavicini, „Erinnerungen“, in: Erika Patka, *Friedrich von Berzeviczy-Pallavicini. Poesie der Inszenierung*, Wien, 1988.

1949–65

New York and his female clientele

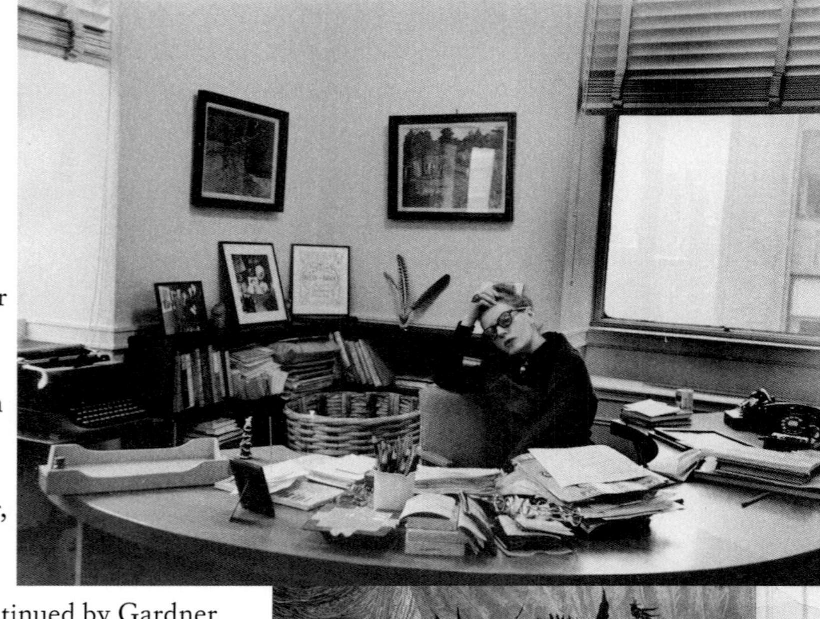

Upon arriving in New York, Pallavicini works with Fleur Cowles on the magazine *Flair*, which publishes its first issue in February 1950. *Flair* is far ahead of its time in terms of design and production, and a pioneering model for the next generation of graphic designers. Its content reflects the tastes and themes of New York's upper classes. The magazine, elaborately produced with postcard inserts, die-cut covers, brochures, and fold-outs, has 90,000 subscribers and a circulation of 200,000. Each issue deals with a specific topic and features contributions from famous artists such as Salvador Dalí or Saul Steinberg. However, the initially acclaimed magazine experienced a decline in advertising revenue from the autumn of 1950 onwards and was officially discontinued by Gardner Cowles in January 1951, after twelve issues and a pilot issue (published in a limited edition in autumn 1949) due to its costly production. Pallavicini moves to *Look*, where he works as a stylist and set designer. Alongside his professional career as a graphic designer, he produces a variety of costumes and props for Hollywood. He also makes a name for himself as a visual artist through exhibitions at renowned galleries on the East Coast. One of his first New York exhibitions takes place in 1951 at the Hugo Gallery, founded by Robert Rothschild, Elizabeth Arden, and Maria dei Principi Ruspoli Hugo and run by Alexander Iolas. Iolas provides a platform for the Surrealists exiled in America, but also for the contemporary New York avant-garde. He later opened his own gallery in New York. Fleur Cowles introduces Pallavicini to the upper echelons of New York society. In 1955 he works as art director for Elizabeth Arden and designs the window displays for her stores. In 1956 he joins Helena Rubinstein, who shares his opulent tastes. He not only decorates her beauty salons and designs her packaging, but also her numerous private apartments around the world, primarily with murals. For the New York department store Lord & Taylor he designs a mechanical wonderland display, which is featured on Austrian television. In 1956, following the death of her aunt Anna Demel, Klára Berzeviczy takes over the Demel confectioners. Around that time, while in Europe for Helena Rubinstein, Pallavicini redesigns the confectioners' stores. He removes his own decorations from the 1930s and replaces them with Neoclassical furnishings.
His mural motifs feature frequently as backdrops in *Vogue* photo shoots between 1957 and 1959, while home accessories designed by Pallavicini are also promoted as gift ideas, for example in the pre-Christmas issue of *Vogue* in November 1957.

Oben / Above: Fleur Cowles in ihrem Büro bei / in her office at *Look* magazine, um / c. 1950
Unten / Below: Helena Rubinstein vor einer Wandmalerei von / in front of a painting by Federico Pallavicini in ihrer New Yorker Wohnung / in her New York apartment. Abbildung / photograph in *Milwaukee Sentinal*, January 26, 1958

1950s

In 1950, Jackson Pollock presents his allover paintings in New York. Shortly afterwards, New York's Abstract Expressionists make their international breakthrough.
In the mid-1950s, the art world's focus shifts increasingly toward New York, which is taking over from Paris as the world's premier art city.
In Kassel, at the initiative of the artist and curator Arnold Bode, the first documenta takes place in 1955, a documentation of modern art that was inaccessible to Germans during the Nazi era. The second documenta in 1959 highlights contemporary art's international status. Abstraction dominates.

1949–65

New York und Berzeviczy-Pallavicinis Auftraggeberinnen

Als Pallavicini nach New York kommt, arbeitet er mit Fleur Cowles am Magazin *Flair*, das im Februar 1950 seine erste Ausgabe publiziert. *Flair* ist in Gestaltung und Design seiner Zeit weit voraus und wegweisendes Vorbild für die nachkommende Generation von Grafikerinnen und Grafikern. Die Zeitschrift, die Postkarten-Einlagen, vorgestanzte Einbände, Broschüren und Faltblätter enthält, erzielt 90.000 Abonennten und eine Auflage von 200.000 Stück. Jede Ausgabe behandelt ein spezielles Thema und enthält Beiträge namhafter Künstler*innen wie Salvador Dalí oder Saul Steinberg. Inhaltlich bedient es den Geschmack und die Themen der New Yorker Upperclass. Das anfänglich gefeierte Magazin erfährt ab Herbst 1950 einen Rückgang an Werbeeinnahmen und wird offiziell aufgrund der kostspieligen Produktion bereits im Januar 1951 nach zwölf Ausgaben und einem Prototyp (herausgegeben in einer limitierten Ausgabe im Herbst 1949) von Gardner Cowles eingestellt. Pallavicini wechselt zu *Look*, um dort als Stylist und Setdesigner zu arbeiten.

Neben seiner beruflichen Karriere als Grafikdesigner und Gestalter produziert er für Hollywood verschiedene Kostüme und Designarbeiten. Außerdem macht er sich als bildender Künstler durch Ausstellungen in renommierten Galerien an der Ostküste einen Namen. Eine seiner ersten Ausstellungen in New York findet 1951 in der Galerie Hugo statt, die 1945 von Robert Rothschild, Elizabeth Arden und Maria dei Principi Ruspoli Hugo gegründet wird und unter der Leitung von Alexander Iolas steht. Iolas stellt die ins amerikanische Exil geflüchteten Surrealisten, aber auch die damalige New Yorker Avantgarde aus und eröffnet später seine eigene Galerie in New York. Durch Fleur Cowles wird Pallavicini in die gehobenen Kreise der New Yorker Society eingeführt. So arbeitet er 1955 als Art Director für Elizabeth Arden und gestaltet die Auslagen ihrer Geschäfte. 1956 wechselt er zu Helena Rubinstein, die seinen Geschmack für das Opulente teilt. Er schmückt nicht nur ihre Schönheitssalons und entwirft ihre Verpackungen, sondern dekoriert auch ihre privaten Wohnungen und Salons auf der ganzen Welt, vorwiegend mit Wandmalereien. Für das New Yorker Kaufhaus Lord & Taylor entwirft er u. a. eine mechanisch bewegte Wunderwelt, die in einer Auslage präsentiert wird und über die das österreichische Fernsehen berichtet.

Im Jahr 1956 übernimmt Klára Berzeviczy nach dem Tod ihrer Tante Anna Demel die Geschäftsleitung der Konditorei Demel. Als sich Berzeviczy um 1956 für Helena Rubinstein in Europa aufhält, gestaltet er die Salons der Zuckerbäckerei um. Er lässt seine eigenen Dekorationen aus den 1930er-Jahren entfernen und ersetzt sie durch eine neoklassizistische Einrichtung.

Als angesagter „Murals Painter" entwirft er zwischen 1957 und 1959 öfter Hintergründe bei Fotoshootings für die *Vogue*. Aber auch von Pallavicini entworfene Einrichtungsaccessoires werden zum Beispiel in der Vorweihnachtsausgabe der *Vogue*, im November 1957, als Geschenkidee angepriesen.

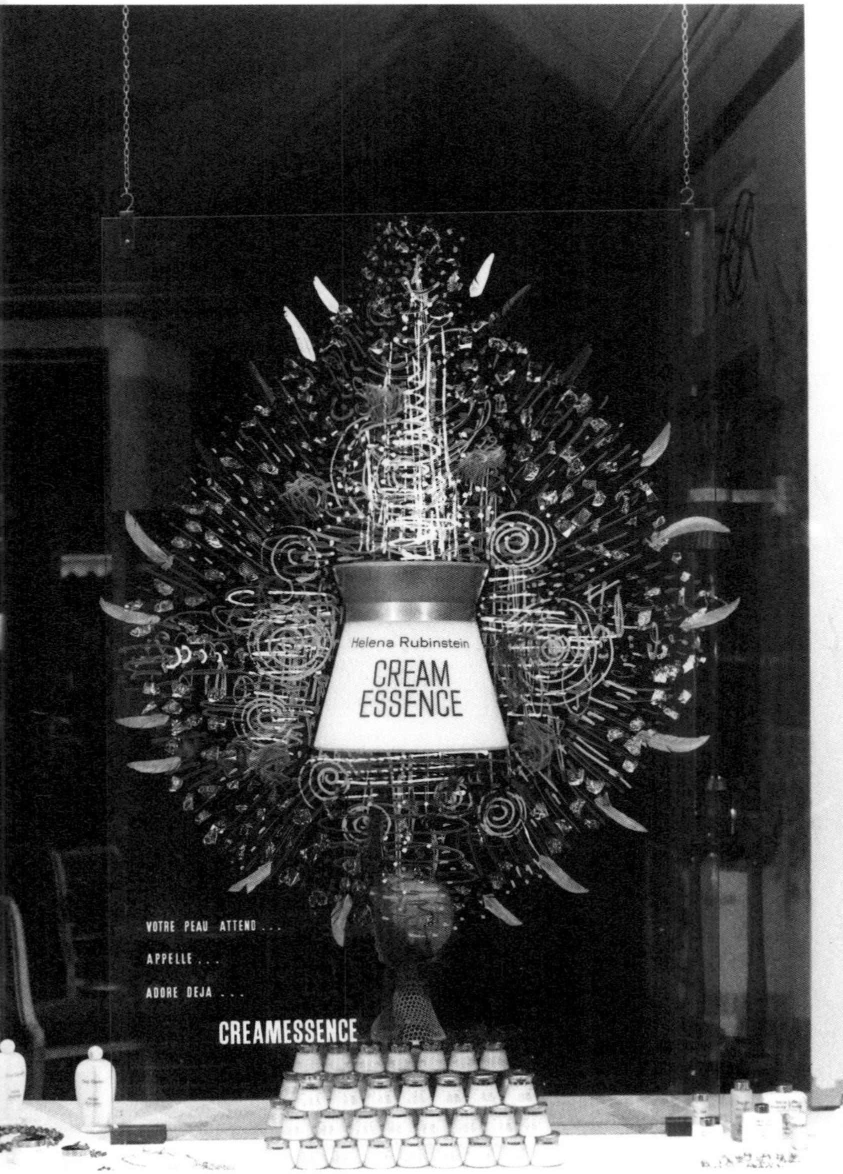

Schaufenster in einem Salon von Helena Rubinstein, gestaltet von Federico Pallavicini / Window display in a Helena Rubinstein salon designed by Federico Pallavicini, undatiert / undated

1960s

In the UK, Pop Art is increasingly preoccupied with perception and its appearance in pictures. In New York, Pop Art and Environmental Art split from the dominant Abstract Expressionism and attempt to reintegrate art into ordinary life. The artists come from the world of advertising and consumerism; they design window displays and work as graphic designers and illustrators in advertising. Traditional painterly materials are cast aside.
Eduard Wimmer-Wisgrill dies on December 25, 1961, in Vienna. Berzeviczy-Pallavicini travels to Vienna shortly afterwards.
Helena Rubinstein dies on April 1, 1965, at the age of 94. Right up until her death she runs the business herself. The Helena Rubinstein brand becomes part of L'Oréal in 1988.

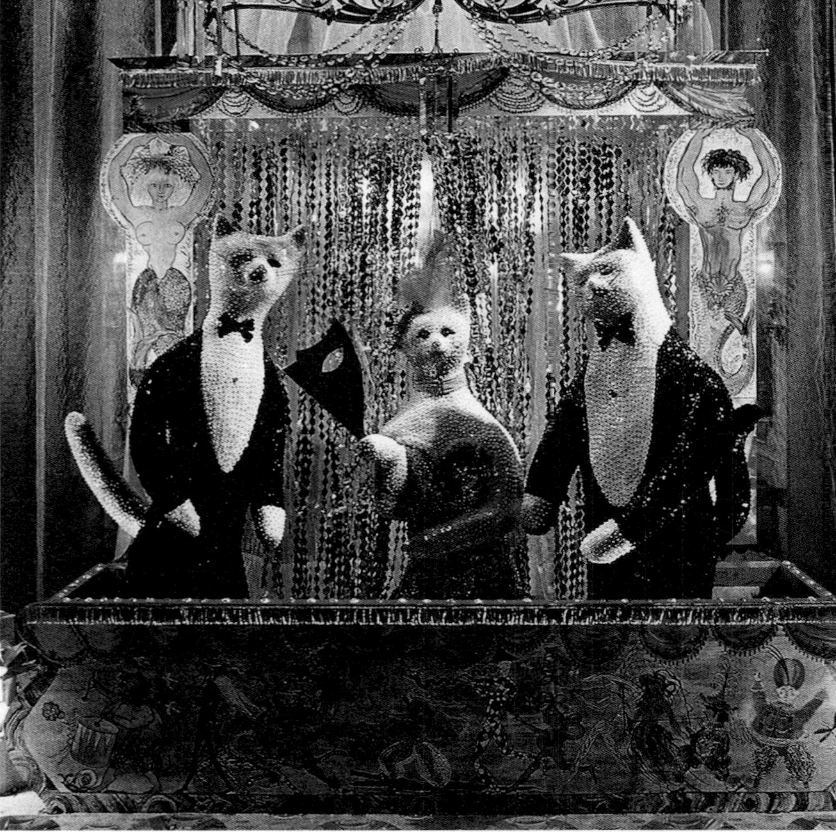

Schaufenster im Demel, gestaltet von Friedrich von Berzeviczy-Pallavicini / Window display at Demel designed by Friedrich von Berzeviczy-Pallavicini, *In der Opernloge, Katzendame und Katzenkavaliere / In the Opera Box: Lady Cat and Cavalier Cats*, 1965–72

1965
Director of Demel

When his wife Klára dies in 1965, Federico Pallavicini returns to Vienna and takes over the running of the business. He sets up a studio on one of the upper floors of the Demel building. There he creates a 1:1 model of the store window to prepare his famous window displays. These rapidly gain widespread acclaim among the Viennese public and become known as "theater of the street." Among the artist's close friends during this period in Vienna are the author and journalist Hilde Spiel and the actor Michael Heltau.
In 1967, he donates a rug, two wall hangings, seventy-nine design sketches, three floral pieces, and a folding screen to the library of the Academy of Applied Arts.
However, the high costs of his displays for Demel get him into deep water with the tax office, and he is also finding it difficult to reconcile 1960s Vienna with his memory of the city.
In 1972, Berzeviczy-Pallavicini therefore decides to sell the Demel business. It is sold via an intermediary to a company in Switzerland which, it later transpires, belongs to Udo Proksch.

1972–89
Return to New York, acknowledgement in Vienna

His pride wounded, Berzeviczy-Pallavicini returns to New York. In October 1975, a retrospective dedicated to his work is held at Galerie Würthle in Vienna. In the same year, the book titled *Die K. u. K. Hofzuckerbäckerei Demel: Ein Wiener Märchen* is published by Brandstätter, containing numerous illustrations by Berzeviczy, which today adorn the Italian wallpaper on the upper floor of the Demel store. In 1976, a limited edition of 3,000 numbered copies of the book is printed.
In 1978, the Vienna State Opera commissions Berzeviczy-Pallavicini to design the set and costumes for the comic opera *Der junge Lord* (The Young Lord), produced by Gustav Rudolf Sellner. It premieres in Vienna on June 9, 1978, and runs for eight performances until March 1979. Berzeviczy-Pallavicini works on this project in Vienna, using the Stöckl building owned by his good friend Michael Heltau as his studio.
In spring 1982, the exhibition *Die verlorenen Österreicher 1918–1938* (The Lost Austrians: 1918–1938), curated by Oswald Oberhuber, is held at the Zentralsparkasse und Kommerzialbank Wien, featuring, among others, works by Berzeviczy-Pallavicini from his time at the School of Applied Arts. The artist, who is in Vienna at the time, visits the exhibition and afterwards also the University of Applied Arts and is deeply moved.

1950er

1950 stellt Jackson Pollock seine All-over-Paintings in New York aus. Kurz darauf erfolgt der internationale Durchbruch der New Yorker abstrakten Expressionisten.
Mitte der 1950er-Jahre verlagert sich das Interesse der Kunstwelt immer mehr auf New York, das Paris den Rang als Weltstadt der Kunst abläuft.
1955 findet auf Initiative des Künstlers und Kurators Arnold Bode die erste documenta in Kassel statt – eine Dokumentation moderner Kunst, die den Deutschen während der Zeit des Nationalsozialismus nicht zugänglich war. Auf der zweiten documenta 1959 wird bereits der internationale Stand der Gegenwartskunst aufgezeigt – die Abstraktion dominiert.

1960er

In England setzt sich die Pop Art immer mehr mit der Wahrnehmung und ihrem Erscheinen in Bildern auseinander. In New York lösen Pop Art und Environment Art den dominierenden abstrakten Expressionismus ab und versuchen, die Kunst wieder in die Normalität des Lebens einzubinden. Die Künstler*innen kommen aus dem Bereich der Reklame und des Konsums, sie dekorieren Auslagen, sind Werbegrafiker*innen und Illustrator*innen. Die herkömmlichen Handwerksmaterialien der Maler*innen werden beiseitegelegt.
Eduard Wimmer-Wisgrill stirbt am 25. Dezember 1961 in Wien. Berzeviczy-Pallavicini reist kurz darauf nach Wien.
Helena Rubinstein stirbt am 1. April 1965 im Alter von 94 Jahren. Bis zu ihrem Tod leitet sie ihr Unternehmen selbst. Seit 1988 gehört die Marke Helena Rubinstein zum L'Oréal-Konzern.

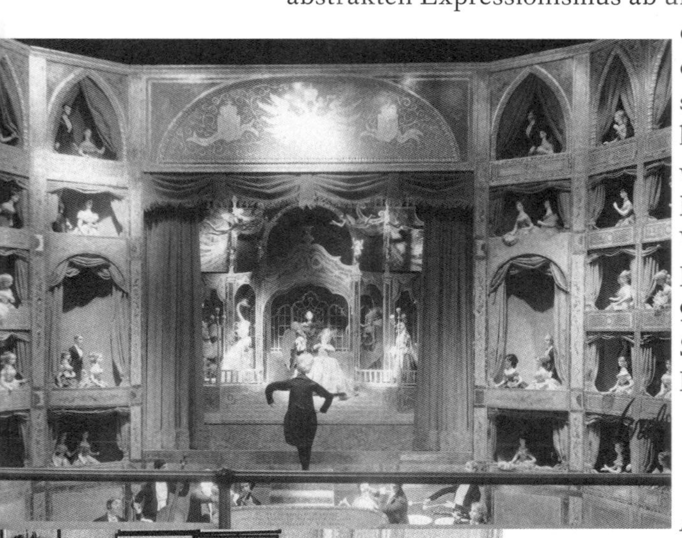

1965

Geschäftsführer im Demel

Als 1965 seine Frau Klára stirbt, kehrt Federico Pallavicini nach Wien zurück und übernimmt die Geschäftsführung des Demel.
Er richtet sich in einem oberen Stockwerk des Hauses ein Atelier ein. Dort stellt er ein 1:1-Modell der Auslage auf, um seine berühmten Schaufensterinszenierungen vorzubereiten. Diese finden beim Wiener Publikum bald großen Anklang und gehen als „Theater auf der Straße" in die Geschichte ein. Wichtige Bezugspersonen in dieser Zeit in Wien sind für ihn u. a. die Schriftstellerin und Journalistin Hilde Spiel und der Schauspieler Michael Heltau.
1967 übergibt er der Bibliothek der Akademie für angewandte Kunst einen Teppich, zwei Wandbehänge sowie 79 Entwürfe, drei Blumenstücke und einen Paravent.
Da ihm das Finanzamt aufgrund der hohen Ausgaben für die Demel-Auslagen einen Strich durch die Rechnung macht und Berzeviczy-Pallavicini Wien nicht mehr so sehen kann, wie er es in Erinnerung hat, entschließt er sich 1972 zum Verkauf des Demel. Dieser findet über eine Mittelsfrau an eine Schweizer Gesellschaft statt, hinter der, wie sich später herausstellt, Udo Proksch steckt.

Schaufenster im Kaufhaus Lord & Taylor gestaltet von Friedrich von Berzeviczy-Pallavicini / Window display at the department store Lord & Taylor designed by Friedrich von Berzeviczy-Pallavicini, New York City, 1967

Friedrich von Berzeviczy-Pallavicini in seiner Wohnung in Wien / in his apartment in Vienna, 1969

1972–89

Rückkehr nach New York, Würdigung in Wien

In seinem Stolz gekränkt, kehrt er nach New York zurück. Im Oktober 1975 findet in der Galerie Würthle in Wien eine ihm gewidmete Retrospektive statt. Im selben Jahr erscheint das Buch *Die K. u. K. Hofzuckerbäckerei Demel. Ein Wiener Märchen* im Brandstätter Verlag, das zahlreiche Illustrationen von Berzeviczy enthält, die heute auf italienischen Wandtapeten das Obergeschoss des Demel schmücken. 1976 erscheint eine auf 3.000 nummerierte Exemplare limitierte Auflage des Buchs.

In December 1982, Berzeviczy-Pallavicini is the first person to receive the newly founded Honorary Membership of the University of Applied Arts Vienna. In 1986 and 1987, Berzeviczy-Pallavicini donates the majority of his paintings, drawings, designs, and pattern samples to the art collection of the University of Applied Arts.

In 1988, the then head of the collection, Erika Patka, curates a solo exhibition on Friedrich von Berzeviczy-Pallavicini, titled *Poesie der Inszenierung*, which runs from April to May at the Heiligenkreuzer Hof exhibition center in Vienna. Berzeviczy-Pallavicini attends the opening. A publication accompanies the exhibition, containing written recollections by the artist, as well as numerous illustrations and essays on art history. In 1994, the exhibition travels to the Museum of Applied Arts in Budapest in a slightly adapted form.

Berzeviczy-Pallavicini writes his memoirs in the late 1980s; unfortunately they are never published in full. The manuscript has never been found.

In April 1989, he is awarded an Honorary Professorship by the Federal Ministry of Education, Arts and Sports.

On November 11, 1989, Friedrich von Berzeviczy-Pallavicini dies in his New York apartment.

At the initiative of Irene Haerdtl, daughter-in-law of Oswald and Camela Haerdtl, a homage to Berzeviczy-Pallavicini is held at the picture framing shop of Christine Ernst in Vienna in April 1996.

In 2009, Fleur Cowles dies in the UK. Her estate is dissolved and in the following years several works by Berzeviczy-Pallavicini enter the art market.

With a total of 519 objects, the Collection and Archive of the University of Applied Arts Vienna probably has the most extensive collection of works by Friedrich von Berzeviczy-Pallavicini.

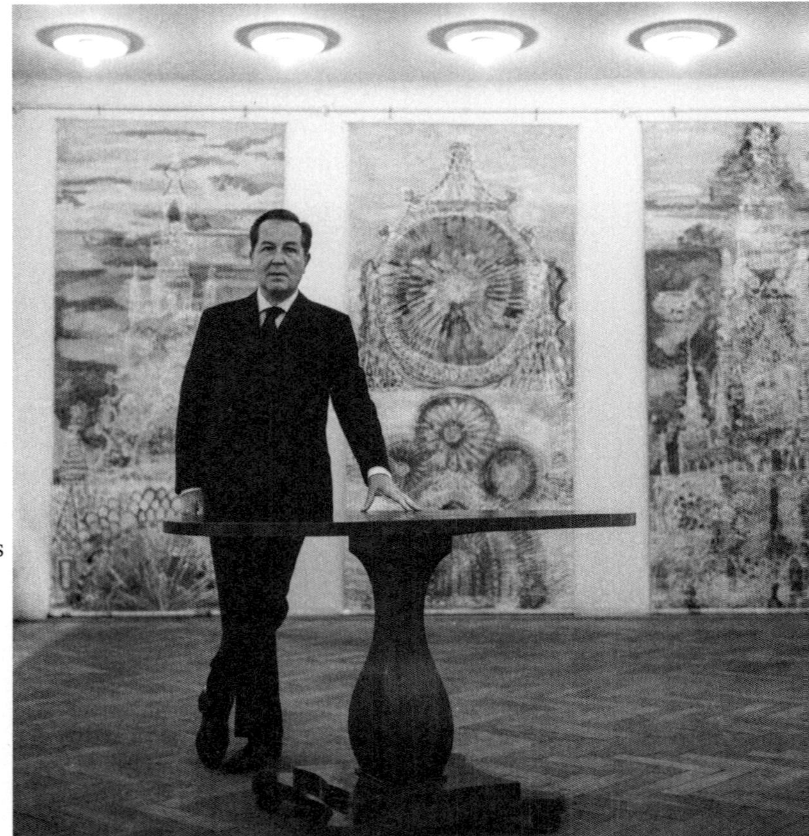

Friedrich von Berzeviczy-Pallavicini in seiner Ausstellung in der Galerie Würthle Wien / at his exhibition at Würthle Gallery Vienna, 1975

This biography is primarily informed by:
the publication for the exhibition of the same name, *Friedrich von Berzeviczy-Pallavicini: Poesie der Inszenierung*, ed. Erika Patka (Vienna, 1988);
the master's thesis *EINE ANDERE WELT: Friedrich von Berzeviczy-Pallavicini—sein Wiener Frühwerk der Zwischenkriegszeit* by Waltraud Kaufmann (Vienna, 2010);
the chronology from the exhibition catalogue *Helena Rubinstein: Die Schönheitserfinderin / Pioneer of Beauty*, eds. Iris Meder and Danielle Spera (Vienna, 2017);
the *Catalogue of the Fleur Cowles Library*, published by Henry Sotheran Limited;
the essay by Christian Witt-Dörring in *Der andere Blick: Lesbischwules Leben in Österreich*, eds. Wolfgang Förster, Tobias G. Natter, and Ines Rieder (Vienna, 2001);
the article "A Flair for Living" by Amy Fine Collins published in *Vanity Fair*, October 1996;
the tape recordings, autographs, and archives of Berzeviczy-Pallavicini, held at the University of Applied Arts Vienna, Art Collection & Archive;
as well as personal conversations with friends and acquaintances of the artist.

1978 beauftragt ihn die Wiener Staatsoper mit der Ausstattung für das komische Stück *Der junge Lord* von Hans Werner Henze. Berzeviczy-Pallavicini entwirft die Kostüme und das Bühnenbild für die von Gustav Rudolf Sellner inszenierte Oper, die in Wien am 9. Juni 1978 ihre Premiere feiert und bis März 1979 in acht Aufführungen an der Staatsoper gespielt wird. Berzeviczy-Pallavicini arbeitet an diesem Projekt in Wien, als Atelier nutzt er das Stöckl-Gebäude seines guten Freundes Michael Heltau.
Im Frühling 1982 findet in der Zentralsparkasse und Kommerzialbank Wien die von Oswald Oberhuber kuratierte Ausstellung *Die verlorenen Österreicher 1918–1938* statt, in der auch Arbeiten von Berzeviczy-Pallavicini aus seiner Zeit an der Kunstgewerbeschule gezeigt werden. Berzeviczy-Pallavicini befindet sich zu dieser Zeit in Wien, besucht die Ausstellung und daraufhin auch die Hochschule für angewandte Kunst und ist tief berührt.
Im Dezember 1982 erhält Berzeviczy-Pallavicini als Erster die neu geschaffene Ehrenmitgliedschaft der Hochschule für angewandte Kunst Wien.
1986 und 1987 überlässt Berzeviczy-Pallavicini einen Großteil seiner Gemälde, Zeichnungen, Entwürfe und Probemuster der Kunstsammlung an der Hochschule für angewandte Kunst Wien.
1988 kuratiert die damalige Leiterin der Kunstsammlung, Erika Patka, eine Einzelausstellung zu Friedrich von Berzeviczy-Pallavicini mit dem Titel *Poesie der Inszenierung*, die von April bis Mai im Ausstellungszentrum Heiligenkreuzer Hof in Wien stattfindet. Berzeviczy-Pallavicini ist bei der Eröffnung anwesend. Eine Publikation begleitet die Werkschau, die schriftliche Erinnerungen des Künstlers sowie zahlreiche Abbildungen und kunsthistorische Texte beinhaltet. Die Ausstellung wandert 1994 in etwas abgeänderter Form an das Kunstgewerbemuseum Budapest.
Berzeviczy-Pallavicini schreibt in den späten 1980er-Jahren an seinen Memoiren, die leider nie vollständig veröffentlicht werden. Das Manuskript ist heute nicht auffindbar.
Im April 1989 wird ihm die Ehrenprofessur vom Bundesministerium für Unterricht, Kunst und Sport verliehen.
Am 11. November 1989 stirbt Friedrich von Berzeviczy-Pallavicini in seiner New Yorker Wohnung. Im April 1996 findet eine Hommage an Berzeviczy-Pallavicini in der Rahmenhandlung Christine Ernst in Wien statt, die von Irene Haerdtl, der Schwiegertochter von Oswald und Camela Haerdtl, initiiert worden ist. Als Fleur Cowles 2009 in England stirbt und ihre Wohnung aufgelöst wird, gelangen etliche Kunstwerke von Berzeviczy-Pallavicini auf den Kunstmarkt.
Kunstsammlung und Archiv besitzen mit insgesamt 519 Objekten die wohl ausführlichste Sammlung von Werken von Friedrich von Berzeviczy-Pallavicini.

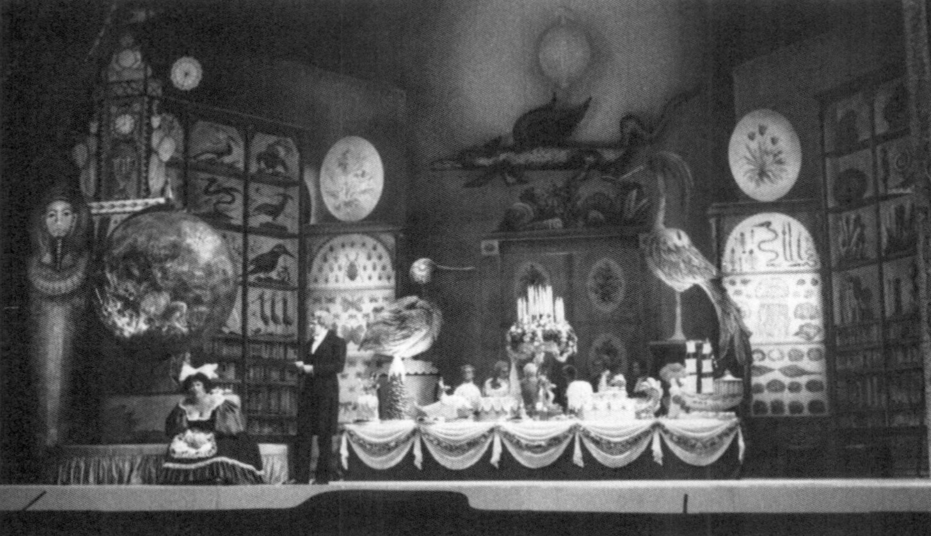

Szenenbild der Oper *Der Junge Lord* von Hans Werner Henze, Bühnenbild von / Set design for the opera *Der Junge Lord* by Hans Werner Henze, stage design by Friedrich von Berzeviczy-Pallavicini, Wiener Staatsoper / Vienna State Opera, premiere 9. Juni / June 9, 1978

Diese biografische Darstellung stützt sich primär auf:
die Publikation zur gleichnamigen Ausstellung *Friedrich von Berzeviczy-Pallavicini. Poesie der Inszenierung*, hg. von Erika Patka, Wien 1988;
die Diplomarbeit *EINE ANDERE WELT: Friedrich von Berzeviczy-Pallavicini – sein Wiener Frühwerk der Zwischenkriegszeit* von Waltraud Kaufmann, Wien 2010;
die Chronologie im Ausstellungskatalog *Helena Rubinstein. Die Schönheitserfinderin / Pioneer of Beauty*, hg. von Iris Meder und Danielle Spera, Wien 2017;
den *Catalogue of the Fleur Cowles Library*, veröffentlicht von Henry Sotheran Limited;
den Beitrag von Christian Witt-Dörring in: *Der andere Blick. Lesbischwules Leben in Österreich*, hg. von Wolfgang Förster, Tobias G. Natter und Ines Rieder, Wien 2001;
dem Artikel *A Flair for Living* von Amy Fine Collins veröffentlicht in der Vanity Fair im Oktober 1996;
den Tonbandaufzeichnungen, Autographen und Archivalien Berzeviczy-Pallavicinis in den Beständen der Universität für angewandte Kunst Wien, Kunstsammlung & Archiv;
sowie auf persönliche Gespräche mit Freund*innen und Bekannten des Künstlers.

Entwurf für ein Krinolinenkleid in Schwarz und Weiß / Design for a crinoline dress in black and white, 1927
Bleistift, Tusche, Aquarell auf Papier / pencil, India ink, and watercolor on paper, 39 × 27,2 cm, IN 5033

Entwurf für ein Kostüm mit Lendenschurz und rot-schwarzem Cape / Design for a costume with loincloth and red-and-black cape, 1928
Bleistift, Tusche, Aquarell auf Papier / pencil, India ink, and watercolor on paper, 35 × 25 cm, IN 5031

Entwürfe für Möbel / Furniture designs, 1929
Bleistift auf Papier, Dimensionen variabel / pencil on paper, variable dimensions, ca. / c. 29 × 22,9 cm, IN 1269, 1270, 1271, 1272, 1536, 1538, 1684, 1685, 1687, 1688

Vorhang mit gestickten Tüll-intarsien für / Drape with embroidered tulle inlay for *Boudoir einer mondänen Dame / Boudoir for a Cosmopolitan Lady*, 1929
Tüll, Voile, Tüllstickerei, Seidenapplikationen / tulle, voile, tulle embroidery, silk appliqué, 236 × 168 cm, IN 198/O/T

Paravent für / Folding screen for *Boudoir einer mondänen Dame / Boudoir for a Cosmopolitan Lady*, 1929
verschiedene Seiden, Metallfäden, Glasperlen, Applikationsstickereien, 5-teilig, jeweils / various silks, metal threads, glass beads, appliqué embroidery, 5 panels, each 122 × 79 cm, IN 201/O/T

Bodenteppich für / Rug for *Boudoir einer mondänen Dame / Boudoir for a Cosmopolitan Lady*, 1929
Ripsbänder, in ein fertiges Gewebe eingezogen, Kunstseide, Baumwolle / rep ribbon woven into a rug, artificial silk, cotton, 171 × 96 cm, IN 200/O/T

Wandspiegel für / Mirror for *Boudoir einer mondänen Dame / Boudoir for a Cosmopolitan Lady*, 1929
Holzrahmen, Lederschlaufen, Metallketten / wood frame, leather loops, metal chains, Ø 92 cm, IN 10.637/O

Bestickter Tüllvorhang für / Embroidered tulle drape for *Boudoir einer mondänen Dame / Boudoir for a Cosmopolitan Lady*, 1929
Tüll / tulle, 284 × 260 cm, IN 6991/O/T

Vorhang für / Curtain for, *Boudoir einer mondänen Dame / Boudoir for a Cosmopolitan Lady*, 1929
Tüll und Applikationen aus Seide / tulle and silk applications, 137 × 391 cm, IN 10.632/O/T

Teppichentwürfe / Rug designs, 1929
Bleistift, Tempera auf Papier / pencil, tempera on paper, ca. / c. 29 × 22,5 cm, IN 2328/1-4, 1693, 1275, 1694

Paravent / Folding screen, um / c. 1929
Holzrahmenkonstruktion, mit Leinwand bespannt bzw. überzogen, Collagen aus bemalten Papierformen, 6-teilig, jeweils / wood frame covered with canvas, collages composed of painted paper shapes, six panels, each 150 × 33,5 cm, IN 10.363/O

Runde Tischdeckchen (für Demel) / Round table coverlet (for Demel), 1932
Stickerei auf Leinen / embroidery on linen, Ø: 63,5 cm, IN 6329/T, 6326/T, 6325/T, 6323/ T, 6327/T, 6342/T, 6341/T

Entwurf Gymnasium der Dame / Design for a lady's gymnasium (*Raum und Mode*), 1932
Feder, Deckfarben auf Transparentpapier / ink and gouache on transparent paper, 35,5 × 40 cm, IN 4933

Entwurf Gymnasium der Dame / Design for a lady's gymnasium (*Raum und Mode*), 1932
farbige Tusche, Aquarell auf Papier / colored India ink, watercolor on paper, 31,5 × 42,5 cm, IN 4935

Entwurf für einen Wandbehang / Design for a wall hanging, 1932
blaue Tinte auf Papier / blue ink on paper, 29 × 22,5 cm, IN 157

Entwürfe für Handschuhe / Designs for gloves, ohne Datierung / undated
Bleistift, Tempera auf Papier / pencil and tempera on paper, 29 × 22,5 cm, IN 150, 151, 152, 153

Entwurf / Design for the *Madonna mit Sternenkranz / Madonna with a Wreath of Stars*, 1932
Aquarell, Tempera auf braunem Papier, Papierspitze und Silberfolie, collagiert auf weißen Karton montiert / watercolor and tempera on brown paper, doilies and silver foil, collage mounted on white cardboard, 56,6 × 43 cm, IN 7030

Madonna mit Sternenkranz / Madonna with a Wreath of Stars, 1932
Seidenstickerei / silk embroidery, 52 × 46 cm (mit Rahmen / with frame), IN 5047/O/T

Hafen (Wolgalandschaft) / Harbor (Volga Landscape), 1932
Stickerei auf roter Seide / Embroidery on red silk, 31 × 39 cm, IN 4888/O/T/3

Entwurf für ein Bühnenkostüm zu / Design for a costume for *Madama Butterfly*, 1932
Tusche, Aquarell, Tempera auf Papier / India ink, watercolor, and tempera on paper, 42 × 26,5 cm, IN 175

Entwurf für ein Bühnenkostüm zu / Design for a costume for Jean Giraudoux' *La Guerre de Troie n'aura pas lieu*, 1932
Feder, Aquarell auf Papier / ink and watercolor on paper, 48,3 × 28,5 cm, IN 184

Entwürfe für Demel-Verpackungspapiere / Designs for Demel packaging, 1932–38
Tusche, Tempera auf Papier, Dimensionen variabel / India ink and tempera on paper, variable dimensions, IN 10.911/5, 10.911/9, 10.911/15, 10.912/7, 5037/6, 5037/7, 5038, 5098, 5099, 5100, 6414, 6417

Entwurf für einen Wandbehang / Design for a wall hanging, 1933
Gouache auf Japanpapier / gouache on Japan paper, 27,4 × 17,5 cm, IN 1689

Entwurf für einen Gobelin / Design for a tapestry, 1933
Feder, Aquarell und Goldfarbe auf Japanpapier / ink, watercolor, and gold paint on Japan paper, 25,5 × 21 cm, IN 169

Entwurf für einen Gobelin / Design for a tapestry, 1934
Tusche, Aquarell auf Papier / India ink and watercolor on paper, 20 × 25,5 cm, IN 158

Entwurf für einen Gobelin / Design for a tapestry, 1934
Tusche, Aquarell auf Papier, auf Karton montiert / India ink and watercolor on paper, mounted on cardboard, 21,6 × 18,4 cm, IN 164

Entwurf für einen Gobelin / Design for a tapestry, 1934
Feder, Aquarell auf Papier / ink and watercolor on paper, 18,4 × 16 cm, IN 165

Entwurf für einen Gobelin / Design for a tapestry, 1935
Feder, Aquarell auf Papier / ink and watercolor on paper, 20,8 × 20,5 cm, IN 162

Entwurf für einen Gobelin / Design for a tapestry, 1935
Feder, Aquarell auf Papier / ink and watercolor on paper, 16,5 × 21 cm, IN 163

Fliese mit dem Motiv / Tile with the motif *Kniende, in den Spiegel schauende Dame, Brieftaube / Kneeling Woman Looking in the Mirror, Carrier Pigeon*, um / c. 1936
Porzellan, Druck in Schwarz, Email-Lichtblau, Rosa und Gold / porcelain, printed in black, enameled in pale blue, pink, and gold, 12,5 × 12,5 cm
Leihgabe / on loan from Wiener Porzellanmanufaktur Augarten – Porzellanmuseum

Vase *Bogenschütze und Falknerin / Archer and Falconer*, 1937
Porzellan, Blumen und Blüten in Goldzeichnung, graviert auf Kobalt-Fond, Goldrand / porcelain, flowers and blossoms rendered in gold, engraved on a cobalt background, gold rim, 25 cm, Ø 15 cm
Leihgabe / on loan from Wiener Porzellanmanufaktur Augarten – Porzellanmuseum

Entwurf für einen Gobelin / Design for the tapestry *Die Vier Jahreszeiten / The Four Seasons*, 1937
Tempera und Gouache auf Papier / tempera and gouache on paper, 315 × 331 cm, IN 1837

Entwurf für einen Gobelin / Design for the tapestry *Zauberwald des Papageno / Papageno's Enchanted Forest*, 1937
Tempera und Gouache auf Papier / tempera and gouache on paper, 309 × 349 cm, IN 1836

Maskenkostüm (Jacke mit Hose) / Fancy dress costume (jacket and trousers), 1937
naturfarbenes Leinen mit rotem und blauem Druck / natural-colored linen printed in red and blue, IN KM 3615 a, b

Entwurf für ein Bühnenbild im Akademietheater / Design for a stage set at the Akademietheater, *Aimée*, 1937–38
Tusche, Tinte, Aquarell auf Papier / India ink, ink, and watercolor on paper, 48 × 57 cm, IN 5025

Dekorstoff / decorative fabric *Venini*, 1943
Baumwolle / cotton, 98 × 100 cm, IN 5254/O/T/2

Thee und Kaffee / Tea and Coffee, 1943
Dekorstoff, Ausführung für Manufaktur Campisotta / decorative fabric for Campisotta, 126 × 88 cm, IN 5256/O/T/1

Modezeichnung für die Zeitschrift / Fashion drawing for the magazine *Bellezza*, 1943
Tusche, Aquarell auf Zeichenpapier / India ink and watercolor on paper, 33 × 49 cm, IN 7256

Kleiderstoff / dress fabric *Marie Barkirtdeff*, 1945
Seide / silk, 47 × 90 cm, IN 5255/O/T/1

Triompho della Guerra, um / c. 1945
Feder, Aquarell auf Karton / ink and watercolor on paper, 39,1 × 30,5 cm, IN 7003

Flair, 1950–51
Magazin / magazine, 33,1 × 24,9 cm, IN 18.976/1/ Q – 18.976/12/Q

Ohne Titel / Untitled, Blumenkomposition / floral composition, 1952
Öl auf Wachstuch / oil on wax cloth, 190 × 120 cm, IN 1833/B

Doblando, 1955
Öl auf Leinwand / oil on canvas, 90 × 120 cm, IN 6316/B

Kostümentwürfe für / Costume designs for *Gigi (nach Colette) / (after the novel by Colette)*, um / c. 1957
Tusche, Aquarell auf Karton / India ink and watercolor on cardboard, 45,5 × 61 cm, IN 6890/1 6890/2 6890/3

In der Opernloge, Katzendame und Katzenkavaliere / In the Opera Box: Lady Cat and Cavalier Cats, 1965–72
Styropor, Pailletten, Stecknadeln, Dimensionen variabel / polystyrene, sequins, pins, variable dimensions, ca. / c. 95,5 × 40 × 37 cm, IN 14.315/1/O, 14.315/2/O, 14.315/3/O

Auslagendekoration für Demel / Window display decoration for Demel, um / c. 1970
Applikation aus Seidenpapieren, Pailletten, Bildchen, Perlen, Maschen etc. auf Tüll, 2-teilig / appliqué tissue paper, sequins, pictures, beads, bows etc. on tulle, 2 sections, 300 × 60 cm, IN 11.305/O/T

Originalentwürfe für die Publikation / Original designs for the publication *Die K. u. K. Hofzuckerbäckerei Demel. Ein Wiener Märchen / The Imperial and Royal Confectioners Demel: A Viennese Fairytale*, 1975
Dimensionen variabel / variable dimensions, ca. / c. 12,4 × 31 cm, IN 5206/1–8

Damenbüste auf Rollwagen mit Hut und Häusern / Female bust on a trolley with hat and houses, um / c. 1980
Tusche, Aquarell auf Papier / India ink and watercolor on paper, 60 × 48 cm, IN 5015/1

Ohne Titel / Untitled, undatiert / undated
Öl auf Holz / oil on wood, um / c. 1950, 150,5 × 122,5 cm, IN 15.765/B

Frau mit drei Gesichtern / Woman with three faces, undatiert / undated
Bleistift, Kugelschreiber auf Papier / pencil and ballpoint pen on paper, 60 × 48 cm, IN 5015/2

Zwei Damenbüsten / Two female busts, undatiert / undated
schwarzer Kugelschreiber auf Papier / black ballpoint pen on paper, 60,5 × 48 cm, IN 5019/2

Vogel mit zwei Gesichtern / Bird with two faces, undatiert / undated
Tusche auf Papier / India ink on paper, 22,5 × 17 cm, IN 5949

Bildnis einer jungen Dame / Portrait of a Young Woman, undatiert / undated
Öl auf Leinwand / oil on canvas, 60,5 × 45,3 cm
Leihgabe / loan from Demel K. u. K. Hofzuckerbäckerei Wien / Vienna

Maquette for the Alphabet Book, undatiert / undated
26 Zeichnungen und 24 Kalligrafien, Wasserfarbe, Tinte, Tusche auf Papier, jeweils / 26 drawings and 24 examples of calligraphy, watercolor, ink, and India ink on paper, each ca. / c. 35 × 26 cm, IN 19.027/1-50/Ma

Werkliste Ausstellung /
List of Other Exhibited Works

Kamilla Bischof und / and
Laura Welker
Victoria's Secret Subtenants, 2018
Video, full color HD, 8:38 min,
IN 18.959/AV/O

Kamilla Bischof und / and
Laura Welker
Victoria's Secret Subtenants, 2018
Zwei Stühle, Kissen bemalt, Flasche, Gläser / two chairs, painted cushions, bottle, glasses 41 × 58 × 65 cm
Privatbesitz / private collection

Kamilla Bischof
Mitgift / Dowry, 2019
Acryl auf Leinwand / acrylic on canvas, 70 × 100 cm
Galerie Sandy Brown, Berlin,
IN 19.048/B

Kamilla Bischof
Hollywood-Schaukel / Hollywood Swing, 2019
Öl auf Leinwand / oil on canvas,
250 × 200 cm
Courtesy die Künstlerin / of the artist

Kamilla Bischof
Aloe Vera, 2019
Öl auf Leinwand / oil on canvas,
150 × 180 cm
Courtesy die Künstlerin / of the artist

Kamilla Bischof
Priesterweg, 2019
Acryl und Öl auf Leinwand / acrylic and oil on canvas, 250 × 200 cm
Courtesy die Künstlerin / of the artist

Kamilla Bischof
Double Hot Plate, 2019
Öl auf Leinwand / oil on canvas,
150 × 180 cm
Courtesy die Künstlerin / of the artist

Kamilla Bischof
Teppich / Rug, 2019
Öl, Arcyl auf Auslegeware / oil and acrylic on carpet,
70 × 120 cm, IN 19.072/O/T

Otto Breuer
Tischlampe / Table lamp, 1937
gehämmertes Silber mit Schirm aus Serpentin, Schalter und Stecker aus Silber, Silberpunzen / hammered silver with serpentine shade, silver switch and plug, silver hallmarks,
34,5 × 12 × 13 cm, IN 5050/O

Verena Dengler
*Lech mich am Arlberg / Kiss My Arlberg**, 2011
Gips, Blumentopf, Schnürsenkel, Wolle, Perlen / plaster, flowerpot, shoelaces, wool, beads,
30 × 40 × 20 cm
Galerie Meyer Kainer, Wien / Vienna
*Lech is in Vorarlberg, so the title contains a double pun.

Verena Dengler
Gmundner Keramik, Paravents für den Fantastischen Sozialismus / Gmunden Ceramics, Folding Screens for Fantastic Socialism, 2013
Zwei Paravents, Foto, Tapete, Spanplatte, Fotodruck auf Leinwand, Acryl, jeweils / two folding screens, photo, wallpaper, chipboard, photographic print on canvas, acrylic, each 200 × 160 cm
Galerie Meyer Kainer, Wien / Vienna

Josef Frank
Couchtisch / Coffee table,
um / c. 1925
Holz (Nuss) / wood (walnut),
56 cm, Ø 67 cm, IN 15.869/M

Josef Frank
Stoffmuster / Fabric pattern
Kirschzweige / Cherry Branches,
1925–30
Leinen, bunt bedruckt / linen, printed in bright colors,
40 × 58 cm, IN 26215/O/T

Josef Frank
Stoffmuster / Fabric pattern
Primavera, undatiert / undated
65,5 × 130 cm, IN 4796/1/O/T

Josef Frank
Stoff / Fabric design *Worry Bird*,
um / c. 1944
Modeldruck auf Baumwolle / block printing on cotton, ca. 80 × 100 cm, IN 14.497/O/T

Josef Frank
verschiedene Stoffmuster / various fabric designs
Mirakel, Primavera, Mistral, Semiramis, 1925–40
Leinen, bunt bedruckt, Dimensionen variabel / linen, printed in bright colors, variable dimensions,
IN 26215/O/T, 14.499/1-3/O/T, 14.500/O/T, 14.505/O/T

Julian Göthe
Les Feux d'Artifice pour le Spectacle 3, 2016
Bleistiftzeichnung auf Karton / pencil on cardboard, 84 × 59,5 cm
Courtesy of Galerie Buchholz, Köln-Berlin-New York / Cologne-Berlin-New York

Julian Göthe
Möbelentwurf / Furniture Design,
Vitrinen-Skulptur / vitrine sculpture,
2019
Metall, Holz, Lack, Acrylglas / metal, wood, lacquer, acrylic glass, ca. / c. 150 × 100 × 100 cm,
IN 19.026/M

Hans Hollein
Österreichisches Verkehrsbüro, Hauptverkaufssitz Opernringhof Wien / Main sales center of the Austrian tourism group at Opernringhof, Vienna, 1976–78
Ansichten / views
Auftraggeber / commissioned by the Österreichisches Verkehrsbüro GmbH, Wien / Vienna
Foto / photo: Jerzy Survillo
Foto, Reproduktion / photo, reproduction, 20 × 30 cm
Privatarchiv / private archive of Hans Hollein

Elisabeth Karlinsky
Kostümentwurf / Costume design,
1923–24
Tempera, Kohle, Goldfarbe auf Papier / tempera, charcoal, and gold paint on paper, 31,9 × 22,6 cm,
IN 14.774/8

Elisabeth Karlinsky
Kostümentwurf / Costume design
Läufer / Runner, 1923–24
Tempera, Kohle auf Papier / tempera and charcoal on paper,
26,7 × 19,8 cm, IN 14.774/16

Elisabeth Karlinsky
Kostümentwurf / Costume design,
1923–24
Tempera, Goldfarbe auf Papier / tempera and gold paint on paper,
33,1 × 24,9 cm, IN 14.774/19

Amy Lien und / and Enzo Camacho
mit / with Ilya Lipkin
Fotoserie für Starship /
Photo series for Starship, 2015
Arts & Foods (spaghetti al pomodoro)
Arts & Foods (due caffè, grazie)
Arts & Foods (il gusto)
Arts & Foods (selection of fresh fish)
Arts & Foods (bookshelf)
Barytfoto, 5 Bilder von 14 / baryta photos, 5 images of 14,
20 × 30 cm, 40 × 30 cm, Edition 3/1

Lucy McKenzie
Painted boxes, Table III, 2017
Objekte / Objects: Öl auf Leinwand, Öl auf Holz, Metall, Farbe, Glas / oil on canvas, oil on wood, metal, paint, glass, 120 × 120 × 116 cm
Galerie Buchholz, Berlin-Köln-New York / Berlin-Cologne-New York

Ulrike Müller
Others, 2017
Glasemail auf Stahl / glass enamel on steel, 39,4 × 30,5 cm
Courtesy of Galerie Meyer Kainer, Wien / Vienna, und Privatbesitz / and private collection

Oswald Oberhuber
Rednerpult / Lectern, um / c. 1980
Eiche, Spanplatte / oak, chipboard,
123 × 81 × 52 cm, IN 10.941/M

Dagobert Peche
Rundes Deckchen / Round lace doily,
um / c. 1920
Klöppelspitze / bobbin lace, Ø 26 cm,
IN 2387/O

Dagobert Peche
Tischvitrine / Vitrine table, 1917
Holz, Glas / wood, glass,
84 × 50 × 30,5 cm, IN 5247/M

Dagobert Peche
Deckeldose / Box and cover,
um / c. 1916
Keramik, weißer Scherben,
elfenbeinfarbene Glasur,
goldfarbenes Reliefdekor / ceramic,
white body, ivory glaze, gold relief
decor, 20 cm, Ø unten / base 13 cm,
Ø oben / top 18 cm, IN 3780/O

Marianne My Ullmann
Kostümentwurf für / Costume design
Shawl for the *Bunte Laterne*
carnival ball, 1933
Tempera, Kohle auf
Transparentpapier / tempera and
charcoal on transparent paper,
29,4 × 20,9 cm, IN 11.616/1

Marianne My Ullmann
Kostümentwurf für einen
Handschuh / Costume design for
a glove, 1933
Tempera, Kohle auf
Transparentpapier / tempera and
charcoal on transparent paper,
29,6 × 20,8 cm, IN 8977/1

Marianne My Ullmann
Kostümentwurf / Costume design
Zipp, 1933
Tempera, Kohle auf Seidenpapier /
tempera and charcoal on silk paper,
29,5 × 20,8 cm, IN 8980

Yves Saint Laurent
Untitled, 1965
Tusche und Pastellzeichnung auf
Papier / India ink and pastel on paper,
41 × 32 cm
Galerie Neu, Berlin

Jack Smith
Untitled, 1968
Filzstift und Collage auf Papier /
felt tip pen and collage on paper,
41 × 32 cm
Privatbesitz / private collection,
Berlin

Jack Smith
Untitled, Big Hotel, 1968
Fotokopie / photocopy, 41 × 32 cm
Privatbesitz / private collection,
Berlin

Eduard Wimmer-Wisgrill
Tisch / Table, undatiert / undated
Holz (Eiche), Textil, Glas /
wood (oak), fabric, glass,
80 × 80 × 41,5 cm, IN 3303/M

Eduard Wimmer-Wisgrill,
Oswald Oberhuber
*Ohne Titel (Männlicher Halbakt
in Gelb) / Untitled (Male Semi-Nude
in Yellow)*,
um / c. 1938, um / c. 1980
Öl auf Karton / oil on cardboard,
67,9 × 48,6 cm, IN 10.901/B

Eduard Wimmer-Wisgrill
*Ohne Titel (Stehender männlicher
Halbakt) / Untitled (Standing Male
Semi-Nude)*,
um / c. 1955
Mischtechnik auf Karton /
mixed media on cardboard,
69,7 × 50 cm, IN 11.549/B/1

Amelie von Wulffen und / and
Nico Ihlein
Ohne Titel / Untitled, 2019
Ton, Muscheln, Ölfarbe /
pottery, shells, oil paint
Courtesy die Künstler / of the artists

Katharina Wulff
Dr. Ruppel, 2001
Siebdruck gerahmt / framed screen
print, 1/20, 63 × 80 cm
Galerie Neu, Berlin

Katharina Wulff
Graf Stromboli, 2002
Öl auf Leinwand / oil on canvas,
69 × 58 cm
Privatbesitz / private collection

Min Yoon
Ohne Titel / Untitled, 2019
Leder, Faden / leather, threads,
137 × 54 cm, IN 19.007/O

Autor*innenbiografien / Authors' biographies

MANUELA AMMER ist Kuratorin am Museum moderner Kunst Stiftung Ludwig Wien, wo sie Ausstellungen wie *Steve Reinke: Butter* (2020), *Pattern and Decoration: Ornament als Versprechen* (2019), *Bruno Gironcoli: In der Arbeit schüchtern bleiben* (2018), *Painting 2.0: Malerei im Informationszeitalter* (2016, gemeinsam mit Achim Hochdörfer, David Joselit und Tonio Kröner), *Ulrike Müller: The old expressions are with us always and there are always others* und *Always, Always, Others: Unklassische Streifzüge durch die Moderne* (2015, gemeinsam mit Ulrike Müller) verantwortete.
MANUELA AMMER is a curator at the Museum moderner Kunst Stiftung Ludwig Wien, where she has been responsible for exhibitions such as *Steve Reinke: Butter* (2020), *Pattern and Decoration: Ornament as Promise* (2019), *Bruno Gironcoli: Shy at Work* (2018), *Painting 2.0: Expression in the Information Age* (with Achim Hochdörfer, David Joselit, and Tonio Kröner), *Ulrike Müller: The old expressions are with us always and there are always others* and *Always, Always, Others: Non-Classical Forays into Modernism* (2015, with Ulrike Müller).

GERALD BAST, Studium der Rechts- und Wirtschaftswissenschaften an der Johannes Kepler Universität Linz, von 1980 bis 1999 im Bundesministerium für Bildung und Forschung, seit 2000 Rektor der Universität für angewandte Kunst Wien. Mitglied der Europäischen Akademie der Wissenschaften und Künste, stv. Vorsitzender des Dachverbandes der österreichischen Universitäten, Kuratoriumsmitglied Europäisches Forum Alpbach. Autor und Vortragender insbesondere zu Bildungs- und Kulturpolitik sowie zur Verbindung von Wissenschaft, Kunst und Innovation.
GERALD BAST, studied law and economics at Johannes Kepler University Linz, worked between 1980 and 1999 at the Austrian Federal ministry for Higher Education and Research, since 2000 rector of the University of Applied Arts Vienna. Member of the European Academy of Sciences and Arts, deputy chairman of the umbrella organisation of Austrian universities, member of the board of trustees of the European Forum Alpbach. Author and lecturer especially on educational and cultural policy and on the connection between science, art and innovation.

ANKE DYES ist Künstlerin und Autorin. Sie lebt in Berlin. Zuletzt erschien: *A Substantive Theory of Harm* (im Eigenverlag).
ANKE DYES is an artist and author. She lives in Berlin. Her most recent publication is titled: *A Substantive Theory of Harm* (self-published).

BRIGITTE FELDERER ist Kuratorin und Kulturwissenschaftlerin. Sie lehrt an der Universität für angewandte Kunst Wien, leitet das Masterstudium „Social Design – Arts As Urban Innovation" und hat zahlreiche medien- und kulturhistorische Ausstellungsprojekte und Publikationen realisiert, zuletzt *Der Hände Werk*, Schallaburg 2019.
BRIGITTE FELDERER is a curator and cultural theorist. She teaches at the University of Applied Arts Vienna, directs the master's degree program "Social Design – Arts As Urban Innovation," and has realized numerous media and cultural-historical exhibition projects and publications, most recently *Der Hände Werk*, Schallaburg 2019.

MICHAEL FRANZ ist Künstler und lebt in Berlin.
MICHAEL FRANZ is an artist living in Berlin.

ANETTE FREUDENBERGER ist Leiterin der Galerie der Stadt Schwaz in Tirol und unterrichtet an der Universität für angewandte Kunst in Wien. Sie war am Kunstverein für die Rheinlande und Westfalen Düsseldorf, an der Wiener Secession sowie freiberuflich tätig und kuratierte Ausstellungen mit Marc Camille Chaimowicz, Amelie von Wulffen, Isa Genzken, Anita Leisz, Hans-Christian Lotz, Min Yoon, Julian Göthe, Juliette Blightman u. a.
ANETTE FREUDENBERGER is director of the Galerie der Stadt Schwaz in Tyrol and teaches at the University of Applied Arts in Vienna. She has worked at the Kunstverein für die Rheinlande und Westfalen Düsseldorf, at the Vienna Secession, as well as freelance and has curated exhibitions with Marc Camille Chaimowicz, Amelie von Wulffen, Isa Genzken, Anita Leisz, Hans-Christian Lotz, Min Yoon, Julian Göthe, Juliette Blightman, and others.

YUKI HIGASHINO ist ein in Wien lebender Künstler. Er stellte unter anderem aus in Last Tango, Zürich, kunstbuero, Wien, Contemporary Art Factory, Kyoto, The Living Art Museum, Reykjavik und Le BBB centre d'art, Toulouse. Seine Texte wurden in Zeitschriften wie ArtForum, Texte zur Kunst und The Avery Review veröffentlicht.
YUKI HIGASHINO is an artist based in Vienna. He has exhibited at Last Tango, Zurich, kunstbuero, Vienna, Contemporary Art Factory, Kyoto, The Living Art Museum, Reykjavik, and Le BBB centre d'art, Toulouse, among other venues. His writing has been published in journals such as *ArtForum*, *Texte zur Kunst* and *The Avery Review*.

TONIO KRÖNER arbeitet als Künstler in Berlin.
TONIO KRÖNER works as an artist in Berlin.

SOFIE MATHOI lebt als Autorin und Kuratorin in Wien. Sie arbeitet als Senior Scientist an der Universität für angewandte Kunst Wien, Kunstsammlung und Archiv. 2015 bis 2017 Kuratorin Neue Galerie Innsbruck, 2015 Leitung Krinzinger Projekte Wien, 2012 und 2013 kuratorische Assistentin am Kölnischen Kunstverein. Sie schreibt über zeitgenössische Kunst sowie Essays und Textbeiträge für Ausstellungskataloge.
SOFIE MATHOI is an author and curator living in Vienna. She works as Senior Scientist at the Collection and Archive of the University of Applied Arts Vienna. 2015 to 2017 curator at the Neue Galerie Innsbruck. 2015 director of the Krinzinger project space Vienna. 2012 and 2013 curatorial assistant at the Kölnischer Kunstverein. She writes about contemporary art and contributes essays and text for exhibition catalogues.

INKA MEISSNER ist Künstlerin in Berlin.
INKA MEISSNER is an artist living in Berlin.

ROBERT MÜLLER ist Künstler und lebt in Berlin und Wien. Er ist Redakteur des Online-Magazins *The Critical Ass* (mit Anke Dyes und Niklas Lichti). Seit 2013 organisiert er die Ausstellungsreihe *NOUSMOULES* in Wien.
ROBERT MÜLLER is an artist living in Berlin and Vienna. He is coeditor of the online publication *The Critical Ass* (with Anke Dyes and Niklas Lichti). Since 2013 he has been organizer of the exhibition series *NOUSMOULES* in Vienna.

COSIMA RAINER ist Kuratorin und Leiterin von Kunstsammlung und Archiv der Universität für angewandte Kunst Wien. Von 2013 bis 2018 war sie Direktorin der Galerie der Stadt Schwaz. 2011 war sie als Kuratorin des Belvedere mitverantwortlich für die Eröffnung des 21er-Haus in Wien. Als wissenschaftliche Mitarbeiterin war sie von 2012 bis 2018 an der Akademie der bildenden Künste Wien tätig und von 2011 bis 2013 Mitglied im Board des *Artist-in-Residence-Programm* der Sammlung Lenikus. Cosima Rainer studierte Theater- Film und Medienwissenschaft an der Universität Wien und ist Absolventin des internationalen Curatorial Training Programme, Stiftung De Appel Amsterdam, 1996–97.
COSIMA RAINER is curator and director of the Collection and Archive of the University of Applied Arts Vienna. From 2013–18 she was director of the Galerie der Stadt Schwaz. In 2011, as curator of the Belvedere, she was jointly responsible for the opening of the 21er-Haus in Vienna. From 2012–18 she worked as a research assistant at the Academy of Fine Arts Vienna and from 2011–13 she was a member of the board of the Artist-in-Residence Program of the Lenikus Collection. Cosima Rainer studied theatre, film, and media at the University of Vienna and is a graduate of the international Curatorial Training Programme, Foundation De Appel Amsterdam, 1996–97.

ANNE-KATRIN ROSSBERG, geboren in Berlin, Studium der Kunstgeschichte in Wien. Forschungen zur Interieur- und Möbelgeschichte, speziell zu geschlechtsspezifischen Räumen. Bis 2003 Kuratorin im MAK – Museum für angewandte Kunst Wien und Lehrbeauftragte an der Universität Wien bzw. der Universität für angewandte Kunst Wien. Langjährige Mitarbeiterin der Künstlergruppe Gelitin. Forschungen zur Gebrauchsgrafik der Kunstblättersammlung im MAK Wien, ab 2016 in der Sammlung Metall und Wiener-Werkstätte-Archiv tätig, seit 2018 als deren Leiterin.

ANNE-KATRIN ROSSBERG, born in Berlin, studied art history in Vienna. Research on the history of interiors and furniture, especially on gender-specific spaces. Until 2003 curator at MAK – Museum of Applied Arts Vienna and lecturer at the University of Vienna and the University of Applied Arts Vienna. For many years she was a member of the artist group Gelitin. Research on the commercial art of the Kunstblättersammlung at the MAK Vienna. Since 2016 she has been working at the Metal Collection and Wiener Werkstätte Archive, since 2018 as its director.

INGA CHARLOTTE THIELE ist freischaffende Autorin und Kuratorin. Seit 2018 lebt und arbeitet sie in Wien und absolviert ihr Masterstudium in Critical Studies an der Akademie der bildenden Künste. Zuletzt realisierte sie die Reiseausstellung *I am a City of Habits* in Düsseldorf (Ædt – Am Ende des Tages), Hamburg (Come over Chez Malik's) und Berlin. Sie schrieb (autotheoretische/poetische) Ausstellungs- sowie Katalogtexte und Reviews für u. a. Croy Nielsen, Hugo Zorn, Kuba Paris.
INGA CHARLOTTE THIELE is a freelance author and curator. She has been living and working in Vienna since 2018 and is studying for her Masters in Critical Studies at the Academy of Fine Arts Vienna. Most recently she produced the traveling exhibition *I am a City of Habits* in Düsseldorf (Ædt – Am Ende des Tages), Hamburg (Come over Chez Malik's), and Berlin. She has written (auto-theoretical/poetic) exhibition and catalogue texts and reviews for Croy Nielsen, Hugo Zorn, Cuba Paris, and others.

Künstler*innenbiografien / Artists' Biographies

KAMILLA BISCHOF

(geb. / b. 1986 Graz, lebt und arbeitet / lives and works in Berlin). Ausgewählte Einzelausstellungen und Projekte / Selected solo exhibitions at Boltenstern.Raum, Galerie Meyer Kainer, Wien / Vienna (2020), Künstlerhaus – Halle für Kunst & Medien, Graz (2019), Fonda, Leipzig (2019), FIAC, Paris (2018), Sandy Brown, Berlin (2017), Halle für Kunst, Lüneburg (2017), Degraw Social Club, New York (2016), Bar du Bois, Wien / Vienna (2014).
Ausgewählte Gruppenausstellungen u. a. / Selected group shows include *Paint, also known as blood*, Museum of Modern Art, Warschau / Warsaw (2019), *Kamilla Bischof, Hélène Fauquet, Till Megerle, Evelyn Plaschg*, cur. Melanie Ohnemus, Galleria Acappella, Napoli (2019), *An Order of Things*, Gregor Staiger, Zürich / Zurich (2019), *Jugend ist Trunkenheit ohne Wein*, BIKINI, Basel (2018), *Condo New York*, Sandy Brown and Koppe Astner at Rachel Uffner Gallery, New York (2017), *How far to open up?*, Forum Stadtpark, Graz (2017), *Der Funke soll in dir sein*, cur. André Butzer, Salon Dahlmann, Berlin (2016), *Schmerz Schmerz Schmerz*, Ve.Sch, Wien / Vienna (2013), *Fuzzy Sets*, After the Butcher, Berlin (2010).

VERENA DENGLER

(geb. / b. 1981 in Wien; lebt und arbeitet / lives and works in Vienna). Ausgewählte Einzelausstellungen und Projekte / Selected solo exhibitions at Secession, Wien / Vienna (2020), STRABAG Kunstforum, Wien / Vienna (2019), *Mar-a-Lago (Marlene Streeruwitz) / Revolt. She Said. Revolt. Again (Alice Birch)*, Bühnenbild und Kostüme / costumes and stage design (gemeinsam mit / with Dominique Wiesbauer), Berliner Ensemble (2018), Kunsthalle Bern (2016), Zabriskie Point, Genf / Genève (2016), Thomas Duncan Gallery, Los Angeles (2015), Galerie Meyer Kainer, Wien / Vienna (2014), Sala Terrena, Belvedere, Wien / Vienna (2014), MAK Galerie, Wien / Vienna (2013), Mumok, Wien / Vienna (2013), Boltenstern.Raum, Galerie Meyer Kainer, Wien / Vienna (2012)
Ausgewählte Gruppenausstellungen u. a. / Selected group shows include *Hate Speech: Aggression and Intimacy*, KHM – Künstlerhaus, Halle für Kunst & Medien, Graz (2019), *Since Last We Met*, curated by Debra Singer, Simon Lee Gallery, New York (2019), *Wiener Raum*, Heiligenkreuzer Hof, Univeritätsgalerie der Universität für angewandte Kunst, Wien / Vienna (2018), *Oh ... Jakob Lena Knebl and the mumok Collection*, Mumok, Wien / Vienna (2017), *Sie sagen, wo Rauch ist, ist auch Feuer*, Kunsthaus Glarus, Glarus, Schweiz / Switzerland (2017), *To lie in the cheese, to smile in the butter*, Kunstsäle, Berlin (2016), *Surround Audience*, New Museum Triennial, New York (2015), *New Needs*, Haus Wittmann by Johannes Spalt, Etsdorf/Kamp (2015), *The Vienna Complex* (kuratiert von / curated by Cosima Rainer), Austrian Cultural Forum New York (2013), *Freak out*, Greene Naftali Gallery, New York (2013), *NOA NOA* (kuratiert von / curated by Alexander Ferrando), Metro Pictures, New York (2013), *Town-Gown Conflict*, Kunsthalle Zürich, Zürich (2011), *Pro Choice in Schattendorf* (Kur. / cur. Will Benedict & Lucie Stahl), Kunstverein Schattendorf, Schattendorf (2010).

JOSEF FRANK

(geb. / b. 1885 in Baden bei Wien, gest. / d. 1967 in Stockholm). Ausgewählte Ausstellungen und Retrospektiven u. a. / Selected shows and retrospectives included Österreichische Kunstausstellung (1900–24), Künstlerhaus Wien (1924), *Exposition internationale des arts décoratifs et industriels modernes* (1925), *Neues Bauen*, Hofburg Wien (1929), Österr. Werkbundausstellung, Wien / Vienna (1930), Werkbundsiedlung internationale Ausstellung, Wien / Vienna (1932), Weltausstellung / World Fair Paris (1937), *Josef Frank*, Nationalmuseum / National Museum Stockholm (1952), *Josef Frank*, Österr. Gesellschaft für Architektur / Society for Architecture, Wien / Vienna (1965), *Josef Frank*, MAK, Wien / Vienna (1981), *Josef Frank 100 Jahre Jubiläumsausstellung / 100 years anniversary exhibition*, Svenskt Tenn, Stockholm (1985), *Josef Frank, Architect and Designer*, Bard Graduate Center, New York (1996), *Josef Frank*, Jewish Museum Stockholm (2007), *Josef Frank, Against Design*, MAK Wien / Vienna (2016).

JULIAN GÖTHE

(geb. / b. 1966 in Berlin, lebt und arbeitet / lives and works in Berlin). Ausgewählte Einzelausstellungen und Projekte / Selected solo exhibitions and projects at Kunstverein München (2020), Galerie der Stadt Schwaz (2019), Galerie Buchholz, Berlin (2016), *Don Giovanni*, Bühnenbild und Kostüme / costumes and stage design, Volkstheater Rostock (2014), Fürstenberg Zeitgenössisch, Donaueschingen (2013), kestnergesellschaft, Hannover (2011), Cabinet, London (2008), Galerie Daniel Buchholz, Köln / Cologne (2007), Sorcha Gallery, Glasgow (2006), Galerie Meerrettich, Berlin (2005).
Ausgewählte Gruppenausstellungen u. a. / Selected group shows include *Klassentreffen: Werke aus der Sammlung Gaby und Wilhelm Schürmann*, mumok – Museum Moderner Kunst Stiftung Ludwig, Wien / Vienna (2018), *Material Traces*, Charim Galerie, Wien / Vienna (2017), *Drawing. The Bottom Line*, S.M.A.K. Stedelijk Museum voor Actuele Kunst, Gent (2015), *Abandon the Parents*, Statens Museum for Kunst, Kopenhagen / Copenhagen (2014), *The Stairs*, Algus Greenspon, New York (2013), *The Collection*, 21er Haus, Wien / Vienna (2012), *Kalte Gesellschaft*, curated by Judith Hopf, KW Institute for Contemporary Art, Berlin (2011), *While Bodies Get Mirrored*, Migros Museum, Zürich (2010), *Empfindungen oder in der Nähe der Fehler liegen die Wirkungen*, Augarten Contemporary, Belvedere, Wien / Vienna (2009), Von *Abts bis Zmijewski – Neue Werke aus der Sammlung Gegenwartskunst*, Pinakothek der Moderne, München / Munich (2007), *Eine Person allein in einem Raum mit Coca-Cola-farbenen Wänden*, Grazer Kunstverein, Graz (2006), *Imagination Becomes Reality – Part II: Painting Surface Space*, Sammlung Goetz, München / Munich (2005), *The Future Has A Silver Lining: Genealogies of Glamour*, Migros Museum, Zürich / Zurich (2004).

HANS HOLLEIN

(geb. / b. 1934 in Wien, gest. / d. 2014 in Wien)
Architekt und Designer, Bildhauer, Ausstellungsgestalter und Architekturtheoretiker / Architect, designer, sculptor, exhibition designer, and architectural theorist.
Ausgewählte Projekte, Tätigkeiten und Ausstellungen u. a. / Selected projects and shows include Herausgeber der Zeitschrift / editor of the journal *Bau* (1965–70), Professor Staatliche Kunstakademie Düsseldorf (1967–76), *Tod*, Städtisches Museum Mönchengladbach (1970), *Werk und Verhalten. Leben und Tod. Alltägliche Situationen*, XXXVI Biennale di Venezia (1972), Architekt / architect Städtisches Museum Abteiberg, Mönchengladbach (1972–82), Leiter / director Meisterklasse Industrial Design, Universität für angewandte Kunst Wien (1974–79), Architekt / architect Österreichisches Verkehrsbüro, Wien (1976), *MAN transFORMS*, Cooper-Hewitt Museum, New York (1976), *documenta VI*, Kassel (1977), Leiter / director Meisterklasse Architektur, Universität für angewandte Kunst Wien (1979–2002), Architekt / architect Museum für

Moderne Kunst, Frankfurt (1983–91), Architekt / architect *Haas-Haus*, Wien (1985–90), *Traum und Wirklichkeit*, Künstlerhaus Wien (1985), *Hans Hollein retrospective: Métaphores et Métamorphoses*, Centre Pompidou, Paris (1987), Direktor der Sektion Architektur, Architektur-Biennale Venedig / Director of the Architecture Section of the Venice Architecture Biennale (1994–96), Architekt / architect Österreichische Botschaft, Berlin (1997–2001), Architekt / architect Albertina-Flugdach (Soravia Wing), Wien / Vienna (2003), *Car Building*, Skulptur beim Zentrum für Kunst und Medientechnologie in Karlsruhe (2011), *Hans Hollein*, Neue Galerie Graz am Universalmuseum Joanneum, Graz (2011).

NICO IHLEIN
(geb. / b. 1972 in Neckarsulm, D, lebt und arbeitet / lives and works in Berlin).
Ausgewählte Einzelausstellungen u. a. / Selected solo shows at Neuer Essener Kunstverein, Essen (2017), Schiefe Zähne, Berlin (2017), Halle für Kunst, Lüneburg (2015), Marquise Dance Hall, Istanbul (2016), *based in berlin*, Evas Arche zeigt, Berlin (2011), Nice & Fit, Berlin (2007), Apotheke, Berlin (2004), Galerie Antique, Berlin (2003).
Ausgewählte Gruppenausstellungen u. a. / Selected group shows include *glazed & confused*, fonda, Leipzig (2020), *Omnibus* (m. / w. Honey Suckle Company), ICA, London (2019), *Bedmanners*, Kunstpunkt, Berlin (2019), *Piusstrasse 36*, HOSPITALITY, Köln / Cologne (2018), *Authentizität*, Halle für Kunst, Lüneburg (2017), *Gefäße*, Galerie Cruise & Callas, Berlin (2016), *1.–3. Person singular*, Verein für zeitgenössische Kunst, Leipzig (2016), *Gebärden und Ausdruck* (m. / w. Honey Suckle Company), Halle für Kunst, Lüneburg (2016), *How long is tomorrow?*, Galerie im Turm, Berlin, *freier Fall – Magazin für Befindlichkeit*, Badischer Kunstverein, Karlsruhe (2009), *Palisadenparenchym*, Danese Gallery, New York (2007), *non est hic* (m. / w. Honey Suckle Company), Kunsthalle Basel (2006), *ohnend* (m. / w. Honey Suckle Company), Cubitt Gallery, London (2005), *Es werde* in *Der Reigen*, Künstlerhaus Stuttgart (2003), *Neu West End* in *Children of Berlin* (m. / w. Honey Suckle Company), PS1 Contemporary Art, New York (1999).

ELISABETH KARLINSKY-SCHERFIG
(geb. / b. 1904 in Kasten, gest. / d. 1994 in Graested).
Ausgewählte Ausstellungen, Projekte und Retrospektiven u. a. / Selected shows, projects, and retrospectives include: Internationale Kunstausstellung / International Art Exhibition, Paris (1925), Ausstellung / exhibition in Dänemark / Denmark (1932), regelmäßige Ausstellungsbeteiligungen der Künstlervereinigung / regular participation in exhibitions of the artists' association CORNER (ab / from 1935/36), Lobmeyer-Preis für kinetische Glasfenster / Lobmeyer Award for kinetic glass windows (1926), Raumausstattung für den Weltfrauenkongress / Interior design for the World Congress of Women Kopenhagen / Copenhagen (1953), *Zwischen den Kriegen – Österreichische Künstler 1918–1938*, Leopold Museum Wien / Vienna (2007), *Bedrohung & Idylle – Das Menschenbild in Österreich. 1918–1938*, Schloss Bruck (2009), *DYNAMIK! Kubismus / Futurismus / KINETISMUS*, Universität für angewandte Kunst Wien, Belvedere Wien / Vienna (2011), *Stadt der Frauen. Künstlerinnen in Wien von 1900 bis 1938*, Belvedere Wien / Vienna (2019).

AMY LIEN
(geb. / b. 1987 in Dallas)
ENZO CAMACHO
(geb. / b. 1985 in Manila).
Ausgewählte Einzelausstellungen u. a. / Selected solo shows at NTU Center for Contemporary Art, Singapore (2019), Cordova, Barcelona (2018), Kunstverein Freiburg, Freiburg im Breisgau, (2018), CCS Bard Hessel Museum, Annandale-on-Hudson, New York (2018), 47Canal, New York (2018), Goethe-Institut Shanghai, Schanghai / Shanghai (2017), Mannanganal, various locations, Berlin (2016), NTU Center for Contemporary Art, Singapur / Singapore (2015), Mathew Gallery, Berlin (2014), Pablo Fort, Taguig (2012), Republikha Art Gallery, Quezon City (2011), Mo Space, Taguig (2009).
Ausgewählte Gruppenausstellungen u. a. / Selected group shows include *Motions of this Kind: Propositions & Problems of Belatedness*, Brunei Gallery, SOAS University of London, London (2019), *Diaspora, Ma Homey*, Space_31, Berlin (2018), *Produktion. Made in Germany Drei*, Kestner Gesellschaft, Hannover (2017), *The New Normal*, Ullens Center for Contemporary Art, Peking / Beijing (2017), *Urban Aspiration, The Physics Room*, Christchurch, Neuseeland / New Zealand (2016), *Not with nothing but. With nothing.*, Project Native Informant, London (2015), *Whose Subject am I?*, Kunstverein Düsseldorf, Düsseldorf (2015), *Lynda, Robert, Amy, Enzo und die Anderen*, Künstlerhaus Bremen, Bremen (2014), *MIND RVIDXR*, Station/3001 Gallery, USC ROSKI School of Art and Design, Los Angeles (2013), *Queer Manila*, Manila Contemporary, Makati (2012), *Grand Opening*, Mathew Gallery, Berlin (2011), *Survivalism*, Light and Space Contemporary, Quezon City (2011), *Latent/ Lubricious*, Adams ArtSpace, Cambridge (2009).

ILYA LIPKIN
(geb. / b. in 1983 in Riga, lebt und arbeitet / lives and works in Berlin).
Ausgewählte Einzelausstellungen / Selected solo exhibitions at Svetlana Gallery, New York (2019, 2018), Beach Office, Berlin (2017), kim?, Contemporary Art Centre, Riga (2017), Lars Friedrich, Berlin (2016), Nousmoules, Wien / Vienna (2015).
Ausgewählte Gruppenausstellungen u. a. / Selected group shows include *EMOTION IS AN UNLIMITED RESOURCE*, Stadtgalerie Bern (2019), *Elevations*, Galerie Emanuel Layr, Wien / Vienna (2018), *Relevelations*, Emanuel Layr Gallery, Roma, *Elevator to Mezzanine (E-M)*, Cleopatras, New York (2017), *Periodico 001 02 17 and Four Proposals for Future Covers*, Mavra, Berlin (2017), *Stuttgart*, Galerie Francesca Pia, Zürich (2016), *Hybrids in Purgatory*, Autocenter, Berlin (2014), *Imitiation of Life*, screening at Haus der Kulturen der Welt, Berlin (2013), *Downstairs Productions Presents*, with Joen Vedel, Overgaden Institute for Contemporary Art, Kopenhagen / Copenhagen (2013), *Collaborative Art Show*, New York (2012), *Based In Berlin*, Hamburger Bahnhof, Berlin (2011).

LUCY MCKENZIE
(geb. / b. 1977, Glasgow; lebt und arbeitet in Brüssel / lives and works in Brussels).
Ausgewählte Einzelausstellungen / Selected solo exhibitions at Museum Brandhorst, München / Munich (2020), Cabinet, London (2019), Fondazione Bevilacqua la Masa, Venedig / Venice (2017), Galerie Buchholz, Berlin (2015), The Art Institute of Chicago, Chicago (2014), Stedelijk Museum, Amsterdam (2013), MoMA, New York (2008), SFMoMA, San Francisco (2007), Metro Pictures, New York (2005), Tate Britain, London (2003), Inverleith House, Edinburgh (2001).
Ausgewählte Gruppenausstellungen u. a. / Selected group shows include *Atelier E.B: Passer-by*, Garage, Moskau / Moscow (2020), Lafayette Anticipations, Paris (2019), Serpentine Galleries, London (2018), *‚33– ‚29– ‚36*, Galerie UM, Academy of Arts, Architecture and Design, Prag / Prague (2016), *Painting Now*, Tate Britain (2013), *Te Kust en te Keur*, Mu.ZEE, Oostende (2012), *A Bigger Splash*, Tate Modern, London (2012), *Town-Gown Conflict*, Kunsthalle Zürich, Zürich / Zurich (2011), 50th Venice Biennale, Venice (2003), *The Best Book About Pessimism I Ever Read*, Kunstverein Braunschweig (2002), *Charisma Presents: It May Be a Year of Thirteen Moons, But it's Still the Year of Culture* Transmission, Glasgow (2000).

ULRIKE MÜLLER
(geb. / b. 1971 in Brixlegg, lebt und arbeitet / lives and works in New York).
Ausgewählte Einzelausstellungen u. a. / Selected solo shows at International Pavillion, 58. Biennale di Venezia (2019), Kunstverein für Rheinlande und Westfalen, Düsseldorf (2018), Callicoon Fine Arts, New York (2016), mumok, Wien / Vienna (2015), Kunstraum Lakeside, Klagenfurt (2014), Kairo Biennale (2010), Steinle Contemporary, München / Munich (2010), O'Connor Art Gallery, Chicago (2008), Aktualisierungsraum, Hamburg (2007), Temporary Art Space at Hotel Chelsea, New York (2005).
Ausgewählte Gruppenausstellungen u. a. / Selected group shows include *Straying from the Line*, Schinkel Pavillon, Berlin (2019), *The Carnegie International*, Carnegie Museum of Art, Pittsburgh (2018), *Trigger: Gender as a Tool and a Weapon*, New Museum, New York (2017), *The Whitney Biennial*, The Whitney Museum of American Art, New York (2017), *The Cypress Broke*, Rodeo, London (2016), *Painting 2.0: Expression in the Information Age*, mumok, Wien / Vienna (2016) und / and Museum Brandhorst, München / Munich (2015), *The Little Things Could be Dearer*, MoMa PS1, New York (2014), *Descartes' Daughters*, Swiss Institute, New York (2013), *Dance/Draw*, ICA Boston (2011), *Held Up By Columns*, Renwick Gallery, New York (2010), *Undigested Kernel*, General

Public, Berlin (2009), *The Sound of Things: Unmonumental Audio*, New Museum, New York (2008), *Shared Women*, LACE, Los Angeles (2007), *Reality/Play*, Orchard, New York (2006), *I Beg Your Pardon*, Vera List Center of Art and Politics at the New School, New York (2005).

OSWALD OBERHUBER
(geb. / b. 1931 in Meran / Merano, gest. / d. 2020 in Wien / Vienna). Ausgewählte Einzelausstellungen u. a. / Selected solo shows at KOW, Berlin (2016), 21er Haus, Wien / Vienna (2016), Galerie Altnöder, Salzburg (2014), Eiserner Vorhang, Staatsoper Wien / Vienna (2013), Galerie der Stadt Schwaz (2013), Galerie Ernst Hilger, Wien / Vienna (2009), Orangerie, Unteres Belvedere, Wien / Vienna (2009), Landesmuseum Joanneum, Graz (2006), Secession, Wien / Vienna (2006), Tiroler Landesmuseum Ferdinandeum, Innsbruck (2006), steirischer herbst, Galerie Kunst & Handel, Graz (2004), MAK – Österreichisches Museum für angewandte Kunst, Wien / Vienna (1999), Galerie Thoman, Innsbruck (1999), Kunsthalle Wien / Vienna (1994), BAWAG Foundation, Wien / Vienna (1994). Ausgewählte Gruppenausstellungen u. a. / Selected group shows include *Die Nacht im Zwielicht: Kunst von der Romantik bis heute*, Unteres Belvedere und Orangerie, Wien / Vienna (2012), *Der nackte Mann*, Lentos Kunstmuseum Linz (2012), *The excitment continues – Zeitgenössische Kunst aus der Sammlung Leopold II*, Leopold Museum, Wien / Vienna (2011), *Ich weiß gar nicht, was Kunst ist – Einblicke in eine private Sammlung*, MARTa Museum für zeitgenössische Kunst, Herford (2010), *Fine Line*, Georg Kargl Fine Arts, Wien / Vienna (2010), *Malerei: Prozess und Expansion – von den 1950er Jahren bis heute*, Museum Moderner Kunst, Stiftung Ludwig, Wien / Vienna (2010), *Klein aber oho! Plastiken aus der Sammlung*, Museum der Moderne Salzburg – Rupertinum (2009), *documenta XII, Herbert Fuchs VERBALE (Die Filme)*, Kassel (2007), *50 Jahre documenta*, Kunsthalle Fridericianum, Kassel (2005), *documenta VII*, Kassel (1982), *documenta VI*, Kassel (1977), XXXVI Biennale di Venezia (1972), *Surrealismus ohne Surrealisten; Kunst ohne Künstler*, Galerie nächst St. Stephan, Wien / Vienna (1969).

DAGOBERT PECHE
(geb. / b. 1887 in Sankt Michael im Lungau, gest. / d. 1923 in Mödling). Ausgewählte Ausstellungen, Projekte und Retrospektiven u. a. / Selected shows, projects, and retrospectives include Internationale Kunstausstellung Rom / International Art Exhibition Rome (1914), Werkbundausstellung Köln / Cologne (1914), Modeausstellung im k. k. Österreichisches Museum für Kunst und Industrie Wien / Fashion exhibition at the Austrian Museum for Art and Industry Vienna (1915), Leitung Zürcher Filiale / Director Zurich Branch of the Wiener Werkstätte (1916–19), Kunstschau Wien / Vienna (1920), Gestaltung Ausstellungsstand Wiener Werkstätte für Wiener international Messe / Design of the Wiener Werkstätte exhibition stand at the International Exhibition in Vienna (1921), Gewerbeschau München / Industrial Exhibition Munich (1922), *Dagobert-Peche-Gedächtnisausstellung*, Wien / Vienna (1923), *Dagobert Peche*, Paris (1925), *Die Überwindung der Utilität: Dagobert Peche und die Wiener Werkstätte* MAK Wien (1998), *Beyond Utility: Dagobert Peche and the Wiener Werkstätte*, Neue Galerie New York (2002), *Yearning for Beauty: The Wiener Werkstätte and Palais Stoclet*, Center for Fine Arts Brussels, Brüssel (2006).

YVES SAINT LAURENT
(geb. / b. 1936 in Oran, DZA, gest. / d. 2008 in Paris).
Couturier, Kostümbildner, Assistent (1955–57) und künstlerischer Leiter / Fashion and costume designer, assistant, and artistic director at Dior (1958–60), Gründer des gleichnamigen Modelabels / founder of the fashion brand Yves Saint Laurent (YSL) in Paris (Erste Kollektion / first collection 1962).
Wichtige Kollektionen u. a. / Important collections include *Autumn-Winter collection of 1965* (hommage to Piet Mondrian), *Autumn-Winter collection of 1966* (hommage to Pop Art), *Spring-Summer collection of 1968* (safari-jacket, jumpsuit), *Autumn-Winter collection of 1969* (w. Claude Lalanne), *Libération / Quarante* collection (1971), *Opéras – Ballets russes* collection (1976), *Broadway Suit* collection (1978), Arbeiten für Theater, Ballet und Film / projects for theater, ballet, and film include, *La Chaloupée*, Ballet m. / w. Roland Petit, Opera of Copenhagen (1961), *Les Forains*, Ballet m. / w. Roland Petit (1961), *The Pink Panther*, R. / dir. Blake Edwards (1963), *Zizi Jeanmaires Show*, Music Hall Revue m. / w. Roland Petit, Théâtre National de Chaillot (1963), *Notre Dame de Paris*, Ballet m. / w. Roland Petit, Palais Garnier, Paris (1965), *Arabesque*, R. / dir. Stanley Donen (1966), *Belle de Jour*, R. / dir. Luis Buñuel (1967), *La Chamade* (Heartbeat), R. / dir. Alain Cavalier (1968), *La Sirène du Mississipi (Mississippi Mermaid)*, R. / dir. François Truffaut (1969).
Retrospektiven u. a. / Retrospective exhibitions include
Bowes Museum, Barnard Castle, County Durham/UK, 2015, Denver Art Museum, Denver/CO, 2012, Centre Georges Pompidou, Paris (2002), Musée des Arts de la Mode, Paris (1986), Tretyakov Gallery, Moskau / Moscow (1986), Metropolitan Museum of Art, New York 1983.

JACK SMITH
(geb. / b. 1932 in Columbus (OH), gest. / d. 1989 in New York).
Filmografie (Auswahl) u. a. / Selected filmography includes
No President (1967–70), *Song For Rent* (1969), *Jungle Island* (1967), *Normal Love* (1963), *Overstimulated* (1959–63), *Scotch Tape* (1959–62), *The Yellow Sequence* (1963–65), *Flaming Creatures* (1962–63), *Respectable Creatures* (1950–66), *Buzzards Over Bagdad* (1951).
Happenings, Performances, und / and Screenings u. a. / included *Death of a Penguin* (1985), *I Was a Male Yvonne De Carlo for the Lucky Landlord Underground* (1982), *What's Underground About Marshmallows* (1981), *Art Crust on Crab Lagoon* (1981), *I Was a Mekas Collaborator* (1978), *Secret of Rented Island* (1976–77), *Shows Brassieres of Atlantis* (1969).
Retrospektiven, Ausstellungen u. a. / Retrospectives include
Jack Smith: Art Crust of Spiritual Oasis, Artists Space, New York (2018), *Jack Smith: Theater and Performance Works*, Gladstone Gallery Brussels, Brüssel (2014), *Rituals of Rented Island: Object Theater, Loft Performance, and the New Psychodrama—Manhattan, 1970–1980*, Whitney Museum of American Art, New York (2013), *Jack Smith: Normal Love*, MoMA PS1, New York (2012), *Jack Smith: Thanks for Explaining Me*, Gladstone Gallery New York (2011), *Jack Smith: Films and Publications*, Galerie Buchholz, Köln / Cologne (2000), *Jack Smith: Flaming Creature: His Amazing Life and Times*, The Institute for Contemporary Art/P.S.1 Museum, New York, Pittsburg/PA, Berkeley/CA (1997).

MARIANNE MY ULLMANN
(geb. / b. 1905 in Wien / Vienna, gest. / d. 1995 in Konstanz).
Ausgewählte Ausstellungen, Projekte und Retrospektiven u. a. / Selected shows, projects and retrospectives include: internationale Ausstellungen der Čižek-Klasse, gemeinsam mit / international exhibitions of the Čižek class, together with Erika Giovanna Klien und / and Elisabeth Karlinsky (1921–25), *Exposition internationale des arts décoratifs et industriels modernes* (1925), *Künstler im Kunsthandwerk und in der Industrie*, k. k. Österreichisches Museum für Kunst und Industrie / Austrian Museum of Art and Industry (1925), entwarf zahlreiche Gobelins, Vorhangstoffe und Teppiche / designed numerous tapestries, curtain fabrics, and carpets (1927–29), Bühnen- und Kostümbildnerin am Münchner Stadttheater / set and costume designer at the Munich City Theatre (1930), Ausstattung für die Festlichen Spiele in Luzern / scenography for the Lucerne Festival (1931), Ausstattung des Faschingsballs *Die bunte Laterne* der Berliner Kunstgewerbeschule / design for the carnival ball *Die bunte Laterne* of the Berlin School of Applied Arts (1933), in Berlin als Malerin, Bühnenbildnerin und Reklameleiterin / painter, stage designer, and art director in advertising (ab / from 1933/34), *Farbenlust und Formgedanken*, Baden bei Wien, Klagenfurt, Wien / Vienna (2000), *Zeit des Aufbruchs. Budapest und Wien zwischen Historismus und Avantgarde*, Budapest (2004), *Der Kinetismus: Wien entdeckt die Avantgarde*, Wien Museum, Wien / Vienna (2006), *DYNAMIK! – Kubismus / Futurismus / KINETISMUS*, Belvedere, Wien / Vienna (2011), *Das ist Österreich! Bildstrategien und Raumkonzepte 1914–1938*, Vorarlberg Museum (2015), *Years of Disarray. Art of the Avantgarde in Central Europe 1908–1928*, International Cultural Centre, Krakau / Krakow (2019), *Schall und Rauch*, Kunsthaus Zürich (2020).

AMELIE VON WULFFEN
(geb. / b. 1966, Breitenbrunn, D, lebt und arbeitet / lives and works in Berlin).
Ausgewählte Einzelausstellungen u. a. / Selected solo shows at KW, Kunst-Werke, Berlin (2020), Kunsthalle Bern (2019), Radio Athènes (2019), Reena Spaulings, New York (2018), Liszt, Berlin (2018), Gió Marconi Mailand / Milan (2018), Studio Voltaire, London (2017), Galerie Barbara Weiss, Berlin (2016), Pinakothek der Moderne, München / Munich (2015), Galerie Meyer Kainer, Wien / Vienna (2015),

Freedman Fitzpatrick Gallery, Los Angeles (2015), Portikus, Frankfurt (2013), Aspen Art Museum, Aspen (2012), Kunstraum Innsbruck (2009), Kunstverein Düsseldorf (2006), Centre Pompidou, Paris (2005), Museum für Gegenwartskunst, Basel (2005).
Ausgewählte Gruppenausstellungen u. a. / Selected group shows include *1. COLOR 2. HOLE AND 3. JOKE*, Galerie Meyer Kainer, Wien / Vienna (2020), *Feelings. Kunst und Emotion*, Pinakothek der Moderne, München / Munich, (2019), *Liebe und Ethnologie*, Haus der Kulturen der Welt, Berlin (2019), *Knock Knock*, South London Gallery, London (2018), *Infected Foot*, Greene Naftali Gallery, New York (2017), *Sputterances*, Metro Pictures, New York (2017), *Raw and Delirious*, Kunsthalle Bern (2015), *Call and Response*, Gavin Brown's Enterprise, New York (2015), *Summer Sweatshop*, Liverpool Biennial (2014), *A TOP-HAT, A MONOCLE, AND A BUTTERFLY*, etablissement d'en face, Brüssel / Brussels (2013), *Malerei in Fotografie*, Städel Museum, Frankfurt (2012), *Compass in Hand*, The Museum of Modern Art, New York (2009), *Form und Grund*, Augarten Contemporary, Österreichische Galerie Belvedere, Wien / Vienna (2008), *Manifesta 5* (2005), *3. Berlin Biennale* (2004), 50. Biennale di Venezia, Venedig / Venice (2003).

LAURA WELKER
(geb. / b. 1985 in Amsterdam, lebt und arbeitet / lives and works in Berlin).
Ausgewählte Ausstellungen und Projekte u. a. / Selected exhibitions and projects include: *Unter Flaschen: Die Fledermaus in der Bar du Bois*, Heiligenkreuzer Hof, Wien / Viena (2020), *3hd*, HAU 2, Berlin (2019), *Creamcake* (table dance performance Michelle Woods, Berlin (2019), *Klosterruine*, FIAC (m. / w. Sandy Brown Gallery), Paris (2018), *Jugend ist Trunkenheit ohne Wein*, BIKINI, Basel (2018), *Fundraiser & Hors d'Oevre*, Stations, Berlin (2017).
Weitere Projekte u. a. / Further projects include *Hotlegs* Kerzenständer / candlestick (available w. Rani Bageria, Wien / Vienna), *Badeanzüge / Swimsuits* m. / w. Ehsan Morshed Sefat (Velvetesque.com), *LVMM shoes* m. / w. Arielle de Pinto.

EDUARD WIMMER-WISGRILL
(geb. / b. 1882 in Wien / Vienna, gest. / d. 1961 in Wien / Vienna).
Ausgewählte Ausstellungen, Projekte, Positionen und Retrospektiven u. a. / Selected shows, projects, positions and retrospectives include: Kunstschau Wien / Vienna (1908), Internationale Kunstschau Wien / Vienna (1909), Internationale Kunstschau Rom / International Art Exhibition Rome (1911), Werkbundausstellung Köln / Cologne (1914), Leiter der Werkstätte für Mode und Modezeichnen an der Kunstgewerbeschule Wien / director of the workshop for fashion and fashion drawing at the School of Applied Arts Vienna (1918–21), Theaterausstellung / Theatre Exhibition London (1922), Leiter der Kunstgewerbe- und Modeklasse am Art Institute in Chicago / head of the applied arts and fashion class at the Art Institute in Chicago (1923–25), Leiter der Meisterklasse für Mode und der Werkstätte für Textilarbeiten an der Kunstgewerbeschule Wien / head of the masterclass for fashion and the workshop for textile work at the School of Applied Arts Vienna (1925–55), *Les Arts décoratifs* Paris (1925), Kunstschau im k. k. Österreichischen Museum für Kunst und Industrie / Austrian Museum for Art and Industry (1927), Werkbundausstellung Wien / Vienna (1930), Innendekoration des Österreichischen Pavillons bei der Weltausstellung in Paris / interior design of the Austrian pavilion at the World's Fair in Paris (1937), *Eduard Josef Wimmer-Wisgrill – Modeentwürfe 1912–1927 aus dem Besitz der Hochschule für angewandte Kunst in Wien*, Festsaal der Hochschule für angewandte Kunst in Wien (1983), *Wiener Werkstätte 1903–1932: The Luxury of Beauty*, Neue Galerie New York (2017).

KATHARINA WULFF
(geb. / b. 1968 in Berlin, lebt und arbeitet in Berlin und Marrakesch / lives and works in Berlin and Marrakesh).
Ausgewählte Einzelausstellungen u. a. / Selected solo shows at Brighton CCA, Brighton (2020), Haus Mödrath, Kerpen (2019), Galerie Daniel Buchholz, Köln / Cologne (2017), Greene Naftali Gallery, New York (2016), Fürstenberg Zeitgenössisch, Donaueschingen (2014), San Francisco Museum of Modern Art (2012), Galerie Neu, Berlin (2008), The Douglas Hyde Gallery, Dublin (2006), Galerie Bleich-Rossi, Graz (2002), Bonner Kunstverein und / and Kunstverein Göttingen (1999), Galerie Christian Nagel, Köln / Cologne (1998).
Ausgewählte Gruppenausstellungen u. a. / Selected group shows include *Maskulinitäten*, Bonner Kunstverein, Kölnischer Kunstverein und / and Kunstverein für die Rheinlande und Westfalen, Düsseldorf (2019), *An Uncanny Likeness*, Simon Lee, New York (2017), *These Strangers … Painting and People*, S.M.A.K., Gent (2016), *Works on Paper*, Greene Naftali Gallery, New York (2015), *The Sea*, Mu.ZEE, Oostende (2014), Queen Size, Collectors Room Berlin (2014), *Abandon the Parents*, curated by Henrik Olesen, Daniel Buchholz and Christopher Müller, Statens Museum for Kunst, Kopenhagen / Copenhagen (2014), *Play What's Not There*, Raven Row, London (2014), *The Happy Fainting of Painting*, Zwinger Galerie, Berlin(2013), *Head-Wing (Portrait of an Exhibition), selected by Paulina Olowska*, Camden Arts Centre, London (2009), *The Subversive Charm of the Bourgeoisie*, Van Abbemuseum, Eindhoven (2006), *Optik Schröder. Werke aus der Sammlung Schröder*, Kunstverein Braunschweig (2006), *actionbutton*, Hamburger Bahnhof, Berlin (2003).

MIN YOON
(geb. / b. 1986, Cheon, KOR; lebt und arbeitet in Wien / lives and works in Vienna).
Ausgewählte Einzelausstellungen / Selected solo shows at Galerie Meyer Kainer, Wien / Vienna (2019), Aquarium, Wien / Vienna (2018), Galerie der Stadt Schwaz (2017), Lars Friedrich, Berlin (2016), Maladie D'amour, Grenoble (2015), Bar du Bois, Wien / Vienna (2014), HHDM, Wien / Vienna (2013).
Ausgewählte Gruppenausstellungen / Selected group shows include *Chaisson, Driver, Charmer*, Commercial Street, Los Angeles (2018), *Der Verdienst. 2014–2017*, Oracle, Berlin (2017), *Piscine—The Conference*, Kunsthal Aarus, Aarhus (2016), *Dead Letter Office* (org. by Anna Sophie Berger), JTT Gallery, NewYork (2016), *More Anecdotes* (cur. by Tenzing Barshee), *Wellwellwell*, Wien / Vienna (2015), *Playtime*, 9800 Sepulveda Blvd., Los Angeles (2015), *New Needs*, Haus Wittmann, Etsdorf (2015), *Painting, Poetry, Pottery*, Tobias Naehring, Leipzig (2014), *Verbrecher und Dekorateure*, Galerie Senn, Wien / Vienna (2012).

Bildnachweis / Image Credits

UaK, KA = Universität für angewandte Kunst Wien, Kunstsammlung und Archiv / University of Applied Arts Vienna, Collection and Archive
FB-P = Friedrich Berzeviczy-Pallavicini

Cover
FB-P, Entwurf für ein Schränkchen / Design for a small cabinet, 1929, Bleistift auf Papier / pencil on paper, 29 × 22,6 cm, UaK, KA, IN 1685
Entwurf Ausstellungsplakat Alexander Nussbaumer FONDAZIONE Europa

Cover Innen / Cover Inside
FB-P, Entwurf für einen Gobelin / Design for the tapestry, *Zauberwald des Papageno / Papageno's Enchanted Forest*, 1937, Tempera und Gouache auf Papier / tempera and gouache on paper, 309 × 349 cm, Uak, KA, IN 1836

Die Kraft des Ephemeren / The Force of the Ephemeral
S. / p. 18: Foto / photo: James Godbold, Cowles Magazine Inc., Uak, KA IN 18.976/11/Q; S. / p. 21: Cover Einladungskarte / invitation card Hugo Gallery New York, 1951, Druck auf Papier / print on paper, 15,7 × 17,4 cm, Reproduktion / reproduction: kunst-dokumentation.com, Manuel Carreon Lopez, UaK, KA, IN 10.641/2/Q; S. / p. 24: FB-P, *Fürst Rehrücken*, Originalentwurf für das Buch / original designs for the publication *Die K. u. K. Hofzuckerbäckerei Demel. Ein Wiener Märchen / The Imperial and Royal Confectioners Demel: A Viennese Fairytale*, 1975, Tinte auf Karton / ink on cardbord, 30,5 × 12,5 cm, Reproduktion / reproduction: kunst-dokumentation.com, Manuel Carreon Lopez, UaK, KA, IN 5206-5;

Wie im Champagnerglas / As if in a Champagne Glass
S. / p. 26: Foto / photo: D'Ora-Benda, Atelier, Österreichische National-bibliothek Wien / Austrian National Library, IN 205.401-B; S. / p. 29: Foto / photo: Julius Scherb, UaK, KA, IN 11.319/FW/1; S. / p. 30: FB-P, Paravent für / Folding screen for *Boudoir einer mondänen Dame / Boudoir for a Cosmopolitan Lady*, 1929, verschiedene Seiden, Metallfäden, Glasperlen, Applikationsstickereien, 5-teilig, jeweils / various silks, metal threads, glass beads, appliqué embroidery, 5 panels, each 122 × 79 cm, UaK, KA, IN 201/O/T; S. / p. 31: FB-P, Bodenteppich für / Rug for *Boudoir einer mondänen Dame / Boudoir for a Cosmopolitan Lady*, 1929, Ripsbänder, in ein fertiges Gewebe eingezogen, Kunstseide, Baumwolle / rep ribbon woven into a rug, artificial silk, cotton, 171 × 96 cm, UaK, KA, IN 200/O/T; S. / p. 32: FB-P, Wandbehang für / tapestry for *Boudoir einer Dame / Boudoir for a Cosmopolitan Lady*, 1929, verschiedene Seiden, Metallfäden, Glasperlen, Applikationsstickereien / various silks, metal threads, glass beads, appliqué embroidery, 228 × 88 cm, UaK, KA, IN 199/O/T; S. / p. 33 links / left: Otto Lendecke, *Preis Nebensache / Price is No Object*, Illustration in: *Simplicissmus*, 2. April 1918, S. / p. 12., Österreichische Nationalbibliothek Wien / Austrian National Library Vienna; S. / p. 33 rechts / right: Otto Lendecke, *Der Tag bricht an / Daybreak*, Illustration in: *Die Damenwelt*, April 1917, © MAK Wien / Vienna, BI 18815-1917-4; S. / p. 34 links / left: Dagobert Peche, Salon in der 45. Ausstellung der Wiener Secession, 1913, in: *Deutsche Kunst und Dekoration* (34), 1914, S. 214, © MAK Wien / Vienna, BI 12337-1914-214; S. / p. 34 rechts / right: Christa Ehrlich, *Ecke in einem Damensalon*, in: *Moderne Bauformen*, Mai-Heft, 1927, S. / p. 1 (21), UaK, KA, IN ON494; S. / p. 35: Fotografie / photography, UaK, KA, IN 11.318/FW/1; S. / p. 36: *Innendekoration* (44), 1933, S. 47, © MAK Wien / Vienna; S. / p. 38: *Moderne Bauformen*, 1933, S. / p. 156, © MAK Wien / Vienna, BI 17860-1933-156; S. / p. 40: FB-P, Entwurf Gymnasium der Dame / Design for a lady's gymnasium (*Raum und Mode*), 1932, Feder, Deckfarben auf Transparentpapier / ink and gouache on transparent paper, 35,5 × 40 cm, UaK, KA, IN 4933; S. / p. 40 links / left: Katalog zur Ausstellung / exhibition catalogue, 1929, S. / p. 49, © MAK Wien / Vienna, Ausstell. I 1219; S. / p. 40 rechts / right: © MAK Wien / Vienna, IN KI 14178-22; S. / p. 41: *Architectural Digest*, Mai / May 1978, S. / p. 89. Foto / photo: Hans Mayr, *Architectural Digest*, UaK, KA, IN M-BERZ 2;

ABCs im Klassenkampf / ABCs and Class Struggle
S. / p. 42, 45, 46, 47: FB-P, Maquette for the Alphabet Book, Buchstaben / letters R, H, B, Z, Y, T, undatiert / undated, Wasserfarbe, Tinte, Tusche auf Papier / watercolor, ink, and India ink on paper, ca. / c. 35 × 26 cm, Reproduktion / reproduction: kunst-dokumentation.com, Manuel Carreon Lopez, UaK, KA, IN 19.027/18/Ma, IN 19.027/8/Ma, IN 19.027/2/Ma, IN 19.027/26/Ma, IN 19.027/25/Ma, IN 19.027/20/Ma; S. / p. 48: Cover *Flair*, Ausgabe / issue September 1950, Cowles Magazine Inc., New York, 1950, Zeitschrift / magazine, 33,2 × 24,8 cm, Reproduktion / reproduction: kunst-dokumentation.com, Manuel Carreon Lopez, UaK, KA, IN 18.976/11/Q; S. / p. 49 links / left: Cover *Flair*, Ausgabe / issue Februar / February 1950, Cowles Magazine Inc., New York, 1950, Zeitschrift / magazine, 33,2 × 24,8 cm, Reproduktion / reproduction: kunst-dokumentation.com, Manuel Carreon Lopez, UaK, KA, IN 18.976/1/Q; S. / p. 49 rechts / right: Cover *Flair Annual*, Cowles Magazine Inc., New York, 1953, 34 × 25,5 cm, Reproduktion / reproduction: kunst-dokumentation.com, Manuel Carreon Lopez, UaK, KA, IN 5027/Q; S. / p. 51: FB-P, *ohne Titel / Untitled*, Vase mit Blättern und Federn / vase with leafs and feathers, um / c. 1950, Öl auf Hartfaserplatte / oil on hardboard, 126,7 × 63,5 cm, Reproduktion / reproduction: kunst-dokumentation.com, Manuel Carreon Lopez, UaK, KA, IN 6312/B; S. / p. 52: *ohne Titel / Untitled*, Fantastische Blumen / fantastic flowers, 1952, Öl auf Hartfaserplatte / oil on hardboard, 126,5 × 63,7 cm, Reproduktion / reproduction: kunst-dokumentation.com, UaK, KA, IN 7132/B; S. / p. 54: Porträt von / of FB-P vor einem Paravent in der / in front of a folding screen at Iolas Gallery, New York, 1953, Foto / photo: *Look* Magazine, in: *Friedrich von Berzeviczy-Pallavicini. Poesie der Inszenierung*, 1988, S. / p. 14, UaK, KA; S. / p. 55 links / left: Einladungskarte zur Ausstellung von / Invitation card for the exhibition by Friedrich von Berzeviczy Pallavicini bei / at Zodiac Gallery, New York, 1956, Reproduktion / reproduction: kunst-dokumentation.com, Manuel Carreon Lopez, UaK, KA, IN 10.641/3/Q; S. / p. 55 rechts / right: FB-P, Innenseite der Einladungskarte / Inside of the invitation card, Hugo Gallery New York, 1951, Druck auf Papier / print on paper, 15,7 × 17,4 cm, Reproduktion / reproduction: kunst-dokumentation.com, Manuel Carreon Lopez, UaK, KA, IN 10.641/2/Q; S. / p. 56: FB-P, *Die 12 Sternzeichen / The 12 signs of the zodiac*, Virgo, ca. 1956, Mischtechnik auf Sperrholz / mixed technique on plywood, 63,5 × 53 cm, Foto / photo: Dorotheum Wien / Vienna, Auktionskatalog / auction catalogue 2012; S. / p. 57: FB-P, *Die 12 Sternzeichen / The 12 signs of the zodiac*, Gemini, Scorpio, Leo ca. 1956, Mischtechnik auf Sperrholz, Glasperlen / Mixed technique on plywood, glass beads, 63,5 × 53 cm, Foto / photo: Dorotheum Wien / Vienna, Auktionskatalog / auction catalogue 2012; S. / p. 58 und / and 59: Andy Warhol, Ralph Thomas Ward, *Ladies' Alphabet*, 1953, Tinte auf Riverside-Bondpapier / ink on Riverside bond paper, 27,9 × 21,6 cm, The Andy Warhol Museum, Pittsburgh; Founding Collection, Contribution The Andy Warhol Foundation for the Visual Arts, Inc. 1998.1.1880, 1998.1.1885, 1998.1.1886, © The Andy Warhol Foundation for the Visual Arts, Inc. / licensed by Bildrecht, Wien 2020; Andy Warhol, Ralph Thomas Ward, *A Is an Alphabet*, 1953, Tinte und Graphit auf Strathmore Seconds-Papier / ink and graphite on Strathmore Seconds paper, 26,7 × 16,2 cm, The Andy Warhol Museum, Pittsburgh, Founding Collection, Contribution The Andy Warhol Foundation for the Visual Arts, Inc., 1998.1.1357, 1998.1.1371, 1998.1.1382, © The Andy Warhol Foundation for the Visual Arts, Inc. / licensed by Bildrecht, Wien 2020; S. / p. 60 links / left: Illustration eines Fingeralphabets / Illustration of a finger alphabet in: *Flair Annual*, S. / p. 17, Cowles Magazine Inc., 1953, Reproduktion / reproduction: kunst-dokumentation.com, Manuel Carreon Lopez, UaK, KA, IN 5027/Q; S. / p. 60 rechts / right: The Musical Alphabet in: *Flair Annual*, S. 33, Cowles Magazine Inc., 1953, Reproduktion / reproduction: kunst-dokumentation.com, Manuel Carreon Lopez, UaK, KA, IN 5027/Q; S. / p. 63: FB-P, *ohne Titel / Untitled*, Blumen-Parterre / Flower Parterre, 1952, Öl auf Hartfaserplatte / oil on hardboard, 63,7 × 121,5 cm, Reproduktion / reproduction: kunst-dokumentation.com, Manuel Carreon Lopez, UaK, KA, IN 6315/B; S. / p. 66: Modell in einem Leinen-Hemd und Rock vor einer Wandmalerei von / Model in a linen shirt and skirt in front of a mural by Federico Pallavicini, in: *Vogue*, Mai / May 01, 1958, Foto / photo: Karen Radkai, *Vogue* © Conde Nast IN CN00033510; S. / p. 68: Modell in einem Rogers Abendkleid vor einer Wandmalerei von / Model in Rogers evening gown in front of mural by Federico Pallavicini in: *Vogue*, November 01, 1959, Foto / photo: William Bell, Vogue © Conde Nast IN CN00033767; S. / p. 69: Stilleben von / Still Life of Federico Pallavicini, *Katze und Tassen / Cat and Cups*, 1957, Foto / photo: Horst P. Horst, *Vogue* © Conde Nast IN CN00033603; S. / p. 70: Andy Warhol, *25 Cats Name[sic!] Sam and One Blue Pussy*, 1954, Künstlerbuch, Offsetdruck auf Papier, handkoloriert / artist's book, offset print on paper, hand-colored, 23,3 × 15,6 × 1 cm (Buch geschlossen / book closed), Udo und Anette Brandhorst Sammlung / Udo and Anette Brandhorst Collection, Foto / Photo: Haydar Koyupinar, Bayerische Staatsgemäldesammlungen, München / Munich, © The Andy

Warhol Foundation for the Visual Arts, Inc. / licensed by Bildrecht, Wien 2020; S. / p. 71: FB-P, *Chat I*, undatiert / undated, Tinte und Metallfarbe auf Metall / ink and metallic paint on metal, Foto / photo: christies.com;

Ausstellungsansichten / Exhibition Views
detaillierte Angaben zu den einzelnen abgebildeten Werken siehe Werkliste / see list of works for detailed information on the individual works shown.
S. / p. 76, 78–79, 80–81, 82–83, 88–89, 99: Ausstellungsansicht / exhibiton view, *Der Hausfreund. Eine Wiederentdeckung des exzentrischen Werks von Friedrich von Berzeviczy-Pallavicini / Der Hausfreund. A Rediscovery of the Eccentric Work of Friedrich von Berzeviczy-Pallavicini*, Universitätsgalerie Heiligenkreuzer Hof Wien, 02.05.-01.06.2019, 2019, Foto / photo: Amelie Proché, © UaK, KA;
S. / p. 84–85, 86–87, 90–91, 92–93, 94–95, 96–97, 98: Ausstellungsansicht / exhibiton view, *Der Hausfreund. Eine Wiederentdeckung des exzentrischen Werks von Friedrich von Berzeviczy-Pallavicini / Der Hausfreund. A Rediscovery of the Eccentric Work of Friedrich von Berzeviczy-Pallavicini*, Universitätsgalerie Heiligenkreuzer Hof Wien, 02.05.-01.06.2019, 2019, Foto / photo: Till Martin, © Uak, KA;

Ciphers of Regression
S. / p. 101, 102–103, 104: Foto / photo: Martina Lajczak, © Klasse für Malerei / Painting Department, Universität für angewandte Kunst Wien / University of Applied Arts Vienna

S. / p. 106, 108–131: Ausstellungsansicht / exhibiton view, *Der Hausfreund. Eine Wiederentdeckung des exzentrischen Werks von Friedrich von Berzeviczy-Pallavicini / Der Hausfreund. A rediscovery of the eccentric work of Friedrich von Berzeviczy-Pallavicini*, Österreichisches Kulturforum Berlin, 13.09.-25.10.2019, 2019, Foto / photo: Timo Ohler, © UaK, KA;
Reproduktionen / reproductions: detaillierte Angaben zu den einzelnen abgebildeten Werken siehe Werkliste / see list of works for detailed information on the individual works shown.
S. / p. 132–135: Foto / photo: © Uak, KA; S. / p. 136–143: Reproduktion / reproduction: kunst-dokumentation.com, Manuel Carreon Lopez, © UaK, KA; S. / p. 144: Reproduktion / reproduction: kunst-dokumentation.com, Manuel Carreon Lopez, © Bildrecht, Wien 2020; S. / p. 145–149: Reproduktion / reproduction: kunst-dokumentation.com, Manuel Carreon Lopez, © UaK, KA; S. / p. 150–151: Foto / photo: © Uak, KA;

Künstler*innen der Ausstellung / Artists at the Exhibition
detaillierte Angaben zu den einzelnen abgebildeten Werken siehe Werkliste / see list of works for detailed information on the individual works shown.
S. / p. 154: Foto / photo: Amelie Proché, © Uak, KA und die Künstlerinnen / and the artists;
S. / p. 155: Foto / photo: Ilya Lipkin, © die Künstler*innen / the artists;
S. / p. 156: Foto / photo: © Galerie Meyer Kainer, Wien / Vienna;
S. / p. 157: Foto / photo: Amelie Proché, © UaK, KA; S. / p. 158: Foto / photo: © Galerie Buchholz, Berlin-Köln-New York / Berlin-Cologne-New York und die Künstlerin / and the artists;
S. / p. 159: Foto / photo: © Galerie Meyer Kainer, Wien / Vienna und die Künstlerin / and the artist;
S. / p. 160 links / left: Foto / photo: © Sammlung / Collection Schröder Berlin; S. / p. 160 rechts / right: Foto / photo: © Galerie Neu, Berlin und die Künstlerin / and the artist; S. / p. 161, 162: Reproduktion / reproduction: kunst-dokumentation.com, Manuel Carreon Lopez © UaK, KA;

Eine Chronologie / A Chronology
S. / p. 164: Foto / photo: unbekannt / unknown, UaK, KA, IN 19.047/FP;
S. / p. 165: Foto / photo: Seifert Wien / Vienna, Uak, KA, IN 11.321/FP/2; S. / p. 166: Foto / photo: Julius Scherb, Wien / Vienna, UaK, KA, IN 11.148/FW/4; S. / p. 167 oben / above: Foto / photo: unbekannt / unknown, UaK, KA, IN 15.232/FP;
S. / p. 167 unten / below: Foto / photo: Julius Scherb, Wien / Vienna, Uak, KA, IN 11.319/FW/7; S. / p. 168 oben / above: Foto / photo: Ing. Franz Mayer, Wien / Vienna, Uak, KA, IN 11.318/FW/2; S. / p. 168 unten / below: Foto / photo: Skall Wien / Vienna, UaK, KA, IN 11.314/FP/11;
S. / p. 169: Foto / photo: Maria Wölfl, Wien / Vienna, UaK, KA, IN 11.314/FW/6; S. / p. 170 oben / above: Foto / photo: Maria Wölfl, Wien / Vienna, UaK, KA, IN 11.314/FW/8; S. / p. 170 unten / below: Foto / photo: Dora Horowitz, 1937, UaK, KA, IN 11.315/FP; S. / p. 171 oben / above: Foto / photo: Otto Skall, Österreichische Nationalbibliothek Wien, Austrian National Library Vienna; S. / p. 171 unten / below: Foto / photo: unbekannt / unknown, UaK, KA; S. / p. 172: Reproduktion / reproduction: kunst-dokumentation.com, Manuel Carreon Lopez UaK, KA, IN 10.639/Q/1; S. / p. 173: Reproduktion / reproduction: kunst-dokumentation.com, Manuel Carreon Lopez, UaK, KA, IN 10.641/1/Q;
S. / p. 174 oben / above: Foto / photo: unbekannt / unknown, Harry Ransom Center Texas; S. / p. 174 unten / below: Foto / photo: unbekannt / unknown, Uak, KA, IN 16.711/FP; S. / p. 175: Foto / photo: unbekannt / unknown, UaK, KA, IN 11.317/FW/1; S. / p. 176: Foto / photo: Franz Hubmann, Uak, KA, IN 13.982/2/FW; S. / p. 177 oben / above: Foto / photo: unbekannt / unknown, UaK, KA, IN 11.317/FW/1; S. / p. 177 unten / below: Foto / photo: Franz Hubmann, IMAGNO Nr. 00137495; S. / p. 178: Foto / photo: Barbara Pflaum, IMAGNO Nr. 00680679;
S. / p. 179: Foto / photo: Barbara Pflaum, IMAGNO Nr. 00680680;

Wenn nicht anders in den Bildunterschriften angegeben sind alle abgebildeten Werke von Friedrich von Berzeviczy-Pallavicini / Unless indicated otherwise in the captions, all depicted works are by Friedrich von Berzeviczy-Pallavicini.

Falls zu einzelnen Abbildungen trotz eingehender Recherche der korrekte Bildnachweis nicht erbracht werden konnte, ersuchen wir in diesen Fällen um Verständnis und bitten um Hinweis für künftige Nennungen. / If in spite of our thorough research any individual illustrations have not been correctly attributed or acknowledged, we offer our apologies and would appreciate any information that will allow us to rectify the matter in future editions.

Impressum / Colophon

Universität für angewandte Kunst Wien, Kunstsammlung und Archiv /
University of Applied Arts Vienna, Collection and Archive
Leitung / Director: Cosima Rainer

Der Hausfreund.
Eine Wiederentdeckung des exzentrischen Werks
von Friedrich von Berzeviczy-Pallavicini
A Rediscovery of the Eccentric Work
of Friedrich von Berzeviczy-Pallavicini

[s'ʌmmlung
Universität für angewandte Kunst Wien
University of Applied Arts Vienna

dɪ:'ʌngewʌndtə
Universität für angewandte Kunst Wien
University of Applied Arts Vienna

Ausstellung / Exhibition

Universistätsgalerie Heiligenkreuzer Hof Wien / Vienna
Eröffnung / Opening: 30. April 2019
Dauer / Duration: 2. Mai bis 1. Juni / May 2 to June 1, 2019

Österreichisches Kulturforum / Austrian Cultural Forum Berlin
Eröffnung / Opening: 12. September 2019
Dauer / Duration: 13. September bis 25. Oktober /
September 13 to October 25, 2019
Förderung durch das Bundeskanzleramt Kunst und Kultur Österreich
supported by the Arts and Culture Department of the
Austrian Bundeskanzleramt

Konzept / Concept: Cosima Rainer
Ausstellungsgestaltung / Exhibition design: Robert Müller
Kuratoren / Curators: Cosima Rainer, Robert Müller
Projektleitung / Project managment: Sofie Mathoi (Wien / Vienna),
Robert Müller (Berlin)
Projektteam / Project team: Sofie Mathoi, Silvia Herkt, Lukas Kaufmann,
Judith Burger, Nathalie Feitsch, Elisabeth Frottier, Johanna Enzersdorfer-Konrad, Natalia Gustavson
Aufbau / Installation: Christian Schneider und / and Team,
Lukas Kaufmann, Sebastian Doplbaur (Wien / Vienna)
Lukas Kaufmann, Nicolas Bakowski, Jan Stradtmann, Vera Lutz (Berlin)
Grafik (Ausstellung) / Graphic design (exhibition):
FONDAZIONE Europa

Leihgeber / Lenders:
Archiv Hans Hollein, Wien / Vienna
Wiener Porzellanmanufaktur Augarten – Porzellanmuseum
Demel K. u. K. Hofzuckerbäckerei Wien / Vienna
Galerie Buchholz, Köln – New York – Berlin
Galerie Meyer Kainer, Wien / Vienna
Galerie Neu, Berlin
Galerie Sandy Brown, Berlin
Rodeo, London
ungenannte Privatbesitze / unnamed private collections

Besonderer Dank an / With special thanks to:
Dorothea Apovnik, Thomas Ballot, Judith Burger, Daniel Buchholz,
Christian Brandstätter, BillyBoy, Patrizia Dander, Brigitte Felderer,
Nathalie Feitsch, Lars Friedrich, Katharina Forero de Mund,
Elisabeth Frottier, Petra Gold, Friederike Gratz, Erhard F. Grossnig,
Silvia Herkt, Michael Heltau, Lilli Hollein, Axel Hubmann,
Renate Kainer, Lukas Kaufmann, Tonio Kröner, Antonia Kühnel,
Claudia Lehner-Jobst, Minnie McIntyre, Birgit Megerle, Christian Meyer,
Christopher Muller, Martin Anton Müller, Erika Patka, Gerald Piffl,
Alexander Schröder, Anja Seipenbusch, Christoph Simon,
Eva Maria Stadler, Janis Staggs, Li Tasser, Viktoria Wagner,
Michael Weintraub, Thilo Wermke, Rosmarie Zechmeister,
Heimo Zobernig.

österreichisches kulturforumber

Bundeskanzleramt

Publikation / Publication

Diese Publikation erscheint anlässlich der Ausstellung *Der Hausfreund. Eine Wiederentdeckung des exzentrischen Werks von Friedrich von Berzeviczy-Pallavicini* in der Universitätsgalerie Heiligenkreuzer Hof Wien (2. Mai – 1. Juni 2019) und im Österreichischen Kulturforum Berlin (13. September – 25. Oktober 2019).
This catalogue was published for the exhibition *Der Hausfreund: A Rediscovery of the Eccentric Work of Friedrich von Berzeviczy-Pallavicini* at the University Gallery Heiligenkreuzer Hof Vienna (May 2 – June 1, 2019) and at the Austrian Cultural Forum Berlin (September 13 – October 25, 2019).

Herausgegeben von / Edited by Cosima Rainer, Robert Müller
Universität für angewandte Kunst Wien, Kunstsammlung und Archiv / University of Applied Arts Vienna, Collection and Archive
Postgasse 6, A-1010 Wien / Vienna

Konzept / Concept: Cosima Rainer
Redaktion / Editorial management: Sofie Mathoi
Werkliste / List of Works: Sofie Mathoi
Produktion / Production: Sofie Mathoi, Robert Müller, Cosima Rainer
Bildredaktion / Picture editing: Sofie Mathoi
Biografien der Künstler*innen / Artist's biographies: Sofie Mathoi, Robert Müller
Grafisches Konzept, Layout und Satz / Graphic design, layout and typesetting: HIT
Deutsches Lektorat / German copy-editing: Johannes Payer, Esther Pirchner
Englisches Lektorat / English copy-editing: Betti Moser
Übersetzungen / Translations: Rebecca Law, Nick Sommers, Jessica West, Signe Rose
Gesamtherstellung / Produced by: Medialis Offsetdruck GmbH, Berlin
Lithografie / Lithography: Medialis Offsetdruck GmbH, Berlin
Papier / Paper: Omni Bulk 1.3
Auflage / Print run: 800

Autor*innen / Authors:
Manuela Ammer, Gerald Bast, Anke Dyes, Brigitte Felderer, Michael Franz, Anette Freudenberger, Yuki Higashino, Tonio Kröner, Sofie Mathoi, Inka Meißner, Robert Müller, Cosima Rainer, Anne-Katrin Rossberg, Inga Charlotte Thiele

Cover / Cover:
Friedrich von Berzeviczy-Pallavicini, Entwurf für ein Schränkchen / Design for a Cabinet, 1929, IN 1685

Erschienen im / Published by
Verlag der Buchhandlung Walther König, Köln
Ehrenstraße 4
D-50672 Köln
www.buchhandlung-walther-koenig.de

Printed in Germany

Vertrieb / Distribution

Europe
Buchhandlung Walther König
Ehrenstraße 4
D-50672 Köln
Tel. +49 (0) 221 / 20 59 6 53
verlag@buchhandlung-walther-koenig.de

UK and Ireland
Cornerhouse Publications Ltd. – HOME
2 Tony Wilson Place
UK – Manchester M15 4FN
Tel. +44 (0) 161 212 3466
publications@cornerhouse.org

Outside Europe
D.A.P. / Distributed Art Publishers, Inc.
75 Broad Street, Suite 630
USA – New York, NY 10004
Tel. +1 (0) 212 627 1999
orders@dapinc.com

Buchhandelsausgabe / Trade edition
ISBN: 978-3-96098-713-0